ove hope dreams achievement **SYMBOLS OF COMMUNICATION**

and gestured at what he had
and a water glass. It was a globe, comp
used to be champion that," Ali
Suddenly, I fel the na
was boxing ld, would
You either li his way o
get beat. orch. And yo
Ali said th Ali, of all peo
"You c much more tha
ments at the kind of gi
knack–Sonny Liston, Joe Frazi
Foreman—but the true
w instinctively what to do
glory were his. No hiding behin
morphing into the monster tha
and out of sports. That would
chose no easy paths in his life o
He shed the name Cassius Cl
ter's shackles, he found peace in
the heartland's sensibilities, and
a country that hadn't come lo
free man in every sense,
cans when pride bec
My punch that
m, there was nowh
Something happ
to knock his head

BLACK BOOK
Illustration
NINETEEN 99

THE BLACK BOOK

10 Astor Place, Sixth Floor
New York, New York 10003
Tel: 212.539.9800 or
800.841.1246
Fax: 212.539.9801
www.BlackBook.com

BLACK BOOK ILLUSTRATION **NINETEEN99**

Publisher David Shaffer
President & Chief Operating Officer Laura Branchini

Design & Production

Director of Design & Production Christina Holbrook
Senior Production Coordinator Tracy Russek
Production Coordinator Mary Prevosti
Traffic & Graphic Coordinator Jane Helmick
Production Staff Cathy Citarella, Fiona L'Estrange, Sherman Sussman

Circulation & Listings

Circulation & Listings Manager Paul Szymanski
Circulation Coordinator Natalie Bousigard
Listings Editor Barbara Goldman
Research Assistants Lily Lau, Robin Lau

Marketing

Marketing Manager & AR100 Coordinator Linda Maglionico

Administration

IS Manager & Webmaster David Messig
Sales Administration Coordinator Maggie Kenny 415.255.1202
Sales Administration Coordinator Tosca Marcy 212.539.9817
Receptionist Jean Walker

Accounting

Accounting Manager Christopher Cole
Senior Accountant/Office Manager Frances Llano
Staff Accountant Farida Dhanji

Marketing Consultants

East
Illustration Valerie Frasca 212.539.9822
Becky Raveson 800.841.1246
Photography Michael Mazzola 212.539.9826

Midwest
Illustration Adrian Johnson 847.836.9015
Photography Jennifer Faber 800.493.0030

South
Illustration Becky Raveson 800.841.1246
Photography Ellen Afflick 888.734.0866

West
Illustration Sharon Bates 888.404.9378
Photography Debra Weiss 800.981.8388

Publication designed by:
McDaniel Design Associates, Inc.
2 North Finley Avenue
Basking Ridge, NJ 07920
Voice: 908.766.2130
Facsimile: 908.766.2131
www.mcdaniel-design.com

The Guide to Creative Specialties designed by Beth Crowell, Cheung/Crowell Design.

Printed in Singapore by Toppan Printing Company. Color Separations through Print Pro Ltd., Hong Kong.

Black Book Illustration is distributed in the U.S. by The Black Book. Outside the U.S. contact: Corporate Office: RotoVision S.A., 7 rue du Bugnon, 1299 Crans, Switzerland. Tel: 41 22 776 05 11 Fax: 41 22 776 08 89 Sales Office: RotoVision S.A., Sheridan House, 112-116 Western Road, Hove, East Sussex BN3 1DD England. Tel: 44 1273 727268 Fax: 44 1273 727269 E-Mail: BRIANM@ROTOVISION.COM.

ISBN 0-942454-59-6 ISSN 1093-6513.

New York Times
3M BUF PUF
Black Book
Penguin USA

How important is imagery? From the pre-historic cave drawings of Lascaux, to the hieroglyphs of ancient Egypt, to today's multi-million dollar advertising campaigns, images are the most basic and powerful symbols of communication. A picture is worth a thousand words, so the saying goes, and in this year's Black Book Illustration you'll find the talent and the imagery you need to convey a multitude of ideas -- and to get your message across. For a quick, visual reference to Black Book Illustration talent by subject, flip to the back of the book and explore our new "Guide to Creative Specialties." Black Book Illustration 1999 celebrates the art of visual communication and the vital role of Black Book artists in creating the images that persuade us, enlighten us, and influence our vision of the world.

never give up while there is still hope

HOPE
SPRINGS
ETERNAL

NINETEEN 99 SHOWCASED ILLUSTRATORS

dreams THEO RUDNAK

power ALEX HACKWORTH

achievement NINA BERKSON

hope LORI LOHSTOETER

money STEVEN HOGAN

love PAULA PERTILE

Index To Advertisers

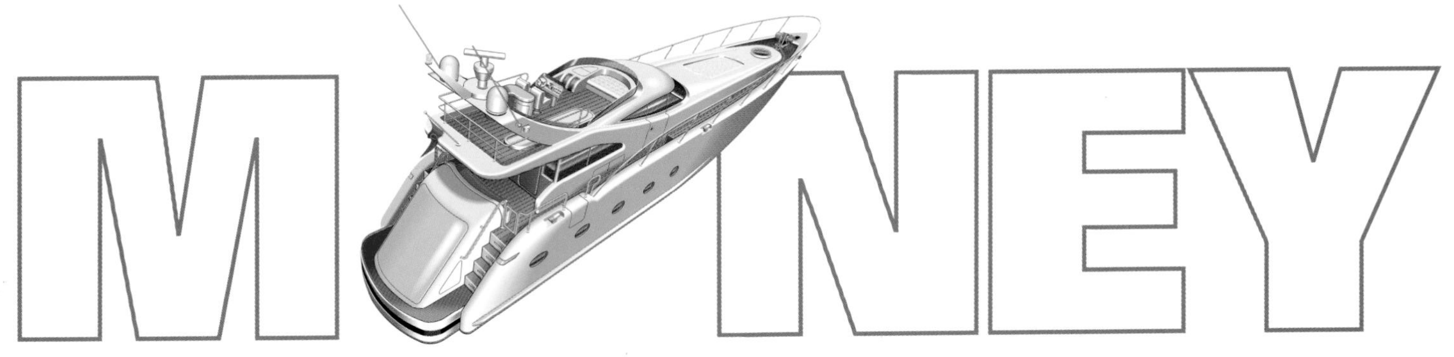

Index To Advertisers

Index To Advertisers

christine m. schneider

785.838.7630

Susan Gross
illustrations & monotypes
415.751.5879
www.susangross.com

Clients include: Levi-Strauss, Chronicle Books, Adobe, Joe Boxer, Beringer Vineyards, Nordstrom, Harper Collins, & Psychology Today.

Susan Gross

illustrations & monotypes
415.751.5879
www.susangross.com

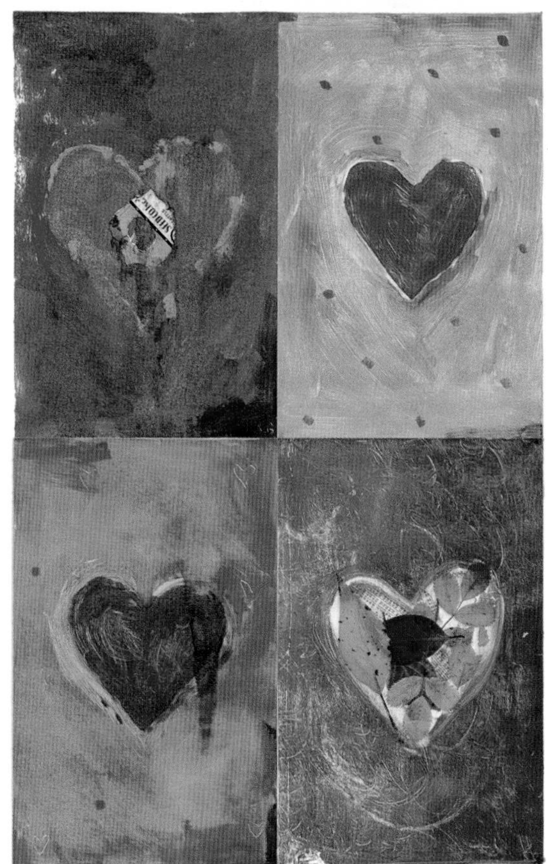

Clients include: PCW Communications, Marcel Schurman, Family Circle Magazine, W. W. Norton Publishing, Nobleworks, & Sybex, Inc.

JIM FRAZIER ILLUSTRATION 214 340-9972

EVAN SCHWARZE
708 445 0154

Tuko Fujisaki Illustration

Studio 800.208.2456

San Francisco
Jane Klein Represents
1.888.ART.1008

Studio
505.466.4741
800.208.2456

St. Louis
Teenuh Foster
314.647.7377

TUKO FUJISAKI ILLUSTRATION

STUDIO 800.208.2456

SAN FRANCISCO
JANE KLEIN REPRESENTS
1.888.ART.1008

STUDIO
505.466.4741
800.208.2456

ST. LOUIS
TEENUH FOSTER
314.647.7377

BARBARA HRANILOVICH

PHONE/FAX (517) 321-2917

WWW.NGEXPLORER.COM
FLY BALL
CAMERON CLEMENT
501.646.7734
IN AR.OK.KS.MO.TX OR L.A. ☎ SUZANNE CRAIG @ 918.749.9424

MONA DALY

Studio **888.220.3909** http://members.aol.com/mweirdaly

Represented by **Carrie Perlow 310.540.5958** fx **310.792.9161**

michael s. wertz illustration
tel 415.824.5542 **email** michael@wertzateria.com **www.**wertzateria.com

ROGER HILL

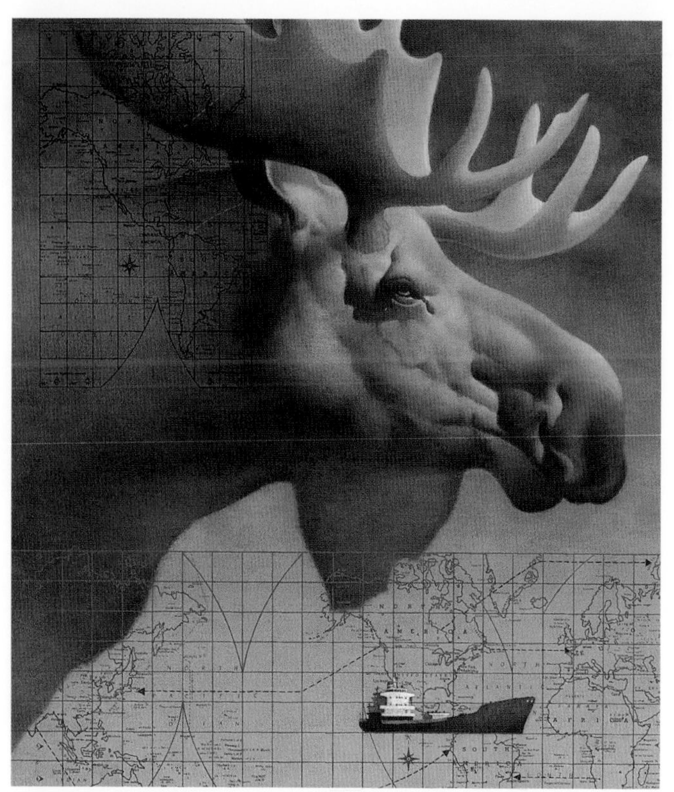

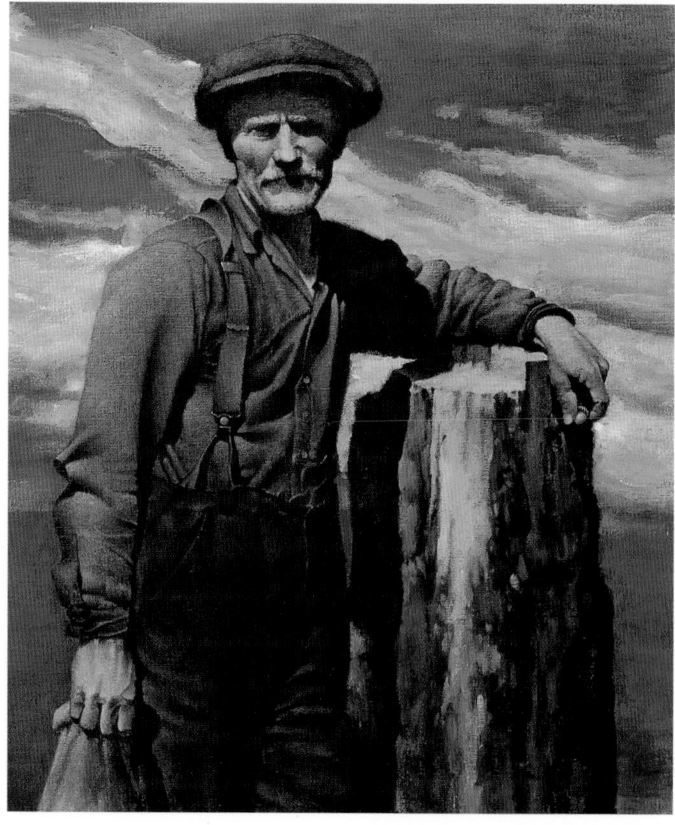

63A YORKVILLE AVE. TORONTO/ONTARIO/CANADA/M5R-1B7 PHONE/FAX (416) 923-5933

ROGER HILL

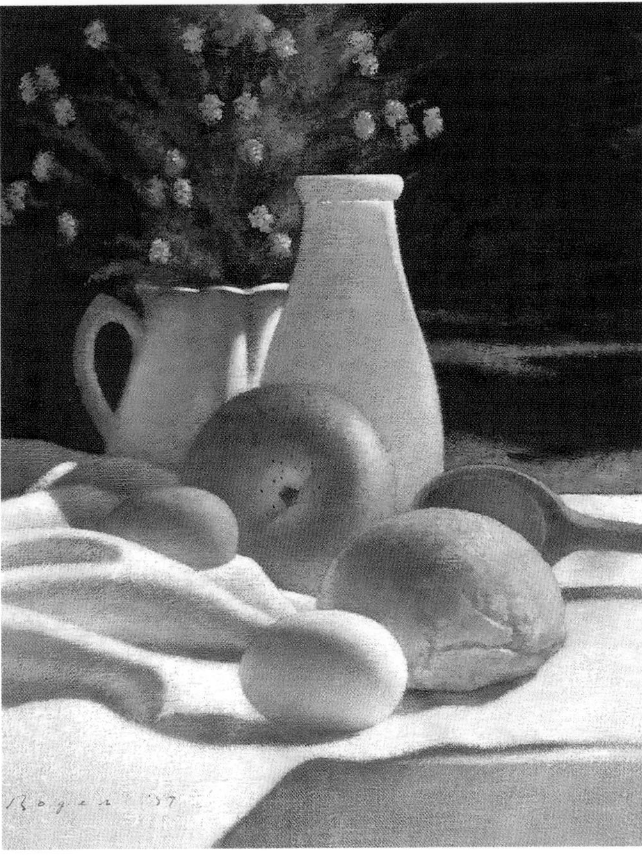

63A YORKVILLE AVE. TORONTO/ONTARIO/CANADA/M5R-1B7 PHONE/FAX (416) 923-5933

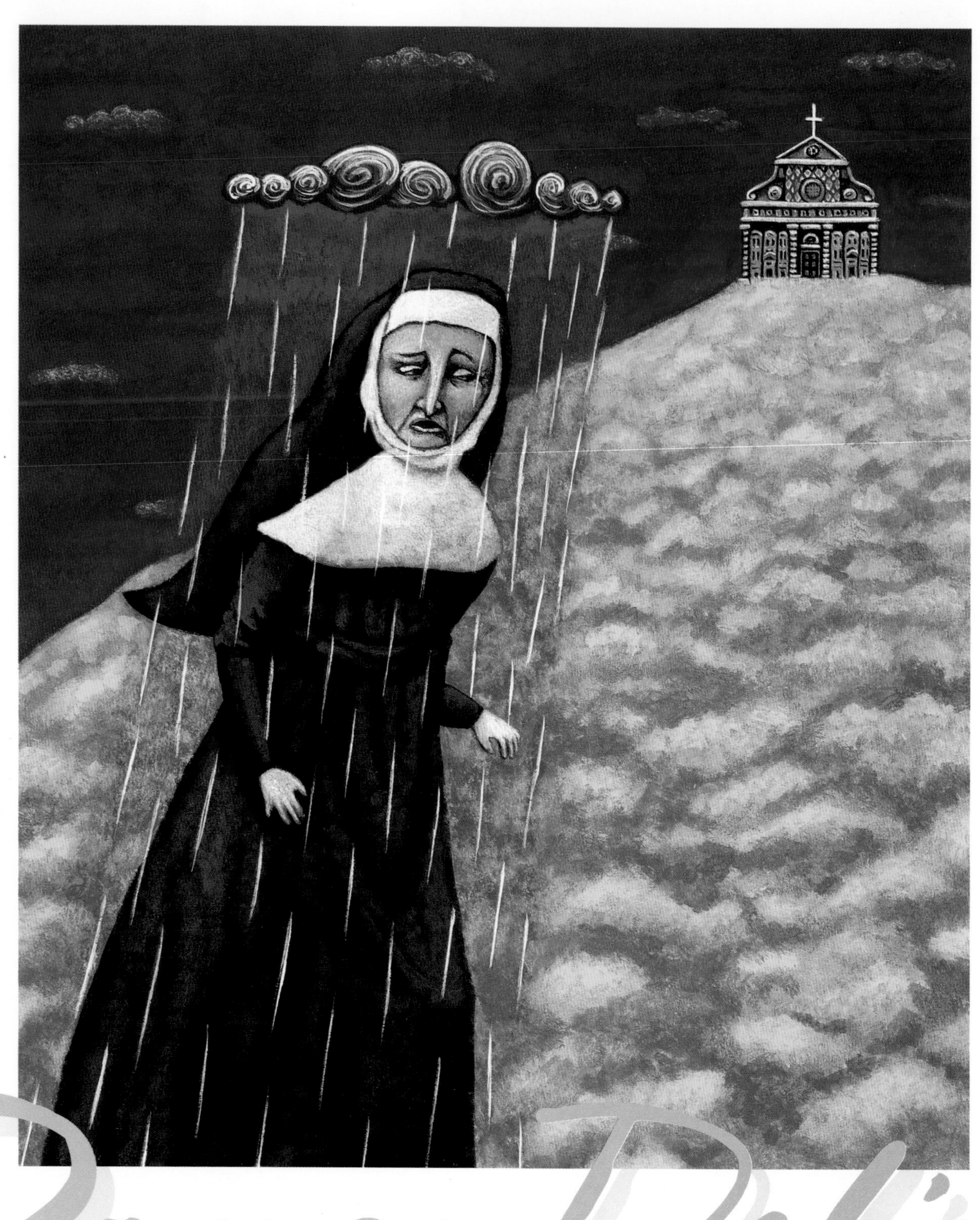

Donna Delich

DONNA DELICH
889 WILLIAMS PLACE
HARTSVILLE, PA 18974
PHONE: 215.674.2506
FAX: 215.674.8670

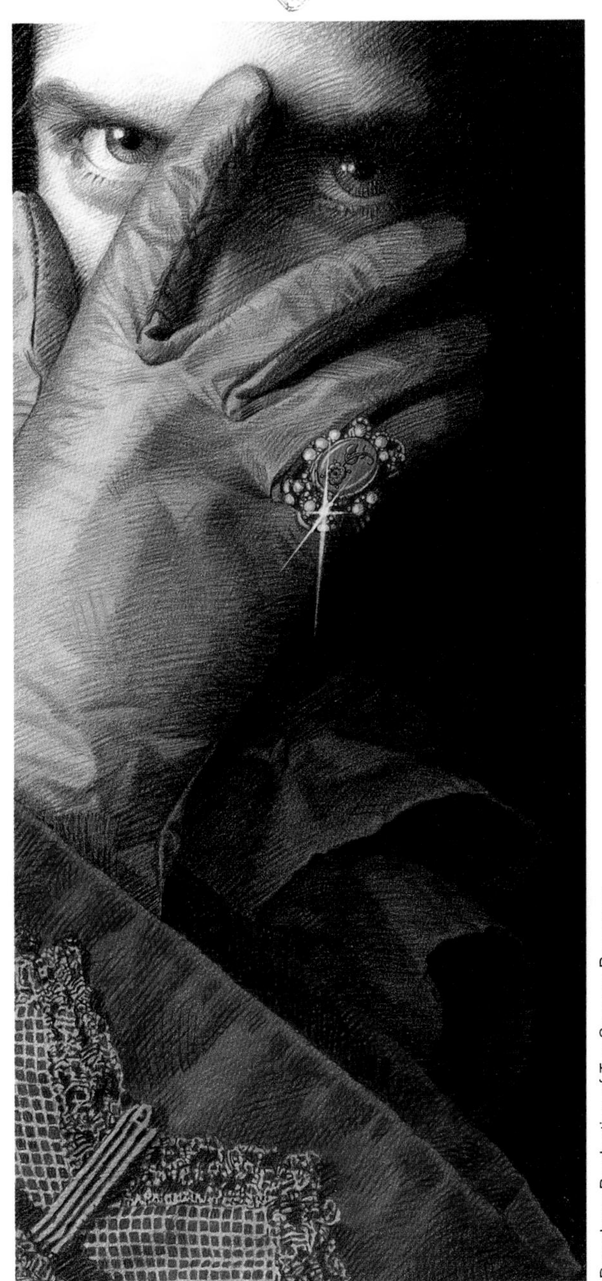

Broadway Production of The Scarlet Pimpernel

ScrippsHealth

LINDA FENNIMORE 212-866-0279

808 WEST END AVE. #801 NEW YORK, NEW YORK 10025

er doodles for Nickalodeon.

spot thingy for U.S. News & World Report

something for Adobe Magazine

ROBERT ZIMMERMAN
(828) 252-9689

On the world wide web at
www.zimm.net

Check out the web site for Zimm products like Ceramic Pet Ware, Wallets, Greeting Cards, Journals, T-Shirts, Bubble Watches, School Binders and various other whacked out stuff.

zimm@circle.net

Clancy Gibson

REPRESENTED BY LINK 416 530 1500 FAX 416 530 1401

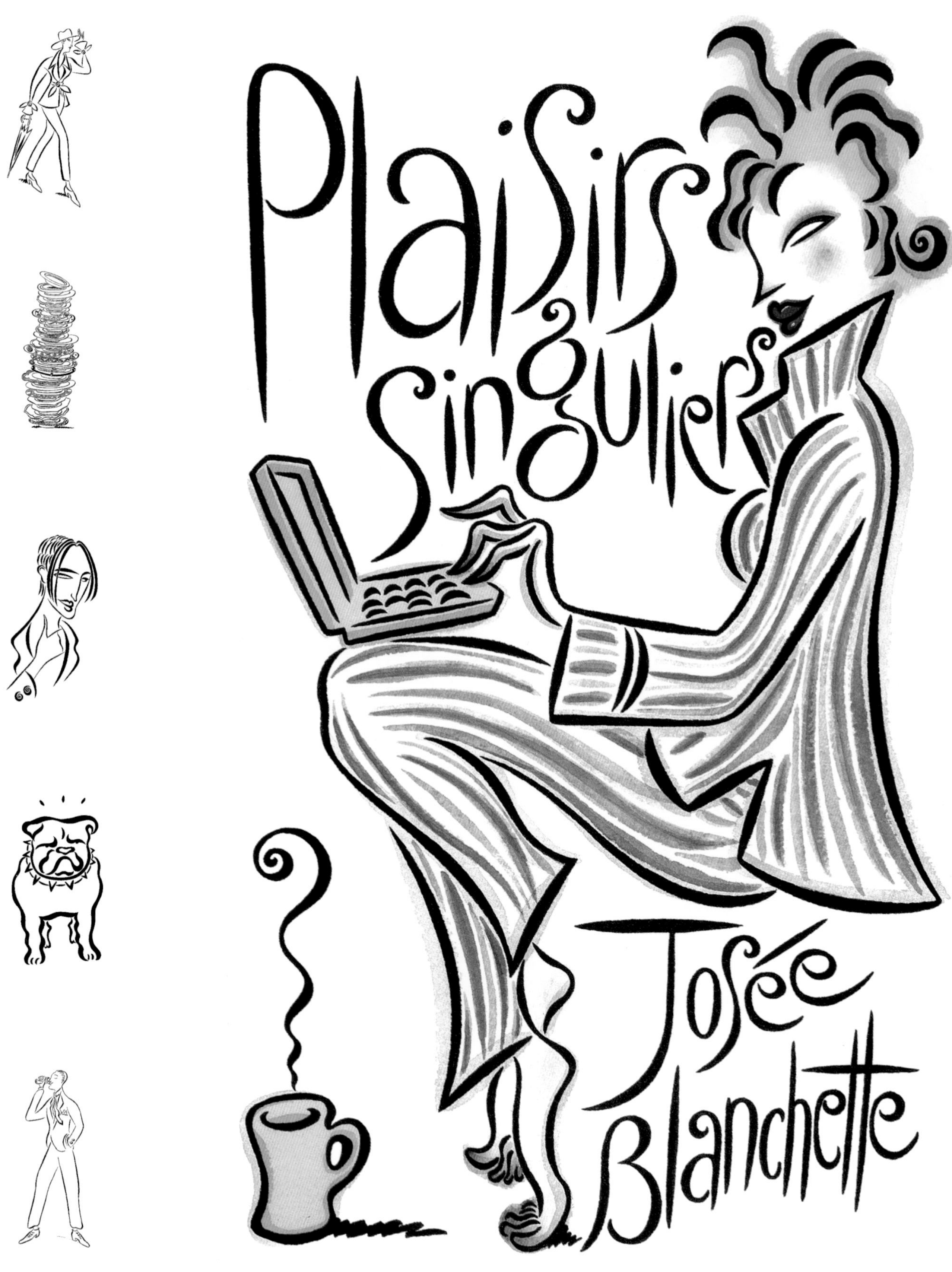

Nina Berkson

REPRESENTED BY LINK 416 530 1500 FAX 416 530 1401

jennifer riegler
c h i c a g o
773.327.7489

TAYLOR BRUCE

755 TZABACO CREEK RD
GEYSERVILLE, CA. 95441
PHONE & FAX 707.857.3373

m
MARLENA AGENCY
TELEPHONE: 212•289•5514 / 609•252•9405 / FAX: 609•252•1949

MARLENA TORZECKA REPRESENTS **ISTVAN OROSZ**
TELEPHONE: 212•289•5514 / 609•252•9405 / FAX: 609•252•1949

Istvan Orosz

Giuseppe Verdi
DER TROUBADOUR
Großes Haus
ab 05, Oktober 1995
VOLKS THEATER ROSTOCK
design: István Orosz

A poster for Verdi's opera Trubadour.

MARLENA TORZECKA REPRESENTS **GERARD DUBOIS**
TELEPHONE: 212•289•5514 / 609•252•9405 / FAX: 609•252•1949

GERARD DUBOIS

The rethinking of corporate govemance in France; a new revolution.

MARLENA TORZECKA REPRESENTS **JACQUES COURNOYER**
TELEPHONE: 212•289•5514 / 609•252•9405 / FAX: 609•252•1949

J. Cournoyer

New technique of treating kidney stones with shock waves rather than surgery.

MARLENA TORZECKA REPRESENTS **MARC MONGEAU**
TELEPHONE: 212•289•5514 / 609•252•9405 / FAX: 609•252•1949

Marc Mongeau

From the top left:

- Like luggage, we carry our words
- Flaming bird;
  celebrating St. Jean Baptiste Day in Quebec.
- Changing the face of the neighbourhood;
  from factories and offices into residential buildings.

MARLENA TORZECKA REPRESENTS **PAUL ZWOLAK**
TELEPHONE: 212•289•5514 / 609•252•9405 / FAX: 609•252•1949

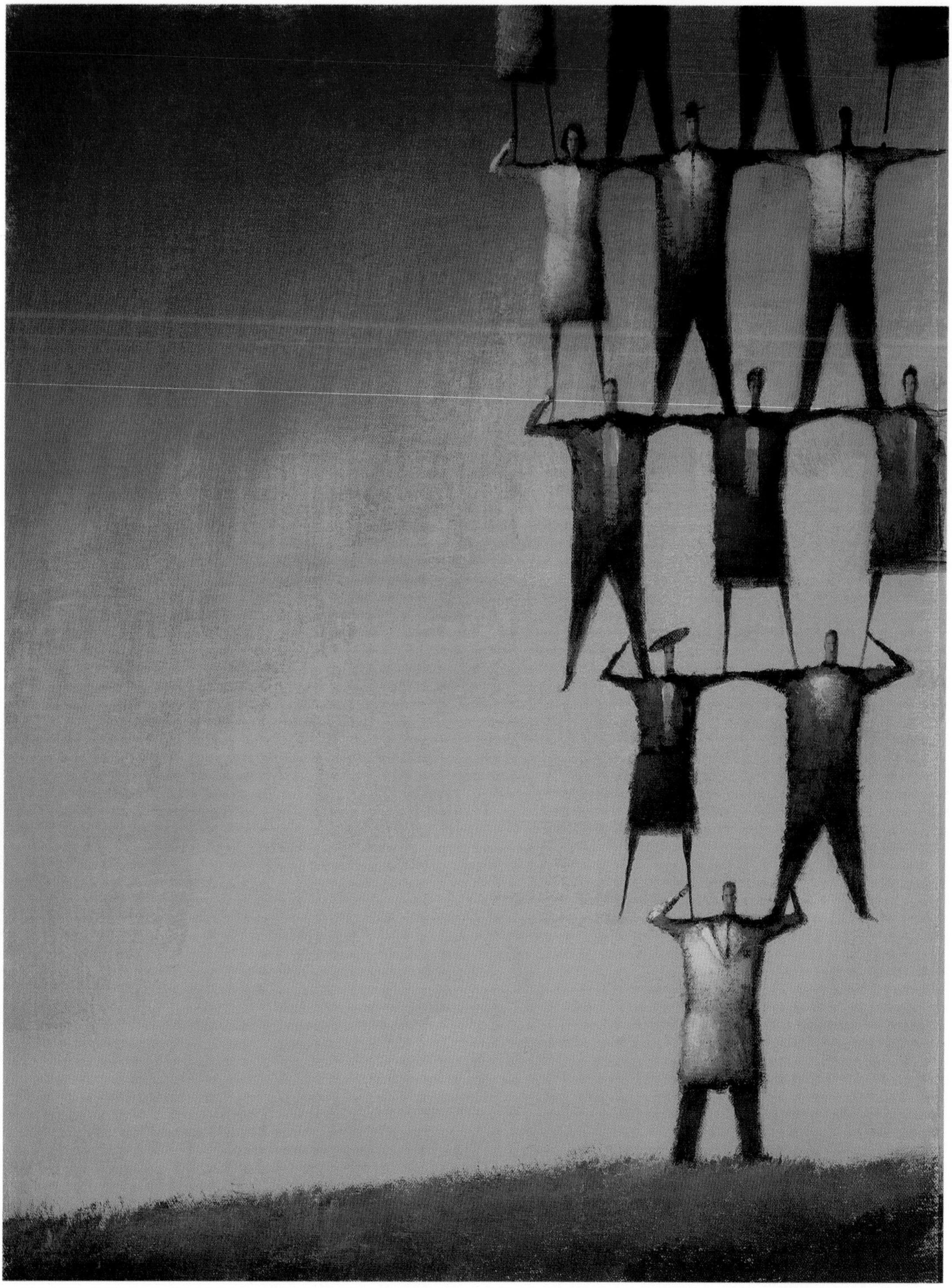

Selling insurance to doctors

PAUL ZWOLAK

MARLENA TORZECKA REPRESENTS **FERRUCCIO SARDELLA**
TELEPHONE: 212•289•5514 / 609•252•9405 / FAX: 609•252•1949

Ferruccio

Community support. A poster for Volunteer Day in Orange County, California.

MARLENA TORZECKA REPRESENTS **MICHAEL WOLOSCHINOW**
TELEPHONE: 212•289•5514 / 609•252•9405 / FAX: 609•252•1949

Michael Woloschinow

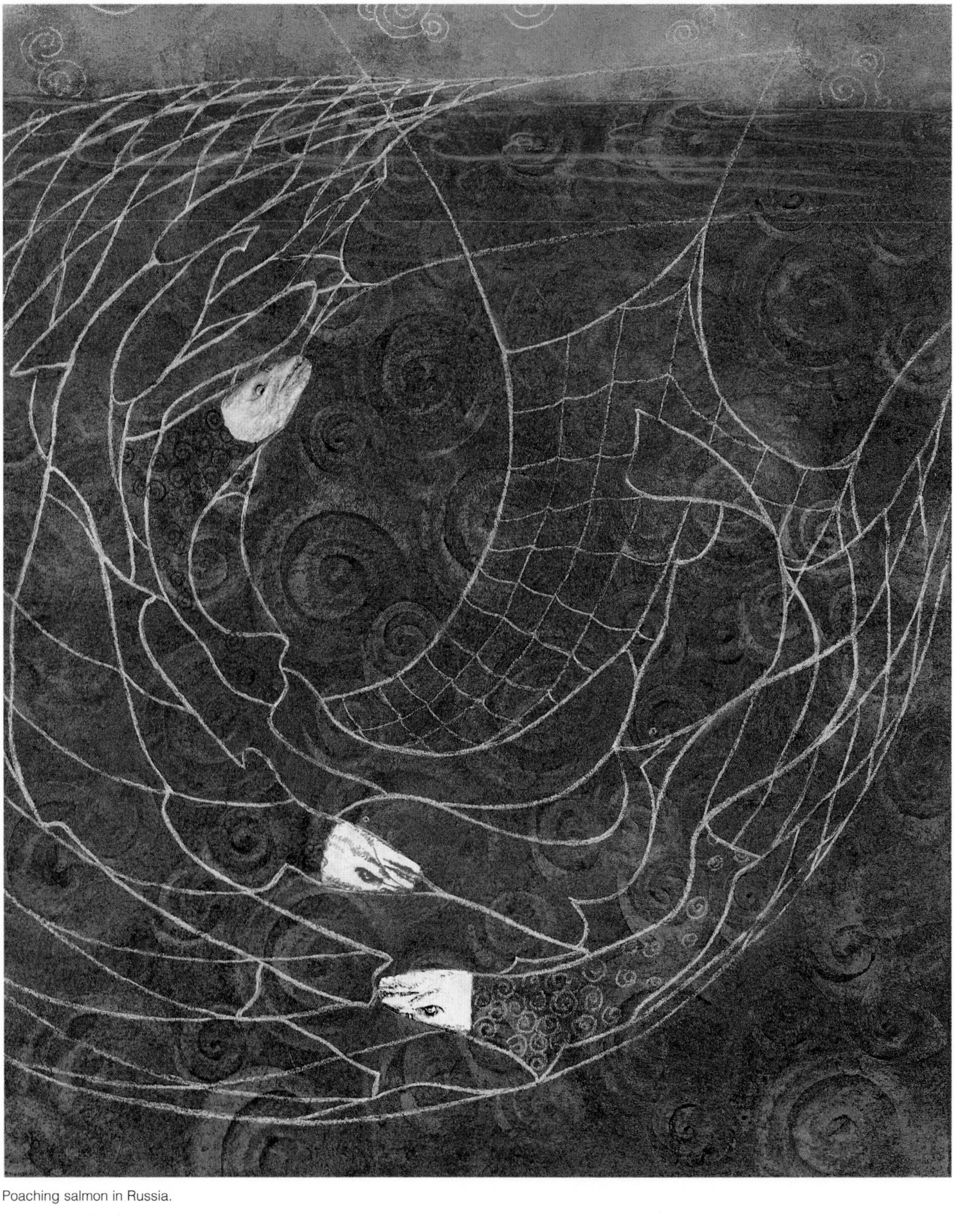

Poaching salmon in Russia.

MARLENA TORZECKA REPRESENTS **NORMAND COUSINEAU**
TELEPHONE: 212•289•5514 / 609•252•9405 / FAX: 609•252•1949

CouSiNeAu

Strategy for a growing global economy.

KAREN LAURENCE

PHONE: 212-751-8215

FAX: 212-759-0511

The Steelmaker *oil on canvas 28"x 22"*

Gulliver arrives in Lilliput *oil on canvas 14"x 40"*

JOHN RUSH

123 Kedzie St., Evanston, IL 60202

(847) 869-2078

DAVID SAWYER
303·666·5581

Precise technical, conceptual and educational illustration. Ghosted and cutaway views from engineering drawings, photos or verbal briefing. See also Black Book 1997, 1998.

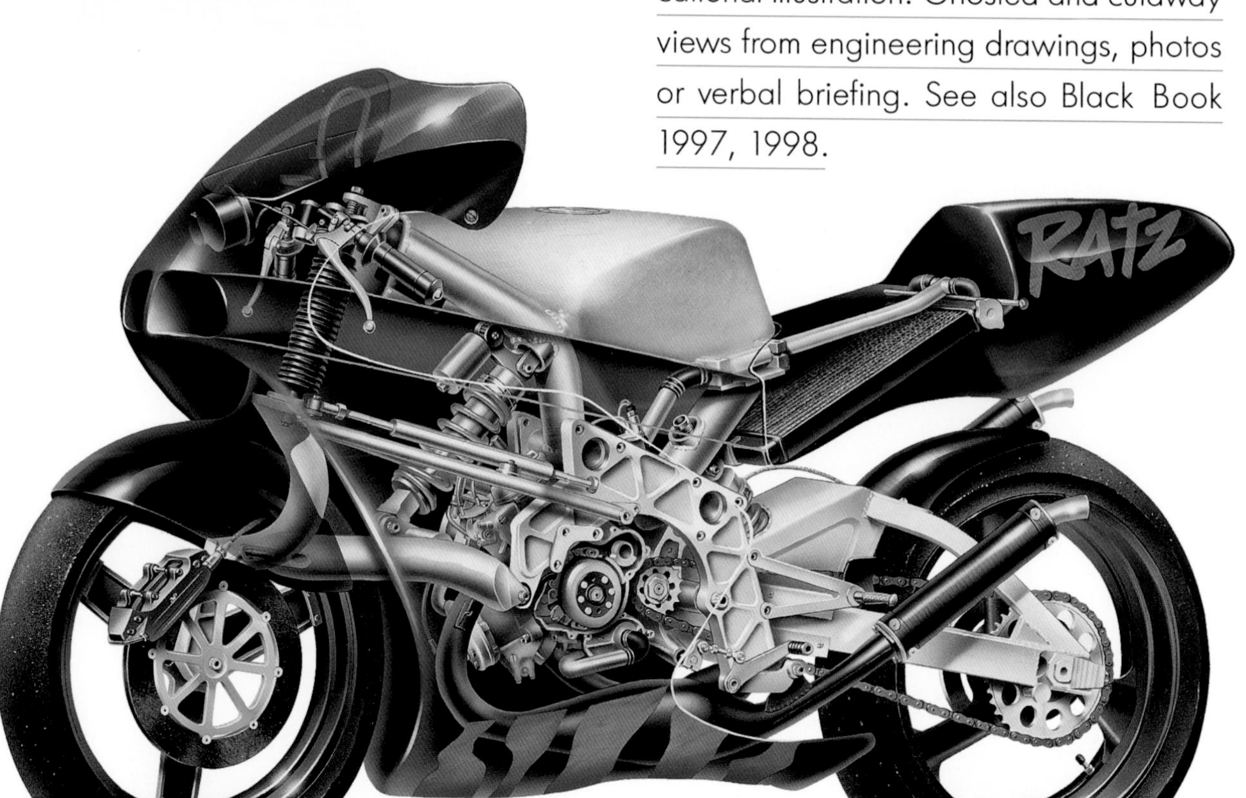

COMING SOON
ATOMIC
the SHERIFF
the PROFESSOR
the MOVIE STAR
THE GIRL
CHIHUAHUA
AARON MESHON
1 (800) 753-7513
free call

Brenda Weeks

35 jane st, suite 5

toronto, ont, canada

m6s 3y3

Illustration

tel (416) 766 2942

fax (416) 766 9315

Holly Dickens Design, Inc. **312.280.0777** Fax 312.280.1725 e-mail HolDickens@aol.com

Pizzazz!

ANDERSON FLOORING

I would become fluent in French.

FIDELITY INVESTMENTS

GUINNESS

Better than Milk?

BRISTOL-MEYERS

PLANTERS

Relax. Go Nuts

NABISCO

WILD THINGS

A JOHN McNAUGHTON FILM

Pace
PACE. THE REAL DEAL.

CAMPBELL SOUP COMPANY

KRAFT FOODS

Imagine yourself in a Mercury

MERCURY

DENIM BLUES RETAIL

BEST
BUY
Now that's a great idea!

BEST BUY

INTEL

Digital Output Available

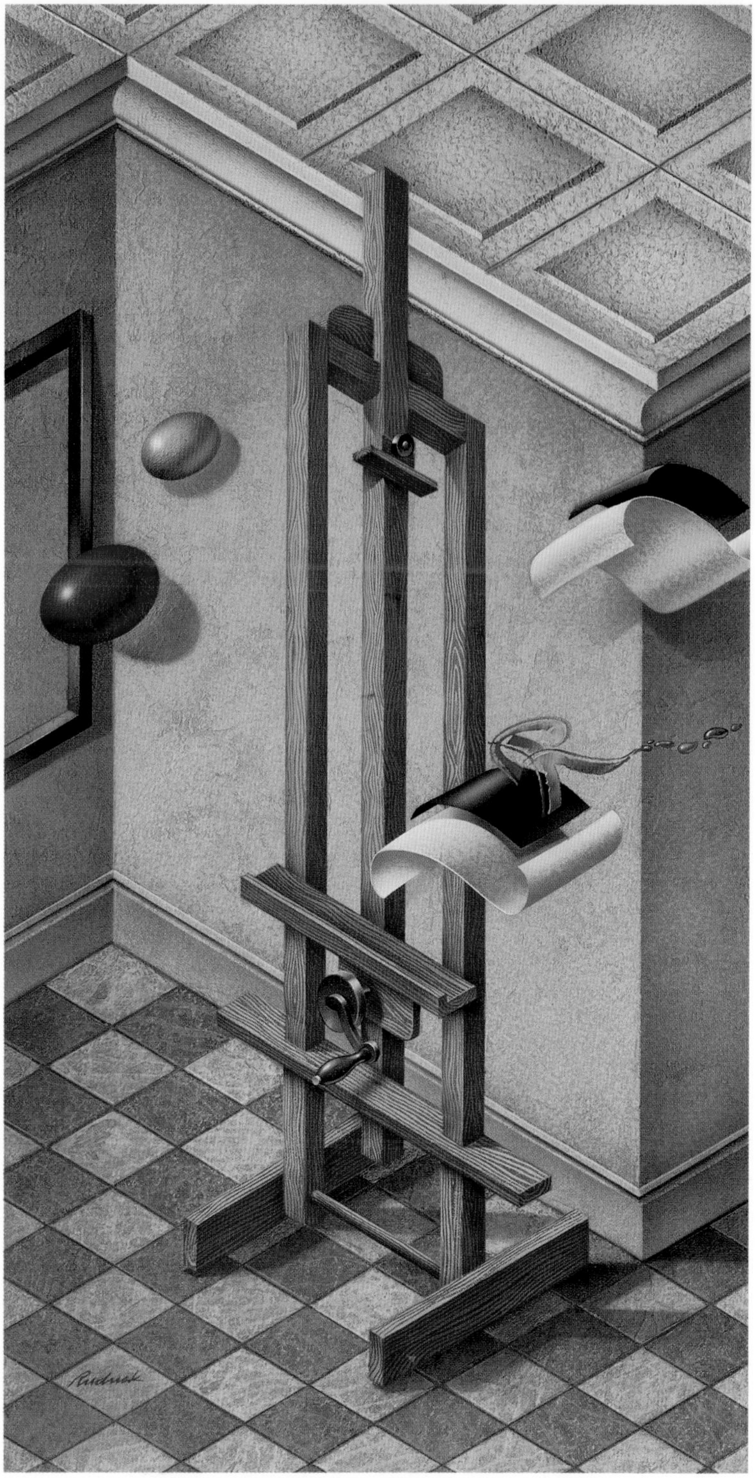

RENARD
REPRESENTS
212.490.2450
FAX697.6828
WWW.RENARDREPRESENTS.COM

THEO RUDNAK

RENARD REPRESENTS TEL: 212-490-2450 • FAX: 212-697-6828 • www.renardrepresents.com

RENÉ MILOT

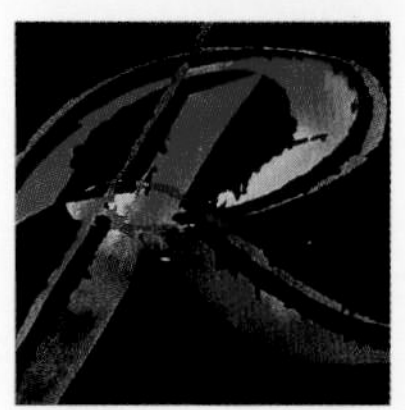

RENARD REPRESENTS
Tel: (212) 490-2450
Fax:(212) 697-6828

www.renardrepresents.com

KAZUHIKO SANO

RENARD REPRESENTS
Tel: (212) 490-2450
Fax:(212) 697-6828

www.renardrepresents.com

ROB BROOKS

RENARD REPRESENTS
Tel: (212) 490-2450
Fax: (212) 697-6828

www.renardrepresents.com

STÉPHAN DAIGLE

RENARD REPRESENTS
Tel: (212) 490-2450
Fax: (212) 697-6828

www.renardrepresents.com

DAN GARROW

RENARD REPRESENTS
Tel: (212) 490-2450
Fax:(212) 697-6828

www.renardrepresents.com

MATSU

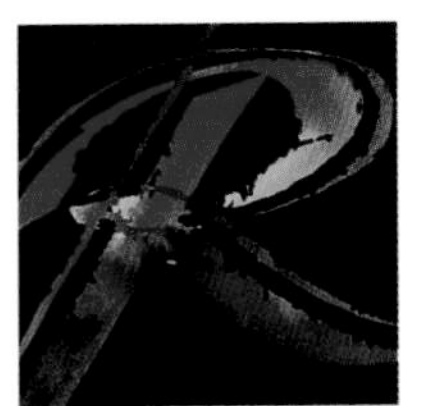

RENARD REPRESENTS
Tel: (212) 490-2450
Fax:(212) 697-6828

www.renardrepresents.com

ROBERT RODRIGUEZ

RENARD REPRESENTS
Tel: (212) 490-2450
Fax: (212) 697-6828

www.renardrepresents.com

TIM LEE

RENARD REPRESENTS
Tel: (212) 490-2450
Fax:(212) 697-6828

www.renardrepresents.com

STEVE BJÖRKMAN

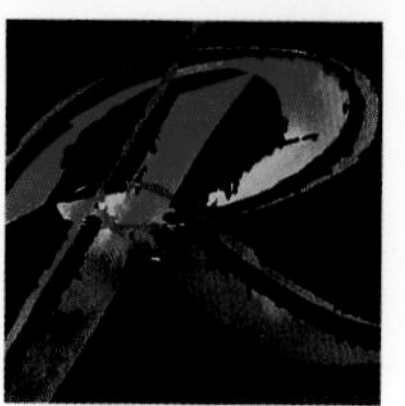

RENARD REPRESENTS
Tel: (212) 490-2450
Fax: (212) 697-6828

Björkman

www.renardrepresents.com

BILL CIGLIANO

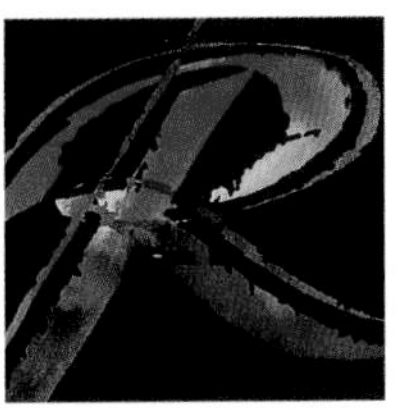

RENARD REPRESENTS
Tel: (212) 490-2450
Fax: (212) 697-6828

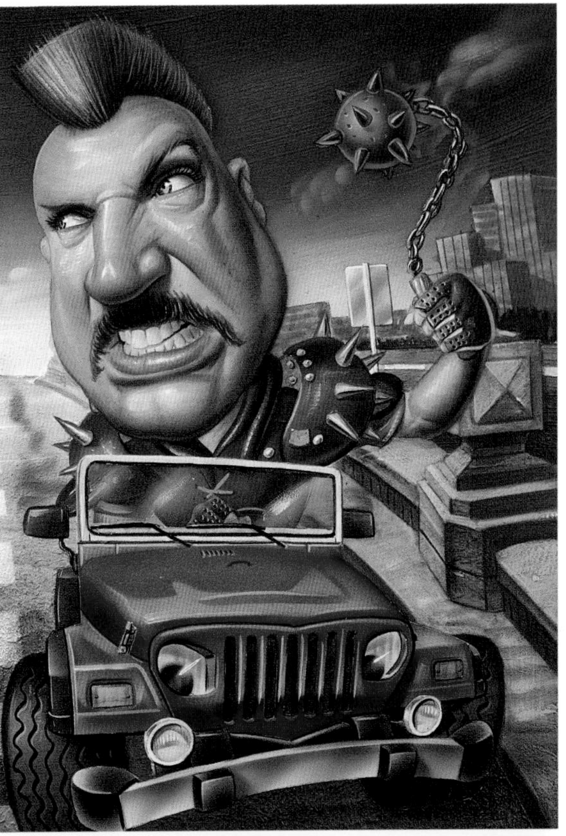

www.renardrepresents.com

MATTHEW HOLMES

RENARD REPRESENTS
Tel: (212) 490-2450
Fax: (212) 697-6828

www.renardrepresents.com

JONATHAN HERBERT

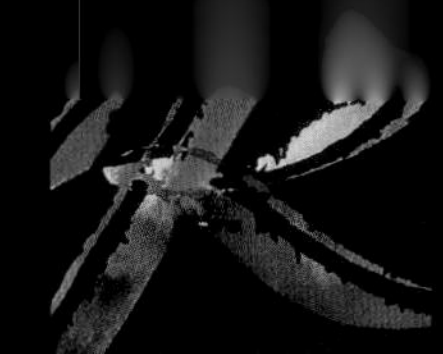

RENARD REPRESENTS
Tel: (212) 490-2450
Fax: (212) 697-6828

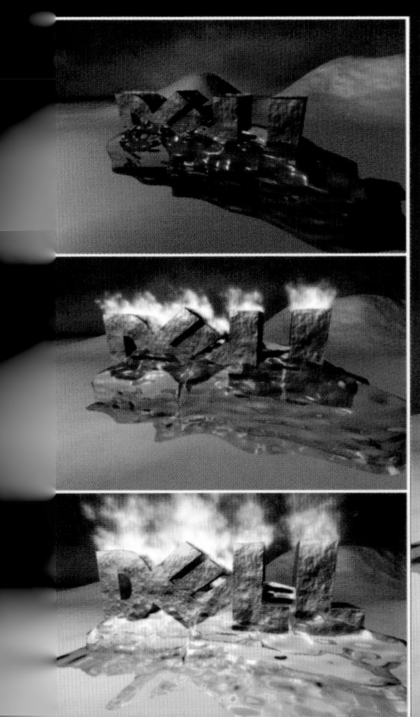

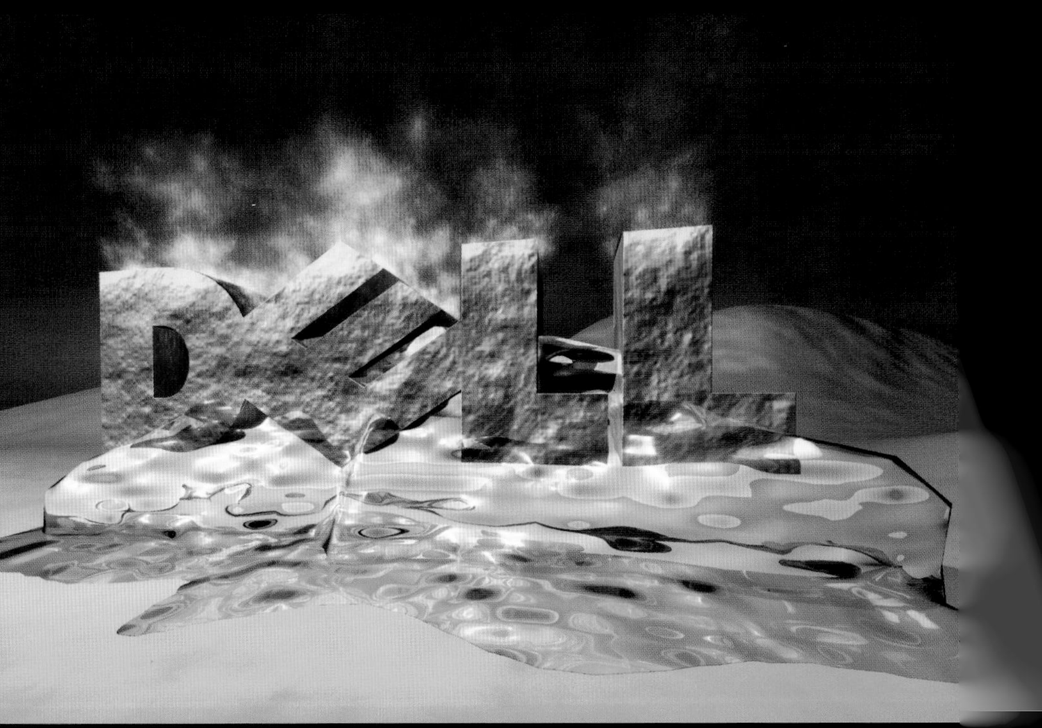

STATE • OF • THE • ART 3D MODELING FOR PRINT AND ANIMATION CALL FOR BOOK OR REEL

GARY ELDRIDGE

RENARD REPRESENTS
Tel: (212) 490-2450
Fax:(212) 697-6828

www.renardrepresents.com

VALERIE SINCLAIR

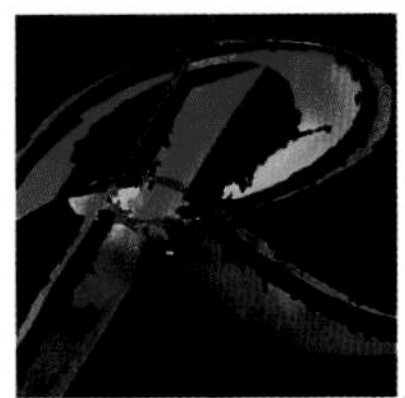

RENARD REPRESENTS
Tel: (212) 490-2450
Fax: (212) 697-6828

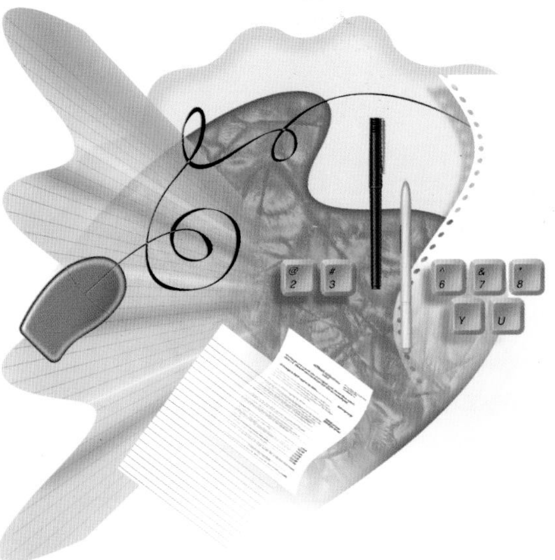

www.renardrepresents.com

MICHAEL McGURL

RENARD REPRESENTS
Tel: (212) 490-2450
Fax: (212) 697-6828

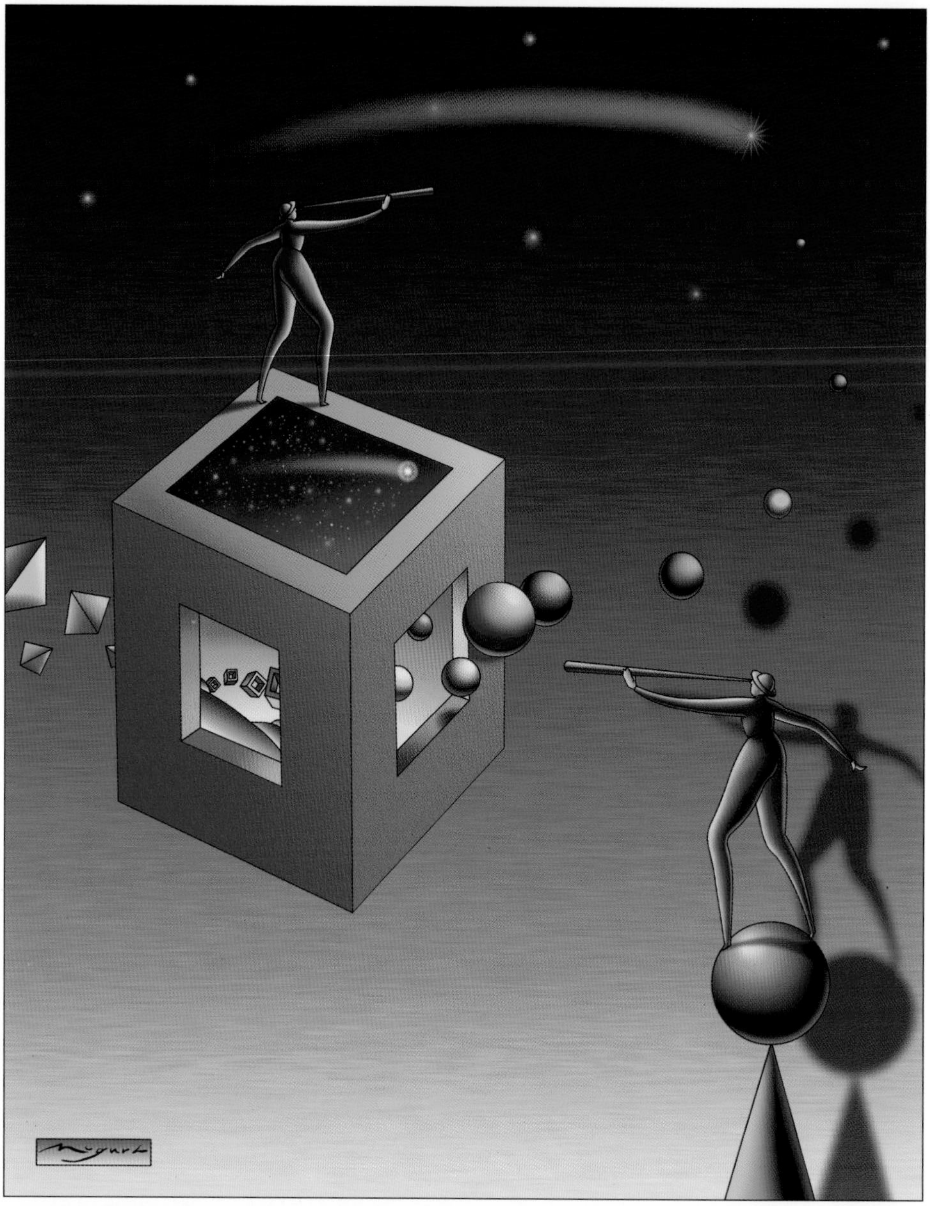

www.renardrepresents.com

WENDY GROSSMAN

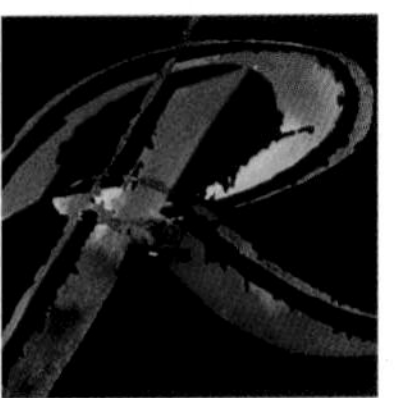

RENARD REPRESENTS
Tel: (212) 490-2450
Fax:(212) 697-6828

www.renardrepresents.com

JEFFREY PELO

RENARD REPRESENTS
Tel: (212) 490-2450
Fax: (212) 697-6828

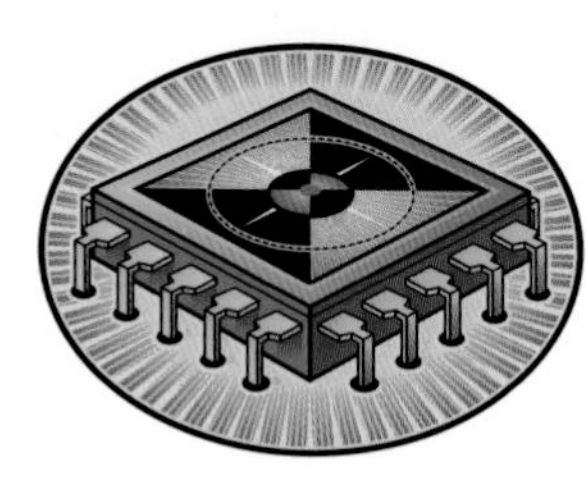

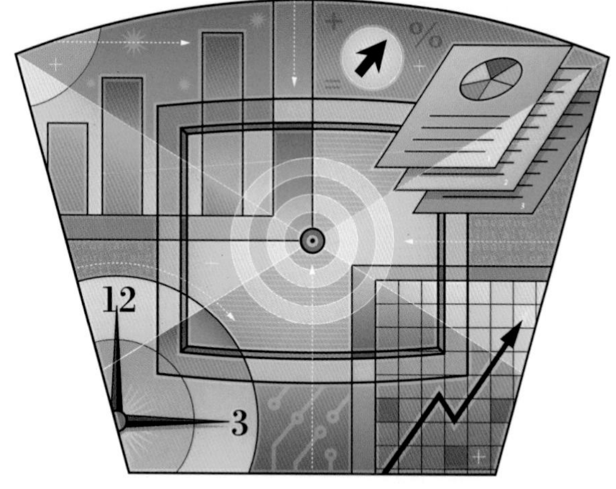

www.renardrepresents.com

JOHN MACDONALD

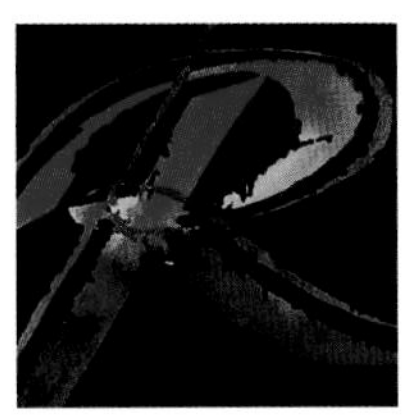

RENARD REPRESENTS
Tel: (212) 490-2450
Fax:(212) 697-6828

www.renardrepresents.com

KEVIN POPE

RENARD REPRESENTS
Tel: (212) 490-2450
Fax:(212) 697-6828

The always important follow up call from the temp agency

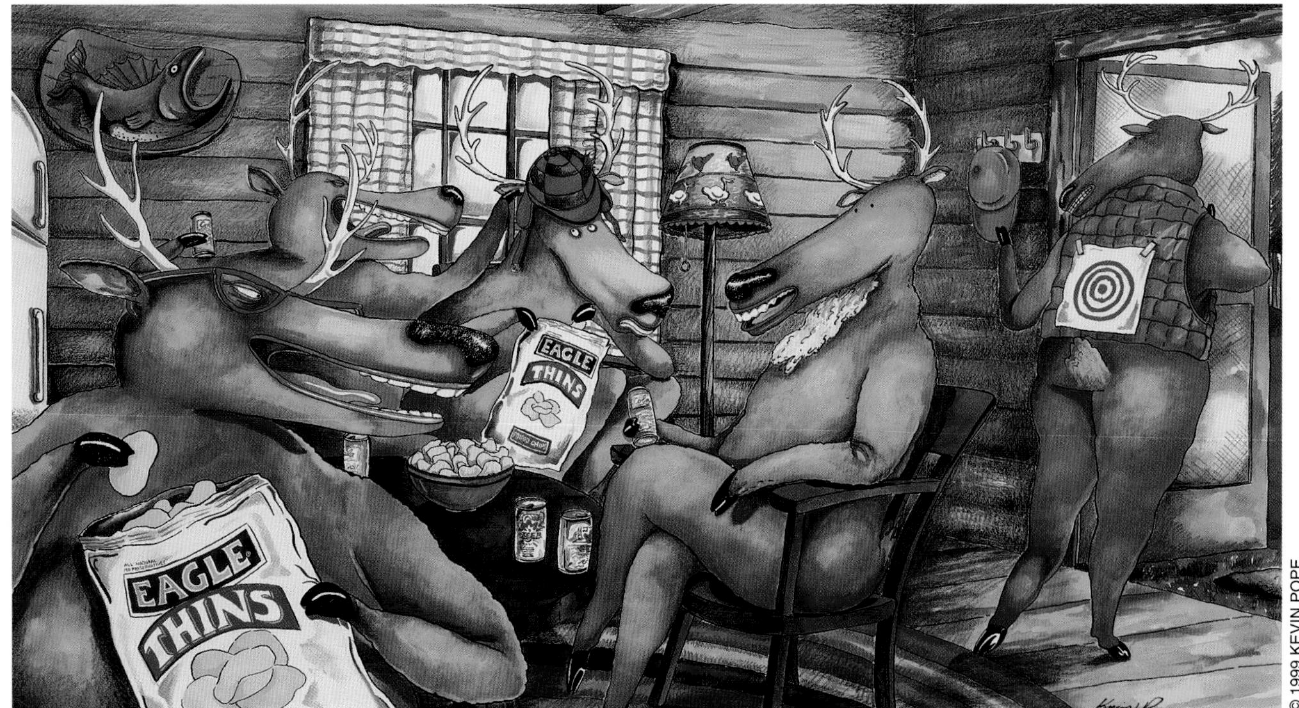

www.renardrepresents.com

www.renardrepresents.com

Corey Wilkinson

855 Joyce Avenue • Melrose Park, Illinois • 60164

708-562-2512

WILKINSON
©Corey Wilkinson 1998

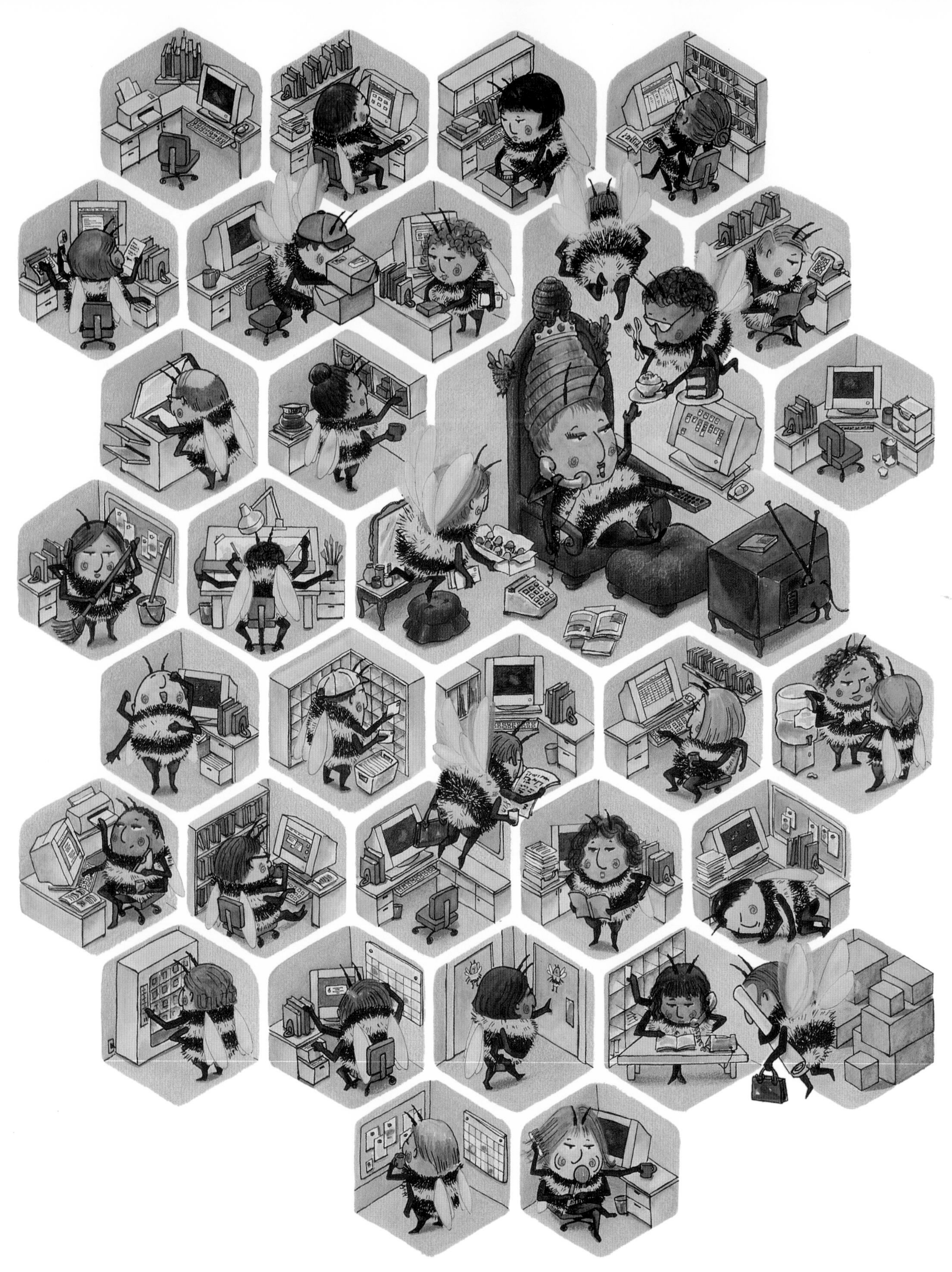

PAULA PERTILE DESIGN & ILLUSTRATION 419 22ND AVENUE SAN FRANCISCO, CA 94121
phone.**415.668.7156** fax.**668.0883** or **415.668.8545** email.**ppertile@aol.com**

HATLEY

COMPUTER ILLUSTRATIONS

500-442-2428

HOFKIN

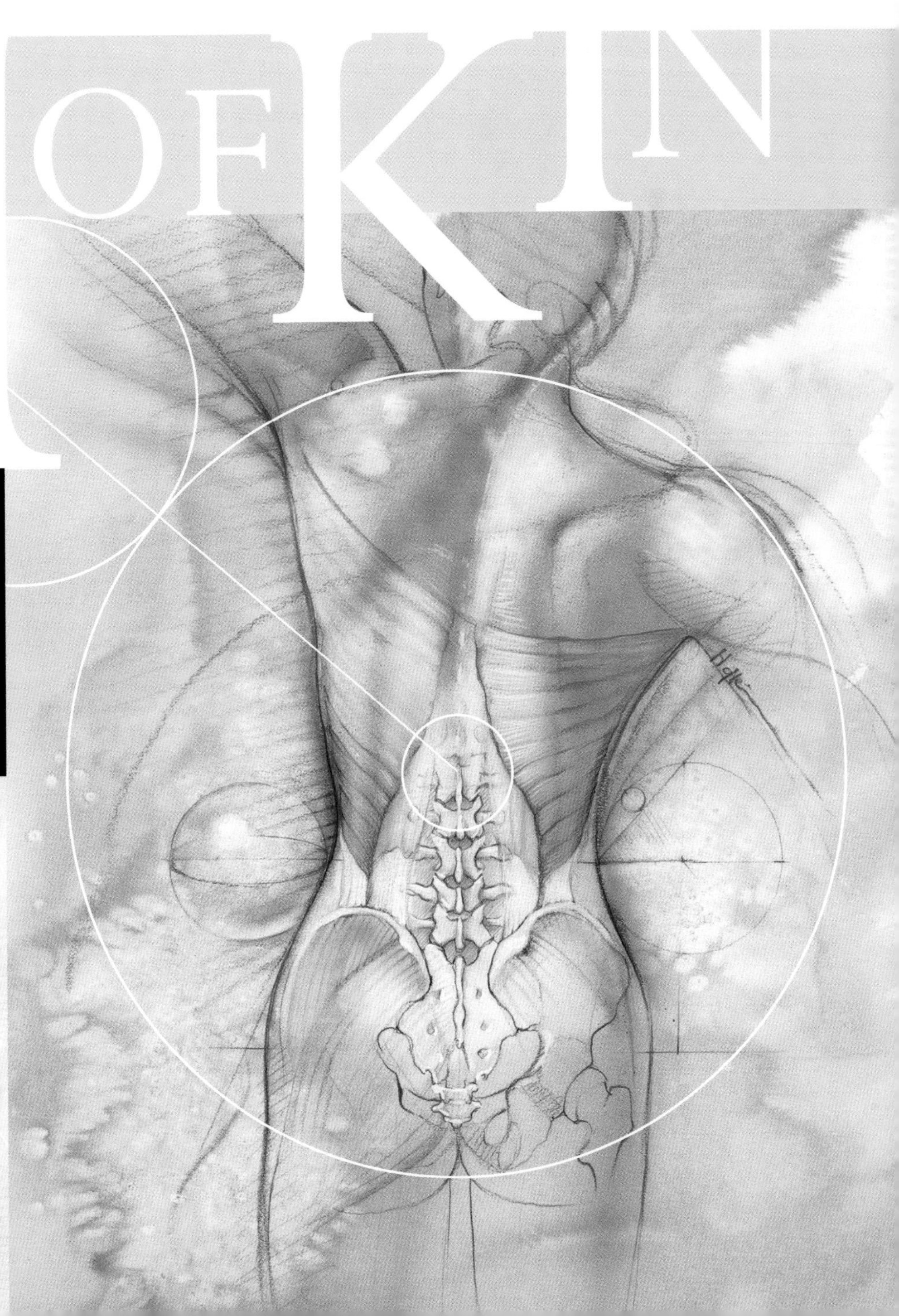

BONNIE HOFKIN

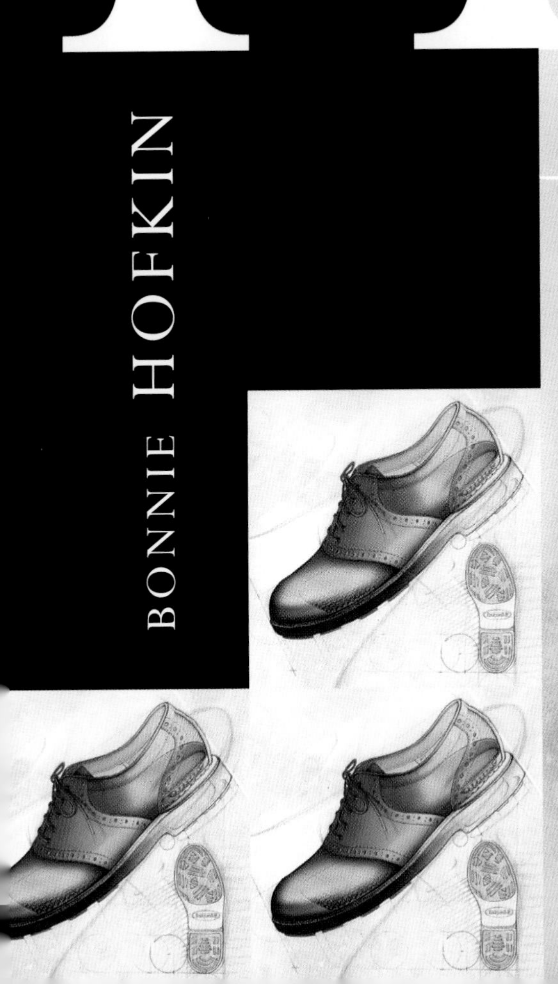

JOANNE PALULIAN
REPRESENTATIVE
TEL 212.581.8338
203.866.3734
FAX 203.857.0842

Trip Park
908-522-0167
Represented By
Joanne Palulian
212 581-8338 or 203 866-3734
Fax 203-857-0842

SUBJECT
DEPRESSION

MEDIUM
ACRYLA GOUACHE ON PAPER

BACKGROUND
PEOPLE CAN BECOME DEPRESSED WHEN THEY SPEND TOO MUCH TIME IN THEIR MINDS IN THE PAST OR IN THE FUTURE. BEING IN THE PAST CAN CREATE FEELINGS OF REGRET AND FEAR, AND BEING IN THE FUTURE CAN CREATE FEELINGS OF FEAR AND WORRY. BEING IN THE NOW (THE OVERLAPPING PART OF THE ILLUSTRATION) GIVES YOU THE OPTION TO JUST BE PRESENT TO WHAT IS. THE FLOWERS SYMBOLIZE GROWTH, GROWTH OF THE SOUL, SPIRIT, EMOTIONS.

Gayle Kabaker

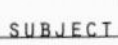

SUBJECT
SPA

MEDIUM
ACRYLA GOUACHE ON PAPER

BACKGROUND
WHAT YOU DON'T SEE BEHIND THE SCENES HERE IS THE INCREDIBLE FOOD, THE SOFT COMFORTABLE BEDS THAT YOU CAN STAY IN ALL DAY AND READ IF YOU WANT, THE INCREDIBLE 2 HOUR MASSAGES DONE BY 2 PEOPLE AT ONCE WITH THEIR HANDS DRIPPING WITH OIL THAT IS SCENTED WITH ALL KINDS OF AROMATIC HERBS, THE EARLY MORNING HIKES THROUGH THE WOODS, THE LONG SWIMS IN THE RIVER OR SOAKING IN BEAUTIFUL NATURAL POOLS OF HOT, STEAMING WATER. SOUNDS GOOD, HUH?

SUBJECT
MASSAGE

MEDIUM
ACRYLA GOUACHE ON PAPER

BACKGROUND
WHEN A WOMAN TAKES CARE OF HERSELF—TAKES TIME OUT OF HER BUSY LIFE FOR HERSELF—SHE FEELS GOOD, SHE'S NICER, EASIER TO GET ALONG WITH, HAS MORE PATIENCE WITH THE CHILDREN, AND SHE HAS MORE ENERGY. IN THE LONG RUN IT BENEFITS MORE THAN JUST HER.

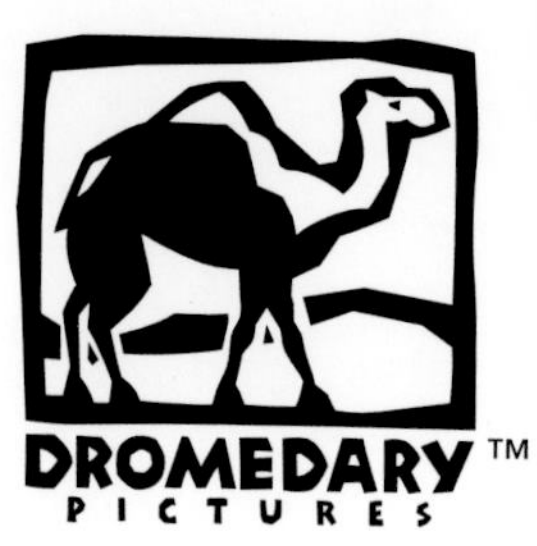

NANCY DONIGER ▪ 718.399.8666 ▪ email: doniger@earthlink.net ▪ www.shadow.net/~jerryd

Beata Szpura

(718)424-8440

barbara Samanich

studio 602·966·3070 fax 602·966·6082

East and Midwest: Vargo Bockos Phone 312.661.1717 Fax 312.661.0043
West and Southwest: Marla Matson Phone 602.252.5072 Fax 602.252.5073

JEAN HOLMGREN

ILLUSTRATOR
phone. 901.527.3396
fax. 901.527.3404

REPRESENTED BY
The Pred Group
phone. 913. 438. 7733
fax. 913. 438. 7734
WWW. PREDGROUP. COM

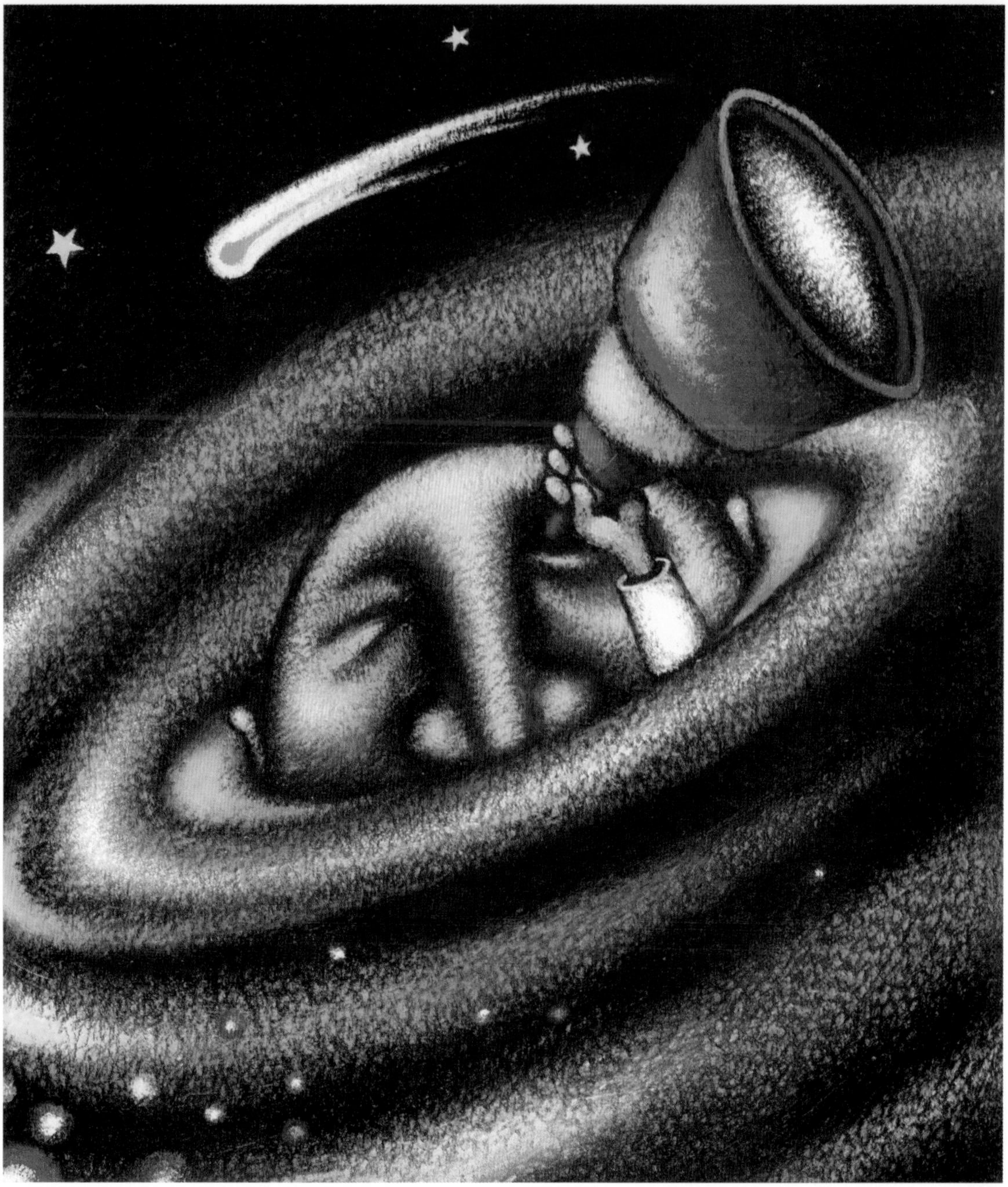

Angela Moore 212.690.7011 tel + fax
The Pred Group 913.438.7733 www.predgroup.com

CALL: 816-561-8045 **JIM PAILLOT** **FAX: 816-561-6201**

e-mail: paillot@gvi.net
web: www.jimpaillot.com

REPRESENTED IN THE MIDWEST BY THE PRED GROUP 913-438-7733 WEB: www.predgroup.com

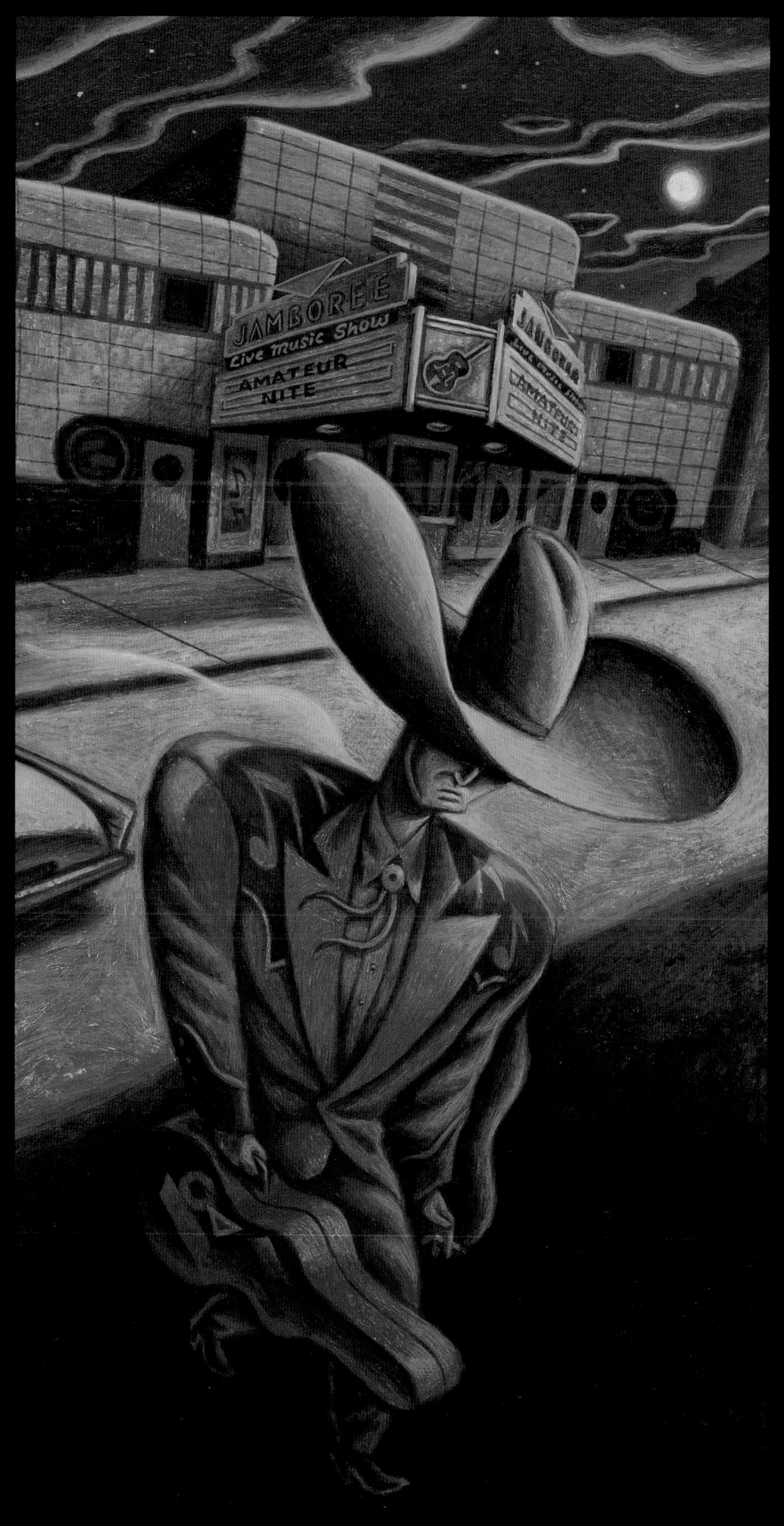
JAMBOREE
Live Music Show
AMATEUR
NITE

JUGULAR

HEMOGLOBIN

PHARYNX

STERNUM

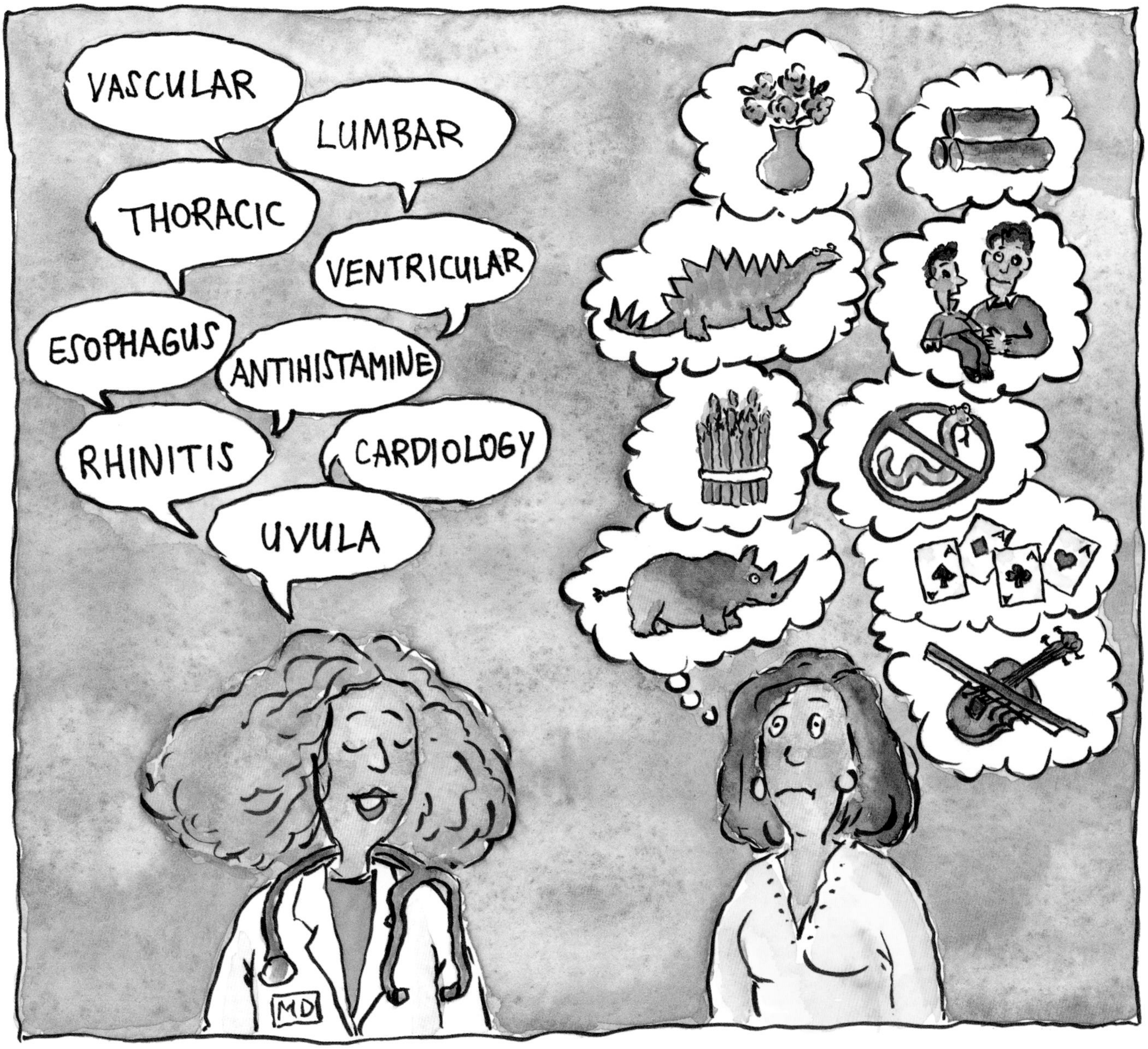

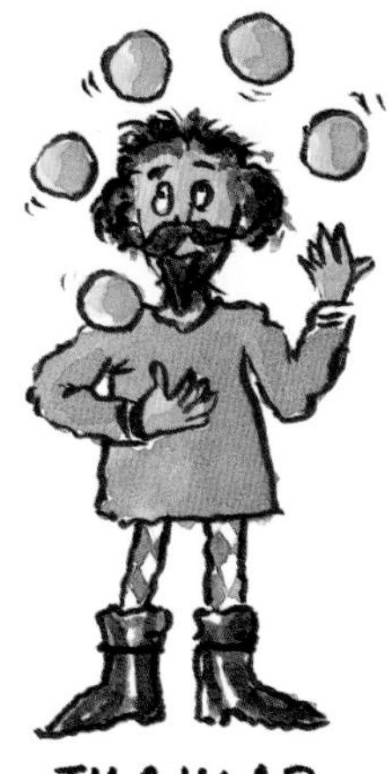

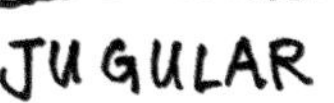

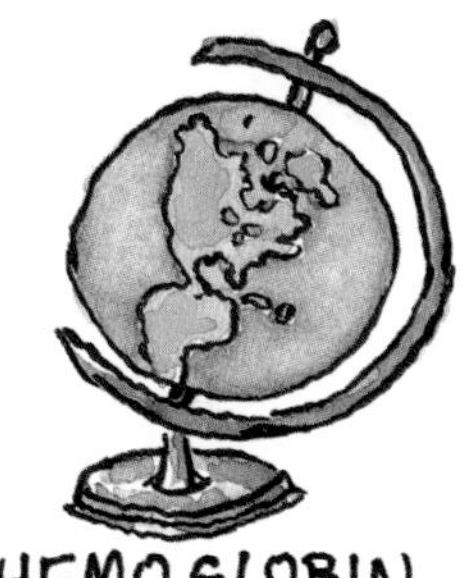

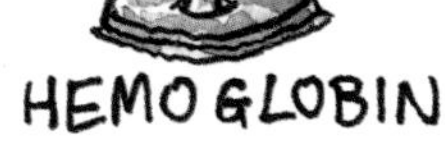

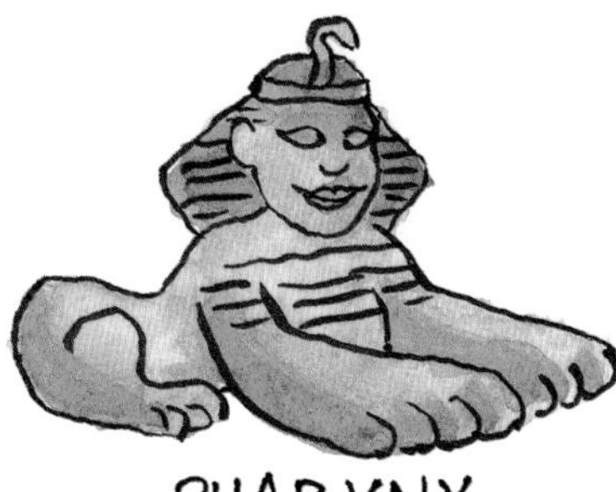

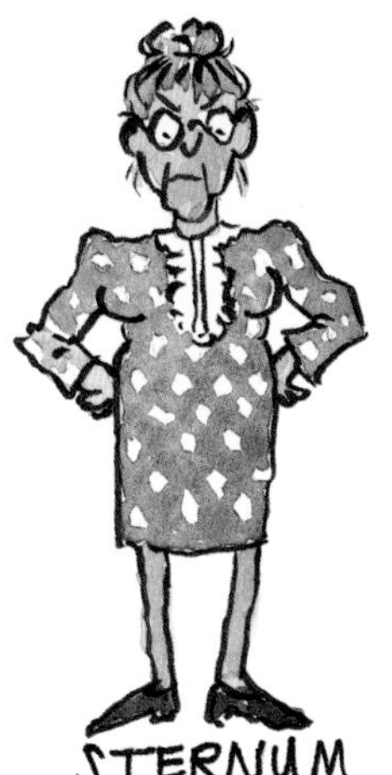

HEDY KLEIN

ILLUSTRATION FOR WHAT AILS YOU

718-793-0246

THE BRITISH ISLES

NORTH SEA

ATLANTIC OCEAN

MK

Map Illustrations 651.698.6960 Fax.651.698.7144 maphero@aol.com

MATT KANIA

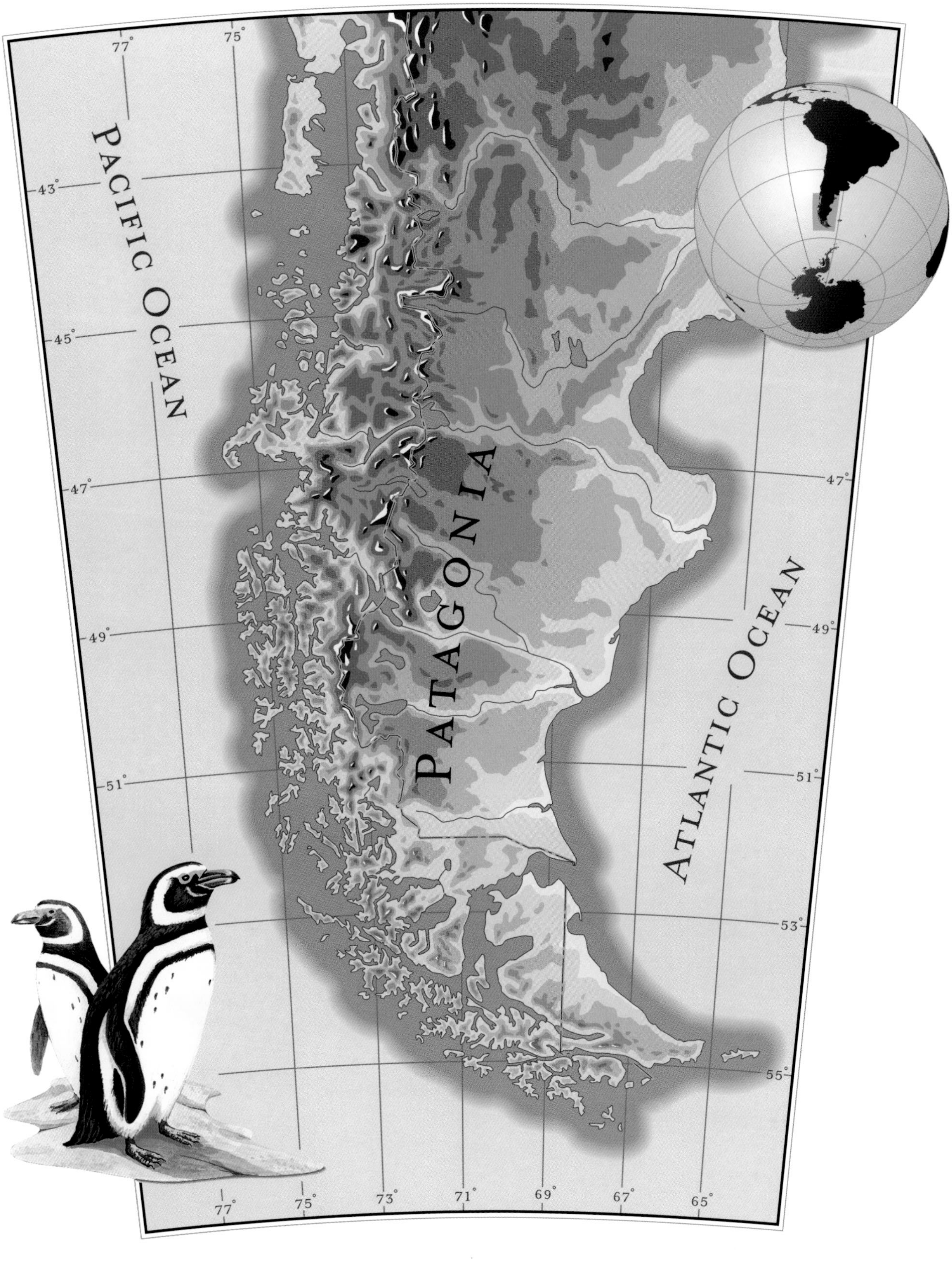

PACIFIC OCEAN

PATAGONIA

ATLANTIC OCEAN

77° 75° 73° 71° 69° 67° 65°

43° 45° 47° 49° 51° 53° 55°

Map Illustrations **651.698.6960** Fax.651.698.7144 maphero@aol.com

ROBIN MORO

REPRESENTED BY:
LAURIE LAMBERT AND ASSOCIATES
2870 ROMANA COURT
CINCINNATI, OH 45209
513-841-0073
513-841-0017 FAX

Amanda Haley
Teen angels...
groovy...
girl power!
Soda
What's going on here...
represented by
Laurie Lambert
(513) 841-0073 FAX (513) 841-0017

ANIMATION
ILLUSTRATION
STEPHEN FOSTER, INC.
894 GROVE STREET
GLENCOE, ILLINOIS 60022
800-944-1109 rep
847-835-2741 studio
847-835-2783 fax
www.do-dah.com

mark tellok

represented by ***Anna Goodson*** *- phone : 514.983.9020 - fax : 514.482.0686*

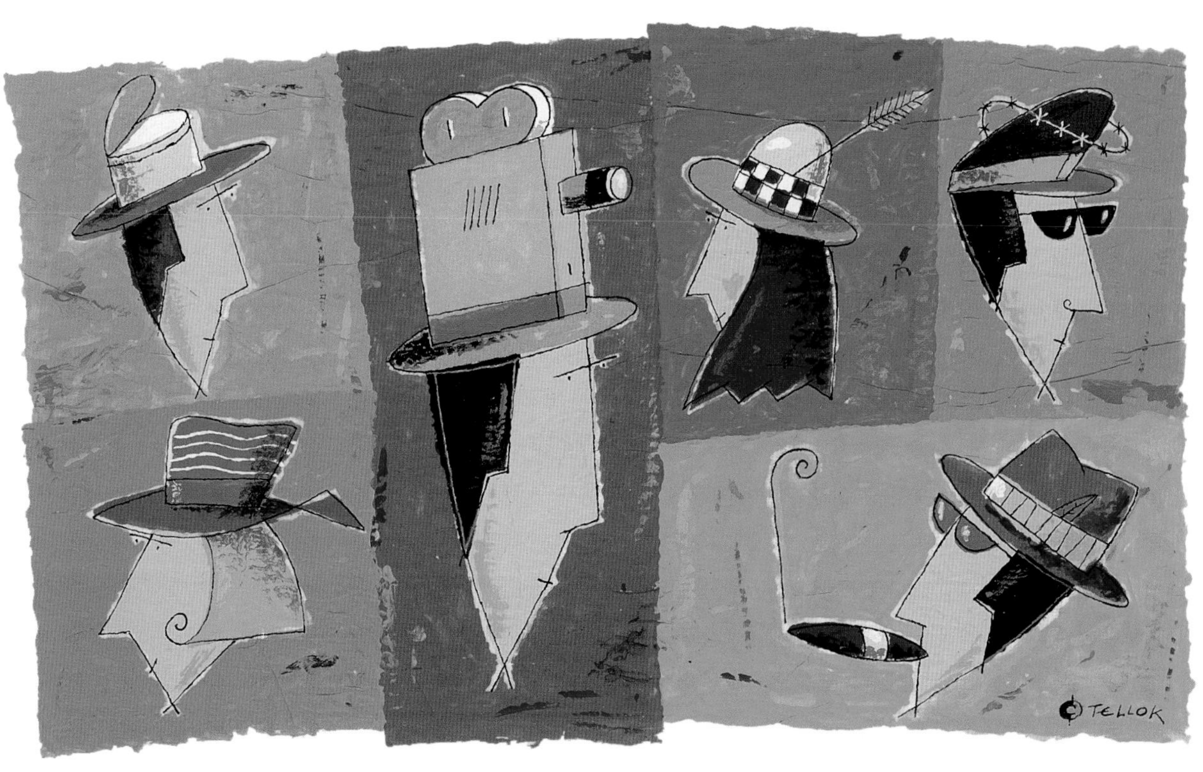

John Etheridge  Illustration

Tel 905 828 2879 • Fax 905 828 0283

FITZGERALD

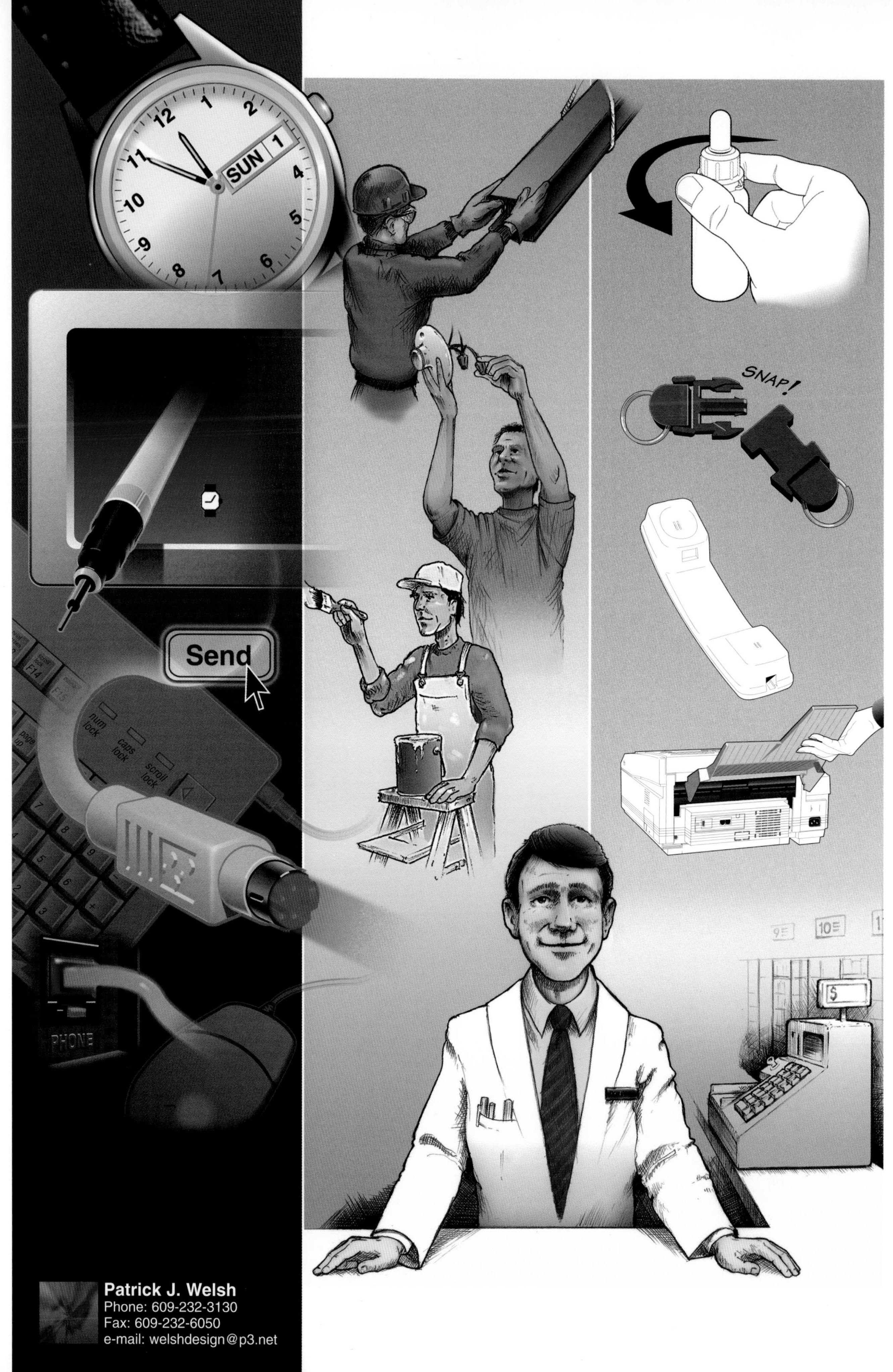

Patrick J. Welsh
Phone: 609-232-3130
Fax: 609-232-6050
e-mail: welshdesign@p3.net

jackie urbanovic

420 n. 5Th st,suite 950, Mpls., Mn 55401
ph612-673-9323 fax612-333-4823

www.stockillustrated.com

lindgren & smith

www.lindgrensmith.com

regan dunnick

joseph daniel fiedler

douglas fraser

joe & kathy heiner

jennifer herbert

miles hyman

jeff jackson

kim johnson

susan leopold

lori lohstoeter

bill mayer

jonny mendelsson

vince mcindoe

yan nascimbene

christopher o'leary

212.397.7330

pat lindgren

piper smith

tricia weber

www.stockillustrated.com

lindgren & smith

www.lindgrensmith.com

bruno paciulli

michael paraskevas

rick peterson

charles pyle

tim raglin

steven salerno

marti shohet

valerie sokolova

robert gantt steele

j.w. stewart

bethann thornburgh

pol turgeon

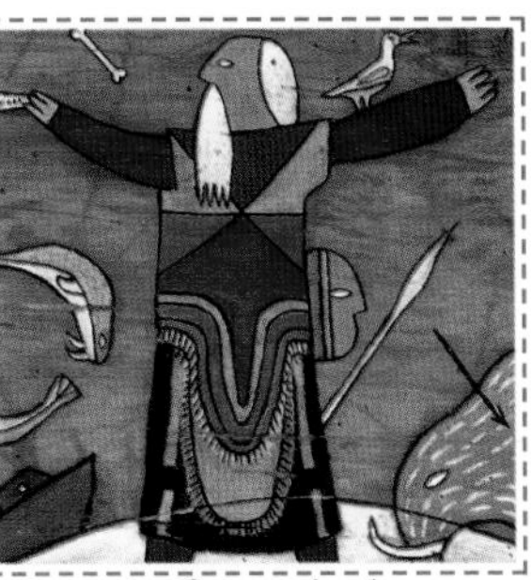

stefano vitale

jean wisenbaugh

brian zick

212.397.7330

pat lindgren

piper smith

tricia weber

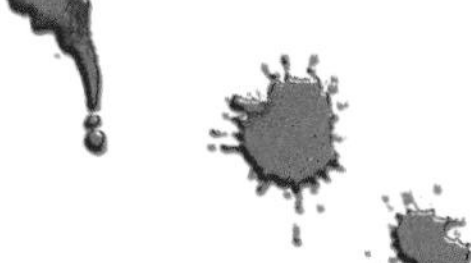

doug fraser

lindgren & smith

212.397.7330 ››› patricia lindgren / piper smith / tricia weber
www.lindgrensmith.com / outside the northeast jan collier 415.383.9026

doug fraser

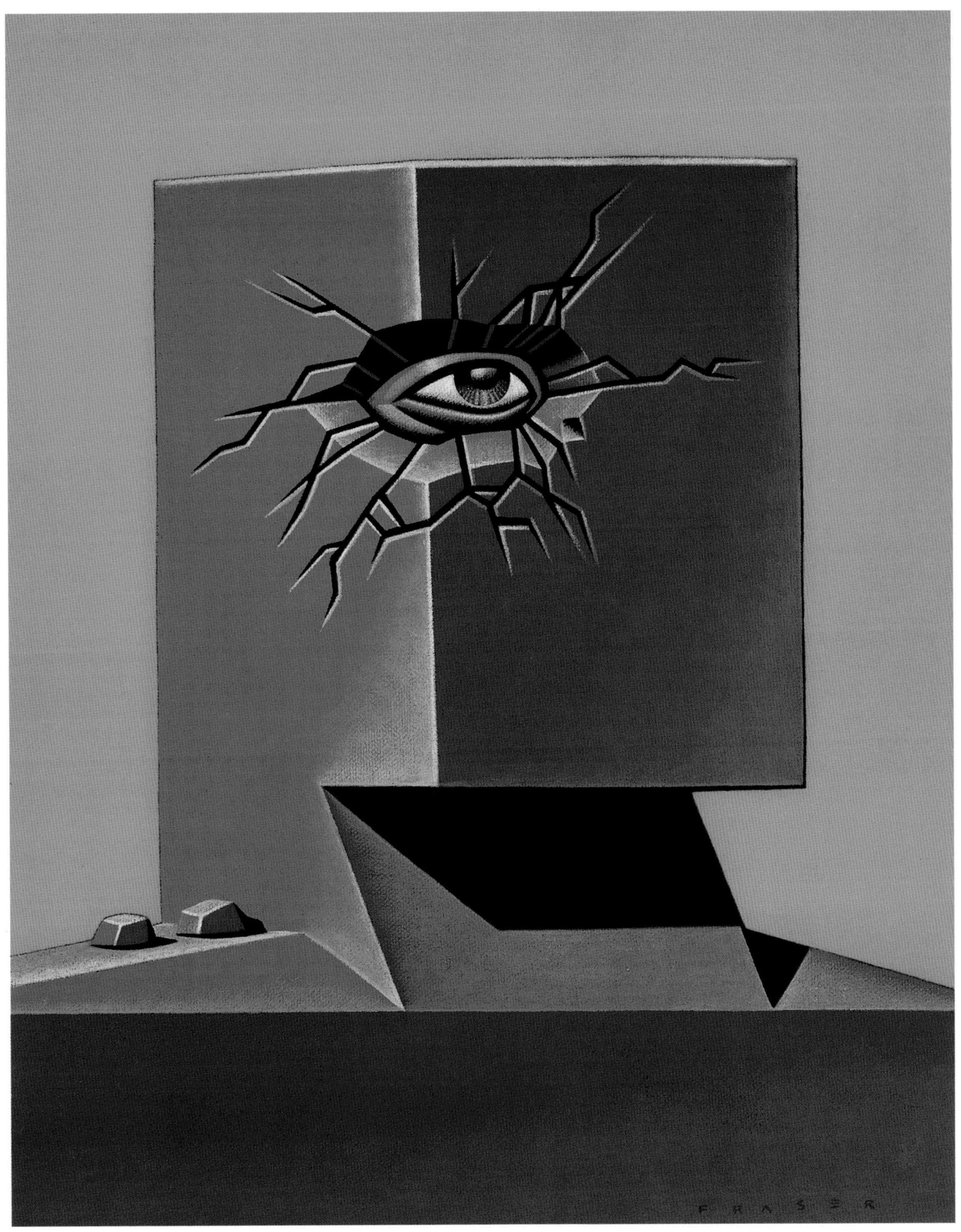

chuck pyle

lindgren & smith

representatives ››› patricia lindgren / piper smith / tricia weber
new york 212.397.7330 / www.lindgrensmith.com / san francisco 415.788.8552

vince mcindoe
GLEN ELLEN
lindgren & smith

lori lohstoeter

lindgren & smith

representatives ››› patricia lindgren / piper smith / tricia weber
new york 212.397.7330 / www.lindgrensmith.com / san francisco 415.788.8552

lindgren & smith

representatives ››› patricia lindgren / piper smith / tricia weber
new york 212.397.7330 / www.lindgrensmith.com / san francisco 415.788.8552

stefano vitale

susan leopold

kim johnson

miles hyman

pol turgeon

chris o'leary

j.w. stewart

lindgren & smith

representatives ››› patricia lindgren / piper smith / tricia weber
new york 212.397.7330 / www.lindgrensmith.com / san francisco 415.788.8552

rick peterson

bruno paciulli

marti shohet

lindgren & smith

representatives ››› patricia lindgren / piper smith / tricia weber
new york 212.397.7330 / www.lindgrensmith.com / san francisco 415.788.8552

mickey paraskevas

robert gantt steele

jennifer herbert

lindgren & smith

representatives ››› patricia lindgren / piper smith / tricia weber
new york 212.397.7330 / www.lindgrensmith.com / san francisco 415.788.8552

francis livingston

Thank you... Please come again...... Who's Next...Thank You...
Dressing Room
HAT SALE
RONDA
PAT. PEND.
1 2 3 4
5 6 7 8 9
Charge
Cash
thornburgh

BT.

RETURNS
Thornburgh

GREAT TO SEE YOU... UH...SU... UH, JA...UH.. MA... HA, HA... UHHHH...

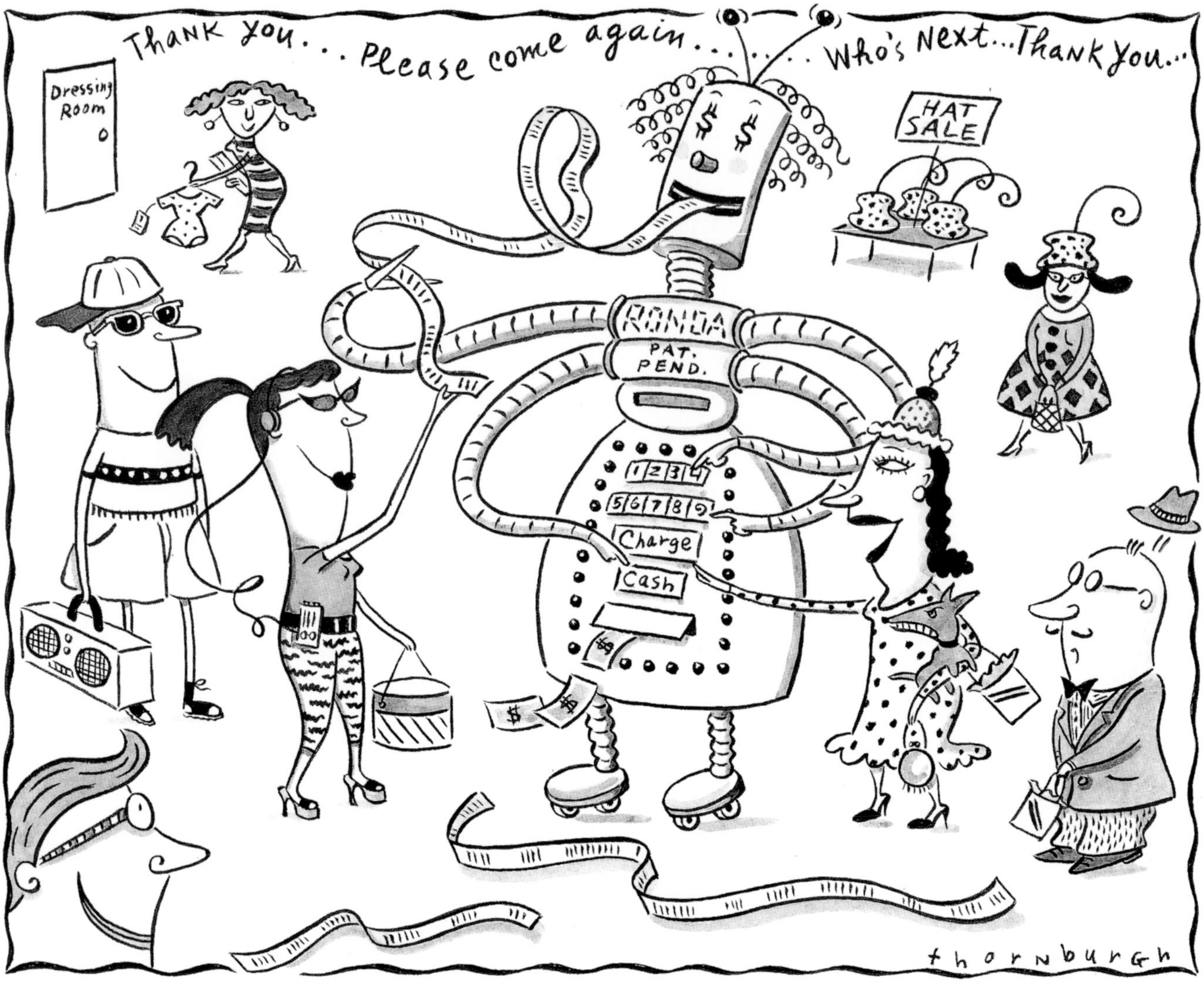

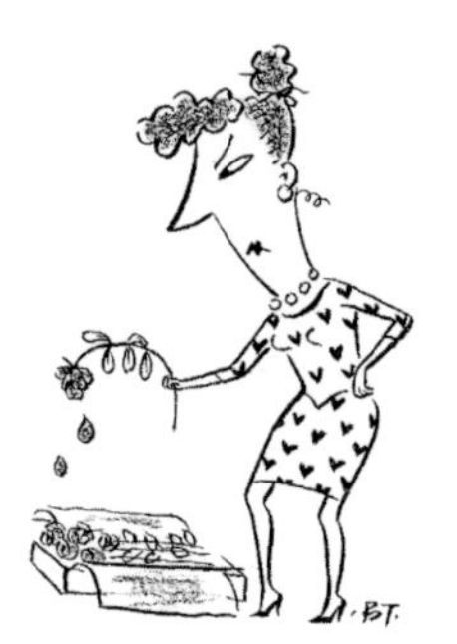

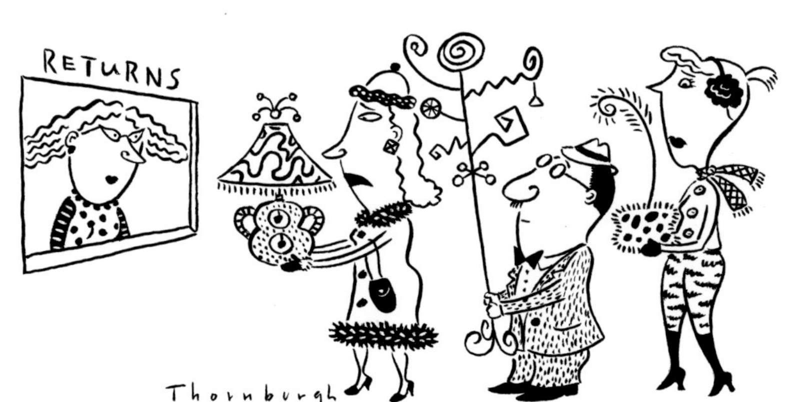

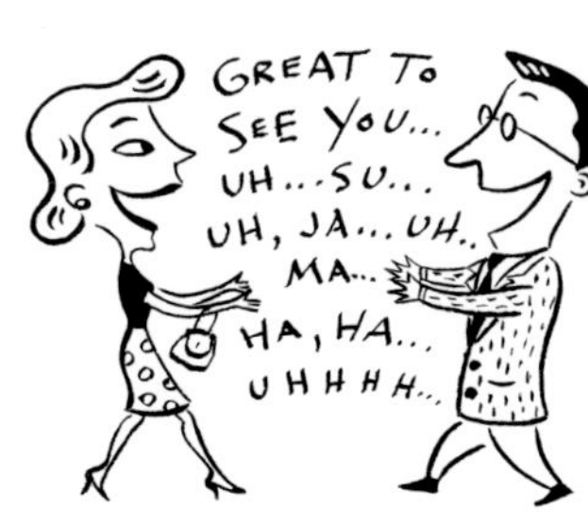

robert wagt

jeff jackson

lindgren & smith

representatives ››› patricia lindgren / piper smith / tricia weber
new york 212.397.7330 / www.lindgrensmith.com / san francisco 415.788.8552

valerie sokolova

lindgren & smith

representatives >>> patricia lindgren / piper smith / tricia weber
new york 212.397.7330 / www.lindgrensmith.com / san francisco 415.788.8552

SHAKESPEARE
SHAKESPEARE
AGATHA CHRISTIE
N or M?
AGATHA CHRISTIE
Fontana Books 2/6
Mills & Boon
ROMANCE
Intangible Dream
PATRICIA WILSON
Bridget Jones's diary
Helen Fielding

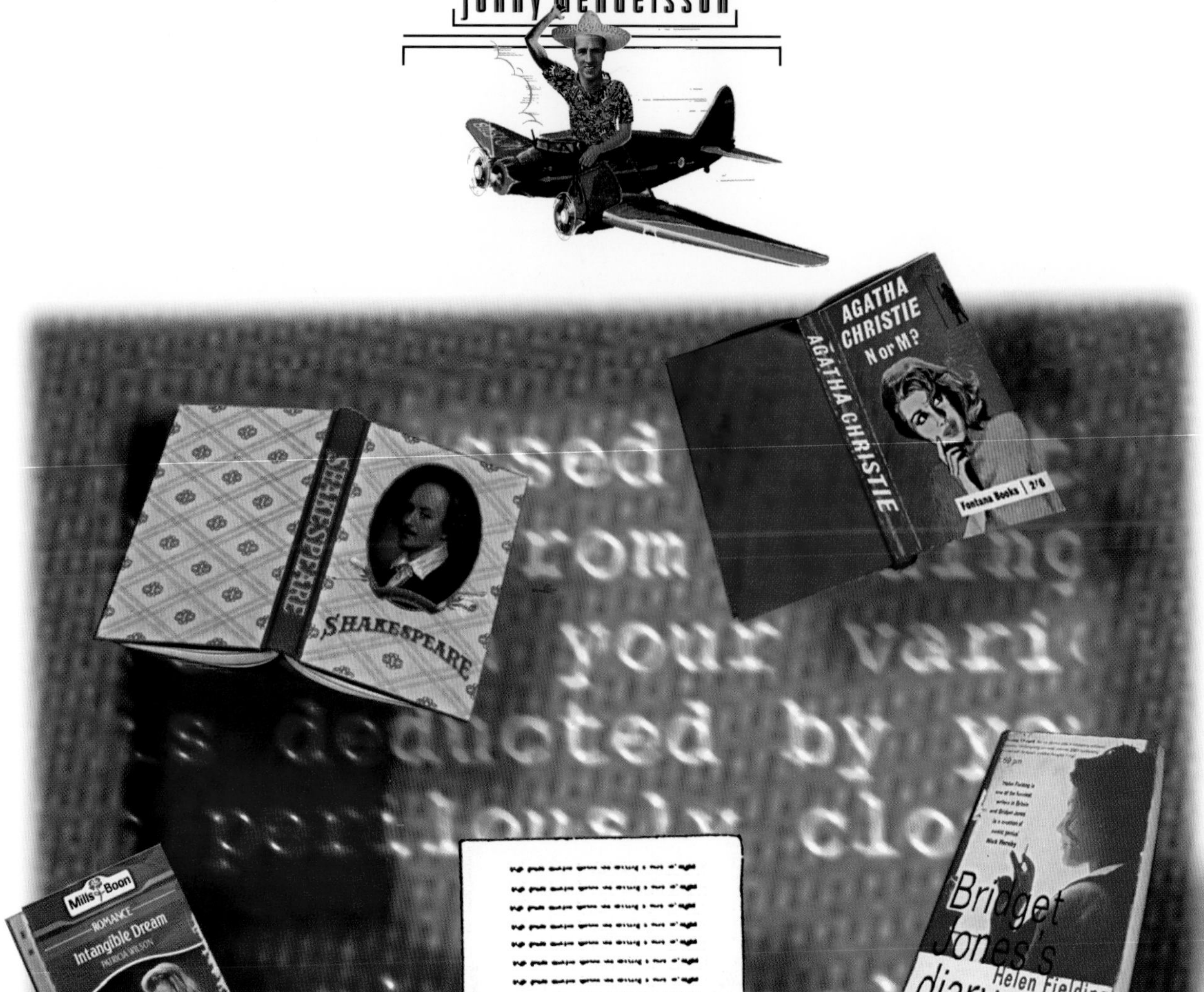

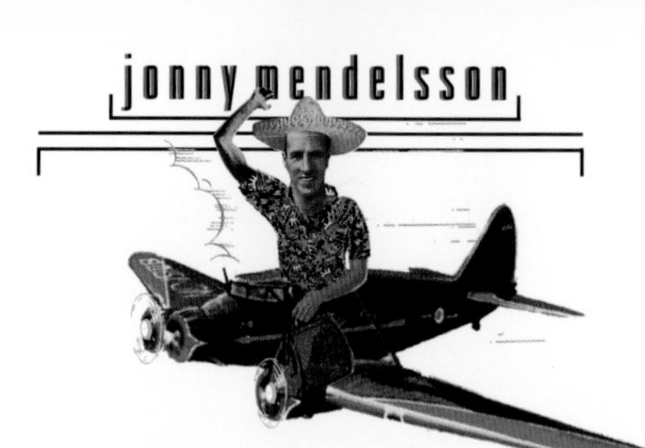

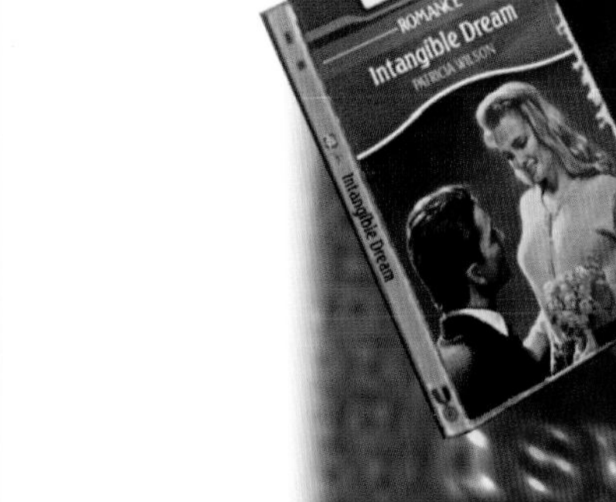

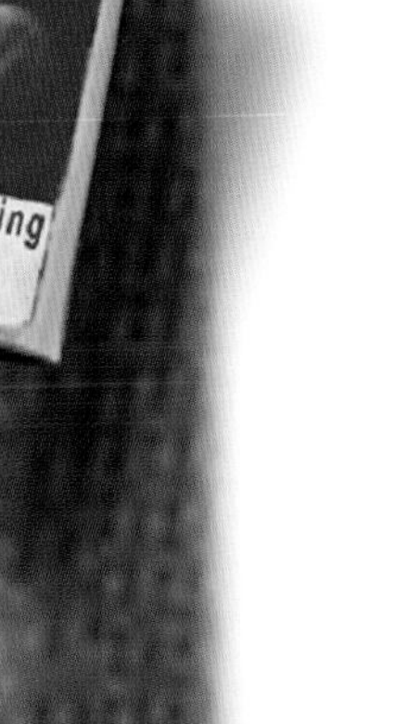

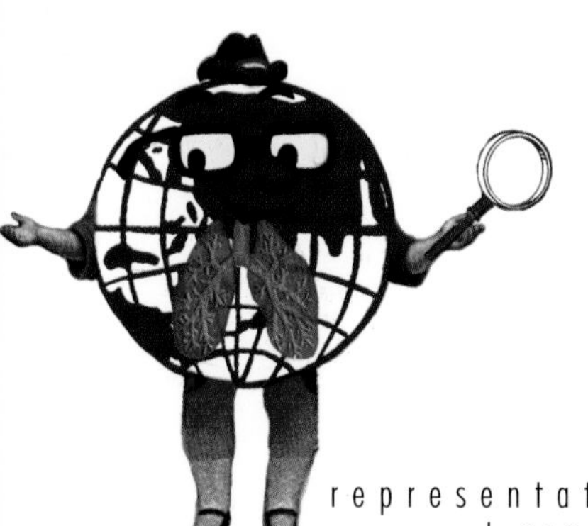

yan nascimbene

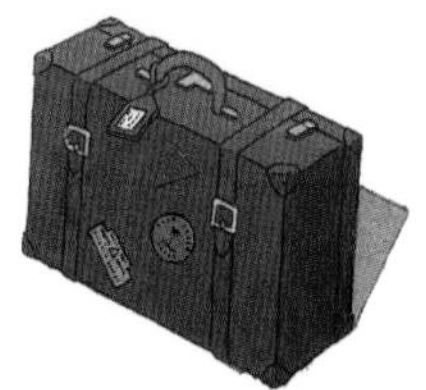

lindgren & smith

representatives ››› patricia lindgren / piper smith / tricia weber
new york 212.397.7330 / www.lindgrensmith.com / san francisco 415.788.8552

joe & kathy heiner

lindgren & smith

212.397.7330 ››› patricia lindgren / piper smith / tricia weber / www.lindgrensmith.com
in los angeles martha productions 310.390.8663 / in chicago joel harlib assoc. 312.573.1370

putien richard
516 marine view avenue
belmont, ca 94002
fon/fax 650.591.2341
email putien@pacbell.net

Paul-Emile Fequiere
407-772-0081
Pager: 407-623-6512

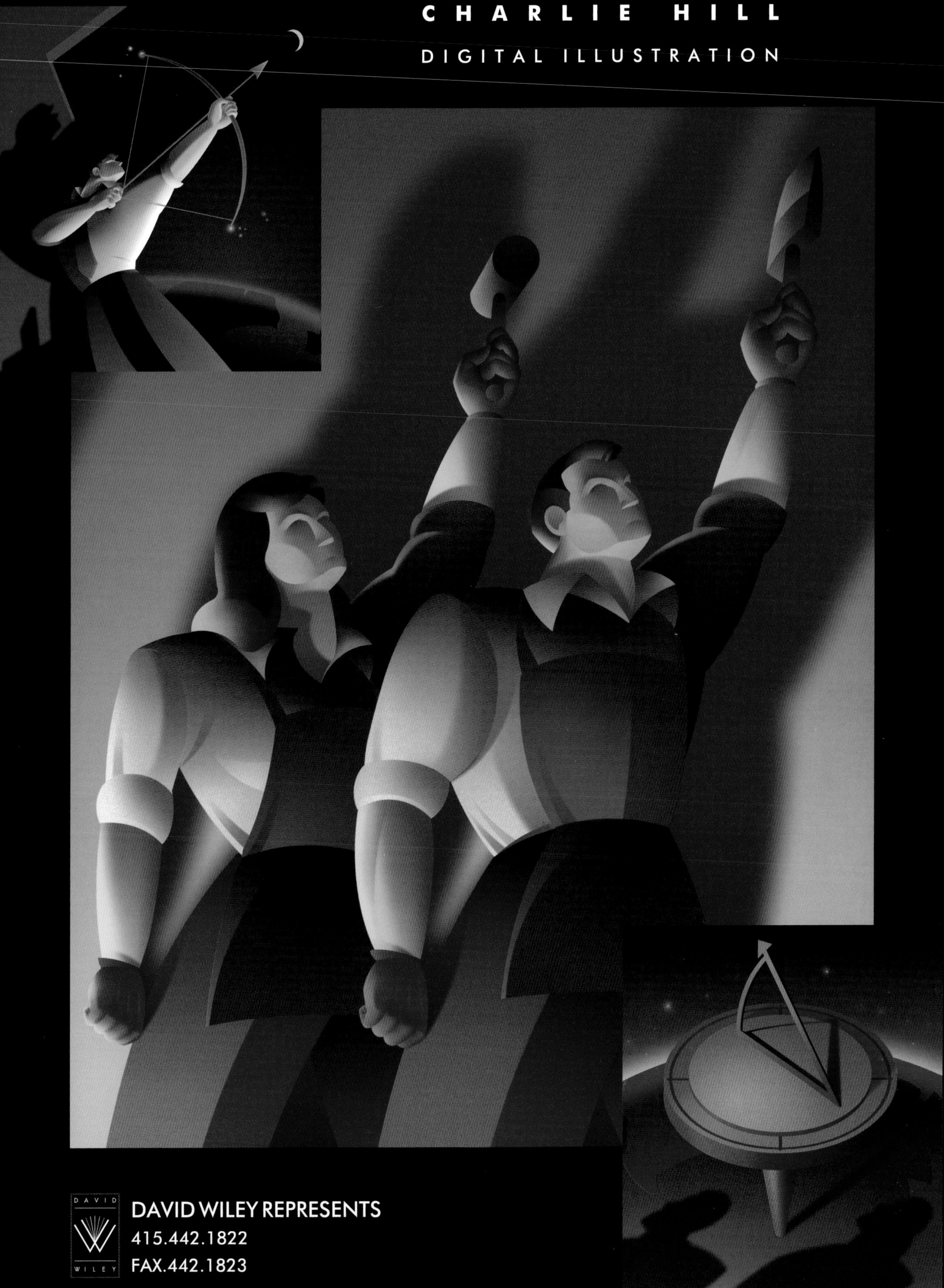
CHARLIE HILL
DIGITAL ILLUSTRATION
DAVID WILEY
DAVID WILEY REPRESENTS
415.442.1822
FAX.442.1823

RAT UNDER PAPER

❶❷❸ & ❹ **PUBLICATION:** SLATE, **CREATIVE DIRECTION:** KATHLEEN KINCAID. ❺ **PUBLICATION:** TV GUIDE, **CREATIVE DIRECTION:** KEN FEISEL. ❻ **PUBLICATION:** FORBES FYI, **CREATIVE DIRECTION:** PENNY BLATT/HELLO STUDIO. DON'T WALK AWAY, RENÉE.

AMANDA DUFFY 135 PRESLEY AVENUE TORONTO CANADA M1L 3P9 (416) 755-4447

KEN TOYAMA

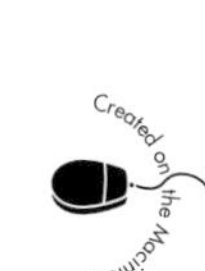

DAVID WILEY REPRESENTS

TEL 415 442-1822 FAX 415 442-1823

registration
website icons - series

group online - internet

seminars & events - info

e-mail contacts

stock image

Matt Foster

Studio: 602.595.7950 fax: 595.7955 email: artgun@aol.com

stock image

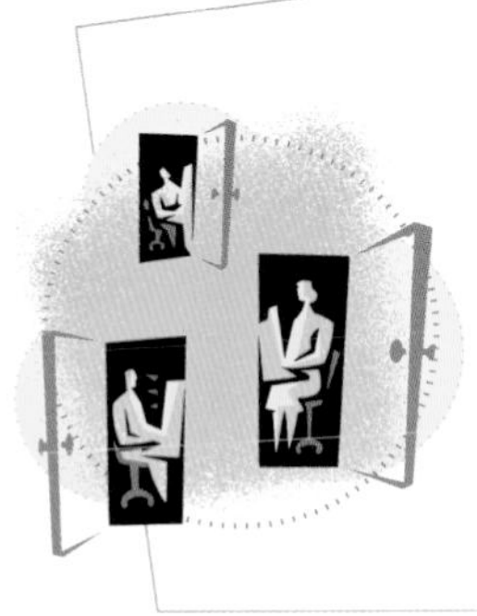

virtual networks

information week – series

fibre channels

extended ERP

3rd-party outsourcing

Matt Foster

email: artgun@aol.com 602.595.7950 fax: 595.7955

KRIS WILTSE

RAUL COLON

NICHOLAS GAETANO

DAHL TAYLOR

STEAM

JOYCE PATTI

JOANIE SCHWARZ

KAREN BLESSEN

DAVE CALVER

TOM CHRISTOPHER

NANETTE BIERS

WILLIAM LOW

ELIZABETH ROSEN

ROBERT SAUBER

WENDY WRAY

BEPPE GIACOBBE

THE ART OF COMMUNICATION

LISA MANNING
978 927 9990

REPRESENTED IN NEW ENGLAND BY  LEIGHTON & COMPANY 978 921 0887

http://www.leightonreps.com

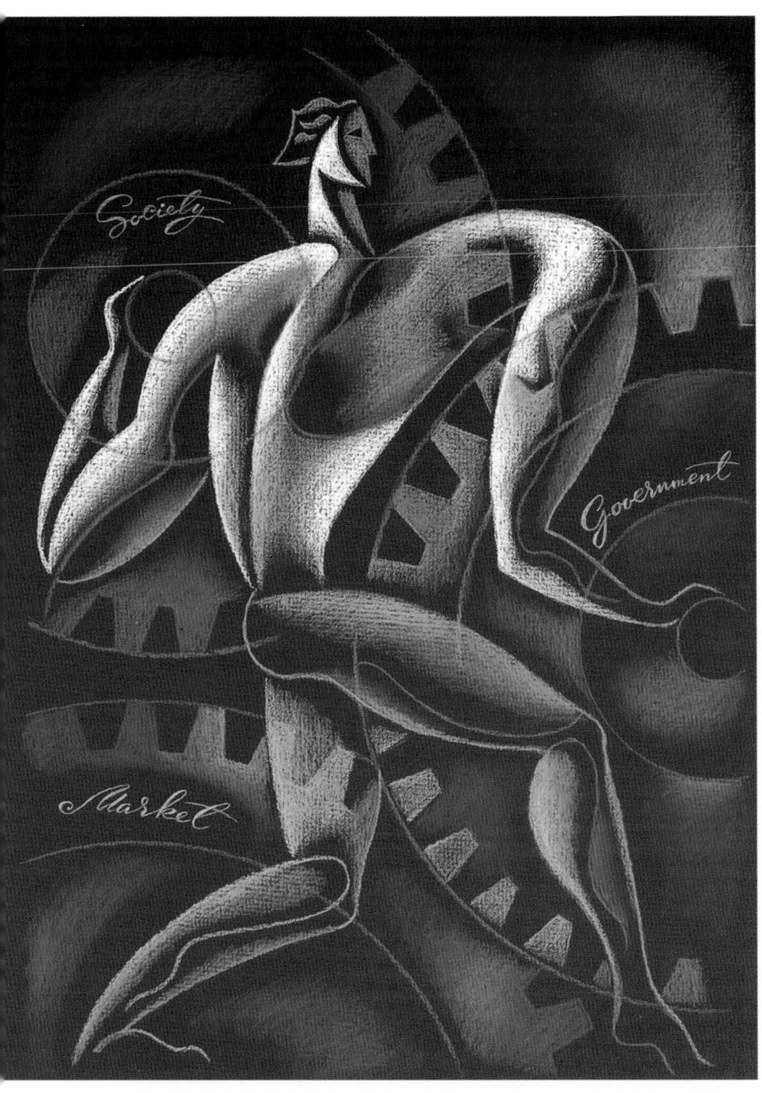

Leon Zernitsky

Tel: (416) 638-9271
Fax: (416) 638-9271

FREDERIQUE BERTRAND

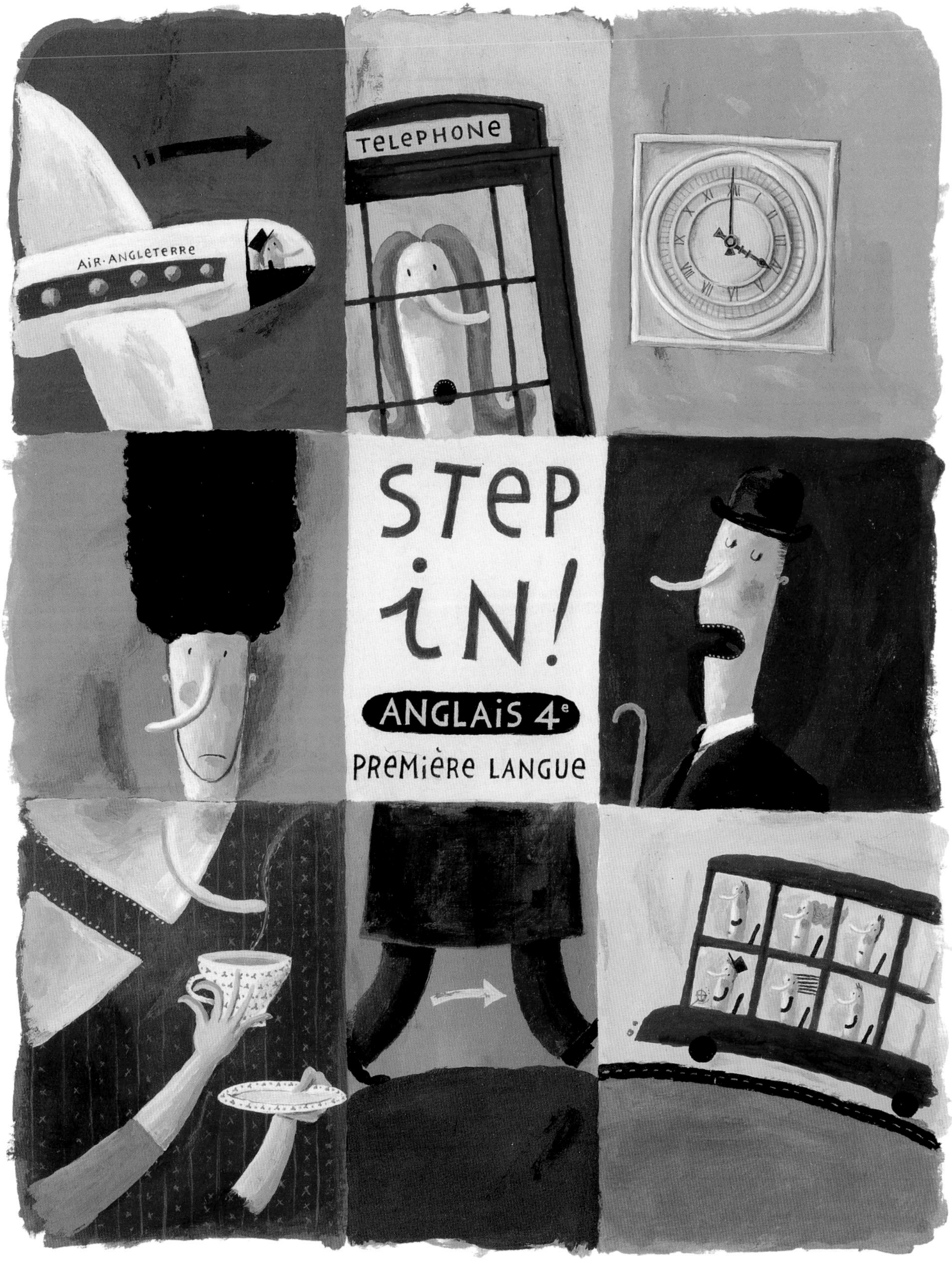

TELEPHONE

AIR·ANGLETERRE

STEP IN!

ANGLAIS 4^e

PREMIÈRE LANGUE

REPRESENTED  WANDA NOWAK 

PHONE 212·535·0438 FAX 212·535·1624

doug ross

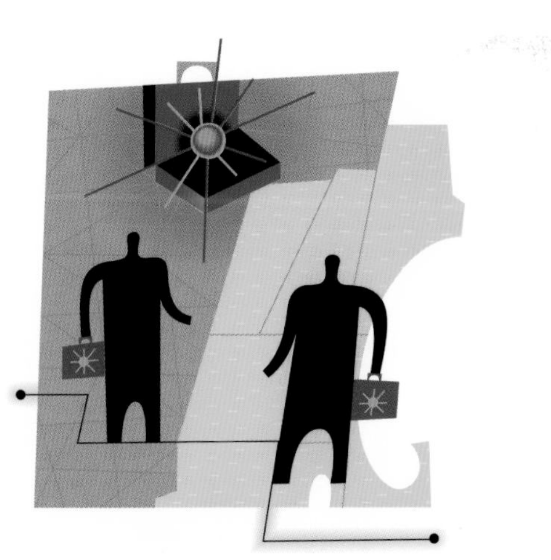

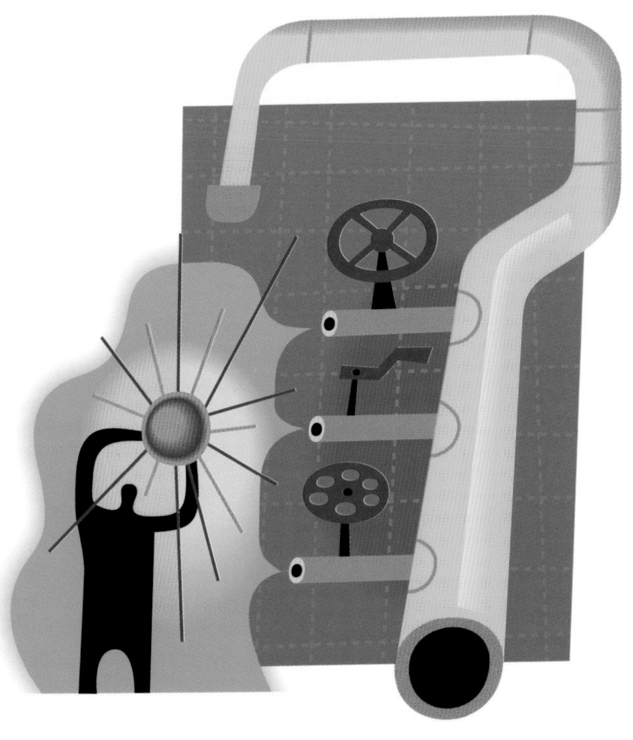

Lori Nowicki & Associates
212 243 5888
web: www.lorinowicki.com
:email lori@lorinowicki.com

joe veno

antonio

508) 872-8180

31 Magnolia Street
Framingham, MA 01701
Phone/Fax: (508) 872-8180

415/433-1222
FAX 415/433-9560
Sweet Represents
REPRESENTED BY RON SWEET

ANATOLY

MIKE BLATT

CHARLEY BROWN

DICK COLE

JONATHAN COMBS

ROBERT EVANS

RANDY GLASS

KENT LEECH

RACHAEL McCAMPBELL

DEREK MUELLER

WILL NELSON

JAMES NICHOLS

STEVEN NOBLE

TODD NORDLING

BRUCE WOLFE

RON SWEET 716 MONTGOMERY STREET SAN FRANCISCO CA 94111
Sweet Represents

TODD NORDLING

415/433-1222 FAX 415/433-9560

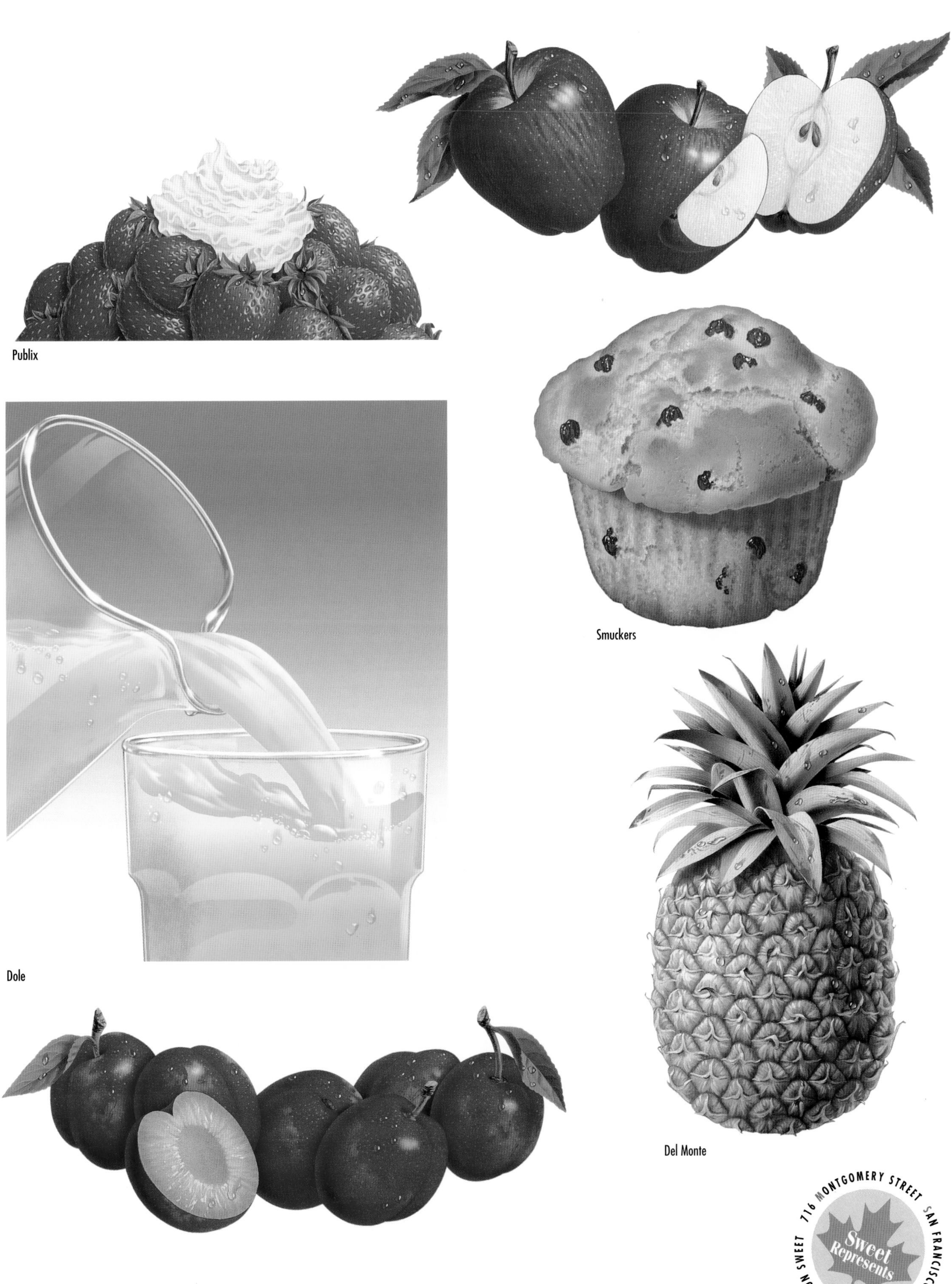

Publix

Smuckers

Dole

Del Monte

415/433-1222 FAX 415/433-9560

ROBERT EVANS

Sutter Home Winery

Annheiser-Busch

The Ironworker Annual Report

RON SWEET 716 MONTGOMERY STREET SAN FRANCISCO CA 94111

Sweet Represents

STEVEN NOBLE

415/433-1222 FAX 415/433-9560

S&W Tri Valley Growers

Coors Logo

Francisco Bread

John F. Kennedy: scratchboard

Cakebread Cellars

STEVEN NOBLE

415/433-1222 FAX 415/433-9560

Animatek, Computer Package

Time Life

State of Wyoming

Sun Brand

WILL NELSON

415/433-1222 FAX 415/433-9560

Road & Track

Kent Leech 925.254.5748

Textron Automotive

Represented by Ron Sweet 415/433-1222 Fax 415/433-9560
Sweet Represents

Michael Powditch 805.497.0069 Mendola Ltd. 212.986.5680 Joel Harlib 312.573.1370

James Nichols
Jain Painter Studios
Icons
Paintings
Digital
Traditional
Ron Sweet 716 Montgomery Street San Francisco CA 94111
Sweet Represents
James Nichols
RON: 415/433-1222 FAX 415/433-9560
STUDIO: 707/762-4455 FAX 707/762-6699 WWW.JNPAINTER.COM

Sweet Represents
RON SWEET 716 MONTGOMERY STREET SAN FRANCISCO CA 94111
JAMES NICHOLS
RON: 415/433-1222 FAX 415/433-9560
STUDIO: 707/762-4455 FAX 707/762-6699 WWW.JNPAINTER.COM

Tel:612-823-7630 Fax:612-824-8421 Web: www.tomlochray.com

GREGORY DYE ILLUSTRATION

Studio
303.933.0340
Fax
303.904.2909

Chicago
Tom Maloney
312.704.0500

James Swanson Tele. (708) 352 - 3081 Fax (708) 352 - 3082

James Swanson
tele.
(708) 352-3081
fax
(708) 352-3082

GREG HARGREAVES
MICHAEL FISHER
CAROL GUENZI AGENTS
PHONE: 303•820•2599 FAX: 303•820•2598
1•800•417•5120
SEE PORTFOLIOS AT WWW.ARTAGENT.COM
RYLE SMITH
TONITE! BIG MAC
YAY!
BRAVO!
MORE!
DON SULLIVAN

TOM WARD
MARC BROWN
CAROL GUENZI AGENTS
PHONE: 303•820•2599 FAX: 303•820•2598
1•800•417•5120
SEE PORTFOLIOS AT WWW.ARTAGENT.COM
DAN BULLEIT
JOE McDERMOTT

LORIO

LORI OSIECKI
123 WEST SECOND STREET
MESA ARIZONA 85201
PHONE & FAX 602-962-5233

Dan McGeehan

HUMOROUS ILLUMINOUS

Koralik Associates · 312/944-5680 PH · 312/421-5948 FX

Koralik

Koralik Associates
represents **DENNIS SODERSTROM**
Tel: 312-944-5680 Fax: 312-421-5948

© Walt Disney

© The Coca Cola Comp

© The Keebler Company

Koralik
represents ILENE ROBINETTE
Tel: 312-944-5680 Fax: 312-421-5948
© Ilene Robinette

BORIS ЛЮБНЕР
БОРИС LYUBNER

TEL: 435 649 2129

FAX: 435 649 8803

Armstrong Ind.

MacWorld Expo•98

Ernst & Young

VAR Business

Ernst & Young

BORIS ЛЮБНЕР
БОРИС LYUBNER

TEL: 435 649 2129

FAX: 435 649 8803

Training & Development

(212) 677-9100 / FAX: 353-0954

Carol Chislovsky Design Inc
853 Broadway New York, New York, 1000

CHISLOVSKY

SANDRA SHAP

CHRIS GALL

GIL ADAMS

Mick Rosolek
Illustration and Design

Represented by: Lexington Ashworth House 414.290.4313 www.lexash.com mick@lexash.com

JEANETTE ADAMS

Scott Peck

2701 THORNDALE CIRCLE

PLANO, TEXAS 75074

(972) 422-7438 ◀ PHONE

FOR MORE SAMPLES

SEE BLACK BOOK

ILLUSTRATION 1993-1998

all that glitters
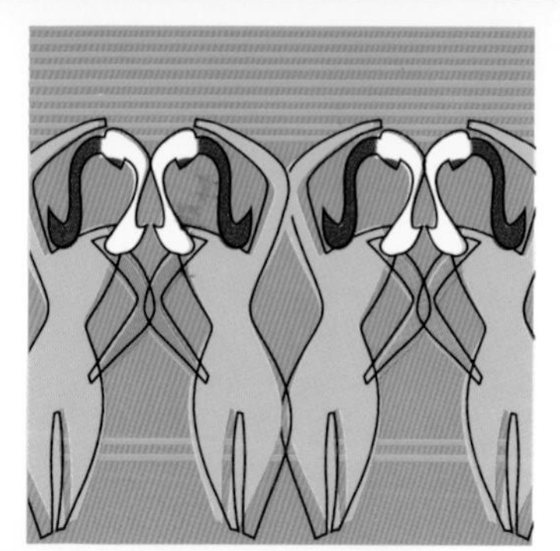

La Boheme

Don Sebesky
a tribute to
Bill Evans

HAIR
TODAY...
GONE
TOMORROW

SUNDAY
NITE
LINE
UP
NEXT
NICK at NITE
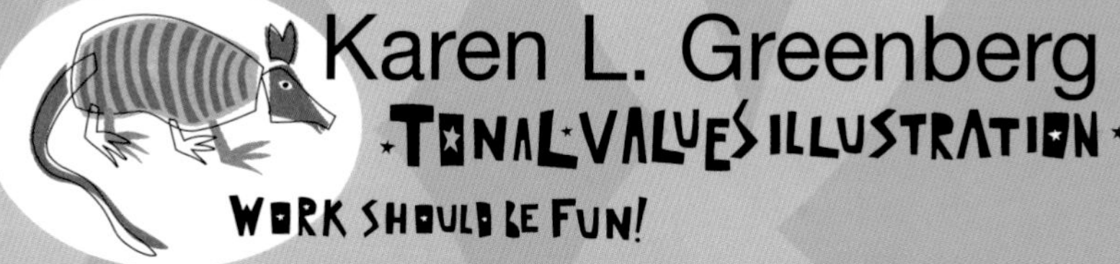
Karen L. Greenberg
TONAL VALUES ILLUSTRATION
WORK SHOULD BE FUN!

Jane Mjolsness

TONAL VALUES ILLUSTRATION

WORK SHOULD BE FUN!

Tel: 214.943.2569 Fax: 214.942.6771

E-Mail: tonalvalues@mindspring.com Toll free: 800.484.8592 code 2787

MARGERY MINTZ

Studio 617-332-8858

In Midwest Call:

Tom Maloney

312-704-0500 (phone)

312 704 0501 (fax)

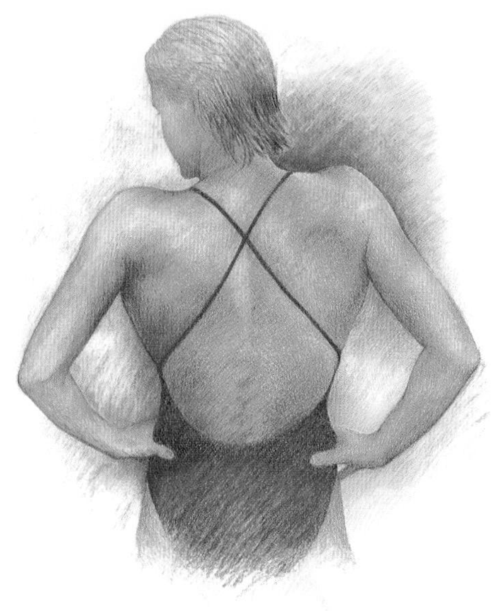

☎ 773-264-1152

FAX 773-264-0916

STUDIO 505-983-9706

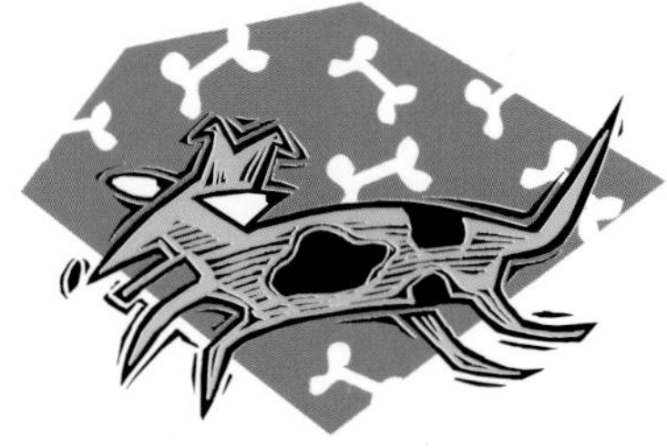

IN SAN FRANCISCO CALL JANE KLEIN 1-888-ART-1008

Longhorn
Angus
Hereford
A GREENHORN'S
LEXICON
OR, HOW TO TALK LIKE A COWBOY
YOUR PEERS:
PARD, DUDE, WRANGLER,
BUCKARETTE, HOMBRE
WHISTLE THESE TUNES:
Happy Trails, BUFFALO GALS,
BACK IN THE SADDLE AGAIN
YOUR HERD: CRITTERS,
BEEVES, DOGIES, STEERS
AVOID THESE: RATTLERS,
BADGER HOLES, mosquitoes
BLACK FLIES, RUSTLERS
YOUR HANGOUTS: CORRAL,
BUNKHOUSE, HOOSEGOW,
CHUCKWAGON, SALOON
BUFFALO BILL
OL' PAINT
ANNIE OAKLEY
CAROLYN FISHER
(800) 585-4096
IN SAN FRANCISCO
CALL JANE KLEIN
(888) ART-1008

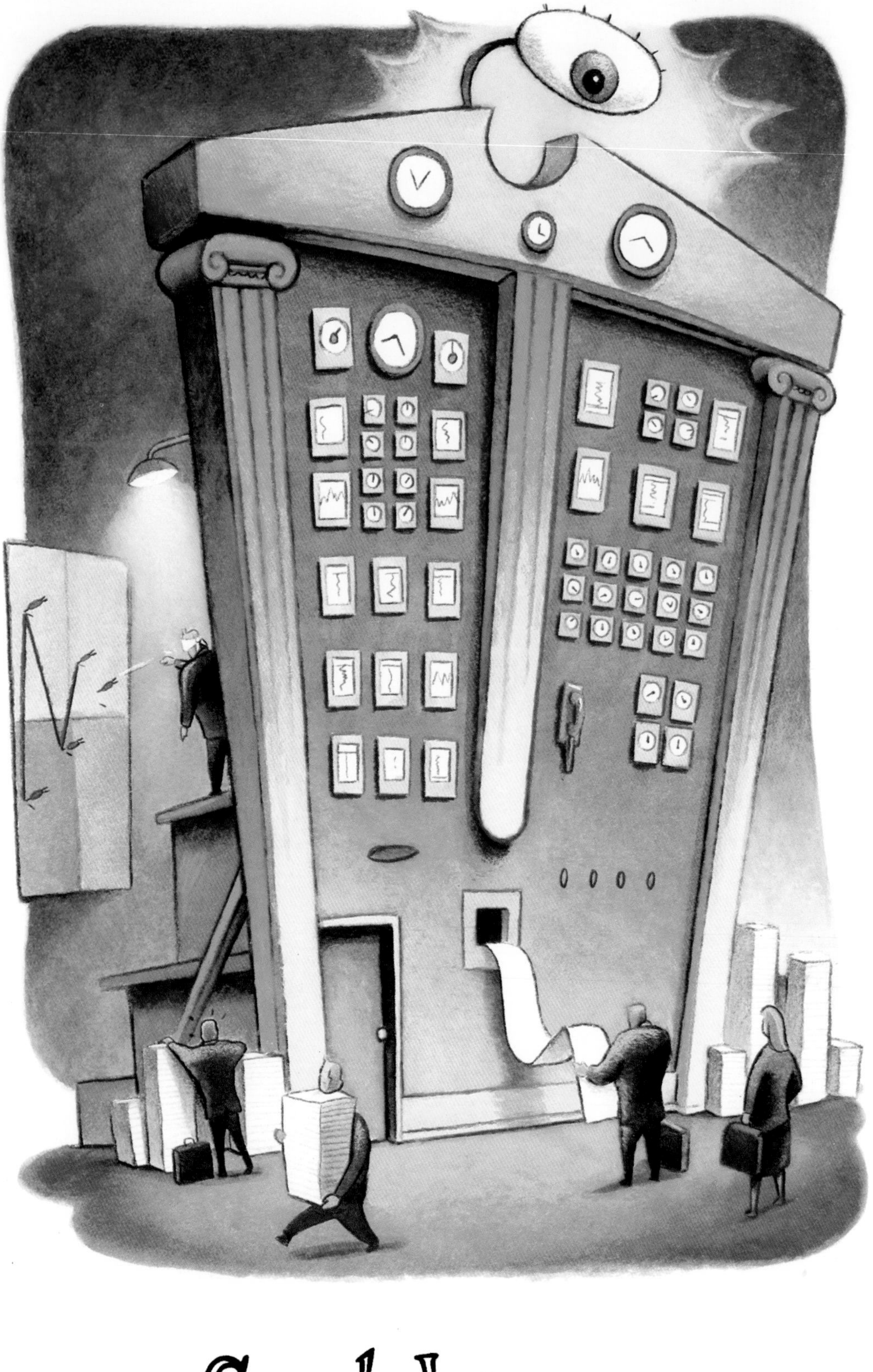

Carl Wiens

613.476.2500
http://home.ican.net/~wiens

PRINT & WEB ILLUSTRATION

American
Artists

American Artists

Looking for Stock Illustration?

We'll send you low-res files of your search results via e-mail!

Contact: (212) 682-2462 • Fax (212) 582-0090

www.amerartists.com • e-mail info@amerartists.com

Keith Batcheller
★
Don Bishop
★
Steve Celmer
★
John Churchman
★
Gary Ciccarelli
★
Andrew Condron
★
Bob Depew
★
Jim Effler
★
Jacques Fabre
★
Russell Farrell
★
Ian Flemming Associates
★
Kent Gamble
★
Bill Garland
★
Garth Glazier
★
Scott Grimando
★
Doug Henry
★
John Holm
★
Hom & Hom
★
Michael Jaroszko
★
Maurice Lewis
★
Jerry LoFaro
★
Alan Male
★
Shawn McKelvey
★
Jean-Claude Michel
★
Dave Miller
★
Shawn Murphy
★
Tony Randazzo
★
Bot Roda
★
Joe Scrofani
★
Jim Starr
★
Rod Vass
★
Rhonda Voo
★
Stan Watts
★
Jonathan Wright
★
Eddie Young

353 West 53rd St 1W
Tel: (212)682-2462
info@amerartists.com

New York, NY 10019
Fax: (212)582-0090
www.amerartists.com

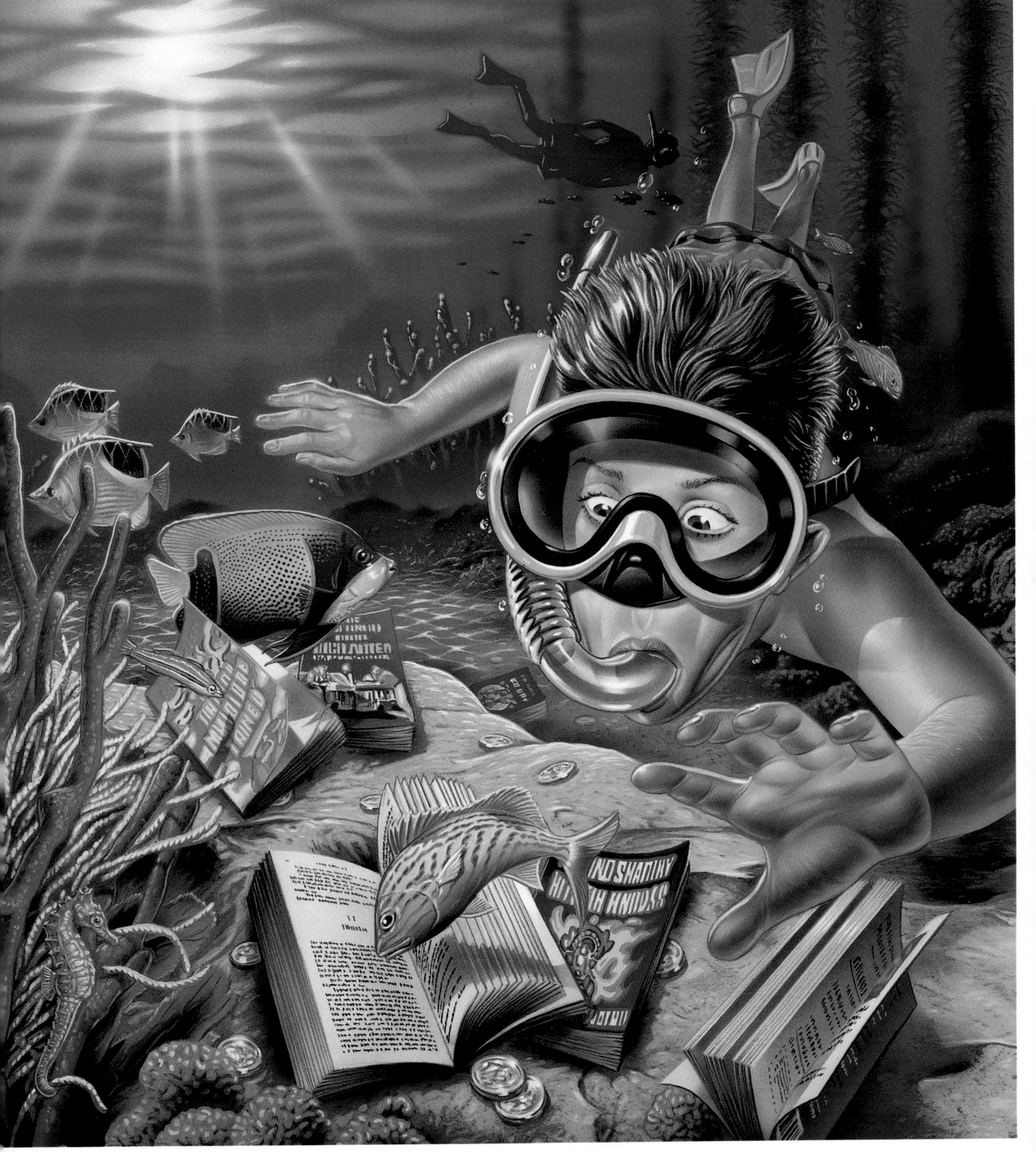

GARY CICCARELLI

353 West 53rd St 1W
Tel: (212)682-2462
info@amerartists.com

American Artists

New York, NY 10019
Fax: (212)582-0090
www.amerartists.com

National Geographic/Lewis Galoob Toys

JERRY LoFARO

353 West 53rd St 1W
Tel: (212)682-2462
info@amerartists.com

New York, NY 10019
Fax: (212)582-0090
www.amerartists.com

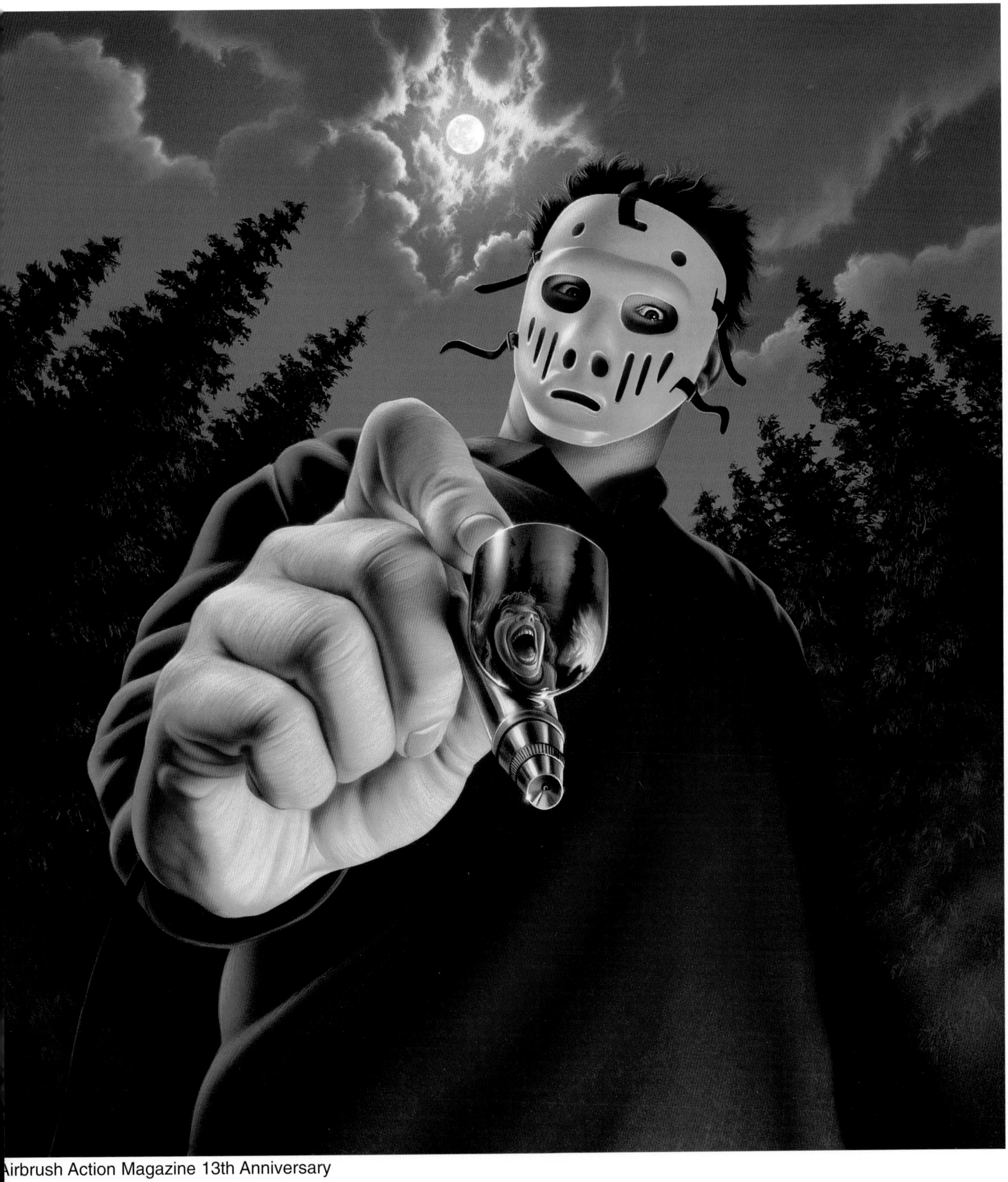

Airbrush Action Magazine 13th Anniversary

JERRY LoFARO

353 West 53rd St 1W
Tel: (212)682-2462
info@amerartists.com

New York, NY 10019
Fax: (212)582-0090
www.amerartists.com

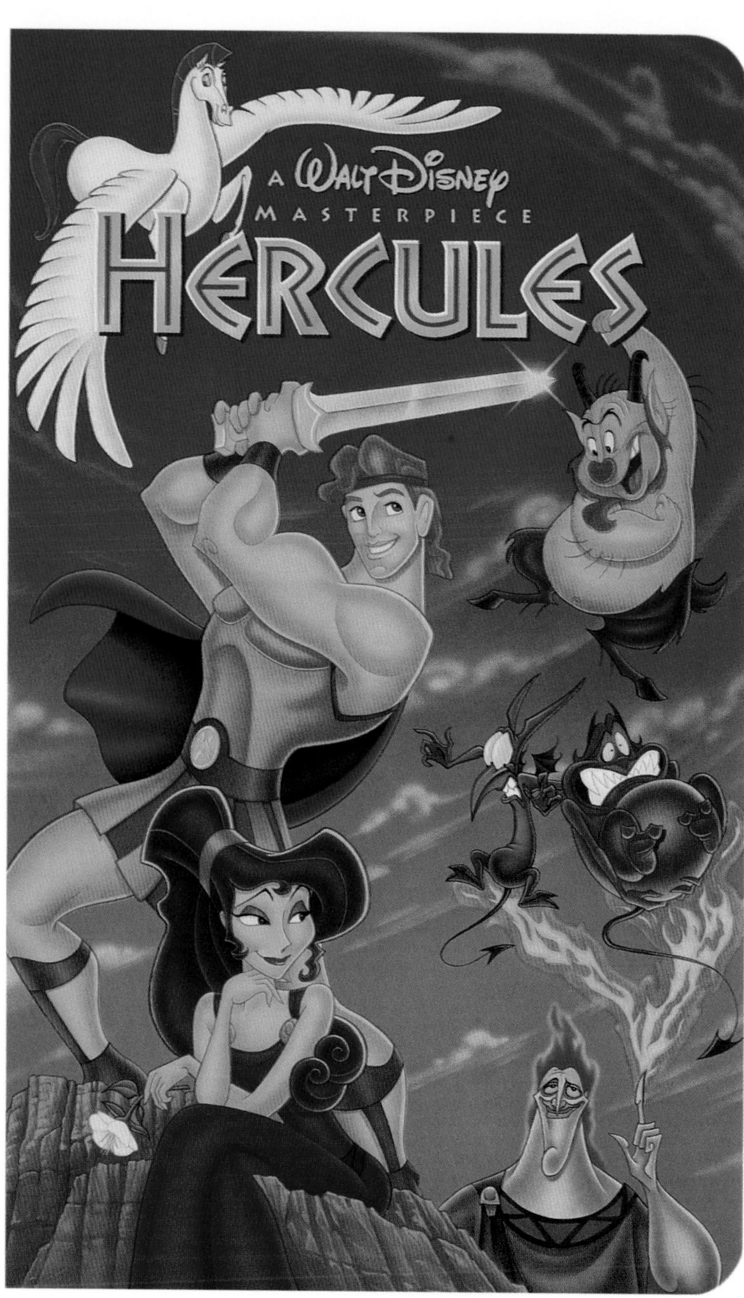

KEITH BATCHELLER

353 West 53rd St 1W
Tel: (212)682-2462
info@amerartists.com

American Artists

New York, NY 10019
Fax (212) 582-0090
www.amerartists.com

GARTH GLAZIER

353 West 53rd St 1W
Tel: (212)682-2462
info@amerartists.com

American Artists

New York, NY 10019
Fax: (212)582-0090
www.amerartists.com

JACQUES FABRE

353 West 53rd St 1W
Tel: (212)682-2462
info@amerartists.com

American Artists

New York, NY 10019
Fax: (212)582-0090
www.amerartists.com

DOUG HENRY

353 West 53rd St 1W
Tel: (212)682-2462
info@amerartists.com

American Artists

New York, NY 10019
Fax: (212)582-0090
www.amerartists.com

JOHN HOLM

353 West 53rd St 1W
Tel: (212)682-2462
info@amerartists.com
American Artists
New York, NY 10019
Fax (212) 582-0090
www.amerartists.com
JOHN CHURCHMAN

353 West 53rd St 1W
Tel: (212)682-2462
info@amerartists.com

American Artists

New York, NY 10019
Fax: (212)582-0090
www.amerartists.com

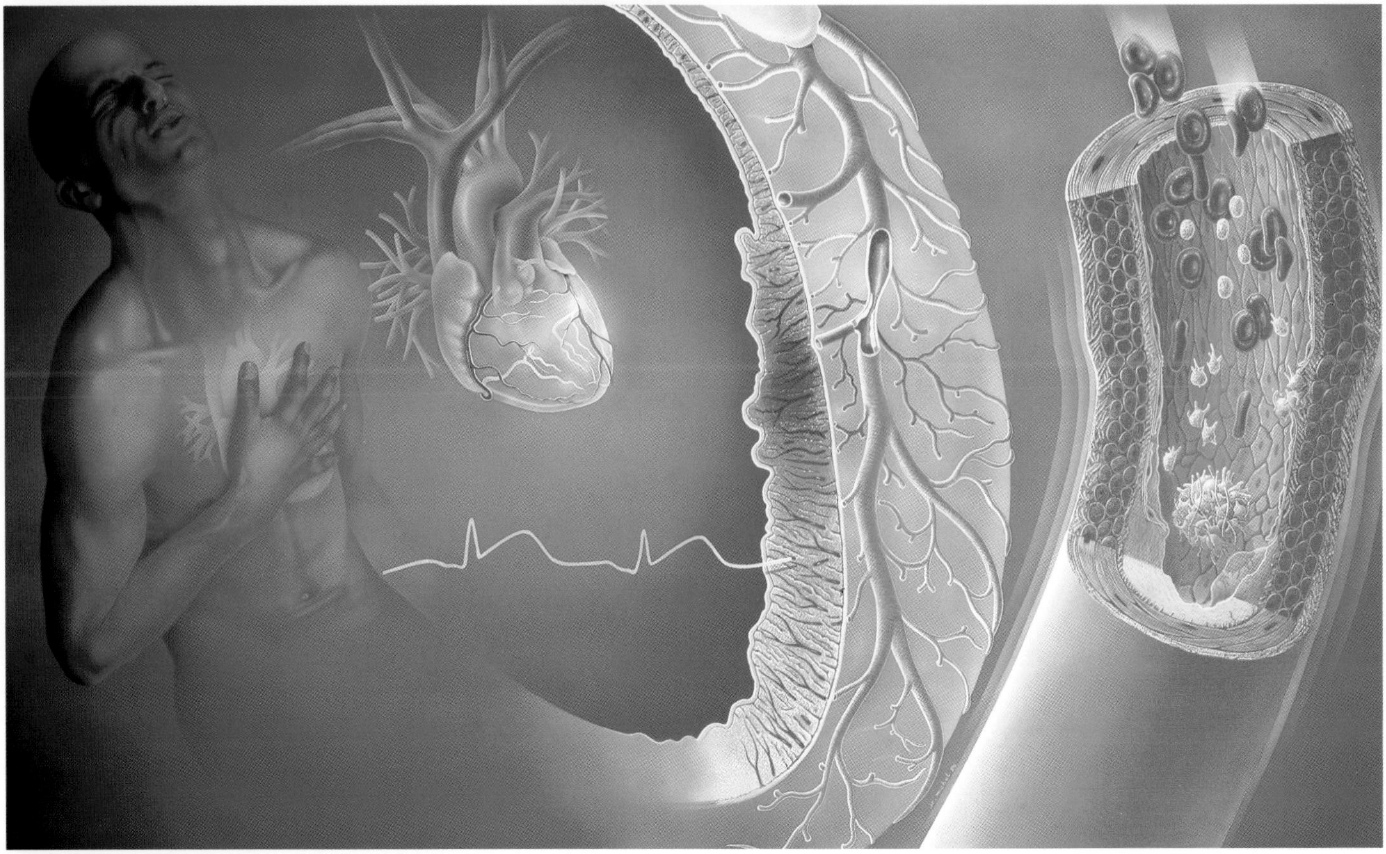

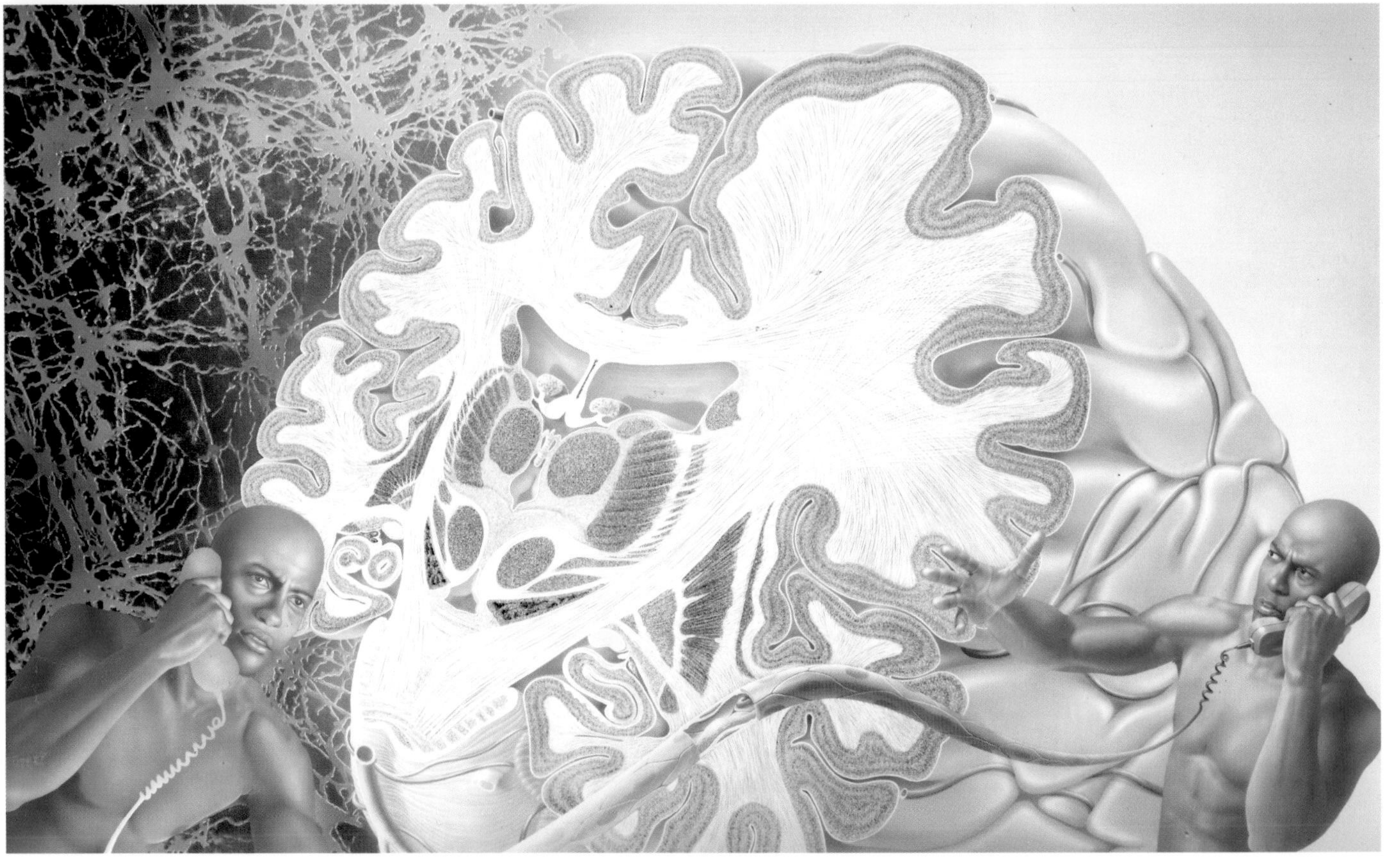

JEAN-CLAUDE MICHEL

353 West 53rd St 1W
Tel: (212)682-2462
info@amerartists.com

American Artists

New York, NY 10019
Fax: (212)582-0090
www.amerartists.com

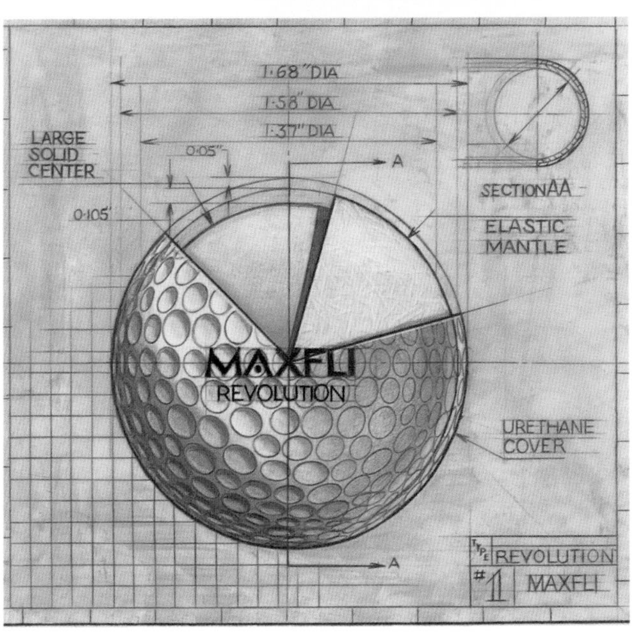

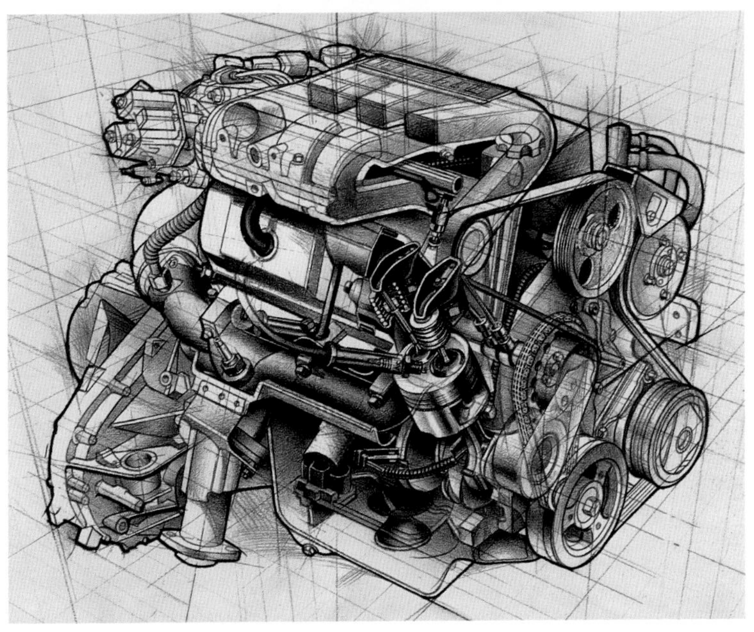

JONATHAN WRIGHT

353 West 53rd St 1W
Tel: (212)682-2462
info@amerartists.com

American Artists

New York, NY 10019
Fax: (212)582-0090
www.amerartists.com

JIM EFFLER

353 West 53rd St 1W
Tel: (212)682-2462
info@amerartists.com

American Artists

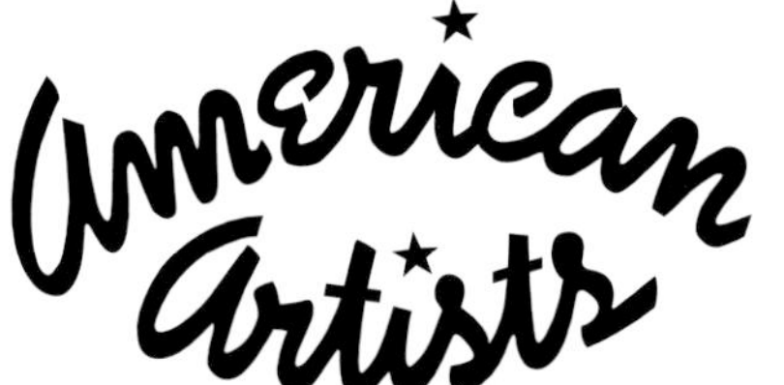

New York, NY 10019
Fax: (212)582-0090
www.amerartists.com

Stock Art Available

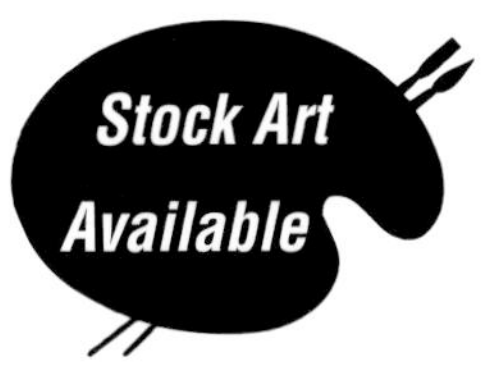

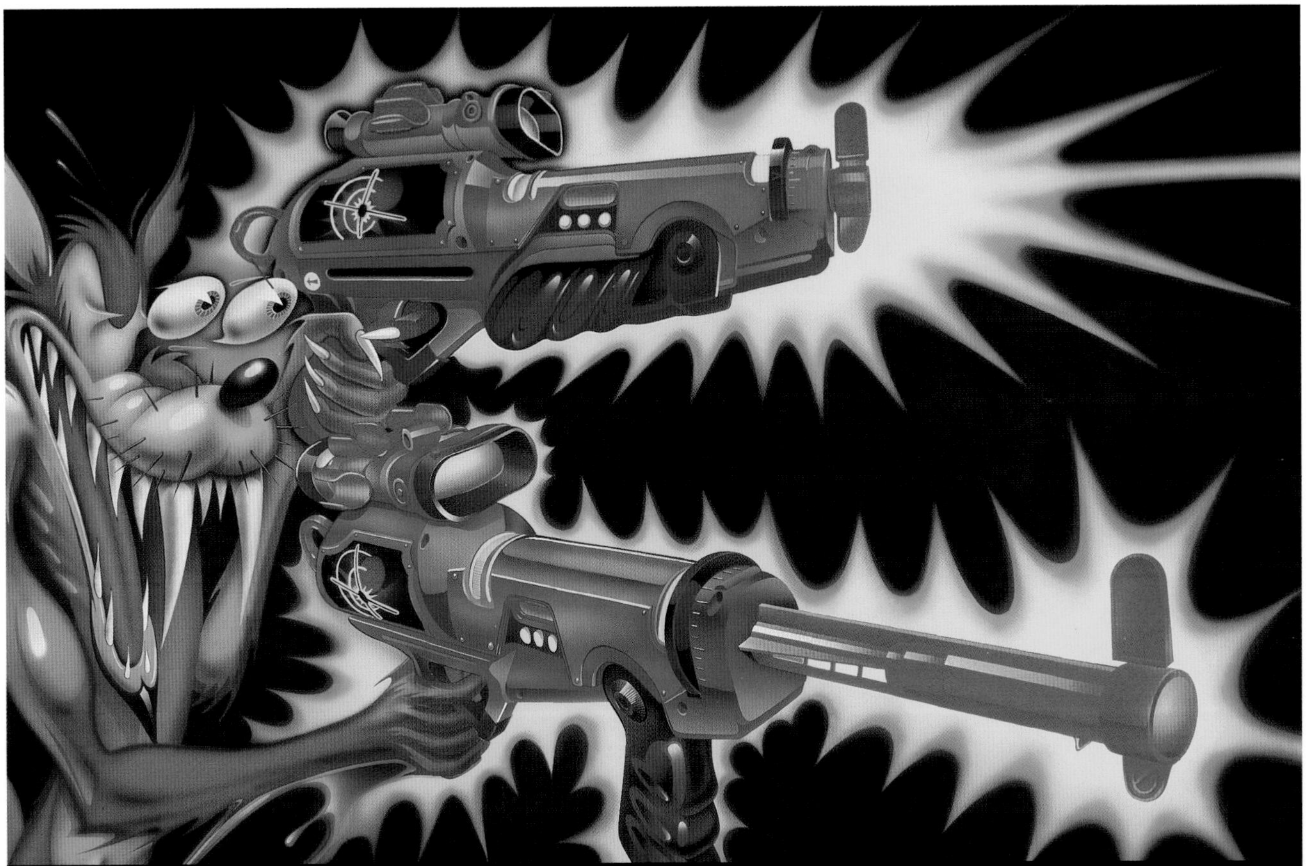

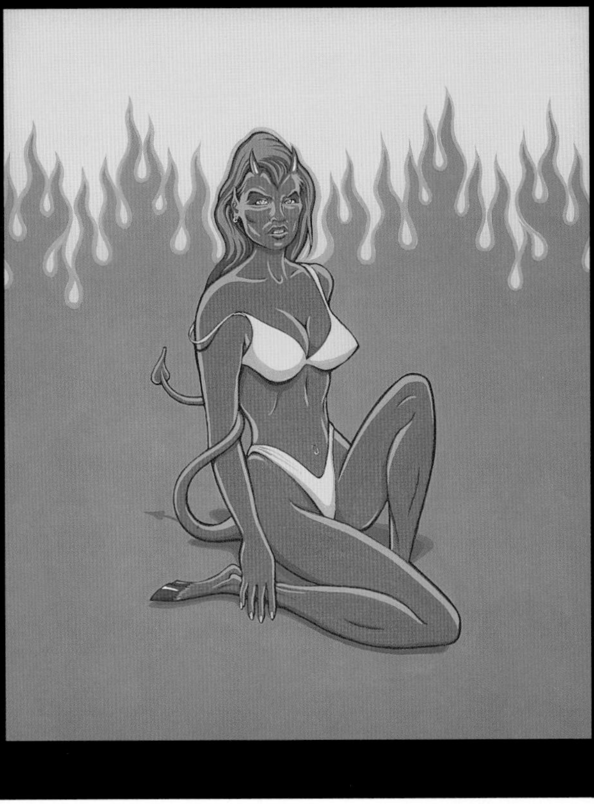

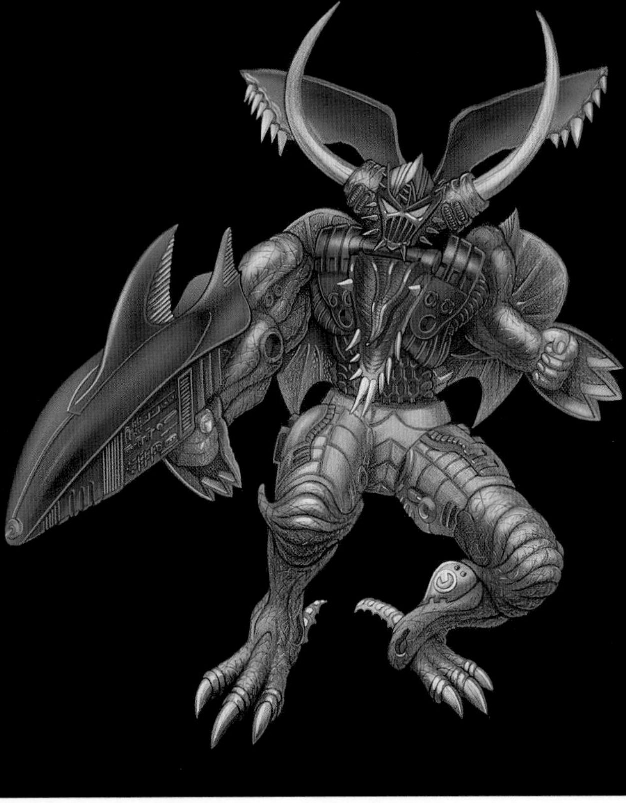

DAVE MILLER

Stock Art Available

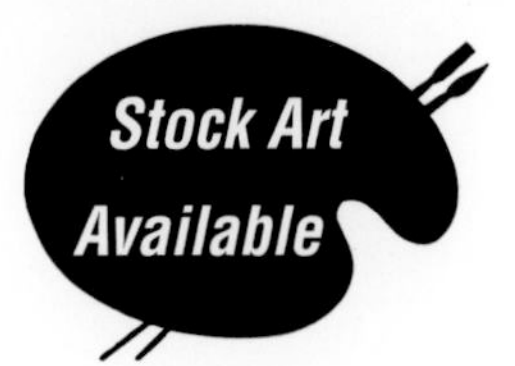

353 West 53rd St 1W
Tel: (212)682-2462
info@amerartists.com

American Artists

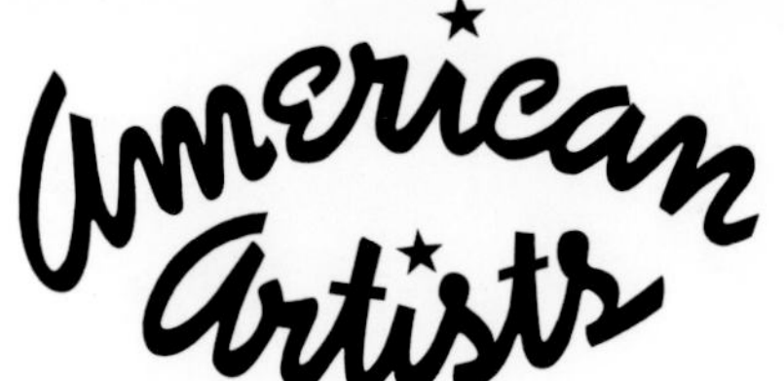

New York, NY 10019
Fax: (212)582-0090
www.amerartists.com

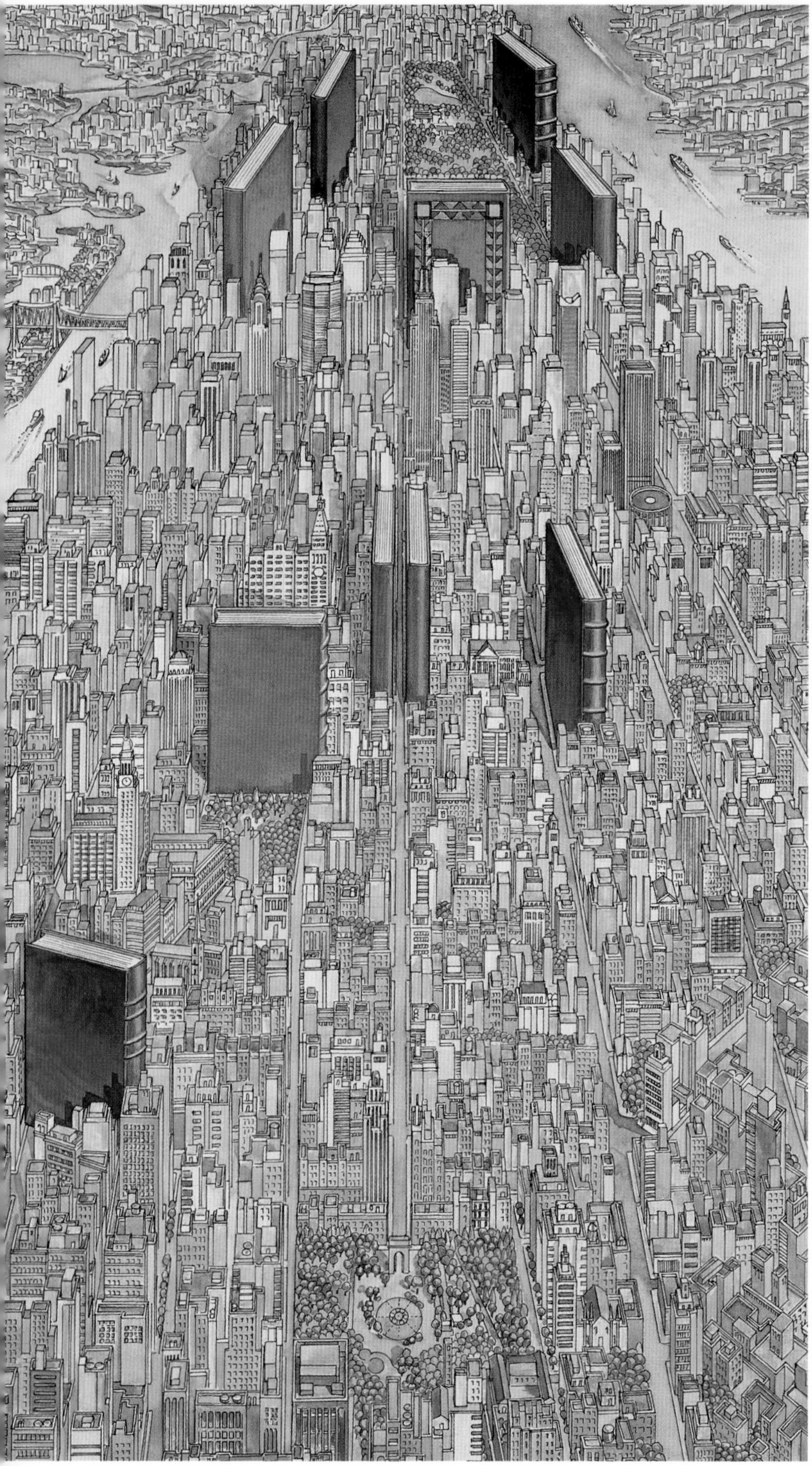

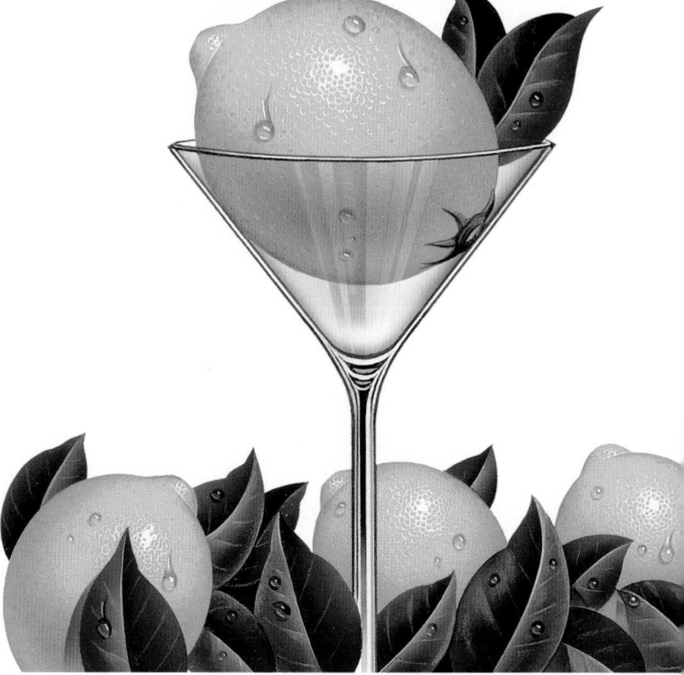

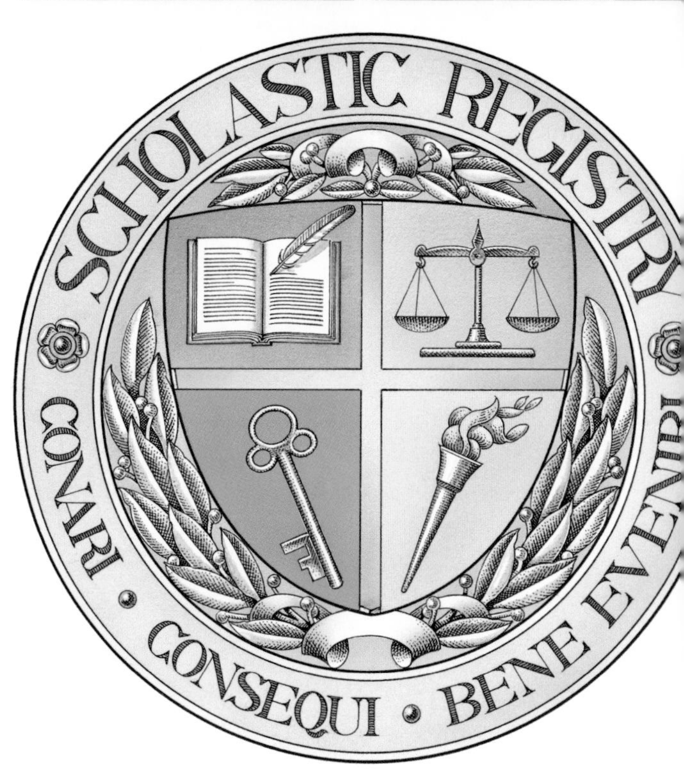

JOE SCROFANI

353 West 53rd St 1W
Tel: (212)682-2462
info@amerartists.com

American Artists

New York, NY 10019
Fax: (212)582-0090
www.amerartists.com

HOM & HOM

353 West 53rd St 1W
Tel: (212)682-2462
info@amerartists.com

American Artists

New York, NY 10019
Fax: (212)582-0090
www.amerartists.com

JIM STARR

353 West 53rd St 1W
Tel: (212)682-2462
info@amerartists.com

American Artists

New York, NY 10019
Fax: (212)582-0090
www.amerartists.com

RUSSELL FARRELL

353 West 53rd St 1W
Tel: (212)682-2462
info@amerartists.com

American Artists

New York, NY 10019
Fax: (212)582-0090
www.amerartists.com

SHAWN MURPHY

353 West 53rd St 1W
Tel: (212)682-2462
info@amerartists.com

American Artists

New York, NY 10019
Fax: (212)582-0090
www.amerartists.com

MAURICE LEWIS

353 West 53rd St 1W
Tel: (212)682-2462
info@amerartists.com

American Artists

New York, NY 10019
Fax: (212)582-0090
www.amerartists.com

DON BISHOP

353 West 53rd St 1W
Tel: (212)682-2462
info@amerartists.com

American Artists

New York, NY 10019
Fax: (212)582-0090
www.amerartists.com

the EXTREME ADVENTURES of WACKY WILLIE

Studio: Ph:562 429-2513 Fx: 429-1400
E-Mail: youngeddie@earthlink.net

eddie young
Builds good characters

353 West 53rd St 1W
Tel: (212)682-2462
info@amerartists.com

American Artists

New York, NY 10019
Fax: (212)582-0090
www.amerartists.com

MICHAEL JAROSZKO

353 West 53rd St 1W
Tel: (212)682-2462
info@amerartists.com

American Artists

New York, NY 10019
Fax: (212)582-0090
www.amerartists.com

ALAN MALE

353 West 53rd St 1W
Tel: (212)682-2462
info@amerartists.com

American Artists

New York, NY 10019
Fax: (212)582-0090
www.amerartists.com

BOB DEPEW

353 West 53rd St 1W
Tel: (212)682-2462
info@amerartists.com

American Artists

New York, NY 10019
Fax (212) 582-0090
www.amerartists.com

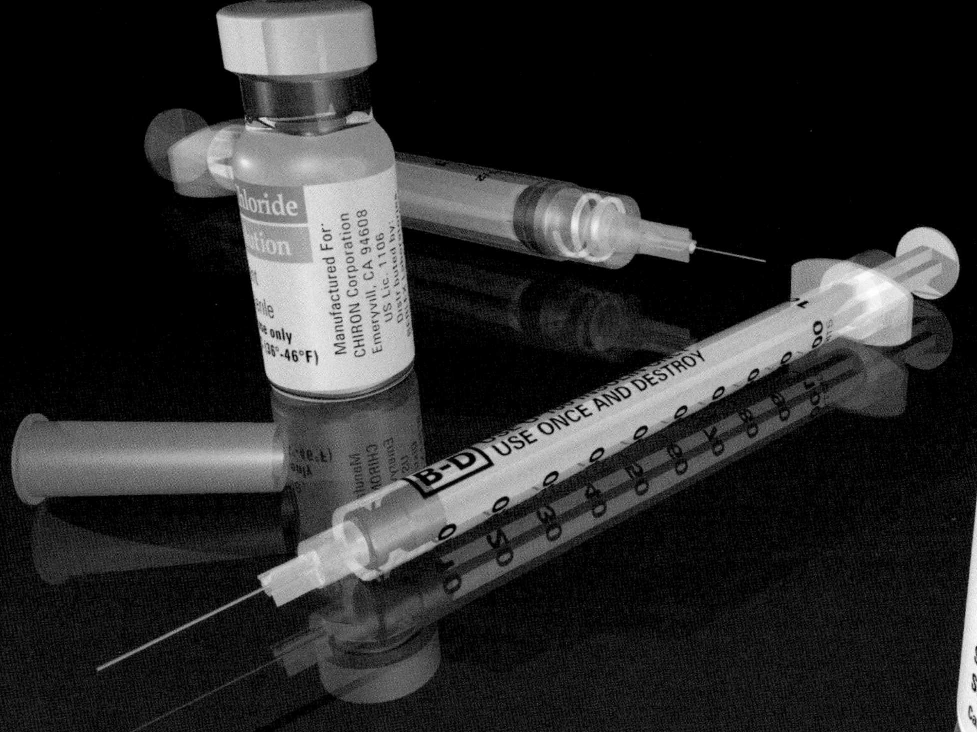

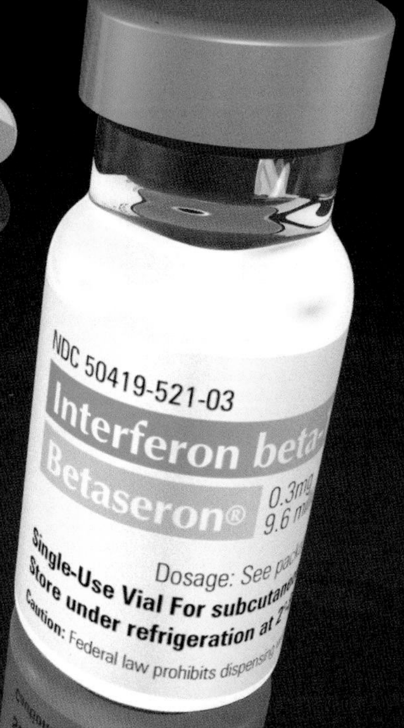

STEVE CELMER

353 West 53rd St 1W
Tel: (212)682-2462
info@amerartists.com

American Artists

New York, NY 10019
Fax: (212)582-0090
www.amerartists.com

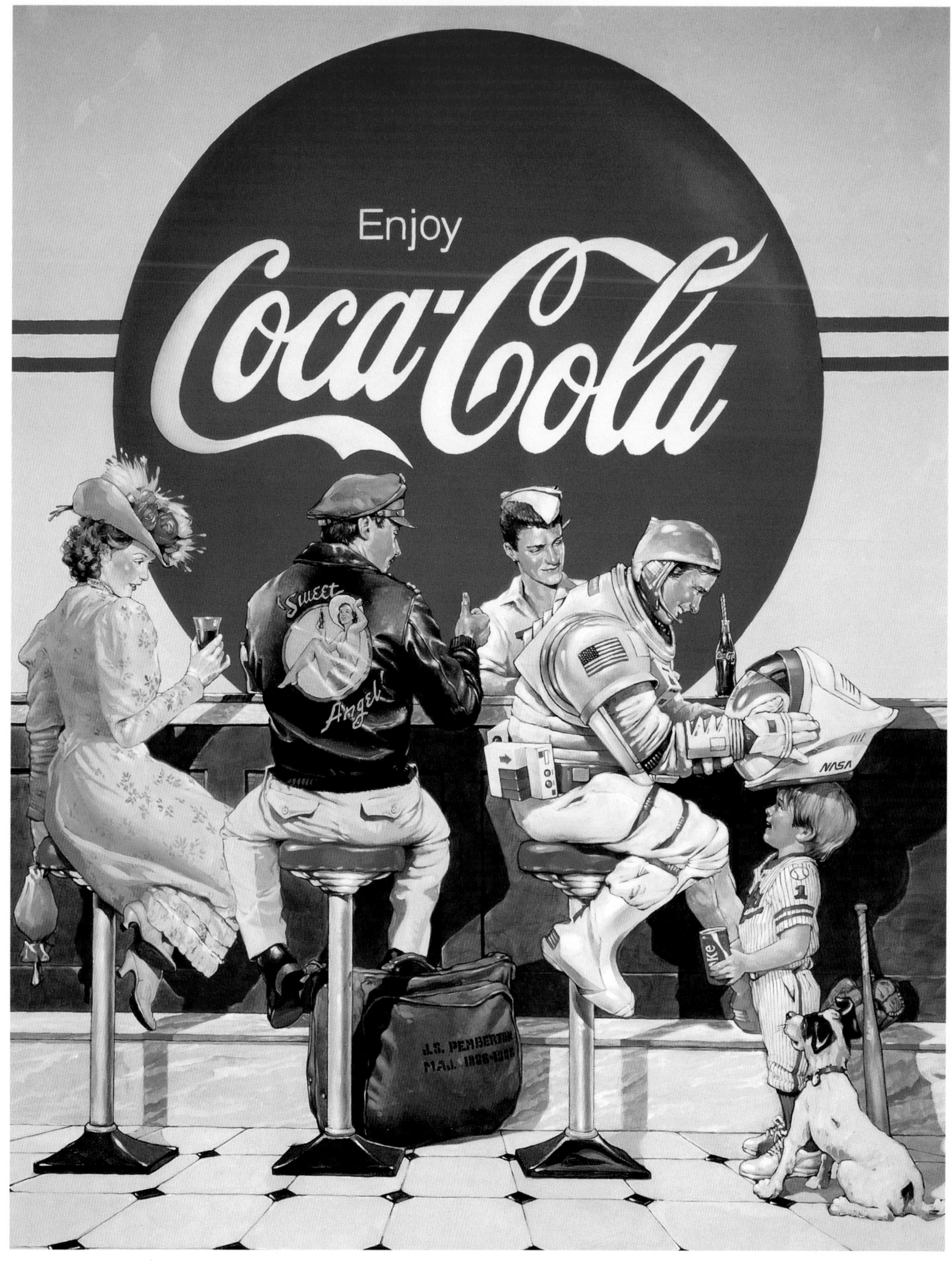

BILL GARLAND

353 West 53rd St 1W
Tel: (212)682-2462
info@amerartists.com

American Artists

New York, NY 10019
Fax (212) 582-0090
www.amerartists.com

SCOTT GRIMANDO

Scott Grimando

Digital illustration with a foundation in traditional painting

353 West 53rd St 1W
Tel: (212)682-2462
info@amerartists.com

New York, NY 10019
Fax: (212)582-0090
www.amerartists.com

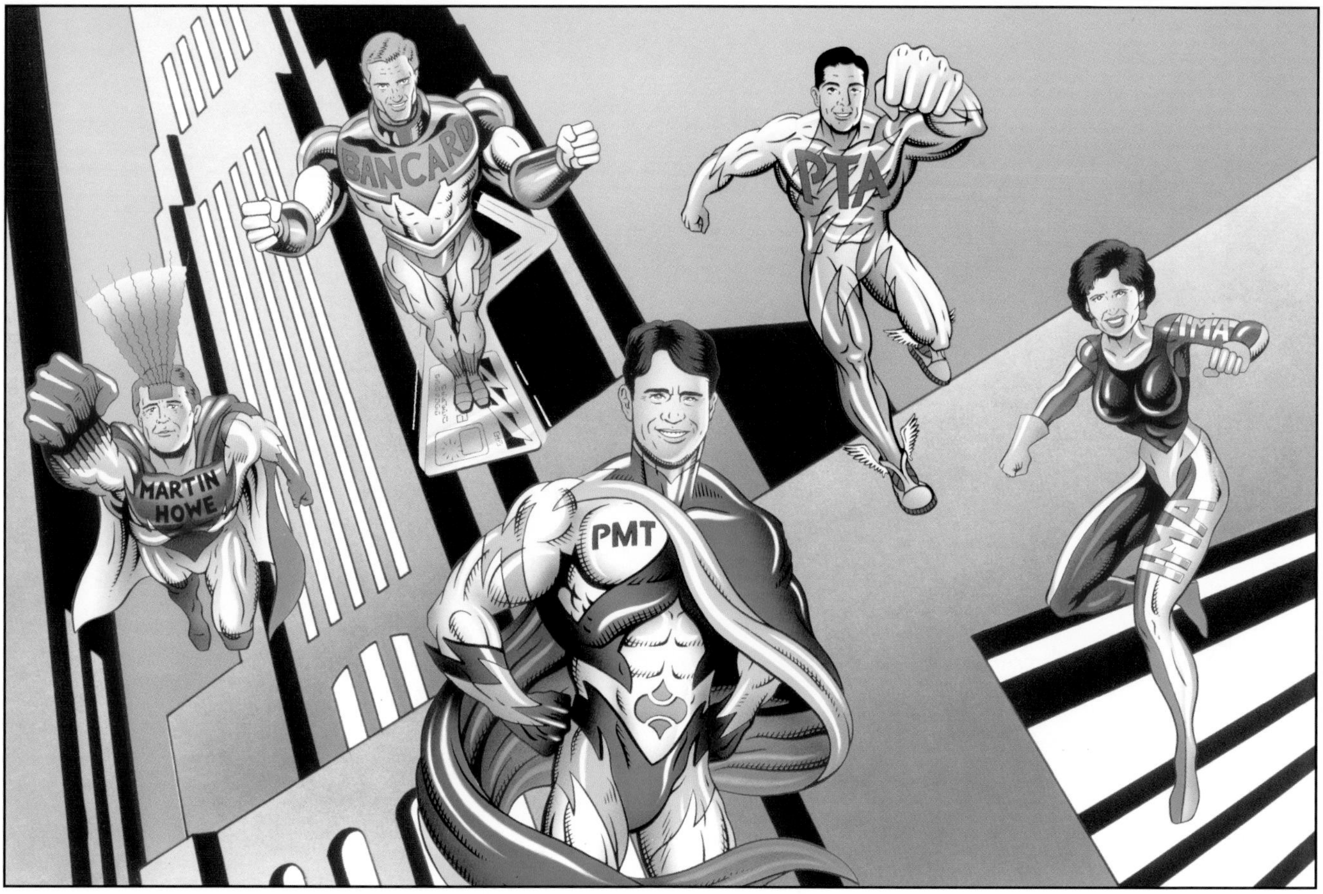

ROD VASS

353 West 53rd St 1W
Tel: (212)682-2462
info@amerartists.com

American Artists

New York, NY 10019
Fax: (212)582-0090
www.amerartists.com

Stock Art Available

ANDREW CONDRON

353 West 53rd St 1W
Tel: (212)682-2462
info@amerartists.com

American Artists

New York, NY 10019
Fax (212) 582-0090
www.amerartists.com

BOT RODA

353 West 53rd St 1W
Tel: (212)682-2462
info@amerartists.com

New York, NY 10019
Fax: (212)582-0090
www.amerartists.com

In Atlanta Area:

Cary & Company
(404) 296-9666
Fax: 296-1537

SHAWN McKELVEY

353 West 53rd St 1W
Tel: (212)682-2462
info@amerartists.com

New York, NY 10019
Fax: (212)582-0090
www.amerartists.com

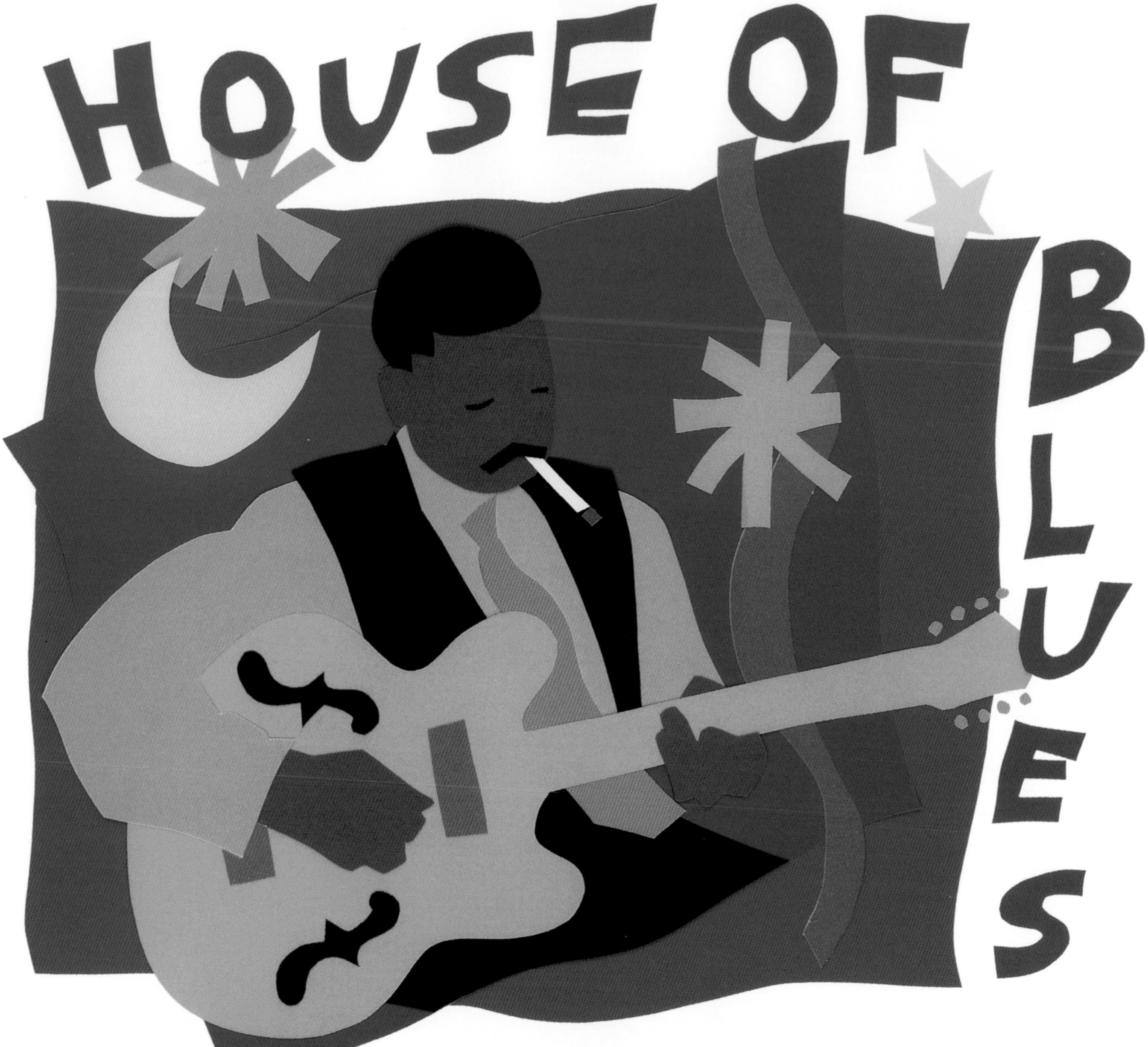

HOUSE OF BLUES

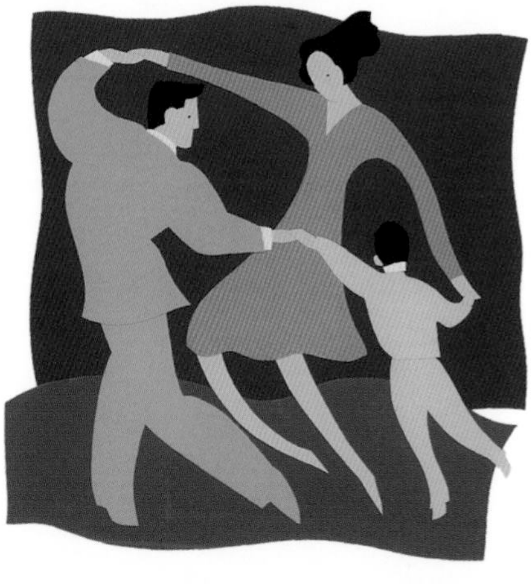

RHONDA VOO

353 West 53rd St 1W
Tel: (212)682-2462
info@amerartists.com

American Artists

New York, NY 10019
Fax: (212)582-0090
www.amerartists.com

Liam O'Farrell

Trevor Smith

Julia Whatley

Brian McIntyre

Robert Edward

Carl Melegari

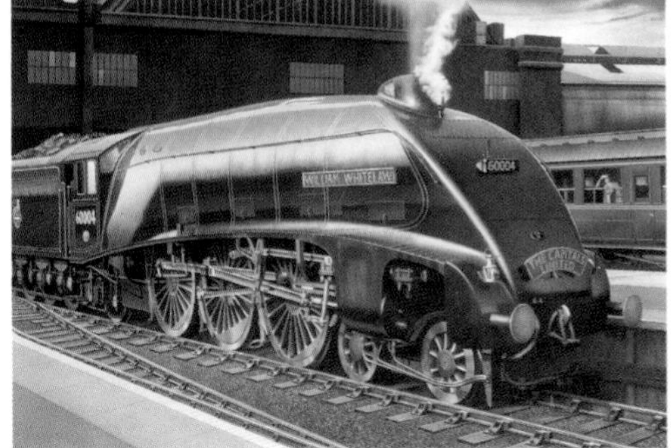
Paul Higgins

Paul Shorrock

IAN FLEMMING ASSOCIATES

353 West 53rd St 1W
Tel: (212)682-2462
info@amerartists.com

American Artists

New York, NY 10019
Fax: (212)582-0090
www.amerartists.com

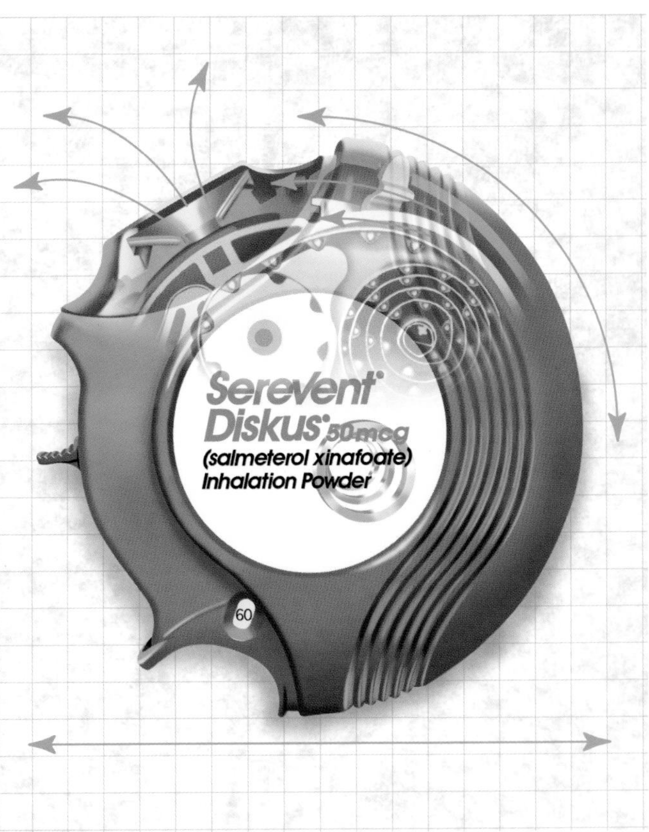

TONY RANDAZZO

353 West 53rd St 1W
Tel: (212)682-2462
info@amerartists.com

American Artists

New York, NY 10019
Fax: (212)582-0090
www.amerartists.com

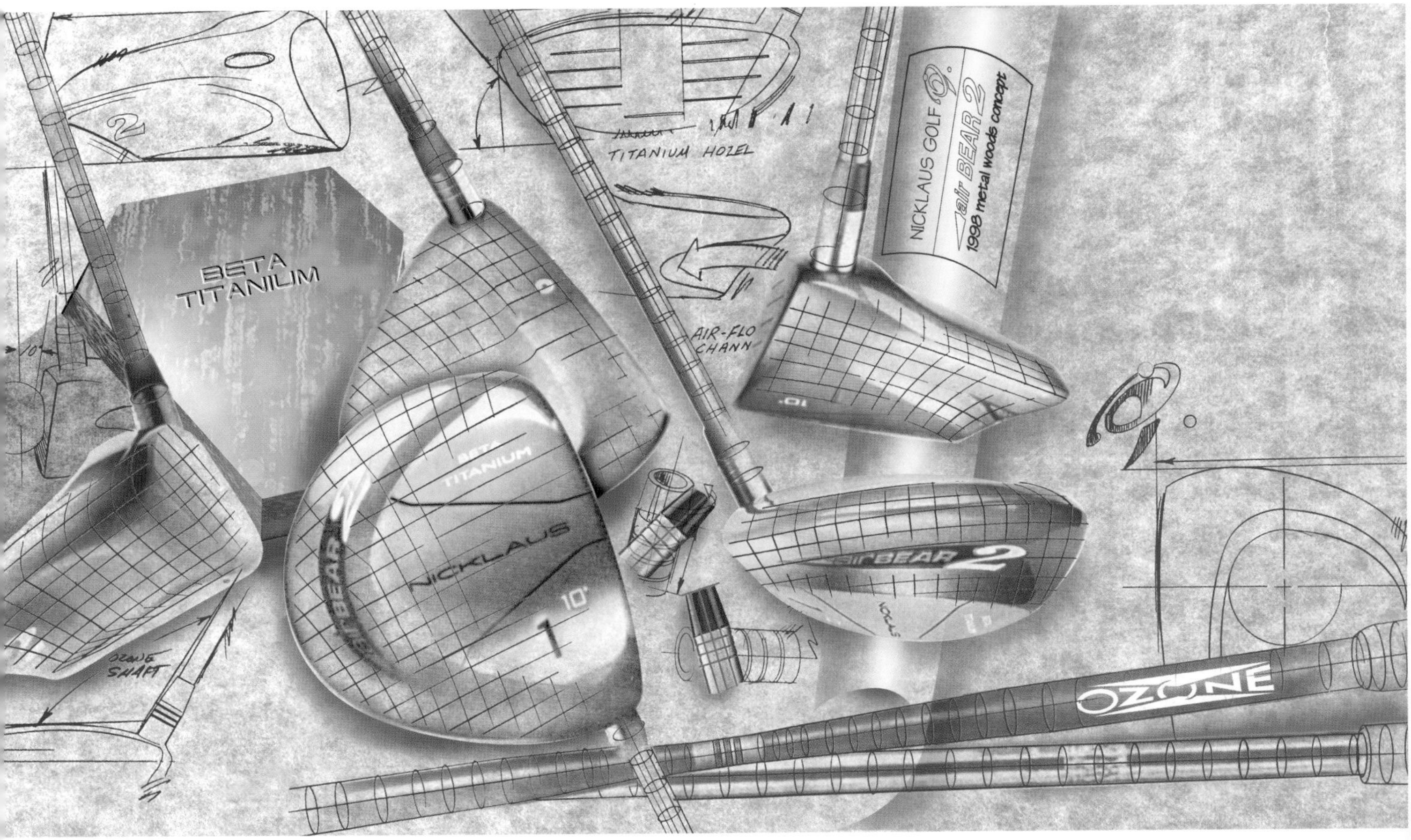

TONY RANDAZZO

Stock Art Available

353 West 53rd St 1W
Tel: (212)682-2462
info@amerartists.com

American Artists

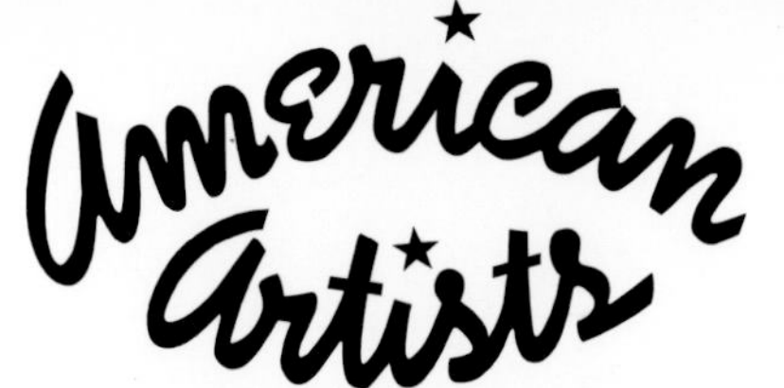

New York, NY 10019
Fax: (212)582-0090
www.amerartists.com

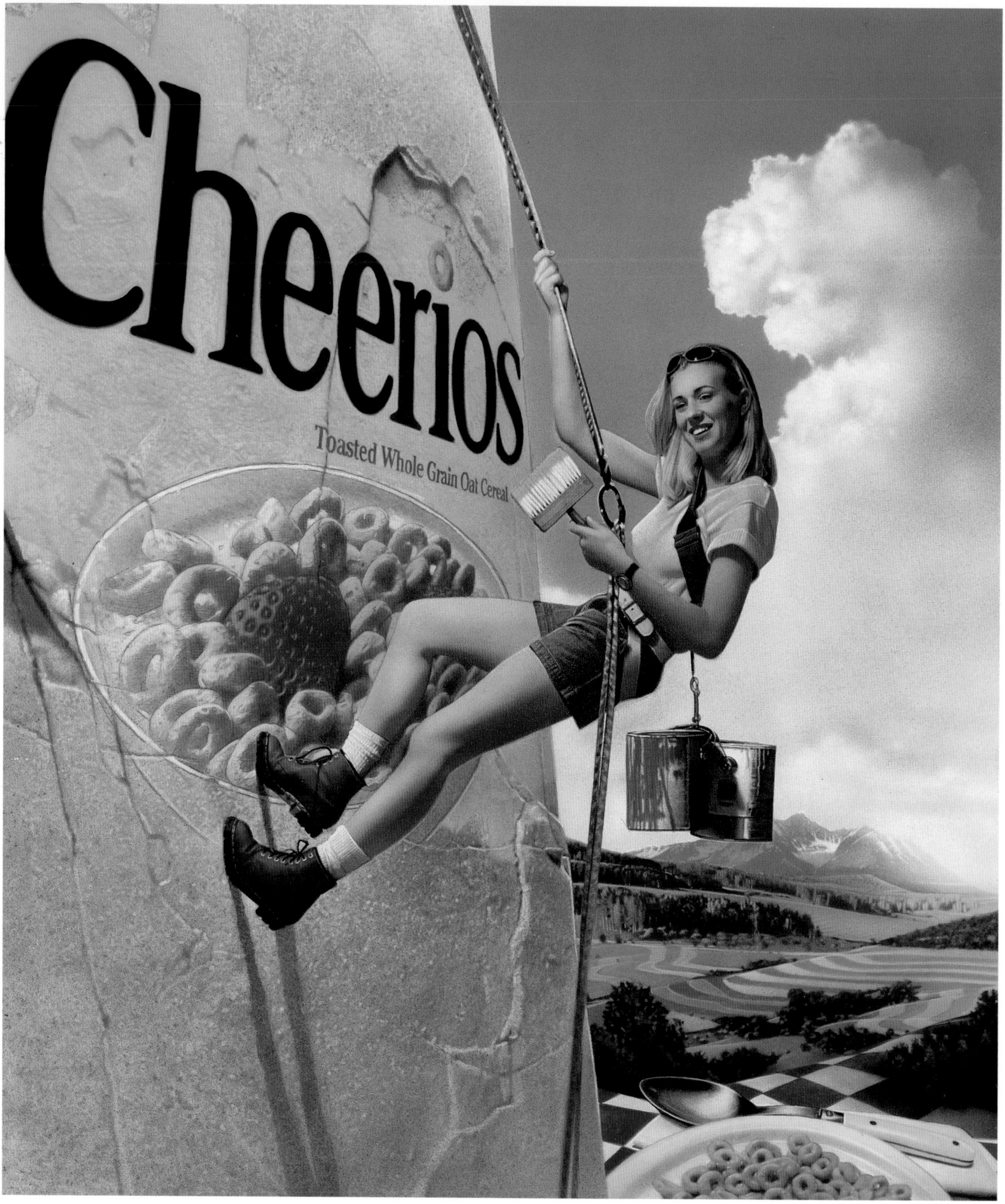

STAN WATTS

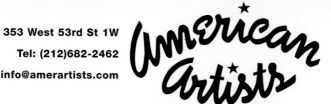

353 West 53rd St 1W
Tel: (212)682-2462
info@amerartists.com

American Artists

New York, NY 10019
Fax: (212)582-0090
www.amerartists.com

KENT GAMBLE

elizabeth sayles

(914) 267-4127
60 brookside ave, valley cottage, ny 10989

the hartford courant

new video

orient express

represented in the children's market by: CORNELL & McCARTHY
(203) 454-4210

DAVID UHL Studios

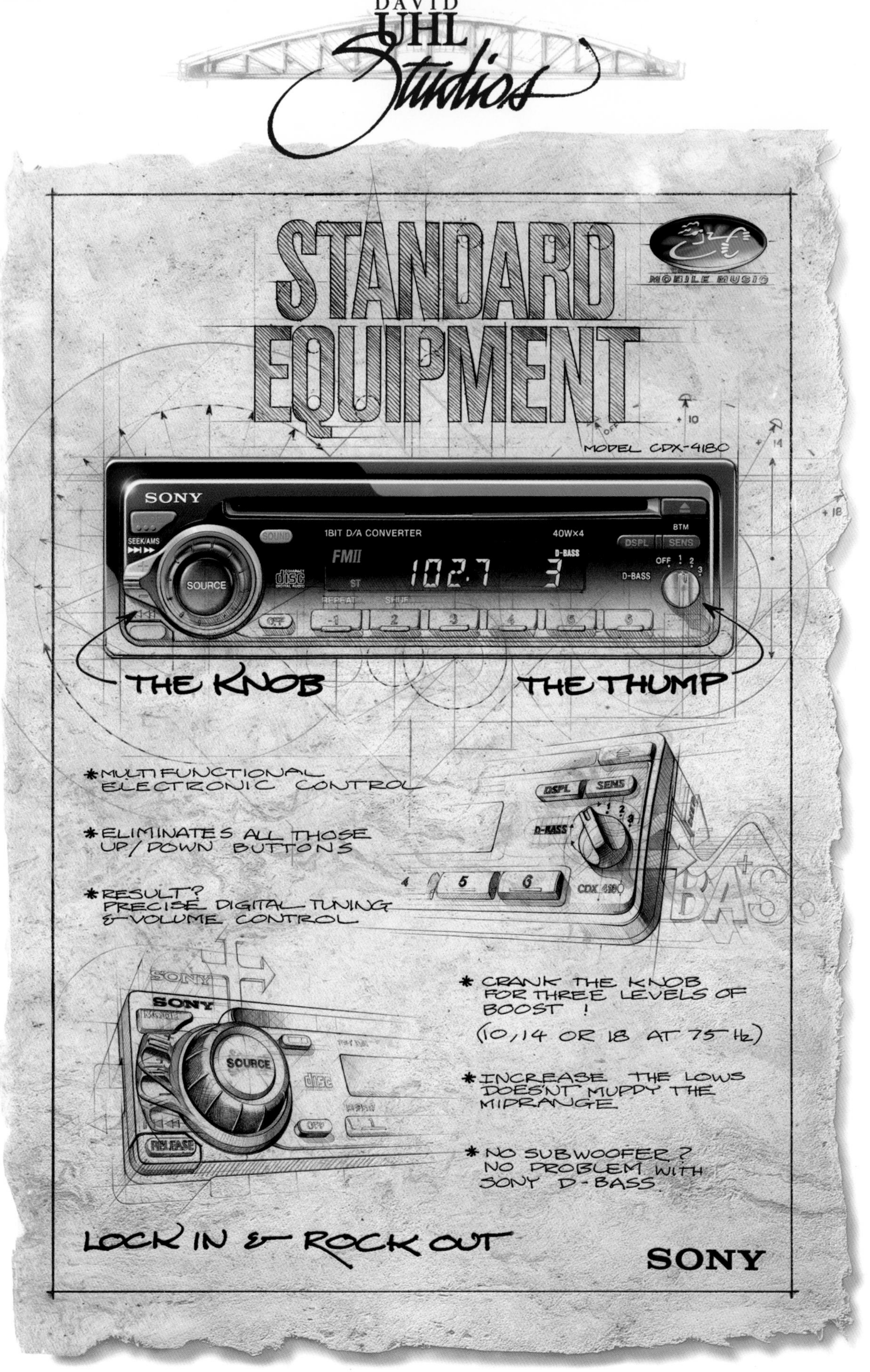

1261 Delaware St. Denver, Colorado 80204 • 303.534.2054 • Fax 303.534.2056
email daviduhl@sni.net

DAVID
UHL
Studios

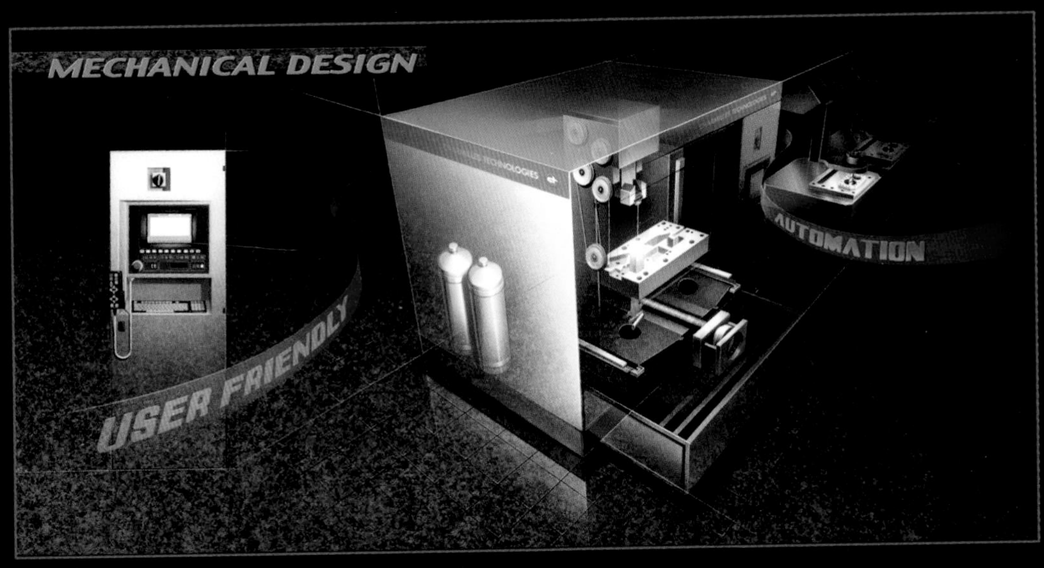
MECHANICAL DESIGN
AUTOMATION
USER FRIENDLY

Name: Monica Torrejon
Past history: Obsessive illustration
Health card number: (416) 878-6225
Web Page: home.istar.ca/~alterna
e-mail: alterna@istar.ca
Nationality: Planet Torrejon
Medication: Daily reality pil
Diagnosis: Severe compulsive creativity
SALSA

nancy
FREEMAN
FABRIC
ILLUSTRATION
PHONE & FAX
707•745•5228
L.L.Bean®
SEATTLE WATER
BETTE'S TO GO
BETTE'S
TO GO
548-9494
BAKE SHOP
DELICATESSEN
NLF

ANATOLY CHERNISHOV

201-327-2377

FAX 201-236-9469

A&I STUDIO
4 WILLOWBANK COURT
MAHWAH • NJ • 07430

SOUTHEAST
ALEXANDER/
POLLARD
404 875 1363

NEW YORK
MUNRO
GOODMAN
212 691 2667

WASHINGTON D.C.
ALLAN COMPORT
W/C STUDIO INC.
410 349 8669

CAROLINAS
KERRY REILLY
704 372 6007

MIDWEST
DAN SELL, INC
312 578 8844

CALIFORNIA
TAMI GORDON
213 887 8958

EUROPE
LAURENCE FAURE
33 1 46 06 29 36

www.theispot.com

SALLY WERN COMPORT

SALLY WERN COMPORT

REPRESENTED BY ALEXANDER | POLLARD

800.347.0734 ATLANTA 404.875.1363 FAX 404.875.9733

MARK WEAKLEY

"DEVIL JACK" HAYS
Texas Ranger 1840

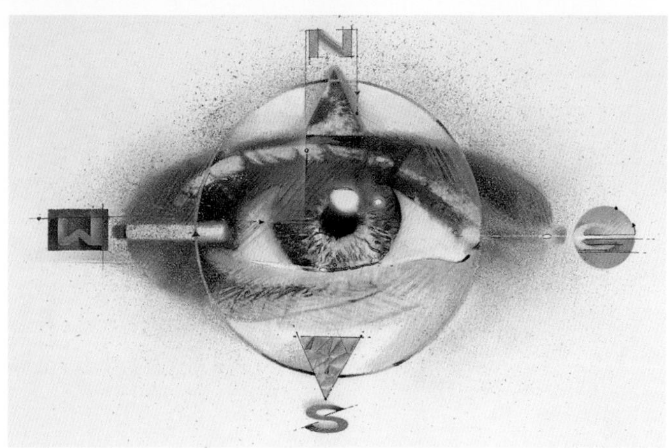

THOMAS GONZALEZ

REPRESENTED BY ALEXANDER | POLLARD

800.347.0734 ATLANTA 404.875.1363 FAX 404.875.9733

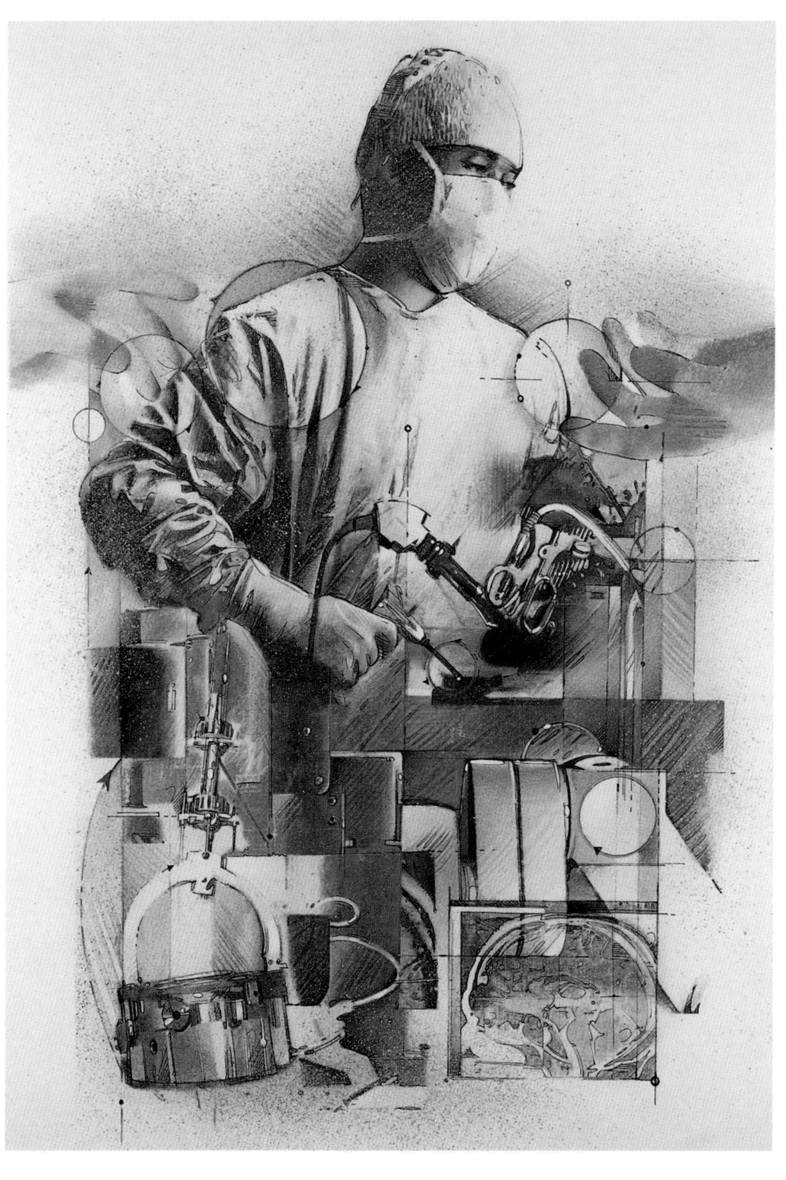

REPRESENTED BY ALEXANDER | POLLARD

800.347.0734 ATLANTA 404.875.1363 FAX 404.875.9733

NIP ROGERS

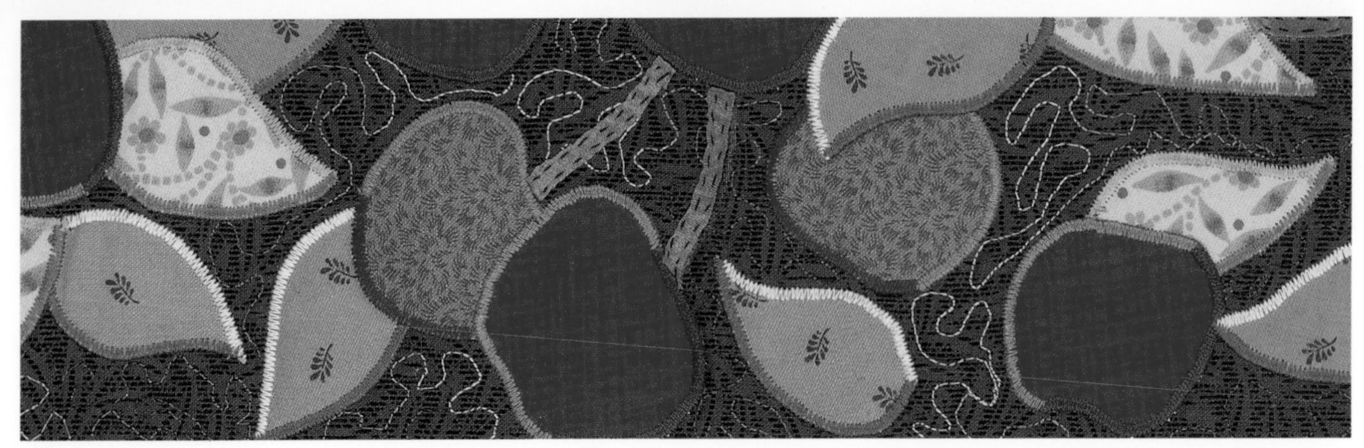

Kathy Lengyel

REPRESENTED BY ALEXANDER | POLLARD

800.347.0734 ATLANTA 404.875.1363 FAX 404.875.9733

THE
EARTH
WAS NOT
GIVEN TO
YOU BY
YOUR
PARENTS

REPRESENTED BY ALEXANDER | POLLARD

800.347.0734 ATLANTA 404.875.1363 FAX 404.875.9733

DIANE BOROWSKI

Discover
MEXICO

STEPHEN WELLS

REPRESENTED *east of the Mississippi* BY ALEXANDER | POLLARD

800.347.0734 ATLANTA 404.875.1363 FAX 404.875.9733

west of the Mississippi BY KAREN WELLS 800.778.9076 *ph/fx* 281.579.3220*

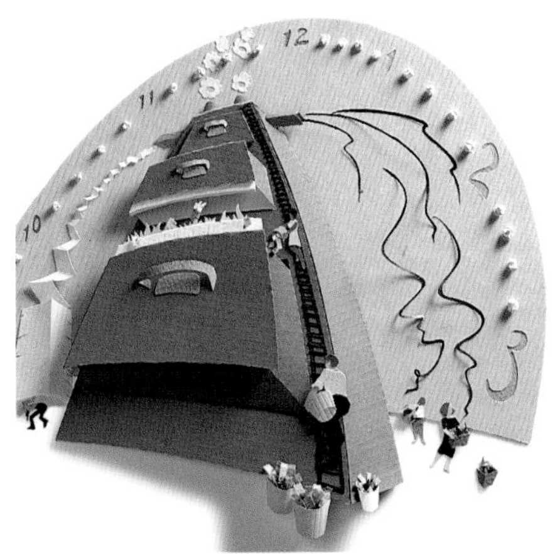

Karen Strelecki

Represented by Alexander | Pollard

800.347.0734 Atlanta 404.875.1363 Fax 404.875.9733

DAN KANGAS
(905) 726-4226 dkangas@interlog.com
HIRAM WALKER
FROZEN
HURRICANES

1928D6
SUZUKI
1998
specializing in:
• photo Realistic Illustration
• Design
• web graphics and Animation
L5
Level 5 Limited
2722 Munson Street • Wheaton, Maryland • 20902
Phone: 301-933-6203 • Fax: 301-942-4590
Email: level_5_ltd@earthlink.net

KRISTIN MOUNT

2123 West Warner Ave. • Chicago, IL • 60618
800-455-9717

Industrial • Technical • Product Illustration

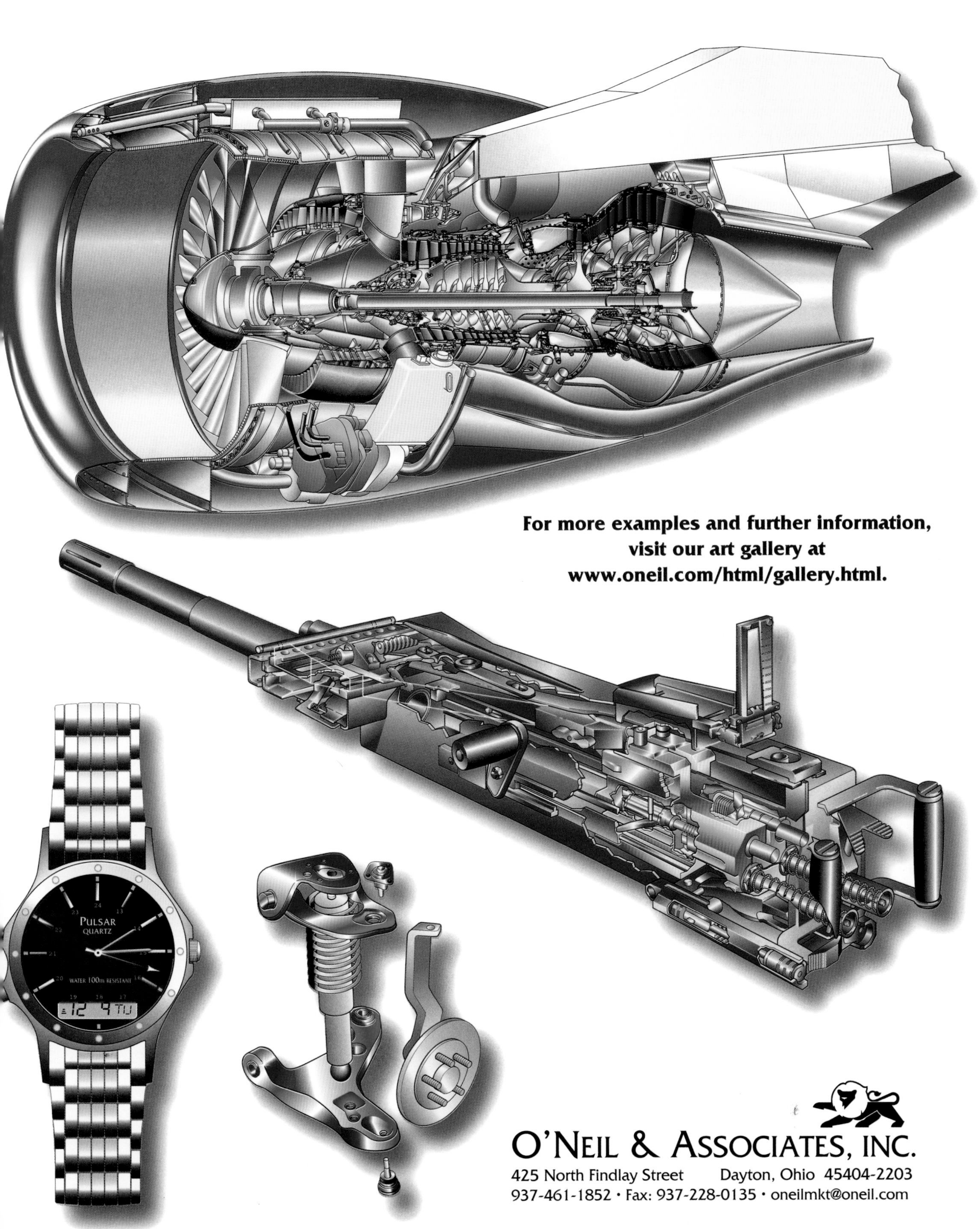

Rob Collinet can add "illustrationality"

to anything you do

Rob Supplies Everything

From conceptual thinking to handsome roughs to beautiful finished illustrations delivered to you on disk by courier or via the internet! As Rob's customer you will receive quality finished artwork done to your exacting specifications in the format you need. No muss! No fuss!

If you would like a sampling of Rob's unique and fanciful illustrational style mailed directly to your home or office, call the phone number at the bottom of this page. NOW!

Samples & Games FREE

If you're looking for even more samples, fresh new ideas or a jolly distraction from work, why not visit **Mr. Rob's Funsite™** You'll find novel games and delightful amusements plus plenty of other useful information, all at no expense to you.

rhob@sentex.net

www.splashworks.com/rob

416.469.1092

Bill BOYKO

SHARPSHOOTER
CREATIVE REPRESENTATION INC.

Phone 416.703.5300 | *Fax* 416.703.0762
email shooter@the-wire.com

Stephanie CARTER

Phone 416.703.5300 | *Fax* 416.703.0762

email shooter@the-wire.com

Frederic EIBNER

SHARPSHOOTER
CREATIVE REPRESENTATION INC.

Phone 416.703.5300 | Fax 416.703.0762
email shooter@the-wire.com

Nancy Ruth JACKSON

SHARPSHOOTER
CREATIVE REPRESENTATION INC.

Phone 416.703.5300 | Fax 416.703.0762
email shooter@the-wire.com

JACOBSON/FERNANDEZ

Represented in the U.S. by Susan Gomberg

SHARPSHOOTER
CREATIVE REPRESENTATION INC.

Phone 416.703.5300 *Fax* 416.703.0762
email shooter@the-wire.com

Olena KASSIAN

Phone 416.703.5300 | *Fax* 416.703.0762

email shooter@the-wire.com

J.C. KNAFF

JANUaRY
M T W T F S S
1 2 3 4
5 6 7 8 9 10 11
12 13 14 15 16 17 18
19 20 21 22 23 24 25
26 27 28 29 30 31

mArCH
M T W T F S S
1
2 3 4 5 6 7 8
9 10 11 12 13 14 15
16 17 18 19 20 21 22
23 24 25 26 27 28 29
30 31

Stuart McLACHLAN

Gordon SAUVÉ

Laura WALLACE

SHARPSHOOTER
CREATIVE REPRESENTATION INC.

Phone 416.703.5300 | *Fax* 416.703.0762
email shooter@the-wire.com

Jeff Slemons

2555 Walnut Street
Suite LF
Denver, CO 80205
303-298-0807

Mary Ross

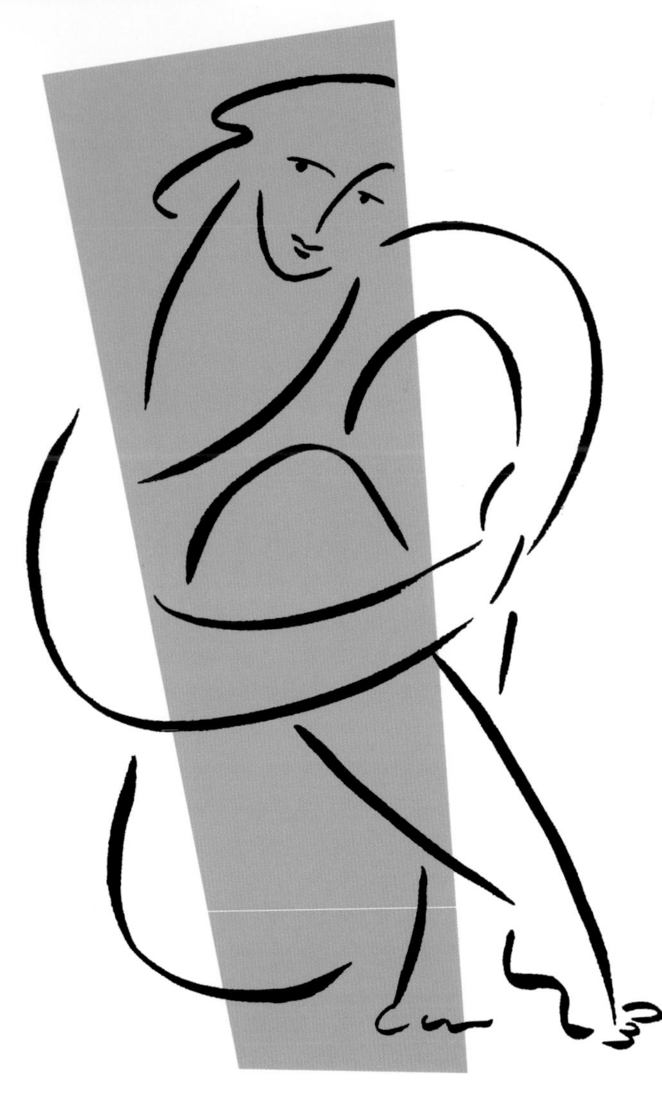

RITA GATLIN REPRESENTS

Digital Illustration · *Animation Reel Available*

USA 800.924.7881 · **SF** 415.924.7881 · **FAX** 415.924.7891 · www.ritareps.com

RITA GATLIN

R E P R E S E N T S

Jack Lutzow

Elizabeth Hinshaw

Anne Crosse

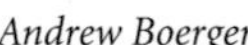
Andrew Boerger

Russell Charpentier

John Pirman

Tom Hennessy

Tana Powell

Mary Ross

This is just a sampling of the many talented artists we represent. Please call for a sample package of the entire group.

USA 800.924.7881 · SF 415.924.7881 · FAX 415.924.7891 · www.ritareps.com

Farida Zaman

USA: (973) 744 9377 • CANADA: (416) 489 3769
e-mail: fzaman@cybernex.net

JOANNE KOLTES
represents

KATHLEEN
ROGNESS
ILLUSTRATION

PHONE (612) 884-4045 FAX (612) 884-3450
www.dimensioncreative.com

JOANNE KOLTES
represents

MEG SMITH
ILLUSTRATION

PHONE (612) 884-4045 FAX (612) 884-3450
www.dimensioncreative.com

JOY
of ILLUSTRATION

Joy Massen Shidla
6037 11th Avenue South
Minneapolis, MN 55417
P/F 612~866~0358

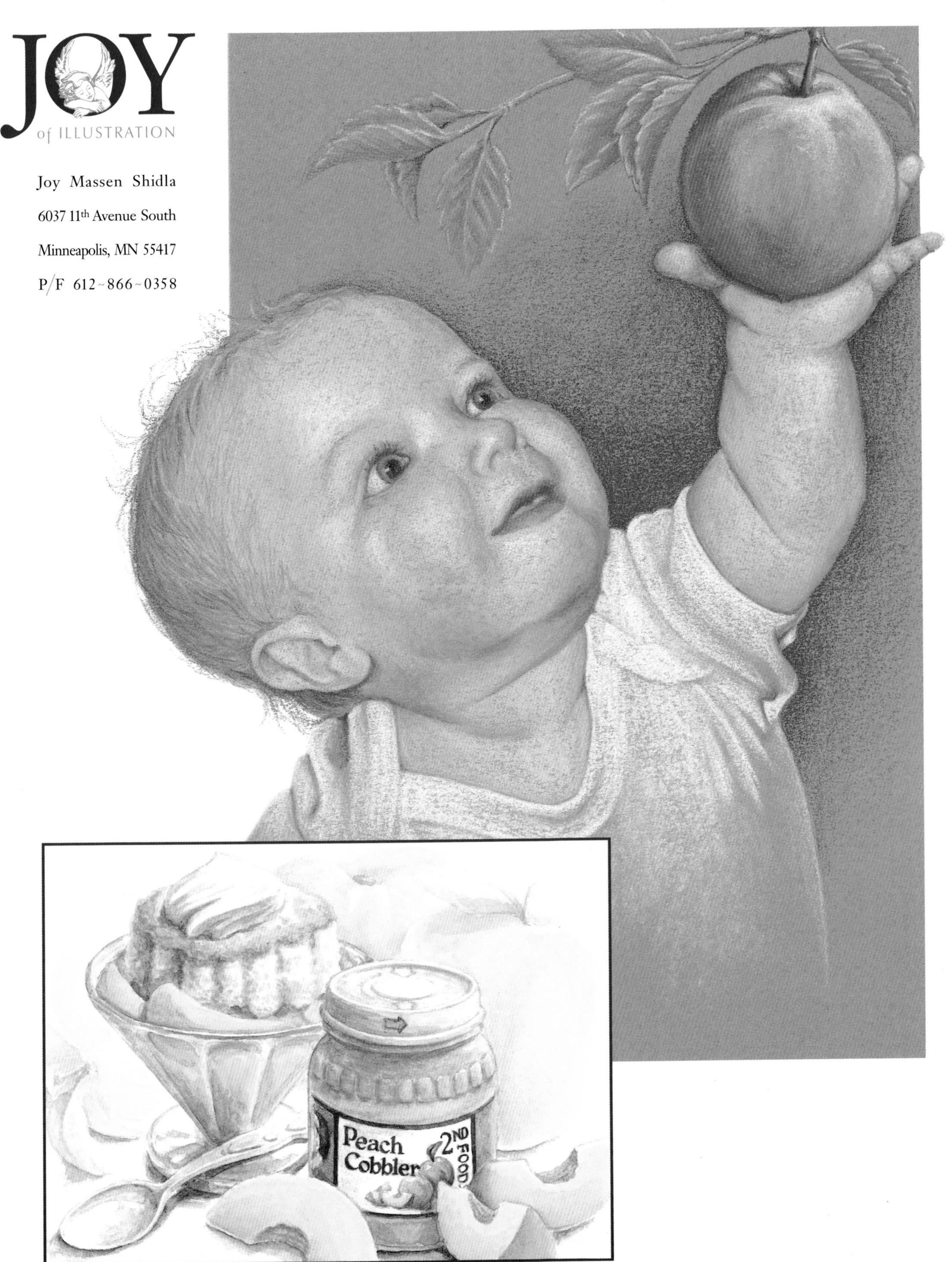

STEPHEN BAUER

LINDA CANE

PAUL DEMPSEY

JEFF FITZ-MAURICE

PATRICK GNAN

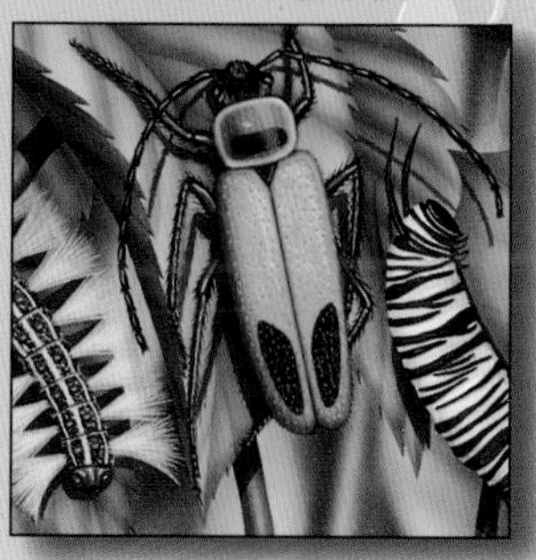

STEVE GREENBERG

MARIANNE HUGHES

LYNN JEFFERY

JOSEPH PAGE KOVACH

DEAN KUBE

JEFF LeVAN

BARBARA McADAMS

J.T. MORROW

731 N 24TH ST PHILA PA 19130 www.deborahwolfeltd.com 215.232.6666 fax 232.6585

Laura Stutzman

100 G Street Mtn. Lake Park MD 21550
V. 301 334-4086 F. 301 334-4186
eloqui@aol.com Eloqui www.eloqui.com

Eloqui is a studio devoted exclusively to illustration

AFIS

Tyndale Publishing

Consultant Pharmacist

Pocket Books

Mick Coulas Candace Lourdes

416-698-3304

416-698-3304
Mick
Coulas
Candace
Lourdes

CLOR
3-D Illustration
Computer Imaging
Chris Clor / Represented by Mike Iezzi
phone 248.583.5540 fax 248.583.3216
cclor@aol.com

METRO NEWSLAND!

Cottage Country
Ottawa
Georgian Bay
METRO TORONTO NEWS
Kingston
Barrie
Lake Huron
Toronto
Cobourg
Lake Ontario
Kitchener
QEW
401
London
Brantford
St Catharines
Lake Erie
Windsor

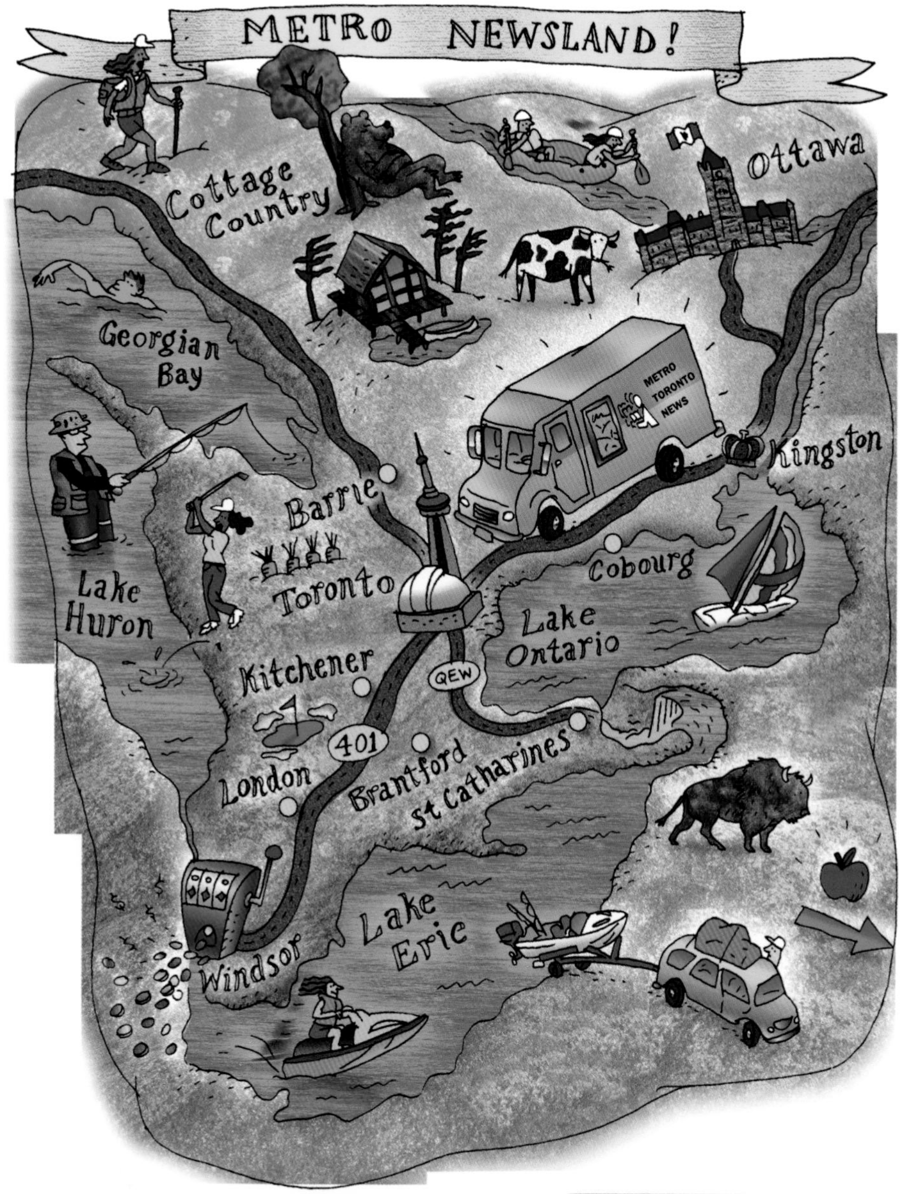

Stephen MacEachern T 905 271 7410 F 905 271 5922 E quack@inforamp.net

Matthews Griffith
music
Art Hill on the b&w line: (503)590-6767
represented by Deborah
R410
Brough Superior
COSINA
LOVE RIDE
11
HARLEY-DAVIDSON OF GLENDALE
©1998 Art Hill

Greg Mably (416) 410-8744

digital Illustration

represented by

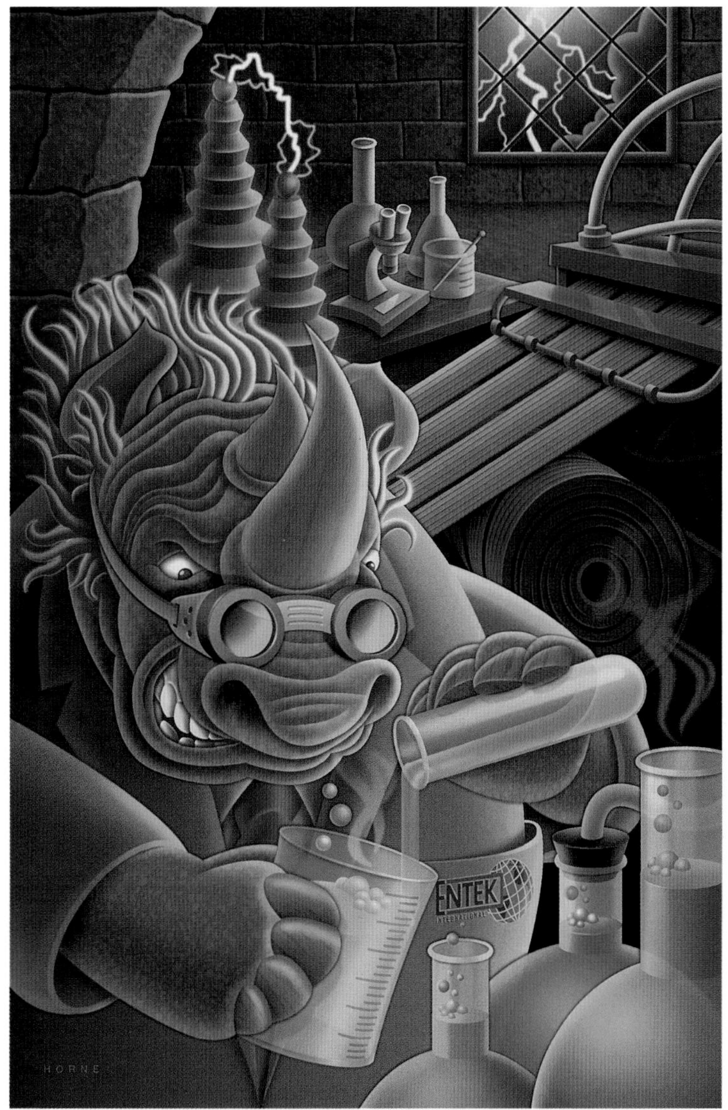

Please contact Christine

p 503.658.7070
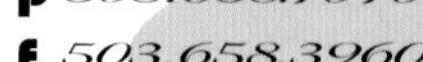
f 503.658.3960

artist studio *doug horne*
phone 602.553.8438
fax 602.956.6919

represented by

christine prapas

stephen **HOGAN**

Please contact Christine

p 503.658.7070
f 503.658.3960

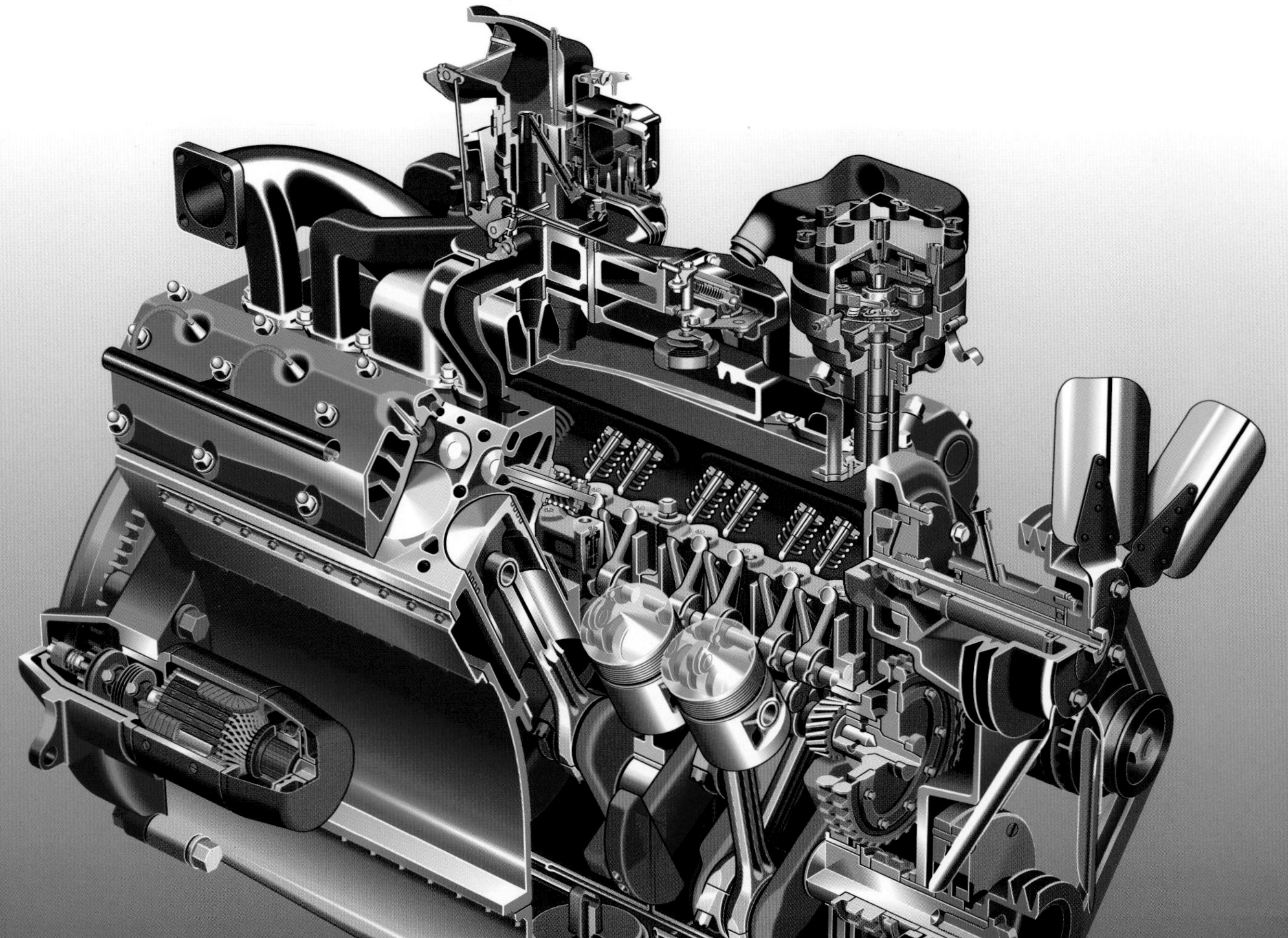

Technical digital illustrations created in Adobe Illustrator

artist studio *stephen hogan*
phone 914.737.4304
fax 914.736.6524

jeff **FOSTER**

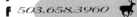

Einstein Bros. poster /mixed media and hand lettering on board

Esco earth moving poster /mixed media on board

represented by

christine prapas

Please contact Christine

p 503.658.7070
f 503.658.3960

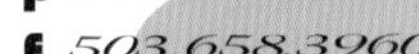

Northwest Natural Gas business campaign / airbrush on board

Chronicle book cover, "Food Lovers Companion to Portland" /mixed media

studio jeff foster
phone 503.223.1884
fax 503.221.2483

represented by

see also: Blackbook '95, '96, '97, '98

partial client list includes:
L A Times Magazine
Harcourt Brace & Co.
Puffin Books
Random House
Utne Reader Magazine
Playboy
Polygram Records
NEC Computers
Candlewick Press
Phillips Interactive
Sybase
Hewlett Packard
Killian's Irish Red Beer

Please contact Christine

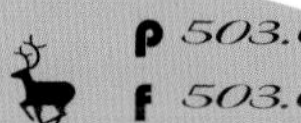

p 503.658.7070
f 503.658.3960

brad WEINMAN

"Sex, Symbols, and the Stars" book cover for The Book Tree — oil on paper

"Smart Dog" book cover for Harcourt Brace & Co. — oil on paper

Advertisement for MEKOS Corporation — oil on paper

brad's studio hotline:

phone 818.342.9984
fax 818.342.9985
e-mail: brado@linkonline.net

dan **BROWN**

represented by

christine prapas

Please contact Christine

p 503.658.7070
f 503.658.3960

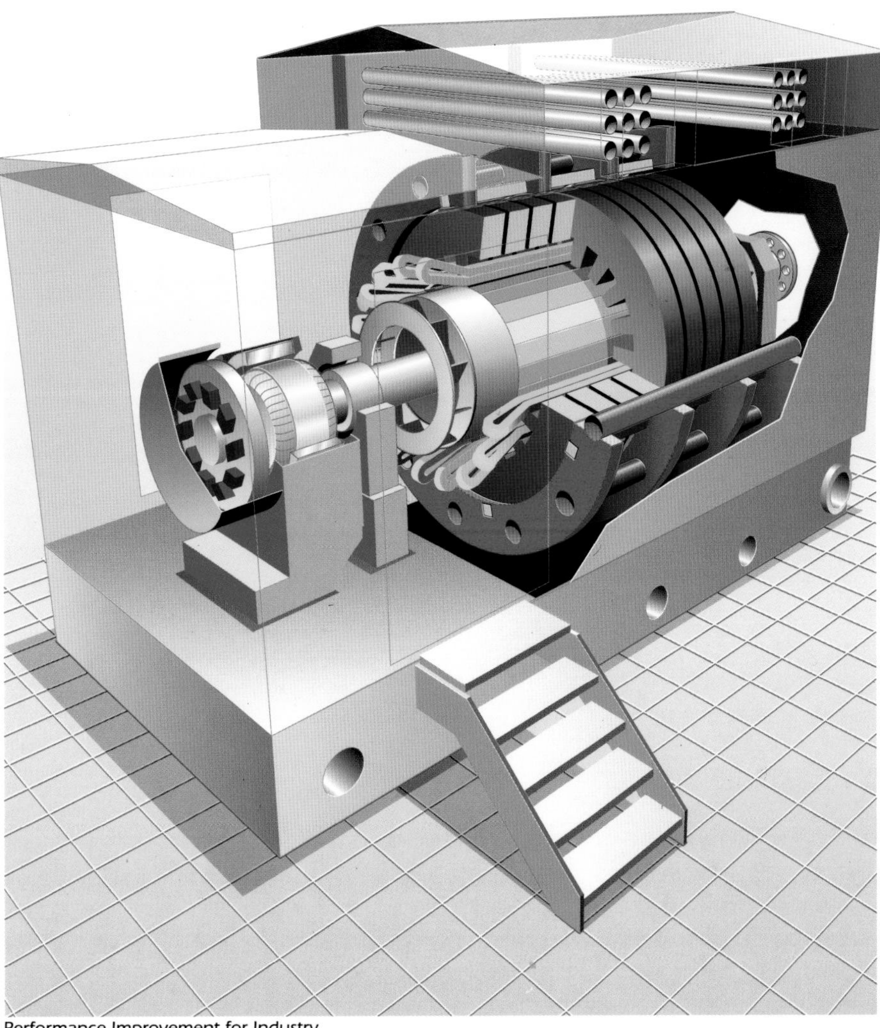

Performance Improvement for Industry

Computer Illustration on a PC.

- Editorial
- Technical
- Black and White

More examples at
http://www.pacifier.com/~danbrown

See also Black Book 96, 97, 98

artist studio dan brown
phone 360.737.9920
e-mail danbrown@pacifier.com

represented by

kim **MALEK**

Please contact Christine

p 503.658.7070
f 503.658.3960

Telemark/digital final

Hewlett-Packard/digital

Paccess/digital final

artist studio *kim malek*
phone 503.223.4250
fax 503.223.2719

malekstudio@id-inc.com

steve **ELLIS**

represented by

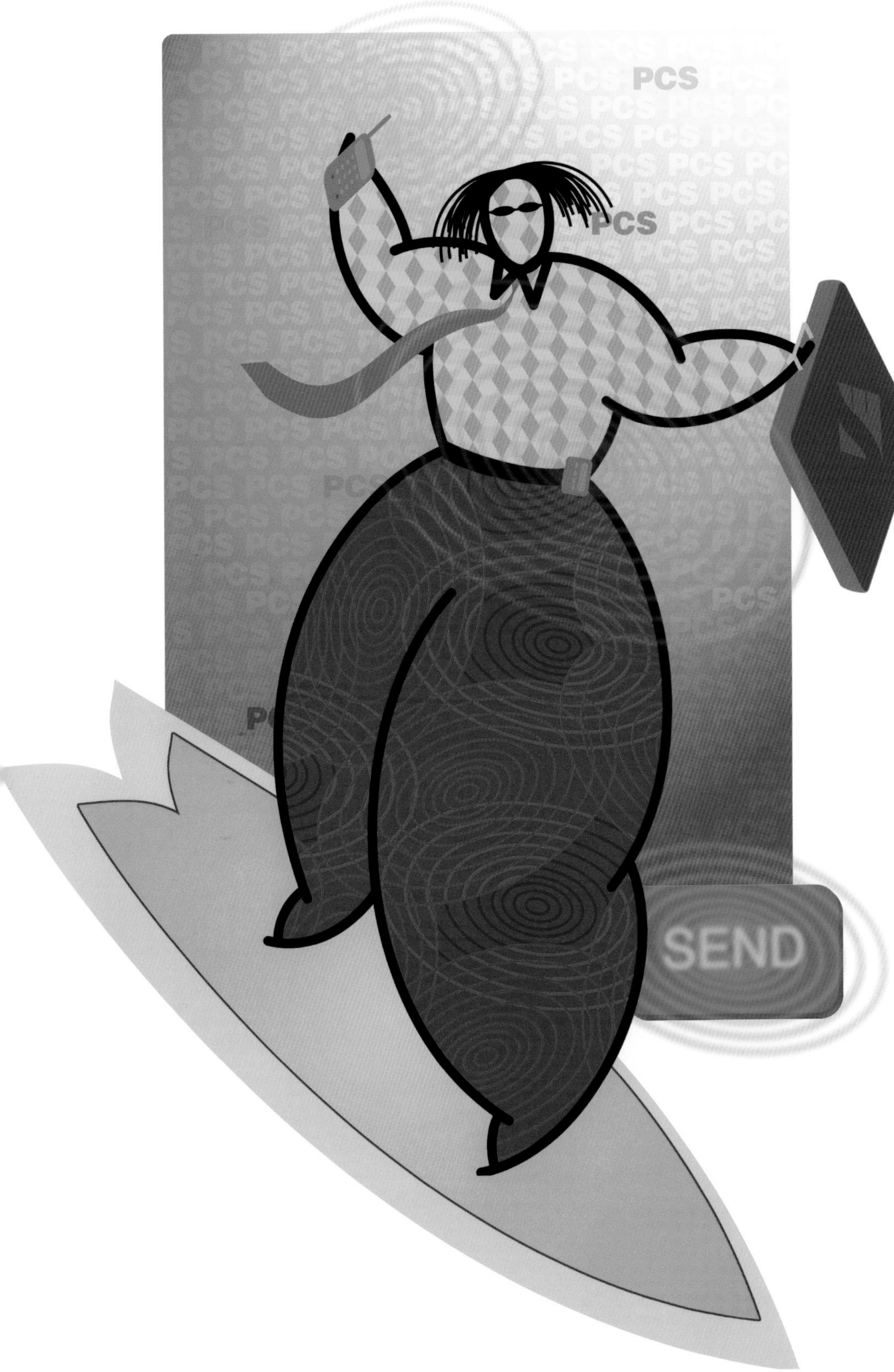

Please contact Christine

artist studio *steve ellis*
phone 310.792.1888
fax 310.318.9079

east coast *penny and stermer group*
phone 212.505.9342
fax 212.505.1844

represented by

christine prapas

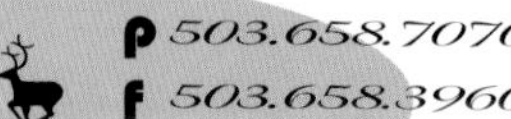

michael **CARROLL**

Illustration for children's story "Sillyville"

Please contact Christine

p *503.658.7070*
f *503.658.3960*

Traditional and digital techniques

NetPro Software

chicago *steven edsey*
phone 312.527.0351
fax 312.527.5468

http://www.studiomike.com
phone 708.386.6197
fax 708.386.6125

phoenix *marla matson*
phone 602.252.5072
fax 602.252.5073

OLIVIA

represented by

Honda

Please contact Christine

p 503.658.7070
f 503.658.3960

Call for mini-portfolio!

Pacific Lending

Hewlett Packard

Stock

Arnerich Massena

artist studio olivia
phone 505.471.8300
fax 505.471.3959 • email: MacBruja@aol.com

RON BOMBA STUDIO
INDUSTRIAL, TECHNICAL &
PRODUCT ILLUSTRATION
206-286-1277
1
2
3
4
5
6
7
8
9
FLEXOR
DRYFINGER
DRYFINGER
HOBERMAN
MINI SPHERE™
HOBERMAN
Moon Glow™
MINI
SPHERE™
Transforming Globe
Magically Unfolds
from 5½" to 12"
Visualize your project in stunning full color realism.
At Ron Bomba Studio we can transform your ideas, blueprints or prototypes into high resolution 3-D images, suitable for printing, advertising, exhibit, animation or web site.

JOHN AMOSS • ILLUSTRATION

(404) 636-0275 FAX(404) 633-2628 • 1177 Willivee Dr. Decatur, GA 30033 • http://www.mindspring.com/~amoss

Available in Photoshop.eps, Adobe Illustrator or Aldus Freehand.
GUIDE BOOK

Clients include AT&T, Lucent Technologies, Prudential Securities, New York Times, Washington Post, McCall's Magazine, Family Circle, Children's Television Workshop and others.

Illustration for Print and the Web

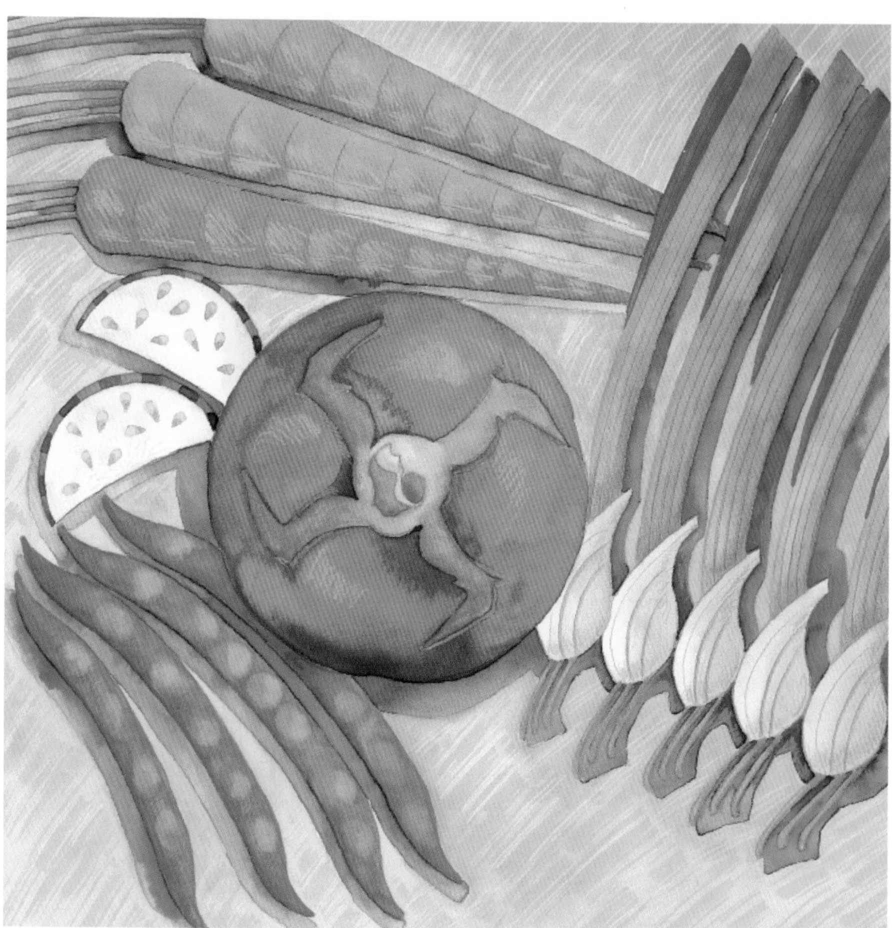

TEL: 415-893-9292 FAX: 415-893-9464 WEB: studionorthnet.com

HEATHER GRAHAM
416 536 1543

KAREN ALBANESE CAMPBELL
Illustration

614-268-2175
155 OAKLAND PARK AVENUE
COLUMBUS, OHIO 43214

Jeff **Kronen**

Philippe **Collot**

Bob **Towner**

Jerry **Vivit**

Meridee **Mandio**

Lee **Wilson**

Shannon **Hogan**

Duff **Moses**

Trevor **Goring**

Shari **Wickstrom**

Collin **Grant**

Gary **Ciccati**

FAMOUS FRAMES

Mark **Yates**

Mark **Millicent**

<u>S T O R Y B O A R D S</u>

<u>A N I M A T I C S</u>

<u>C O M P S</u>

LA **310.642.2721**

NY **212.980.7979**

800.530.3375

www.**famousframes.com**

Portfolio available upon request.

Alex **Morris**

Rod **Dryden**

lex **McOwan**

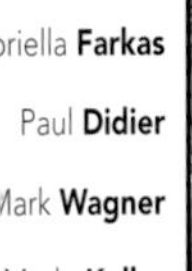

riella **Farkas**

Paul **Didier**

lark **Wagner**

Merle **Keller**

nnifer **Baker**

Michael **Lee**

nnie **Brenno**

an **Pavlovits**

Paul **Binkley**

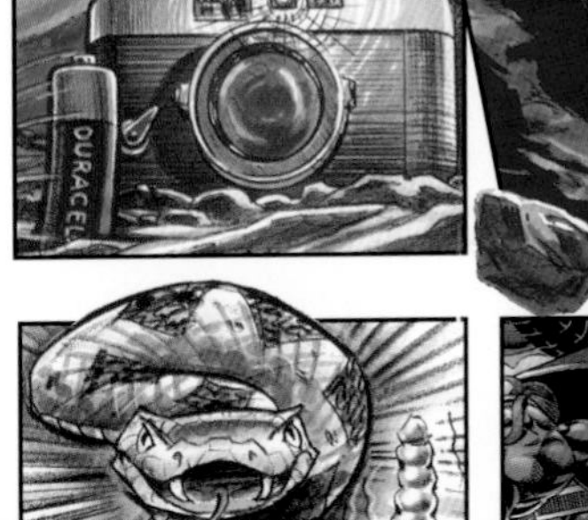

Walter **Lee**

interbottom

Luis **Molina**

illian **Nelson**

cott **Ownbey**

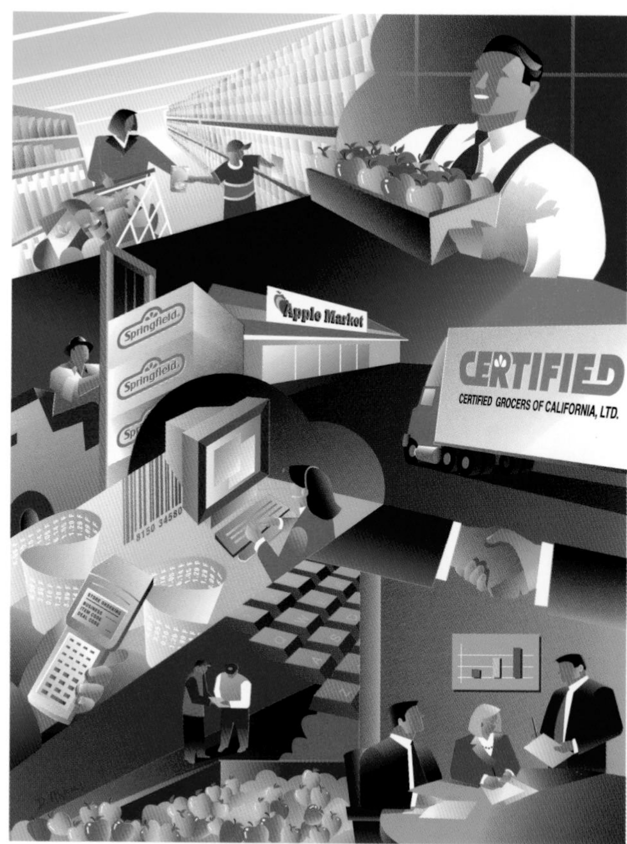

E-MAIL: harmsillst@earthlink.net WEBSITE http://home.earthlink.net/~harmsillst

DENNIS HARMS 847-304-9952

ILLUSTRATION FAX-304-9953

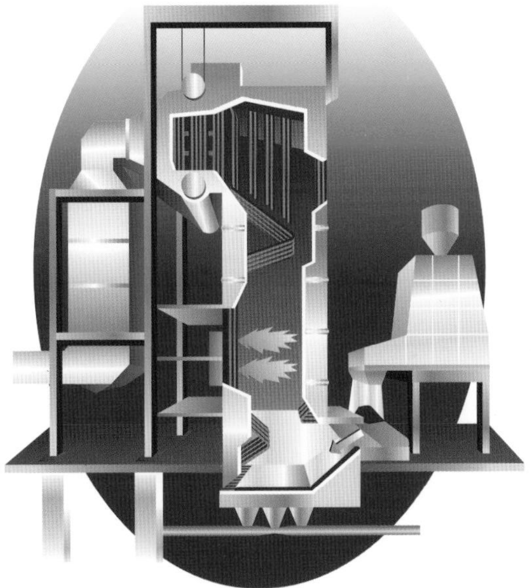

E-MAIL: harmsillst@earthlink.net WEBSITE http://home.earthlink.net/~harmsillst

DENNIS HARMS 847-304-9952

ILLUSTRATION FAX-304-9953

SCOTT **POLLACK** 516 921 1908

john Francis

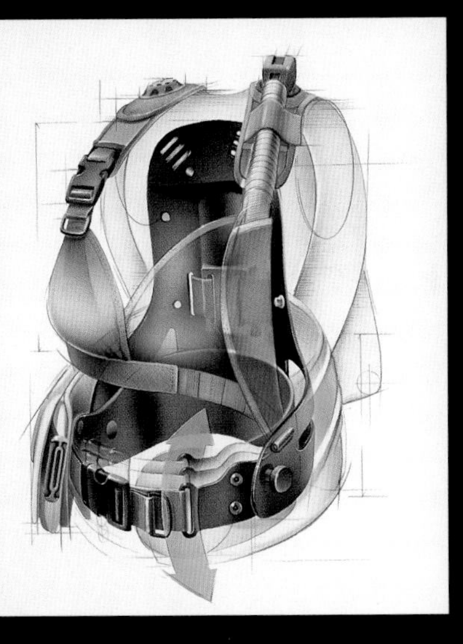

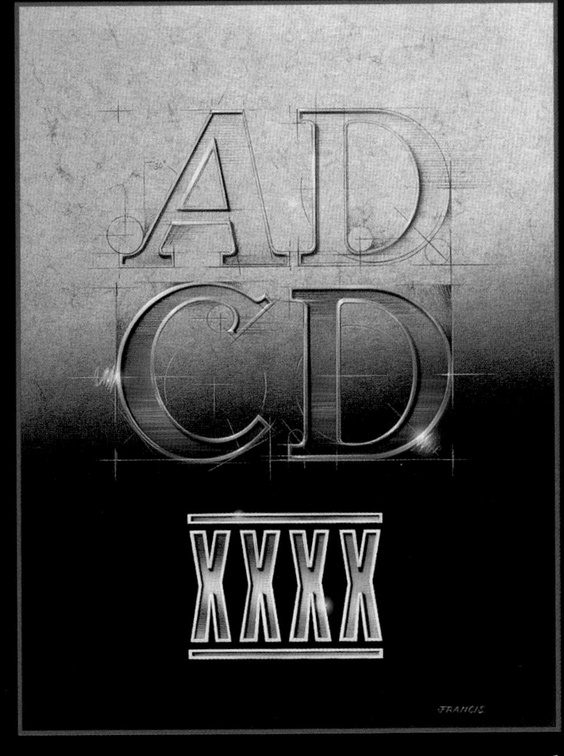

1610 Wynkoop Suite 600 Denver,Colorado. 80202
303 595 3805 fax 595 3808 www.jfrancis.com

J u l i e J o h n s o n

Recent client list: Walt Disney Publishing, Simon & Schuster, United Airlines, L'Oreal, Jean Paul Gaultier, Bauer Publishing, New York Jazz Festival.

represented by

Anita Grien
voice 212.697.6170
fax 212.697.6177
www.anitagrien.com

Midwest:
Roger Johnson
voice 765.497.7504
fax 765.497.2180

roger johnson

associates

LANE DUPONT

DIGITAL ILLUSTRATION

JOHN BREWSTER CREATIVE SERVICES 203·226·4724 fax 203·454·9904
visit us at www.brewstercreative.com

LANE DUPONT

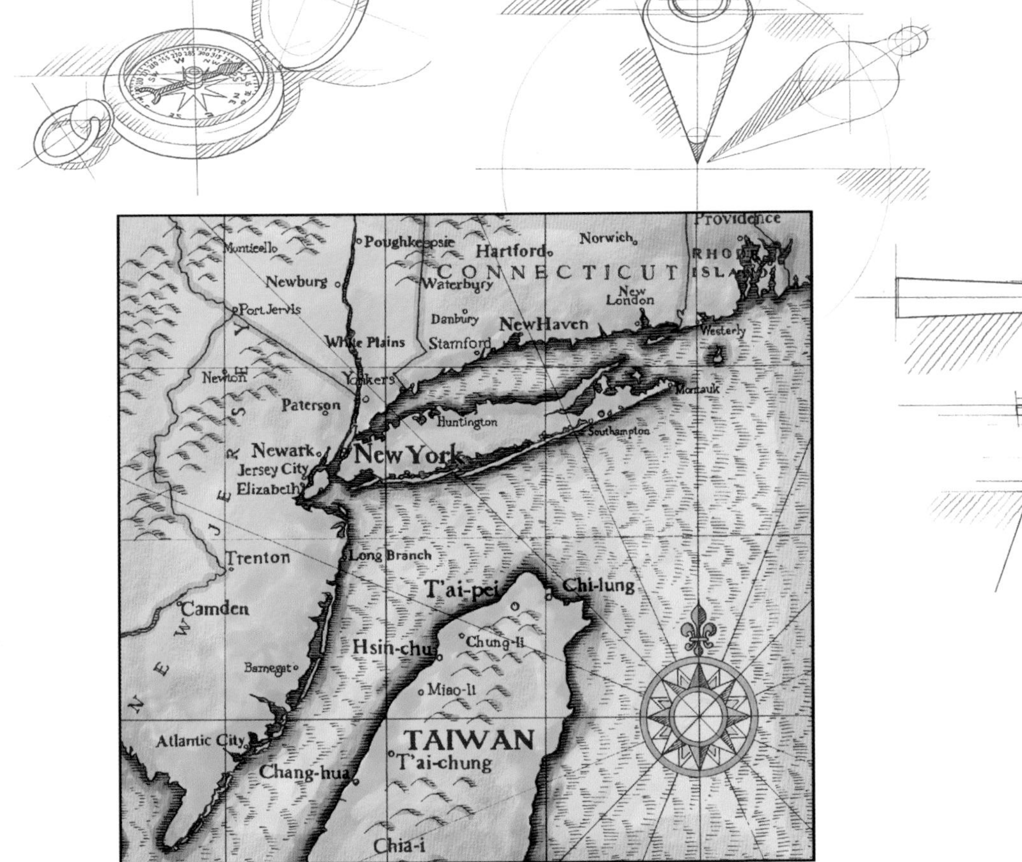

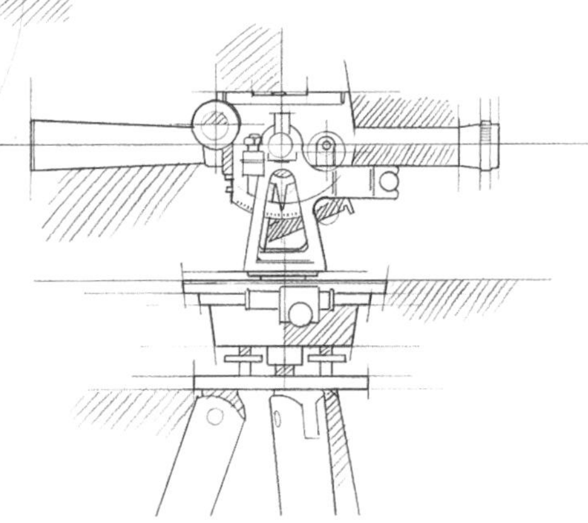

JOHN BREWSTER CREATIVE SERVICES 203·226·4724 fax 203·454·9904
visit us at www.brewstercreative.com

Robert L. Prince

JOHN BREWSTER CREATIVE SERVICES 203·226·4724 fax 203·454·9904
visit us at www.brewstercreative.com

RM SCHNEIDER

JOHN BREWSTER CREATIVE SERVICES 203·226·4724 fax 203·454·9904
visit us at www.brewstercreative.com

Miles Parnell
JOLLY ROGER
RUM

Roger Chandler

Represented by John Brewster Creative Services
203 226.4724 fax 454.9904 www.brewstercreative.com
studio 619 551.1135

GORAN BILLINGSKOG

DIGITAL ILLUSTRATION

JOHN BREWSTER CREATIVE SERVICES 203·226·4724 fax 203·454·9904
visit us at www.brewstercreative.com

S E T H   L A R S O N

DIMENSIONAL ILLUSTRATION

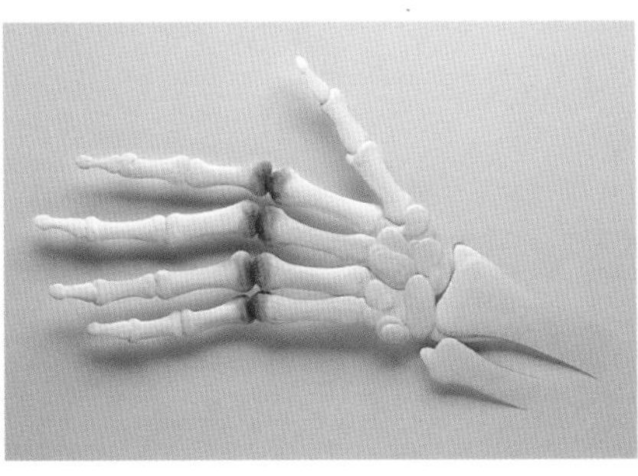

JOHN BREWSTER CREATIVE SERVICES 203·226·4724 fax 203·454·9904
visit us at www.brewstercreative.com

Debbie
Tilley
subway map
Studio (760) 432-6282 fax (760) 738-8019
Represented by Richard Salzman
Phone (415) 285-8267 fax (415) 285-8268

eye catching art • clever ideas • bold design • on ti

ILLUSTRATION

[619] 296.9323

GRAHAM SMIT

illustration • design • packaging • collateral • fashion collections • products • san diego c

Joe Boxer®

CARPENTER PANTS

Joe Boxer®

Corduroy Carpenter Pants

TOOL POCKET

HAMMER LOOP

SMILEY LOGO

PREMIUM

CP

The original joe boxer brand corduroy carpenter pants

• EXTRA POCKETS
• EXTRA WIDE
• EXTRA COOL
• EXTRA QUALITY
• TRADE MARK

Established When We Had Time

AUTHENTIC JOE BOXER DESIGN

ENGINEERED FOR GOOD LOOKS AND STYLE

PREMIUM QUALITY CORDUROY CARPENTER PANTS

JOE BOXER

ROBERT STOCK COMPANY

REGISTERED RS BRAND

CONGRATULATIONS ON PURCHASING GENUINE ROBERT STOCK QUALITY CLOTHING PRODUCTS.

ROBERT STOCK

OVERSIZED

DOUBLE BARREL

EXTRA-WIDE

RSCO

TRADE MARK

EXTRA-WIDE

ROBERT STOCK COMPANY

WWW.ARTMASTERS.NET

cool type • logos • labels • screenprints • mega genius & nice guy • call now

happy clients • Levi Strauss & Co • Gotcha • Joe Boxer • OshKosh B'gosh • Disney
GRAHAM SMITH
art on disk
[619] 296.9323
ILLUSTRATIONS
GRAHAM SMITH
WWW.ARTMASTERS.NET
ART MASTERS
ILLUSTRATION & DESIGN

TERRI SCHWARZ
(314) 644-0091

HOTEL
RITA LASCARO
DIGITAL DRAWINGS
TEL 212.677.6494
FAX 212.260.6076
EMAIL britonia@aol.com
e
A
29
USA

I HAVE ALSO DRAWN BUFFALOES, BUNNIES, BUSINESSMEN, CARS, KIDS, WAGONS, TREES, TRAINS, PLANES, VANS, SCIENTISTS, SOFAS, SPIES, STUDENTS, SUITCASES, JUDGES, LAWYERS, OUTLAWS, MAZES, PUSHPINS, BALD GUYS, AND LOTS OF OTHER THINGS FOR AAA, THE ABA, THE AHA, BUDGET, GTE, HEWLETT PACKARD, MARCEL SCHURMAN, MCDONALD'S, NATION'S RESTAURANT NEWS, QUAKER, TARGET, TRAVELERS INSURANCE, UNITED AIRLINES, AND OTHER FINE FOLKS.

FLORIDA

Tampa

Miami

N

W

E

S

BERNEY KNOX

ILLUSTRATION

THE NEIS GROUP

ILLUSTRATION • DESIGN • PHOTOGRAPHY

11440 OAK DRIVE • P.O. BOX 174 • SHELBYVILLE, MICHIGAN 49344
TELEPHONE 616-672-5756 • FAX 616-672-5757 • www.neisgroup.com

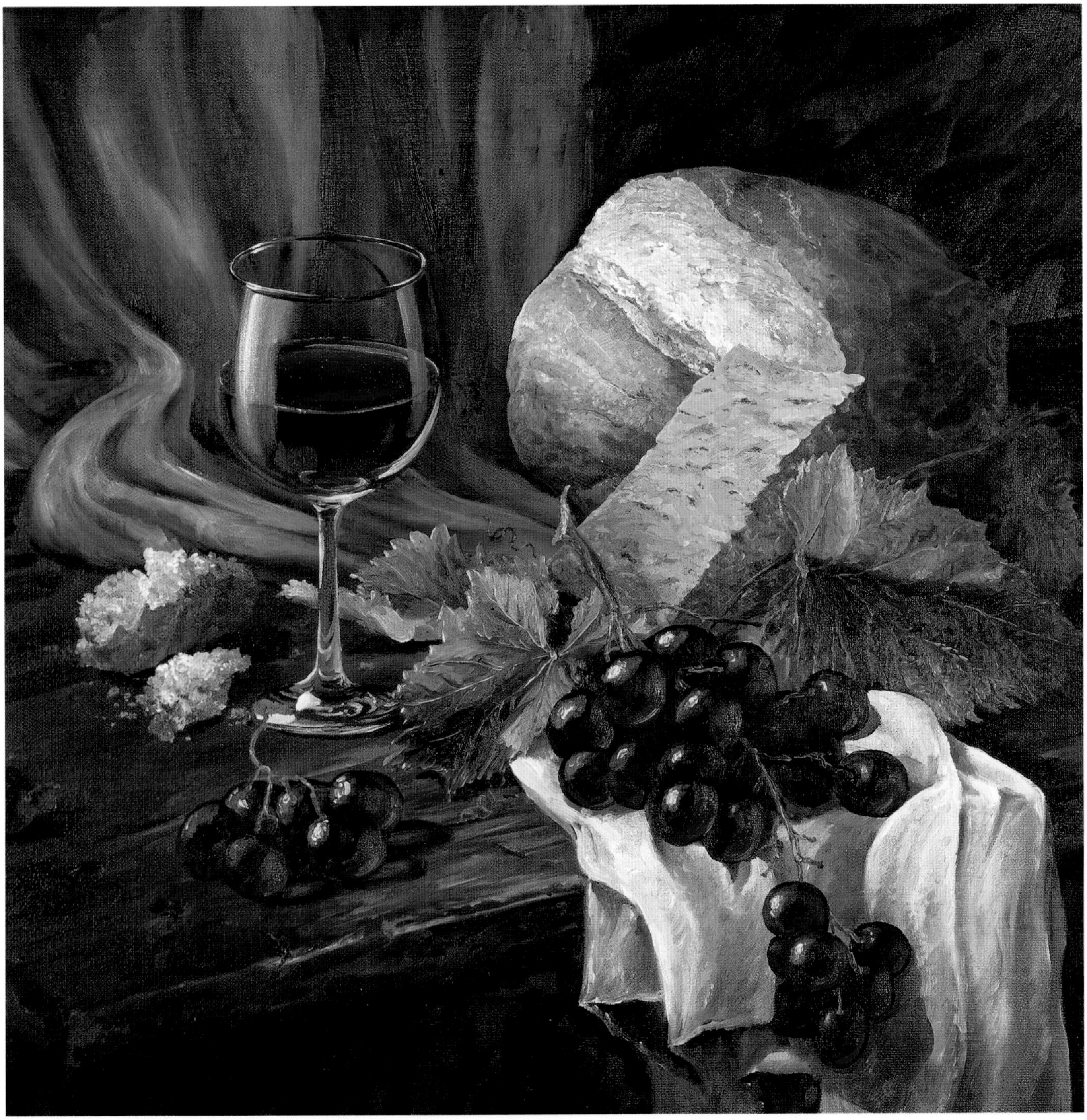

CLINT HANSEN

ILLUSTRATION

THE NEIS GROUP

ILLUSTRATION • DESIGN • PHOTOGRAPHY

11440 OAK DRIVE • P.O. BOX 174 • SHELBYVILLE, MICHIGAN 49344
TELEPHONE 616-672-5756 • FAX 616-672-5757 • www.neisgroup.com

ERIKA LeBARRE
ILLUSTRATION

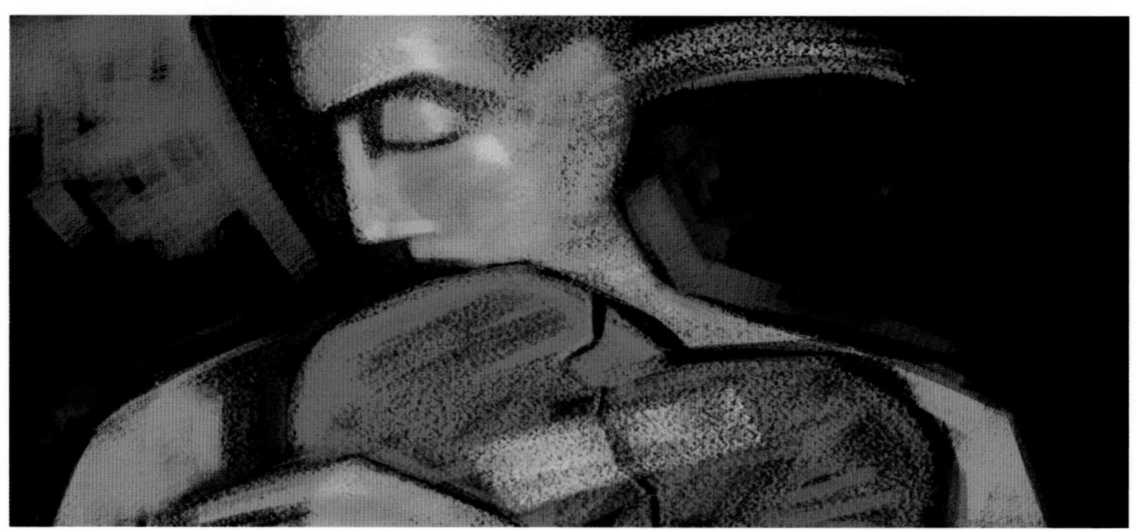

PAUL LACKNER
ILLUSTRATION

THE NEIS GROUP
ILLUSTRATION • DESIGN • PHOTOGRAPHY

11440 OAK DRIVE • P.O. BOX 174 • SHELBYVILLE, MICHIGAN 49344
TELEPHONE 616-672-5756 • FAX 616-672-5757 • www.neisgroup.com

J O H N   W H I T E

I L L U S T R A T I O N

THE NEIS GROUP

ILLUSTRATION • DESIGN • PHOTOGRAPHY

11440 OAK DRIVE • P.O. BOX 174 • SHELBYVILLE, MICHIGAN 49344
TELEPHONE 616-672-5756 • FAX 616-672-5757 • www.neisgroup.com

Cub Scouts Rule!

Cub Scouts ONLY!

CHIPS

ICE

GARRY COLBY

ILLUSTRATION

THE NEIS GROUP

ILLUSTRATION • DESIGN • PHOTOGRAPHY

11440 OAK DRIVE • P.O. BOX 174 • SHELBYVILLE, MICHIGAN 49344
TELEPHONE 616-672-5756 • FAX 616-672-5757 • www.neisgroup.com

Fa·la la la la·laaa··la la la·laaa

L I Z   C O N R A D

I L L U S T R A T I O N

THE NEIS GROUP

ILLUSTRATION • DESIGN • PHOTOGRAPHY

11440 OAK DRIVE • P.O. BOX 174 • SHELBYVILLE, MICHIGAN 49344

TELEPHONE 616-672-5756 • FAX 616-672-5757 • www.neisgroup.com

P E G   M A G O V E R N

I L L U S T R A T I O N

THE NEIS GROUP

ILLUSTRATION • DESIGN • PHOTOGRAPHY

11440 OAK DRIVE • P.O. BOX 174 • SHELBYVILLE, MICHIGAN 49344
TELEPHONE 616-672-5756 • FAX 616-672-5757 • www.neisgroup.com

MATT LeBARRE

ILLUSTRATION

THE NEIS GROUP

ILLUSTRATION • DESIGN • PHOTOGRAPHY

11440 OAK DRIVE • P.O. BOX 174 • SHELBYVILLE, MICHIGAN 49344
TELEPHONE 616-672-5756 • FAX 616-672-5757 • www.neisgroup.com

Patty O'Friel!
FEBRUARY
DON'T SQUEEZE ME!
10%
900
VINO Red
NEWS
PRESS
KEEP OUT!
PRIVATE PROPERTY
BEWARE OF LAWYER
Fresh
FONE & FAX NO.
Chicago 773 384 3496
Wanna see more? Check out black books 7, 8, & 9!

MICHELE NIDENOFF

416-482-5348 FAX 416-932-9297

Lite

Miller Time

STUDIO 212°

STUDIO 212° • DALLAS • CONTACT BILL JENKINS • PHONE 214 744 4421 • FAX 214 720 0080

Lite
Miller Time
Miller Lite
Lite
Miller Time
STUDIO 212°
STUDIO 212° • DALLAS • CONTACT BILL JENKINS • PHONE 214 744 4421 • FAX 214 [illegible]20 0080

JOSEPH
TAYLOR
CALL DAVID MONTAGANO 312-527-3283
STUDIO 847-328-2454
When it's more than OK, It's
O-KE-DOKE
CHEESE
FLAVORED POPCORN
Jays
FAT FREE
33% LESS SODIUM
THINS
BAKED PRETZELS
Jays
Can't stop eating 'em
Potato Chips
VIVA los Cabos
IMPORTED
100% FINE JAMAICAN RUM
WORLD FAMOUS
MYERS'S RUM
Original Dark
Ashland
UNLEADED
PLUS
ISDN
ISDN
ISDN

MARY • JONES

REPRESENTED BY
David Montagano
TELEPHONE 312.527.3283
FACSIMILE 312.527.2108

JEFF CLINE'S
HUMOROUS ILLUSTRATION
FACTORY
PHONE/FAX: (800) 770-4089
I'D LIKE A CHICKEN WITH GLASSES.
RAW HUMOR
INK
RING RING
SHIPPING DEPT.

Kodak Professional
CYAN
MAGENTA
YELLOW
BLACK
opyright © 1998, Eastman Kodak Company
l Rights Reserved
eveloped by Camlight Systems, NYC
Surge Graphix LLC
ph 212-995-5290 fax 212-388-0276
fusion@escape.com www.surgegraphix.com
3D Illustration, Multimedia, Medical, Real Estate,
Animation, Video, Lingo Programming, Charts & Graphs

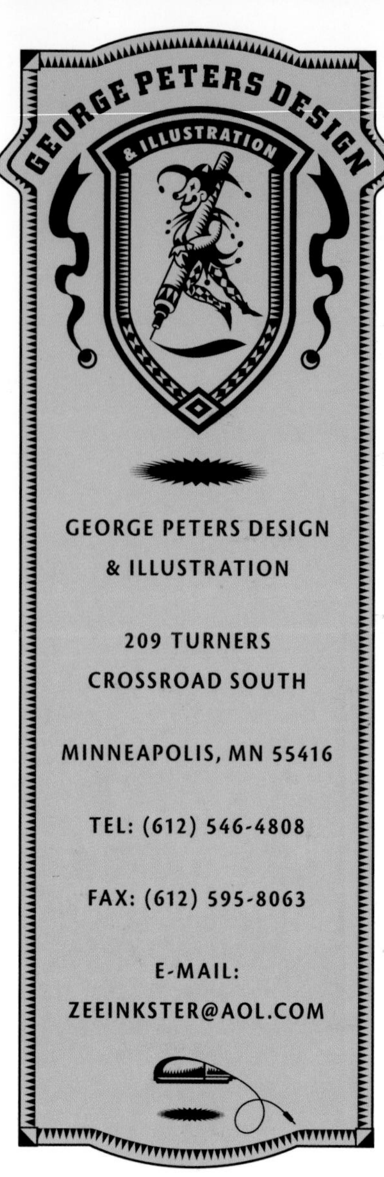

GEORGE PETERS DESIGN
& ILLUSTRATION

209 TURNERS
CROSSROAD SOUTH

MINNEAPOLIS, MN 55416

TEL: (612) 546-4808

FAX: (612) 595-8063

E-MAIL:
ZEEINKSTER@AOL.COM

Comfort
FOOD

The maximum dosage of digital humor allowed by law!

GERBER STUDIO/Tradigital Illustration

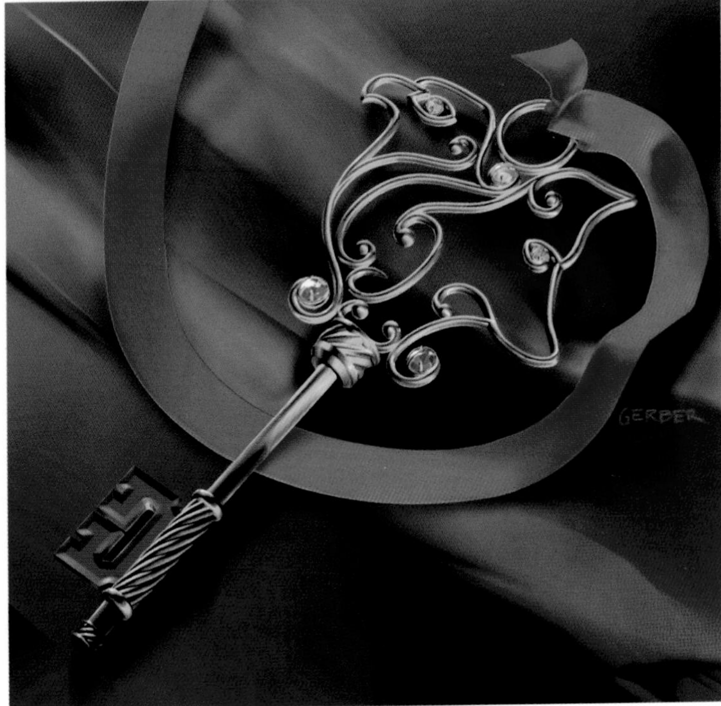

Represented by
Pat Heroux Goudreau

Phone: 413.967.9855
Fax: 413.967.3293

Roc Goudreau

Represented by
Pat Heroux Goudreau

PG REPRESENTATIVES
VISUAL COMMUNICATION

Phone: 413.967.9855
Fax: 413.967.3293

Chuck Primeau

© Hasbro, Inc.

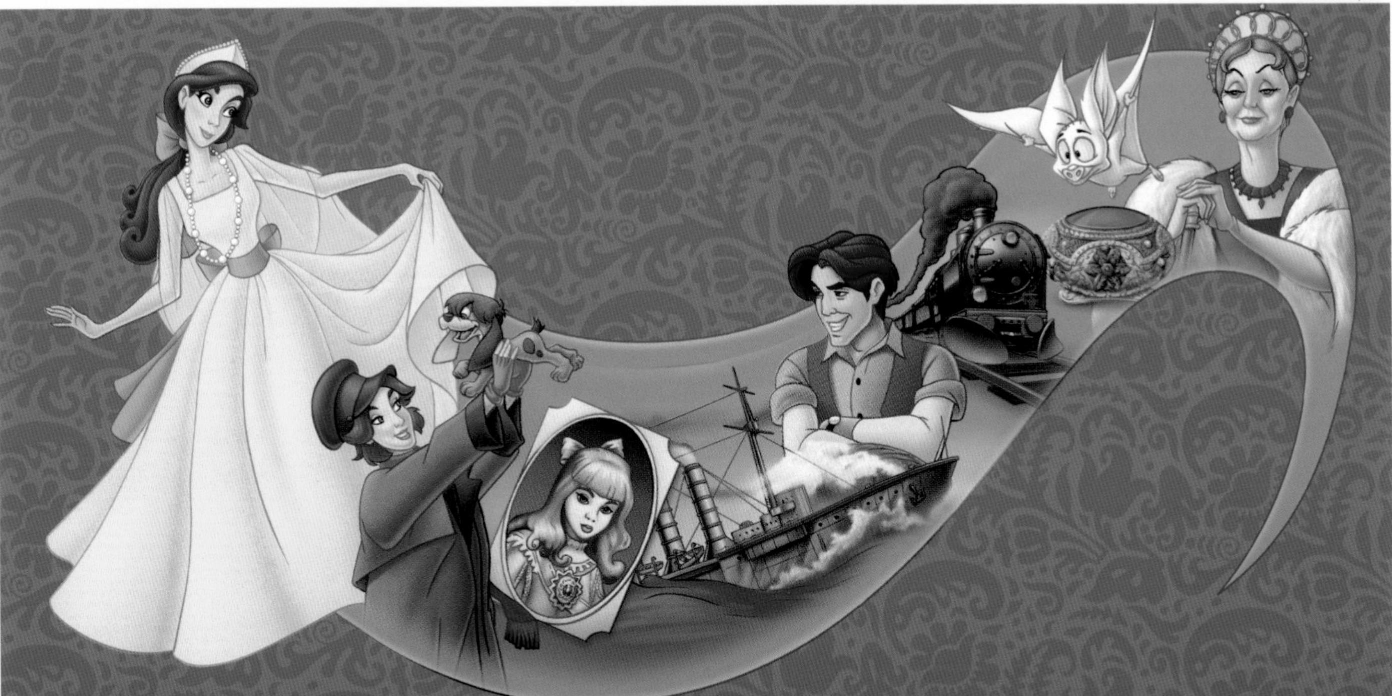

© &™ Fox Animation Studio, Inc.

© Disney

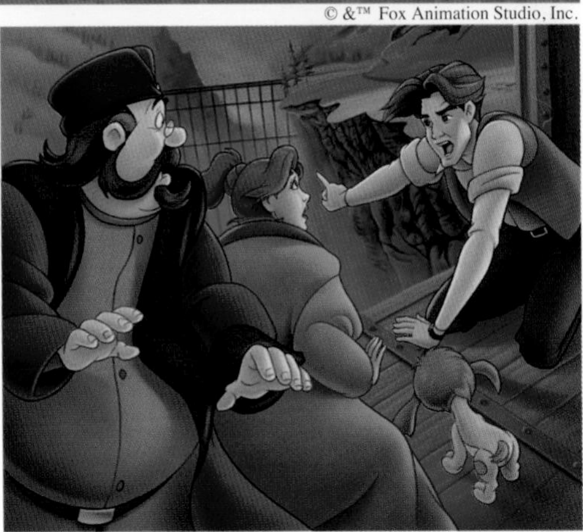

© &™ Fox Animation Studio, Inc.

Represented by
Pat Heroux Goudreau

Phone: 413.967.9855
Fax: 413.967.3293

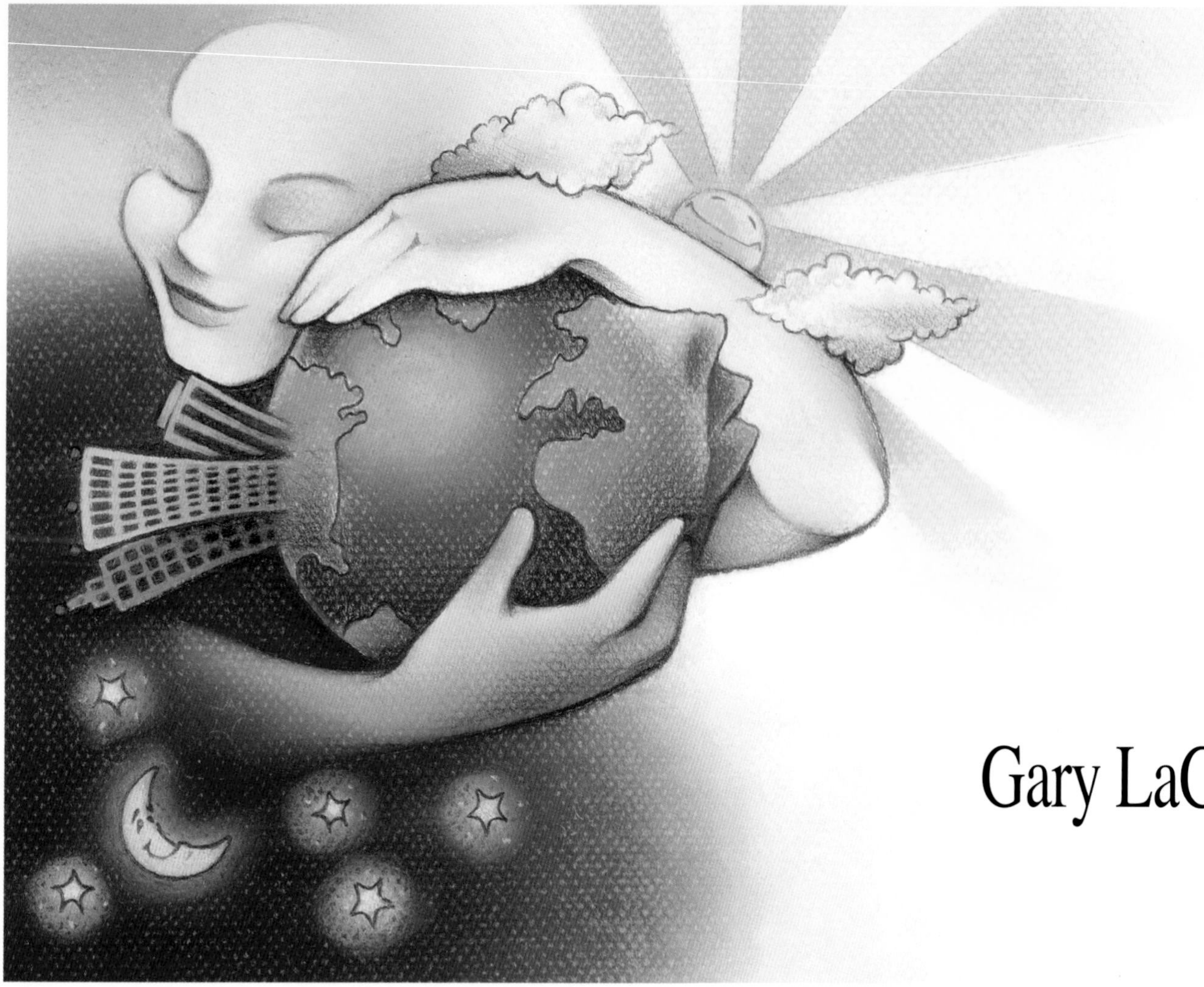

Gary LaCoste

Image created with Adobe Photoshop.®

Represented by
Pat Heroux Goudreau

Phone: 413.967.9855
Fax: 413.967.3293

Robbie Short

▼ Represented by Pat Heroux Goudreau
▼ Phone: 413.967.9855 ▼ Fax: 413.967.3293

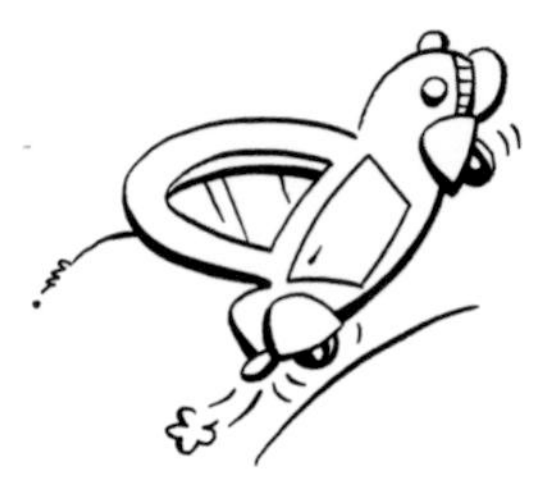

Jackie Snider
(705) 924-1487

Stephen Snider

(705) 924-1487

Also see Creative Illustration Book 1994 pg. 538, Creative Illustration Book 1995 pg. 395, Black Book Illustration 1996 pg. 389 and Black Book Illustration 1997 pg. 306.

THE ILLUSTRATION LAB

Andrew Peycha

91 Cowan Ave., Toronto, ON M6K 2N1

Studio (416) 725-8122 / Fax (416) 516-8104

ERIC DEVER

New Work ILLUSTRATION

represented by MICHELE MANASSE

Playboy, Japan

Le cimetière du Père-Lachaise

MATTHEW TRUEMAN

represented by MICHELE MANASSE

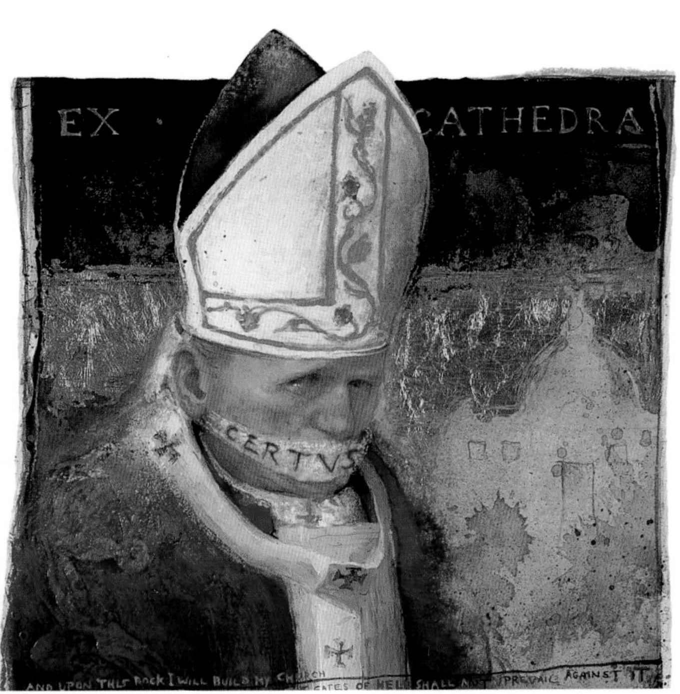

"The Silence"

"www.st.sebastian.com"

ph 215.862.2091 fax 215.862.2641 e-mail mmanasse@new-work.com web www.voicenet.com/~mmanasse

represented by MICHELE MANASSE

Pace Communications

Avon Books

National Geographic Traveler

ph 215.862.2091 fax 215.862.2641 e-mail mmanasse@new-work.com web www.voicenet.com/~mmanasse

MAXINE BOLL-HUGHES

represented by MICHELE MANASSE

The City of Fort Lauderdale

Asahi Wines, Japan

Moët & Chandon

Food & Wine Books

ph 215.862.2091 fax 215.862.2641 e-mail mmanasse@new-work.com web www.voicenet.com/~mmanasse

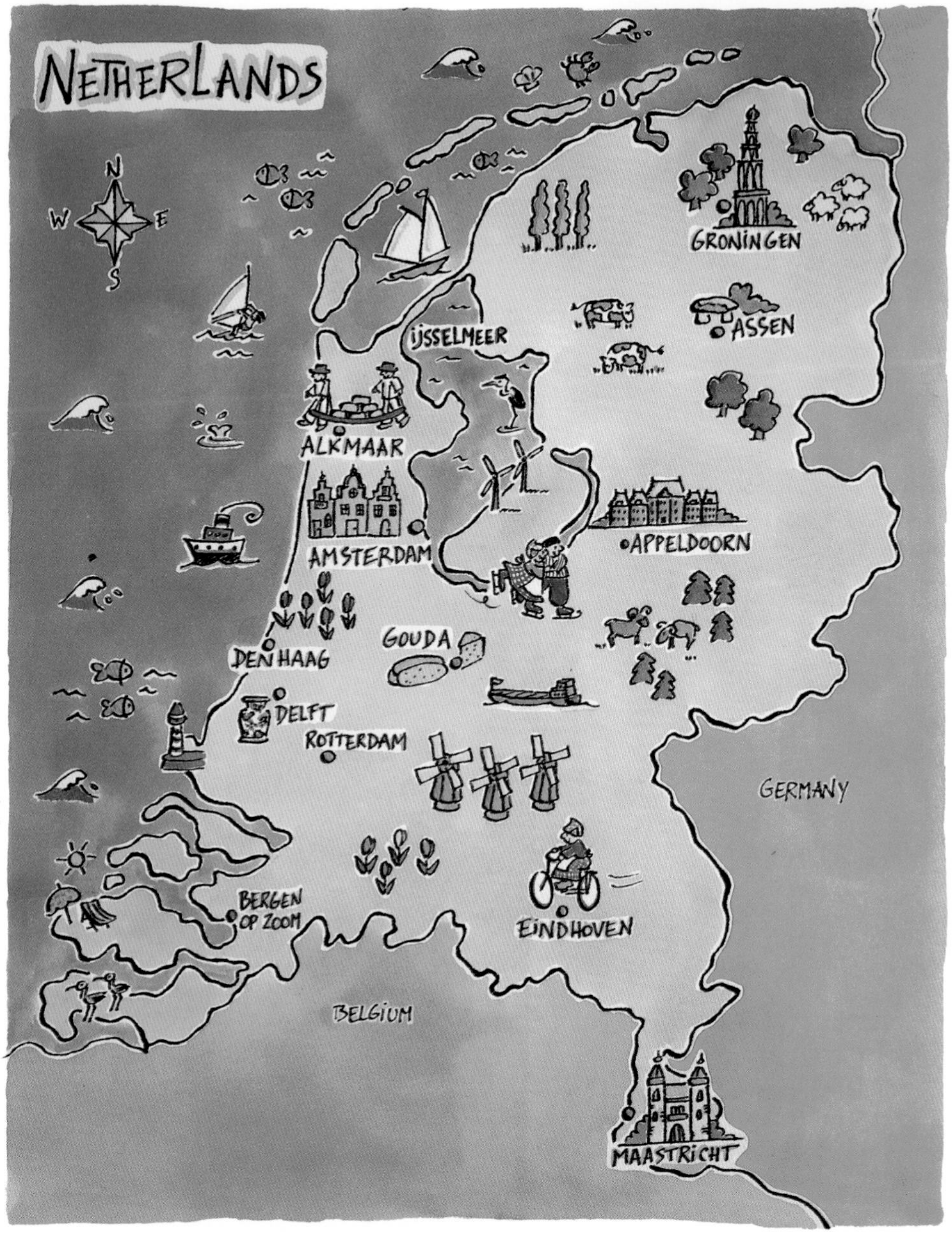

NETHERLANDS
N
W
E
S
GRONINGEN
IJSSELMEER
ASSEN
ALKMAAR
AMSTERDAM
APPELDOORN
GOUDA
DEN HAAG
DELFT
ROTTERDAM
GERMANY
BERGEN OP ZOOM
EINDHOVEN
BELGIUM
MAASTRICHT

ph 215.862.2091 fax 215.862.2641 e-mail mmanasse@new-work.com web www.voicenet.com/~mmanasse

TERRY WIDENER

represented by MICHELE MANASSE

Dow Jones/The Wall Street Journal/Europe

The San Diego Union-Tribune

ph 215.862.2091 fax 215.862.2641 e-mail mmanasse@new-work.com web www.voicenet.com/~mmanasse

SHELDON GREENBERG

NEW Work ILLUSTRATION

represented by MICHELE MANASSE

"Christmas Dog"

Dow Jones/The Wall Street Journal

The San Diego Union-Tribune

ph 215.862.2091 fax 215.862.2641 e-mail mmanasse@new-work.com web www.voicenet.com/~mmanasse

CAROL INOUYE

represented by MICHELE MANASSE

A TRUE 360° COCA-COLA LANDSCAPE

ph 215.862.2091 fax 215.862.2641 e-mail mmanasse@new-work.com web www.voicenet.com/~mmanasse

HIGH FIDELITY
Matcho
ILLUSTRATION
8899

Try Me!

MARK MATCHO
ILLUSTRATION

ENTERTAINMENT WEEKLY
GENTLEMEN'S QUARTERLY
TIME
NEWSWEEK
ESQUIRE
THE ATLANTIC
DETAILS
THE NEW YORK TIMES
PREMIERE
and
MODERN PLUMBER

510.836.4462

Oakland, Ca.

510★836★4462

Matcho

PURVEYOR *of* CURIOUS ILLUSTRATIONS

OAKLAND, CA •

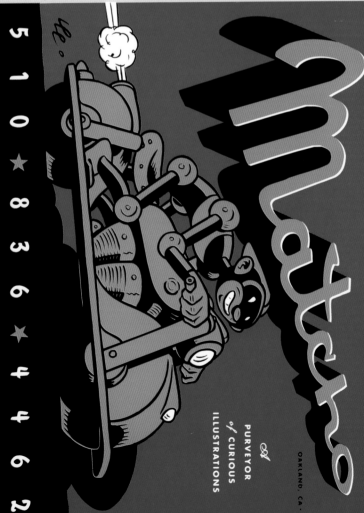

DAVE WINTER IS REPRESENTED BY DAVE WINTER 312-527-3900

Mark Bremmer
303.932.8759

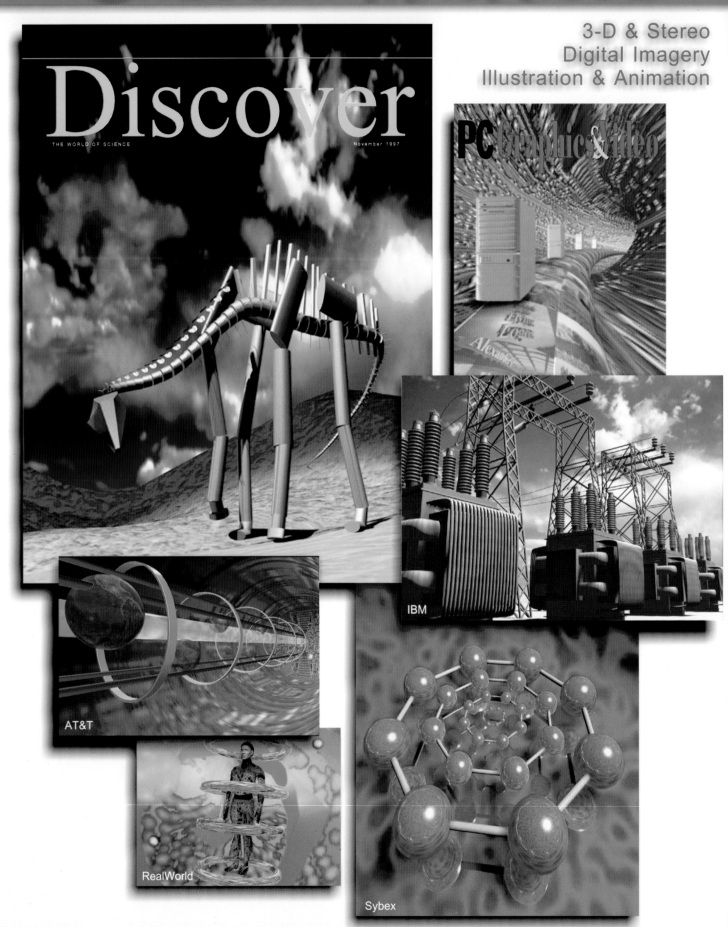

MARK WICKART

6293 SURREY RIDGE RD • LISLE, IL 60532
PHONE (630) 369-0164 • FAX (630) 369-4004

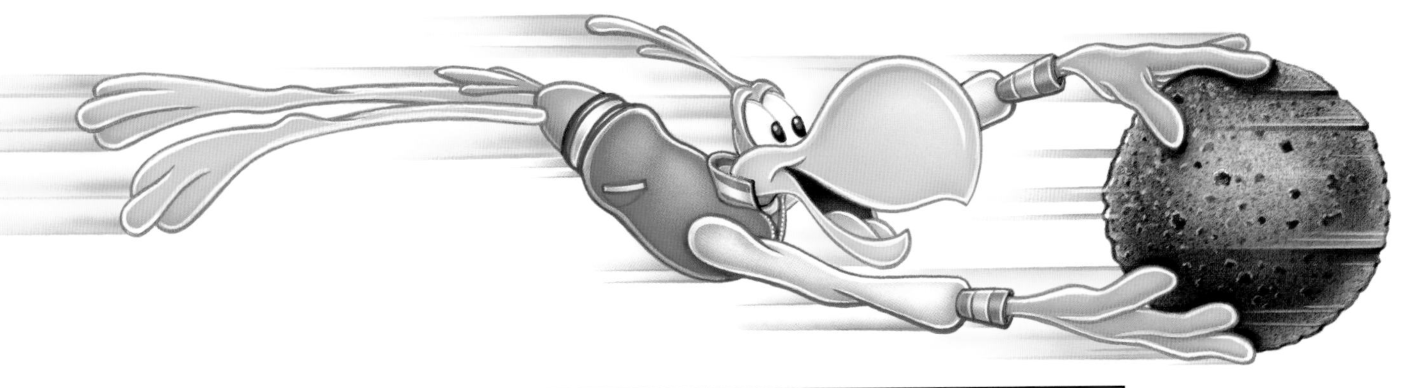

THE ROLAND GROUP

PHOTOGRAPHERS
ILLUSTRATORS
FILM DIRECTORS

MICHAEL
crampton

GARTH
glazier

MAX
altekruse

KURT
krebs

RALPH
hughes

We're your style. Whatever it is. Call Rochel Roland © **301.718.7955.** therolandgroup.com

We're your style. Whatever it is. Call Rochel Roland ✆ 301.718.7955. therolandgroup.com

Mark **weber**

Paul **manz**

Tungwai **chau**

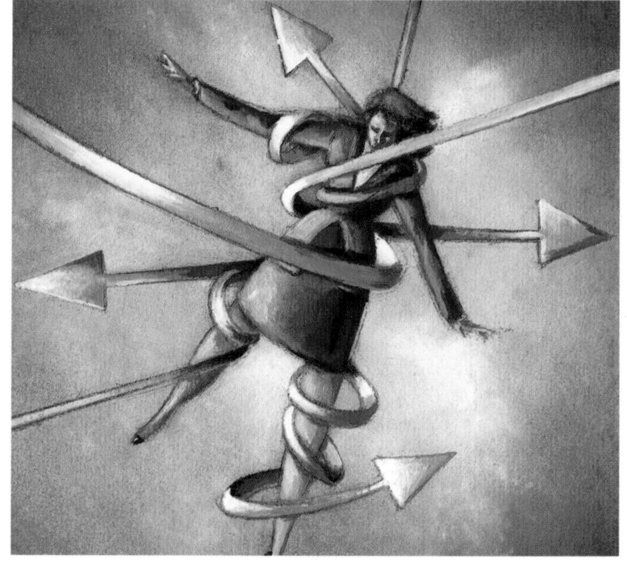

Karen **stolper**

THE ROLAND GROUP

PHOTOGRAPHERS
ILLUSTRATORS
FILM DIRECTORS

Brian White Electronic Illustration
2108 Sul Ross • Houston, TX 77098 • Studio 713-522-4220 • Fax 713-522-4220
E-mail brian@twinpix.com • Website www.twinpix.com

Brian White

Craig White

Craig White Digital Illustration
161 Lower Terrace • San Francisco, CA 94114 • 415-522-1875 • Fax 415-522-1912
E-mail craig@twinpix.com • Website www.twinpix.com

ISP
BOOT CAMP
©LAYMEYER
ILLUSTRATOR
601.969.5720
MONOPOLY
BLAKE'S
BOWS+ARROWS
MISSISSIPPI COLLEGE
OPERA STUDIO
THUNDER
CHICKEN
CRAZY
COW
Jimmy
the FISH
DōBie's
CORNER BAR
Evelyn
Dearest Peruser,
If the stuff here doesn't ting-tang your walla-walla-bing-bang, you might want to check out my website by clicking on this link right here:
www.claymeyer.com
(go ahead, click on it.)
(Well--go get your mouse then!)
(Okay, just nevermind.)
You'll find other styles, more samples and other fun stuff that hopefully you'll get a kick out of. Thank ye.

MERLE NACHT 374 MAIN ST. WETHERSFIELD, CT. 06109 (860) 563-7993

The Washington Post
Too young for a concert?

The Wall Street Journal
Leaving home for the holidays

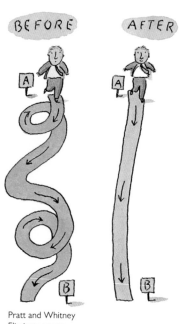

Pratt and Whitney
Eliminate waste

MERLE NACHT 374 MAIN ST. WETHERSFIELD, CT. 06109 (860) 563-7993

Nissan Japan/Dyna Search
Calendar: March

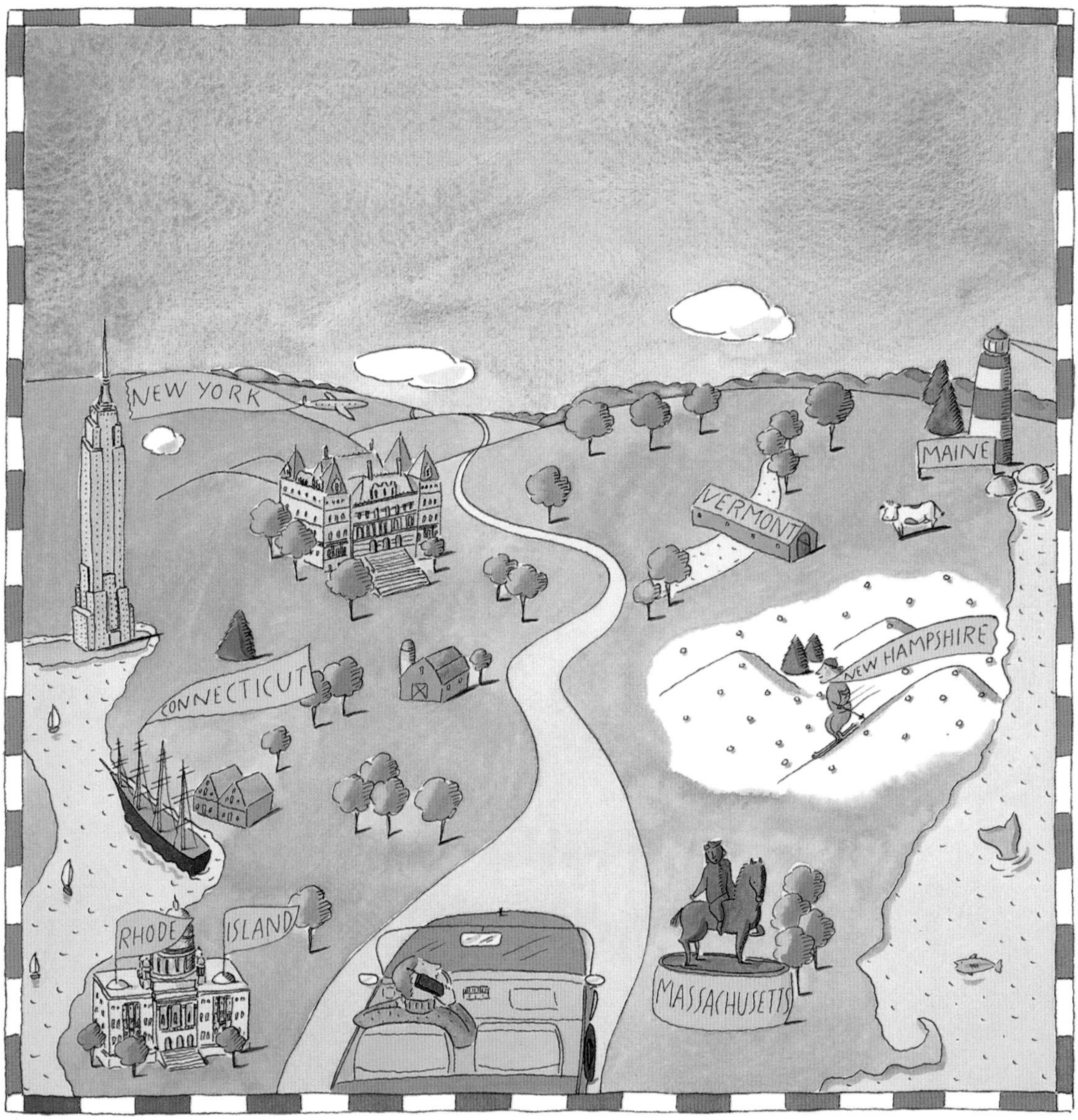

Bell Atlantic Nynex Mobile/Bozell Worldwide
Seven states, one home rate

jeff shelly

2330 San Marco Dr. Los Angeles, CA 90068 • (800)318-3244 • (213)460-4604 • Fax (213)464-6630

STEVE MCAFEE

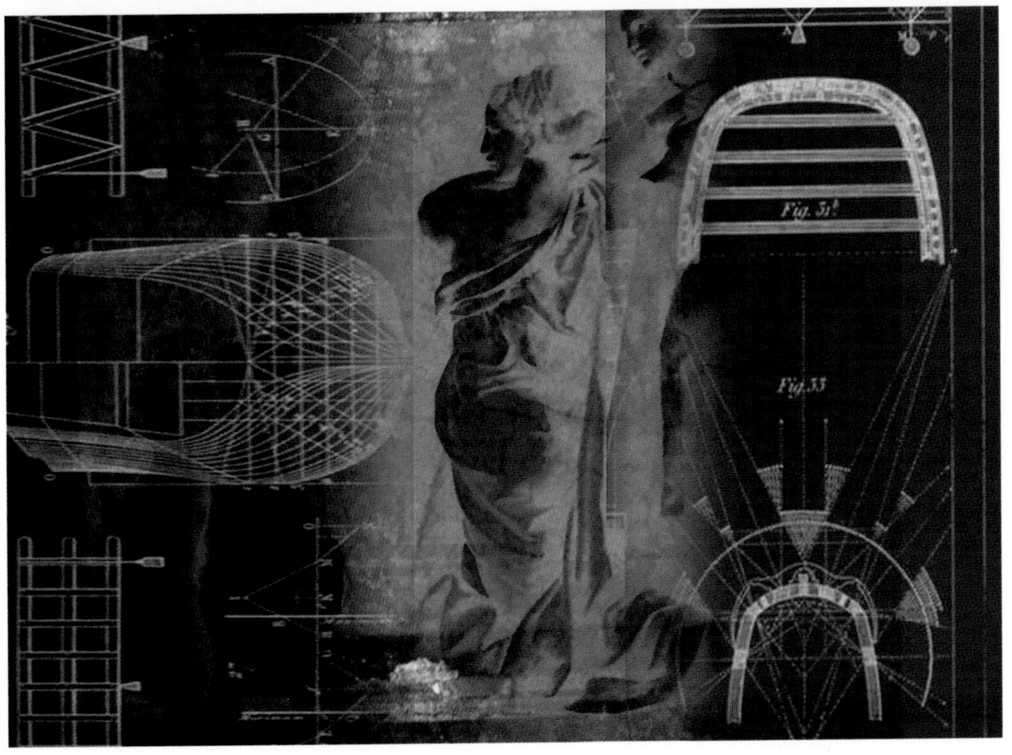

(770) 925-2481 ▪ P.O. BOX 54272 ▪ ATLANTA, GA ▪ 30308

SAL BARRACCA ASSOCIATES

JOHN ZIELINSKI

212 889 2400
FAX 889 2698
GERALD T COUNIHAN
RIKKE ANDERSEN

J I M M Y   H O L D E R

SAL BARRACCA ASSOCIATES
381 PARK AVE. SOUTH NEW YORK N.Y. 10016 TEL. 212 889 2400 FAX 212 889 2698

HUGO DI PIETRO

SAL BARRACCA ASSOCIATES
381 PARK AVE. SOUTH NEW YORK N.Y. 10016 TEL. 212 889 2400 FAX 212 889 2698

HUGO DI PIETRO

SAL BARRACCA ASSOCIATES

381 PARK AVE. SOUTH NEW YORK N.Y. 10016 TEL. 212 889 2400 FAX 212 889 2698

CYNTHIA WATTS CLARK

bob tedesco

D DIGITAL ILLUSTRATION CONCEPT DESIGN 8 PAYNE ROAD BETHEL CT 06801 203 778 3206 GREYCHEEK@AOL.COM

Clients include:
McCann Erickson, MTV, Kirshenbaum and Bond, Cartoon Network, Sega, Snapple, Phillips Interactive, Broderbund, Henry Holt, Time Magazine, Atlantic Monthly, Sports Illustrated, Forbes, Outside, Discover, New Media, Wired ... and you?

JOLT
PIZZA
N1B6202
DARYL STEVENS
digital illustration
©1998 D.Stevens

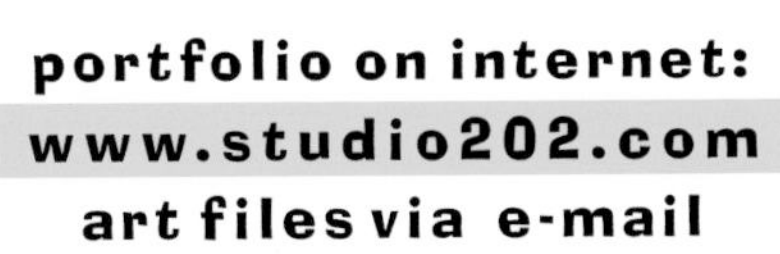

New York Studio

digital illustration

dara
goldman
978.440.8636
fax 978.440.9709

DAVID WINK

· DAVID WINK INC · 678 KING AVE. MARION, OHIO 43302 · STUDIO: (740) 387-8267 · FAX: (740) 383-4040 ·
· E-MAIL: DAVEWINK@ON-RAMP.NET ·

shelly meridith

55 mercer street floor 4

nyc 10013

212 941 1905 fax 212 226 3227

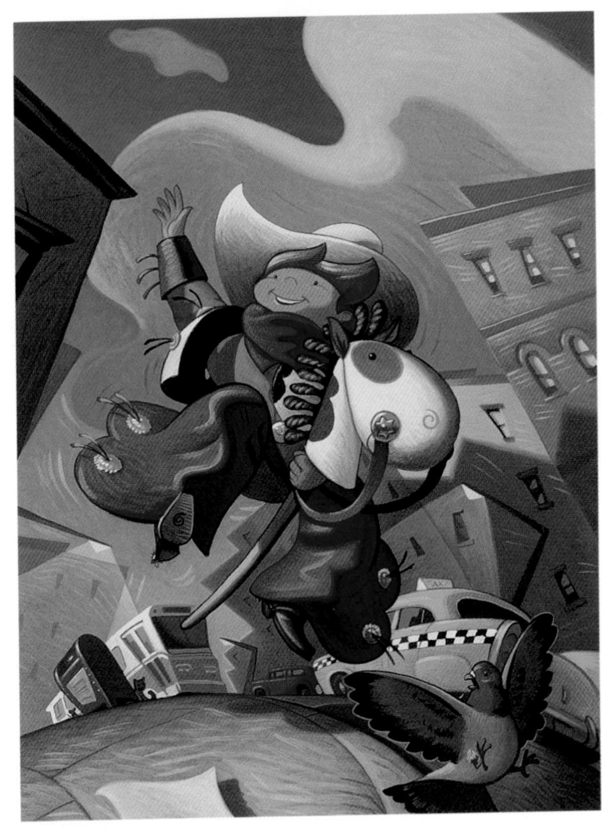

KENNETH SPENGLER

2668 17TH STREET SACRAMENTO, CA 95818 (916)441-1932 FAX(916)441-3490

BILL MAYER INC., 240 FORKNER DRIVE, DECATUR, GA 30030 404-378-0686 FAX 404-373-1759

© BILL MAYER 1999

JANET WOOLLEY

MATILDA HARRISON

ALAN LYNCH, ARTISTS REPRESENTATIVE
TEL (908) 813-8718 / FAX (908) 813-0076

REPRESENTED IN EUROPE BY ARENA:
TEL +44 171-267 9661 / FAX +44 171-284 0486

BRIGID COLLINS

SIMON BARTRAM

ALAN LYNCH, ARTISTS REPRESENTATIVE
TEL (908) 813-8718 / FAX (908) 813-0076

REPRESENTED IN EUROPE BY ARENA:
TEL +44 171-267 9661 / FAX +44 171-284 0486

JENNY TYLDEN-WRIGHT

ALAN LYNCH, ARTISTS REPRESENTATIVE
TEL (908) 813-8718 / FAX (908) 813-0076

REPRESENTED IN EUROPE BY ARENA:
TEL +44 171-267 9661 / FAX +44 171-284 0486

DAVID HITCH

JOHN CLEMENTSON

DANIEL TORRES

ALAN LYNCH, ARTISTS REPRESENTATIVE
TEL (908) 813-8718 / FAX (908) 813-0076

REPRESENTED IN EUROPE BY ARENA:
TEL +44 171-267 9661 / FAX +44 171-284 0486

JARED D. LEE
513-932-2154
FAX (513)932-9389
2942 Hamilton Rd./Lebanon, OH 45036
satisfying clients for over 28 years

TEL.: 212 227 7863
E-MAIL : NIKOLAIP@AOL.COM

REPRESENTED BY CHIP CATON 860 523 4562

FOR PORTFOLIO AND STOCK IMAGES SEE: http://www.nikolaiillustration.com

Mark Shaver

REPRESENTED BY

LIZ SANDERS AGENCY
TELEPHONE: (714) 495-3664 FACSIMILE: (714) 495-0129

For Editorial: MARK SHAVER
TELEPHONE: (310) 450-4336 FACSIMILE: (310) 392-9978

Mark Andresen

Ted Burn

Chad Cameron

Dave Clegg

Elaine Dillard

John Findley

Alex Hackworth

Matt Phillips

Represented by Susan Wells & Associates / Atlanta / 404.255.1430 / Fax 404.255.3449 / 888.255.1490

DAVE CLEGG

A♯ Guy

P-770-887-6306
F-770-781-5780
dcleggo@mindspring.com

Represented by Susan Wells & Associates / Atlanta / 404.255.1430 / Fax 404.255.3449 / 888.255.1490

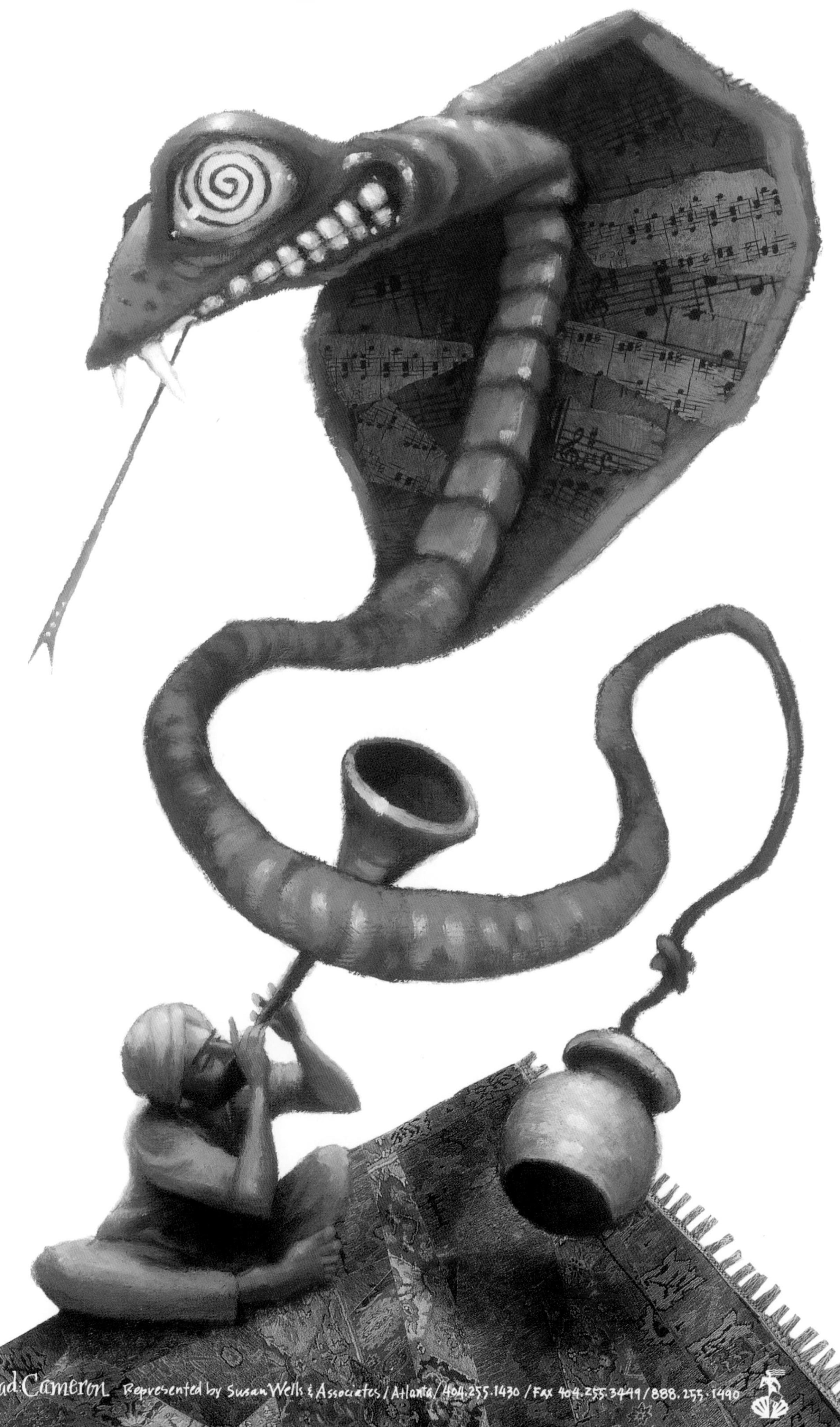
Chad Cameron
Represented by Susan Wells & Associates / Atlanta / 404.255.1430 / Fax 404.255.3449 / 888.255.1490

©Mark Andresen Represented by Susan Wells & Associates / Atlanta / 404.255.1430 / Fax 404.255.3449 / 888.255.1490

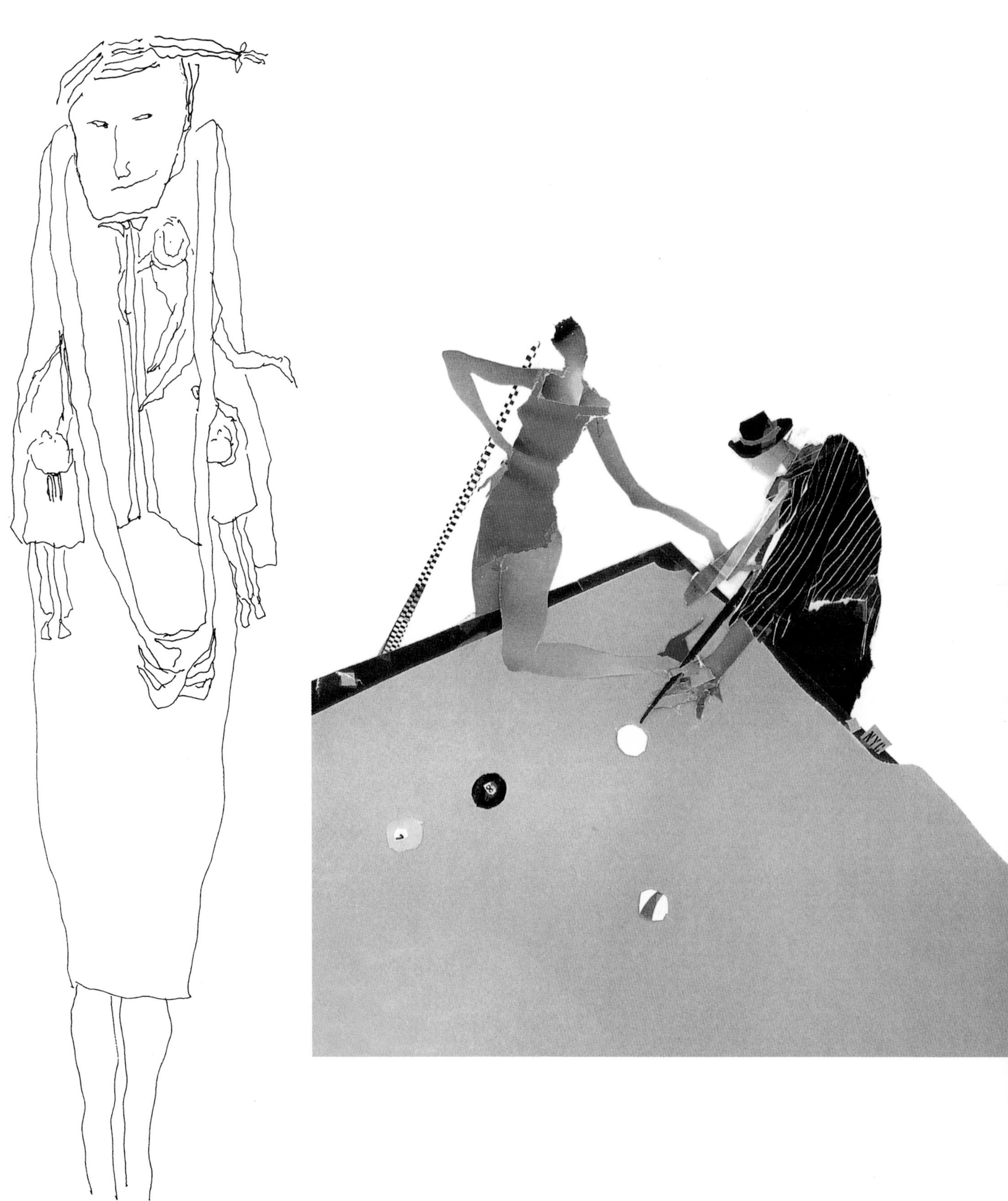

Alex Hackworth Represented by Susan Wells & Associates / Atlanta / 404.255.1430 / Fax 404.255.3449 / 888.255.1490

Matt Phillips Represented by Susan Wells & Associates / Atlanta/ 404.255.1430 / Fax 404.255.3449/888.255.1490

Elaine Dillard

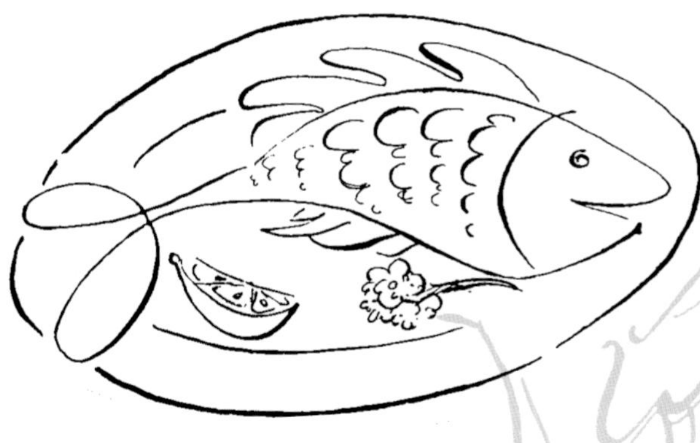

Divali Festival
paintings

Our neighborhood has
what most others don't.

A pulse.

Santa
Fe

Represented by Susan Wells & Associates / Atlanta / 404.255.1430 / Fax 404.255.3449 / 888.255.1490

Ted Burn Represented by Susan Wells & Associates / Atlanta / 404.255.1430 / Fax 404.255.3449 / 888.255.1490

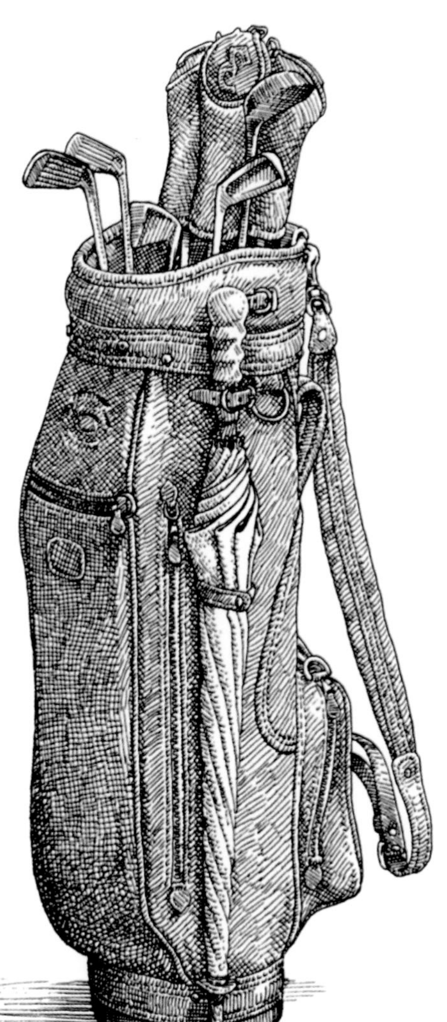

TEX ARCANA
©1984 John Findley
Meets the Toast of Europe
Part 14
THE OLD CLAIM JUMPER
NIGHT HAS FALLEN AND IN THE DESERT THAT LIES TO THE WEST OF THE TOWN OF HANGMAN'S CORNERS, THE SHERIFF AND HIS SEARCH PARTY ARE GRAPPLING WITH CONCEPTS AND CHALLENGES THAT ARE AS FAR BEYOND THEIR COMPREHENSION AS THE HARD TWINKLE-LESS STARS THAT BURN OVERHEAD....

WULL...I BEEN STUDYIN' ON IT, SHERIFF, AN' I'LL TELL YA WHAT... I DON'T B'LIEVE THEM LI'L FELLERS ARE OF THIS-HERE WORLD!
(TINKLE)

DAMNATION!
SPLATTER!

TH' WORLD'S TH' WORLD, ROGER, AN' THERE AIN'T BUT ONE OF 'EM.
YOU PLUMB LOCO, ER WHAT?
HOL' ON, THERE, JED. COULD BE ROGER'S GOT HIM A POINT.

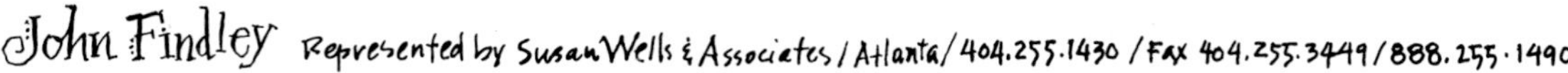
John Findley Represented by Susan Wells & Associates / Atlanta / 404.255.1430 / Fax 404.255.3449 / 888.255.1490

ILLUSTRATION/ CARTOONING

JIM HUMMEL
3023 DELTA ROAD
SAN JOSE, CA 95135-1012
PHONE AND FAX 408 270 2349
E-Mail k2it@pacbell.net

Susan Williams
Phone: 612-824-6103
Fax: 612-824-2896
DIGITAL ILLUSTRATION

Alec Syme Illustration

Digital Illustration and Animation

Represented in Minneapolis by Geoffrey Stewart **(612) 824-8914** e-mail: geo@scc.net
Online portfolio: www.stewartartists.com

digital & traditional illustrations

gary KEITH

ph 650.358.9398 fax 650.358.9327

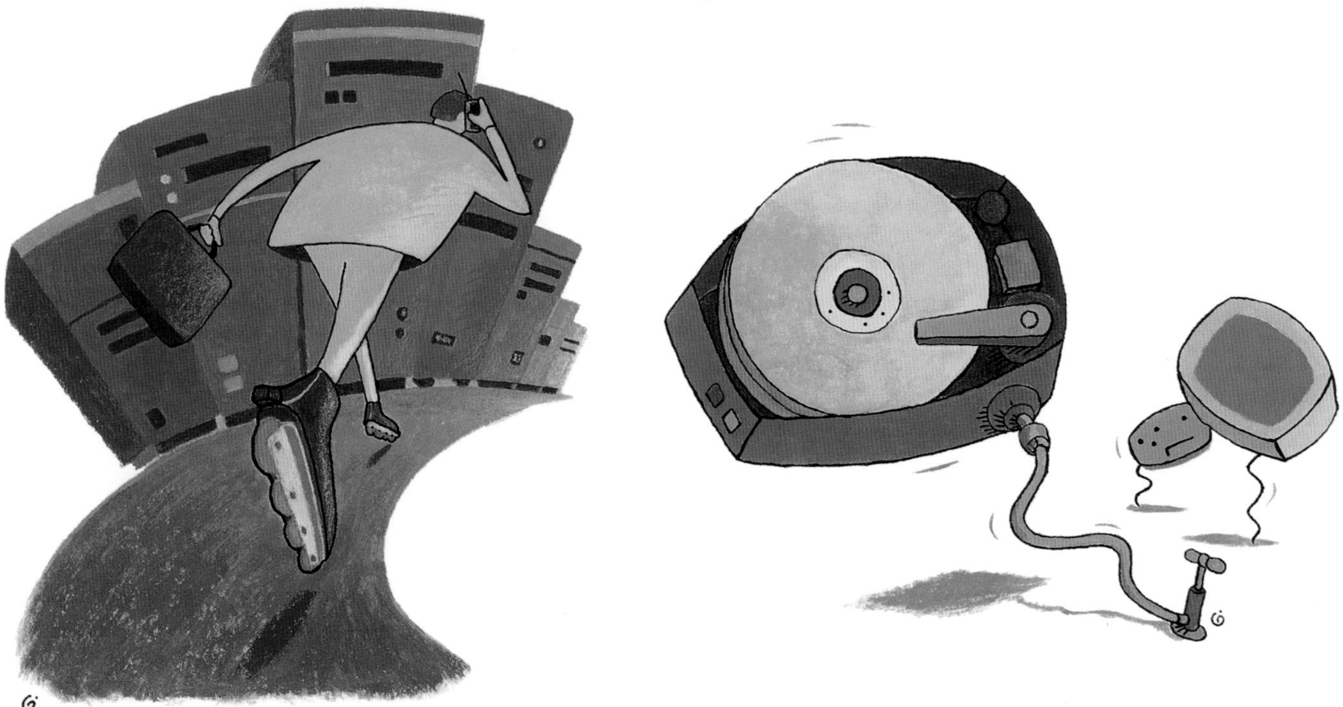

email gary@tintoycreative.com

visit my web portfolio at www.tintoycreative.com

member graphic artists guild

KARL EDWARDS
Phone (831) 647-9100 FAX (831) 647-9110
www.karledwards.com
BANK

Westbrook illustration

phone/fax 202.328.8593

ericwestbrook

2325 42nd St., NW
Suite 419
Washington, DC
20007

Annie Lunsford

TRADITIONAL AND DIGITAL ILLUSTRATION 703-527-7696 FAX 703-527-3099

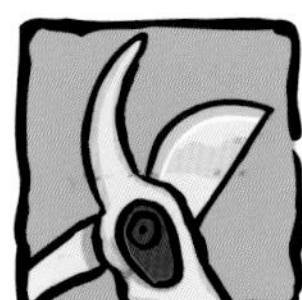

E-mail: fredbell@execpc.com
Web Site: http://www.execpc.com/~fredbell
Fax: 414-771-6352

All drawings
delivered on disk
or e-mailed ready to
drop into your document.

FRED BELL
414-771-0472

Mike Lester ©

studio
706
234
7733

fax
706
234
0086

portfolio
www.mikelester.com

More good stuff in animation, animals, black/white & humor in the Specialty Index

studio: 706-234-7733
fax: 706-234-0086
www.mikelester.com
I'D RATHER BE FISHING
TARTAR SAUCE
Mike Lester.

Fresh hot talent!

Bruce MacPherson

Dale Rutter

Artists' Rep

(301) 384-8925 ☎ FAX (301) 879-9854

www.aaarrt.com/donnasgallery

ROB JOHNSON

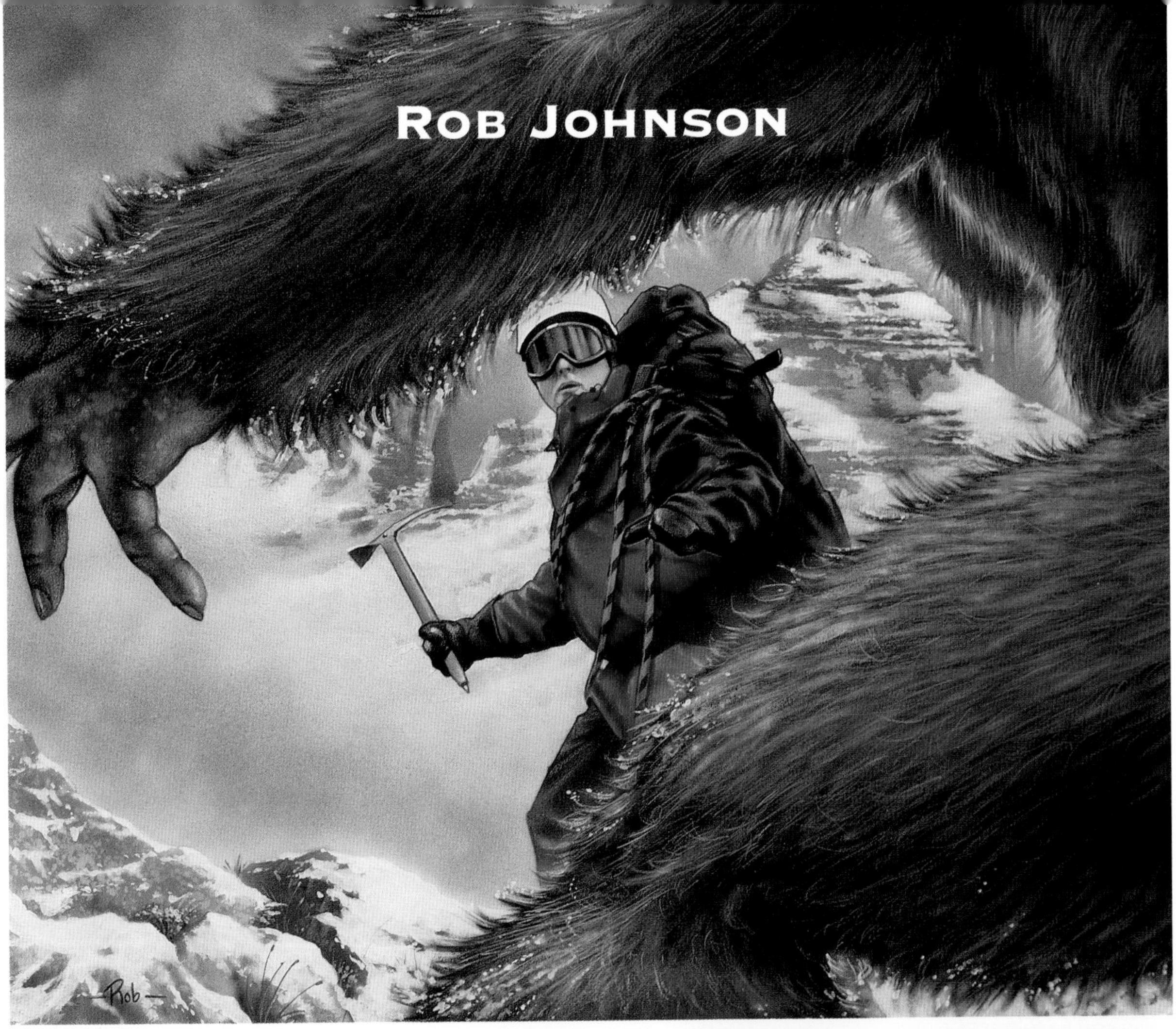

ARTISTS' REP

(301) 384-8925 ☎
FAX (301) 879-9854
www.aaarrt.com/donnasgallery

Matthew Baek

The Great Pretender

Waiting for the Moon

Shop Lifting

Half The Man I Used To Be

Donna Rosen
ARTISTS' REP

(301) 384-8925 ☎ FAX (301) 879-9854
www.aaarrt.com/donnasgallery

STEVE PICA

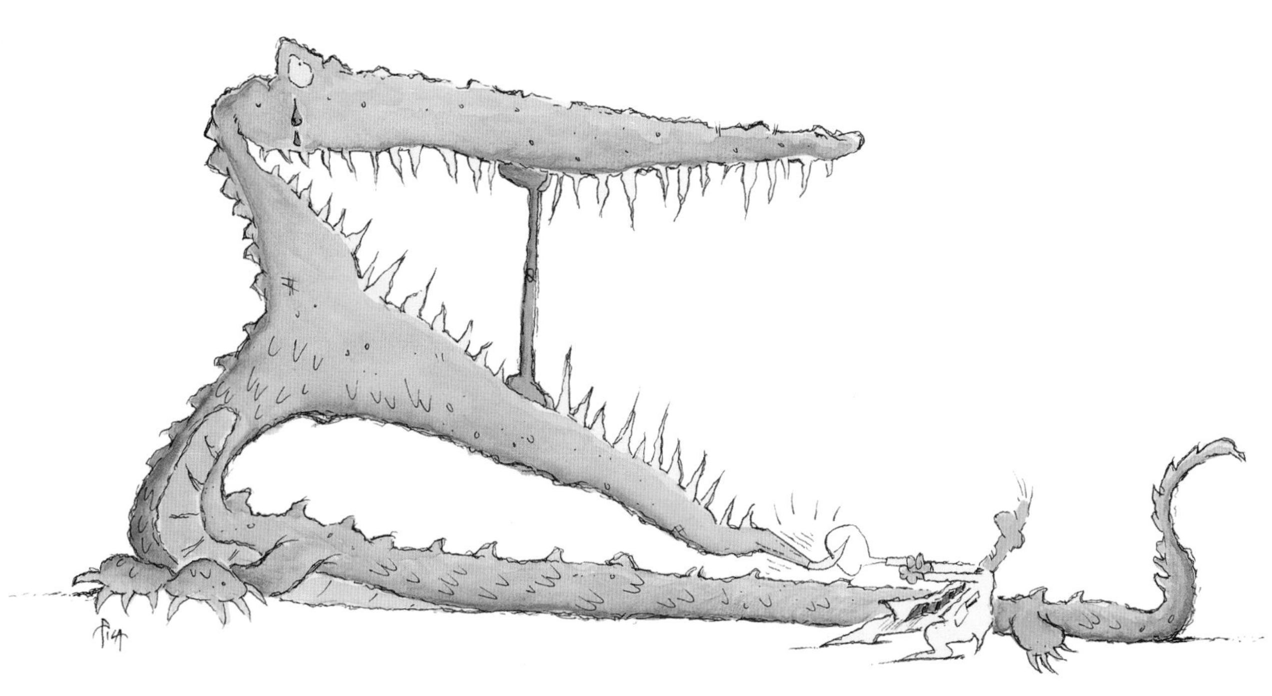

(301) 384-8925 ☎ FAX (301) 879-9854

www.aaarrt.com/donnasgallery

Jim Haynes
ILLUSTRATION

(301) 384-8925 ☎ FAX (301) 879-9854

www.aaarrt.com/donnasgallery

JO RIVERS

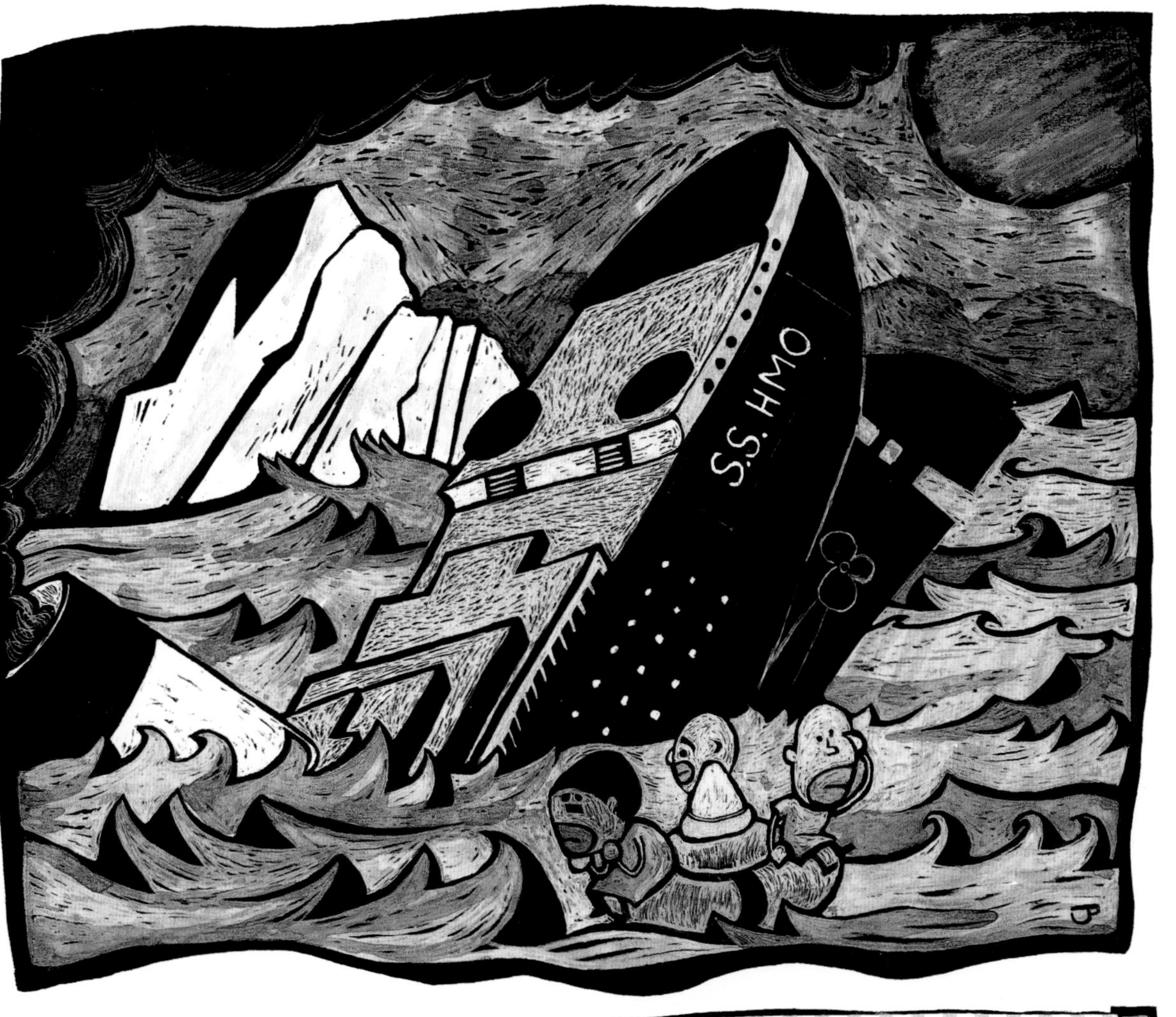

(301) 384-8925 ☎ FAX (301) 879-9854

www.aaarrt.com/donnasgallery

Sean Dawdy

I don't think that playing like this is fun.

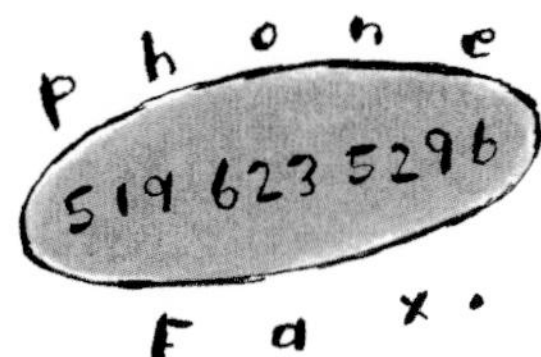

Marian Nixon
+ new numbers!
(773)588-8640
(FAX)588-7640
sky blue

stephanie langley illustration **650.857.9539**
fax.857.0445 *619 maybell avenue palo alto, ca 94306*

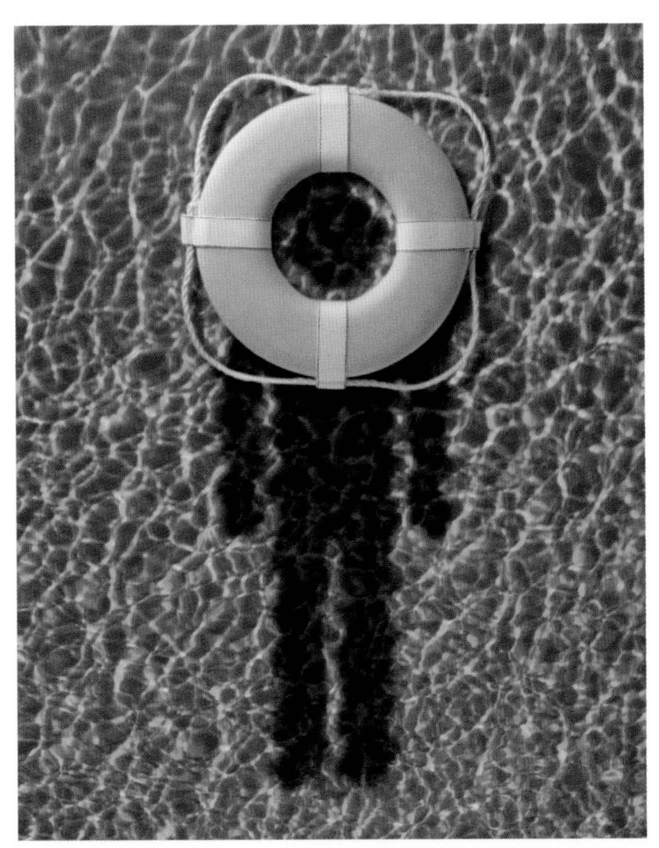

617 482 1604
chris jagmin illustration
home sweet home
www.jagart.com

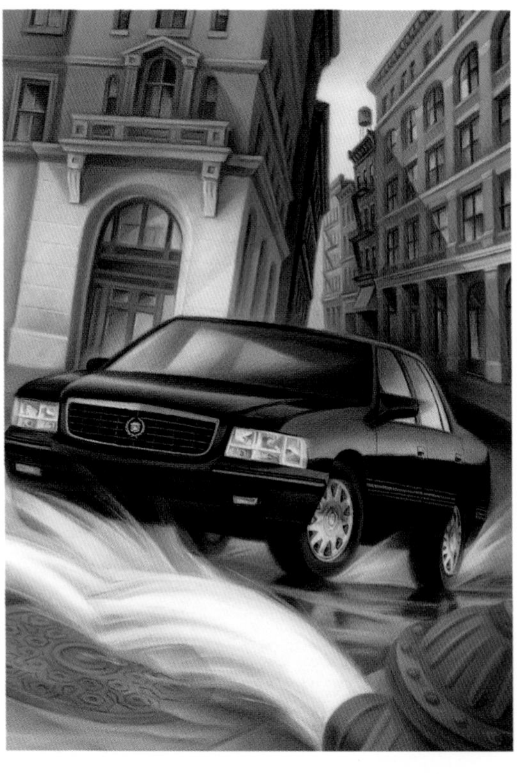

KATHY PETRAUSKAS

312 642 • 4950 • FAX 312 642 • 6391

David Plunkert

(P)

DAN KROVATIN

2157 PENNINGTON ROAD, EWING, NJ 08638
TELEPHONE AND FAX: (609) 882-6181

visit www.erols.com/okstraub
Matt Straub
212.995.9359

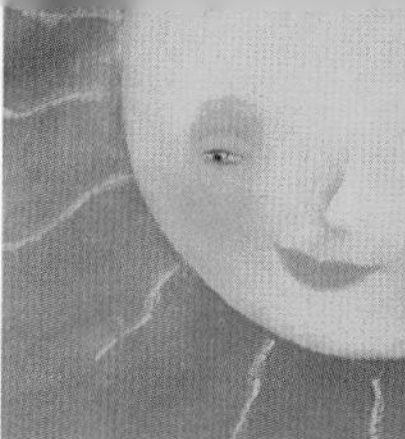

V I R G I N I A
H A L S T E A D

4336 GAYLE DRIVE

TARZANA, CA 91356

PHONE/FAX

818.705.4353

Illustrations from the book, *Daughter Have I told You*, by Rachel Coyne, ©1998 by Henry Holt & Co., New York. Original paintings are available for sale.
Other clients include AT&T, Bantam Doubleday Dell, Harcourt Brace, Kimberly-Clark, MTV Networks, Simon & Schuster, Time-Warner Cable, Weight Watchers, Workman Publishing.

james bozzini 1. 888. 269. 9464. nyc

Guide to Creative Specialties

Black Book Illustration 1999

Guide to Creative Specialties

The *Guide to Creative Specialties* will simplify your search for the best in illustration. The *Guide*, featuring Black Book illustrators, offers a wide range of categories organized alphabetically – so whether you're looking for children, food, maps, or even wildlife you'll find it quickly and easily.

The *Guide to Creative Specialties* is found directly following the artists' ad pages of Black Book Illustration. A page number that refers back to the artist's full page ad and the information you'll need for contacting the artist appears above each image. Or you can flip to the listings for addresses and phone numbers. The *Guide* is also available as an individual volume. Contact information for each artist is located by referring directly to the listings pages at the back of the volume.

You will find that the *Guide to Creative Specialties* is a refreshing way to locate talent – let us know how it works for you!

Daryll Collins PAGE 354

Mary Ross/Rita Gatlin Represents PAGE 242

Mike Lester PAGE 390, 391

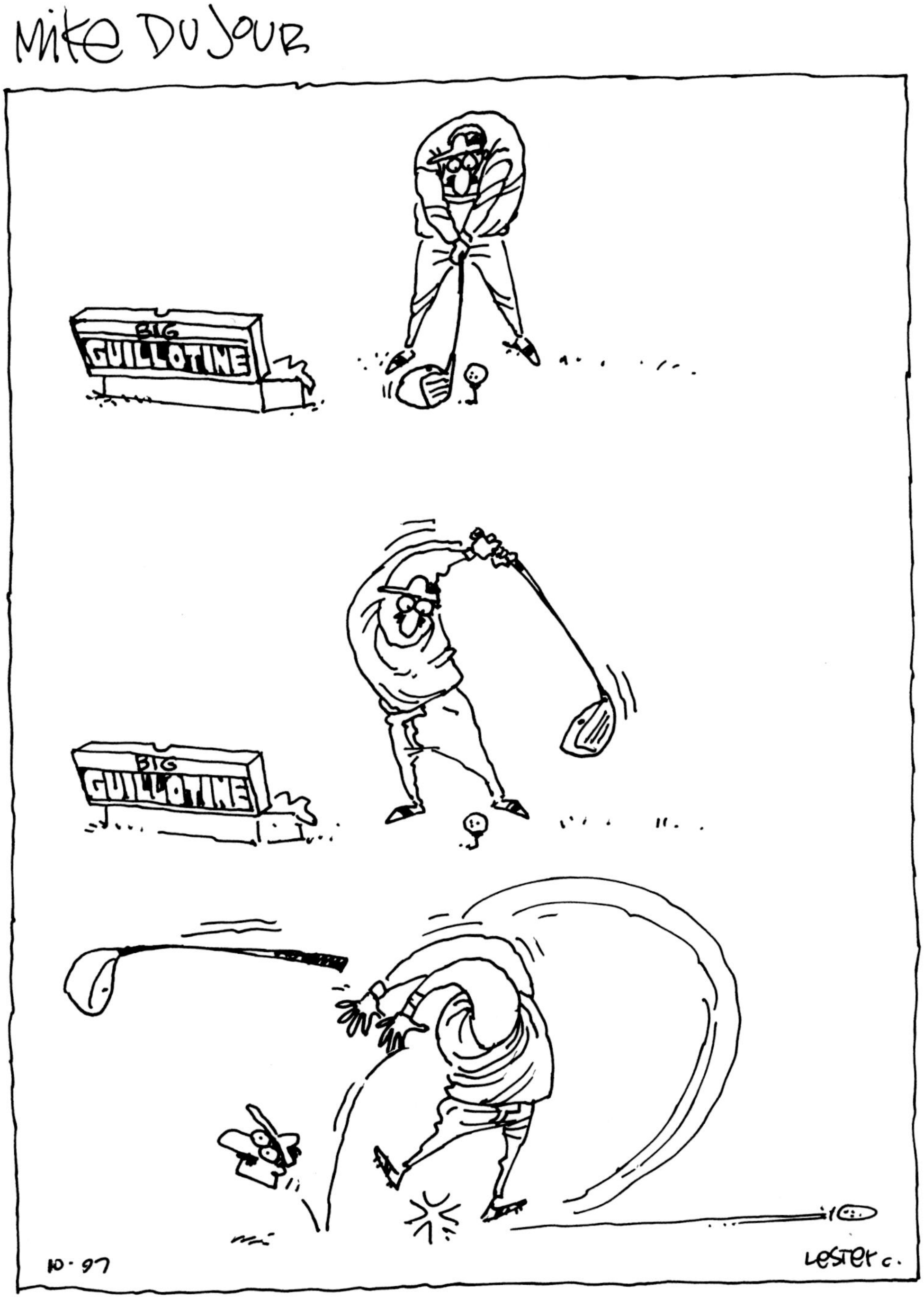

MIKE DU JOUR

BIG GUILLOTINE

BIG GUILLOTINE

10·97

LESTER c.

Margery Mintz PAGE 162

Eric Dever/Michele Manasse PAGE 325

Alex Hackworth/Susan Wells & Associates PAGE 377

Mike Lester PAGE 390, 391

Karen Laurence PAGE 32

Bill Cigliano/Renard Represents PAGE 49

Redgrafix PAGE 128

Fred Bell PAGE 389

Daryll Collins PAGE 354

George Peters PAGE 316

Mmmm, Meatloaf...

Jim Hummel PAGE 382

Trip Park/Joanne Palulian PAGE 66

Steve Björkman/Renard Represents PAGE 48

Erika LeBarre/The Neis Group PAGE 302

Michele Nidenoff PAGE 309

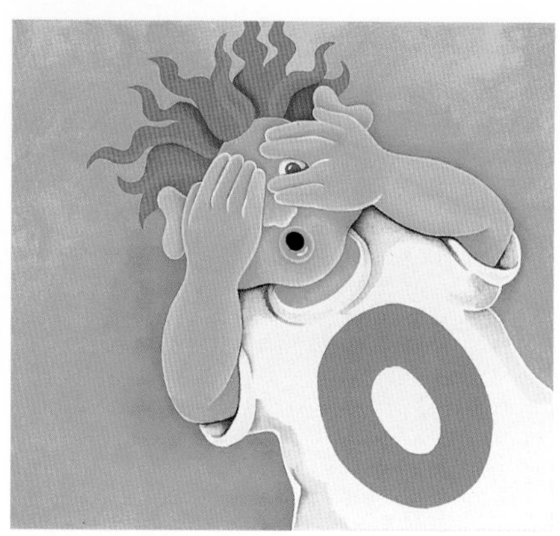

Liz Conrad/The Neis Group PAGE 305

Terri Schwarz PAGE 296

Mary Ross/Rita Gatlin Represents PAGE 242

Susan Gross PAGE 2, 3

Chad Cameron/Susan Wells & Associates PAGE 375

Redgrafix PAGE 128

Shelly Meridith PAGE 362

Garry Colby/The Neis Group PAGE 304

Alex Hackworth/Susan Wells & Associates PAGE 377

RM Schneider/John Brewster Creative Services PAGE 287

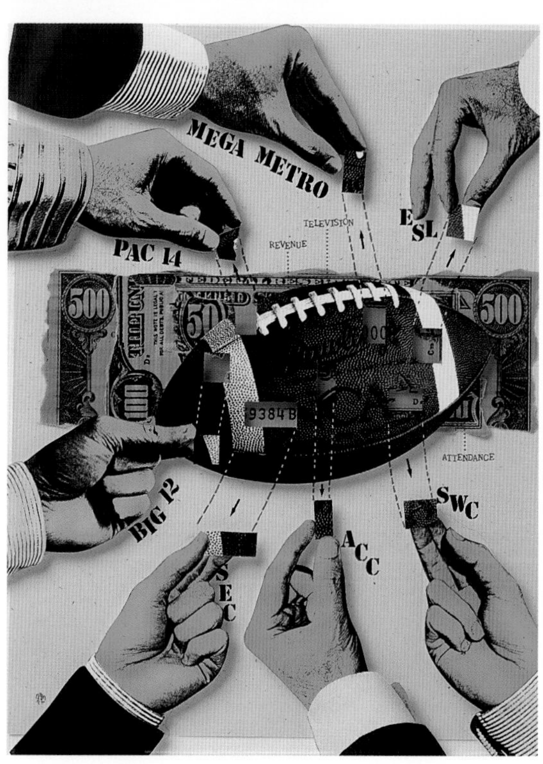

Seth Larson/John Brewster Creative Services PAGE 292

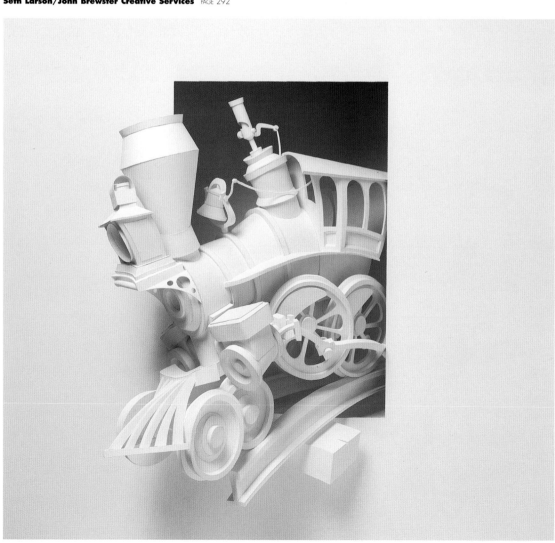

Mark Andresen/Susan Wells & Associates PAGE 376

Jo Rivers/Donna Rosen PAGE 399

Doug Ross/Lori Nowicki & Associates PAGE 130

Corey Wilkinson PAGE 60, 61

Goran Billingskog/John Brewster Creative Services PAGE 291

Jim Cohen PAGE 403

Dan Garrow/Renard Represents PAGE 44

Eric Westbrook PAGE 387

Gary Eldridge/Renard Represents PAGE 52

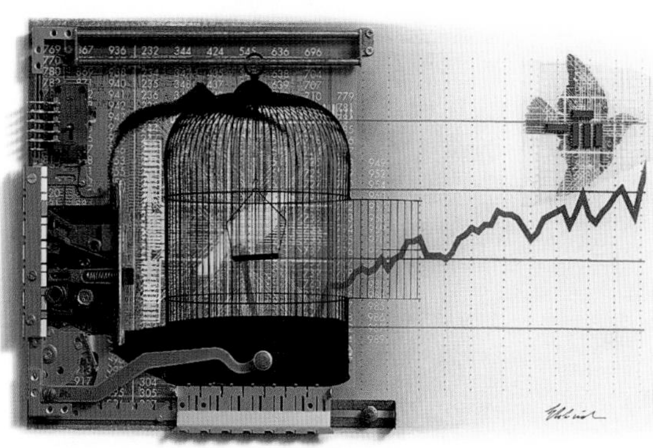

Rob Brooks/Renard Represents PAGE 42

Nip Rogers/Alexander Pollard PAGE 219

Michael McGurl/Renard Represents PAGE 54

Joe Veno/Lori Nowicki & Associates PAGE 131

Stéphan Daigle/Renard Represents PAGE 43

Theo Rudnak/Renard Represents PAGE 38, 39

Sally Wern Comport PAGE 214, 215

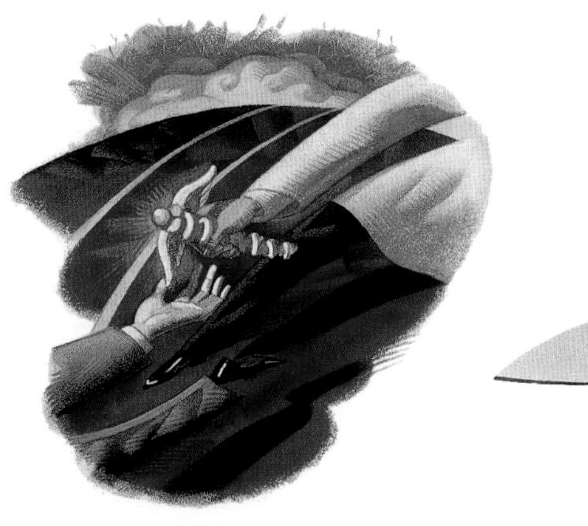

Valerie Sinclair/Renard Represents PAGE 53

Virginia Halstead PAGE 410

Tim Lee/Renard Represents PAGE 47

Matthew Baek/Donna Rosen PAGE 396

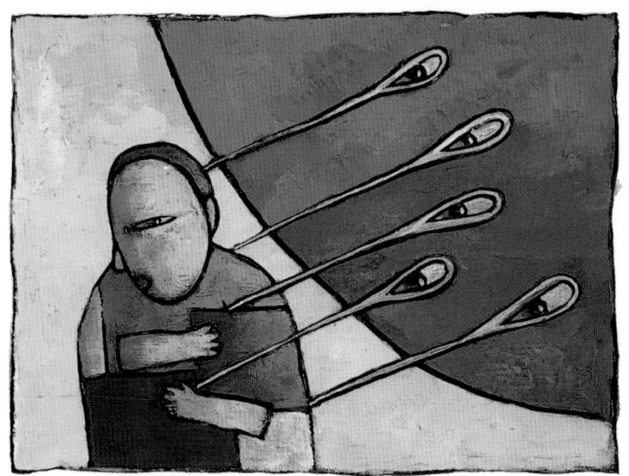

Kim Malek/Christine Prapas PAGE 268

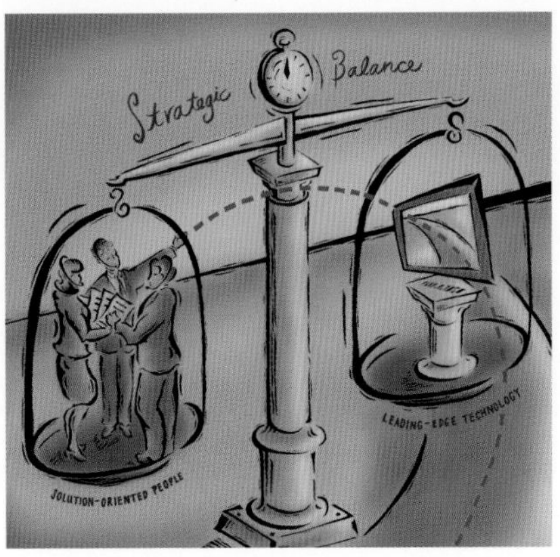

Roger Chandler/John Brewster Creative Services PAGE 290

RM Schneider/John Brewster Creative Services PAGE 287

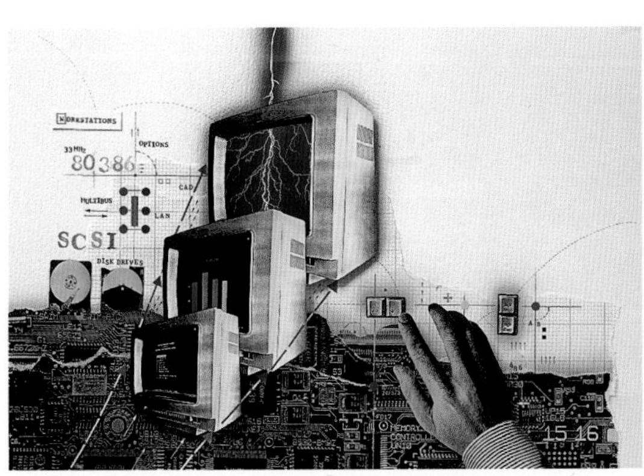

Matthew Baek/Donna Rosen PAGE 396

Putien Richard PAGE 116

Doug Horne/Christine Prapas PAGE 263

Jonathan Herbert/Renard Represents PAGE 51

James Nichols/Sweet Represents PAGE 140, 141

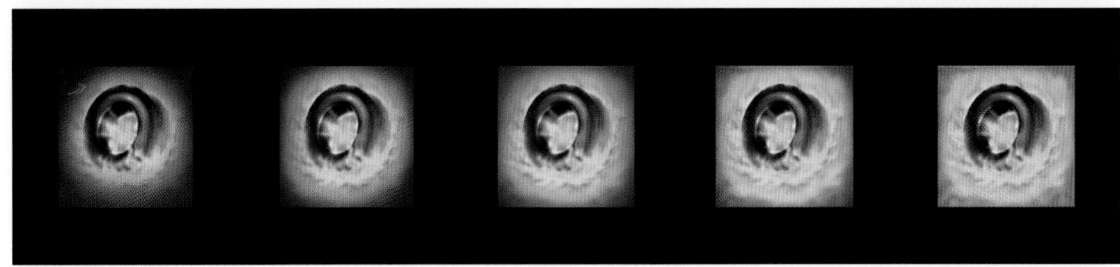

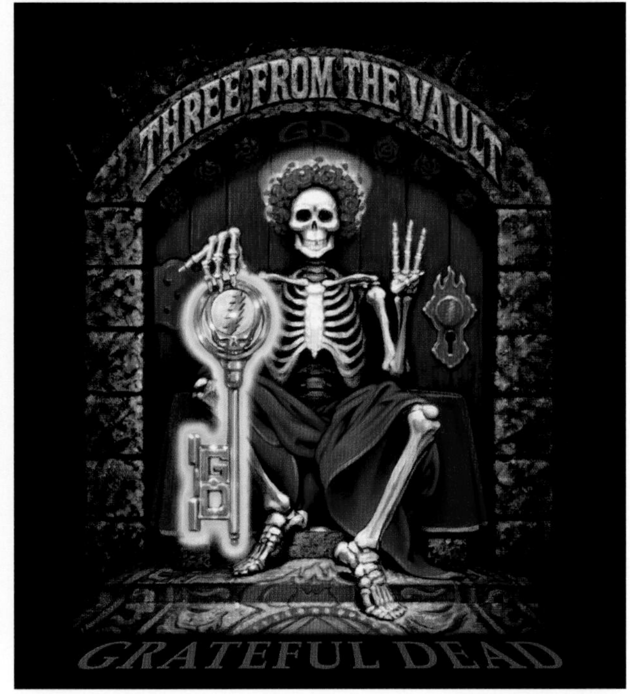

Studio 212 PAGE 310, 311

John Findley/Susan Wells & Associates PAGE 381

Steve Ellis/Christine Prapas PAGE 269

Chris Jagmin PAGE 404

Robert Zimmerman PAGE 16, 17

Doug Ross/Lori Nowicki & Associates PAGE 130

Mark Shaver PAGE 372

Roger Chandler/John Brewster Creative Services PAGE 290

Susan Williams PAGE 383

Matt LeBarre/The Neis Group PAGE 307

Matsu/Renard Represents PAGE 45

Mick Coulas PAGE 256

Jeffrey Pelo/Renard Represents PAGE 56

Jim Cohen PAGE 403

Todd Nordling/Sweet Represents PAGE 134

CAPRI SUN
ALL NATURAL™ JUICE DRINK

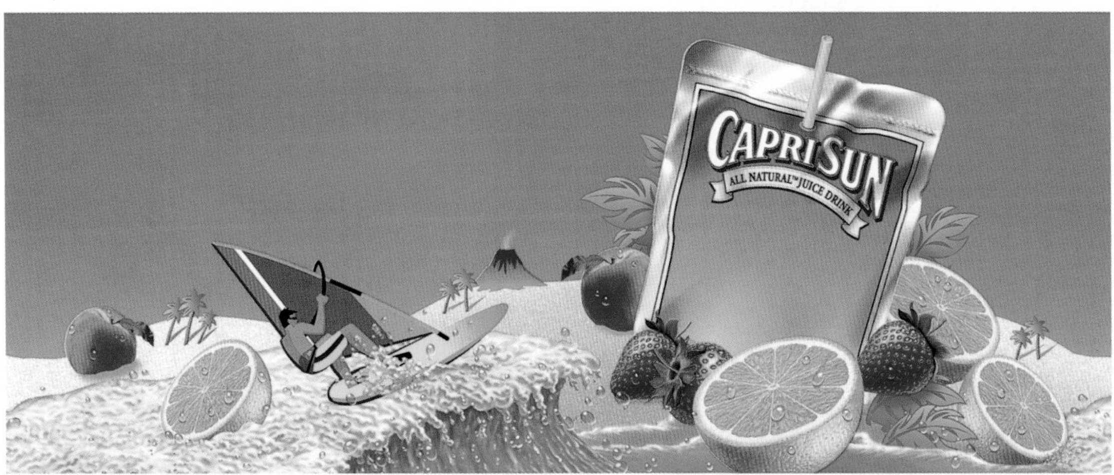
CAPRI SUN
ALL NATURAL™ JUICE DRINK

CAPRI SUN
ALL NATURAL™ JUICE DRINK

Daryl Stevens PAGE 358, 359

Nikolai Punin PAGE 371

Wendy Grossman/Renard Represents PAGE 55

Clor Imaging PAGE 258

Nikolai Punin PAGE 371

Brenda Weeks PAGE 36

Jim Cohen PAGE 403

Chad Cameron/Susan Wells & Associates PAGE 375

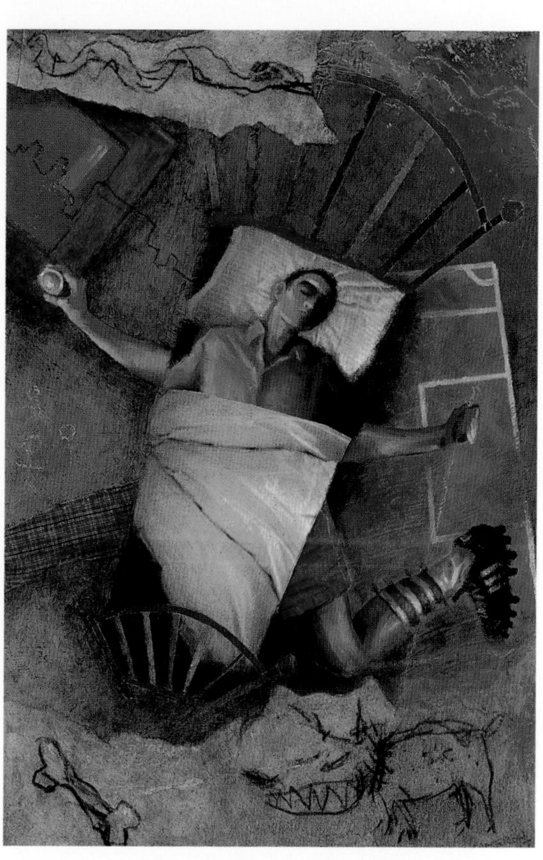

Matthew Baek/Donna Rosen PAGE 396

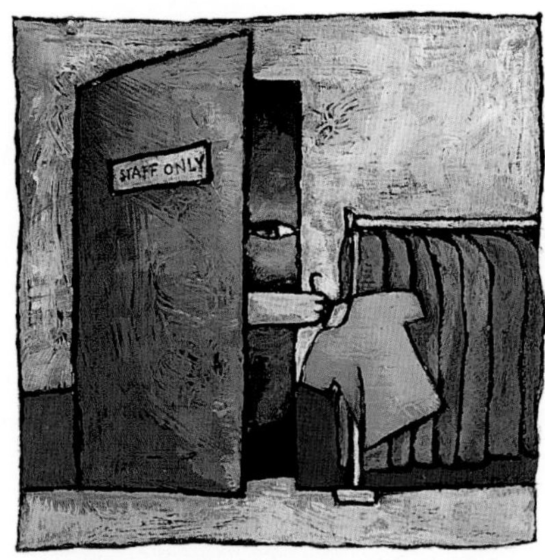

Joe Veno/Lori Nowicki & Associates PAGE 131

Terri Schwarz PAGE 296

Terri Schwarz PAGE 296

Susan Williams PAGE 383

Clay Meyer PAGE 341

Rob Johnson/Donna Rosen PAGE 395

Gayle Kabaker/Joanne Palulian PAGE 67

Gary Keith PAGE 385

Andrew Peycha PAGE 324

Eric Westbrook PAGE 387

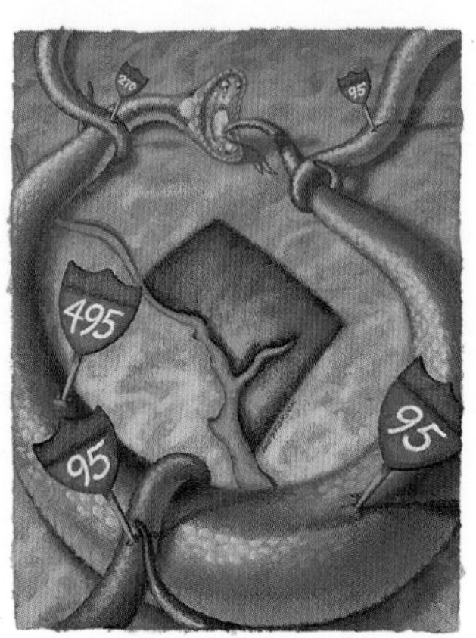

Jo Rivers/Donna Rosen PAGE 399

Chris Jagmin PAGE 404

Daryll Collins PAGE 354

Miles Parnell/John Brewster Creative Services PAGE 288

Daryl Stevens PAGE 358, 359

Linda Fennimore PAGE 15

Margery Mintz PAGE 162

Clint Hansen/The Neis Group PAGE 301

Ted Burn/Susan Wells & Associates PAGE 380

Brenda Weeks PAGE 36

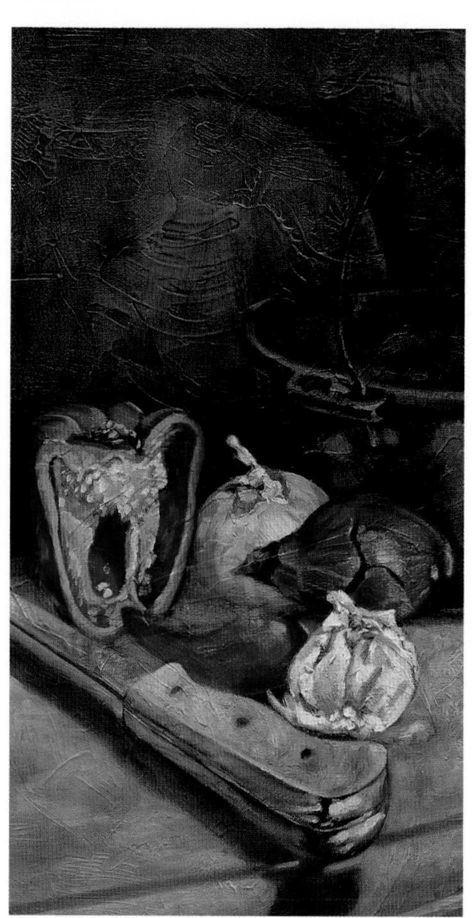

Jennifer Riegler PAGE 20

Susan Williams PAGE 383

Patty O'Friel PAGE 308

John White/The Neis Group PAGE 303

Terri Schwarz PAGE 296

Jon & Georgina Rosenbaum/John Brewster Creative Services PAGE 289

Mick Rosolek PAGE 157

Redgrafix PAGE 128

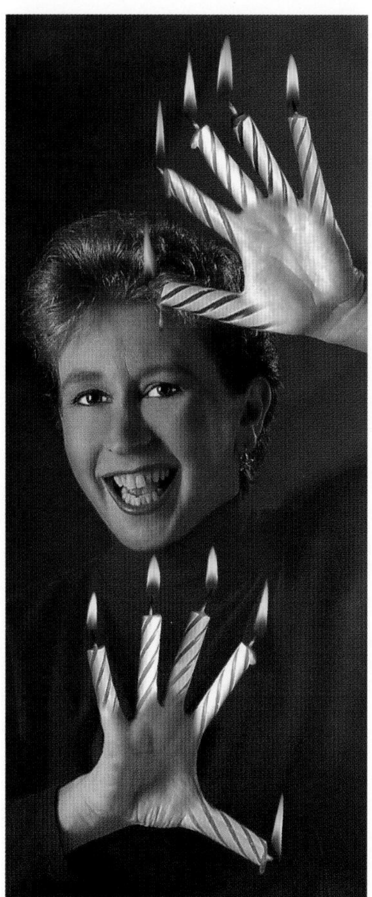

Brenda Weeks PAGE 36

Margery Mintz PAGE 162

Shelly Meridith PAGE 362

Jared D. Lee PAGE 370

Mary Ross/Rita Gatlin Represents PAGE 242

Jim Paillot/The Pred Group PAGE 73

Matt Phillips/Susan Wells & Associates PAGE 378

Jeff Shelly PAGE 344

Robert L. Prince/John Brewster Creative Services PAGE 286

Steve Pica/Donna Rosen PAGE 397

Robert Zimmerman PAGE 16, 17

Daryll Collins PAGE 354

Bruce MacPherson/Donna Rosen PAGE 393

Annie Lunsford PAGE 388

Clay Meyer PAGE 341

Steve Björkman/Renard Represents PAGE 48

Kevin Pope/Renard Represents PAGE 58, 59

Mick Coulas PAGE 256

Trip Park/Joanne Palulian PAGE 66

Mike Lester PAGE 390, 391

Dave Clegg/Susan Wells & Associates PAGE 374

Karl Edwards PAGE 386

Jennifer Riegler PAGE 20

Nikolai Punin PAGE 371

Clay Meyer PAGE 341

Mary Ross/Rita Gatlin Represents PAGE 242

Diane Borowski/Alexander Pollard PAGE 221

Mark Weakley/Alexander Pollard PAGE 217

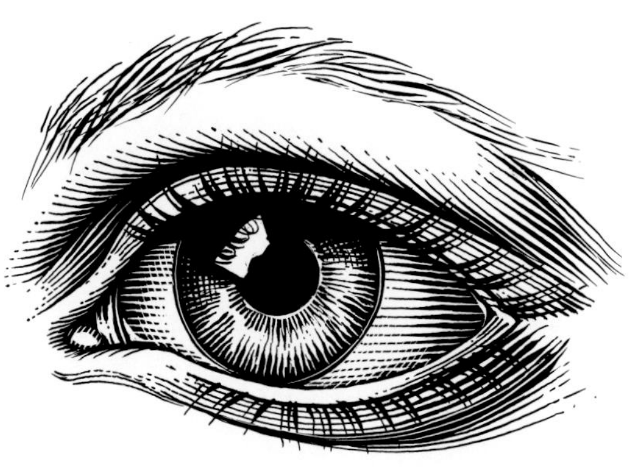

Redgrafix PAGE 128

Shelly Meridith PAGE 362

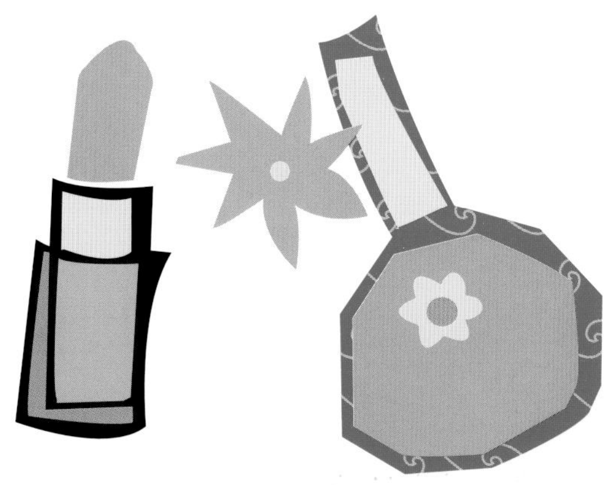

Studio North PAGE 274

Patty O'Friel PAGE 308

Susan Williams PAGE 383

Chris Jagmin PAGE 404

Robert Zimmerman PAGE 16, 17

Corey Wilkinson PAGE 60, 61

Elaine Dillard/Susan Wells & Associates PAGE 379

Aborigine
wall art

Lane Dupont/John Brewster Creative Services PAGE 284, 285

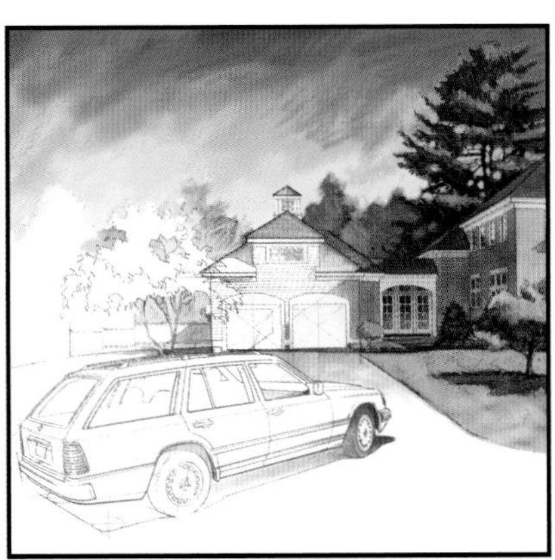

Normand Cousineau/Marlena Agency PAGE 31

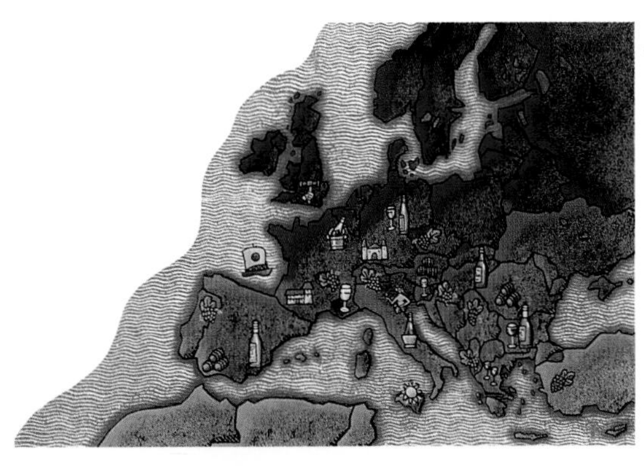

Berney Knox/The Neis Group PAGE 300

Jim Haynes/Donna Rosen PAGE 398

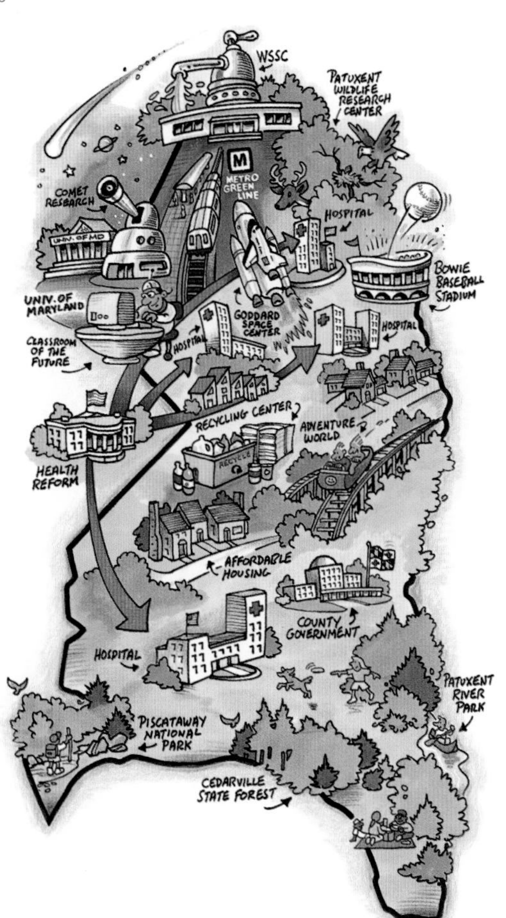

Matt Kania PAGE 76, 77

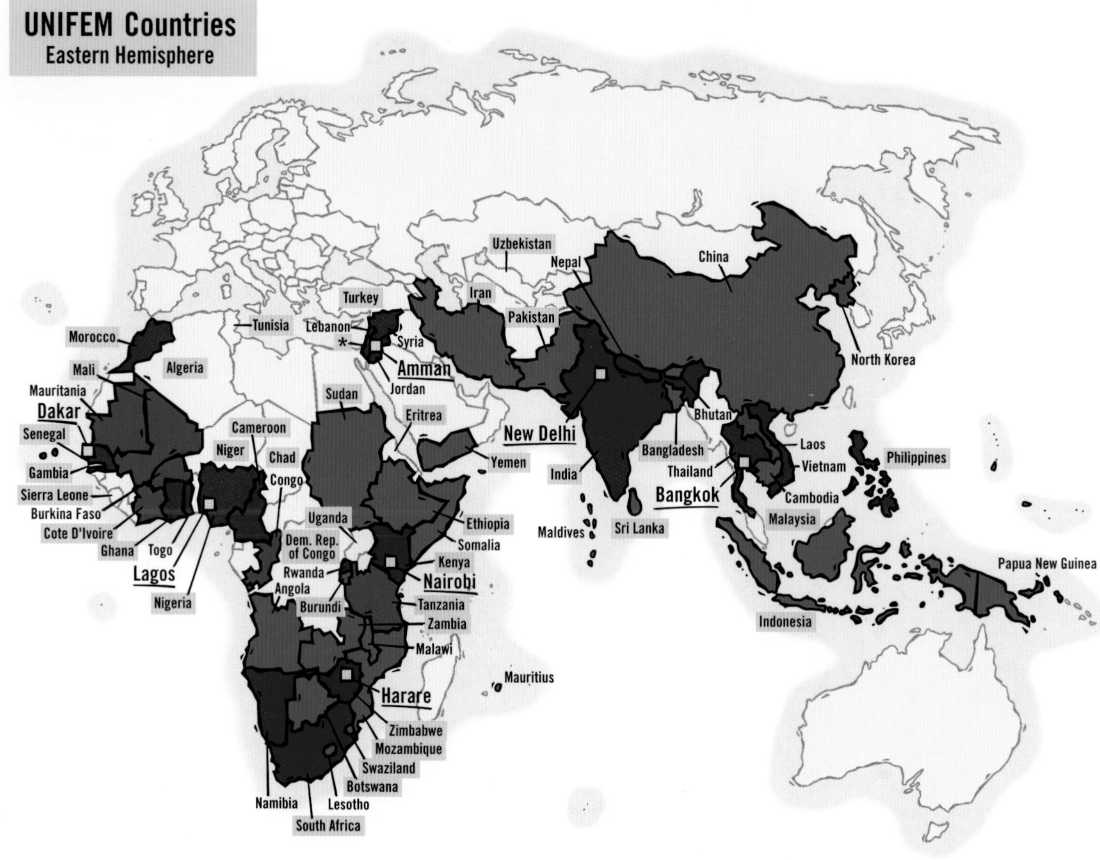

Mike Reagan/Michele Manasse PAGE 326

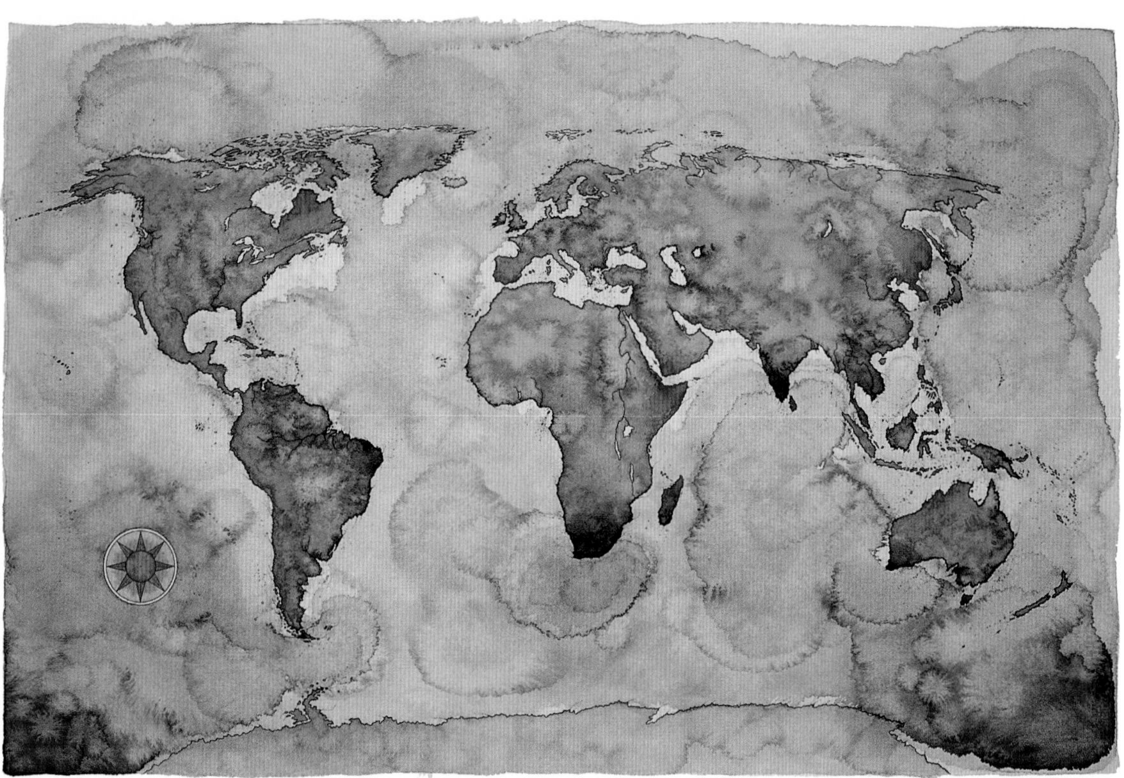

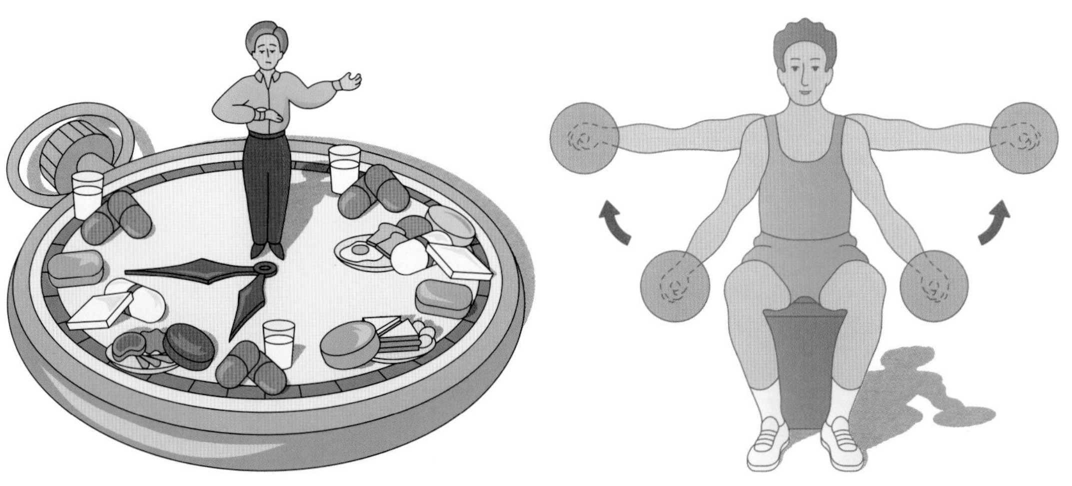

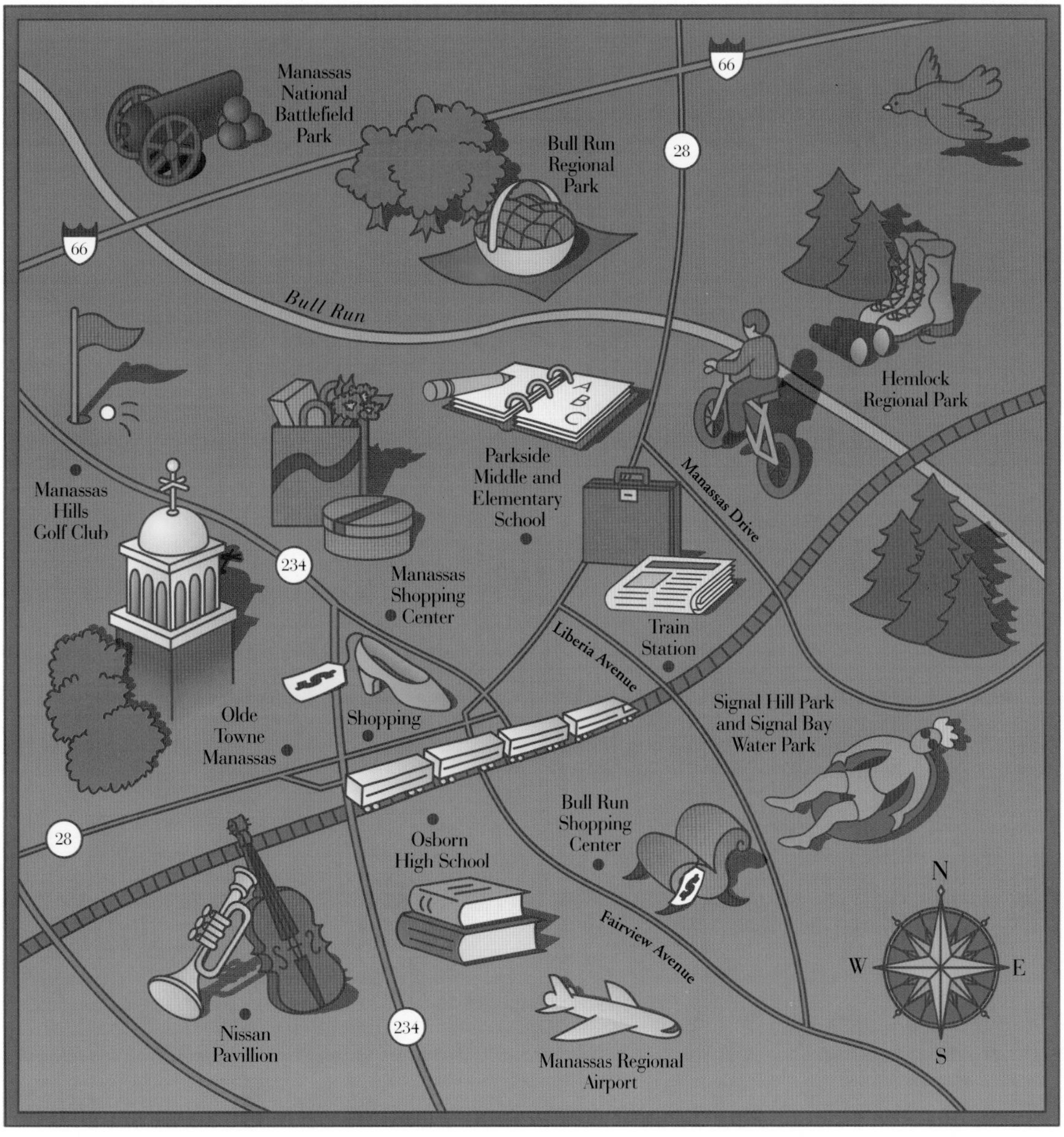

Manassas National Battlefield Park
Bull Run Regional Park
66
28
Bull Run
Hemlock Regional Park
Parkside Middle and Elementary School
Manassas Drive
Manassas Hills Golf Club
234
Manassas Shopping Center
Liberia Avenue
Train Station
Signal Hill Park and Signal Bay Water Park
Olde Towne Manassas
Shopping
Bull Run Shopping Center
Osborn High School
Fairview Avenue
N
W
E
S
Nissan Pavillion
Manassas Regional Airport

Jennifer Riegler PAGE 20

Chris Jagmin PAGE 404

Mark Andresen/Susan Wells & Associates PAGE 376

Linda Fennimore PAGE 15

Laura Stutzman PAGE 255

Lane DuPont/John Brewster Creative Services PAGE 284, 285

Peg Magovern/The Neis Group PAGE 306

Mick Coulas PAGE 256

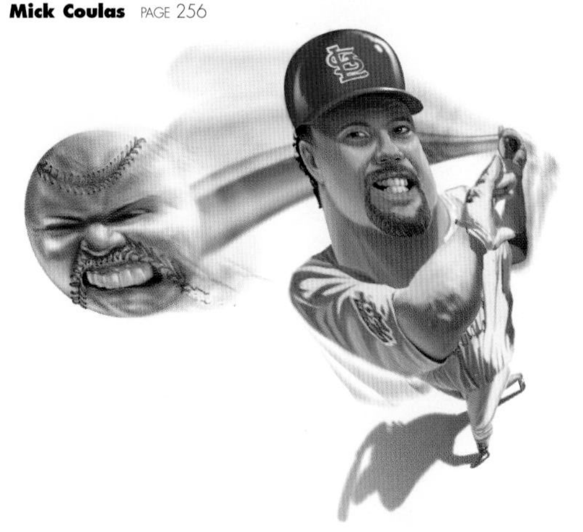

John Findley/Susan Wells & Associates PAGE 381

Mark Stutzman PAGE 254

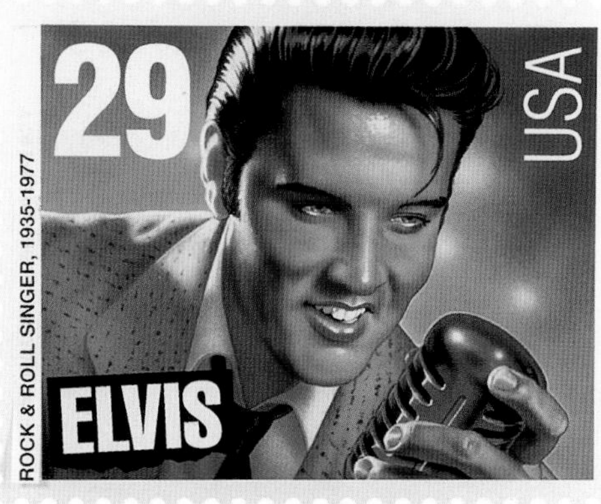

Paul-Emile Fequiere PAGE 118

Corey Wilkinson PAGE 60, 61

Eric Westbrook PAGE 387

Brad Weinman/Christine Prapas PAGE 266

Brenda Weeks PAGE 36

Margery Mintz PAGE 162

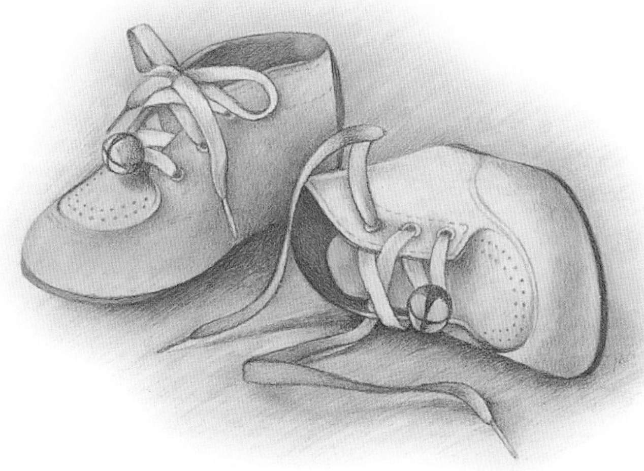

John Findley/Susan Wells & Associates PAGE 381

Rob Johnson/Donna Rosen PAGE 395

Robert Zimmerman PAGE 16, 17

Matthew Holmes/Renard Represents PAGE 50

Mark Stutzman PAGE 254

Robert Rodriguez/Renard Represents PAGE 46

John Etheridge PAGE 82

John MacDonald/Renard Represents PAGE 57

Mark Weakley/Alexander Pollard PAGE 217

Corey Wilkinson PAGE 60, 61

Diane Borowski/Alexander Pollard PAGE 221

Nikolai Punin PAGE 371

Ron Bomba PAGE 272

Kristin Mount PAGE 226

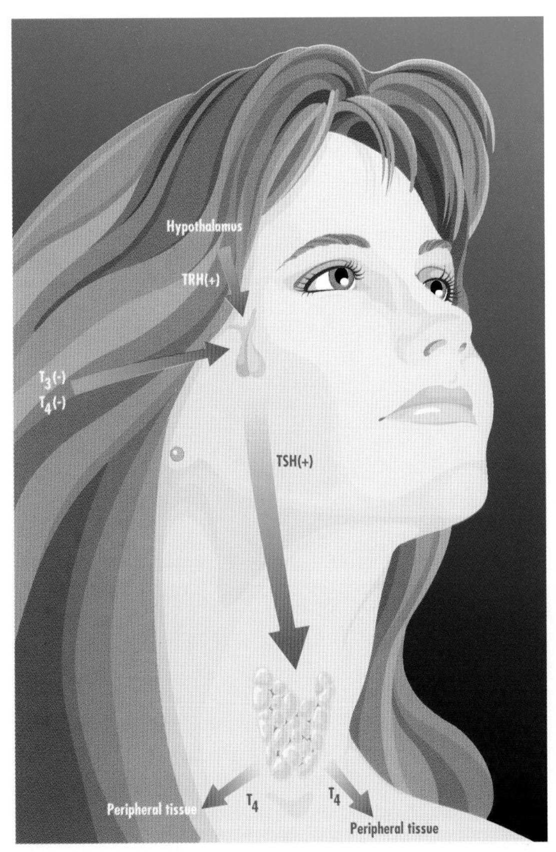

Bonnie Hofkin/Joanne Palulian PAGE 65

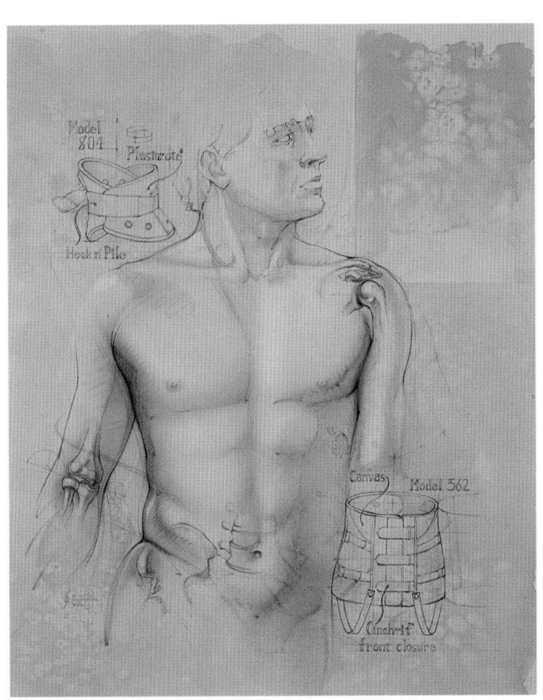

Stephen Hogan/Christine Prapas PAGE 264

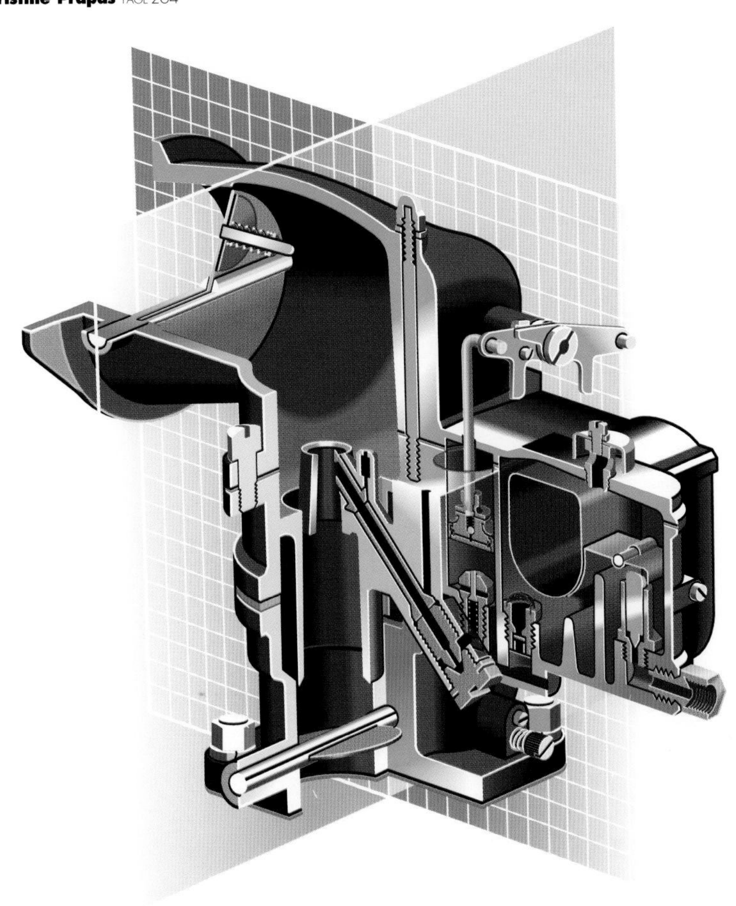

Laura Stutzman PAGE 255

Kazuhiko Sano/Renard Represents PAGE 41

Margery Mintz PAGE 162

Stephen Wells/Alexander Pollard PAGE 222

René Milot/Renard Represents PAGE 40

Ted Burn/Susan Wells & Associates PAGE 380

Eric Westbrook PAGE 387

Rob Johnson/Donna Rosen PAGE 395

Patty O'Friel PAGE 308

Jim Cohen PAGE 403

Shelly Meridith PAGE 362

Terri Schwarz PAGE 296

Annie Lunsford PAGE 388

Patty O'Friel PAGE 308

Stephen Wells/Alexander Pollard PAGE 222

Dave Clegg/Susan Wells & Associates PAGE 374

Mike Lester PAGE 390, 391

ILLUSTRATORS

Aagaard, Gary 159 Warren Street #2, Brooklyn, NY 11201 . . . . . (718) 694-0458
Abbey, Shannon 2425 17th Street #3, San Francisco, CA 94110 . . . . . (415) 252-0199
Abe, George Y. 21531 NE 144th Place, Woodinville, WA 98072 . . . . . (425) 788-5304
Abraham, Daniel 372 Fifth Avenue, Brooklyn, NY 11215 . . . . . (718) 499-4006
Abraham, Pascale 5421 Monkland, Montreal, PQ Canada H4A 1C5 . . . . . (514) 488-1084
Abramowitz, M.D. 884 Washington Street, Canton, MA 02021 . . . . . (781) 575-0063
Accornero, Franco 620 Broadway, New York, NY 10012 . . . . . (212) 674-0068
Represented By: Jerry Leff Associates, Inc. . . . . . (212) 697-8525
Ackison, Wendy Wassink Represented By: Berendsen & Associates . . . . . (513) 861-1400
Acuna, Ed Represented By: Artco . . . . . (212) 889-8777
Adam, Winky 370 Central Park West, New York, NY 10025 . . . . . (212) 423-0746
Adams, Beth 440 W 24th Street #16-C, New York, NY 10011 . . . . . (212) 987-8700
Adams, Cheryl 2124 NW 139th Street, Des Moines, IA 50325 . . . . . (515) 223-7174

ADAMS, GIL Page 156
Represented By: Carol Chislovsky Design, Inc. **(212) 677-9100**
Specialties: Conceptual; Corporate; Editorial; Greeting Cards; Oil; Still Life; Stock

Adams, Kathryn Represented By: Three in a Box . . . . . (416) 367-2446
Adams, Lisa 40 Harrison Street #29F, New York, NY 10013 . . . . . (212) 385-8189
Adams, Lynn Represented By: Evelyne Johnson Associates . . . . . (212) 532-0928
Adel, Daniel 50 W 22nd Street, 6th Flr., New York, NY 10024 . . . . . (212) 989-6114
Adler, Steven Represented By: Steven Kenny . . . . . (800) 789-9389
Agrell, Lewis 430 Hillcrest Drive, Prescott, AZ 86304 . . . . . (520) 445-7038
Aiello, Susan 120 W Illinois Street, Chicago, IL 60610 . . . . . (312) 527-3533
Aikins, David Represented By: Berendsen & Associates . . . . . (513) 861-1400
Aikman, Geraldine Represented By: Creative Connection . . . . . (410) 360-5981
Aikman, Pauline Represented By: Creative Connection . . . . . (410) 360-5981
Air Hero's Studio 30 Duke Street, St. Catherines, ON Canada L2R 5W5 . . . . . (905) 984-6140
Aire Apparent Studio 76 State Street #206, Newburyport, MA 01950 . . . . . (508) 462-1948
Aizawa, Kaz Represented By: Irmeli Holmberg . . . . . (212) 545-9155
Ajhar, Brian Represented By: Pamela Korn & Associates . . . . . (717) 595-9298
Akgulian, Nishan Represented By: David Goldman Agency . . . . . (212) 807-6627
Akimoto, George 6389 Embarcadero Drive, Stockton, CA 95219 . . . . . (209) 476-1564
Akins, Charles 2276 Virginia Place NE #C, Atlanta, GA 30305 . . . . . (404) 231-1312
Akins, Kelly 29023 Rolando Road, Lake Elsinore, CA 92530 . . . . . (909) 674-6124
Akopyan, Loudvik Represented By: Shannon Associates . . . . . (212) 831-5650
Alain, Luc 30 Dela Roseraie, Hull, PQ Canada J9A 2R8 . . . . . (819) 595-8941
Alanen, Erkki 161 Country Club Road, El Paso, TX 79932 . . . . . (915) 581-2272
Alavezos, Gus 19050 Merrymen Circle, Monument, CO 80132 . . . . . (719) 488-9078
Represented By: Carol Guenzi Agents, Inc. . . . . . (800) 417-5120
Alberg, Kari 11125 Kane Trail, Northfield, MN 55057 . . . . . (507) 645-2272
Albers, Dave Represented By: Scott Hull Associates . . . . . (937) 433-8383
Alcorn, Jo Lynn 290 Grandview Terrace, Hartford, CT 06114 . . . . . (860) 956-8529
Alcorn, Stephen 112 W Main Street, Cambridge, NY 12816 . . . . . (518) 677-5798
Alder, Kelynn Z. 19 Valley-Wood Court E, St. James, NY 11780 . . . . . (516) 584-6505
Aldredge, Vaughn Represented By: Jaz & Jaz . . . . . (206) 633-3445
Aldrich, David 143 Amelia Street, Toronto, ON Canada M4X 1E6 . . . . . (416) 960-6005
Alex, Leon Represented By: Carol Bancroft & Friends . . . . . (203) 748-4823
Alexander & Turner Represented By: Artco . . . . . (212) 889-8777
Alfano, Wayne Represented By: Bill & Maurine Klimt . . . . . (212) 799-2231
Alfonso, Gary 189 Delaware Avenue, Toronto, ON Canada M6H 2T2 . . . . . (416) 534-8522
Alion, Jeffrey Represented By: Carol Bancroft & Friends . . . . . (203) 748-4823
Allen, Dave 18108 Martin Avenue #2F, Homewood, IL 60430 . . . . . (708) 798-3283
Allen, Gina Minor 7755 S Kingston #2N, Chicago, IL 60649 . . . . . (773) 734-6418
Allen, Julian Represented By: The Newborn Group . . . . . (212) 260-6700
Allen, Mark Venice, CA 90291 . . . . . (310) 396-6471
New York, NY 10011 . . . . . (212) 243-4508
Allen, Pat 4510 Alpine Road, Portola Valley, CA 94028 . . . . . (650) 851-3116
Allen, Rick 2222 E Third Street, Duluth, MN 55812 . . . . . (218) 724-4861
Represented By: Jae Wagoner . . . . . (310) 392-4877
Allen, Terry 84 Campfire Road, Chappaqua, NY 10514 . . . . . (914) 238-1422

Allen, Victoria 1714 Bolton Street, Baltimore, MD 21217 . . . . . (410) 383-0893
Alley, R.W. Represented By: Publishers' Graphics . . . . . (203) 797-8188
Allison, Martyna 160 Spadina Road #206, Toronto, ON Canada . . . . . (416) 532-6587
Allport, Sophie Represented By: Sally Heflin . . . . . (212) 366-1893
Alma, Ray 42-32 215th Street, Apt. 3, Bayside, NY 11361 . . . . . (718) 631-0531
Almquist, Don Represented By: American Artists . . . . . (212) 682-2462
Alpert, Olive 9511 Shore Road #111, Brooklyn, NY 11209 . . . . . (718) 833-3092
Alphonso, Gary 189 Delaware Avenue, Toronto, ON Canada M6H 2T2 . . . . . (416) 534-8522

ALTEKRUSE, MAX Pages 338-339
Represented By: The Roland Group **(301) 718-7955**
Website: www.therolandgroup.com • Specialties: Acrylic; Oil; Realism; Water Color

Altera, Bina Represented By: Edana Reps . . . . . (617) 437-9760
Alton, Jeffrey Represented By: Carol Bancroft & Friends . . . . . (203) 748-4823
Alvin, John Represented By: The Pate Company . . . . . (805) 529-8111
Aly Illustration 14165 Garfield Drive, Spring Lake, MI 49456 . . . . . (616) 847-1630
Amatrula, Michele 259 W 10th Street, New York, NY 10014 . . . . . (212) 255-7413
Ambler, Barbara J. Hoopes 2769 Nipoma Street, San Diego, CA 92106 . . . . . (619) 222-7535
Ambre, Matthew 743 W Brompton Avenue, Chicago, IL 60657 . . . . . (773) 935-5170
Represented By: Dolby Represents . . . . . (312) 855-9336
Ambroson, Rodd 141 N State Street, Lake Oswego, OR 97034 . . . . . (503) 635-6238
Represented By: Spencer Church . . . . . (206) 860-9239
Amedee Illustration 126 Fifth Avenue, 13th Flr., New York, NY 10011 . . . . . (212) 620-0728
Amos, Jack & Son 18 E Main Street, Richmond, VA 23219-2110 . . . . . (804) 780-0993

AMOSS, JOHN Page 273
1177 Willivee Drive, Decatur, GA 30033 • Fax (404) 633-2628 **(404) 636-0275**
Website: www.mindspring.com/~amoss • Specialties: Computer; Digital; Editorial

Ampel, Kenneth Robert 1014 Black Oak Drive, Medford, OR 97504 . . . . . (541) 779-3859
Anatoly Represented By: Sweet Represents . . . . . (415) 433-1222
Anderian, Raffi 25 The Esplanade #2713, Toronto, ON Canada M5E 1W5 . . . . . (416) 362-5673
Anderson, A. Richard Represented By: Joel Harlib Associates, Inc. . . . . . (312) 573-1370
Anderson, Bryan Represented By: Nancy Bacher . . . . . (612) 786-1200
Anderson, David 27 Atlantic Avenue, Toronto, ON Canada M6K 3E7 . . . . . (416) 533-2188
Anderson, Kat Represented By: Tiffany Represents . . . . . (206) 441-7701
Anderson, Lori Represented By: Carol Bancroft & Friends . . . . . (203) 748-4823
Anderson, Mark 8222 SW Hawthorne Lane, Vashon Island, WA 98070 . . . . . (206) 567-4514
Anderson, Paul 182 Christie Avenue, Clifton, NJ 07011 . . . . . (973) 340-4914
Represented By: Conrad Represents, Inc. . . . . . (415) 921-7140
Anderson, Richard 490 Bleeker Avenue, Mamaroneck, NY 10543 . . . . . (914) 381-2682
Represented By: Joel Harlib Associates, Inc. . . . . . (312) 573-1370
Anderson, Robert Clyde 48 Green Street, 4th Flr, New York, NY 10013 . . . . . (212) 925-4222
Represented By: Art Department . . . . . (212) 925-4222
Anderson, Terry Represented By: Rosenthal Represents . . . . . (818) 222-5445
Anderson, Tim Represented By: Scott Hull Associates . . . . . (937) 433-8383
Anderson Design, Michael 28202 Cabot Road, Ste. 300, Laguna Niguel, CA 92677-1249 . . . . . (714) 831-3501
Anderson Illustration, Mark 4 E Ohio Street #7, Chicago, IL 60611 . . . . . (312) 654-8999
Andreasen, Dan Represented By: Publishers' Graphics . . . . . (203) 797-8188

ANDRESEN, MARK Pages 373,376,427,458
6417 Gladys Street, Metairie, LA 70003 **(504) 888-1644**
Represented By: Susan Wells & Associates **(404) 255-1430**
e-mail: AndresenM@aol.com • Specialties: Black & White; Conceptual; Line Art; People

Andrews, Bob Represented By: Skidmore, Inc. . . . . . (248) 353-7722
Andrews, Martin Represented By: Alan Lynch Artists . . . . . (908) 813-8718
Ang, Thom 766 N Mentor Avenue, Pasadena, CA 91104 . . . . . (818) 553-5166
Represented By: Allen Spiegel & Associates . . . . . (408) 372-4672
Angel Ink 343 Dumfries Avenue, Kitchner, ON Canada N2H 2E9 . . . . . (519) 578-9373
Angelini, George Represented By: Artco . . . . . (212) 889-8777
Angelo 1449 Longfellow Avenue, Bronx, NY 10459 . . . . . (718) 617-2907
Angle, Scott 21051 Barbados Circle, Huntington Beach, CA 92646 . . . . . (714) 960-8485
Represented By: Carole Newman & Associates . . . . . (310) 394-5031

Angrisani, Chris 6095 N Ninth Road, Arlington, VA 22205 . . . . . (703) 241-3739
Angry Cow 164 Colbeck Street, Toronto, ON Canada M6S 1V9 . . . . . (416) 767-6035
AnimationFX, Inc. P.O. Box 771025, Coral Springs, FL 33077-1025 . . . . . (954) 718-0600
Annino, Michael 1700 North Park, Apt. 4F, Chicago, IL 60614 . . . . . (312) 255-0850
Annis, Scott 26099 McCiver Circle, Conifer, CO 80433 . . . . . (303) 674-1151
Anthony, Tony 718 S Philip Street, Philadelphia, PA 19147 . . . . . (215) 238-9550
Antonios, Tony Represented By: Bernstein & Andriulli, Inc. . . . . . (212) 682-1490
Anzalone, Lori 35-02 Berdan Avenue, Fair Lawn, NJ 07410 . . . . . (201) 796-5588
Apel, Eric Represented By: Woody Coleman Presents, Inc. . . . . . (216) 661-4222
Apice, Michael P.O. Box 397, Oceanside, NY 11572 . . . . . (516) 678-3735
apJones, Todd Represented By: Joanie Bernstein Art Rep . . . . . (612) 374-3169
Aponte, Carlos Represented By: Art Department . . . . . (212) 925-4222
Appleoff, Sandy 2029 Custer Parkway, Richardson, TX 75080 . . . . . (972) 761-0500
Represented By: Ravenhill Represents . . . . . (816) 333-0744
Appleton, Diana Minisci 488 Fern Street W, Hartford, CT 06107 . . . . . (860) 521-4745
Represented By: Chip Caton . . . . . (860) 523-4562
Appleton, Wayne Represented By: Skidmore, Inc. . . . . . (248) 353-7722
Archambault, Matthew Represented By: Hankins & Tegenborg Ltd. . . . . . (212) 867-8092
Archer, Doug Represented By: Penny & Stermer Group . . . . . (212) 505-9342
Archey, Rebecca 63 Madrone Avenue, Larkspur, CA 94939 . . . . . (415) 924-2424
Represented By: Nadine Hunter . . . . . (415) 456-7711
Arday Illustration, Don 616 Arbor Creek Drive, DeSoto, TX 75115 . . . . . (972) 223-6235
Represented By: Photocom Inc. . . . . . (214) 720-2272
Arenson, Roberta 1647 Oregon Avenue, Prescott, AZ 86301 . . . . . (520) 776-8128
Argus Represented By: Lori Nowicki & Associates . . . . . (212) 243-5888
Arion, Katherine 1162 N Orange Grove Avenue, West Hollywood, CA 90046 . . . . . (213) 654-6252
Arkle, Dave 1 La Ramada Place, Pomona, CA 91766-4782 . . . . . (909) 865-2967
Represented By: Hall & Associates . . . . . (213) 962-2500
Represented By: Storyboards . . . . . (310) 581-4050
Armson, Michael Represented By: Alan Lynch Artists . . . . . (908) 813-8718
Armstrong, Bruce Represented By: Berendsen & Associates . . . . . (513) 861-1400
Armstrong, Jayne 19331 Centre Street, Box 610, Mount Albert, ON Canada L0G 1M0 . . . . . (905) 473-3181
Armstrong, Rene 916 Olive, Ste. 300, St. Louis, MO 63101 . . . . . (314) 231-6800
Armstrong, Shelagh 120 Mavety Street, Toronto, ON Canada M6P 2L9 . . . . . (416) 536-1636
Arnold, Mike 225 Park Place, Brooklyn, NY 11238 . . . . . (718) 398-9039
Arrasmith, Patrick 309 Sixth Street, Brooklyn, NY 11215 . . . . . (718) 499-4101
Arrco Medical Art & Design 909 Beacon Street, Boston, MA 02215 . . . . . (617) 266-2680
Arroyo, Fian 901 Surfside Boulevard, Miami, FL 33154 . . . . . (305) 866-6370
Arruda, Richard Represented By: Repertory . . . . . (213) 931-7449
Arsenault, Melina 284 St. Helens Avenue #217, Toronto, ON Canada . . . . . (416) 530-4440
Art Gecko 2500 State Street, Dallas, TX 75201 . . . . . (214) 855-1264
Represented By: Those 3 Reps . . . . . (214) 871-1316
Art Staff, Inc. 1000 John R Road #201, Troy, MI 48083 . . . . . (248) 583-6070
Arthurs, Madeleine Hope 206 W 104th Street #45, New York, NY 10025 . . . . . (212) 678-5703
Artifx 3000 Carlisle #203, Dallas, TX 75204 . . . . . (214) 969-6911
Represented By: Those 3 Reps . . . . . (214) 871-1316
Artman Represented By: Those 3 Reps . . . . . (214) 871-1316
Artonweb P.O. Box 1160, Wayne, IL 60184 . . . . . (630) 289-6262
Arturo Represented By: Shooting Star . . . . . (213) 469-2020
Aru, Agnes 498 Manning Avenue, Toronto, ON Canada M6G 2V7 . . . . . (416) 532-9861
Asami, Daiji Represented By: Envoy Creative Consultants . . . . . (703) 706-5729
Asbaghi, Zita 104-40 Queens Boulevard, Forest Hills, NY 11375 . . . . . (718) 275-1995
Ascencios, Natalie 918 Metropolitan Avenue #1-L, Brooklyn, NY 11211 . . . . . (718) 388-7931
Ashby, Gil Represented By: Mendola Ltd. . . . . . (212) 986-5680
Represented By: Ken Barboza . . . . . (212) 505-8635
Asher, Terri 21800 Schoenborn Street #162, Canoga Park, CA 91304 . . . . . (818) 348-4278
Aska, Warabe 1019 Lorne Park Road, Mississauga, ON Canada L5H 2Z9 . . . . . (905) 271-6474
Aspinall, Neal 1255 Martha Washington Drive, Wauwatosa, WI 53213 . . . . . (414) 774-3808
Athanas, Charlie Evanston, IL 60202 . . . . . (847) 332-2136
Atkins, Bill 485 Bent Street, Laguna Beach, CA 92651 . . . . . (714) 494-5899
Atkinson, Janet 584 Broadway #608, New York, NY 10012 . . . . . (212) 941-1710
Atkinson, Steve 3408 Meridian Drive, Minneapolis, MN 55422 . . . . . (612) 522-7756
Represented By: Leighton & Company, Inc. . . . . . (978) 921-0887
Ator, Robin Represented By: The Art Agency . . . . . (503) 203-8300
Atteberry, Kevan J. P.O. Box 40188, Bellevue, WA 98015-4188 . . . . . (425) 453-6010

Attebery, Craig Represented By: Frank & Jeff Lavaty . . . . (212) 427-5632
Attiliis, Andy 9710 Days Farm Drive, Vienna, VA 22182 . . . . (703) 759-4283
Aubrey, Meg Represented By: Cornell & McCarthy, LLC . . . . (203) 454-4210
Auckland, Jim Represented By: Liz Sanders Agency . . . . (714) 495-3664
August, Robert Represented By: Melissa McCallum . . . . (847) 441-8993
Austin, Carolyn 169 Beatrice Street, Toronto, ON Canada M6G 3E9 . . . . (416) 588-9040
Austin, Cary Represented By: Creative Freelancers . . . . (800) 398-9544
Represented By: Shannon Associates . . . . (212) 831-5650
Austin, Steve Fresno, CA 93710 . . . . (209) 323-6939
Avanti Studios 2305 Ashland Street #C, Ashland, OR 97520 . . . . (800) 435-6509
Aveto, Michael Represented By: Irmeli Holmberg . . . . (212) 545-9155
Avishai, Susan Represented By: Barbara Gordon Associates Ltd. . . . . (212) 686-3514
Awad, Macy 56 Roxborough Street W, Toronto, ON Canada M5R 1P8 . . . . (416) 929-0964

AYERS, ALAN Pages 350-351
Represented By: Sal Barracca Associates **(212) 889-2400**
Website: www.alanayers.com • Specialty: Digital

Azakami, Makiko Represented By: Lilla Rogers Studio . . . . (781) 641-2787
Azpiri Represented By: Alan Lynch Artists . . . . (908) 813-8718
Azubike, Jenny 7430 Milan Avenue, St. Louis, MO 63130 . . . . (314) 726-5013
Azzinaro, Lew Represented By: Donna Rosen Artists' Rep . . . . (301) 384-8925
Azzuolo, Elia 7185 Louis-Hemon, Montreal, PQ Canada H2E 2T8 . . . . (514) 729-1741
Bach, Del-Bouree Represented By: Buck & Kane . . . . (212) 631-0009
Bachem, Paul Represented By: Artworks . . . . (212) 627-1554
Bachtell, Tom 220 S State Street, 19th Flr., Chicago, IL 60604 . . . . (312) 939-6603
Backes, Nick Represented By: Barb Hauser . . . . (415) 647-5660
Represented By: Joel Harlib Associates, Inc. . . . . (312) 573-1370
Backhaus, Kenn Represented By: Mason Illustration . . . . (612) 729-1774
Backhouse, Colin Represented By: Alan Lynch Artists . . . . (908) 813-8718
Backus, Michael Represented By: Joel Harlib Associates, Inc. . . . . (312) 573-1370
Badaracco, Gonz 8500 E Indian School Road, Scottsdale, AZ 85251 . . . . (602) 994-0098
Badenhop, Mary Represented By: Creative Connection . . . . (410) 360-5981
Badkerhanian, Genetta 1825 W Eighth Avenue, Ste. 207, Vancouver, BC Canada V6J 1V9 . . . . (604) 733-7329
Baehr, Richard C. Represented By: Frank & Jeff Lavaty . . . . (212) 427-5632

BAEK, MATTHEW J. Pages 392,396,429,430,440
Represented By: Donna Rosen Artists' Rep **(301) 384-8925**
e-mail: djrosen@erols.com • Website: www.aaarrt.com/donnasgallery
Specialties: Advertising; Annual Report; Conceptual; Corporate; Editorial

Baer, Roxanna 850 Amsterdam Avenue #13-C, New York, NY 10025 . . . . (212) 865-2183
Baggs, Mike 160 E 38th Street #20G, New York, NY 10016 . . . . (800) 49B-AGGS
Bailey, Adrian 11940-104 Street, Apt. 2, Alberta, BC Canada T5G 2L2 . . . . (403) 471-9160
Bailey, John 7709 W Lisbon Avenue, Milwaukee, WI 53222 . . . . (414) 442-1367
Bailey, R.C. 225 Westward Drive, Miami Springs, FL 33166
Baker, Bradley 284 St. Helens Avenue #217, Toronto, ON Canada . . . . (416) 530-4440
Baker, Don Represented By: Kolea Baker Artists Representative . . . . (206) 784-1136
Baker, Garin 478 Union Avenue, New Windsor, NY 12553 . . . . (914) 562-7802

BAKER, JENNIFER Page 277
Represented By: Famous Frames **(310) 642-2721**
e-mail: info@famousframes.com • Website: www.famousframes.com • Specialties: Animation; Storyboards

Baker, Joe 35 Wooster Street, Studio 2F, New York, NY 10013 . . . . (212) 925-6555
Baker, Louise M. 223 W Erie Street, Chicago, IL 60610 . . . . (312) 915-0570
Baker, Skip Represented By: Deborah Wolfe . . . . (215) 232-6666
Baker, Susan 315 West Side Drive #303, Gaithersburg, MD 20878-3046 . . . . (301) 258-0126
Balbes, Sydney 9740 Sepulveda Boulvard, Ste. 17, North Hills, CA 91343 . . . . (818) 891-1370
Baldwin, Christopher Represented By: Jaz & Jaz . . . . (206) 633-3445
Baldwin, Scott Represented By: Jacqueline Dedell, Inc. . . . . (212) 741-2539
Balkcum, Gregg 13519 Krislyn Woods Place, Charlotte, NC 28278 . . . . (704) 588-7278
Ball, John Represented By: Skidmore, Inc. . . . . (248) 353-7722
Ballard Visual Comm., Dan P.O. Box 85187, Seattle, WA 98145 . . . . (206) 634-0084
Ballsun, John 7711 Reseda Boulevard #32, Reseda, CA 91316 . . . . (818) 343-1542

Balnave, Jack Represented By: Dane Sonneville. . . . . (973) 744-4465
Balouch, Kristen 57 Norman Avenue #4R, Brooklyn, NY 11222 . . . . . (718) 349-2311
Bamundo, David 146 Chandler Avenue, Staten Island, NY 10314. . . . . (718) 370-7726
Band, William 815 Fletcher Valley Crescent, Mississauga, ON Canada L5J 2X6. . . . . (905) 823-1537
Bandera, Emilio 99 Woodpark Place, Newmarket, ON Canada L3Y 3P5. . . . . (905) 898-1759
Bandle, Johnna 7726 Noland Road, Lenexa, KS 66216 . . . . . (913) 962-9595
Bandsuch, Matt 497 Prentis Street #4, Detroit, MI 48201 . . . . . (313) 831-7324
Banek, Yvette Represented By: Cornell & McCarthy, LLC . . . . . (203) 454-4210
Banfield, Elliot 341 E 10th Street, New York, NY 10009 . . . . . (212) 473-6772
Banta, Susan 17 Magazine Street, Cambridge, MA 02139 . . . . . (617) 876-8568
RR #1 Box 101, Brookfield, VT 05036 . . . . . (802) 276-3248
Banthien, Barbara 127 Leland Way, Tiburon, CA 94920. . . . . (415) 381-0842
Represented By: Jan Collier Represents, Inc. . . . . . (415) 383-9026
Banyai, Istvan Represented By: Betsy Hillman . . . . . (415) 381-4728
Bapp, Kevin Represented By: Carol Chislovsky Design, Inc. . . . . . (212) 677-9100
Baquero, George Represented By: Steve Edsey & Sons . . . . . (312) 527-0351
Baradat, Sergio 210 W 70th Street #1606, New York, NY 10023. . . . . (212) 721-2588
Barbaria, Steve 1990 Third Street #400, Sacramento, CA 95814 . . . . . (916) 442-3200
Barber, David Represented By: Sheryl Beranbaum . . . . . (401) 737-8591
Barber, Julia Redwood, 92 Charles Close, Wroxham, Norwich, England NR12 8TT 44 160 378 4444
Barbour, Karen P.O. Box 1210, Point Reyes Stn., CA 94956 . . . . . (415) 663-1100
Bardell, Graham 448 Spadina Road #408, Toronto, ON Canada M5P 2W4. . . . . (416) 488-7514
Barker, Tim 3248 Minnesota Avenue, Costa Mesa, CA 92626 . . . . . (714) 850-1935
Barlowe, Wayne 7 Allen Street, Rumson, NJ 07760 . . . . . (908) 758-1035
Barnard, Bryn 432 Point Caution Drive, Friday Harbor, WA 98250 . . . . . (360) 378-6355
Barner, Bob 65 Mount Vernon Street, Boston, MA 02108 . . . . . (617) 523-0953
Represented By: Kirchoff/Wohlberg, Inc.. . . . . (212) 644-2020
Barnes, Karen 17 Pinewood Street, Annapolis, MD 21401. . . . . (410) 266-6550
Barnes, Kim 3000 Chestnut Avenue, Ste. 6, Baltimore, MD 21211 . . . . . (410) 243-1951
Barnes, Melanie Represented By: Irmeli Holmberg . . . . . (212) 545-9155
Barnes, Michelle Represented By: David Goldman Agency. . . . . (212) 807-6627
Barnes, Suzanne 22 Pleasant Street, Salem, MA 01970. . . . . (508) 740-9150
Barnes, Tim Represented By: Artco . . . . . (212) 889-8777
Barnes-Murphy, Rowan Represented By: Mendola Ltd. . . . . (212) 986-5680
Barnet, Nancy P.O. Box 9, Elk Grove, CA 95759-0009 . . . . . (916) 685-4147
Barnett, Deborah 46 Harbord Street, Toronto, ON Canada M5S 1G2. . . . . (416) 977-0769
Barolini, Nicoletta 110 High Street, Hastings-on-Hudson, NY 10706. . . . . (914) 478-7119
Barr, Ken Represented By: Jerry Leff Associates, Inc. . . . . (212) 697-8525
Barr, Marilynn P.O. Box 8787, Greensboro, NC 27419 . . . . . (336) 851-1743
Barrall, Tim 372 Bleecker Street, New York, NY 10014. . . . . (212) 243-9003
Barrett, Robert Represented By: Pema Browne Ltd. . . . . (914) 985-2936
Barrett, Ron Represented By: HK Portfolio. . . . . (212) 675-5719
Barrett, Tom 81 Mt. Vernon Street, Boston, MA 02108. . . . . (617) 523-4072
Barry, Ron Represented By: Barbara Gordon Associates Ltd. . . . . (212) 686-3514
Barsky, Alexander Represented By: Irmeli Holmberg. . . . . (212) 545-9155
Barson, Jeff Represented By: Hankins & Tegenborg Ltd. . . . . (212) 867-8092
Bartalos, Michael 30 Ramona Avenue #2, San Francisco, CA 94103. . . . . (415) 863-4569
Bartek, Shelly 8522 Izard Street, Omaha, NE 68114 . . . . . (402) 399-5251
Represented By: Carol Guenzi Agents, Inc. . . . . . (800) 417-5120
Represented By: Mary Holland & Company . . . . . (602) 263-8990
Bartholomew, Sandra Steen 136 Bennington Road, Charlottesville, VA 22901 . . . . . (804) 979-8252
Barto, Renzo Represented By: American Artists . . . . . (212) 682-2462
Barton, Kent Represented By: Richard Solomon . . . . . (212) 683-1362

BARTRAM, SIMON Pages 366-367
Represented By: Alan Lynch Artists **(908) 813-8718**
Represented By: Arena **44 171 267 9661**

Baruffi, Andrea 341 Hudson Terrace, Piermont, NY 10968 . . . . . (914) 359-9542
Baseman, Gary Represented By: Jan Collier Represents, Inc.. . . . . (415) 383-9026

BATCHELLER, KEITH Pages 168,172
Represented By: American Artists **(212) 682-2462**
e-mail: info@amerartists.com • Website: www.amerartists.com
Specialties: Advertising; Airbrush; Cartoon; Character; Entertainment

Batelman, Kenneth 47-16 39th Avenue, Sunnyside, NY 11104 . . . . . (718) 392-3483
Bateman, Aaron Represented By: Barbara Gordon Associates Ltd. . . . . . (212) 686-3514
Bates, Harry Represented By: Carol Chislovsky Design, Inc. . . . . . (212) 677-9100
Battles, Brian 2245 Yucca Hill Drive, Alpine, CA 91901 . . . . . (619) 445-3045
Bauer, Ann Represented By: Skidmore, Inc.. . . . . . (248) 353-7722
Bauer, Carla 156 Fifth Avenue, Ste. 1100, New York, NY 10010 . . . . . (212) 807-8305
Bauer, Frank 301 N Water Street, Milwaukee, WI 53202 . . . . . (414) 271-3171

BAUER, STEPHEN Pages 252-253
Represented By: Deborah Wolfe **(215) 232-6666**
Website: www.deborahwolfeltd.com • Specialties: Advertising; Airbrush; Conceptual; Editorial; Mixed Media; Stock

Baughman, Christi 467 Clearfield, Garland, TX 75043 . . . . . (972) 270-5925
Baumgart Studio 2425 Mountain Avenue, La Crescenta, CA 91214 . . . . . (818) 957-1071
Bautista, Vincent 1302 Lyndon Street #7, South Pasadena, CA 91030 . . . . . (626) 403-9124
Baviera, Rocco 41 King William Street #210, Hamilton, ON Canada L8R 1A2 . . . . . (905) 570-0004
Baynham, John Represented By: Flannery Lane Ltd. . . . . . (914) 631-1413
BC Communications 1626 Eastern Parkway, Louisville, KY 40204. . . . . . (502) 459-0295
Beach, Lou 900 S Tremaine Avenue, Los Angeles, CA 90019 . . . . . (213) 934-7335
Beach, Pearl 4939 Sycamore Terrace, Los Angeles, CA 90042 . . . . . (213) 256-2170
Beale, Chris 1527 16th Street, Flr. A, Santa Monica, CA 90404 . . . . . (310) 828-3999
Beards, Richard Represented By: Jacqueline Dedell, Inc. . . . . . (212) 741-2539
Beauchamp, Joe Represented By: Yolanda Burnett Represents . . . . . (770) 967-0039
Represented By: Wilson-Zumbo Illustration . . . . . (414) 271-3388
Beaudoin, Mario 4675 Patineau Avenue, Montreal, PQ Canada H2H 1V4. . . . . . (514) 523-6109
Beavers, Sean Represented By: Lott Representatives. . . . . . (212) 953-7088
Bechtold, Glory 22 N Morgan #113, Chicago, IL 60607 . . . . . (312) 666-9494
Beck, Dave Represented By: Scott Hull Associates. . . . . . (937) 433-8383
Becker, Neesa Represented By: Carol Bancroft & Friends . . . . . (203) 748-4823
Becker, Pamela Represented By: Cliff Knecht. . . . . . (412) 761-5666
Becker, Paula 6017 Ebonwood, Corpus Christi, TX 78412 . . . . . (512) 993-0164
Becker, Polly 156 W Newton Street, Boston, MA 02118 . . . . . (617) 247-0469
Bedwell, Clem 968 Watkins Street NW, Atlanta, GA 30318. . . . . . (404) 881-1101
Represented By: Yolanda Burnett Represents . . . . . (770) 967-0039
Represented By: Langley & Associates. . . . . . (847) 670-0912
Bee, Johnee Represented By: Liz Sanders Agency. . . . . . (714) 495-3664
Beecham, Greg Represented By: Jerry Leff Associates, Inc. . . . . . (212) 697-8525
Beecham, Tom Represented By: Jerry Leff Associates, Inc. . . . . . (212) 697-8525
Beeke, Tiphanie Represented By: HK Portfolio . . . . . (212) 675-5719
Beerworth, Roger 1723 S Crescent Heights Blvd., Los Angeles, CA 90035 . . . . . (213) 933-9692
Begin, Mary Jane Represented By: Jerry Leff Associates, Inc.. . . . . . (212) 697-8525
Bego, Dolores Represented By: Anita Grien Represents . . . . . (212) 697-6170
Beha, Philippe Represented By: Joanne Palulian . . . . . (212) 581-8338
Behm, Kim Represented By: Leyden Diversified . . . . . (215) 663-0587
Behnke, Brian Represented By: Lisa Freeman. . . . . . (317) 920-0068
Beilfuss, Kevin Represented By: Mendola Ltd. . . . . . (212) 986-5680
Beise, Sarah Represented By: Harriet Kastaris & Associates . . . . . (314) 773-2600
Belcher, Steven Represented By: Artco . . . . . (212) 889-8777
Belden, Linda Represented By: Creative Connection . . . . . (410) 360-5981

BELL, FRED Pages 389,423
212 N 77th Street, Milwaukee, WI 53213 • Fax (414) 771-6352 **(414) 771-0472**
e-mail: fredbell@execpc.com • Website: www.execpc.com/~fredbell
Specialties: Advertising; Cartoon; Digital; Editorial; Graphic Design/Illustration; Humour; People; Poster; Whimsical

Bell, Julie Represented By: Joel Harlib Associates, Inc. . . . . . (312) 573-1370
Bell, Karen 1700 Decker Canyon Road, Malibu, CA 90265. . . . . . (310) 457-3943
Bell, Ron Represented By: Clare Jett & Associates . . . . . (502) 228-9427
Bell, Tom 1831 W Roscoe #2, Chicago, IL 60657. . . . . . (773) 248-8190
Bella, Joset Represented By: Irmeli Holmberg . . . . . (212) 545-9155
Bellantuono, Jeffrey 292 Britannia Street, Ste. A, Meriden, CT 06450 . . . . . (203) 639-0665
Bellemare, Sylvain 2970 St. Emil, Montreal, PQ Canada H1L 5M5. . . . . . (514) 493-1704
Bello, Jean 67-52 Demorman Ville, Montreal, PQ Canada H1S 2C1 . . . . . (514) 279-4039
Belmore, Jay 215 AVA Road, Toronto, ON Canada M6C 1N9 . . . . . (416) 423-8262

Bemus, Bart Represented By: American Artists . . . . (212) 682-2462
Represented By: Sharon Dodge/Illustration Works . . . . (206) 284-4701
Ben-Ami, Doron Represented By: Artco . . . . (212) 889-8777
Bendell, Norm Represented By: David Goldman Agency . . . . (212) 807-6627
Bender, Cherie 455 NE 10th Street, Boca Raton, FL 33432 . . . . (561) 368-5722
Represented By: Liz Sanders Agency . . . . (714) 495-3664
Bender, Mark Represented By: Cliff Knecht . . . . (412) 761-5666
Bendis, Keith Represented By: David Goldman Agency . . . . (212) 807-6627
Benfanti, Russell Represented By: Mendola Ltd. . . . . (212) 986-5680
Benger, Brent Represented By: Mendola Ltd. . . . . (212) 986-5680
Bengoechea, Fernando Represented By: Bernstein & Andriulli, Inc. . . . . (212) 682-1490
Benjamin, Bernard 1763 Second Avenue, Apt. 37-K, New York, NY 10128 . . . . (212) 722-7773
Bennet, Gary 3308 Startan Court, Louisville, KY 40220 . . . . (502) 458-2067
Bennett, Dianne 424 Rancho Drive, Ventura, CA 93003 . . . . (805) 641-1670
Represented By: Robin Ogden Represents . . . . (612) 925-4174
Represented By: Daniele Collignon . . . . (212) 243-4209
Bennett, James Represented By: Richard Solomon . . . . (212) 683-1362
Bennett, Jamie Represented By: Reactor Art & Design Ltd. . . . . (416) 703-1913
Bennett, Joe Represented By: Glass House Graphics . . . . (304) 232-5641
Bennett, Lynn Represented By: Shooting Star . . . . (213) 469-2020
Bennett, Tom 84 Withers Street, 5th Flr., Brooklyn, NY 11211 . . . . (718) 349-2477
Benny, Mike 2600 Lake Austin Boulevard, #5108, Austin, TX 78703 . . . . (512) 860-3224
Benoit Represented By: Riley Illustration . . . . (212) 989-8770
Benson, Linda 150 Union Street, Ridgewood, NJ 07450 . . . . (201) 652-1940
Bensusen, Sally J. 932 S Walter Reed Drive, CPAS- 2nd Flr., Arlington, VA 22204 . . . . (703) 979-3931
Bentz, Charles 110 W 40th Street, New York, NY 10018 . . . . (212) 302-9088
Berasi, Teresa 427 Third Street, Brooklyn, NY 11215 . . . . (718) 965-2231
Berendt, Eric 1989A Santa Rita Road #307, Pleasanton, CA 94566 . . . . (510) 462-6809
Bereznickas, Ilja Represented By: Wanda Nowak . . . . (212) 535-0438
Berg, John 110 Cottage Street, Buffalo, NY 14201 . . . . (716) 884-8003
Berg, Ron Represented By: Mendola Ltd. . . . . (212) 986-5680
Bergendoff, Roger Represented By: American Artists . . . . (212) 682-2462
Bergherr, Mary Represented By: Nancy Bacher . . . . (612) 786-1200
Berglund, Cindy 5275 E Lake Beach Court, Shoreview, MN 55126 . . . . (612) 490-5141
Bergman, Eliot 362 W 20th Street #201, New York, NY 10011 . . . . (888) 266-5749
Berkey, John Represented By: Frank & Jeff Lavaty . . . . (212) 427-5632

BERKSON, NINA Pages 18-19
Represented By: Link **(416) 530-1500**
Specialty: Fashion

Berlin, Rose Represented By: Cornell & McCarthy, LLC . . . . (203) 454-4210
Bernal, Richard Represented By: Carol Bancroft & Friends . . . . (203) 748-4823
Bernardi, Barry 77 Davisville Avenue #1603, Toronto, ON Canada M4S 1G4 . . . . (416) 487-9601
Bernardin, James 6836 16th Avenue NE, Seattle, WA 98115 . . . . (206) 517-4953
Represented By: Christina Tugeau . . . . (203) 438-7307
Bernasconi, Jay 10 Dresden Street #2, Jamaica Plain, MA 02130 . . . . (617) 675-7992
Bernatchez, Patrick 4398 Garnier, Montreal, PQ Canada H2J 3S2 . . . . (514) 523-0689
Bernetti, Larry Represented By: Art Source/Diane Barkley . . . . (914) 747-2220
Berran, Bob Represented By: Hankins & Tegenborg Ltd. . . . . (212) 867-8092
Berrett, Randy Represented By: Sweet Represents . . . . (415) 433-1222
Berrit, Grynan 1125 Landwehr Road, Northbrook, IL 60062 . . . . (708) 498-8936
Berry, Fanny Mellet Represented By: Anita Grien Represents . . . . (212) 697-6170
Bertin, Marie 1204 Chenin Lausanne, Rimouski, PQ Canada G5L 8Y9 . . . . (418) 722-7953

BERTRAND, FREDERIQUE Page 129
Represented By: Wanda Nowak **(212) 535-0438**
Specialties: Advertising; Children; Collage; Conceptual; Editorial; Lettering; Whimsical

Beshwaty, Steve 4425 Messier Street, Montreal, PQ Canada H2H 2H8 . . . . (514) 525-9687
Besser Digital Studio 423 N Cuyler, Oak Park, IL 60302 . . . . (708) 660-9720
Betula Design 8340 San Marcos, Atascadero, CA 93422 . . . . (805) 461-4171
Betz, Marti 922 Melvin Road, Annapolis, MD 21403 . . . . (410) 268-1191
Beylon, Cathy Represented By: Evelyne Johnson Associates . . . . (212) 532-0928
Biber, Hugh Represented By: HK Portfolio . . . . (212) 675-5719

Biddel Perry Studio 160 Via Paraiso, Monterey, CA 93940 . . . . . . (408) 373-7443
Biddell, Meg 160 Via Paraiso, Monterey, CA 93940 . . . . . . (408) 373-7443
Bieck, Kathy Represented By: Famous Frames . . . . . . (310) 642-2721
Biellis, Jim Represented By: Famous Frames . . . . . . (310) 642-2721
Bierig, Brian 225 Ridge Road, Marshfield, MA 02050 . . . . . . (781) 834-0142
Biernot, Tad 510 Front Street W, Unit 400, Toronto, ON Canada M5V 1B8 . . . . . . (416) 924-1945

BIERS, NANETTE
Pages 124-125
Represented By: Vicki Morgan Associates
(212) 475-0440
e-mail: vmartrep@aol.com • Website: www.vickimorganassociates.com
Specialties: Architecture; Landscape; Oil; Period Settings; People; Realism; Still Life; Stock

Biffignandi, Alessandro Represented By: Pat Foster . . . . . . (212) 661-4557
Bignaud, Pierre 8301 rue Foucher, Montreal, PQ Canada H2P 2B . . . . . . (514) 388-7771
Bikadoroff, Roxanna Represented By: Reactor Art & Design Ltd. . . . . . . (416) 703-1913
Billin-Frye, Paige Represented By: Publishers' Graphics . . . . . . (203) 797-8188

BILLINGSKOG, GORAN
Pages 283,290-291,427
Represented By: John Brewster Creative Services
(203) 226-4724
e-mail: creative.svcs@snet.net • Website: www.brewstercreative.com • Specialties: Conceptual; Digital

Billout, Guy Represented By: Conrad Represents, Inc. . . . . . . (415) 921-7140
Bilter, Lori Represented By: W/C Studio, Inc./Allan Comport . . . . . . (410) 349-8669
Binder, Eric 1528 A Cherry Avenue, Charlottesville, VA 22903 . . . . . . (888) 374-2278
Binder, Pat 2108 Loch Haven Drive, Dallas, TX 75023 . . . . . . (972) 596-5275
Binkley, Gina 209 10th Avenue S #214, Nashville, TN 37203 . . . . . . (615) 256-1110

BINKLEY, PAUL
Page 277
Represented By: Famous Frames
(310) 642-2721
e-mail: info@famousframes.com • Website: www.famousframes.com • Specialties: Animation; Storyboards

Biomedical Communications Univ. of Toronto/Med. Sci Bldg, Toronto, ON Canada M5S 1A8 . . . . . . (416) 978-2659
Birchman, Fred Represented By: Jorgensen & Barrett Reps . . . . . . (206) 634-1880
Birdsong, Keith Represented By: Pat Foster . . . . . . (212) 661-4557
Birdsong, Stephanie K. 2009 Canal Street, Venice, CA 90291 . . . . . . (310) 822-3509

BIRKEY, RANDAL
Page 153
Represented By: Connie Koralik Associates Represents
(312) 944-5680
e-mail: rbirkey@birkey.com • Website: www.birkey.com
Specialties: Advertising; Architecture/Interiors; Corporate; Industrial; Technical

Birling, Paul Represented By: Art Source/Diane Barkley . . . . . . (914) 747-2220
Birmingham, Christian Represented By: Sally Heflin . . . . . . (212) 366-1893
Birmingham, Lloyd P. 500 Peekskill Hollow Road, Putnam Valley, NY 10579 . . . . . . (914) 528-3207
Birnbaum, M. Dianne 17301 Elsinore Circle, Huntington Beach, CA 92647 . . . . . . (714) 847-7631
Bishop, David 610 22nd Street #311, San Francisco, CA 94107 . . . . . . (415) 558-9532

BISHOP, DON
Pages 168,188
Represented By: American Artists
(212) 682-2462
e-mail: info@amerartists.com • Website: www.amerartists.com

Bixby, Mark Represented By: Nachreiner Boie Art Factory . . . . . . (414) 785-1940

BJORKMAN, STEVE
Pages 48,423,450
Represented By: Renard Represents
(212) 490-2450
e-mail: renardreps@earthlink.net • Website: www.renardrepresents.com
Specialties: Cartoon; Conceptual; Humour; Illustrative

Black, Brad Represented By: Three in a Box . . . . . . (416) 367-2446
Black, Dave Represented By: Bruck & Moss . . . . . . (212) 980-8061
Black, Rebecca 7680 Johnstown Road, Mount Vernon, OH 43050 . . . . . . (614) 393-0206
Black, Richard 205 Foxridge Drive, Kettering, OH 45429 . . . . . . (937) 293-9001
BlackDog 330 Sir Francis Drake Blvd., Ste. A, San Anselmo, CA 94960 . . . . . . (415) 258-9663
Blackshear, Thomas 220 Elm Circle, Colorado Springs, CO 80906 . . . . . . (719) 636-5009
Represented By: France Aline Associates . . . . . . (213) 933-2500

Blair, Dru Represented By: Pat Foster . . . . . (212) 661-4557
Blair Design P.O. Box 14054, High Point, NC 27263. . . . . (336) 434-1941
Blais, Richard 8777 Albanel, St. Leonard, PQ Canada . . . . . (514) 234-2774
Blake, Marty 2043 Jamesville Terrace, Box 266, Jamesville, NY 13078 . . . . . (315) 492-1332
Blakey, Paul Represented By: Tania Kimche . . . . . (212) 529-3556
Blalke, Gary Represented By: Carol Bancroft & Friends . . . . . (203) 748-4823
Blanchard, Marie 69 White Heather Boulevard, Toronto, ON Canada M1V 1P7 . . . . . (416) 292-3527
Blandino, Carmelo 1535 Sherbrooke W, 3rd Flr., Montreal, PQ Canada H3G 1L7 . . . . . (514) 934-5583
Blaney, Muriel 145 Canada Street, Hamilton, ON Canada L8P 1P4 . . . . . (905) 577-0590
Blank, Jerry 1048 Lincoln Avenue, San Jose, CA 95125 . . . . . (408) 289-9095
Blasutta, Mary Lynn 156 Huguenot Street, New Paltz, NY 12561 . . . . . (914) 256-0830
Blatt, Mike Represented By: Sweet Represents . . . . . (415) 433-1222
Bleck, Cathie Represented By: Jacqueline Dedell, Inc. . . . . . (212) 741-2539
Bleck, John 3636 N Bosworth, Chicago, IL 60613 . . . . . (773) 975-8232

BLESSEN, KAREN Pages 124-125
Represented By: Vicki Morgan Associates **(212) 475-0440**
e-mail: vmartrep@aol.com • Website: www.vickimorganassociates.com
Specialties: Advertising; Collage; Computer; Conceptual; Digital; Editorial; Greeting Cards; Icons; Lettering; Still Life

Bliok, Leo 25 Old Colony Lane, Great Neck, NY 11023 . . . . . (516) 466-8879
Bliss, Harry 45 Washington Street, Nyack, NY 10960 . . . . . (914) 358-8690
Bliss, Jim 22 Briggs Avenue, Fairport, NY 14450 . . . . . (716) 377-1609
Bliss, Philip 22 Briggs Avenue, Fairport, NY 14450. . . . . (716) 377-9771
Bloch, Anthony 854 W 181st Street #6D, New York, NY 10033 . . . . . (212) 927-6856
Blondon, Herve Represented By: Wanda Nowak . . . . . (212) 535-0438
Bloom, Mark Represented By: Famous Frames . . . . . (310) 642-2721
Bloss, Larry 4387 Spruce Avenue, Burlington, ON Canada L7L 1L7. . . . . (905) 681-7041
Blubaugh, Susan M. 511 E 81st Street #17, New York, NY 10028 . . . . . (212) 570-6731
Blumstein, Paul Represented By: Hankins & Tegenborg Ltd. . . . . . (212) 867-8092
Boatwright, Phil 2342 Stillwater Drive, Mesquite, TX 75181 . . . . . (972) 222-7571
Boban Represented By: Leyden Diversified . . . . . (215) 663-0587
Bobnick, Dick 9801 Dupont Avenue S, Ste. 165, Bloomington, MN 55431 . . . . . (612) 881-1008
Bocci, Michael 1529 First Street, Simi Valley, CA 93065 . . . . . (805) 581-4936
Boddy, Joe 5375 Skyway Drive, Missoula, MT 59804. . . . . (406) 251-3587
Boehm, Roger Represented By: Corey Graham Represents . . . . . (415) 956-4750
Boer, Jan-Willem Represented By: Nancy Bacher. . . . . (612) 786-1200

BOERGER, ANDREW Page 243
Represented By: Rita Gatlin Represents **(800) 924-7881**
Website: www.ritareps.com • Specialties: Architecture/Interiors; Conceptual; Landscape; Pastels

Bogusalav, Rafael Represented By: Katherine Tise . . . . . (212) 570-9069
Bohn Illustration 14 N First Avenue, Ste. 1410, St. Charles, IL 60174 . . . . . (630) 513-1269
Boie, Chuck Represented By: Nachreiner Boie Art Factory . . . . . (414) 785-1940
Boies, Alex 126 N Third Street, Minneapolis, MN 55401 . . . . . (612) 333-2418
Boise, Kathyjean 1233 De Haro Street, San Francisco, CA 94107 . . . . . (415) 285-3014
Bolesky, John 431 NW Flanders, Ste. 201, Portland, OR 97209 . . . . . (503) 241-7324
Boll, Tom 9500 Wyoming Avenue S, Bloomington, MN 55438. . . . . (612) 942-6119

BOLL-HUGHES, MAXINE Page 327
Represented By: Michele Manasse **(215) 862-2091**
e-mail: mmanasse@new-work.com • Website: www.voicenet.com/~mmanasse
Specialties: Advertising; Food; Lettering; Painterly; Poster; Product; Water Color

Boller, David Represented By: Marvel Entertainment . . . . . (212) 696-0808
Bolling, Bob 2395 NE 185th Street, Miami, FL 33180 . . . . . (305) 931-0104
Bollinger, Kristine Represented By: Evelyne Johnson Associates . . . . . (212) 532-0928
Bollinger, Peter Represented By: Shannon Associates . . . . . (212) 831-5650
Bollman, Angela 2305 Ashland Street #C, Ashland, OR 97520 . . . . . (800) 435-6509
Bolster, Rob Represented By: Leighton & Company, Inc.. . . . . (978) 921-0887
Bolten, Jennifer Represented By: Clare Jett & Associates . . . . . (502) 228-9427
Bolton, Andrea 400 Merrimac Way #36, Costa Mesa, CA 92626 . . . . . (714) 435-0150
Bolton, Suzannah 19585 Grand View Drive, Los Angeles, CA 90290 . . . . . (310) 455-2671

BOMBA STUDIO, RON Pages 272,464
1900 W Emerson Place #106, Seattle, WA 98119 **(206) 286-1277**
Specialties: Industrial; Medical; Product; Realism; Technical

Bond, Jocelyne 158 Connaught Avenue N, Hamilton, ON Canada L8L 6Z3 . . . . . (905) 547-7756
Bondurant, Steve Represented By: Tom Maloney . . . . . (312) 704-0500
Bonforte, Lisa Represented By: Evelyne Johnson Associates . . . . . (212) 532-0928
Bongrazio 116 W Illinois Street, 5th Flr., Chicago, IL 60610 . . . . . (312) 527-2389
Bonilla, Michael Dayton, OH 45481 . . . . . (513) 435-5058
Bonin, Diana Rice Represented By: The Art Agency . . . . . (503) 203-8300
Bono, Mary 288 Graham Avenue, Brooklyn, NY 11211 . . . . . (718) 387-3774
Bono, Peter 63 Stark Road, Columbia, NJ 07832 . . . . . (908) 496-8524
Booker, George Represented By: Famous Frames . . . . . (310) 642-2721
Bookwalter, Tom Represented By: Image Mill . . . . . (515) 490-6110
Boonthanskit, Ted Represented By: Motion Artists, Inc. . . . . . (213) 851-7737
Booth, Martha Anne P.O. Box 208, Montara, CA 94037 . . . . . (650) 728-8332
Borda, Juliette 114 Carnegie Place, Pittsburgh, PA 15208 . . . . . (412) 441-7188
Borge, Rich Represented By: Jan Collier Represents, Inc. . . . . . (415) 383-9026
Borgert, Tim 45 S Ludlow Street, Dayton, OH 45402 . . . . . (513) 225-2386
Borgman, Harry Represented By: R. Fischer & Company . . . . . (312) 368-1441
Borhi, Michael 28 Seventh Street, Roxboro, PQ Canada H8Y 1E8 . . . . . (514) 684-4188
Borovsky, Paul Represented By: Square Moon . . . . . (510) 253-9451

BOROWSKI, DIANE Pages 216,221,452,463
675 30th Avenue N, St. Petersburg, FL 33704 • Fax (813) 898-3088 **(813) 822-7836**
Represented By: Alexander/Pollard, Inc. **(800) 347-0734**
e-mail: chstudio@aol.com • Specialties: Black & White; Food; Graphic Design/Illustration; Greeting Cards; Icons; Lettering; Scratchboard; Stock; Wildlife; Woodcut

Borrillo, Angelo 12 Cecil Road, Peterborough, Cambs, England PE1 3PU
Botana, Federico Represented By: Reactor Art & Design Ltd. . . . . . (416) 703-1913
Bote, Tivadar Represented By: Irmeli Holmberg . . . . . (212) 545-9155
Represented By: Adrienne Arbour Artist Rep . . . . . (416) 410-9828
Botelho, Clemente 229 Beatrice Street, Toronto, ON Canada M6G 3E9 . . . . . (416) 535-0945
Botzis, Ka Represented By: Melissa Turk & The Artist Network . . . . . (914) 368-8606
Bourin, Coni Represented By: Black Inc. Creative Rep. . . . . . (602) 381-1332
Bovy, Deb Represented By: Leyden Diversified . . . . . (215) 663-0587
Represented By: Image Mill . . . . . (515) 490-6110
Bower, Joel 6417 Summit Street, Kansas City, MO 64113 . . . . . (816) 822-1409
Bower, Tim Brooklyn, NY 11201 . . . . . (718) 834-8974
Bowers, David Represented By: Scott Hull Associates . . . . . (937) 433-8383
Bowles, Bruce 1045 Sansome Street #306, San Francisco, CA 94111 . . . . . (415) 362-4478
Bowser, Ken 922 Camellia Avenue, Winter Park, FL 32789 . . . . . (407) 644-9888
Boyajian, Ann Represented By: Lilla Rogers Studio . . . . . (781) 641-2787
Boyd, David Represented By: Will Sumpter & Associates . . . . . (770) 460-8438
Boyer, Bill HCR 2 Box 850-316, Tucson, AZ 85735 . . . . . (520) 822-9320

BOYKO, BILL Page 230
Represented By: Sharpshooter Creative Representation, Inc. **(416) 703-5300**
e-mail: shooter@the-wire.com • Website: www.portfolios.com/illustrators
Specialties: Advertising; Annual Report; Collage; Mixed Media; Montage; Photoillustration; Poster; Sports; Still Life; 3D

BOZZINI, JAMES Page 411
New York, NY **(888) 269-9464**
Represented By: Renard Represents **(212) 490-2450**
e-mail: renardreps@earthlink.net • Website: www.renardrepresents.com
Specialties: Advertising; Conceptual; Editorial; Mixed Media; Oil; People; Photography

Brace, Eric Represented By: Publishers' Graphics . . . . . (203) 797-8188
Bracke, Chuck Represented By: Steve Edsey & Sons . . . . . (312) 527-0351
Bracken, Carolyn 43 E 19th Street, New York, NY 10003 . . . . . (212) 254-4996
Bradford, Stuart 508 San Anselmo Avenue #19, San Anselmo, CA 94960 . . . . . (415) 485-6903
Bradshaw, Anne Represented By: Creative Connection . . . . . (410) 360-5981
Braganza, Alan 108 Kirk Drive, Thornhill, ON Canada L3T 3L2 . . . . . (905) 731-4266

Bragg, Shokie 234 Philadelphia Pike, Ste. 11, Wilmington, DE 19809 . . . . . (302) 762-2285
Represented By: Iconomics . . . . . (800) 297-7658
Bralds, Bradlt 13 Herrada Court, Santa Fe, NM 87505 . . . . . (505) 466-3603
Bramhall, William Represented By: Riley Illustration. . . . . (212) 989-8770
Bramman, Michael 104 Dudley Court, London, England W1H 7PJ 44 171 723 3564
Bramsen, David 644 N Hope Avenue, Santa Barbara, CA 93110. . . . . (805) 687-6864
Brandes Illustration, Robin 130 Meadowcroft Drive, San Anselmo, CA 94960 . . . . . (415) 454-0787
Brandon, Bill Represented By: Tania Kimche . . . . . (212) 529-3556
Brandt, Elizabeth 35 ½ W Eighth Street, Holland, MI 49423 . . . . . (616) 394-4240
Brandt, Kim Wilson 219 Crescent Avenue, San Francisco, CA 94110 . . . . . (415) 824-2055
Brandtner, Al 1304 W Cornelia, Chicago, IL 60657 . . . . . (773) 588-1860
Brassard, France 4052 rue Cartier, Montreal, PQ Canada H2Y 4G4 . . . . . (514) 529-6183
Braught, Mark 767 N Parkwood Road, Decatur, GA 30030. . . . . (404) 373-7430
Braukmann-Towns, Krista 6 N 777 Palomino Drive, St. Charles, IL 60175 . . . . . (630) 513-9525
Braun, David 12104 Greenway Court, Fairfax, VA 22033
Braun, Marty 265 Pleasant Avenue, Peaks Island, ME 04108 . . . . . (207) 766-9726
Brautigam, Don Represented By: Artists Associates . . . . . (941) 756-8445
Represented By: Bernstein & Andriulli, Inc. . . . . . (212) 682-1490
Brawner, Dan Represented By: Clare Jett & Associates . . . . . (502) 228-9427
Brazeal, Lee Lee Represented By: Brooke & Company. . . . . (214) 352-9192
Bredemeier, Bob Represented By: Susan & Company . . . . . (206) 232-7873
Breen, Jerry 816-A Cinnamon Ridge Place, Cockeysville, MD 21030 . . . . . (410) 683-1562

BREMMER, MARK — Page 335
7155 W Walden Place, Littleton, CO 80128 — **(303) 932-8759**
Specialties: Cars; Editorial; People; Product

Brennan, Neil Represented By: Bernstein & Andriulli, Inc. . . . . . (212) 682-1490
Brennan, Steve Represented By: Mendola Ltd.. . . . . (212) 986-5680
Brennan Illustration, Dan 1919 W Berteau Avenue, Chicago, IL 60613 . . . . . (312) 822-0887

BRENNO, VONNIE — Page 277
Represented By: Famous Frames — **(310) 642-2721**
e-mail: info@famousframes.com • Website: www.famousframes.com • Specialties: Animation; Storyboards

Brewer, Allen Represented By: Joanie Bernstein Art Rep . . . . . (612) 374-3169
Briant, Ed Represented By: Jacqueline Dedell, Inc. . . . . . (212) 741-2539
Brice, Jeff Represented By: Kolea Baker Artists Representative . . . . . (206) 784-1136
Brickman, Robin Represented By: Barbara Gordon Associates Ltd.. . . . . (212) 686-3514
Bridges, Gregory Represented By: Bernstein & Andriulli, Inc.. . . . . (212) 682-1490
Bridy, Dan Represented By: Irmeli Holmberg . . . . . (212) 545-9155
Brierly, Louise Represented By: Bernstein & Andriulli, Inc. . . . . . (212) 682-1490
Brigell, Ian 531 King Street #400, Toronto, ON Canada M5V 1K4. . . . . (416) 581-1075
Brigham, Derek 4512 Harriet Avenue S, Minneapolis, MN 55409 . . . . . (612) 827-3431
Brignell, Ian 511 King Street W #400, Toronto, ON Canada M5V 1K4 . . . . . (416) 581-1075
Brill, Jackie 29 Clifton Street, Cambridge, MA 02140 . . . . . (617) 868-9697
Bringham, Sherry 1804 Arlington, El Cerrito, CA 94530 . . . . . (510) 235-2859
Brinkman, Mark 1512 W 35th Street #200, Austin, TX 78731. . . . . (512) 302-0734
Brinkman, Paula 417 W 43rd Street #12, New York, NY 10036 . . . . . (212) 757-9497
Brion, David 58 Glenville Street, Greenwich, CT 06831 . . . . . (203) 531-9381
Brissette & Gendron 417 St. Pierre #301, Montreal, PQ Canada H2Y 2M4 . . . . . (514) 278-1784
Britt, Stephanie P.O. Box 818, Hanalei, HI 96714 . . . . . (808) 828-0069
Britt, Tracy Represented By: Scott Hull Associates . . . . . (937) 433-8383
Broad, David 100 Golden Hinde Boulevard, San Rafael, CA 94903 . . . . . (415) 479-5505
Broda, Ron Represented By: Jerry Leff Associates, Inc. . . . . . (212) 697-8525
Brodie, Cindy Represented By: Square Moon . . . . . (510) 253-9451
Brodner, Steve Represented By: Shannon Associates . . . . . (212) 831-5650
Broeck, Fabricio Vanden Represented By: Gwen Walters-Goldstein . . . . . (781) 235-8658
Brokaw, Tanya 633 Ocean Avenue #13, Santa Monica, CA 90402 . . . . . (310) 394-8456
Bronson, Linda Represented By: Leighton & Company, Inc.. . . . . (978) 921-0887
Brook Trout Studio 439 Loveman Avenue, Columbus, OH 43085 . . . . . (614) 885-4889 • (800) 484-5419
Brookens, Suzanne Represented By: Corporate Art Planning. . . . . (212) 242-8995
Brooker, Krysten Represented By: Fortuni Illustration . . . . . (414) 964-8088
Brooker, Philip 117 Palmetto Drive, Miami Springs, FL 33166 . . . . . (305) 887-8821
Represented By: Tonal Values . . . . . (214) 943-2569

Brooks, Andrea Represented By: Corey Graham Represents . . . . . (415) 956-4750
Brooks, Hal 730 Columbus Avenue #15B, New York, NY 10025 . . . . . (212) 531-0255
Brooks, Kelly Represented By: Rep Art. . . . . (604) 684-6826
Brooks, Lou Glen Ellen, CA 95442 . . . . . (707) 996-2688
New York, NY 10019 . . . . . (212) 245-3632
Brooks, Nan Represented By: Holly Hahn Artist Rep (H2 + Co.) . . . . . (312) 633-0500

BROOKS, ROB Pages 42, 428
Represented By: Renard Represents **(212) 490-2450**
e-mail: renardreps@earthlink.net • Website: www.renardrepresents.com
Specialties: Advertising; Conceptual; Corporate; Editorial; Oil; People; Stock

Brothers, Barry 1920 E 17th Street, Brooklyn, NY 11229 . . . . . (718) 336-7540
Brown, Charley Represented By: Sweet Represents. . . . . (415) 433-1222
Brown, Craig 1615 S Tejan #3, Colorado Springs, CO 80906. . . . . (719) 636-9025
Brown, Dan Represented By: Artworks . . . . . (212) 627-1554

BROWN, DAN Page 267
3815 Falk Road, Vancouver, WA 98661 **(360) 737-9920**
Represented By: Christine Prapas **(503) 658-7070**
e-mail: danbrown@pacifier.com • Website: www.pacifier.com/~danbrown
Specialties: Black & White; Computer; Digital; Editorial; Technical

Brown, Greg 1025 Conkey Street, Hammond, IN 46320. . . . . (219) 931-1164
Brown, Helen 20 Avenue Road, Abergavenny, South Wales, England NP7 7DA 44 187 385 2820

BROWN, MARC Pages 146-147
Represented By: Carol Guenzi Agents, Inc. **(800) 417-5120**
e-mail: artagent@artagent.com • Website: www.artagent.com
Specialties: Architecture/Interiors; Computer; Digital; Icons; Mixed Media; People; Product; Realism; Sports; Still Life

Brown, Rick 16635 Howard Circle, Omaha, NE 68118 . . . . . (402) 697-1962
Represented By: Joel Harlib Associates, Inc. . . . . . (312) 573-1370
Represented By: Bernstein & Andriulli, Inc. . . . . . (212) 682-1490
Brown, Rick P.O. Box 341, Furlong, PA 18925 . . . . . (215) 794-8186
Brown, Ryan Represented By: PG Representatives . . . . . (413) 967-9855
Brown, William L. Represented By: Donna Rosen Artists' Rep . . . . . (301) 384-8925
Brown Jr., R. P.O. Box 8533, Universal City, CA 91618 . . . . . (213) 882-6926
Browning, Vivian Wu 12640 A Springbrook Drive, San Diego, CA 92128 . . . . . (619) 486-8185
Bruce, Donnie 501 Oakes Boulevard, San Leandro, CA 94577. . . . . (510) 639-1978
Bruce, Sandra 13997 Emerald Court, Grass Valley, CA 95945. . . . . (530) 477-1909

BRUCE, T. TAYLOR Page 21
755 Tzabaco Creek Road, Geyserville, CA 95441 • Fax (707) 857-3373 **(707) 857-3373**
Specialties: Children; Editorial; Food; Greeting Cards; People; Product; Still Life; Water Color

Bruce, Tim 5850 Brookway Drive, Winston-Salem, NC 27105 . . . . . (910) 767-8890
Brugger, Bob Represented By: Robin Ogden Represents. . . . . (612) 925-4174
Represented By: Martha Productions. . . . . (310) 390-8663
Brunettin, Alan Represented By: Lulu Creatives . . . . . (612) 825-7564
Bruning, Bill 118 E 26th Street, Minneapolis, MN 55404 . . . . . (612) 871-4539
Represented By: Ceci Bartels Associates . . . . . (314) 781-7377
Represented By: Oasis Art Studio. . . . . (612) 927-0955
Brunnick, Jeannie Manhattan Beach, CA 90266 . . . . . (310) 798-2771
Brunz, Robert 600 Seventh Avenue #523, Seattle, WA 98104 . . . . . (206) 255-5809
Bryan, Mike Represented By: Fox Art, Inc. . . . . . (213) 662-0020

BRYANT, AMY Page 213
3420 Timberview Road, Dallas, TX 75229 • Fax (214) 357-8406 **(214) 357-7669**
Represented By: Repertoire **(972) 761-0500**
Specialties: Black & White; Computer; Woodcut

Bryant Illustration, Web 9310 Coronado Terrace, Fairfax, VA 22031 . . . . . (703) 359-1039
Bryn, Barnard Represented By: Dane Sonneville
Buchanan, Nigel Represented By: Tonal Values . . . . . (214) 943-2569

Buchanan, Yvonne 18 Lincoln Place, Brooklyn, NY 11217 . . . . . (718) 783-6682
Buchart, Greta P.O. Box 959, 7 Ivy Hill Road, Ridgefield, CT 06877 . . . . . (203) 438-8386
Buchs, Thomas Represented By: Nachreiner Boie Art Factory . . . . . (414) 785-1940
Buchschacher, Scott Represented By: Deborah Snyder Creative Representative . . . . . (612) 922-3462
Buckingham, Lesley Represented By: Bernstein & Andriulli, Inc. . . . . . (212) 682-1490
Buckley, Jim Represented By: Shekut Communications Network . . . . . (312) 977-9171
Buckley, Marjory Represented By: Rosenthal Represents . . . . . (818) 222-5445
Bucky Boy Group Represented By: Ann Koeffler Represents . . . . . (213) 957-2327
Budai, Kathy Represented By: Virginia Boggie & Associates . . . . . (604) 943-6414
Budd, Don 8776 W Tierra Buena Lane, Peoria, AZ 85382 . . . . . (602) 815-1210
Budgen, Dennis 64 Capri Avenue NW, Calgary, AB Canada T2L 0H1 . . . . . (403) 282-0031
Buehler, David 2218 16th Street, Cuyahoga Falls, OH 44223-1934 . . . . . (216) 929-9418
Buelow, Alicia Represented By: Jacqueline Dedell, Inc. . . . . . (212) 741-2539
Bull, Michael 2350 Taylor Street, San Francisco, CA 94133 . . . . . (415) 776-7471

BULLEIT, DAN Pages 146-147
Represented By: Carol Guenzi Agents, Inc. **(800) 417-5120**
e-mail: artagent@artagent.com • Website: www.artagent.com • Specialties: Computer; Conceptual

Bunn, Christine Represented By: Sharpshooter Creative Rep Inc. . . . . . (416) 703-5300
Burch, Allan M. 404 Red Maple, Kirbyville, MO 65679 . . . . . (417) 335-2410
Burchard, Michelle 2269 India Street, Los Angeles, CA 90039 . . . . . (213) 664-5036
Burckhardt, Marc 112 W 41st Street, Austin, TX 78751 . . . . . (512) 458-1690
Burgard, Tim Represented By: Motion Artists, Inc.. . . . . . (213) 851-7737
Burgard, W.C. 2785 Heather Way, Ann Arbor, MI 48104 . . . . . (734) 971-3014
Burger, Robert 145 Kingwood Stockton Road, Stockton, NJ 08559 . . . . . (609) 397-3737
Burgess, Jeff Represented By: Rep Art . . . . . (604) 684-6826
Burgio, Trish 8205 Santa Monica Boulevard, Los Angeles, CA 90046 . . . . . (310) 274-5787
Burgos, George Represented By: Skidmore, Inc. . . . . . (248) 353-7722
Burgoyne, John T. 26 Statler Road, Belmont, MA 02178 . . . . . (781) 489-4960
Burke, Kelly Represented By: Freda Scott, Inc.. . . . . . (415) 398-9121
Burke, Leland 215 W 83rd Street #15-A, New York, NY 10024 . . . . . (212) 580-8724
Burleson, Joe Represented By: Hankins & Tegenborg Ltd. . . . . . (212) 867-8092
Burman, Harry Represented By: Artworks . . . . . (212) 627-1554
Burman, Rob Represented By: Skidmore, Inc. . . . . . (248) 353-7722

BURN, TED Pages 373,380,444,466
Represented By: Susan Wells & Associates **(404) 255-1430**
e-mail: TEBurn@concentric.net • Specialties: Animals; Children; Food; Painterly; Pastels; Water Color

Burnett, Lindy 476 Loridans Drive, Atlanta, GA 30346-3406 . . . . . (404) 531-0541
Represented By: Alexander/Pollard, Inc. . . . . . (800) 347-0734
Burns, Jim Represented By: Alan Lynch Artists . . . . . (908) 813-8718
Burns, Rhonda Represented By: Repertory . . . . . (213) 931-7449
Burr, Dan Represented By: Hankins & Tegenborg Ltd. . . . . . (212) 867-8092
Burris, Priscilla Represented By: Christina Tugeau . . . . . (203) 438-7307
Burrows, Diane 35 S Maple Street, Corning, NY 14380 . . . . . (607) 962-2769
Burzynski, Mary 1535 N Western Avenue, Chicago, IL 60622. . . . . . (773) 227-6755
Busacca, Mark 2150 Hyde Street #1, San Francisco, CA 94109 . . . . . (415) 776-4247
Busbee, Elisha Ann Baltimore, MD 21201 . . . . . (410) 426-2593
Bush, D.J. 5120 N St. Louis Avenue, Chicago, IL 60625 . . . . . (773) 463-5775
Buske, Gregory A. Represented By: Penny & Stermer Group. . . . . . (212) 505-9342
Bustamante, Gerald 2400 Kettner Boulevard #227, San Diego, CA 92101. . . . . . (619) 234-8803
Represented By: Jan Collier Represents, Inc. . . . . . (415) 383-9026
Butkovich, Anthony 812 Branard #3, Houston, TX 77006 . . . . . (713) 523-0388
Represented By: Schumann & Company . . . . . (512) 481-0907
Butler, Callie 4307 Adler Drive, San Diego, CA 92116 . . . . . (619) 280-2343
Butler, Lynn Represented By: American Artists . . . . . (212) 682-2462
Butler, Ralph 18521 Tarragon Way, Germantown, MD 20874 . . . . . (301) 601-9164
Buttram, Andy Represented By: Scott Hull Associates . . . . . (937) 433-8383
Butvila, Paul Represented By: Berendsen & Associates. . . . . . (513) 861-1400
Buzzworks Studio 231 Mayatt Road, Barrington, RI 02806 . . . . . (401) 245-8438
Bynum, Jane 134 E Candlewyck #424, Kalamazoo, MI 49001 . . . . . (888) 342-0707
Byrd, Bob Represented By: Irmeli Holmberg . . . . . (212) 545-9155
Byrne, Robert 6135 Reseda Boulevard #24, Reseda, CA 91335 . . . . . (818) 342-3766

Byrnes, Pat 3622 N Hamilton, Chicago, IL 60618 . . . . . (773) 472-3649
Bywaters, Lynn 21 Arrowhead Drive, Glastonbury, CT 06033 . . . . . (860) 659-0678
Cable, Annette 2018 Maryland Avenue, Louisville, KY 40205 . . . . . (502) 454-0475
Represented By: Clare Jett & Associates . . . . . (502) 228-9427
Cable, Mark 2018 Maryland Avenue, Louisville, KY 40205 . . . . . (502) 454-0475
Represented By: Clare Jett & Associates . . . . . (502) 228-9427
Cabon, Carlos Represented By: HK Portfolio . . . . . (212) 675-5719

CABOSSEL, JANNINE Page 164
56 Coyote Crossing, Santa Fe, NM 87505 • Fax (505) 983-4026 **(505) 983-9706**
Represented By: Jane Klein **(888) ART-1008**
e-mail: cabo@rt66.com • Specialties: Advertising; Children; Conceptual; Digital; Editorial; Greeting Cards; Humour; Icons; Scratchboard; Whimsical

Cabrera, Marcela 1226 Smithwood Drive #4, Los Angeles, CA 90035 . . . . . (310) 277-1503
Cabry, Cyril Represented By: Marlena Agency . . . . . (609) 252-9405
Cadman, Joel 41-15 50th Avenue #3F, Sunnyside, NY 11104 . . . . . (718) 784-1267
Cadoret, Don Represented By: Carol Bancroft & Friends . . . . . (203) 748-4823
Cahill, Chris Represented By: Mendola Ltd. . . . . . (212) 986-5680
Cain, David 200 W 20th Street #607, New York, NY 10011-3560 . . . . . (212) 633-0258
Cairns, Brian Represented By: Jacqueline Dedell, Inc. . . . . . (212) 741-2539
Calanche, Mague 545 Belvedere Street, San Francisco, CA 94117 . . . . . (415) 664-9511
Calder, Jean 161 Eglinton Avenue E #707, Toronto, ON Canada M4P 1J5 . . . . . (416) 484-6349
Calder, Jill Represented By: Jerry Leff Associates, Inc. . . . . . (212) 697-8525
Caldwell, Kirk Represented By: Tania Kimche . . . . . (212) 529-3556
Calitri, Susan Represented By: Publishers' Graphics . . . . . (203) 797-8188
Call, Greg Represented By: Shannon Associates . . . . . (212) 831-5650
Call, Ken Represented By: Buck & Kane . . . . . (212) 631-0009
Callahan, Kevin 26 Frances Street, Nowalk, CT 06851 . . . . . (203) 847-2046
Callanan, Brian Represented By: Jerry Leff Associates, Inc. . . . . . (212) 697-8525
Calsoni, Laurel A. 3130 Webster #24, San Francisco, CA 94123

CALVER, DAVE Pages 124-125
Represented By: Vicki Morgan Associates **(212) 475-0440**
e-mail: vmartrep@aol.com • Website: www.vickimorganassociates.com
Specialties: Cartoon; Corporate; Editorial; Fantasy; Fashion; Greeting Cards; Humour; Icons; People; Whimsical

Calver, Lewis E. 10627 Royal Club Lane, Dallas, TX 75229 . . . . . (214) 648-4699
Calvetti, Leonello Represented By: Bernstein & Andriulli, Inc. . . . . . (212) 682-1490
Calviello, Joseph 23-35 Bell Boulevard #6J, Bayside, NY 11360 . . . . . (718) 423-3797
Cam's Happy Pencil Studio 1819 Fiske Avenue, Pasadena, CA 91104 . . . . . (626) 797-8890
Camarro, Paul 36 Bank Street, Sussex, NJ 07461 . . . . . (973) 875-2092
Cameneti, Michael 7358 Genesta Avenue, Van Nuys, CA 91406 . . . . . (818) 705-2738

CAMERON, CHAD Pages 373,375,425,440
Atlanta, GA **(500) 443-0333**
Represented By: Susan Wells & Associates **(404) 255-1430**
e-mail: chadwick@mindspring.com • Specialties: Children; Editorial

Camp, Barbara 52 W 85th Street, Apt. 3F, New York, NY 10024 . . . . . (212) 877-0201
Campbell, Annie 5650 Fitzgerald Road, Trumansburg, NY 14886 . . . . . (607) 387-9086
Campbell, D.J. 2809 Folsom Lane, Bowie, MD 20715 . . . . . (301) 262-3062
Campbell, Franklin Represented By: Peter Kuehnel & Associates . . . . . (312) 642-6499
Campbell, Harry 17 Plainfield Avenue, Metuchen, NJ 08840 . . . . . (732) 548-7544
Campbell, Jenny Represented By: Deborah Wolfe . . . . . (215) 232-6666
Campbell, Jim Represented By: Mendola Ltd. . . . . . (212) 986-5680

CAMPBELL, KAREN ALBANESE Page 276
155 Oakland Park Avenue, Columbus, OH 43214 **(614) 268-2175**
Specialties: Children; People; Travel; Water Color

Campbell, Laurie 418 Claremont Ave #23, Westmount, PQ Canada . . . . . (514) 487-3366
Campbell, Stephen Represented By: Art Department . . . . . (212) 925-4222
Campbell, Tim Represented By: Connie Koralik Associates Represents . . . . . (312) 944-5680
Campbell Design Studio, Judy 2154 Lillie Road, Jefferson, OH 44047 . . . . . (440) 992-6437

Campbell-Boyd, Alice 4838 Milwee, Houston, TX 77092 . . . . . (713) 681-3172

CANE, LINDA Pages 252-253
Represented By: Deborah Wolfe **(215) 232-6666**
Website: www.deborahwolfeltd.com
Specialties: Advertising; Children; Conceptual; Editorial; Humour; People; Stock; Whimsical

Cane Studios, Eleni 2163 Walnut Street, Baldwin, NY 11510 . . . . . (516) 378-3203 • (800) 854-4602
Canetti, Michel Represented By: Buck & Kane . . . . . (212) 631-0009
Cangemi, Antonio 95 Westhampton Drive, Toronto, ON Canada M9R 1Y1 . . . . . (416) 245-0730
Represented By: Clare Jett & Associates . . . . . (502) 228-9427
Cannon, Joanne Represented By: Evelyne Johnson Associates . . . . . (212) 532-0928
Cannoy, Lynne 755 Brookline Boulevard, Pittsburgh, PA 15226 . . . . . (412) 561-6880
Canny Studios, Thomas 7471 Melrose Avenue, Ste. 14, Los Angeles, CA 90046 . . . . . (213) 653-4421
Cantu, Pavel Represented By: Famous Frames . . . . . (310) 642-2721
Caparosa, Mark Represented By: Hankins & Tegenborg Ltd. . . . . . (212) 867-8092
Caporale, Wende Studio Hill Farm Route 116, North Salem, NY 10560 . . . . . (914) 669-5653
Capstone Studios, Inc. 2820 Westshire Drive, Los Angeles, CA 90068 . . . . . (213) 464-2787 • (888) 888-5060
Carabetta, Natalie Represented By: Evelyne Johnson Associates . . . . . (212) 532-0928
Cardella, Elaine 24 Elizabeth Street, Port Jervis, NY 12771 . . . . . (914) 856-8889
Cardona Studio Represented By: SI International . . . . . (212) 254-4996
Carey 3-D Illustration, Sue 1700 Bush Street #9, San Francisco, CA 94109 . . . . . (415) 441-7046
Caricatures & Cartoons 7126 Via Sendero, Scottsdale, AZ 85258 . . . . . (602) 922-9000
Carlotta Represented By: Kramer + Kramer . . . . . (212) 645-8787
Carlson, Frederick H. 118 Monticello Drive, Monroeville, PA 15146-4837 . . . . . (412) 856-0982
Carlson, Jonathan 3000 Chestnut Avenue #6, Baltimore, MD 21211 . . . . . (410) 467-9172
Carlson, Lisa 407 14th Avenue SW, Rochester, MN 55902 . . . . . (507) 252-0311
Carlson, Rand Represented By: Kimberley Boege . . . . . (602) 265-4389
Carlson, Sue 102 Bonita Road, Waretown, NJ 08758 . . . . . (800) 707-0980
Carmi, Glora Represented By: Carol Bancroft & Friends . . . . . (203) 748-4823
Carmichael, Dennis 19355 Pacific Coast Highway, Malibu, CA 90265 . . . . . (310) 456-5915
Carnabucci, Anthony Represented By: Evelyne Johnson Associates . . . . . (212) 532-0928
Carnes, Bruce Represented By: Liz Sanders Agency . . . . . (714) 495-3664
Carnes, Lorne Represented By: Rep Art . . . . . (604) 684-6826
Carney, Don Represented By: Lisa Freeman . . . . . (317) 920-0068
Carolan, Lana Represented By: Creative Connection . . . . . (410) 360-5981
Caroline S. 143 Ripley Street, San Francisco, CA 94110 . . . . . (415) 558-8760
Carpenter, Carolyn Represented By: Creative Freelancers . . . . . (800) 398-9544
Carpenter, Mia Represented By: Famous Frames . . . . . (310) 642-2721
Carrabotta, Vic Represented By: Famous Frames . . . . . (310) 642-2721
Carreiro, Ron 6 Hillside Drive, Plymouth, MA 02360 . . . . . (508) 224-9290
Carrell, Jeanette 3187 Park Overlook Drive, St. Paul, MN 55126 . . . . . (612) 481-4948
Carroll, Jim Represented By: Harriet Kastaris & Associates . . . . . (314) 773-2600

CARROLL, MICHAEL Page 270
538 Belleforte Avenue, Oak Park, IL 60302 • Fax (708) 386-6125 **(708) 386-6197**
Represented By: Christine Prapas **(503) 658-7070**
Represented By: Steve Edsey & Sons **(312) 527-0351**
Represented By: Marla Matson Represents **(602) 252-5072**
Website: www.studiomike.com • Specialties: Airbrush; Animals; Cartoon; Digital; Pen & Ink

Carruthers, Kevin 305 Spence Street #304, Hawkesbury, PQ Canada . . . . . (540) 553-7875
Carruthers, Roy Represented By: The Newborn Group . . . . . (212) 260-6700
Carsello, Margaret P.O. Box Box G, Hinsdale, IL 60521 . . . . . (630) 794-9120
Represented By: The Pred Group . . . . . (913) 438-7733
Carson, Jim 11 Foch Street, Cambridge, MA 02140 . . . . . (617) 661-3321
Carter, Abby Represented By: HK Portfolio . . . . . (212) 675-5719
Carter, Ben Represented By: Carol Bancroft & Friends . . . . . (203) 748-4823
Carter, Bonnie 200 E 78th Street, New York, NY 10021 . . . . . (212) 570-9069
Carter, Jane 460 W 42nd Street, 2nd Flr., New York, NY 10036 . . . . . (212) 967-6655
Carter, Mary P.O. Box 421443, San Francisco, CA 94142-1443 . . . . . (415) 647-5660
Carter, Mike 32 Oaken Gateway, Toronto, ON Canada M2P 2A1 . . . . . (416) 250-5433
Carter, Penny 12 Stuyvesant Oval, New York, NY 10009 . . . . . (212) 473-7965

CARTER, STEPHANIE Page 231
Represented By: Sharpshooter Creative Representation, Inc. **(416) 703-5300**
e-mail: shooter@the-wire.com • Website: www.portfolios.com/illustrators
Specialties: Advertising; Annual Report; Computer; Conceptual; Corporate; Digital; Food; Illustrative; People; Scratchboard

Cartoon Room P.O. Box 726, Masontown, PA 15461 . . . . . (724) 583-0303 • (888) 478-0502
Caruso, Bob 7925 Dartworth Drive, Parma, OH 44129 . . . . . (440) 885-1669
Case, Kelvin Represented By: Hankins & Tegenborg Ltd. . . . . . (212) 867-8092
Case, Robert 635 W Desert Broom Drive, Chandler, AZ 85226 . . . . . (602) 759-7582
Cashwell, Charles Represented By: Will Sumpter & Associates . . . . . (770) 460-8438
Casmer, Tom 800 Cleveland Avenue S, St. Paul, MN 55116 . . . . . (612) 696-1664
Cassady, Jack P.O. Box 340568, Tampa, FL 33694 . . . . . (813) 264-4346
Cassels, Jean Represented By: Publishers' Graphics . . . . . (203) 797-8188
Cassler, Carl Represented By: Mendola Ltd. . . . . . (212) 986-5680
Castiglione, Janice Represented By: Carol Bancroft & Friends . . . . . (203) 748-4823
Castillito, Mark Represented By: Dane Sonneville
Castillo, Julie Represented By: Bernstein & Andriulli, Inc. . . . . . (212) 682-1490
Castro, Antonio Represented By: Cornell & McCarthy, LLC . . . . . (203) 454-4210
Cat, Stat Represented By: Melissa Hopson . . . . . (214) 747-3122
Catalano, Nick Represented By: Carol Bancroft & Friends . . . . . (203) 748-4823
Catalano, Sal 114 Boyce Place, Ridgewood, NJ 07450 . . . . . (201) 447-5318
Caton, Don Represented By: West End Studio . . . . . (310) 664-9200
Ceballos, John Represented By: Scott Hull Associates . . . . . (937) 433-8383
Ceccarelli Illustrations, Chris 447 Amhurst Circle, Folsom, CA 95630-7952 . . . . . (916) 355-8511
Cecil, Moffitt 214 W 85th Street, New York, NY 10024 . . . . . (212) 580-5320

CELMER, STEVE Pages 168,193
Represented By: American Artists **(212) 682-2462**
e-mail: info@amerartists.com • Website: www.amerartists.com
Specialties: Computer; Photoillustration; Realism

Celusniak, Chris Represented By: Creative Freelancers . . . . . (800) 398-9544
Cepeda, Joe 3340 Ivar Avenue, Rosemead, CA 91770 . . . . . (818) 288-8205
Cericola, Anthony Represented By: Deborah Wolfe . . . . . (215) 232-6666
CGL Multimedia Corp. 133 Cedar Road, East Northport, NY 11731 . . . . . (516) 368-2031
Chabrian, Deborah Represented By: Artworks . . . . . (212) 627-1554
Champie, Zhon 2500 Summit Street, Kansas City, MO 64108 . . . . . (816) 435-2000
Champlin, Dale Represented By: The Art Agency . . . . . (503) 203-8300
Chan, Ron 24 Nelson Avenue, Mill Valley, CA 94941 . . . . . (415) 389-1820
Chandler, Karen 6 Second Street, Locust Valley, NY 11560 . . . . . (516) 671-0388

CHANDLER, ROGER Pages 283,290-291,430,435
Represented By: John Brewster Creative Services **(203) 226-4724**
e-mail: creative.svcs@snet.net • Website: www.brewstercreative.com
Specialties: Annual Report; Computer; Corporate; Digital

Chang, Michelle 36 Third Street #4-L, Brooklyn, NY 11231 . . . . . (718) 797-4427
Chang Illustration, George 54-17 80th Street, Elmhurst, NY 11373 . . . . . (718) 533-7096
Chap, Louis RD 2, Box 1252, Bethel, VT 05032 . . . . . (802) 234-9352
Chapleski, Gerry Represented By: Joel Harlib Associates, Inc. . . . . . (312) 573-1370
Chapman, Lisa Represented By: Mendola Ltd. . . . . . (212) 986-5680
Chapman, Shirley R. 20 Espada Court, Fremont, CA 94539 . . . . . (510) 792-8986
556 Mowry Avenue, Ste. 103, Fremont, CA 94536 . . . . . (510) 505-9702
Chappell, Ellis Represented By: Artworks . . . . . (212) 627-1554
Charlier, Mark 117 S Morgan #300, Chicago, IL 60607 . . . . . (312) 421-2668
Charmatz, Bill 25 W 68th Street, New York, NY 10023 . . . . . (212) 595-3907

CHARPENTIER, RUSSELL Page 243
51 Oakwood Street, San Francisco, CA 94110 • Fax (415) 552-9447 **(415) 553-8943**
Represented By: Rita Gatlin Represents **(800) 924-7881**
Website: www.ritareps.com • Specialties: Architecture/Interiors; Botanical; Conceptual; Corporate; Maps & Charts; Medical; Mixed Media; Pen & Ink; Technical

Chartier, Norm Represented By: Carol Bancroft & Friends . . . . . (203) 748-4823

CHAU, TUNGWAI Pages 338-339
18439 Lost Knife Circle #204, Montgomery Village, MD 20886 • Fax (301) 208-0279 **(301) 208-0279**
Represented By: The Roland Group **(301) 718-7955**
e-mail: tchau244@aol.com • Website: www.therolandgroup.com
Specialties: Advertising; Black & White; Computer; Conceptual; Corporate; Oil; People; Portraiture; Poster; Scratchboard

Chaves, Leslie 121-12 115th Avenue, South Ozone Park, NY 11420 ... (718) 845-4407
Cheese, Cloe Represented By: Bernstein & Andriulli, Inc. ... (212) 682-1490
Chelsea, David 2814 NE 16th Avenue, Portland, OR 97212 ... (503) 284-3512
Chen, David 2211 Newton Drive, Rockville, MD 20850 ... (301) 460-6575
Represented By: Conrad Represents, Inc. ... (415) 921-7140
Cheney, George Represented By: Susan & Company ... (206) 232-7873
Cheng, Fu-Ding 209 Seventh Avenue, Venice, CA 90291 ... (310) 396-1466
Cheng, Judith Represented By: Creative Connection ... (410) 360-5981
Cherish CFO Design 3333 E Camelback Road, Ste. 200, Phoenix, AZ 85018 ... (602) 955-2707
Cherna, Mindy Represented By: Creative Connection ... (410) 360-5981

CHERNISHOV, ANATOLY Page 212
4 Willowbank Court, Mahwah, NJ 07430-2909 • Fax (201) 236-9469 **(201) 327-2377**
e-mail: chern@iname.com • Specialties: Annual Report; Computer; Corporate; Editorial

Cherry, Jim 902 E Palm Lane, Phoenix, AZ 85006 ... (602) 340-0715
Chesak, Lina Represented By: Holly Hahn Artist Rep (H2 + Co.) ... (312) 633-0500
Chesterman, Adriane Represented By: Artworks ... (212) 627-1554
Chestnut, David 415 Carlton Street, Toronto, ON Canada M5A 2M3 ... (416) 921-8700
Cheung, Phil 1335 Pearl Street #E, Alameda, CA 94501 ... (510) 521-6815
Represented By: Conrad Represents, Inc. ... (415) 921-7140
Chewning, Randy Represented By: HK Portfolio ... (212) 675-5719
Chezem, Douglas R. 3613 Cornell Road, Fairfax, VA 22030 ... (703) 591-5424
ChiaNi Represented By: R. Fischer & Company ... (312) 368-1441
Chiaramonte, Vincent Represented By: Yolanda Burnett Represents ... (770) 967-0039
Represented By: Langley & Associates ... (847) 670-0912
Chickinelli, Mark 6348 Pierce Street, Omaha, NE 68106 ... (402) 551-6829
Represented By: Munro Goodman ... (312) 321-1336
Represented By: Those 3 Reps ... (214) 871-1316
Chicko, Terri & Joe Represented By: Cornell & McCarthy, LLC ... (203) 454-4210
Childers, Argus Represented By: Nowicki & Nowicki ... (617) 423-2800
Chironna, Ronald 122 Slosson Avenue, 2nd Flr., Staten Island, NY 10314 ... (718) 720-6142
Cho, Helen 391 Broadway, Costa Mesa, CA 92627 ... (714) 642-7445
Cho, Young Sook Represented By: Scott Hull Associates ... (937) 433-8383
Chodos-Irvine, Margaret 3018 45th Avenue SW, Seattle, WA 98116 ... (206) 935-0901
Chong, Vanessa 65 Scadding Avenue, Ste. 509, Toronto, ON Canada M5A 4L1 ... (416) 955-0656
Chorney, Steven P.O. Box 2160, Moorpark, CA 93021 ... (805) 529-8111
Represented By: Mendola Ltd. ... (212) 986-5680
Chouinard, Roger Represented By: Ellen Knable & Associates, Inc. ... (310) 855-8855
Chow, Jim Represented By: Jaz & Jaz ... (206) 633-3445
Chow, Rita Represented By: Irmeli Holmberg ... (212) 545-9155
Christensen, David 4338 Manchester Place, Cypress, CA 90630 ... (714) 761-3488
Christensen, Kent 325 E 77th Street #3H, New York, NY 10021 ... (212) 744-3050
Christensen, Wendy Represented By: Barbara Gordon Associates Ltd. ... (212) 686-3514
Christie, Greg Represented By: The Arts Counsel ... (212) 777-6777
Christine, Tina 390 Queen Quay W #1614, Toronto, ON Canada M5V 3A6 ... (416) 345-1676

CHRISTOPHER, TOM Pages 124-125
Represented By: Vicki Morgan Associates **(212) 475-0440**
e-mail: vmartrep@aol.com • Website: www.vickimorganassociates.com
Specialties: Editorial; Icons; Murals; People; Poster; Still Life; Stock

Chun, Jeff 4107 W 177th Street, Torrance, CA 90504 ... (310) 793-0290
Chung, Chi Represented By: Carol Bancroft & Friends ... (203) 748-4823
Church, Peter Represented By: Creative Connection ... (410) 360-5981

CHURCHMAN, JOHN Pages 168,177
Represented By: American Artists **(212) 682-2462**
e-mail: info@amerartists.com • Website: www.amerartists.com

Ciardiello, Joseph 2182 Clove Road, Staten Island, NY 10305 .... (718) 727-4757
Cibere, Joe Represented By: West End Studio .... (310) 664-9200

CICCARELLI, GARY — Pages 168-169
317 Elmwood Street, Dearborn, MI 48124 — **(313) 278-3504**
Represented By: American Artists — **(212) 682-2462**
e-mail: info@amerartists.com • Website: www.amerartists.com • Specialties: Action; Airbrush; People; Product

CICCATI, GARY — Page 277
Represented By: Famous Frames — **(310) 642-2721**
e-mail: info@famousframes.com • Website: www.famousframes.com • Specialties: Animation; Storyboards

Cieslawski, Steve Represented By: Mendola Ltd. .... (212) 986-5680

CIGLIANO, BILL — Pages 49, 422
Represented By: Renard Represents — **(212) 490-2450**
e-mail: renardreps@earthlink.net • Website: www.renardrepresents.com • Specialty: Caricature

Cilluffo, Laurent Represented By: Wanda Nowak .... (212) 535-0438
Cimochowski, Barbara Represented By: Evelyne Johnson Associates .... (212) 532-0928
Cirocco, Frank 2042 Casa Mia Drive, San Jose, CA 95124 .... (408) 371-0337
Ciss, Julius 89 Lynnhaven Road, Toronto, ON Canada M6A 2L1 .... (416) 784-1416
CK Design Represented By: SI International .... (212) 254-4996
Clapp, John 4961 Monaco Drive, Pleasanton, CA 94566 .... (510) 462-6444
Clar, David Austin 104 Loyalist Avenue, Rochester, NY 14624 .... (716) 247-2050

CLARK, BRADLEY — Pages 352-353
Represented By: Sal Barracca Associates — **(212) 889-2400**
e-mail: watrpaintr@aol.com • Specialties: Advertising; Architecture/Interiors; Children; Editorial; Food; Greeting Cards; People; Product; Still Life; Water Color

CLARK, CYNTHIA WATTS — Pages 350-351
Represented By: Sal Barracca Associates — **(212) 889-2400**
e-mail: watrpaintr@aol.com • Specialties: Collage; Editorial; Food; People; Still Life; Water Color

Clark, Johnston 1210 Gregory Avenue, Wilmette, IL 60091 .... (847) 251-2444
Clark, Tim 1256 25th Street, Santa Monica, CA 90404 .... (310) 453-7613
Clarke, Bob 127 Rivershore Drive, Seaford, DE 19973 .... (302) 628-1934
Clarke, Greg 844 Ninth Street #10, Santa Monica, CA 90403 .... (310) 395-7958
Classen, Martin 321 E 153rd Street #13H, Bronx, NY 10451 .... (718) 665-7579
Clavette, Don Represented By: Hankins & Tegenborg Ltd. .... (212) 867-8092
Clayton, Christian 135 S LaBrea Avenue #1, Los Angeles, CA 90036 .... (213) 653-2035

CLEGG, DAVE — Pages 373-374,451,468
3571 Aaron Sosebee Road, Cumming, GA 30130 • Fax (770) 781-5780 — **(770) 887-6306**
Represented By: Susan Wells & Associates — **(404) 255-1430**
e-mail: dcleggo@mindspring.com • Specialties: Animals; Cartoon; Digital; Humour; Wildlife

Cleland, Janet 1 Mono Lane, San Anselmo, CA 94960 .... (415) 457-1049

CLEMENT, CAMERON — Page 9
3422 S Fresno, Ft. Smith, AR 72903 • Fax (501) 646-7734 — **(501) 646-7734**
Represented By: Suzanne Craig Represents, Inc. — **(918) 749-9424**
Website: www.ngexplorer.com • Specialties: Advertising; Caricature; Computer; Conceptual; Corporate; Editorial; Greeting Cards; Icons; Scratchboard; Stock

Clement, Gary 52 Arlington Avenue, Toronto, ON Canada M6G 3K8 .... (416) 657-8975

CLEMENTSON, JOHN — Pages 368-369
Represented By: Alan Lynch Artists — **(908) 813-8718**
Represented By: Arena — **44 171 267 9661**

Clemmensen, Denise 10047 Columbus Avenue, Mission Hills, CA 91345 .... (818) 893-3298

Cleveland, Thomas 333 Janisch Road, Houston, TX 77018 . . . . (713) 691-7402

CLINE, JEFF Page 314
7 Primrose Way, Ste. 703, Warren, NJ 07059 **(908) 561-4553 • (800) 770-4089**
e-mail: jeffdcline@aol.com • Website: http://members.aol.com/jeffdcline
Specialties: Advertising; Children; Editorial; Humour

Cline, Richard Represented By: Richard Solomon . . . . (212) 683-1362
Cline, Rob Represented By: Jennifer Embler Represents, Inc. . . . . (954) 760-4195

CLOR PHOTOGRAPHY & IMAGING Pages 258,439
1237 Chicago Road, Troy, MI 48083 • Fax (248) 583-3216 **(248) 583-5540**
Represented By: Mike Iezzi **(248) 583-5540**
e-mail: cclor@aol.com • Specialties: Animation; Collage; Computer;
Digital Imaging/3D; Montage; Photoillustration; Product; Realism

Clownbank Studio PO Box 7709, Santa Cruz, CA 95060 . . . . (408) 426-4247
Clubb Illustrations, Inc., Rick 310 S Hale Street, Wheaton, IL 60187 . . . . (630) 690-5554
Clyne, Dan 6823 N Lakewood, Chicago, IL 60626 . . . . (773) 338-4972
Represented By: Frank Lux & Associates, Inc. . . . . (312) 222-1361
Coates, Peter 41 Worexeter Avenue, Toronto, ON Canada M4K 1J5 . . . . (416) 466-6878 • (800) 685-4673
Cobane, Russell Represented By: Carol Guenzi Agents, Inc. . . . . (800) 417-5120
Cobb, Patricia 37 Stone Drive, Southport, ME 04106 . . . . (207) 741-2505
Cober-Gentry, Leslie 221 Sherwood Farm Road, Fairfield, CT 06430 . . . . (203) 255-9782
Cockrille, Eva Vagreti Represented By: Cornell & McCarthy, LLC . . . . (203) 454-4210
Coconis, Ted P.O. Box 758, Cedar Key, FL 32625 . . . . (352) 543-5720
Cocotos, Tom Nick 397 W 12th Street, New York, NY 10014 . . . . (212) 620-7556
Coe, Wayne 1636 Golf Club Drive, Glendale, CA 91206 . . . . (818) 241-2401
Coffelt, Nancy Represented By: The Art Agency . . . . (503) 203-8300
Coffelt Design/Illus., Ken 22717 la Lane, Woodland Hills, CA 91364 . . . . (818) 224-4274
Cohen, Adam 252 W 17th Street #5B, New York, NY 10011 . . . . (212) 691-4074
Cohen, Elisa 100 Hudson Street #7-B, New York, NY 10013 . . . . (212) 941-7662
Represented By: France Aline Associates . . . . (213) 933-2500
Cohen, Izhar Represented By: Sally Heflin . . . . (212) 366-1893
Cohen, M.E. 357 W 12th Street, New York, NY 10014 . . . . (212) 627-8033
Cohen, Paula 138 E Fifth Street, Brooklyn, NY 11218 . . . . (718) 633-9043

COHEN ILLUSTRATION, JIM Pages 403,427,436,440,467
107 Miller Road, Hawthorn Woods, IL 60047 • Fax (847) 726-8988 **(847) 726-8979**
e-mail: cohenillus@aol.com • Specialties: Conceptual; Digital; Editorial; Fantasy; Whimsical

Coke, E. Browning 609 Graceland Drive SE, Albuquerque, NM 87108 . . . . (505) 256-9130
Coladonato 9104 Deschambault, St. Leonard, PQ Canada H1R 2C5 . . . . (514) 323-0101
Colalillo, Giovannina 19 East Drive, Toronto, ON Canada M6N 2N8 . . . . (416) 604-0057
Colanero, Michael 2701 SE Seventh Street, Pompano Beach, FL 33062 . . . . (954) 946-2693

COLBY, GARRY Pages 299,304,425
Represented By: The Neis Group **(616) 672-5756**
e-mail: neisgroup@wmis.net • Website: www.neisgroup.com • Specialties: Children; Editorial; Humour; Book Jackets

Cole, Dick Represented By: Sweet Represents . . . . (415) 433-1222
Cole, Lo Represented By: Irmeli Holmberg . . . . (212) 545-9155
Colley, Michael Represented By: Brenda Bender . . . . (404) 842-1913
Collicott, Sharleen 201 Ocean Avenue, Ste. 708-B, Santa Monica, CA 90402 . . . . (310) 458-6616
Collier, John Represented By: Richard Solomon . . . . (212) 683-1362
Collier, Mary Represented By: Cornell & McCarthy, LLC . . . . (203) 454-4210

COLLINET, ROB Page 228
849 Broadview Avenue #11 ½, Toronto, ON Canada M4K 2P9 **(416) 469-1092**
Website: www.splashworks.com/rob

COLLINS, BRIGID Pages 366-367
Represented By: Alan Lynch Artists **(908) 813-8718**
Represented By: Arena **44 171 267 9661**

COLLINS, DARYLL Pages 354,419,423,443,449
2969 Ensley Court, Maineville, OH 45039 • Fax (513) 683-9345 **(513) 683-9335**
e-mail: daryllа1c@aol.com • Specialties: Advertising; Animation; Cartoon; Digital; Editorial; Humour

Collins, Martha 11060 Artesia Boulevard #C, Cerritos, CA 90703 . . . . . (562) 809-4560
Represented By: Liz Sanders Agency . . . . . (714) 495-3664
Collins, Matt 30 Black Alder Lane, Wilton, CT 06897 . . . . . (203) 762-8871

COLLOT, PHILIPPE Page 277
Represented By: Famous Frames **(310) 642-2721**
e-mail: info@famousframes.com • Website: www.famousframes.com • Specialties: Animation; Storyboards

Collyer, Frank 10 Knapp Road, Stony Point, NY 10980 . . . . . (914) 947-3050
Colmer, James Buttes House, Les Buttes, Channel Islands, England GY7 9SD

COLON, RAUL Pages 124-125
Represented By: Vicki Morgan Associates **(212) 475-0440**
e-mail: vmartrep@aol.com • Website: www.vickimorganassociates.com
Specialties: Children; Colored Pencil; Conceptual; Corporate; Editorial; Fantasy; Greeting Cards; People; Portraiture; Water Color

Colon, Terry 554 Lombard Street, San Francisco, CA 94133 . . . . . (415) 835-2422
Colorio, Lynn Represented By: Suzanne Craig Represents, Inc. . . . . . (918) 749-9424
Colquhoun, Eric Represented By: Three in a Box . . . . . (416) 367-2446
Colrus, William Represented By: The Ivy League of Artists . . . . . (212) 243-1333
Colvin, Rob 1351 N 1670 W, Farmington, UT 84025 . . . . . (801) 451-6858
Colwell, Kim 535 Rose Avenue, Venice, CA 90291 . . . . . (310) 452-9538
Represented By: Elizabeth Poje . . . . . (310) 556-1439
Combs, Jonathan Represented By: Sweet Represents. . . . . . (415) 433-1222
Comic Art Productions 8 Ninth Street #313, Medford, MA 02155. . . . . . (781) 395-2778
Command, Betsey 15621 N Hillcrest, Eden Prarie, MN 55346. . . . . . (612) 937-2921
Commander, Bob 1565 Village Round Drive, Park City, UT 84098 . . . . . (801) 649-4356

COMPORT, SALLY WERN Pages 214-216,429
Represented By: W/C Studio, Inc./Allan Comport **(410) 349-8669**
e-mail: acomport@aol.com • wcstudio@crosslink.net • Website: www.theispot.com
Specialties: Advertising; Annual Report; Children; Conceptual; Corporate; Editorial

Comstock, Jacqueline 2 Old Ridge Road #2, Warwick, NY 10990 . . . . . (914) 987-8314
Conahan, Jim 822 S Charles Avenue, Naperville, IL 60540 . . . . . (630) 961-1478
Conant, Pat 13 Heritage Lane, Westfield, MA 01085 . . . . . (413) 572-5301
Condon, Ken 126 Ashfield Mountain Road, Ashfield, MA 01330. . . . . . (413) 628-4042

CONDRON, ANDREW Pages 168,197
Represented By: American Artists **(212) 682-2462**
e-mail: info@amerartists.com • Website: www.amerartists.com

Confer, Mitchell Represented By: Jan Collier Represents, Inc. . . . . . (415) 383-9026
Conge, Bob 8600 Giles Road, Wayland, NY 14572-9317 . . . . . (716) 728-3424
Conley, Peg Represented By: Creative Connection . . . . . (410) 360-5981
Connelly, Gwen Represented By: HK Portfolio . . . . . (212) 675-5719
Conner, Eulala Represented By: Publishers' Graphics. . . . . . (203) 797-8188
Conner, Mona 1 Montgomery Place #8, Brooklyn, NY 11215. . . . . . (718) 636-1527
Connolly, Jim 25 Cedar Street, Hingham, MA 02043 . . . . . (781) 749-0825
Connor, Todd Represented By: Jaz & Jaz . . . . . (206) 633-3445
Connor, Tom 912 President Street, Brooklyn, NY 11215. . . . . . (718) 230-0391
Conrad, Alexandra 9955 Yonge Street #8, Richmond Hill, ON Canada L4C 9M6. . . . . . (905) 883-5539

CONRAD, LIZ Pages 299,305,424
Represented By: The Neis Group **(616) 672-5756**
e-mail: neisgroup@wmis.net • Website: www.neisgroup.com • Specialties: Book Jackets; Children; Editorial

Conrad, Melvin 533 Country Club Road, York, PA 17403 . . . . . (717) 843-4768
Conran, Kevin 16426 Moorpark Street, Encino, CA 91436 . . . . . (818) 990-0611
Constable, Mike Represented By: Link . . . . . (416) 530-1500

Constantin, Valerie Represented By: Barbara Gordon Associates Ltd. . . . . (212) 686-3514
Conteh-Morgan, Jane Represented By: Publishers' Graphics . . . . . (203) 797-8188

CONTESTABILE, GREG Page 117
205-B S Haskell Avenue, Dallas, TX 75226 **(214) 823-7103**

Cook, David Represented By: Hankins & Tegenborg Ltd. . . . . . (212) 867-8092
Cook, Donald Represented By: Publishers' Graphics . . . . . (203) 797-8188
Cook, Laura Represented By: Virginia Boggie & Associates . . . . . (604) 943-6414
Cook, Lynette Represented By: Spencer Church . . . . . (206) 860-9239
Cook, Matthew Represented By: Sally Heflin . . . . . (212) 366-1893
Cook, Peter Simpson 5902 Lindenhurst Avenue, Los Angeles, CA 90036 . . . . . (213) 930-0889
Cook, Richard Represented By: Sheryl Beranbaum . . . . . (401) 737-8591
Cook, Timothy 3107 Ravensworth Place, Arlington, VA 22302 . . . . . (703) 820-2049
Cooley, Gary Represented By: Skidmore, Inc. . . . . . (248) 353-7722
Coonen, John 35 E Crystal Lake Avenue, Chrystal Lake, IL 60014 . . . . . (815) 356-6381
Coons, Sean 12222 Moorpark Street #205, Studio City, CA 91604 . . . . . (818) 755-9058
Cooper, Bob Represented By: Will Sumpter & Associates . . . . . (770) 460-8438
Cooper, Cheryl Represented By: Alexander/Pollard, Inc. . . . . . (800) 347-0734
Cooper, Dan 610 S Lincoln, Bloomington, IN 47401 . . . . . (813) 336-0365
Cooper, David 1061 Fair Birch Drive, Mississauga, ON Canada L5H 1M4 . . . . . (905) 271-4460
Cooper, P.D. 610 S Lincoln Street, Bloomington, IN 47401 . . . . . (812) 334-1266
Represented By: Tom Maloney . . . . . (312) 704-0500
Cooper, Rachel 60 Doddington Road, Lincoln, Lincolnshire, England LN6 7EU 44 152 250 0222
Cooper, Robert Represented By: Nancy George . . . . . (805) 688-3772
Copeland, Eric RR#4, Cobourg, ON Canada K9A 4J7 . . . . . (416) 342-3899
Copeland, Greg 1204 Harmon Place #11, Minneapolis, MN 55403 . . . . . (612) 321-9065
Copenhaver, Trevor 3065 Third Avenue #4, San Diego, CA 92103 . . . . . (619) 299-6709
Corbett, Katherine 14682 N 100th Way, Scottsdale, AZ 85260 . . . . . (602) 451-4848
Corey, Lee Represented By: Sheryl Beranbaum . . . . . (401) 737-8591
Corey Animation Design 45 E 30th Street, Ste. 1102, New York, NY 10016 . . . . . (212) 532-0599
Corfield, Robin Bell Represented By: HK Portfolio . . . . . (212) 675-5719
Corkery, Eddie 152 N Myrtle Avenue, Villa Park, IL 60181 . . . . . (630) 834-3039
Represented By: Langley & Associates . . . . . (847) 670-0912
Cornell, Jeff Represented By: Artco . . . . . (212) 889-8777
Cornner, Hayden Represented By: Bernstein & Andriulli, Inc. . . . . . (212) 682-1490
Correll, Cory 11511 Sullnick Way, Gaithersburg, MD 20878 . . . . . (301) 977-7254
Corrigan, Paul Represented By: Suzanne Craig Represents, Inc. . . . . . (918) 749-9424
Cosentino, Carlo 10752 Vianney, Montreal, PQ Canada H2B 1K1 . . . . . (514) 384-9596
Cosgrove, Dan Represented By: Daniele Collignon . . . . . (212) 243-4209
Costantino, Valerie 2037 New Hyde Park Road, New Hyde Park, NY 11040 . . . . . (516) 358-9121
Cote, Genevieve Represented By: Link . . . . . (416) 530-1500
Cote, Martin 1030 St. Alexandre #709, Montreal, PQ Canada H2Z 1P3 . . . . . (514) 875-6723
Cotton, Mary 333 N Michigan Avenue #1410, Chicago, IL 60601 . . . . . (312) 263-0950
Cottone, Dave Represented By: Lori Nowicki & Associates . . . . . (212) 243-5888
Couch, Greg Represented By: Joanne Palulian . . . . . (212) 581-8338

COULAS, MICK Pages 256-257,418,436,450,459
99 Coleman Avenue #208, Toronto, ON Canada M4C 1P8 • Fax (416) 690-0689 **(416) 698-3304**
e-mail: lourdes@netcom.ca • Website: www.zeta-media.com/lourdes
Specialties: Airbrush; Digital; Humour; People

COULAS-LOURDES ILLUSTRATORS Pages 256-257
99 Coleman Avenue #208, Toronto, ON Canada M4C 1P8 • Fax (416) 690-0689 **(416) 698-3304**
e-mail: lourdes@netcom.ca • Website: www.zeta-media.com/lourdes
Specialties: Airbrush; Digital; Humour; People

Coulson, David 1107 Goodman Street, Pittsburgh, PA 15218 . . . . . (412) 243-7064
Coulter Studio, Marty 10129 Conway Road, St. Louis, MO 63124-1239 . . . . . (314) 432-2721

COURNOYER, JACQUES Pages 24-25
Represented By: Marlena Agency **(609) 252-9405**
e-mail: marzena@bellatlantic.net • Website: http://members.bellatlantic.net/~marzena
Specialties: Conceptual; Corporate; Editorial; Whimsical

Courtney, Richard Represented By: SI International . . . . . (212) 254-4996

COUSINEAU, NORMAND Pages 30-31,455
Represented By: Marlena Agency **(609) 252-9405**
e-mail: marzena@bellatlantic.net • Website: http://members.bellatlantic.net/~marzena
Specialties: Conceptual; Corporate; Editorial; Maps & Charts; Whimsical

Coven, John Represented By: Motion Artists, Inc. . . . . . (213) 851-7737
Covington, Nervene K. P.O. Box 648, St. Petersburg, FL 33731 . . . . . (813) 822-1267
Covington & Pettis P.O. Box 648, St. Petersburg, FL 33703 . . . . . (813) 822-1267
Cowdrey, Richard Represented By: Shannon Associates. . . . . . (212) 831-5650
Cox, Bob 4701 Crystal Drive, Columbia, SC 29206 . . . . . (803) 790-0208
Cox, Craig 2305 Ashland Street #C, Ashland, OR 97520 . . . . . (800) 435-6509
Cox, Elaine Represented By: Alan Lynch Artists. . . . . . (908) 813-8718
Cox, H. Ed 1147 S Salisbury Boulevard #5, Salisbury, MD 21801 . . . . . (410) 548-9106
Cox, Mari 107 Berkeley Place #4-F, Brooklyn, NY 11217. . . . . . (718) 783-2247
Cox, Paul Represented By: Richard Solomon . . . . . (212) 683-1362
Cox, Steve Represented By: HK Portfolio . . . . . (212) 675-5719
Cox, Teresa 308 Prince Street, Ste. 322, St. Paul, MN 55101 . . . . . (612) 290-9158
Cox, Tracy 1700 Bush Street #2, San Francisco, CA 94109 . . . . . (415) 673-6461
Cozzolino, Paul New York, NY . . . . . (212) 969-8680
Crabb, Gordon Represented By: Alan Lynch Artists . . . . . (908) 813-8718
Craft, Kinuko Y. 83 Litchfield Road, Norfolk, CT 06058 . . . . . (860) 542-5018
Craig, Casey P.O. Box 1841, Wimberley, TX 78676. . . . . . (512) 847-7008
Craig, Dan 118 E 26th Street #302, Minneapolis, MN 55404 . . . . . (612) 871-4539
Represented By: Bernstein & Andriulli, Inc. . . . . . (212) 682-1490
Craig, John Route 2, Box 2224, Tower Hill Road, Soldiers Grove, WI 54655. . . . . . (608) 872-2371

CRAMPTON, MICHAEL Pages 338-339
25 McKinley Street, Rowayton, CT 06853 **(203) 853-9227**
Represented By: The Roland Group **(301) 718-7955**
e-mail: mcrampton@aol.com • Website: www.therolandgroup.com • Specialties: Fashion; Food; Music; Travel

Crane, Gary 1511 W Little Creek Road, Norfolk, VA 23505 . . . . . (804) 579-2263
Crawford, Denise Represented By: Jerry Leff Associates, Inc.. . . . . . (212) 697-8525
Represented By: Repertoire. . . . . . (972) 761-0500
Crawford, Duke P.O. Box B-80, Los Angeles, CA 90026 . . . . . (213) 482-4889
Crawford, Emma 108 E 16th Street, New York, NY 10003 . . . . . (212) 343-7080
Crawford, K. Michael 6146 ½ Glen Holly Street, Los Angeles, CA 90068. . . . . . (213) 466-7086
Creative Capers Represented By: Bernstein & Andriulli, Inc. . . . . . (212) 682-1490
Creative Force Studio 1235-B Colorado Lane, Arlington, TX 76015 . . . . . (817) 467-1013
Creative Impulse 2611 Eastwood Avenue, Evanston, IL 60201 . . . . . (847) 864-6062
Creative Touch 2456 Matador Drive, Rowland Heights, CA 91748 . . . . . (626) 964-2918
Crehan, Linda Represented By: Leighton & Company, Inc. . . . . . (978) 921-0887
Crespo, George Represented By: Carol Bancroft & Friends . . . . . (203) 748-4823
Cressy, Mike P.O. Box 762, Issaquah, WA 98027-0762 . . . . . (425) 603-9669
Cristos Represented By: Repertory. . . . . . (213) 931-7449
Criswell, Ron 2929 Wildflower Street, Dallas, TX 75229 . . . . . (972) 243-8058
Represented By: Connie Koralik Associates Represents . . . . . (312) 944-5680
Crittenden, Susan 5914 Lakecrest Drive, Garland, TX 75043-6419 . . . . . (972) 226-2196
Crnkovich, Tony 5706 S Narragansett Avenue, Chicago, IL 60638 . . . . . (773) 586-9696
Represented By: Connie Koralik Associates Represents . . . . . (312) 944-5680
Cro, Alex P.O. Box 470818, San Francisco, CA 94147 . . . . . (415) 383-9026
Crockett, Linda 23336 Williams Avenue, Euclid, OH 44123 . . . . . (216) 261-7863
3208 Indian Moon Road, Las Vegas, NV 89129. . . . . . (702) 395-4887
Crofut, Bob 8 New Street, Ridgefield, CT 06877 . . . . . (203) 431-4304
Croll, Carolyn Represented By: HK Portfolio . . . . . (212) 675-5719
Cronin, Brian 682 Broadway, Ste. 4A, New York, NY 10012 . . . . . (212) 254-6312
Crosby, Jeff 242 W 16th Street, 5th Flr., New York, NY 10011 . . . . . (212) 645-4679

CROSSE, ANNE Page 243
105 Hill Street, Santa Barbara, CA 93022 • Fax (805) 649-5812 **(805) 649-2788**
Represented By: Rita Gatlin Represents **(800) 924-7881**
Website: www.ritareps.com • Specialties: Collage; Computer; Digital; Food; Icons

Crossgrove, Cathy P.O. Box 5634, Redwood City, CA 94064 . . . . . (650) 367-0986
Croth, Chuck 5644 Eichelberger, St. Louis, MO 63109 . . . . . (314) 752-0984
Crowell, James R. 218 Madison Avenue #5-F, New York, NY 10016 . . . . . (212) 213-5333
Crowther, Catherine Rose 1732 Hearst Avenue #3, Berkeley, CA 94703-1387 . . . . . (510) 704-8763
Crowther, Will 2400 Suwanee Lakes Trail, Suwanee, GA 30024 . . . . . (707) 513-0738
Crump, Christopher 24 Jersey Drive, Petts Wood, Kent, England BR5 1ER 44 168 981 0111
Cruz, Jose 6321 Bramble Drive, Ft. Worth, TX 76133 . . . . . (817) 292-2418
Cruz, Roger Represented By: Glass House Graphics . . . . . (304) 232-5641
Cruz & Slowik Associates 190 Elm Avenue, Hackensack, NJ 07601 . . . . . (201) 489-3528
Cuddy, Robbin Represented By: SI International . . . . . (212) 254-4996
Cullum, Leo 2900 Valmere Drive, Malibu, CA 90265 . . . . . (310) 456-9315
Culter, Dave Represented By: Friend & Johnson . . . . . (214) 559-0055
Culver, Margaret 4118 Warner Boulevard #C, Burbank, CA 91505 . . . . . (818) 846-2408
Cummings, Terrance P.O. Box 573, New York, NY 10023 . . . . . (212) 586-4193
Cundiff, William Charles 1719 Fairway Drive, Newton, NC 28658 . . . . . (704) 466-0556 • (704) 612-6170
Cunis, Peter Represented By: Carol Guenzi Agents, Inc. . . . . . (800) 417-5120
Cunningham, Dennis Represented By: The Art Agency . . . . . (503) 203-8300
Curl, Steve 460 Everett Avenue, Ste. 1, Palo Alto, CA 94301 . . . . . (650) 328-3499
Curlee, Walt Represented By: Air Studio . . . . . (513) 721-1193
Represented By: Jennifer Embler Represents, Inc. . . . . . (954) 760-4195
Currey, Anna Represented By: HK Portfolio . . . . . (212) 675-5719
Curry, Kevin 210 Harvard Drive SE, Albuquerque, NM 87106 . . . . . (505) 266-2915
Curry, Tom Represented By: Conrad Represents, Inc. . . . . . (415) 921-7140
Cusack, Margaret 124 Hoyt Street, Brooklyn, NY 11217-2215 . . . . . (718) 237-0145
Cusano, Steven R. 80 Talbot Court, Media, PA 19063 . . . . . (610) 565-8829
Custode, Michael Represented By: Patti Shaw . . . . . (416) 361-3184
Custodio, Bernard 20103 Baltar Street, Canoga Park, CA 91306 . . . . . (818) 998-4242
Cutler, Dave 7 W Street, Warwick, NY 10990 . . . . . (914) 987-1705
Cutler, Greg 4144 Park Boulevard, Palo Alto, CA 94306 . . . . . (415) 493-8715
Cutter, David Represented By: American Artists . . . . . (212) 682-2462
Cyber Graphics Studio 3369 Ingram Road, Mississauga, ON Canada L5L 4N4 . . . . . (905) 828-6992
Cymerman, John Emil Represented By: Leyden Diversified . . . . . (215) 663-0587
Cyr, Kurt Represented By: Famous Frames . . . . . (310) 642-2721
Czetela, Chris Represented By: Harriet Kastaris & Associates . . . . . (314) 773-2600
D'Aguanno, Carla Represented By: Hankins & Tegenborg Ltd. . . . . . (212) 867-8092
D'Andrea, Bernard Represented By: Frank & Jeff Lavaty . . . . . (212) 427-5632
D'Andrea, Dominick Represented By: Frank & Jeff Lavaty . . . . . (212) 427-5632
D'Souza, Helen 487 Mortimer Avenue, Toronto, ON Canada M4J 2G6 . . . . . (416) 466-0630
Dabcovich, Meral 77 Pond Avenue #1106, Brookline, MA 02146 . . . . . (617) 566-0299
Dacey, Bob 7213 Woodchuck Hill Road, Fayetteville, NY 13202 . . . . . (315) 637-4614
Dadds, Jerry 1745 Circle Road, Ruxton, MD 21204 . . . . . (410) 296-3751
Represented By: Ivy Glick & Associates . . . . . (925) 944-0304
Represented By: Deborah Wolfe . . . . . (215) 232-6666
Represented By: Sell Inc. . . . . . (312) 578-8844
Daeni, Pino Represented By: Hankins & Tegenborg Ltd. . . . . . (212) 867-8092
Dagenias, Yvan 5938 Falco, Rock Forest, PQ Canada . . . . . (819) 864-9507
Dahlquist, Roland 1149 E Village Circle Drive, Phoenix, AZ 85022 . . . . . (602) 993-9895

DAIGLE, STEPHAN Pages 43,429
Represented By: Renard Represents **(212) 490-2450**
e-mail: renardreps@earthlink.net • Website: www.renardrepresents.com • Specialty: Conceptual

Daigneault, Sylvie 341 Wellesley Street E, Toronto, ON Canada M4X 1H2 . . . . . (416) 961-0681
Dailey, Eileen 4929 Lisette Avenue, St. Louis, MO 63109 . . . . . (314) 832-1335
Daily, Don 57 Academy Road, Bala Cynwyd, PA 19004-2501 . . . . . (610) 664-5729
Daily, Renee Quintal 57 Academy Road, Bala Cynwyd, PA 19004-2501 . . . . . (610) 664-5729
Dakins, Todd Represented By: Nachreiner Boie Art Factory . . . . . (414) 785-1940
Daley, Joann Represented By: Kimberley Boege . . . . . (602) 265-4389
Dallas Graphics 806 Fig Tree Lane, Brandon, FL 33511 . . . . . (813) 681-6505 • (800) 872-3367
Daly, Bob Represented By: Three in a Box . . . . . (416) 367-2446
Daly, Carla Represented By: Alan Lynch Artists . . . . . (908) 813-8718
Daly, Jim Represented By: Carol Bancroft & Friends . . . . . (203) 748-4823

DALY, MONA Page 10
2388 Silver Ridge Drive, Reno, NV 89509 • Fax (702) 825-4592 **(702) 826-3862 • (888) 220-3909**
Represented By: Das Grup **(310) 540-5958**
e-mail: mweirdaly@aol.com • Website: http://members.aol.com/mweirdaly
Specialties: Digital; Food; Icons; People

Dammer, Mike 350 W Ontario Street, Chicago, IL 60610 . . . . . (312) 943-4995
Represented By: Steve Edsey & Sons . . . . . (312) 527-0351
Dandy, Jim 36 W Palmdale Drive, Tempe, AZ 85282 . . . . . (602) 829-8992
Represented By: Irmeli Holmberg . . . . . (212) 545-9155
Represented By: Ceci Bartels Associates . . . . . (314) 781-7377
Represented By: Kimberley Boege . . . . . (602) 265-4389
Dangelico, Vittorio Represented By: Hankins & Tegenborg Ltd. . . . . . (212) 867-8092
Daniels, Sid Represented By: Jennifer Embler Represents, Inc. . . . . . (954) 760-4195
Daniels & Daniels Represented By: Carol Chislovsky Design, Inc. . . . . . (212) 677-9100
Danisi, Joe Represented By: Hankins & Tegenborg Ltd. . . . . . (212) 867-8092
Dann, Penny Represented By: Sally Heflin . . . . . (212) 366-1893
Dannenburg, Thomas 407 Mill Street, Richmond Hill, ON Canada L4C 4C1 . . . . . (905) 884-9166
Danz, David Represented By: Sandy Danz . . . . . (530) 622-3218
Darby, Janet Represented By: Cliff Knecht . . . . . (412) 761-5666
DaRold, Dave P.O. Box 5000, Davis, CA 95617 . . . . . (530) 758-1379
216 F Street #145, Davis, CA 95616
Darrow, David 532 N Rosemary Lane, Burbank, CA 91505-3255. . . . . . (618) 972-9968 • (800) 597-9132
Daste, Larry Represented By: Evelyne Johnson Associates . . . . . (212) 532-0928
Daugavietis, Ruta 5301 N Lakewood Avenue, Chicago, IL 60640. . . . . . (773) 334-8213
Daugherty, John Represented By: Spencer Church . . . . . (206) 860-9239
Davalos, Felipe Represented By: Publishers' Graphics . . . . . (203) 797-8188
Davick, Linda 4805 Hilldale Drive, Knoxville, TN 37914 . . . . . (423) 546-1020
Davidson, Andrew Represented By: Sally Heflin . . . . . (212) 366-1893
Davidson, Dennis Represented By: SI International . . . . . (212) 254-4996
Davidson Graphics 18551 Cocqui Road, Apple Valley, CA 92307 . . . . . (760) 242-4635
Davidson/Dogstar, Rodney 626 54th Street S, Birmingham, AL 35212 . . . . . (205) 591-BARK
Davies, Jim Represented By: Suzanne Craig Represents, Inc. . . . . . (918) 749-9424
Davies, Simon Old School Whitecross, Cornwall, England TR20 8BT 44 173 674 1105
Davis, Allen Represented By: SI International . . . . . (212) 254-4996
Davis, Dennas 904 Sutton Hill Road, Nashville, TN 37204. . . . . . (615) 386-0444
Davis, Gary One Cedar Place, Wakefield, MA 01880 . . . . . (781) 245-2628
Davis, Jack E. Represented By: Richard Solomon . . . . . (212) 683-1362
Davis, Michael Represented By: Mendola Ltd. . . . . . (212) 986-5680
Davis, Nancy Represented By: Jacqueline Dedell, Inc. . . . . . (212) 741-2539
Represented By: Sharon Dodge & Associates . . . . . (206) 284-4701
Davis, Nelle 20 E 17th Street, 4th Flr., New York, NY 10003 . . . . . (212) 807-7737
Davis, Paul 14 E Fourth Street #504, New York, NY 10012. . . . . . (212) 420-8789
Davis, Will New York, NY 10019 . . . . . (212) 582-0023
Represented By: American Artists . . . . . (212) 682-2462

DAWDY, SEAN Page 400
73 Bruce Street, Cambridge, ON Canada N1R 2E6 • Fax (519) 623-5296 **(519) 623-5296**
Specialties: Advertising; Children; Editorial

Dawson, Henk 3519 170th Place NE, Bellevue, WA 98008 . . . . . (425) 882-3303
Dawson, John Represented By: Fran Seigel . . . . . (212) 486-9644
Day, Brant Represented By: Kolea Baker Artists Representative. . . . . . (206) 784-1136
Day, Bruce 6080 Arney Lane, Boise, ID 83703 . . . . . (208) 853-8336
Day, Danny 14428 Janal Way, San Diego, CA 92129 . . . . . (619) 672-2528
Day, Douglas 240 Ocho Rios Way, Oak Park, CA 91301-5539 . . . . . (818) 879-1431
Day, Larry 5325 Cumnor Road, Downers Grove, IL 60515. . . . . . (630) 969-2368
Represented By: Christina Tugeau . . . . . (203) 438-7307
Day, Rob Indianapolis, IN 46220 . . . . . (317) 253-9000
Day, Sam P.O. Box 4425, Seattle, WA 98104 . . . . . (206) 382-7413
Dayal, Antar 1666 Las Canoas Road, Santa Barbara, CA 93105 . . . . . (805) 965-5988
Represented By: Shelley Flanders . . . . . (805) 682-6775
De Amicis, John 35 S Durst Drive, Milltown, NJ 08850 . . . . . (732) 249-4937
De Angelis, Tom 862 Dovington Court, Hoffman Estates, IL 60194 . . . . . (847) 843-0653
De Cerchio, Joseph Represented By: Creative Freelancers . . . . . (800) 398-9544

De Groat, Diane 1350 Avenue of the Americas, New York, NY 10019 . . . . (212) 261-6500
De Kiefte, Kees Represented By: Publishers' Graphics . . . . (203) 797-8188
De La Hoz, D'Ann 6995 NW 82nd Avenue #32, Miami, FL 33166 . . . . (305) 592-6887
De Luz, Tony 8102 N Madrid Drive, Tucson, AZ 85704 . . . . (520) 531-9113
Represented By: Hedge Graphics . . . . (818) 244-0110
De Michiell, Robert 250 W 85th Street, New York, NY 10024 . . . . (212) 769-9192
De Musee, Christina 4224 Glencoe Avenue, Marina Del Ray, CA 90292 . . . . (310) 397-1119
De Seve, Peter 25 Park Place, Brooklyn, NY 11217 . . . . (718) 398-8099
Dea, Patrick 372 Ste-Catherine Quest #419, Montreal, PQ Canada H3B 1A2 . . . . (514) 875-1301
Deadpan Studios 1719 Fairway Drive, Newton, NC 28658 . . . . (704) 612-6170 • (704) 466-0556
Deal, Jim Represented By: SI International . . . . (212) 254-4996
Dean, Bruce 23211 Leonora Drive, Woodland Hills, CA 91367 . . . . (818) 716-5632
Represented By: Nancy George . . . . (805) 688-3772
Dean, Glenn 530 Route 517, Sussex, NJ 07461 . . . . (201) 827-7350
Dean, Mike 2001 Sul Ross, Houston, TX 77098 . . . . (713) 527-0295
Represented By: Joel Harlib Associates, Inc. . . . . (312) 573-1370
DeAnda, Ruben Represented By: Lehmen/Dabney, Inc. . . . . (206) 325-8595
Dearstyne, John 10 La Purisima Rancho, Santa Margarita, CA 92688 . . . . (714) 589-6447
Represented By: Rhyne Represents . . . . (303) 871-9166
Represented By: Nancy Bacher . . . . (612) 786-1200
Dearth, Greg Represented By: Scott Hull Associates . . . . (937) 433-8383
Dearwater Illustration 5650 Kirby Drive #255, Houston, TX 77005 . . . . (713) 660-8513
Deas, Michael 39 Sidney Place, Brooklyn Heights, NY 11201 . . . . (718) 852-5630
New Orleans, LA 70130 . . . . (504) 524-3957
DeCarlo, Dan 1570 First Avenue, Ste. 6C, New York, NY 10028 . . . . (212) 879-8660
Decoster, Jeffrey 3530 A 22nd Street, San Francisco, CA 94114 . . . . (415) 206-9430
DeCristoforo, Jennifer Represented By: Square Moon . . . . (510) 253-9451
Deeter, Catherine P.O. Box 401, Templeton, CA 93465-0401 . . . . (805) 434-2741
Represented By: Betsy Hillman . . . . (415) 381-4728
DeFelice, Ron Represented By: Hankins & Tegenborg Ltd. . . . . (212) 867-8092
Defreitas, Peter Represented By: Irmeli Holmberg . . . . (212) 545-9155
Degen, Paul Represented By: Riley Illustration . . . . (212) 989-8770
DeGrace, John 3643 N Lakewood Street, Chicago, IL 60613 . . . . (773) 935-7306
Deigan, Jim Represented By: Cliff Knecht . . . . (412) 761-5666
Dekle, Merritt Represented By: Alan Lynch Artists . . . . (908) 813-8718
Del Rossi, Ken 25 Ninth Avenue, Farmingdale, NY 11735 . . . . (516) 499-7756
Del Rossi, Ric 156 Fifth Avenue, Ste. 617, New York, NY 10010 . . . . (212) 243-1333
DeLancey, Alison 2305 Ashland Street #C, Ashland, OR 97520 . . . . (800) 435-6509
DeLapine, Jim Represented By: Creative Freelancers . . . . (800) 398-9544
Delessert, Etienne Box 1689, Lakeville, CT 06039 . . . . (860) 435-0061
Delhomme, Jean-Philippe Represented By: Barbara Schlager, Inc. . . . . (212) 941-1777

DELICH, DONNA — Page 14
889 Williams Place, Hartsville, PA 18974 • Fax (215) 674-8670 — **(215) 674-2506**
Specialties: Acrylic; Editorial

Dellorco, Chris 32220 Oakshore Drive, Westlake Village, CA 91361 . . . . (818) 889-7003
Represented By: Mendola Ltd. . . . . (212) 986-5680
Represented By: Ceci Bartels Associates . . . . (314) 781-7377
Represented By: Rita Gatlin Represents . . . . (800) 924-7881
Delmonte, Steve 328 W Delavan Avenue, Buffalo, NY 14213 . . . . (716) 883-6086
DeLouise, Dan 15 Youngs Road, Gloucester, MA 01930 . . . . (978) 282-1379
DeLoy, Dee 8166 Jellison Street, Orlando, FL 32825 . . . . (407) 273-8365
Delsol, Lenin Represented By: Peter Kuehnel & Associates . . . . (312) 642-6499
DeMarco, Kim Represented By: Lilla Rogers Studio . . . . (781) 641-2787
Demers, Don Represented By: Frank & Jeff Lavaty . . . . (212) 427-5632

DEMPSEY, PAUL — Pages 252-253
Represented By: Deborah Wolfe — **(215) 232-6666**
Website: www.deborahwolfeltd.com • Specialties: Advertising; Computer; Digital; Editorial; Lettering; Product; Realism; Still Life; Technical; 3D

DeMusee, Christina Represented By: Kolea Baker Artists Representative . . . . (206) 784-1136
DeMuth, Roger 59 Chenango Street, Cazenovia, NY 13035 . . . . (315) 655-8599
Denise & Fernando Represented By: Mendola Ltd. . . . . (212) 986-5680

Densmore, Dee Represented By: Buck & Kane . . . . . (212) 631-0009
Deodato, Mike Represented By: Glass House Graphics . . . . . (304) 232-5641
DePalma, Mary Newell 45 Bradfield Avenue, Boston, MA 02131 . . . . . (617) 327-6241

DEPEW, BOB Pages 168,192
Represented By: American Artists **(212) 682-2462**
e-mail: info@amerartists.com • Website: www.amerartists.com • Specialty: Digital

Dervaux, Isabelle Represented By: Riley Illustration . . . . . (212) 989-8770
Desaix, Deborah Represented By: Kirchoff/Wohlberg, Inc. . . . . . (212) 644-2020
DeSantis, Laura Represented By: Leighton & Company, Inc. . . . . . (978) 921-0887
Design Sense Studios 341 Van Buren Street, North Babylon, NY 11703 . . . . . (516) 587-0623
Designation Inc. 53 Spring Street, 5th Flr., New York, NY 10012 . . . . . (212) 226-6024
Desktop Staffing, Inc. 1904 Capri, Schaumburg, IL 60193 . . . . . (847) 352-4340
Detrich, Susan 253 Baltic Street, Brooklyn, NY 11201 . . . . . (718) 237-9174
Detwiler, Darius 5018 Fawn Lake, San Antonio, TX 78244 . . . . . (210) 662-0603
DeVaney, Richard 460 W 42nd Street, 2nd Flr., New York, NY 10036 . . . . . (212) 967-6655
Devarj Associates, Inc., Silva 116 W Illinois #7E, Chicago, IL 60610 . . . . . (312) 266-1358
Devaud, Jacques Represented By: Carol Guenzi Agents, Inc. . . . . . (800) 417-5120

DEVER, ERIC Pages 325,420
Represented By: Michele Manasse **(215) 862-2091**
e-mail: mmanasse@new-work.com • Website: www.voicenet.com/~mmanasse • Specialties: Advertising; Architecture/Interiors; Black & White; Collage; Editorial; Mixed Media; People; Portraiture; Realism; Water Color

Dever Designs/Fresh Art 1054 W Street, Laurel, MD 20707 . . . . . (301) 776-2812 • (800) 373-7438
DeVito, Grace 170 E Fourth Street, New Castle, DE 19720 . . . . . (302) 322-1224
DeVries, Dave Represented By: Shannon Associates . . . . . (212) 831-5650
Dewar, Ken Represented By: Link . . . . . (416) 530-1500
Dewar, Nick Represented By: Kate Larkworthy Artist Rep. Ltd. . . . . . (212) 633-1310
DeWatt & Associates 210 E Michigan #403, Milwaukee, WI 53202 . . . . . (414) 276-7990
Dey, Lorraine 45 Johnson Lane N, Jackson, NJ 08527 . . . . . (732) 928-5510
Di Marco, Anthony 301 Aris Avenue, Metairie, LA 70005 . . . . . (504) 833-3122

DI PIETRO, HUGO Pages 348-349
Represented By: Sal Barracca Associates **(212) 889-2400**
Specialties: Digital; Caricature; Humour

Diamond, Donna Represented By: Hankins & Tegenborg Ltd. . . . . . (212) 867-8092
Diaz, Cindy Ann 1126 Rodman, Apt. 1B, Philadephia, PA 19147 . . . . . (215) 238-0475
Diaz, David 1697 Robin Place, Carlsbad, CA 92009 . . . . . (760) 438-0070 • (800) 474-ICON
DiCesare, Joe 27 Sterling Place, Brooklyn, NY 11217 . . . . . (718) 622-4157

DICKENS DESIGN, INC., HOLLY Page 37
50 E Bellevue #402, Chicago, IL 60611 • Fax (312) 280-1725 **(312) 280-0777**
e-mail: HolDickens@aol.com • Specialty: Lettering & Design

Dickenson, Rebecca Represented By: Carol Bancroft & Friends . . . . . (203) 748-4823
Dickert, Sheryl Represented By: Ceci Bartels Associates . . . . . (314) 781-7377

DIDIER, PAUL Page 277
Represented By: Famous Frames **(310) 642-2721**
e-mail: info@famousframes.com • Website: www.famousframes.com • Specialties: Animation; Storyboards

Didion, Nancy Represented By: Melissa Turk & The Artist Network . . . . . (914) 368-8606
Diefendorf, Cathy Represented By: Mendola Ltd. . . . . . (212) 986-5680
Diercksmeier, Robert J. 550 E McKellips Road Ste. 2072, Mesa, AZ 85203 . . . . . (602) 962-4864
Dietz, James 2203 13th Avenue E, Seattle, WA 98102 . . . . . (206) 325-1151
Dietz, Mike Represented By: Shannon Associates . . . . . (212) 831-5650
Diez-Luckie, Cathy 6278 Clive Avenue, Oakland, CA 94611 . . . . . (510) 482-5600
DiFate, Vincent 12 Ritter Drive, Wappingers Falls, NY 12590 . . . . . (914) 297-6842
Diffenderfer, Ed 32 Cabernet Court, Lafayette, CA 94549 . . . . . (510) 284-8235
DiFilippi, Thomas 710 Horatio Avenue, Franklin Square, NY 11010 . . . . . (516) 489-2449
DiGennaro, Robert 10 Godfrey Road W, Weston, CT 06883 . . . . . (203) 454-9658
Digital Art 3166 E Palmdale Boulevard #120, Palmdale, CA 93550 . . . . . (805) 265-8092

DILLARD, ELAINE
P.O. Box 1171, Monroe, GA 30655
Represented By: Susan Wells & Associates
Specialties: Calligraphy; Lettering
Pages 373,379,454
(770) 267-8786
(404) 255-1430

Dillon, Kathleen 3710 Murworth Drive, Houston, TX 77025 . . . . . (713) 661-5205
Dillon, Leo & Diane 221 Kane Street, Brooklyn, NY 11231 . . . . . (718) 624-0023
DiMare, Paul Represented By: Frank & Jeff Lavaty . . . . . (212) 427-5632
Dimensional Illustrators, Inc. 362 Second Street Pike, Southampton, PA 18966 . . . . . (215) 953-1415
Dinges, Michael 53 W Jackson #340, Chicago, IL 60604 . . . . . (312) 663-3933
Represented By: Jim Hanson Artist Agent . . . . . (312) 337-7770
Dinham, Sian 14 Beechdale Road, Newport, South Wales, England NP9 8AE 44 163 327 8035
Dininno, Steve Represented By: David Goldman Agency . . . . . (212) 807-6627
Dinser, John 9308 Merrill Road, Whitmore Lake, MI 48189 . . . . . (734) 449-5969
Dinyer, Eric Represented By: Harriet Kastaris & Associates . . . . . (314) 773-2600
Represented By: Repertoire . . . . . (972) 761-0500
Dionisi, Sandra 37 Hanna Avenue #13A-200, Toronto, ON Canada M6K 1W9 . . . . . (416) 588-4588
Diorio Associates 2829 Timmons #163, Houston, TX 77027 . . . . . (713) 960-0393
DiPietro, Lisa 40 Kings Place, Brooklyn, NY 11223 . . . . . (718) 376-8097
Dirkes, Jessica 4223 Hymount Avenue, Sarasota, FL 34231 . . . . . (941) 924-7255
DiRubbio, Jennifer 19 Prairie Lane, Levittown, NY 11756 . . . . . (516) 579-1872
Dismukes, John Taylor Represented By: Mendola Ltd. . . . . . (212) 986-5680
Dixon, Debra Spina Represented By: Freda Scott, Inc. . . . . . (415) 398-9121
Dixon, Don 2519 Cedar Avenue, Long Beach, CA 90806 . . . . . (562) 426-1644
Dodge, Bill Represented By: Hankins & Tegenborg Ltd. . . . . . (212) 867-8092
Dodge, Larry Represented By: Skidmore, Inc. . . . . . (248) 353-7722
Dodson, Bert Represented By: Publishers' Graphics . . . . . (203) 797-8188
Doheny, Dennis Represented By: Jae Wagoner . . . . . (310) 392-4877
Doktor, Patricia Represented By: Renee Kalish . . . . . (847) 864-6127
Dolack Gallery, Monte 139 W Front Street, Missoula, MT 59802 . . . . . (406) 549-3248
Dolobowsky, Mena Represented By: Carol Bancroft & Friends . . . . . (203) 748-4823
Dombrowski, Bob Represented By: Artworks . . . . . (212) 627-1554
Domingo, Ray Represented By: Kelly Reps . . . . . (813) 871-3929
Doney, Todd Represented By: Pema Browne Ltd. . . . . . (914) 985-2936

DONIGER, NANCY
109 Eighth Avenue, Brooklyn, NY 11215 • Fax (718) 399-8498
e-mail: doniger@earthlink.net • Website: www.shadow.net/~jerryd
Specialties: Advertising; Children; Corporate; Digital; Editorial
Page 68
(718) 399-8666

Donley, Scott 2734 Rothgeb Drive, Raleigh, NC 27609 . . . . . (919) 781-4695
Donnelly, Martha 131 NW 4th Street, Ste. 223, Corvalis, OR 97330 . . . . . (541) 753-3148
Donner, Carol Represented By: Renard Represents . . . . . (212) 490-2450
Donovan, Cash Represented By: Famous Frames . . . . . (310) 642-2721
Donovan, John 1456 N Dayton, Chicago, IL 60622 . . . . . (312) 649-9144
Doody, Jim Represented By: Hall & Associates . . . . . (213) 962-2500
Dooling, Michael 161 Wyoming Avenue, Audubon, NJ 08106 . . . . . (609) 546-6507
Doolittle, Troy Represented By: Image Mill . . . . . (515) 490-6110
Doquilo, Jesse James 1512 Alaskan Way, Seattle, WA 98101 . . . . . (206) 682-6221
Doret, Michael Hollywood, CA 90068 . . . . . (213) 467-1900
Dorsey, Bob Represented By: Pema Browne Ltd. . . . . . (914) 985-2936
Doty, Eldon Represented By: HK Portfolio . . . . . (212) 675-5719
Dotzler Creative Arts 4202 S 90th Street, Omaha, NE 68127 . . . . . (402) 592-1901
Doucet, Bob 4181 Rose Crescent, West Vancouver, BC Canada V7V 2N6 . . . . . (604) 925-6693
Douglas, Nancy Represented By: Mark Sherrah . . . . . (416) 972-6161
Dowd, Jason Represented By: Mendola Ltd. . . . . . (212) 986-5680
Dowd, Ken 9322 Olive Boulevard, St. Louis, MO 63132 . . . . . (314) 997-2655
Dowling, Mike 1729 S Wayland Avenue, Sioux Falls, SD 57105 . . . . . (605) 336-1745
Downing, Julie 1674 Page Street, San Fransisco, CA 94117 . . . . . (415) 252-9594
Downing, Ray Represented By: Artco . . . . . (212) 889-8777
Downs, Richard 15394 Wet Hill Road, Nevada City, CA 95959 . . . . . (530) 470-0435
Doyle, John Carroll 354 ½ King Street, Charleston, SC 29401 . . . . . (803) 723-3269
Doyle, Pat 333 N Michigan Avenue #932, Chicago, IL 60601 . . . . . (312) 263-2065
Drawson, Blair 14 Leuty Avenue, Toronto, ON Canada M4E 2R3 . . . . . (416) 693-7774
Represented By: Reactor Art & Design Ltd. . . . . . (416) 703-1913

Dreibelbis, Ellen Represented By: Carol Bancroft & Friends . . . . . (203) 748-4823
Dreier, Kyle Dallas, TX 75206 . . . . . (214) 874-0407
Drescher, Henrik Represented By: Reactor Art & Design Ltd. . . . . . (416) 703-1913
Dressel, Peggy 11 Rockaway Avenue, Oakland, NJ 07436 . . . . . (201) 337-2143
Drew, Kim 4033 Aurora Avenue N, Seattle, WA 98103 . . . . . (206) 633-3445
Drew/Brook/Cormack Represented By: Melissa Turk & The Artist Network. . . . . (914) 368-8606
Drobek, Carol 1260 Broadway #106, San Francisco, CA 94109 . . . . . (415) 776-6188
Droppa, Jill Represented By: Evelyne Johnson Associates . . . . . (212) 532-0928
Drovetto, Richard Represented By: Claudia Miller Artists Unlimited . . . . . (561) 995-9444
Drucker, Mort Represented By: Artco. . . . . . (212) 889-8777
Dryden, Jim Represented By: The Schuna Group . . . . . (612) 631-8480
Dryden, Patty Represented By: Famous Frames . . . . . (310) 642-2721

DRYDEN, ROD Page 277
Represented By: Famous Frames **(310) 642-2721**
e-mail: info@famousframes.com • Website: www.famousframes.com • Specialties: Animation; Storyboards

Dubin, Jill Represented By: Evelyne Johnson Associates . . . . . (212) 532-0928
Dubisch, Michael 15 Sieber Road, Kerhonkson, NY 12446. . . . . . (914) 626-4386

DUBOIS, GERARD Pages 24-25
Represented By: Marlena Agency **(609) 252-9405**
e-mail: marzena@bellatlantic.net • Website: http://members.bellatlantic.net/~marzena
Specialties: Corporate; Conceptual; Editorial; Whimsical

Dubois, Tom Represented By: David Montagano & Associates. . . . . . (312) 527-3283
Dubrowski, Ken 845 Moraine Street, Marshfield, MA 02050 . . . . . (617) 837-3457
Ducak, Danilo Represented By: Hankins & Tegenborg Ltd. . . . . . (212) 867-8092
Dudash, C. Michael RR #1, Box 2803, Moretown, VT 05660 . . . . . (802) 496-6400
Dudley, Don 2055 Magnolia Avenue, Petaluma, CA 94952 . . . . . (707) 763-5809
Dudzinski, Andrzej 54 E 81st Street, New York, NY 10028 . . . . . (212) 772-3098

DUFFY, AMANDA Page 120
Rat Under Paper, Inc., 135 Presley Avenue, Toronto, ON Canada M1L 3P9 • Fax (416) 750-0083 **(416) 755-4447**
e-mail: ratsite@earthlink.net • Specialties: Caricature; Conceptual; Corporate;
Editorial; Humour; Lettering; Mixed Media; People

Duffy, Daniel Represented By: Sally Heflin . . . . . (212) 366-1893
Duggan, Lee 3780 Schooner Ridge, Alpharetta, GA 30202 . . . . . (770) 664-1609
Duilio, Mario 5088 W Colonial Courts, Greenfield, WI 53220. . . . . . (414) 541-9221
Duillo, Elaine 146 Dartmouth Drive, Hicksville, NY 11801-3423 . . . . . (516) 681-8820
Duke, Chris Represented By: Frank & Jeff Lavaty. . . . . . (212) 427-5632
Duke, Larry Represented By: Joel Harlib Associates, Inc. . . . . . (312) 573-1370
Represented By: Pat Hackett Artist Representative . . . . . (206) 447-1600
Duke, William 610 22nd Street, Ste. 308, San Francisco, CA 94107 . . . . . (415) 487-1477
Dunaway, Joyce 3000 Harkness Drive, Plano, TX 75093 . . . . . (972) 608-0807
Dunbar, Fiona Represented By: HK Portfolio . . . . . (212) 675-5719
Dundee, Angela Represented By: Lindgren & Smith. . . . . . (212) 397-7330
Dunlap, Leslie Represented By: Publishers' Graphics . . . . . (203) 797-8188
Dunlavey, Rob 8 Front Street, South Natick, MA 01760 . . . . . (508) 651-7503
Dunn, Katherine Represented By: Jan Collier Represents, Inc. . . . . . (415) 383-9026

DUNNICK, REGAN Pages 86-87
Represented By: Lindgren & Smith **(212) 397-7330**
e-mail: inquiry@lindgrensmith.com • Website: www.lindgrensmith.com

Dupays, Nicky Represented By: American Artists . . . . . (212) 682-2462

DUPONT, LANE Pages 283-285,455,459
Represented By: John Brewster Creative Services **(203) 226-4724**
e-mail: creative.svcs@snet.net • Website: www.brewstercreative.com • Specialties: Advertising;
Architecture/Interiors; Black & White; Children; Computer; Digital; Editorial; Maps & Charts; Pastels; People: Technical

Durk, Jim 25108 Wolf Road, Bay Village, OH 44140 . . . . . (440) 871-5835
Represented By: SI International. . . . . . (212) 254-4996

Durrell, Julie Represented By: Publishers' Graphics . . . . (203) 797-8188
Dutkiewicz, Michael Represented By: Glass House Graphics . . . . (304) 232-5641
DuVal, Janee 5009 Stanley Drive, The Colony, TX 75056. . . . . (214) 625-6761
Dverin, Anatoly Represented By: Bernstein & Andriulli, Inc.. . . . . (212) 682-1490
Dvorak, Phillip 632 Steiner Street, San Francisco, CA 94117 . . . . (415) 487-1923
Represented By: Chip Caton . . . . (860) 523-4562
Represented By: Marion Moskowitz Represents . . . . (212) 517-4919
Dvorak, Tim 36 Lexington Drive, Croton on Hudson, NY 10520 . . . . (914) 271-7706
Dwyer, Elizabeth Represented By: Creative Connection . . . . (410) 360-5981

DYE, GREGORY Page 143
7952 W Quarto Drive, Littleton, CO 80128 • Fax (303) 904-2909 **(303) 933-0340**
Represented By: Tom Maloney **(312) 704-0500**
Specialties: Advertising; Conceptual; Corporate; Editorial; Pastels

Dyekman, James 738 Peekskill Hollow Road, Putnam Valley, NY 10579 . . . . (914) 528-6545
Dykeman, Sharen Represented By: Carol Bancroft & Friends . . . . (203) 748-4823
Dykes, John S. 515 Hill Farm Road, Fairfield, CT 06430 . . . . (203) 222-8150
Dynamic Duo Studio 95 Kings Highway S, Westport, CT 06880 . . . . (203) 454-4518
Represented By: Comp Art Plus . . . . (212) 279-0800
Dzedzy, John Represented By: Penny & Stermer Group . . . . (212) 505-9342
Dzielak, Dennis 350 W Ontario Street #600, Chicago, IL 60610 . . . . (312) 642-1241
Eagle, Bruce Represented By: Suzanne Craig Represents, Inc.. . . . . (918) 749-9424
Eagle, Cameron 1911 NW 29th Street, Oklahoma City, OK 73106 . . . . (405) 525-6676
Eastman, Bryant Represented By: Hankins & Tegenborg Ltd.. . . . . (212) 867-8092
Eastman, Jody Represented By: Liz Sanders Agency . . . . (714) 495-3664
Eastwood, Matt 28 Shelton, Covent Garden, London, England UK WC2H 44 171 240 2077
Eastwood, Peter 938 N Grove Avenue, Oak Park, IL 60302. . . . . (708) 445-1435
Ebel, Alex 30 Newport Road, Yonkers, NY 10710 . . . . (914) 961-4058
Represented By: Joel Harlib Associates, Inc. . . . . (312) 573-1370
Eberbach, Andrea Represented By: Scott Hull Associates . . . . (937) 433-8383
Ebersol, Rob 734 Clairemont Avenue, Decatur, GA 30030 . . . . (404) 687-8889
Edelson, Wendy Represented By: Susan & Company . . . . (206) 232-7873
Edens, John Represented By: Creative Freelancers . . . . (800) 398-9544
Edgerton, Tom 911 Elizabethan Drive, Greensboro, NC 27410. . . . . (336) 854-2816
Edholm, Michael Represented By: Artco . . . . (212) 889-8777
Edinjiklian, Teddy Represented By: Rosenthal Represents . . . . (818) 222-5445
Edison, Susan Represented By: Connie Koralik Associates Represents . . . . (312) 944-5680
Edmon, Jim 15 Richmond Avenue, Lexington, KY 40502 . . . . (606) 269-8193 • (800) 530-5678
Edmonds, Laurie P.O. Box 1592, Madison Square Station, New York, NY 10159. . . . . (212) 477-5693
Edsey, Michael Represented By: Steve Edsey & Sons. . . . . (312) 527-0351

EDWARD, ROBERT Page 201
Represented By: American Artists **(212) 682-2462**
Represented By: Ian Flemming Associates
e-mail: info@amerartists.com • Website: www.amerartists.com

Edwards, James Represented By: Sheryl Beranbaum. . . . . (401) 737-8591

EDWARDS, KARL Pages 386,451
1109 Ripple Avenue, Pacific Grove, CA 93950 • Fax (831) 647-9110 **(831) 647-9100**
e-mail: illustration@karledwards.com • Website: www.karledwards.com • Specialties: Advertising; Cartoon; Humour

Edwards, Les Represented By: Alan Lynch Artists . . . . (908) 813-8718
Edwards, Ron 73-4685 Kohana Iki #5B, Kai Lua Kona, HI 96740. . . . . (808) 325-0144

EFFLER, JIM Pages 168,180
Represented By: American Artists **(212) 682-2462**
e-mail: info@amerartists.com • Website: www.amerartists.com • Specialties: Animals; Realism

Eggleston-Wirtz, Kate Represented By: Jaz & Jaz. . . . . (206) 633-3445
Egielski, Richard 27 Amsterdam Road, Milford, NJ 08848 . . . . (908) 995-2874

EIBNER, FREDERIC Page 232
Represented By: Sharpshooter Creative Representation, Inc. **(416) 703-5300**
e-mail: shooter@the-wire.com • Website: www.portfolios.com/illustrators
Specialties: Advertising; Annual Report; Conceptual; Corporate; Food; Icons; Illustrative; Landscape; Poster

Eidrigevicius, Stasys 211 E 89th Street, Ste. A-1, New York, NY 10128 .... (212) 289-5514
Eisler, Sarah Represented By: Liz Sanders Agency .... (714) 495-3664
Eiss, Holly Represented By: K&K Art & Associates .... (612) 338-9138
Eitzen, Allan Represented By: Publishers' Graphics .... (203) 797-8188
Eksioglu, Gurbuz 455 W 23rd Street #8D, New York, NY 10011 .... (212) 366-1893

ELDRIDGE, GARY Pages 52,428
Represented By: Renard Represents **(212) 490-2450**
e-mail: renardreps@earthlink.net • Website: www.renardrepresents.com
Specialties: Annual Report; Conceptual; Corporate; Editorial; Montage

Eldridge, Marion 47 Liberty Drive, North Billerica, MA 01862 .... (978) 667-5986
Electric Soup Represented By: Artco .... (212) 889-8777
Represented By: Repertoire .... (972) 761-0500
Electro Entertainment Group 4037 E Independence Boulevard, Charlotte, NC 28205 .... (704) 567-1145
Represented By: Artline .... (704) 376-7609
Elledge, Leslie 6021 Christie Avenue, Emeryville, CA 94608 .... (510) 540-7901
Ellinger, Debra S 4930 Pretty Lake Road, Dousman, WI 53118 .... (414) 965-2221
Elliot, Linda Represented By: Creative Connection .... (410) 360-5981
Elliott, David Represented By: Barbara Gordon Associates Ltd. .... (212) 686-3514
Elliott, JoAnn 700 Seaview Drive, Crystal Beach, FL 34681 .... (972) 231-5332
Elliott, Mark Represented By: Shannon Associates .... (212) 831-5650
Ellis, Jon 1622 Brownsville Road, Langhorne, PA 19047 .... (215) 750-6180

ELLIS, STEVE Pages 269,434
Redondo Beach, CA 90277 • Fax (310) 318-9079 **(310) 792-1888**
Represented By: Christine Prapas **(503) 658-7070**
Represented By: Penny & Stermer Group **(212) 505-9342**
e-mail: steveeboi@aol.com • Specialties: Animals; Character; Computer; Digital;
Graphic Design/Illustration; Lettering; People

Ellis, Victoria 1 Bellevue Cottages, Westbury, Bristol, England BS9 3AQ 44 117 962 0178
Ellis, Wendi Tregiddle Farm, Gunwalloe, Helston, Cornwall, England TR12 7QW 44 132 657 2726
Ellison, Chris Represented By: Will Sumpter & Associates .... (770) 460-8438
Ellison, Jake Represented By: Berendsen & Associates .... (513) 861-1400
Ellison, Pauline Represented By: Bernstein & Andriulli, Inc. .... (212) 682-1490
Ellithorpe, Chris 490 Dover Drive, Roselle, IL 60172 .... (630) 924-7938
Represented By: Alexander/Pollard, Inc. .... (800) 347-0734
Ellsworth, Kevin 2224 N 38th Avenue, Hollywood, FL 33021 .... (954) 967-0409
Elmer, Richard 504 E 11th Street #FE1A, New York, NY 10009 .... (212) 598-4024
Represented By: Conrad Represents, Inc. .... (415) 921-7140
Elmore, Larry Represented By: Woody Coleman Presents, Inc. .... (216) 661-4222

ELOQUI Pages 254-255
100 G Street, Mountain Lake Park, MD 21550 • Fax (301) 334-4186 **(301) 334-4086**
e-mail: eloqui@aol.com • Website: www.eloqui.com • Specialties: Advertising; Corporate; Editorial;
Food; People; Portraiture; Product; Realism; Sports

Elsdale, Bob Represented By: Mendola Ltd. .... (212) 986-5680
Elsner Associates P.O. Box 5363, Takoma Park, MD 20913 .... (301) 270-6970
Elwell, Tristan Represented By: Shannon Associates .... (212) 831-5650
Ember, Dave Represented By: Mary Holland & Company .... (602) 263-8990
Represented By: Carol Guenzi Agents, Inc. .... (800) 417-5120
Ember, Kathi Represented By: HK Portfolio .... (212) 675-5719
Emberley, Ed & Barbara 6 Water Street, Ipswich, MA 01938 .... (508) 356-2805
Emmert, Eva Ashley Represented By: Jae Wagoner .... (310) 392-4877
Emmett, Bruce Represented By: Artworks .... (212) 627-1554
Emmons, Barbara 504 Hilldale Drive, Decatur, GA 30030 .... (404) 377-8950
Emmons, Jean 15648 94th Avenue SW, Vashon Island, WA 98070 .... (206) 567-5458
Endewelt, Jack 50 Riverside Drive, New York, NY 10024 .... (212) 877-0575

Endicott, Jim 3509 N College, Newberg, OR 97132 . . . . (503) 538-5466
Endom Design Services, Charles 395 Railroad Avenue #4, Pittsburgh, PA 94565 . . . . (925) 432-9397
256 MacArthur Avenue, Pittsburgh, CA 94565 . . . . (510) 427-2348
Enfield, Fred Represented By: Claudia Miller Artists Unlimited . . . . (561) 995-9444
Engleman, Jeremy A. 1350 N Hayworth Avenue #4, Los Angeles, CA 90046 . . . . (213) 851-6196
English, John 5844 Fontana Drive, Fairway, KS 66205 . . . . (913) 831-4830
Engstrom, Seth 816 Linden Avenue, Burlingame, CA 94010 . . . . (650) 579-0630
Enik, Ted 24 Charles Street #6, New York, NY 10014 . . . . (212) 924-1076
Enos, Randall 11 Court of Oaks, Westport, CT 06880 . . . . (203) 227-7684
Enriquez, Robert 710 Wilshire Boulevard, Ste. 510, Santa Monica, CA 90401 . . . . (310) 394-6379
Epic Studios 121 S Road, Chester, NJ 07930 . . . . (908) 879-6583
Epkes, Greg Represented By: Hedge Graphics . . . . (818) 244-0110
Epstein, Len Represented By: Leyden Diversified . . . . (215) 663-0587
Epstein-Eagle, Barbara Represented By: Square Moon . . . . (510) 253-9451
Erdogan, Yucel 65 Seventh Avenue #2, Brooklyn, NY 11217 . . . . (718) 789-7834
Erickson, Kerne Box 2175, Mission Viejo, CA 92690-0175 . . . . (714) 364-1141
Erickson, Marc 1045 Sansome Street #306, San Francisco, CA 94111 . . . . (415) 362-1214
Eriksson, Christopher Represented By: Carol Guenzi Agents, Inc. . . . . (800) 417-5120
Erlacher, Bill Represented By: Artists Associates . . . . (212) 755-1365
Ernster, Scott Represented By: Carol Chislovsky Design, Inc. . . . . (212) 677-9100
Ersland, William C. 220 W Poplar, Stillwater, MN 55082 . . . . (612) 430-1878
Escher Illustrations 6630 Lyndale Avenue S, Richfield, MN 55423 . . . . (612) 866-8732
Eskridge, Lynn 2351 W Northwest Highway #1100, Dallas, TX 75220 . . . . (214) 638-7255
Espinosa, Leo 150 W 25th Street #404, New York, NY 10001 . . . . (212) 462-4121
Estes, Kathleen Represented By: Air Studio . . . . (513) 721-1193

ETHERIDGE, JOHN Pages 82,463
4246 Trellis Crescent, Mississauga, ON Canada L5L 2M2 • Fax (905) 828-0283 **(905) 828-2879**
Specialties: Scratchboard; Woodcut

Ettlinger, Doris 10 Imlaydale Road, Hampton, NJ 08827 . . . . (908) 537-6322
Eugster, Diane 8855 Miamoore Avenue, Las Vegas, NV 89117 . . . . (702) 243-8950
Eureka Cartography 654 Pier Avenue, Santa Monica, CA 90405 . . . . (510) 845-6277
Evans, Brian Represented By: Carol Guenzi Agents, Inc. . . . . (800) 417-5120
Evans, Bruce Represented By: Leyden Diversified . . . . (215) 663-0587
Evans, Jan Represented By: Ann Koeffler Represents . . . . (213) 957-2327
Evans, Jonathan Represented By: Sharon Dodge & Associates . . . . (206) 284-4701
Evans, Leslie 15 Bay Street, Watertown, MA 02172 . . . . (617) 924-3058
Evans, Michael 9457 Danbury, Cypress, CA 90630 . . . . (714) 761-1333
Evans, Nate Represented By: Publishers' Graphics . . . . (203) 797-8188

EVANS, ROBERT Pages 133,135
1045 Sansome Street #306, San Francisco, CA 94111 • Fax (415) 397-5322 **(415) 397-5322**
Represented By: Sweet Represents **(415) 433-1222**
Specialties: Airbrush; Digital; Food; Realism

Evans, Shane Warren Represented By: Artco . . . . (212) 889-8777
Evans, Sid Represented By: McLean & Friends . . . . (404) 881-6627
Evanson, Ann 270 Thornhill Court, Barrington, IL 60010 . . . . (847) 277-7700
Everitt, Betsy Represented By: Harriet Kastaris & Associates . . . . (314) 773-2600
Evernden, Graham Represented By: Sally Heflin . . . . (212) 366-1893
Ewing, Carolyn Represented By: Evelyne Johnson Associates . . . . (212) 532-0928
Ewing, Richard 3966 Gaviota Avenue, Long Beach, CA 90807-3740 . . . . (562) 989-9509 • (888) 403-1004
Eyolfson, Norman Represented By: Sharpshooter Creative Rep Inc. . . . . (416) 703-5300

FABRE, JACQUES Pages 168,174
Represented By: American Artists **(212) 682-2462**
e-mail: info@amerartists.com • Website: www.amerartists.com

Fairman, Dolores Represented By: Jacqueline Dedell, Inc. . . . . (212) 741-2539
Fairweather, Sydney 3900 Kings Highway #3A, Brooklyn, NY 11234 . . . . (718) 253-1504
Faist, Rick Represented By: Art Source/Diane Barkley . . . . (914) 747-2220
Falcon Advertising Art P.O. Box 33063, Cleveland, OH 44133-0063 . . . . (216) 621-4327
Falkenstern, Lisa Represented By: Fran Seigel . . . . (212) 486-9644
Fallin, Ken 155 Riverside Drive #1B, New York, NY 10024 . . . . (212) 362-7646

Falls, Mark Represented By: Tonal Values . . . . . (214) 943-2569
Falquet, Joan Perrin Represented By: Hankins & Tegenborg Ltd. . . . . . (212) 867-8092
Fanning, Jim Represented By: Ravenhill Represents . . . . . (816) 333-0744
Faragher-Gomez, Patsy 1198 Santa Ynez, Los Osos, CA 93402 . . . . . (805) 528-4542
Faranak Represented By: Alan Lynch Artists . . . . . (908) 813-8718
Farber, Joan Represented By: Vicki Prentice Associates, Inc. . . . . . (212) 332-3460
Faricy, Patrick Represented By: Mason Illustration . . . . . (612) 729-1774
Represented By: Shannon Associates . . . . . (212) 831-5650

FARKAS, GABRIELLA Page 277
Represented By: Famous Frames **(310) 642-2721**
e-mail: info@famousframes.com • Website: www.famousframes.com • Specialties: Animation; Storyboards

Farley, Malcolm 7590 Indiana Street, Arvada, CO 80007 . . . . . (303) 420-9135
Farnham, Joe Represented By: Leighton & Company, Inc. . . . . . (978) 921-0887
Farquharson, Alexander 15 Heald Street, Pepperell, MA 01463 . . . . . (978) 433-9092
Farrar, David 4167 Ridgeway Lane, Knoxville, TN 37919 . . . . . (423) 588-0624
Farrell, Kevin Represented By: Famous Frames . . . . . (310) 642-2721
Farrell, Rick 3918 N Stevens Street, Tacoma, WA 98407 . . . . . (253) 752-8814

FARRELL, RUSSELL Pages 168,185
Represented By: American Artists **(212) 682-2462**
e-mail: info@amerartists.com • Website: www.amerartists.com

Farrington, Susan Represented By: Lilla Rogers Studio . . . . . (781) 641-2787
Farris, Jason 121 W Sixth Street, Byron, IL 61010 . . . . . (800) 887-7146
Fasolino, Peter 122 Second Street, Brooklyn, NY 11231 . . . . . (718) 834-6276
Fasolino, Teresa Represented By: The Newborn Group . . . . . (212) 260-6700
Fast, Ingo Represented By: Conrad Represents, Inc. . . . . . (415) 921-7140
Fastner & Larson 529 S Seventh Street, Minneapolis, MN 55415 . . . . . (612) 338-0959
Faulkner Illustration, Andrew 3020 Brideway #107, Sausalito, CA 94969 . . . . . (415) 332-3521
Faust, Clifford 322 W 57th Street #42P, New York, NY 10019 . . . . . (212) 581-9461
Faw, Jenny 29 W 19th Street, 4th Flr., New York, NY 10011 . . . . . (212) 633-9063
Febland, David Represented By: Jennifer Embler Represents, Inc. . . . . . (954) 760-4195
Fehlau, Dagmar RR1 Box 118C, Cold Springs, NY 10516 . . . . . (914) 265-6325
Feiza, Anne Represented By: Creative Freelancers . . . . . (800) 398-9544
Feldman, Joey 1139 Titan Street, Philadelphia, PA 19147 . . . . . (215) 551-1960 • (800) 276-5570
Feldman, Steve 1402 W Jackman Street, Lancaster, CA 93534 . . . . . (805) 945-5966
Felker, Robert Represented By: Clare Jett & Associates . . . . . (502) 228-9427
Fell, Dan Represented By: Mendola Ltd. . . . . . (212) 986-5680
Fellman, Lynn Represented By: Deborah Snyder Creative Representative . . . . . (612) 922-3462
Fellows, Kara 1463 Arden Oaks Drive, Arden Hills, MN 55112-6956 . . . . . (612) 482-9578
Fellows, Stan Olsen Represented By: Joanie Bernstein Art Rep . . . . . (612) 374-3169

FENNIMORE, LINDA Pages 15,444,459
808 West End Avenue #801, New York, NY 10025 **(212) 866-0279**
Specialties: Food; Illustrative; People

Fenster, Diane Represented By: Freda Scott, Inc. . . . . . (415) 398-9121

FEQUIERE, PAUL-EMILE Pages 118,460
320 Wymore Road, Apt. 101, Alta Monte Springs, FL 32714 • Pager (407) 623-6512 **(407) 772-0081**
Specialties: Acrylic; Celebrity: Oil; Painterly; Pastels; Pen & Ink; Portraiture

Ferguson, Scott 710 N Tucker #512, St. Louis, MO 63101 . . . . . (314) 241-3811
Fernandes, Eugenie Represented By: Carol Bancroft & Friends . . . . . (203) 748-4823
Fernandes, Kim Represented By: Carol Bancroft & Friends . . . . . (203) 748-4823
Fernandes, Stanislaw 874 Broadway, New York, NY 10003 . . . . . (212) 533-2648
Ferrara, Jon Paul Represented By: Hankins & Tegenborg Ltd. . . . . . (212) 867-8092
Ferreira, Melissa 231 Myatt Road, Barrington, RI 02806 . . . . . (401) 245-8438
Ferster, Gary 756 Marlin Avenue, Ste. 4, Foster City, CA 94404 . . . . . (650) 577-9696
Fiammenghi, Gioia Represented By: Publishers' Graphics . . . . . (203) 797-8188

FIEDLER, JOSEPH DANIEL Pages 86-87
Represented By: Lindgren & Smith **(212) 397-7330**
e-mail: inquiry@lindgrensmith.com • Website: www.lindgrensmith.com • Specialty: Oil

Field, Ann 2910 16th Street, Santa Monica, CA 90405 . . . . . (310) 450-6413
Field, Lori Nelson Represented By: Connie Koralik Associates Represents . . . . . (312) 944-5680
Represented By: Creative Connection . . . . . (410) 360-5981
Fields Studios, Gary 30 Allen Drive, Wayne, NJ 07470 . . . . . (973) 633-8060
Fike, Scott 1200 E Colorado Boulevard #B, Pasadena, CA 91106 . . . . . (818) 405-9219
Filippucci, Sandra 21 Hillside Drive, Sherman, CT 06784 . . . . . (860) 927-1101

FINDLEY, JOHN Pages 373,381,433,460,461
500 Stanyan Street, Apt. 105, San Francisco, CA 94117 • Fax (415) 386-8985 **(415) 386-7292**
Represented By: Susan Wells & Associates **(404) 255-1430**
e-mail: sweaz@aol.com • Specialties: Celebrity; Digital; Portraiture; Product

Fine, Howard Represented By: Shannon Associates . . . . . (212) 831-5650
Finewood, Bill 604 Colton Avenue, Newark, NY 14513 . . . . . (315) 331-2905
Finger, Ronald Represented By: Bernstein & Andriulli, Inc. . . . . . (212) 682-1490
Fiore, Peter Represented By: Artworks . . . . . (212) 627-1554
Fire, Richard Represented By: Ann Koeffler Represents . . . . . (213) 957-2327
Firestone, Bill 4810 Bradford Drive, Annandale, VA 22003 . . . . . (703) 354-0247
Fiscaletti, William 15 E Market Street, Ste. 198, Rhinebeck, NY 12572 . . . . . (914) 876-3070
Fisch, Paul 5111 Coffee Tree Lane, North Syracuse, NY 13212-4402 . . . . . (315) 451-8147
Fischer, Bunny 730 N Franklin, Chicago, IL 60610
Fisher, Bob Represented By: American Artists . . . . . (212) 682-2462

FISHER, CAROLYN Page 165
#1 1028 14th Avenue SW, Calgary, AB Canada T2R 0P1 **(800) 585-4096**
Represented By: Jane Klein **(888) ART-1008**
e-mail: carolynf@cadvision.com

Fisher, Dawn Represented By: Art Bunch, The . . . . . (312) 368-8777
Fisher, Derek Represented By: Marvel Entertainment . . . . . (212) 696-0808
Fisher, Jay Represented By: Art Bunch, The . . . . . (312) 368-8777
Fisher, Jeffrey Represented By: Riley Illustration . . . . . (212) 989-8770

FISHER, MICHAEL Pages 146-147
Represented By: Carol Guenzi Agents, Inc. **(800) 417-5120**
e-mail: artagent@artagent.com • Website: www.artagent.com • Specialties: Digital; People

Fisher, Shell Box 152, Carmel, CA 93921 . . . . . (408) 624-5044
Fishman, Miriam 12 E 14th Street #2-E, New York, NY 10003 . . . . . (212) 633-9126
Fitch, Tony 3620 Queen Mary Drive, Olney, MD 20832 . . . . . (301) 924-0642

FITZ-MAURICE, JEFF Pages 252-253
Represented By: Deborah Wolfe **(215) 232-6666**
Website: www.deborahwolfeltd.com • Specialties: Advertising; Airbrush; Conceptual; Editorial; Realism; Stock

Fitzgerald, Frank 212 E 89th Street, New York, NY 10128 . . . . . (212) 722-6793

FITZGERALD, PATRICK Page 83
45 River Court Boulevard, Toronto, ON Canada M4J 3A3 • Fax (416) 429-2512 **(416) 429-2512**
Specialties: Editorial; Greeting Cards; Oil; Painterly; People; Portraiture; Poster; Realism

Fitzgerald, Royce Represented By: Martha Productions . . . . . (310) 390-8663
Fitzhugh, Greg Represented By: Creative Freelancers . . . . . (800) 398-9544
Fitzpatrick, Jim Represented By: Air Studio . . . . . (513) 721-1193
Flaming, Jon 2200 N Lamar #222, Dallas, TX 75202 . . . . . (214) 922-9757
Flanagan, Kate Represented By: Cornell & McCarthy, LLC . . . . . (203) 454-4210
Flanagan, Sean 816 Grove Street, San Francisco, CA 94117 . . . . . (415) 931-6605
Flavin, Teresa Represented By: Publishers' Graphics . . . . . (203) 797-8188
Flax, Carol Represented By: Salzman International . . . . . (415) 285-8267
Fleming, Dean Represented By: Bernstein & Andriulli, Inc. . . . . . (212) 682-1490
Fleming, Joe Represented By: Jerry Leff Associates, Inc. . . . . . (212) 697-8525

Fleming, Paul Represented By: Brooke & Company . . . . . (214) 352-9192
Fleming, Ron Represented By: Bernstein & Andriulli, Inc. . . . . . (212) 682-1490
Flesher, Vivienne 71 Atwood Avenue, Sausalito, CA 94965 . . . . . (415) 921-2440
Fletcher, Rusty Represented By: Cornell & McCarthy, LLC . . . . . (203) 454-4210
Floca, Brian Represented By: Publishers' Graphics . . . . . (203) 797-8188
Flock Illustration 1 Riverside Road #3A, Riverside, IL 60546 . . . . . (708) 447-4454
Florczak, Robert 1812 Oak Street, South Pasadena, CA 91030 . . . . . (626) 441-1349
Represented By: The Pate Company . . . . . (805) 529-8111
Florentina Illustration 246 Alsace Road, Richmond Hill, ON Canada L4C 2W8 . . . . . (905) 508-0884
Fluharty, Thomas Represented By: Yolanda Burnett Represents . . . . . (770) 967-0039
Represented By: Langley & Associates . . . . . (847) 670-0912
Flynn Studio L Street, Plum Island, Newburyport, MA 01950 . . . . . (978) 465-5971
Foederer, Christine Represented By: Ravenhill Represents . . . . . (816) 333-0744
Fong, Linda P.O. Box 37394, Honolulu, HI 96837 . . . . . (808) 526-0836
Forbes, Alex Represented By: Leyden Diversified . . . . . (215) 663-0587
Forbes, Bart 5510 Nakoma Drive, Dallas, TX 75209 . . . . . (214) 357-8077
Ford, George Represented By: Evelyne Johnson Associates . . . . . (212) 532-0928
Forest, Crista Represented By: Hankins & Tegenborg Ltd. . . . . . (212) 867-8092
Fornalski, Michael 44434 Camellia Drive, Fremont, CA 94539 . . . . . (510) 252-0204
621 River Oaks Parkway, San Jose, CA 95134 . . . . . (408) 434-6434
Forney, Steve Represented By: Wiley Group . . . . . (415) 442-1822
Forsythe, Alison Represented By: Carol Bancroft & Friends . . . . . (203) 748-4823
Forte, Geneva 11805 Cromwell Avenue, Cleveland, OH 44120 . . . . . (216) 791-6148
Fortier, Bob Represented By: Reactor Art & Design Ltd. . . . . . (416) 703-1913
Fortin, Pierre Represented By: Conrad Represents, Inc. . . . . . (415) 921-7140

FOSTER, JEFF — Page 265
320 SW Stark, Ste.421, Portland, OR 97204 • Fax (503) 221-2483 — **(503) 223-1884**
Represented By: Christine Prapas — **(503) 658-7070**
Specialty: Retro

Foster, Lynn Represented By: Alani Represents . . . . . (212) 465-3355

FOSTER, MATT — Pages 122-123
P.O. Box 5366, Carefree, AZ 85377 • Fax (602) 595-7955 — **(602) 595-7950**
7069 E Terrace Estates Circle, Carefree AZ 85377 (overnight mail only)
e-mail: artgun@aol.com • Specialties: Advertising; Black & White; Computer; Conceptual; Corporate; Editorial

Foster, Phil P.O. Box 1314, Murfreesboro, TN 37133-1314 . . . . . (615) 895-1114
Foster, Susan 4800 Chevy Chase Drive #500, Chevy Chase, MD 20815 . . . . . (301) 652-3848
Foster, Travis P.O Box 336, Whites Creek, TN 37189 . . . . . (615) 876-8492
Represented By: Jan Collier Represents, Inc. . . . . . (415) 383-9026

FOSTER, INC., STEPHEN — Page 80
894 Grove Street, Glencoe, IL 60022 • Fax (847) 835-2783 — **(847) 835-2741 • (800) 944-1109**
e-mail: dodah@ripco.com • Website: www.do-dah.com • Specialties: Animation; Humour

Fotheringham, Edwin Represented By: Pat Hackett Artist Representative . . . . . (206) 447-1600
Foty, Tom 3836 Shady Oak Road, Minnetonka, MN 55343 . . . . . (612) 933-5570
Fountain, Linda 8 Windham Hill, Mendon, NY 14506 . . . . . (716) 624-1405
Fournier, Joe 151 N Elmwood Avenue, Oak Park, IL 60302 . . . . . (708) 848-2756
Foust 4534 New Kent Avenue, Richmond, VA 23225 . . . . . (804) 232-3042
Fox, Bill Represented By: Berendsen & Associates . . . . . (513) 861-1400
Fox, Rosemary Represented By: David Goldman Agency . . . . . (212) 807-6627
Fox, Susan 2301 C Street, Eureka, CA 95501 . . . . . (707) 443-1427
Foxx, Kim Represented By: Liz Sanders Agency . . . . . (714) 495-3664
Frampton, Bill 1308 Drexel Avenue #112, Miami Beach, FL 33139 . . . . . (305) 672-3363

FRANCIS, JOHN — Page 281
1610 Wynkoop, Ste. 600, Denver, CO 80202 • Fax (303) 595-3808 — **(303) 595-3805**
Website: www.jfrancis.com • Specialties: Digital; Product; Technical

Francis, Judy 110 W 96th Street #2C, New York, NY 10025 . . . . . (212) 866-7204
Franco, Elizabeth Represented By: Art Source/Diane Barkley . . . . . (914) 747-2220

Franco, Peter 320 E 49th Street #63, New York, NY 10017 . . . . . (212) 751-3046
Frank, Robert Represented By: Melissa Turk & The Artist Network . . . . . (914) 368-8606
Franzen, Dennis Represented By: Steve Edsey & Sons . . . . . (312) 527-0351

FRASER, DOUGLAS Pages 86-89
Represented By: Lindgren & Smith **(212) 397-7330**
Represented By: Jan Collier Represents, Inc. **(415) 383-9026**
e-mail: inquiry@lindgrensmith.com • Website: www.lindgrensmith.com
Specialties: Advertising; Corporate; Digital; Editorial

Frassineti, Lia Represented By: Evelyne Johnson Associates . . . . . (212) 532-0928
Frazee, Marla 1199 N Holliston Avenue, Pasadena, CA 91104 . . . . . (626) 797-0612
Frazier, Craig 90 Throckmorton Avenue #28, Mill Valley, CA 94941 . . . . . (415) 389-1475
Represented By: Jan Collier Represents, Inc. . . . . . (415) 383-9026

FRAZIER, JIM Page 4
221 Lakeridge Drive, Dallas, TX 75218 **(214) 340-9972**
Specialties: Advertising; Black & White; Children; Computer; Conceptual; Corporate; Digital; Editorial; Graphic Design/Illustration; Stock

Freas, Lenwood Represented By: Sam Brody . . . . . (203) 854-0805
Fredericks, Ray 9705 S 52nd Avenue, Oak Lawn, IL 60453 . . . . . (708) 857-8090
Fredrickson, Mark A. 9808 E Rockridge Court, Tucson, AZ 85749 . . . . . (520) 760-5667
Freeman, Laura 208 E 34th Street #4A, New York, NY 10016 . . . . . (212) 679-0812

FREEMAN, NANCY Page 211
125 Warwick Drive, Apt. 27, Benicia, CA 94510 • Fax (707) 745-5228 **(707) 745-5228**
Specialties: Book Jackets; Children; Editorial; Fabric; Food; Greeting Cards; Poster; Travel

Freeman, Robert Represented By: Art Source/Diane Barkley . . . . . (914) 747-2220
Freeman, Sandra 3333 Elm #105, Dallas, TX 75226 . . . . . (214) 871-1956
Freestyle Studio P.O. Box 823554, Dallas, TX 75382-3554 . . . . . (214) 319-5947
French, Martin Represented By: Pat Hackett Artist Representative . . . . . (206) 447-1600
Frenck, Hal Represented By: Hankins & Tegenborg Ltd. . . . . . (212) 867-8092
Frenett, Elaine 1761 Marina Way, San Jose, CA 95125 . . . . . (408) 450-1630
Fretz, John Represented By: Jaz & Jaz . . . . . (206) 633-3445
Frichtel, Linda Represented By: Jacqueline Dedell, Inc. . . . . . (212) 741-2539
Fricke, Bill 487 Drum Point Road, Bricktown, NJ 08723 . . . . . (732) 477-5482
Fricke, Paul Represented By: Mason Illustration . . . . . (612) 729-1774
Fridell, Pat Represented By: Jorgensen & Barrett Reps . . . . . (206) 634-1880
Fried, Janice 459 Ninth Street #38, Brooklyn, NY 11215 . . . . . (718) 832-0881
Frieden, Sarajo 1910 N Serrano Avenue, Los Angeles, CA 90027 . . . . . (213) 462-5045
Friedman, Arthur Represented By: Connie Koralik Associates Represents . . . . . (312) 944-5680
Friedman, Barbara 29 Bank Street, New York, NY 10014 . . . . . (212) 242-4951
Friedman, Drew RR #1 Box 1304, Shohola, PA 18458 . . . . . (717) 296-2483
Friedman, Michael Represented By: Corporate Art Planning . . . . . (212) 242-8995
Friedman, Todd G. 1032 Euclid Avenue, Miami Beach, FL 33139 . . . . . (305) 538-8518
Friesen, Lianne 64 First Avenue, Toronto, ON Canada M4M 1W8 . . . . . (416) 469-3727
Frisari, Frank 240 W 38th Street, New York, NY 10018 . . . . . (212) 840-3211
Frisino, Jim Represented By: Jaz & Jaz . . . . . (206) 633-3445
Fryer, Douglas Represented By: Scott Hull Associates . . . . . (937) 433-8383
Fuchs, Bernie Represented By: Harvey Kahn . . . . . (201) 467-0223
Fujimori, Brian Represented By: Joni Tuke, Inc. . . . . . (312) 787-6826
Represented By: Das Grup . . . . . (310) 540-5958

FUJISAKI, TUKO Pages 6-7
12 Duende Road, Santa Fe, NM 87505 **(505) 466-4741 • (800) 208-2456**
Represented By: Jane Klein **(888) ART-1008**
Represented By: Teenuh Foster Represents **(314) 647-7377**
Specialties: Advertising; Children; Conceptual; Digital; Editorial; Greeting Cards; Humour; Icons; Whimsical

Fujiwara, Kim 1985 W Big Beaver #207, Troy, MI 48084 . . . . . (248) 643-6290
Represented By: Three in a Box . . . . . (416) 367-2446
Fuka, Ted 19224 Schoolhouse Road, Mokena, IL 60448 . . . . . (708) 479-9514
Fuller, Rocky Represented By: Berendsen & Associates . . . . . (513) 861-1400

Fullmer, Howard Represented By: Cary & Company . . . . . (404) 296-9666
Fullmer, Margie McMullin Represented By: Cary & Company . . . . . (404) 296-9666
Fulton, Parker Represented By: Creative Connection . . . . . (410) 360-5981
Fulvimari, Jeffrey Represented By: Art Department . . . . . (212) 925-4222
Funkhouser, Kristen 2431 Third Street #7, Santa Monica, CA 90405 . . . . . (310) 452-4240
Represented By: Salzman International . . . . . (415) 285-8267
Furchgott Scott, Carol 242 Barren Hill Road, Conshohocken, PA 19428 . . . . . (610) 828-3446
Gaadt, David 2103 Tennyson Drive, Greensboro, NC 27410 . . . . . (910) 288-0953
Gaadt, George S. 888 Thorn Street, Sewickley, PA 15143 . . . . . (412) 741-5161
Represented By: American Artists . . . . . (212) 682-2462
Gabbana, Marc 2453 Olive Court, Windsor, ON Canada N8T 3N4 . . . . . (519) 948-2418
Gabel, Kurt 364 Cobblestone Drive, Colorado Springs, CO 80906 . . . . . (719) 576-3523
Gabriele, Antonio J. 931 Deep Lagoon Lane, Ft. Myers, FL 33919 . . . . . (305) 433-3202

GAETANO, NICHOLAS Pages 124-125
Represented By: Vicki Morgan Associates **(212) 475-0440**
e-mail: vmartrep@aol.com • Website: www.vickimorganassociates.com
Specialties: Advertising; Airbrush; Conceptual; Corporate; Editorial; Fantasy; Icons; Lettering; People; Poster

Gagnon, Mark Represented By: Art Department . . . . . (212) 925-4222
Gal, Susan 267 Cambridge Avenue, Kensington, CA 94708 . . . . . (510) 528-9343
Galkin, Simon Represented By: Evelyne Johnson Associates . . . . . (212) 532-0928

GALL, CHRIS Page 156
Represented By: Carol Chislovsky Design, Inc. **(212) 677-9100**
Specialties: Scratchboard; Woodcut

Gallagher, Jack 1281 Riesling Circle, Livermore, CA 94550 . . . . . (510) 449-9169
Galloway, Nixon Represented By: Rosenthal Represents . . . . . (818) 222-5445
Gambino, Fred Represented By: Bernstein & Andriulli, Inc. . . . . . (212) 682-1490

GAMBLE, KENT Pages 168,205
Represented By: American Artists **(212) 682-2462**
e-mail: info@amerartists.com • Website: www.amerartists.com

Garbot, Dave 11369 SW Winterlake Drive, Tigard, OR 97223 . . . . . (503) 579-0663
Garces, A.J. 8427 Bourwell, San Antonio, TX 78250 . . . . . (210) 509-9943
Garcia, Manuel Represented By: Salzman International . . . . . (415) 285-8267
Garcia, Segundo Represented By: SI International . . . . . (212) 254-4996
Garcia, Stephanie 551 Observer Highway #9D, Hoboken, NJ 07030 . . . . . (201) 963-8089
Garcia, Tom Represented By: John Brewster Creative Services . . . . . (203) 226-4724
Garcia Illustration, David V. 806 N Hart Boulevard, Harvard, IL 60033 . . . . . (815) 943-1241
Gardner, Bonnie T. 142 W 19th Street, New York, NY 10011 . . . . . (212) 255-0863
Gardner, Gail 227 Marlborough Street, Boston, MA 02116 . . . . . (617) 266-8626
Gardner, Mike Represented By: Sheryl Beranbaum . . . . . (401) 737-8591
Gardner, Steve Represented By: Artworks . . . . . (212) 627-1554

GARLAND, BILL Pages 168,194
Represented By: American Artists **(212) 682-2462**
e-mail: info@amerartists.com • Website: www.amerartists.com

Garland, Michael 19 Manor Road, RR #2, Patterson, NY 12563 . . . . . (914) 878-4347
Garns, Allen Represented By: Marla Matson Represents . . . . . (602) 252-5072
Represented By: Martha Productions . . . . . (310) 390-8663
Garramone, Rich 49 Ridgedale Avenue, Ste. 201, East Hanover, NJ 07936 . . . . . (973) 887-7234
Garretson, Helen Represented By: Creative Connection . . . . . (410) 360-5981
Garrett, Tom Represented By: Joanie Bernstein Art Rep . . . . . (612) 374-3169
Garrido, Hector Represented By: Mendola Ltd. . . . . . (212) 986-5680
Garrison, Barbara 12 E 87th Street, New York, NY 10128 . . . . . (212) 348-6382
Garrity, Bruce 249 S Broad Street, Penns Grove, NJ 08069 . . . . . (609) 299-3966
Garro, Mark 20 Kent Place, Coscob, CT 06807 . . . . . (203) 661-6922

GARROW, DAN Pages 44, 428
Represented By: Renard Represents **(212) 490-2450**
e-mail: renardreps@earthlink.net • Website: www.renardrepresents.com • Specialties: Cartoon; Conceptual

Garvie, Ben Represented By: Munro Goodman (312) 321-1336
Gast, Josef Represented By: Scott Hull Associates (937) 433-8383
Gauthier, Corbert Represented By: Oasis Art Studio (612) 927-0955
Gaz, Stan Represented By: Jacqueline Dedell, Inc. (212) 741-2539
Gazsi, Edward 12508 Stagecoach Lane, Bayonet Point, FL 34667 (813) 862-9751
Geary, Rick 701 Kettner Boulevard #204, San Diego, CA 92101 (619) 234-0514
Gebert, Warren 2 Hunte Court, Suffern, NY 10901 (914) 354-2536
Geerinck, Manuel Represented By: Jerry Leff Associates, Inc. (212) 697-8525
Gehm, Charles Represented By: Jerry Leff Associates, Inc. (212) 697-8525
Gelb, Jacki 3921 Greenview Avenue, Chicago, IL 60613 (773) 281-5276
Gelen, Michael 68 Dorchester Road, Buffalo, NY 14222 (716) 882-0102
Geltner, Gail Represented By: Reactor Art & Design Ltd. (416) 703-1913
Gem Studio 420 Lexington Avenue, Ste. 220, New York, NY 10170 (212) 687-3460
Gendron, Raymond 5505 St. Laurent #4004, Montreal, PQ Canada H2T 1S6 (514) 597-2812
Genova, Joe Represented By: Bernstein & Andriulli, Inc. (212) 682-1490
Gentleman, David Represented By: HK Portfolio (212) 675-5719
Genzo, John Paul 3 Emily Court, Robbinsville, NJ 08691 (609) 259-6089
Represented By: Frank & Jeff Lavaty (212) 427-5632
Represented By: Rosenthal Represents (818) 222-5445
George, Jeff Represented By: Martha Productions (310) 390-8663
George, William C. 2172 Sunset Crest Drive, Los Angeles, CA 90046 (213) 654-2660
Geras, Audra Represented By: Renard Represents (212) 490-2450
Gerber, John Represented By: Spectrum Studio, Inc. (612) 332-2361

GERBER STUDIO/TRADIGITAL ILLUSTRATION Page 317
Represented By: PG Representatives **(413) 967-9855**
e-mail: gerber1@aol.com • Specialties: Advertising; Computer; Conceptual; Digital; Photoillustration; Product; Realism

Gerhard, Nik 27931 Paseo Nicole, San Juan Capistrano, CA 92675 (714) 493-5596
Germon, Roy 275 Bleecker Street #4, New York, NY 10014 (212) 807-9728
Gerner, Jochen Represented By: Wanda Nowak (212) 535-0438
Gersten, Gerry 177 Newtown Turnpike, Weston, CT 06883 (203) 454-3134
Gesue, Monica 11740 Montana Avenue #405, Los Angeles, CA 90049 (310) 820-8485
Gettier-Street, Renee 13908 Marblestone Drive, Clifton, VA 20124 (703) 631-1650
Geyer, Jackie Represented By: American Artists (212) 682-2462

GIACOBBE, BEPPE Pages 124-125
Represented By: Vicki Morgan Associates **(212) 475-0440**
e-mail: vmartrep@aol.com • Website: www.vickimorganassociates.com
Specialties: Advertising; Computer; Digital; Editorial; Fashion; Icons; Illustrative; Lettering; People; Whimsical

GIANCOLA, DONATO Pages 352-353
Represented By: Sal Barracca Associates **(212) 889-2400**
Specialties: Advertising; Conceptual; Editorial; Fantasy; Greeting Cards; Oil; Portraiture; Realism; Science

Gibbon, Rebecca Represented By: Riley Illustration (212) 989-8770
Gibbons, Anne 125 W 72nd Street, New York, NY 10023 (914) 631-1413
Gibbs, Bradley 1375 Remington Road, Schaumburg, IL 60173 (847) 781-4172
Gibbs, Kerri Represented By: Hankins & Tegenborg Ltd. (212) 867-8092
Gibbs, Michael Represented By: Conrad Represents, Inc. (415) 921-7140
Gibson, Barbara L. 3501 Toddsbury Lane, Olney, MD 20832 (301) 570-9480

GIBSON, CLANCY Pages 18-19
Represented By: Link **(416) 530-1500**

Gibson, Mike 18726 Ludlow Street, Northridge, CA 91326-2426 (818) 368-4952
Giddio, Tobie Represented By: Art Department (212) 925-4222
Giese, William Represented By: Hankins & Tegenborg Ltd. (212) 867-8092
Gieseke, Thomas A. 7909 W 61st Street, Merriam, KS 66202 (913) 677-4593
Giglio, Mark 233 Elizabeth Street #21, New York, NY 10012 (212) 431-8926
Gilbert, Yvonne Represented By: Alan Lynch Artists (908) 813-8718
Gilleran, Norma 8500 Everest Street, Downey, CA 90242 (562) 861-3722
Gilleran, Owen 8500 Everest Street, Downey, CA 90242 (562) 861-3722

Gillies, Chuck Represented By: Skidmore, Inc. . . . . (248) 353-7722
Represented By: Mendola Ltd. . . . . (212) 986-5680
Gilmour, Joni 10A Orchard Terrace, Salem, NH 03079 . . . . . (603) 898-6961
Gin, Byron Represented By: Carolyn Potts . . . . . (312) 944-1130
Ginsburg, Max 40 W 77th Street, New York, NY 10024 . . . . . (212) 787-0628
Ginzinger, Karla Represented By: Frank Lux & Associates, Inc. . . . . . (312) 222-1361
Giovine, Sergio Represented By: Hankins & Tegenborg Ltd. . . . . . (212) 867-8092
Girouard, Patrick Represented By: Publishers' Graphics . . . . . (203) 797-8188
Giroud, Annie France Represented By: American Artists . . . . . (212) 682-2462
Girvin, Tim Represented By: Renard Represents . . . . . (212) 490-2450
Githens, Doug Represented By: Holly Hahn Artist Rep (H2 + Co.) . . . . . (312) 633-0500
Giusti, Robert Represented By: The Newborn Group . . . . . (212) 260-6700
Givan, Gene Represented By: Steve Edsey & Sons . . . . . (312) 527-0351
Glad, Deanna P.O. Box 1962, San Pedro, CA 90733 . . . . . (310) 831-6274
Gladstone, Dale 32 Havemeyer Street #2A, Brooklyn, NY 11211 . . . . . (718) 782-2250
Glaser, Milton 207 E 32nd Street, New York, NY 10016 . . . . . (212) 889-3161
Glasgow & Associates, Dale 448 Hartwood Road, Fredericksburg, VA 22406 . . . . . (540) 286-2539
Glass, Randy 4923 Arcola Avenue, North Hollywood, CA 91601 . . . . . (213) 851-6555
Represented By: Sweet Represents . . . . . (415) 433-1222
Glattauer, Ned 343 E 30th Street, New York, NY 10016-6439 . . . . . (212) 686-6927
Glazer, Ted 28 Westview Road, Spring Valley, NY 10977-1831 . . . . . (914) 354-1524

GLAZIER, GARTH Pages 168,173,338-339
Represented By: American Artists **(212) 682-2462**
Represented By: The Roland Group **(301) 718-7955**
e-mail: info@amerartists.com • Website: www.amerartists.com • therolandgroup.com
Specialties: Advertising; Airbrush; Corporate; Digital

Glisson, Steve 200 St. Johns Place, Apt. 1, Brooklyn, NY 11217 . . . . . (718) 398-2980
Glover, Ann 1308 Factory Place Box 25 #4-B, Los Angeles, CA 90013 . . . . . (213) 623-6203
Glover, Gary 6715 Xana Way, Carlsbad, CA 92009 . . . . . (760) 471-9453

GNAN, PATRICK Pages 252-253
Represented By: Deborah Wolfe **(215) 232-6666**
Website: www.deborahwolfeltd.com • Specialties: Advertising; Airbrush; Computer; Digital; Product; Realism; Science; Technical; Wildlife

Godfrey, Linda Represented By: Nachreiner Boie Art Factory . . . . . (414) 785-1940
Goettemoeller, Cheryl 4319 Wilkinson Avenue, Studio City, CA 91604 . . . . . (818) 766-4929
Goetzinger, Rolf Represented By: Lehmen/Dabney, Inc. . . . . . (206) 325-8595
Goff, Kathy Represented By: Creative Connection . . . . . (410) 360-5981
Goffe, Toni Represented By: Carol Bancroft & Friends . . . . . (203) 748-4823
Goines, David Lance 1703 Martin Luther King Jr Way, Berkeley, CA 94709 . . . . . (510) 549-1405
Gold & Associates 6000-C Saugrass Village Circle, Ponte Vedra Beach, FL 32082 . . . . . (904) 285-5669
Goldammer, Ken 844 W Gunnison #2E, Chicago, IL 60640 . . . . . (312) 635-5555
Goldberg, Richard A. 15 Cliff Street, Arlington, MA 02174 . . . . . (781) 646-1041
Golden, Harriet 217 E 85th Street, New York, NY 10028 . . . . . (212) 249-4194
Golden, Jan 2305 Ashland Street #C, Ashland, OR 97520 . . . . . (800) 435-6509
Goldin, David Represented By: Joanne Palulian . . . . . (212) 581-8338

GOLDMAN, DARA Page 360
430 Dutton Road, Sudbury, MA 01776 • Fax (978) 440-9709 **(978) 440-8636**
Specialties: Advertising; Animals; Cartoon; Children; Editorial; Humour; People; Water Color; Whimsical

Goldsborough, June Represented By: Evelyne Johnson Associates . . . . . (212) 532-0928
Goldsmith, Lloyd Represented By: Square Moon . . . . . (510) 253-9451
Goldstein, Howard 7031 Aldea Avenue, Van Nuys, CA 91406 . . . . . (818) 987-2837
Goldstrom, Robert Represented By: The Newborn Group . . . . . (212) 260-6700
Goliath Studios 16313 Clark Avenue, Bellflower, CA 90706 . . . . . (562) 920-7004
Goloshapov, Sergei 111 First Street #65E, Jersey City, NJ 07302 . . . . . (201) 792-7604
Gomez, Hector Represented By: Glass House Graphics . . . . . (304) 232-5641
Gomez, Ignacio 812 W Kenneth Road, Glendale, CA 91202 . . . . . (818) 243-2838
Gonnella, Rick Represented By: Mason Illustration . . . . . (612) 729-1774
Represented By: Janice Stefanski Represents . . . . . (415) 928-0457
Represented By: Steve Edsey & Sons . . . . . (312) 527-0351

Gonzales, Chuck 611 Broadway #631, New York, NY 10012 . . . . . (212) 477-1041
Represented By: Chris Glenn . . . . . (312) 670-7737
Gonzales, Danilo Represented By: Tiffany Represents . . . . . (206) 441-7701
Gonzalez, Dan 286 Clinton Avenue, Brooklyn, NY 11205 . . . . . (718) 857-7530
Gonzalez, Pedro Julio Represented By: Melissa Turk & The Artist Network . . . . . (914) 368-8606

GONZALEZ, THOMAS Pages 216,218
Represented By: Alexander/Pollard, Inc. **(800) 347-0734**
Specialties: Advertising; Architecture/Interiors; Conceptual; Editorial; Maps & Charts; Medical; Pastels; Realism; Sports; Stock

Goode, Larry 1205 W 43rd Street, Austin, TX 78756 . . . . . (512) 467-7471
Represented By: Schumann & Company . . . . . (512) 481-0907
Goodell Illustration, Brad 605 Arizona Street SE, Albuquerque, NM 87108-3752 . . . . . (505) 255-7889
Goodfellow, Peter Represented By: Alan Lynch Artists . . . . . (908) 813-8718
Goodman, Johanna 222 E 51st Street #4D, New York, NY 10022 . . . . . (212) 759-8215
Goodman, Paula Represented By: The Ivy League of Artists . . . . . (212) 243-1333
Goodman-Willy, April Represented By: Harriet Kastaris & Associates . . . . . (314) 773-2600
Goodrich, Carter 18 Imperial Palace #6E, Providence, RI 02903 . . . . . (401) 272-6094
Goodridge, James Represented By: Bernstein & Andriulli, Inc. . . . . . (212) 682-1490
Goodridge, Lawrence Represented By: Air Studio . . . . . (513) 721-1193
Gordley, Scott Represented By: Penny & Stermer Group . . . . . (212) 505-9342
Gordon, David 337 A-B 41st Street, Oakland, CA 94609 . . . . . (510) 547-1685
Gordon-Lucas, Bonnie 115 N College Avenue, #16, Bloomington, IN 47404 . . . . . (812) 339-6001
Gore, Leonid 1429-A Dahill Road, Brooklyn, NY 11204 . . . . . (718) 627-4952
Gorey, Edward 8 Strawberry Lane, Box 146, Yarmouthport, MA 02675 . . . . . (508) 362-3909

GORING, TREVOR Page 277
Represented By: Famous Frames **(310) 642-2721**
e-mail: info@famousframes.com • Website: www.famousframes.com • Specialties: Animation; Storyboards

Gorman, Kate Represented By: Cornell & McCarthy, LLC . . . . . (203) 454-4210
Gorman, Ron 87186 Kellmore Road, P.O. Box 2233, Eugene, OR 97402 . . . . . (541) 343-3434
Gorman, Stan 217 Santa Rosa Court, Laguna Beach, CA 92651 . . . . . (714) 733-8071
Gothard, David 104 Creek Road, Bangor, PA 18013 . . . . . (610) 588-4937
Gottlieb, Penelope Represented By: Nancy George . . . . . (805) 688-3772
Gottula, Marc Fredric 688 S Santa Fe Avenue #113, Los Angeles, CA 90021 . . . . . (213) 623-3321
Goudey II, Ray J. 4017 Crescent Point Road, Carlsbad, CA 92008 . . . . . (760) 729-8173

GOUDREAU, ROC Page 318
Represented By: PG Representatives **(413) 967-9855**
e-mail: pgreps@aol.com • Specialties: Digital; Computer

Gowdy, Carolyn Represented By: Reactor Art & Design Ltd. . . . . . (416) 703-1913
Graber, Jack Represented By: Rosenthal Represents . . . . . (818) 222-5445
Graef, Renee Represented By: Cornell & McCarthy, LLC . . . . . (203) 454-4210
Graffics 8120 Santa Arminta Avenue, San Diego, CA 92126 . . . . . (619) 578-6385

GRAHAM, HEATHER Page 275
3723 Holden Crescent, Mississauga, ON Canada L5A 2V9 **(416) 536-1543**
Specialties: Food; People; Portraiture

Graham, Jack Represented By: Langley & Associates . . . . . (847) 670-0912
Represented By: Mary Holland & Company . . . . . (602) 263-8990
Graham Studios Represented By: Connie Koralik Associates Represents . . . . . (312) 944-5680
Graham Studios, Mariah Route 52, Box 425, Jeffersonville, NY 12748 . . . . . (914) 482-4036
Grahn, Geoffrey 4054 Madison Avenue, Apt. E, Culver City, CA 90232 . . . . . (310) 838-7824
Graif Design 1330 W Schatz Lane #4, Nixa, MO 65714 . . . . . (417) 725-1091
Grajek, Tim 213 Webber Avenue, North Tarrytown, NY 10591 . . . . . (914) 332-9704
Gran, Eliza 229 Kane Street, Apt. 2, Brooklyn, NY 11231 . . . . . (718) 797-3793
Gran, Julia 3240 Henry Hudson Parkway #6H, Riverdale, NY 10463 . . . . . (718) 601-8820
Grandpre, Mary 2182 Berkeley Avenue, St. Paul, MN 55105 . . . . . (612) 699-0424
Graning, Ken 2602 Williamsburg Circle, Auburn Hills, MI 48326 . . . . . (248) 299-0677
Granner, Courtney 328 N Fifth Street, Patterson, CA 95363 . . . . . (209) 892-2973

GRANT, COLLIN Page 277
Represented By: Famous Frames **(310) 642-2721**
e-mail: info@famousframes.com • Website: www.famousframes.com • Specialties: Animation; Storyboards

Grant, Mel Represented By: SI International. . . . . (212) 254-4996
Grant, Mike 600-1040 Seventh Avenue SW, Calgary, AB Canada T2P 3G9 . . . . . (403) 265-0812
Grant, Renee Represented By: Artworks . . . . . (212) 627-1554
Graphic Moon Design 467 Alvarado Street, Ste. 3, Monterey, CA 93940 . . . . . (408) 649-5276
Graphic Traffic Represented By: Carol Guenzi Agents, Inc. . . . . . (800) 417-5120
Graphic Visions 15A W Main Street, Ste. 3, Bergenfield, NJ 07621 . . . . . (201) 384-9100
Graphics International 15052 Red Hill Avenue #H, Tustin, CA 92680 . . . . . (714) 259-1007
Grasso, Louis P. 1425 Washington Boulevard, Mayfield Heights, OH 44124 . . . . . (216) 449-6653
Graveline, Todd 770 E 73rd Street, Indianapolis, IN 46240 . . . . . (317) 255-1197
Gravelle, Carol 6329 Calle Bodega, Camarillo, CA 93012 . . . . . (805) 987-4879
Represented By: Barbara Mizuno. . . . . (310) 472-1446
Graves, Clane Represented By: Marla Matson Represents . . . . . (602) 252-5072
Graves, David Represented By: Comp Art Plus . . . . . (212) 279-0800
Graves, Linda Represented By: Carol Bancroft & Friends . . . . . (203) 748-4823
Gray, Barbara New York, NY 10021 . . . . . (212) 288-3938
Gray, Gary 10 Highland Drive, Penfield, NY 14526 . . . . . (716) 586-1357
Gray, Lynda Represented By: Bernstein & Andriulli, Inc. . . . . . (212) 682-1490
Gray, Mike Represented By: Wiley Group . . . . . (415) 442-1822
Gray, Steve 119 W Torrance Boulevard, Ste. 5, Redondo Beach, CA 90277 . . . . . (310) 318-3844
Green, Norman 3053 Joaquin Miller Road, Oakland, CA 94602 . . . . . (510) 531-3531

GREENBERG, KAREN L. Page 160
525 W 22nd Street, Apt. 3E, New York, NY 10011 • Fax (212) 645-3582 **(212) 645-7379**
Represented By: Tonal Values **(214) 943-2569**
e-mail: dkingsley@aol.com • tonalvalues@mindspring.com • Website: www.greenbergkingsley.com
Specialties: Children; Graphic Design/Illustration; Greeting Cards; Icons; Illustrative; Lettering; Stock; Still Life; Whimsical

GREENBERG, SHELDON Page 330
Represented By: Michele Manasse **(215) 862-2091**
e-mail: mmanasse@new-work.com • Website: www.voicenet.com/~mmanasse
Specialties: Advertising; Children; Editorial; Fashion; Food; Greeting Cards; People; Poster; Sports; Still Life

GREENBERG, STEVE Pages 252-253
Represented By: Deborah Wolfe **(215) 232-6666**
Website: www.deborahwolfeltd.com • Specialties: Advertising; Collage; Computer; Conceptual; Corporate; Digital; Photography; Stock

Greenblatt, Mitch 65 Atlantic Avenue, Apt. 13, Brooklyn, NY 11201 . . . . . (718) 624-6361
Greene, Carol Heiman Represented By: Nancy George . . . . . (805) 688-3772
Greenhow, Ralph 203 N Wabash, Ste. 1620, Chicago, IL 60601 . . . . . (312) 444-1168
Greenwald, Joe 650 Inca Lane, New Brighton, MN 55512 . . . . . (612) 631-3355
Greger, Shana Represented By: Carol Bancroft & Friends. . . . . (203) 748-4823
Gregerson, Beth 35362A S Turtle Trail, Willoughby, OH 44094 . . . . . (440) 975-0327
Gregoretti, Rob 41-07 56th Street, Woodside, NY 11377 . . . . . (718) 779-7913
Gregori, Leon 400 E 56th Street, New York, NY 10022 . . . . . (212) 758-1662
Gregory, Fran Represented By: Dolby Represents . . . . . (312) 855-9336
Gregory, Lane Represented By: Gwen Walters-Goldstein . . . . . (781) 235-8658
Greif, Gene 114 W 16th Street, Ste. 6E, New York, NY 10011 . . . . . (212) 647-1286
Greifinger, Mel Represented By: Evelyne Johnson Associates . . . . . (212) 532-0928
Grejniec, Michael Represented By: Kirchoff/Wohlberg, Inc. . . . . . (212) 644-2020
Grethen, Donna Marie 2847 Guilderland Avenue, Schenectady, NY 12306 . . . . . (518) 355-8023
Grider, Dick 218 Madison Avenue #5-F, New York, NY 10016. . . . . (212) 213-5333
Griego, Tony Represented By: The Schuna Group . . . . . (612) 631-8480
Griesbach/Martucci 34 Twinlight Terrace, Highlands, NJ 07732 . . . . . (732) 291-5945
Griffel, Barbara 2345 Bell Boulevard, Bayside, NY 11360-2045 . . . . . (718) 631-1753
Griffin, Jim Represented By: Hankins & Tegenborg Ltd. . . . . . (212) 867-8092
Griffo, Joseph 54 North Avenue, New Rochelle, NY 10805. . . . . (914) 633-5734

GRIMANDO, SCOTT Pages 168,195
Represented By: American Artists **(212) 682-2462**
e-mail: info@amerartists.com • Website: www.amerartists.com • Specialties: Digital; Painterly

Grimes Design Inc., Don 5635 Ridgedale, Dallas, TX 75206 . . . . . (214) 821-9590
Grimwood, Brian Represented By: Bernstein & Andriulli, Inc. . . . . . (212) 682-1490
Grinnell, Derek 621 A 42nd Avenue, San Francisco, CA 94121 . . . . . (415) 221-2820
Griswold, Wendy Smith Represented By: Melissa Turk & The Artist Network . . . . . (914) 368-8606
Groen, Tim Represented By: The Arts Counsel . . . . . (212) 777-6777
Groff, David 420 N Liberty Street, Delaware, OH 43015 . . . . . (614) 363-2131
Represented By: Conrad Represents, Inc. . . . . . (415) 921-7140
Represented By: Harriet Kastaris & Associates . . . . . (314) 773-2600
Groover, Susan 980 E Rocksprings Road, Atlanta, GA 30306 . . . . . (404) 875-5295
Represented By: Tonal Values . . . . . (214) 943-2569
Gross, Alex 1727 La Senda Place, South Pasadena, CA 91030 . . . . . (626) 799-4014

GROSS, SUSAN Pages 2-3,425
532 Cabrillo Street, San Francisco, CA 94118 • Fax (415) 751-5876 **(415) 751-5879**
e-mail: susan@susangross.com • Website: www.susangross.com
Specialties: Advertising; Children; Editorial; Lettering; Mixed Media; Product

Grossman, Myron Represented By: Connie Koralik Associates Represents . . . . . (312) 944-5680
Represented By: Those 3 Reps . . . . . (214) 871-1316
Grossman, Rhoda 216 Fourth Street, Sausalito, CA 94965 . . . . . (415) 331-0328

GROSSMAN, WENDY Pages 55,439
Represented By: Renard Represents **(212) 490-2450**
e-mail: renardreps@earthlink.net • Website: www.renardrepresents.com • Specialties: Conceptual; Digital

Grote, Rich 9001 Trolley Lane, Eagleville, PA 19403 . . . . . (610) 630-3356
Grotenhuis, Eric Represented By: K&K Art & Associates . . . . . (612) 338-9138
Grothman, Lisa Represented By: Tania Kimche . . . . . (212) 529-3556
Grove, David 382 Union Street, San Francisco, CA 94133 . . . . . (415) 433-2100
Grove, Keith Represented By: Dimension . . . . . (612) 884-4045
Grubb, Lisa P.O. Box 388, Sparkill, NY 10976 . . . . . (914) 921-4526
Grunewald, Jeff 2120 W Waveland, Chicago, IL 60618 . . . . . (773) 281-5284
Guarnaccia, Steven 31 Fairfield Street, Montclair, NJ 07042 . . . . . (201) 746-9785
Represented By: Reactor Art & Design Ltd. . . . . . (416) 703-1913
Gudynas, Peter Represented By: Alan Lynch Artists . . . . . (908) 813-8718
Guell, Fernando Represented By: SI International . . . . . (212) 254-4996
Guida, Lisa Chauncy Represented By: Mendola Ltd. . . . . . (212) 986-5680
Guidera, Daniel 819 E Broadway, Boston, MA 02127 . . . . . (617) 268-5120
Guip, Amy 91 E Fourth Street, Apt. 6, New York, NY 10003 . . . . . (212) 674-8166
352 Bowery, New York, NY 10012 . . . . . (212) 674-8166
Guitteau, Jud Represented By: Renard Represents . . . . . (212) 490-2450
Gulick, Dorothy Represented By: Sylvia Franks . . . . . (310) 276-5282
Gully, Bethany 109 Kingston Street, Boston, MA 02111 . . . . . (617) 350-3089 • (800) 710-2779
Represented By: Freda Scott, Inc.. . . . . . (415) 398-9121
Gumble, Gary 1316 102nd Avenue NE, Bellevue, WA 98004 . . . . . (425) 688-1961
Gunn, Robert 229 Berkely Street, Boston, MA 02116 . . . . . (617) 266-3858
Represented By: Evelyne Johnson Associates . . . . . (212) 532-0928
Gunsaullus, Marty Represented By: Salzman International . . . . . (415) 285-8267
Gurche, John 1304 Olive Street, Denver, CO 80220 . . . . . (303) 699-4721
Gurney, John Steven 168 Western Avenue, Brattleboro, VT 05301 . . . . . (802) 258-2654
Gurvin, Abe 31341 Holly Drive, Laguna Beach, CA 92677 . . . . . (949) 499-2001
Represented By: Joel Harlib Associates, Inc. . . . . . (312) 573-1370
Gushock, Mike 4450 N 12th Street #106, Phoenix, AZ 85014 . . . . . (602) 650-1810
Represented By: Marla Matson Represents . . . . . (602) 252-5072
Gustafson, Dale 56 Four Brooks Road, Stanford, CT 06903 . . . . . (203) 322-5667
Represented By: Mendola Ltd.. . . . . . (212) 986-5680
Gustafson, Glenn Represented By: Mason Illustration . . . . . (612) 729-1774
Represented By: Repertoire . . . . . (972) 761-0500
Gustafsson, Mats 755 Washington Street, New York, NY 10014 . . . . . (212) 206-0737
Gutermuth, Stefan 426 Union Street, San Francisco, CA 94133 . . . . . (415) 391-1506
Gutierrez, Rudy 340 Haven Avenue, Apt. 1D, New York, NY 10003 . . . . . (212) 568-2848

Guy, Eddie 309 Race Track Road, Ho Ho Kus, NJ 07423 . . . . . (201) 251-7660
Guyer, Terry 1139 San Carlos Avenue #301, San Carlos, CA 94070 . . . . . (415) 596-0363
Guzner, Vlad Represented By: Wanda Nowak . . . . . (212) 535-0438
Gwilliams, Scott 213 Glen Road, Toronto, ON Canada M4W 2X2 . . . . . (416) 929-8432
Hackney, Rick 559 Pacific Avenue #28, San Francisco, CA 94133 . . . . . (415) 982-1319
26 Narragansett Cove, San Rafael, CA 94901 . . . . . (415) 456-9985

HACKWORTH, ALEX Pages 373,377,421,426
1523 W Jackson Boulevard, Chicago, IL 60607 **(312) 563-9476**
P.O. Box 11380, Chicago, IL 60611
Represented By: Susan Wells & Associates **(404) 255-1430**
e-mail: demand5@aol.com • Specialties: Black & White; Collage; Line Art; 3D

Haefele, Steve Represented By: SI International . . . . . (212) 254-4996
Hagel, Mike 1611 141st Avenue, Omaha, NE 68154 . . . . . (408) 691-8682
Hagen, David 5580 Village Center Drive, Centreville, VA 20120 . . . . . (703) 830-4208
Haggerty, Tim P.O. Box 31199, Santa Barbara, CA 93130 . . . . . (805) 687-4848
Hagio, Kunio 125 Table Top Road, Sedona, AZ 86336 . . . . . (520) 282-3574
Hagner, Dirk 27931 Paseo Nicole, San Juan Capistrano, CA 92675 . . . . . (714) 493-5596
Hagy, Jarrett 9 S Johnson, Indianapolis, IN 46219 . . . . . (765) 345-7854
Hahn, Marika 679 Oak Tree Road, P.O. Box 670, Palisades, NY 10964 . . . . . (914) 365-3317
Haight, Sandy 911 Western Avenue, Ste. 525, Seattle, WA 98104 . . . . . (206) 343-0656
Hajek, Olaf Represented By: Kate Larkworthy Artist Rep. Ltd. . . . . . (212) 633-1310
Halbert, Michael 2419 Big Bend Boulevard, St. Louis, MO 63143 . . . . . (314) 645-6480
Represented By: Mendola Ltd. . . . . . (212) 986-5680

HALEY, AMANDA Page 79
Represented By: Laurie Lambert **(513) 841-0073**
Specialties: Advertising; Children; Commercial; Editorial

Hall, Bill Represented By: Lehmen/Dabney, Inc. . . . . . (206) 325-8595
Hall, Jerry 3050 B Spring Hill Parkway, Smyrna, GA 30080 . . . . . (770) 333-9074
Hall, Joan 155 Bank Street #H954, New York, NY 10014 . . . . . (212) 243-6059
Hall, Kate Brennan 301 De Arment Parkway, Pittsburgh, PA 15241 . . . . . (412) 833-9648
Hallgren, Gary 98 Laurelton Drive, Mastic Beach, NY 11951 . . . . . (516) 399-5531
Hally, Greg 248 Edison Street, Salt Lake City, UT 84111 . . . . . (801) 355-5510
Represented By: Das Grup . . . . . (310) 540-5958

HALSTEAD, VIRGINIA Pages 410,429
4336 Gayle Drive, Tarzana, CA 91356 • Fax (818) 705-4353 **(818) 705-4353**
Website: www.goworldnet.com/vhalste.htm • Specialties: Advertising; Annual Report; Conceptual; Editorial; Painterly; Whimsical

Hamagami, John Represented By: American Artists . . . . . (212) 682-2462
Hamagami/Carroll & Associates 1316 Third Street, Promenade #305, Santa Monica, CA 90401 . . . . . (310) 458-7600
Hamann, Brad 330 Westminster Road, Brooklyn, NY 11218 . . . . . (718) 287-6086
Hamblin, George Represented By: Steve Edsey & Sons . . . . . (312) 527-0351
Hamblin, Randy Represented By: Deborah Wolfe . . . . . (215) 232-6666
Hamilton, Ken 16 Helen Avenue, West Orange, NJ 07052 . . . . . (973) 736-6532
Hamilton, Laurie 600 N McClurg #2412A, Chicago, IL 60611 . . . . . (312) 944-3970
Hamilton, Pamela Represented By: Langley & Associates . . . . . (847) 670-0912
Hamlin, Janet 529 Ninth Street #1, Brooklyn, NY 11215 . . . . . (718) 768-3647
Hamlin, Mary Jo 8024 Henry Clay Boulevard, Liverpool, NY 13090 . . . . . (315) 652-7236
Hammer, Claudia Represented By: Clare Jett & Associates . . . . . (502) 228-9427
Hammond, Franklin 5 Rumsey Road, Toronto, ON Canada M4G 1N5 . . . . . (416) 423-9471
Represented By: Scott Hull Associates . . . . . (937) 433-8383
Hammond, Joseph Represented By: Square Moon . . . . . (510) 253-9451
Hampton, Blake Represented By: Creative Freelancers . . . . . (800) 398-9544
Hampton, Gerry 4792 Tiara Drive, Ste. 204, Huntington Beach, CA 92649 . . . . . (714) 840-8239
Hampton, Stacie Philadelphia, PA 19103 . . . . . (215) 563-1875
Hamrick, Chuck 1068 Ridgefield Road, Wilton, CT 06897 . . . . . (203) 761-0388
Hancock, Roberta P.O. Box 7544, Phoenix, AZ 85011 . . . . . (602) 265-4389
Hand, Judy Represented By: Berendsen & Associates . . . . . (513) 861-1400
Represented By: Creative Connection . . . . . (410) 360-5981
Hankels, Margaret 662 ½ Tanion Road, Sante Fe, NM 87501 . . . . . (505) 989-8032
Hankins, Jane Represented By: Carol Bancroft & Friends . . . . . (203) 748-4823

Hanley, Debbie 500 Aurora Avenue, Ste. 405, Seattle, WA 98109 . . . . . (206) 621-0410
Hanley, John 4803 Wyoming Way, Crystal Lake, IL 60012 . . . . . (815) 459-1123
Hanlon, Virginia Represented By: Claudia Miller Artists Unlimited . . . . . (561) 995-9444
Hanna, B. Scott 408 N Gower Street, Los Angeles, CA 90004 . . . . . (213) 463-8471
Hanna, Cheryl Represented By: Carol Bancroft & Friends . . . . . (203) 748-4823
Hanna, Gary Represented By: Creative Freelancers . . . . . (800) 398-9544
Hannah, Halstead 1250 Addison #211B, Berkeley, CA 94702 . . . . . (800) 742-4225
Hannon, Holly Represented By: SI International . . . . . (212) 254-4996

HANSEN, CLINT Pages 299,301,444
Represented By: The Neis Group **(616) 672-5756**
e-mail: neisgroup@wmis.net • Website: www.neisgroup.com • Specialties: Food; Still Life

Hansen, Derek Represented By: Donna Rosen Artists' Rep . . . . . (301) 384-8925
Hanson, Glen Represented By: Three in a Box . . . . . (416) 367-2446
Hanson, Warren Represented By: The Schuna Group . . . . . (612) 631-8480
Hantel, Johanna 1025 Stokes Avenue, 1st Flr., Collingswood, NJ 08108 . . . . . (609) 858-1911
Harbour, Elizabeth Represented By: Alan Lynch Artists . . . . . (908) 813-8718
Hardebeck, George Represented By: Berendsen & Associates . . . . . (513) 861-1400
Harden, Laurie 121 Banta Lane, Boonton, NJ 07005 . . . . . (973) 335-4578
Represented By: Christina Tugeau . . . . . (203) 438-7307
Hardesty, Debra S. 1017 Vallejo Way, Sacramento, CA 95818 . . . . . (916) 446-1824
Hardiman, Miles 2505 W Alamo Avenue, Littleton, CO 80120 . . . . . (303) 794-4449
Hardy, Neil O. 2 Woods Grove Road, Westport, CT 06880 . . . . . (203) 226-4446

HARGREAVES, GREG Pages 146-147
Represented By: Carol Guenzi Agents, Inc. **(800) 417-5120**
e-mail: artagent@artagent.com • Website: www.artagent.com • Specialties: Acrylic; Mixed Media; Humour

Hargreaves, Joe Represented By: Image Mill . . . . . (515) 490-6110
Harlan, Tom 53 W 19th Street, New York, NY 10011 . . . . . (212) 229-1363
Harley, Evaline 312 Maple Avenue, Oakville, ON Canada L6J 2H7 . . . . . (905) 845-1704
Harlin, Greg 17 Pinewood Street, Annapolis, MD 21401 . . . . . (410) 266-6550
Harmon, Traci Represented By: Creative Freelancers . . . . . (800) 398-9544

HARMS, DENNIS Pages 278-279
Barrington, IL 60010 • Fax (847) 304-9953 **(847) 304-9952**
e-mail: harmsillst@earthlink.net • Website: http://home.earthlink.net/~harmsillst
Specialties: Advertising; Computer; Conceptual; Corporate; Digital; Editorial; Graphic Design/Illustration; Illustrative; Stock; Technical

Harper, Mike 15 Waverly Place, Red Bank, NJ 07701 . . . . . (732) 741-0552
Represented By: Sylvia Franks . . . . . (310) 276-5282
Harrell, Rob 628 E 63rd Street, Indianapolis, IN 46220 . . . . . (317) 722-1344
Harrigan, Peggy Represented By: Connie Koralik Associates Represents . . . . . (312) 944-5680
Harrington, Glenn 54 Twin Lear Road, Pipersville, PA 18947 . . . . . (610) 294-8104
Harrington, Stephen 255 Wilton Road W, Ridgefield, CT 06877 . . . . . (203) 431-5854
Represented By: John Brewster Creative Services . . . . . (203) 226-4724
Harris, Greg Represented By: Cornell & McCarthy, LLC . . . . . (203) 454-4210
Harris, Jennifer Beck 7134 Glendora Avenue, Dallas, TX 75230 . . . . . (214) 750-4669
Harris, John Represented By: Alan Lynch Artists . . . . . (908) 813-8718
Harris, Martin Represented By: Spectrum Studio, Inc. . . . . . (612) 332-2361
Harrison, Chris Represented By: Deborah Snyder Creative Representative . . . . . (612) 922-3462
Harrison, Mark Represented By: Fran Seigel . . . . . (212) 486-9644

HARRISON, MATILDA Pages 366-367
Represented By: Alan Lynch Artists **(908) 813-8718**
Represented By: Arena **44 171 267 9661**

Harrison, Nancy 4671 Durham Road, Gardenville, PA 18926 . . . . . (610) 390-4540
Harrison, William Represented By: Renard Represents . . . . . (212) 490-2450
Harritos, Pete Represented By: Scott Hull Associates . . . . . (937) 433-8383
Harrold, Brian Represented By: American Artists . . . . . (212) 682-2462
Harsh, Fred Represented By: Carol Bancroft & Friends . . . . . (203) 748-4823

Hart, John 5906 N Moore Avenue, Portland, OR 97217 . . . . . (503) 289-3477
Represented By: Rita Gatlin Represents . . . . . (800) 924-7881
Hart, Thomas 225 Lafayette Street, Ste. 509, New York, NY 10012 . . . . . (212) 925-2220
Harte, Thomas 88-07 151st Avenue, Howard Beach, NY 11414 . . . . . (718) 843-8559
Hartland, Jessie 165 William Street, New York, NY 10038 . . . . . (212) 233-1413
Hartman, Bill Represented By: Claudia Miller Artists Unlimited . . . . . (561) 995-9444
Hartmann, Jill Von 12 S Fair Oaks Avenue #208, Pasadena, CA 91105 . . . . . (626) 564-8728
Represented By: Rita Marie & Friends . . . . . (312) 222-0337
Hartmann, Robin 8900 Blossom Drive, Cincinnati, OH 45236 . . . . . (513) 793-7701
Harto, David 826 NW 63rd Street, Seattle, WA 98107 . . . . . (206) 783-1550
Represented By: Pat Hackett Artist Representative . . . . . (206) 447-1600
Hartsock, Marcia Represented By: Berendsen & Associates . . . . . (513) 861-1400
Harvey, Amanda Represented By: HK Portfolio . . . . . (212) 675-5719
Harwin, Fred Represented By: Spencer Church . . . . . (206) 860-9239
Harwood, John Represented By: Bernstein & Andriulli, Inc. . . . . . (212) 682-1490
Haskamp, Steve Represented By: SI International . . . . . (212) 254-4996
Hasler, Gino 13630 Muscatine Street, Arleta, CA 91331-6305 . . . . . (818) 782-1736
Hathaway, Margaret Represented By: Reactor Art & Design Ltd. . . . . . (416) 703-1913
Hatlen, Beth Represented By: The Schuna Group . . . . . (612) 631-8480

HATLEY Page 64
1101E N Hamilton Street, Richmond, VA 23221 • Fax (500) 442-2428 **(500) 442-2428**
Specialties: Children; Computer; Editorial; Food; Product

Haverfield, Mary 3104 Cornell Avenue, Dallas, TX 75205 . . . . . (214) 520-2548
Havlicek, Karel Represented By: Joel Harlib Associates, Inc. . . . . . (312) 573-1370
Haworth, Michel 23 rue Black, Valleyfield, PQ Canada J6S 4C8 . . . . . (514) 373-2689
Hayes, Colin 11908 31st Drive SE, Everett, WA 98208 . . . . . (425) 338-5452
Hayes, Connie 301 E 21st Street, New York, NY 10010 . . . . . (212) 674-0649
Hayes, John 2145 N Dayton, Chicago, IL 60614 . . . . . (773) 665-4536
Hayes, Stephen F. 418 SW Washington, Ste. 309, Portland, OR 97204 . . . . . (503) 228-9189
Represented By: The Art Agency . . . . . (503) 203-8300
Hayes, Steve 3229 Glengyle Avenue, Cincinnati, OH 45208 . . . . . (513) 871-2278
Represented By: Liz Sanders Agency . . . . . (714) 495-3664
Haynes, Bryan Represented By: The Pate Company . . . . . (805) 529-8111
Haynes, Michael Represented By: Brooke & Company . . . . . (214) 352-9192

HAYNES, JIM Pages 392,398,455
Represented By: Donna Rosen Artists' Rep **(301) 384-8925**
email: djrosen@erols.com • Website: www.aaarrt.com/donnasgallery
Specialties: Children: Editorial; Humour; Icons; Maps & Charts; Whimsical

Hays, Diane Represented By: Linda De Moreta Represents . . . . . (510) 769-1421
Head, Gary Represented By: Brooke & Company . . . . . (214) 352-9192
Hearn, Diane Dawson 1099 Deerfield Drive NW, Blacksburg, VA 24060 . . . . . (540) 951-2853
Heater, James 283 Mott Street #1F, New York, NY 10012 . . . . . (212) 226-7844
Represented By: Stock Illustration Source . . . . . (212) 691-6400
Heatwole, Marsha 1168 Sugar Creek, Lexington, VA 24450 . . . . . (540) 463-2255
Heavner, Obadinah 10310 Mary Avenue NW, Seattle, WA 98177 . . . . . (206) 789-8899
Heer, Peter 500 Molino Street #306, Los Angeles, CA 90013 . . . . . (213) 617-1282
Hefferan, Rob Represented By: HK Portfolio . . . . . (212) 675-5719
Heffernan, Phil Represented By: Hankins & Tegenborg Ltd. . . . . . (212) 867-8092
Heffron, Joe 529 S Seventh Street, Minneapolis, MN 55415 . . . . . (612) 729-7896
Hehenberger, Shelly Represented By: HK Portfolio . . . . . (212) 675-5719
Heidel, Theresa Represented By: Carol Bancroft & Friends . . . . . (203) 748-4823
Heindel, Bob Represented By: Artists Associates . . . . . (212) 755-1365
Heine, Caren Represented By: Rep Art . . . . . (604) 684-6826
Heine, Mark Represented By: Rep Art . . . . . (604) 684-6826

HEINER, JOE & KATHY Pages 86-87,115,437
Represented By: Lindgren & Smith **(212) 397-7330**
e-mail: inquiry@lindgrensmith.com • Website: www.lindgrensmith.com • Specialties: Digital; People; Product; Realism

Heinz, Joel Represented By: David Montagano & Associates . . . . . (312) 527-3283
Heinz, Laure Represented By: The Art Agency . . . . . (503) 203-8300

Heinze, Mitchell Represented By: Barbara Gordon Associates Ltd. . . . . (212) 686-3514
Represented By: The Neis Group . . . . . (616) 672-5756
Hejja, Attila Represented By: Mendola Ltd. . . . . (212) 986-5680
Hellmann, Margaret 1007 Lewis Circle, Santa Cruz, CA 95062 . . . . . (408) 462-9337
Helpin, T. Scott 712 E Waterloo Court, Bloomington, IN 47401 . . . . . (812) 323-7759
Helton, Lindan Represented By: Marlena Agency . . . . . (609) 252-9405
Henderling, Lisa Represented By: Artco . . . . . (212) 889-8777
Represented By: Susan & Company . . . . . (206) 232-7873
Henderson, David Represented By: Mendola Ltd. . . . . (212) 986-5680
Henderson, Louis 4520 Rising Hill Road, Altadena, CA 91001 . . . . . (626) 797-6754
Henderson, Stephanie 1605 Petrolia, West Bloomfield, MI 48324 . . . . . (248) 360-0531
Henderson + Tyner 315 N Spruce Street, Winston-Salem, NC 27101 . . . . . (910) 748-1364
Hendler, Sandra 1823 Spruce Street, Philadelphia, PA 19103 . . . . . (215) 735-7380
Hendricks, Steve Represented By: Nancy George . . . . . (805) 688-3772
Hendrickson, Kathy P.O. Box 883, New Providence, NJ 07974 . . . . . (908) 665-2192
Hendrix, Bryan 777 Ponce De Leon Terrace, Atlanta, GA 30306 . . . . . (404) 875-4290
Hendrix, Reggie Represented By: Famous Frames . . . . . (310) 642-2721

HENNESSY, THOMAS Page 243
210 Chapman Road, Mill Valley, CA 94941 • Fax (415) 388-9703 **(415) 388-7959**
Represented By: Rita Gatlin Represents **(800) 924-7881**
Website: www.ritareps.com • Specialties: Landscape; Nature; Product; Scratchboard; Wildlife

Henrichsen, Ronda Represented By: Creative Connection . . . . . (410) 360-5981
Represented By: Square Moon . . . . . (510) 253-9451
Henrie, Cary 1659 E Maple Hills Drive, Bountiful, UT 84010 . . . . . (801) 298-2044
Henriquez, Celeste Represented By: Pat Hackett Artist Representative . . . . . (206) 447-1600

HENRY, DOUG Pages 168,175
Represented By: American Artists **(212) 682-2462**
e-mail: info@amerartists.com • Website: www.amerartists.com

Henry, James 5900 Filaree Heights Avenue, Malibu, CA 90265 . . . . . (310) 457-1500
Henry, Paul 46660 N 27th Avenue, New River, AZ 85027 . . . . . (602) 465-5796
Represented By: Bill & Maurine Klimt . . . . . (212) 799-2231
Henson, Dwayne Represented By: Creative Connection . . . . . (410) 360-5981
Hepburn, Steve Represented By: Jaz & Jaz . . . . . (206) 633-3445

HERBERT, JENNIFER Pages 86-87,106
Represented By: Lindgren & Smith **(212) 397-7330**
e-mail: inquiry@lindgrensmith.com • Website: www.lindgrensmith.com

HERBERT, JONATHAN Pages 51,431
Represented By: Renard Represents **(212) 490-2450**
e-mail: renardreps@earthlink.net • Website: www.renardrepresents.com
Specialties: Animation; Digital; Graphic Design/Illustration

Herder, Edwin Represented By: Hankins & Tegenborg Ltd. . . . . (212) 867-8092
Hergert, Greg 901 Burdan Drive, Ports Town, PA 19464 . . . . . (610) 970-1882
Hering, Al 16 Lown Court, Poughkeepsie, NY 12603 . . . . . (914) 471-7326
Herman, Hersch 10669 Harriet Walk, St. Louis, MO 63114 . . . . . (314) 427-3211
Herman, Terry Represented By: Nachreiner Boie Art Factory . . . . . (414) 785-1940
Hernandez, Erasmo Represented By: Evelyne Johnson Associates . . . . . (212) 532-0928
Hernandez, Jorge 1200 83rd Street, Ste. 1, North Bergen, NJ 07047 . . . . . (201) 869-9489
Herrick, David 2425 Musselwhite Avenue, Orlando, FL 32804 . . . . . (407) 898-8921
Herring, Michael Represented By: Hankins & Tegenborg Ltd. . . . . (212) 867-8092
Hersh, Stephen Represented By: Flannery Lane Ltd. . . . . (914) 631-1413
Herzberg, Tom 4128 W Eddy Street, Chicago, IL 60641 . . . . . (773) 736-1089
Heslop, Michael Represented By: Artco . . . . . (212) 889-8777
Hess, Lydia J. 1246 SE 49th Street, Portland, OR 97215 . . . . . (503) 234-4757
Hess, Mark Represented By: The Newborn Group . . . . . (212) 260-6700

HESSELBERTH C/O SPUR DESIGN, JOYCE Pages 406-407
3647 Falls Road, Baltimore, MD 21211 • Fax (410) 235-4674 **(410) 235-7803**
e-mail: joyce@spurdesign.com • Website: www.spurdesign.com
Specialties: Corporate; Editorial; Graphic Design/Illustration; Illustrative

Heu, Michael 1139 Prospect Avenue #1-A, Brooklyn, NY 11218 .... (718) 369-6143
Hewett, Daphne 181 S Edgewood #1, Memphis, TN 38104 .... (901) 274-1214
Represented By: Teenuh Foster Represents .... (314) 647-7377
Represented By: Artworks .... (212) 627-1554
Hewgill, Jody 260 Brunswick Avenue, Toronto, ON Canada M5S 2M7 .... (416) 924-4200
Hewitson, Jennifer 1145 Wotan Drive, Encinitas, CA 92024 .... (760) 944-6154
Hewitt, Margaret Represented By: Liz Sanders Agency .... (714) 495-3664
Heyd Wharton, Jennifer Represented By: Philip M. Veloric Associates .... (610) 520-3470
Heyer, Carol 925 E Avenida de los Arboles, Thousand Oaks, CA 91360 .... (805) 492-3683
Heyer, Marilee 1619 Sixth Street, Los Angeles, CA 93402 .... (805) 528-0161
Hicklin, Laurie A. 8028 Dusenberg Court, Sacramento, CA 95828 .... (916) 689-6725
Hicks, Gail Represented By: Sharon Morris Associates .... (415) 362-8280

HIGGINS, PAUL Page 201
Represented By: American Artists **(212) 682-2462**
Represented By: Ian Flemming Associates
e-mail: info@amerartists.com • Website: www.amerartists.com

High, Greg P.O. Box 460404, Escondido, CA 92046 .... (760) 480-1827
High, Richard Represented By: Jerry Leff Associates, Inc. .... (212) 697-8525
Hilber, Nelson Represented By: Kolea Baker Artists Representative .... (206) 784-1136
Hildebrandt, Tim Represented By: Frank & Jeff Lavaty .... (212) 427-5632
Hilden, Kathy P.O. Box 804, Evanston, IL 60204-0804 .... (847) 475-2954
Hill, Amy 214 E 10th Street #3, New York, NY 10003 .... (212) 473-2423

HILL, ART Page 260
14211 SW Teal, Apt. A, Beaverton, OR 97008 • Fax (503) 590-6471 **(503) 838-3333**
Represented By: Deborah **(503) 590-6767**
e-mail: DebinOR@aol.com • Specialties: Black & White; Lettering

HILL, CHARLIE Page 119
Represented By: Wiley Group **(415) 442-1822**
e-mail: dww@wco.com • Website: www.charliehill.com • Specialty: Digital

Hill, Malcolm Represented By: Art Department .... (212) 925-4222
Hill, Michael 701 Estate Court, Bel Air, MD 21015 .... (410) 893-7620
Represented By: American Artists .... (212) 682-2462
Represented By: Kate Larkworthy Artist Rep. Ltd. .... (212) 633-1310

HILL, ROGER Pages 12-13
63A Yorkville Avenue, Toronto, ON Canada M5R 1B7 • Fax (416) 923-5933 **(416) 923-5933**

Hill, Tracy Represented By: Kimberley Boege .... (602) 265-4389
Hill Creative Services, Norm 3511 N Hall, Ste. 307, Dallas, TX 75219 .... (214) 520-2552
Hilliard, Fred 8146 Coyle Road, Quilcene, WA 98376 .... (360) 765-4009
Represented By: Jerry Leff Associates, Inc. .... (212) 697-8525
Hilliard-Barry, Pat 3742 N 79th Street, Omaha, NE 68134 .... (402) 572-8041
Hillier, Diane 170 Corte Madera Road, Portola Valley, CA 94028 .... (650) 851-9715
Hilscher, Tony Represented By: Spectrum Studio, Inc. .... (612) 332-2361
Hilton-Campbell, Denise 17336 Montero Road, San Diego, CA 92128 .... (619) 485-6771
Represented By: Salzman International .... (415) 285-8267
Hine, Eileen Represented By: Cornell & McCarthy, LLC .... (203) 454-4210
Hines, Jordan 1844 Los Encantos Court, Los Gatos, CA 95032 .... (408) 379-6444
Hines, Norman 719 Flint Way, Sacramento, CA 95818 .... (916) 444-6553
Hinkley, Mary 561 La Loma Road, Pasadena, CA 91105 .... (626) 441-1944
Hinlicky, Gregg P.O. Box 1521, Toms River, NJ 08754 .... (732) 270-4300

HINSHAW, ELIZABETH Page 243
P.O. Box 585, Ashland, OR 97520 **(541) 488-2137**
Represented By: Rita Gatlin Represents **(800) 924-7881**
Website: www.ritareps.com • Specialties: Celebrity; Portraiture

Hinton, Liz 61 Churchill Road, Nailsworth, Stroud, Glos, England GL6 ODE . . . 44 145 383 3727
Hirashima, Jean 166 E 61st Street #5C, New York, NY 10021 . . . (212) 593-9778
Represented By: Lori Nowicki & Associates . . . (212) 243-5888
Hirokawa, Masami 3144 W 26th Avenue, Denver, CO 80211 . . . (303) 455-9613
Hish, Jerry 312 Queens Street, Studio 3, Hamilton, ON Canada L8P 3T5 . . . (905) 527-0321

HITCH, DAVID Pages 368-369
Represented By: Alan Lynch Artists **(908) 813-8718**
Represented By: Arena **44 171 267 9661**

Hite, Michael 11166 W Arbor Drive, Littleton, CO 80127 . . . (303) 979-9527
Ho, David 35884 Carnation Way, Fremont, CA 94536 . . . (510) 742-1772
Hobb/Angry Cow, Dan 164 Colbeck Street, Toronto, ON Canada M65 1V9 . . . (416) 767-6035
Hobbs, Pam 4150 Hana Highway, Haiku, HI 96708 . . . (808) 573-0042
Hobson, Ken 3 Pineburr Court, Greensboro, NC 27455 . . . (336) 282-7789
Hochgertel, Robert Represented By: Leyden Diversified . . . (215) 663-0587
Hodges, Ken 12401 Bellwood Road, Los Alamitos, CA 90720 . . . (562) 431-4343
Hodges, Mike Represented By: Brooke & Company . . . (214) 352-9192
Represented By: Jerry Leff Associates, Inc. . . . (212) 697-8525
Hodgson, Marion RR #7, Orangeville, ON Canada L9W 2Z3 . . . (519) 940-0192
Hoeffner, Deb 538 Cherry Tree Lane, Kinnelon, NJ 07405 . . . (973) 838-5490
Hoff, Ken Represented By: Jaz & Jaz . . . (206) 633-3445
Hoff, Terry Represented By: Jerry Leff Associates, Inc. . . . (212) 697-8525
Hoffar, Baron & Company 11 E Hubbard Street #711, Chicago, IL 60611 . . . (312) 923-1117
Hofflund, Sylvia 909 Loma Avenue, Long Beach, CA 90804-5252 . . . (562) 439-4175
Hoffman, Eugene 1811 12th Street, Greeley, CO 80631 . . . (970) 351-7991
Hoffman, Joanne 740 Bainbridge Street, Philadelphia, PA 19147 . . . (215) 928-9365
Hoffman, Kate P.O. Box 224, Ft. Collins, CO 80522 . . . (970) 493-2168
Hoffmann, Robert 61A Delaware Street, Toronto, ON Canada M6H 2S8 . . . (416) 588-8359

HOFKIN, BONNIE Pages 65,465
Represented By: Joanne Palulian **(212) 581-8338**
Specialties: Medical; Technical

Hogan, Jamie 265 Pleasant Avenue, Peaks Island, ME 04108 . . . (207) 766-9726

HOGAN, SHANNON Page 277
Represented By: Famous Frames **(310) 642-2721**
e-mail: info@famousframes.com • Website: www.famousframes.com • Specialties: Animation; Storyboards

HOGAN, STEPHEN Pages 264,465
1131 Frost Lane, Peekskill, NY 10566 • Fax (914) 736-6524 **(914) 737-4304**
Represented By: Christine Prapas **(503) 658-7070**
Specialties: Digital; Medical; Technical

Hoggan, Pat Represented By: Square Moon . . . (510) 253-9451
Hogue, Michael Represented By: Suzanne Craig Represents, Inc.. . . . (918) 749-9424
Hohmann, Pamela 3225 N Connecticut, Royal Oak, MI 48073 . . . (313) 585-1897
Hokanson/Cichetti 737 E Passyunk Avenue, Philadelphia, PA 19147 . . . (215) 440-8280
Represented By: Fran Seigel . . . (212) 486-9644
Holbrook, Heather 196 Chatham Avenue, Toronto, ON Canada M4J 1K9 . . . (416) 463-7098
Holdcroft, Tina 83 Chine Drive, Scarborogh, ON Canada M1M 2K8 . . . (416) 264-4506

HOLDER, JIMMY Pages 346-347
Represented By: Sal Barracca Associates **(212) 889-2400**
Specialties: Illustrative; Humour

Holder, John Represented By: Philip M. Veloric Associates . . . (610) 520-3470
Holland, Brad 96 Greene Street, New York, NY 10012. . . . (212) 226-3675

Holland, Gay Represented By: Square Moon (510) 253-9451
Holley, Jason 852 Monterey Road, South Pasadena, CA 91030 (818) 403-0152
Hollingworth, Bella 4872 Lorraine Drive, San Diego, CA 92115 (619) 229-0650
Holloman, Kurt 3077 SW Diane Drive, Lake Oswego, OR 97035 (503) 636-4221

HOLM, JOHN Pages 168,176
Represented By: American Artists **(212) 682-2462**
e-mail: info@amerartists.com • Website: www.amerartists.com • Specialties: Conceptual; Humour

Holm, Sharon Represented By: Cornell & McCarthy, LLC (203) 454-4210
Holman, Carolyn 2521 NW Thurman Street, Portland, OR 97210 (503) 224-6010
Holmer, Martie 971 First Avenue #2C, New York, NY 10022 (212) 355-4610
Holmes, David Represented By: Bernstein & Andriulli, Inc. (212) 682-1490

HOLMES, MATTHEW Pages 50,462
Represented By: Renard Represents **(212) 490-2450**
e-mail: renardreps@earthlink.net • Website: www.renardrepresents.com • Specialties: Airbrush; Realism

Holmes, Nigel 544 Riverside Avenue, Westport, CT 06880 (203) 226-2313
Holmes-Landers, Roberta Represented By: Square Moon (510) 253-9451

HOLMGREN, JEAN Page 71
1348 Pidgeon Roost Road, Byhalia, MS 38611 • Fax (901) 527-3404 **(901) 527-3396**
Represented By: The Pred Group **(913) 438-7733**
Website: www.predgroup.com • Specialties: Advertising; Children; Conceptual; Corporate

Holt-Ayriss, Linda Represented By: Susan & Company (206) 232-7873
Holton, Susan 1512 W Jonquil, Chicago, IL 60626 (773) 973-6429
Holtzman, Sandy Represented By: Sandy Danz (530) 622-3218
Holub, Joan Represented By: Publishers' Graphics (203) 797-8188

HOM & HOM ILLUSTRATION Pages 168,183
3197 W Black Hills Court, Westlake Village, CA 91362 • Fax (805) 374-9647 **(805) 374-9634**
26820 Cactus Trail, Calabassa Hill, CA 91301 • Fax (818) 880-1525 **(818) 880-1524**
Represented By: American Artists **(212) 682-2462**
e-mail: info@amerartists.com • Website: www.amerartists.com
Specialties: Advertising; Airbrush; Animation; Cartoon; Children; Computer; Graphic Design/Illustration; Humour; Mixed Media; Realism

Hondros, Art Represented By: Artline (704) 376-7609
Hong, Beverly 4860 Glencairn Road, Los Angeles, CA 90027 (213) 666-0635
Hong, Min Jae 54 Points of View, Warwick, NY 10990 (914) 986-8040
Honikman, Jessica 165 W 91st Street #4C, New York, NY 10024 (212) 769-2757
Hood, Philip Represented By: Alan Lynch Artists (908) 813-8718
Hooks, Mitchell Represented By: Artworks (212) 627-1554
Hopkins, Chris Represented By: The Pate Company (805) 529-8111
Hopkins, Edie Represented By: Creative Connection (410) 360-5981
Horjus, Peter 3647 India Street #1, San Diego, CA 92103 (619) 299-0729

HORNE, DOUG Pages 263,431
3435 E Turney Avenue, Phoenix, AZ 85018 • Fax (602) 956-6919 **(602) 553-8438**
Represented By: Christine Prapas **(503) 658-7070**
e-mail: horneid@ix.netcom.com • Website: www.netcom.com/~horneid
Specialties: Advertising; Computer; Conceptual; Digital; Editorial; Realism; Stock; 3D

Horridge, Peter Represented By: Bernstein & Andriulli, Inc. (212) 682-1490
Horton, Brian Represented By: Allen Spiegel & Associates (408) 372-4672
Horvath, Barbara Represented By: Creative Connection (410) 360-5981
Horvath, Peter 2226 York Avenue, Ste. 3, Vancouver, BC Canada V6K 1C6 (604) 739-5803
Represented By: Patti Shaw (416) 361-3184
Hoston, James 420 Clinton Avenue #2H, Brooklyn, NY 11238 (718) 230-7908
Hotchkiss, Robin Represented By: Deborah Wolfe (215) 232-6666
Houston, Gary 1306 NW Hoyt #203, Portland, OR 97209 (503) 248-0510
Hovland, Gary 74 Brevoorte, Chappaqua, NY 10514 (914) 238-6003
Howa, Frank 4145 Via Marina #215, Marina Del Rey, CA 90292 (310) 301-9794

Howard, Jason 214 W 96th Street, Apt. 2C, New York, NY 10025 . . . . . (212) 866-7568
Howard, John H. Represented By: The Newborn Group . . . . . (212) 260-6700
Howard, Kim Represented By: Square Moon . . . . . (510) 253-9451
Howard, Rob 55 Westland Terrace, Haverhill, MA 01830 . . . . . (508) 372-8915
Howard Stutesman, Deborah 14378 County Road, Lyons, OH 43533 . . . . . (419) 335-3340
Howe, John Represented By: Alan Lynch Artists . . . . . (908) 813-8718
Howe, Philip 540 First Avenue S, Seattle, WA 98104 . . . . . (206) 682-3453
Howell, Van P.O. Box 889, Westhampton Beach, NY 11978-0889 . . . . . (516) 288-2688
Hoyler, Sally Represented By: Creative Connection. . . . . . (410) 360-5981
Hoyt, Richard 333 N Michigan Avenue #1410, Chicago, IL 60601 . . . . . (312) 263-0950
Hrabe, Curt 684 Pleasant Avenue, Highland Park, IL 60035-4832 . . . . . (847) 432-4632

HRANILOVICH, BARBARA Page 8
3422 Ridgefield Road, Lansing, MI 48906 • Fax (517) 321-2917 **(517) 321-2917**
Represented By: Bruck & Moss **(212) 980-8061**

Huang, Benrei Represented By: Publishers' Graphics. . . . . . (203) 797-8188
Huber, Philip Represented By: Buck & Kane . . . . . (212) 631-0009
Hubig, Dan San Francisco, CA 94114 . . . . . (415) 824-0838
Santa Barbara, CA 93109 . . . . . (805) 963-0003
Huerta, Catherine Represented By: Bernstein & Andriulli, Inc. . . . . . (212) 682-1490
Represented By: Rosenthal Represents . . . . . (818) 222-5445
Huey, Kenneth 460 N 39th Street, Seattle, WA 98103 . . . . . (206) 632-3759
Represented By: Susan & Company . . . . . (206) 232-7873
Huffaker, Sandy 60 Laurel Avenue, Kingston, NJ 08528. . . . . . (609) 252-0267

HUGHES, MARIANNE Pages 252-253
Represented By: Deborah Wolfe **(215) 232-6666**
Website: www.deborahwolfeltd.com
Specialties: Advertising; Conceptual; Corporate; Editorial; Mixed Media; Oil; Stock

HUGHES, RALPH Pages 338-339
Represented By: The Roland Group **(301) 718-7955**
Website: www.therolandgroup.com • Specialties: Advertising; Airbrush; Caricature; Cartoon; Fantasy; Mixed Media; People; Product; Wildlife

Hughes, Red Represented By: Leighton & Company, Inc. . . . . . (978) 921-0887
Huhn, Tim 324 W Acacia Street, Altadena, CA 91001 . . . . . (626) 791-1287
Represented By: Carole Newman & Associates. . . . . . (310) 394-5031
Hull, Cathy 180 E 79th Street, New York, NY 10021 . . . . . (212) 772-7743
Hull, John 12922 72nd Avenue NE, Kirkland, WA 98034. . . . . . (425) 814-0303
Hull, Richard Represented By: Pema Browne Ltd. . . . . . (914) 985-2936
Hullinger Illustration Studio 8246 Locust Avenue, Miller, IN 46403 . . . . . (219) 938-2911
Hulsey, Kevin 211 Crest Road, Carmel, CA 93923 . . . . . (408) 625-8100
Represented By: Vikki Hart . . . . . (415) 495-4278
Represented By: Cary & Company. . . . . . (404) 296-9666
Represented By: Melissa McCallum . . . . . (847) 441-8993
Hume, Kelly P.O. Box 10878, Bainbridge Island, WA 98110. . . . . . (206) 780-9000
Represented By: Rita Gatlin Represents . . . . . (800) 924-7881
Represented By: Carol Guenzi Agents, Inc. . . . . . (800) 417-5120
Represented By: Robin Ogden Represents . . . . . (612) 925-4174

HUMMEL, JIM Pages 382,423
3023 Delta Road, San Jose, CA 95135-1012 • Fax (408) 270-2349 **(408) 270-2349**
e-mail: k2it@pacbell.net • Specialties: Caricature; Cartoon; Humour; Illustrative; People

Humpert, Thomas 3530 SE Hawthorne Boulevard #2, Portland, OR 97214. . . . . . (503) 234-0326
Humphrey, Sarah 9 New Windsor Terrace, Cornwall, England TR11 3BX. 44 132 631 5582
Humphries, Michael 11241 Martha Ann Drive, Rossmoor, CA 90720. . . . . . (562) 493-3323
2210 Canehill Avenue, Long Beach, CA 90815 . . . . . (562) 430-9089
Hungaski, James 396 Ashford Avenue, Dobbs Ferry, NY 10522 . . . . . (914) 693-6471
Hunsinger, Rich 606 Summit House, West Chester, PA 19382 . . . . . (610) 431-8808
Hunt, Robert Represented By: The Pate Company . . . . . (805) 529-8111
Hunt, Thomas Represented By: Reactor Art & Design Ltd. . . . . . (416) 703-1913

Hunter, Brian 1421 Setzer Road, Stroudsburg, PA 18360 . . . . . (717) 629-2810
Hunter, Stan Represented By: Frank & Jeff Lavaty . . . . . (212) 427-5632
Hunter, Steve Represented By: Leyden Diversified . . . . . (215) 663-0587
Huntley/Muir Represented By: Reactor Art & Design Ltd. . . . . . (416) 703-1913
Huppert, Andrea Represented By: Creative Connection . . . . . (410) 360-5981
Hurlin, Kristin P.O. Box 452, Glen Arbor, MI 49636 . . . . . (616) 334-3128
Hurt, Sam Represented By: Flannery Lane Ltd. . . . . . (914) 631-1413
Hussey, Tim Represented By: Wanda Nowak . . . . . (212) 535-0438
Huston, Lance 2958 Greenwich Road, Glendale, CA 91206 . . . . . (818) 956-7021
Hutching & Associates 154 Wright Avenue, Toronto, ON Canada M6R 1L2 . . . . . (416) 588-0580
Hutchison, Bruce Represented By: Sharon Kurlansky Associates . . . . . (508) 872-4549
Huxtable, John Represented By: Black Inc. Creative Rep. . . . . . (602) 381-1332
Huynh, Si 1613 Creekside Drive, Nanaimo, BC Canada V9S 5V8 . . . . . (604) 753-7484
Huyssen, Roger 54 Old Post Road, Southport, CT 06490 . . . . . (203) 256-9192
Hyatt, Mitch 201 Stewart Street, Carmi, IL 62821 . . . . . (618) 382-3331

HYMAN, MILES Pages 86-87,97
Represented By: Lindgren & Smith **(212) 397-7330**
e-mail: inquiry@lindgrensmith.com • Website: www.lindgrensmith.com • Specialty: Pastels

Hynes, Robert Represented By: Mendola Ltd. . . . . . (212) 986-5680
I.O. Image Represented By: Carol Guenzi Agents, Inc. . . . . . (800) 417-5120
Iannaccone, Cynthia J. 9 Sandcastle Drive, Rochester, NY 14622 . . . . . (716) 288-0868
Ibusuki, James 13053 Beaver Street, Los Angeles, CA 91342 . . . . . (818) 362-9899
Represented By: Mendola Ltd. . . . . . (212) 986-5680
Ickert, Tom 354 E 83rd Street #5-A, New York, NY 10028 . . . . . (212) 794-9723
Ienco, Raff 11 Oakland Drive, Hamilton, ON Canada L8E 3R4 . . . . . (416) 560-0805
Illustrated Alaskan Moose 5 W Main Street, Westerville, OH 43081 . . . . . (614) 898-5316
Imatani, Paige 335 Rennie Avenue, Venice, CA 90291 . . . . . (310) 396-3111
Indigo Studios 1720 Peachtree Street NW, Ste. 433-N, Atlanta, GA 30309 . . . . . (404) 872-0110
Ingemanson, Donna Represented By: Lilla Rogers Studio . . . . . (781) 641-2787
Ingle, Michael 2121 E Hickory Road, Battle Creek, MI 49017 . . . . . (616) 721-8385
Ingram, Fred Represented By: Anne Albrecht & Associates . . . . . (312) 595-0300
Represented By: Susan & Company . . . . . (206) 232-7873
Ink Tank, The 2 W 47th Street, New York, NY 10036 . . . . . (212) 869-1630
Inkwell Studios 68 Dorchester Road, Buffalo, NY 14222 . . . . . (716) 882-0102
Innerst, Stacy Represented By: Artco . . . . . (212) 889-8777
Innes, Grant Represented By: Link . . . . . (416) 530-1500

INOUYE, CAROL Page 331
Represented By: Michele Manasse **(215) 862-2091**
e-mail: mmanasse@new-work.com • Website: www.voicenet.com/~mmanasse
Specialties: Advertising; Black & White; Children; Editorial; Food; Greeting Cards; Murals; People; Product; Poster

Iofin, Michael 318 21st Avenue #6, San Francisco, CA 94121 . . . . . (415) 386-1984
Ioka, Tak Represented By: Famous Frames . . . . . (310) 642-2721
Iosa, Ann Represented By: Carol Bancroft & Friends . . . . . (203) 748-4823
Isaly, Rosalee O. Represented By: Alani Represents . . . . . (212) 465-3355
Ishida, Jui 2012 Huntington Drive #12, South Pasadena, CA 91030 . . . . . (626) 403-1681
Ishige, Susan Smith 537 Chestnut Street, Needham, MA 02192 . . . . . (617) 449-7761
Ishihara, Kazz 33 Gold Street, Apt. 114, New York, NY 10038 . . . . . (212) 964-9895
Iskra Design 911 Western Avenue #405, Seattle, WA 98104 . . . . . (206) 340-9506
Represented By: Munro/Goodman Reps . . . . . (212) 691-2667
Ivanov, Sergey Represented By: Wanda Nowak . . . . . (212) 535-0438
Ivens, Rosalind 330 Prospect Avenue, Brooklyn, NY 11215 . . . . . (718) 499-8285
Izold, Don 20475 Bunker Hill Drive, Cleveland, OH 44126 . . . . . (440) 333-9988
Jaben, Seth New York, NY 10003 . . . . . (212) 673-5631
Jackson, Barry E. 4118 Beck Avenue, Studio City, CA 91604 . . . . . (818) 769-7321
Represented By: Renee Kalish . . . . . (847) 864-6127

JACKSON, JEFF Pages 86-87,110
Represented By: Lindgren & Smith **(212) 397-7330**
e-mail: inquiry@lindgrensmith.com • Website: www.lindgrensmith.com

Jackson, Lance 19 Los Amigos Court, Orinda, CA 94563 . . . . . (510) 253-3131

JACKSON, NANCY RUTH Page 233
Represented By: Sharpshooter Creative Representation, Inc. **(416) 703-5300**
e-mail: shooter@the-wire.com • Website: www.portfolios.com/illustrators
Specialties: Animals; Black & White; Botanical; Editorial; Historical; Illustrative; Nature; People; Scratchboard; Woodcut

Jacobsen, Ken Represented By: Gretchen Harris & Associates .... (612) 822-0650

JACOBSON/FERNANDEZ Page 234
Represented By: Sharpshooter Creative Representation, Inc. **(416) 703-5300**
Represented By: Susan Gomberg (U.S.) **(212) 206-0066**
e-mail: shooter@the-wire.com • Website: www.portfolios.com/illustrators
Specialties: Advertising; Food; Landscape; Liquor/Glass; Nature; People; Portraiture; Product; Realism; Still Life

Jaekel, Susan 409 Alberto Way, Ste. 6, Los Gatos, CA 95032 .... (408) 354-1555

JAGMIN, CHRIS Pages 404, 434,443,453,458
78 Waltham Street, Apt. 1, Boston, MA 02118 • Fax (617) 482-1467 **(617) 482-1604**
e-mail: jagart@aol.com • Website: www.jagart.com Specialties: Advertising; Cartoon; Computer; Digital; Editorial; Graphic Design/Illustration; Humour; Icons; Illustrative; People

Jakesevic, Nenad Represented By: Barbara Gordon Associates Ltd. .... (212) 686-3514
Jambor, Nancy 2100 Ridge Drive #14, Minneapolis, MN 55416 .... (612) 544-6387
James, Bob Represented By: Scott Hull Associates .... (937) 433-8383
James, Kathy Represented By: Rep Art .... (604) 684-6826
James, aka Artman, Arthur Represented By: Those 3 Reps .... (214) 871-1316
Janovitz, Marilyn 41 Union Square W #920, New York, NY 10003 .... (212) 727-8330
Janssen, Charlotta Represented By: The Arts Counsel .... (212) 777-6777
Represented By: Lisa Grafton Represents .... (714) 582-2081
Janssen, Kim 5019 W 55th Street, Roeland Park, KS 66205 .... (913) 667-0567
Jaramillo, Rocio 1 Ontario Court #478-2, Oak Park, IL 60302 .... (708) 383-0453
Jareaux, Robin 100 Pond Street (JP), Boston, MA 02130 .... (617) 524-3099
P.O. Box 1250, Sagamore Beach, MA 02562 .... (508) 888-6277
Jarecka, Danuta 114 E Seventh Street #15, New York, NY 10009 .... (212) 353-3298

JAROSZKO, MICHAEL Pages 168,190
Represented By: American Artists **(212) 682-2462**
e-mail: info@amerartists.com • Website: www.amerartists.com

Jarrie, Martin Represented By: Marlena Agency .... (609) 252-9405
Jarvis, David 3100 Parkway Boulevard, Kissimmee, FL 34747-4526
Jarvis, Nathan Young Represented By: Gretchen Harris & Associates .... (612) 822-0650
Jasin, Mark 1065 Lafayette Street #2, Denver, CO 80218 .... (303) 837-1888
Jasinski, Terry Represented By: Frank Lux & Associates, Inc. .... (312) 222-1361
Jasper, Jackie Represented By: Barbara Gordon Associates Ltd. .... (212) 686-3514
Jaynes, Bill 12200 Montecito Road #G-202, Seal Beach, CA 90740 .... (562) 596-3316
Jaynes, Natalie Cox 1117 Graybar Lane, Nashville, TN 37204 .... (615) 298-3776
JC Illustrations 4202 S 90th Street, Omaha, NE 68127 .... (402) 592-1901

JEFFERY, LYNN Pages 252-253
Represented By: Deborah Wolfe **(215) 232-6666**
Website: www.deborahwolfeltd.com • Specialties: Advertising; Black & White; Cartoon; Children; Conceptual; Editorial; Humour; Mixed Media; Whimsical

Jeffrey, Megan Represented By: Carol Bancroft & Friends .... (203) 748-4823
Jeffries, Shannon P.O. Box 423914, San Francisco, CA 94142-3914 .... (510) 883-0503
Jeftovic, Cindy 424G Trellis Crescent, Mississauga, ON Canada L5L 2M2 .... (905) 828-2879
Jelinek, Kveta 68 Alderbury Drive, Markham, ON Canada L3S 3G1 .... (905) 472-8242
Jenkins, Leonard Represented By: Ken Barboza .... (212) 505-8635
Jenks, Aleta Represented By: Hankins & Tegenborg Ltd. .... (212) 867-8092
Jensen, Brian Represented By: RKB Studios, Inc. .... (612) 339-7055
Jensen, Mark Represented By: Spectrum Studio, Inc. .... (612) 332-2361
Jepson, Beth 1086 N 1750 West, Provo, UT 84604 .... (801) 374-6179
Jerins, Edgar Represented By: Hankins & Tegenborg Ltd. .... (212) 867-8092
Jermann, Paul Represented By: Ann Koeffler Represents .... (213) 957-2327
Represented By: Lori Nowicki & Associates .... (212) 243-5888

Jerome, Karen A. 56 Pickering Street, Needham, MA 02192 .... (781) 444-4804
Jessell, Tim Represented By: Suzanne Craig Represents, Inc. .... (918) 749-9424
Jester, Tom 4336 Jarboe Street, Kansas City, MO 64111 .... (816) 753-3134
Jew, Flora Represented By: Square Moon .... (510) 253-9451
Jew, Robert 1405 Hillcrest Lane, Fallbrook, CA 92028 .... (760) 731-6416
Jewett-Furlo, Alison Represented By: Square Moon .... (510) 253-9451
Jezierski, Chet Represented By: Creative Freelancers .... (800) 398-9544
Jia, Bo Represented By: Carol Bancroft & Friends .... (203) 748-4823
Jiang, X.B. Represented By: R. Fischer & Company .... (312) 368-1441
Jinks, John 27 W 20th Street #1106, New York, NY 10011 .... (212) 675-2961
Jo Esco Portrait Artist 2613 NE Garfield Street, Minneapolis, MN 55418-3015 .... (612) 781-5009
Johannes, Greg Represented By: Harriet Kastaris & Associates .... (314) 773-2600
Johannsen, Robert 1088 Diamond Court, Mississauga, ON Canada L5V 1J5 .... (905) 567-1493
John, Shane 933 N Madison Avenue, Pasadena, CA 91104 .... (818) 797-4709
Johns, Elizabeth Represented By: Carol Bancroft & Friends .... (203) 748-4823
Johnson, Audean Represented By: Artworks .... (212) 627-1554
Johnson, D.B. 31 Wolf Run, Lebanon, NH 03766 .... (603) 448-1017
Johnson, David Represented By: Richard Solomon .... (212) 683-1362
Johnson, Doug 45 E 19th Street, New York, NY 10003 .... (212) 260-1880
Johnson, Gary Represented By: Jae Wagoner .... (310) 392-4877
Johnson, Iskra 911 Western Avenue #405, Seattle, WA 98104 .... (206) 340-9506
Johnson, Joel Peter Represented By: Bruck & Moss .... (212) 980-8061

JOHNSON, JULIE
106 W Fifth Street, West Liberty, IA 52776
Represented By: Anita Grien Represents
Represented By: Roger Johnson Associates
e-mail: angeldog@netins.net • Website: www.anitagrien.com • Specialty: Editorial
Page 282
(319) 627-2424
(212) 697-6170
(765) 497-7504

JOHNSON, KIM
Represented By: Lindgren & Smith
e-mail: inquiry@lindgrensmith.com • Website: www.lindgrensmith.com • Specialty: Digital
Pages 86-87,96
(212) 397-7330

Johnson, Lonni Sue 96 Route 39 N, Sherman, CT 06784 .... (860) 355-2043
Johnson, Osie Represented By: Berendsen & Associates .... (513) 861-1400
Johnson, Pamela 1415 N Key Boulevard, Arlington, VA 22209 .... (703) 525-5012
Johnson, Paul Represented By: Langley & Associates .... (847) 670-0912

JOHNSON, ROB
Represented By: Donna Rosen Artists' Rep
e-mail: djrosen@erols.com • Website: www.aaarrt.com/donnasgallery
Specialties: Advertising; Editorial; Fantasy; Humour; People; Portraiture; Product; Realism; Whimsical; Wildlife
Pages 392,395,441,461,467
(301) 384-8925

Johnson, Rose Represented By: Mary Holland & Company .... (602) 263-8990
Johnson, Sharon Represented By: Image Mill .... (515) 490-6110
Johnson, Stephen T. Represented By: Shannon Associates .... (212) 831-5650
Johnson, W.B. 476 Collage Avenue, Winnipeg, MB Canada R2W 1M8 .... (204) 582-1686
Johnson & Fancher Illustration 440 Sheridan Avenue S, Minneapolis, MN 55405 .... (612) 377-8728
Johnson Graphic Comm., Matt 107 E 23rd Avenue, Anchorage, AK 99503 .... (907) 276-1725
Johnston, Scott 1751 Reliez Valley Road, Lafayette, CA 94549 .... (925) 256-6700
Joly, Dave Represented By: Dolby Represents .... (312) 855-9336
Jonason, Dave Represented By: Clare Jett & Associates .... (502) 228-9427
Jones, Bob Represented By: Artworks .... (212) 627-1554
Jones, Dan Represented By: Salzman International .... (415) 285-8267
Jones, Danielle 55 Charles Street W, Toronto, ON Canada M5S 2W9 .... (416) 968-6277
Jones, Doug 1408 Brenthaven Drive, Brentwood, TN 37027 .... (615) 370-0212
Jones, Holly Represented By: Cornell & McCarthy, LLC .... (203) 454-4210
Jones, Jack M. 872 Starr Road, Newnan, GA 30263 .... (770) 251-1799
Jones, Janet Represented By: Creative Connection .... (410) 360-5981
Jones, Jeff 7011 N 22nd Way, Phoenix, AZ 85020-5607 .... (602) 331-4599
Jones, John Represented By: Cornell & McCarthy, LLC .... (203) 454-4210
Jones, Larry 3000 Chestnut Avenue, Ste. 110, Baltimore, MD 21211 .... (410) 662-8777

JONES, MARY
Represented By: David Montagano & Associates
Specialties: Editorial; Mixed Media
Page 313
(312) 527-3283

Jones, Phillip Represented By: Evelyne Johnson Associates . . . (212) 532-0928
Jones Humorous Illus., Buck 4313 65th Street, Des Moines, IA 50322 . . . (515) 278-0379
Jones-Moore, Lisa Represented By: Christine Prapas . . . (503) 658-7070
Jonke, Tim 1375 Rebecca Drive, Apt. 314, Hoffman Estates, IL 60195 . . . (847) 670-0912
Jordan, Charles Represented By: Pema Browne Ltd. . . . (914) 985-2936
Jordan, Laurie Represented By: Carol Bancroft & Friends . . . (203) 748-4823
Jorgensen, Bruce 95 Youmans Avenue, Washington, NJ 07882 . . . (908) 689-7776
Jost, Larry 311 NW 77th Street, Seattle, WA 98117 . . . (206) 789-3979
Represented By: Susan & Company . . . (206) 232-7873
Joudrey, Ken 5706 Sprinter Lane, Bonita, CA 91902 . . . (619) 479-2622
Joyce, Tony 2456 Matador Drive, Rowland Heights, CA 91748 . . . (626) 964-2918
Joyce, William 3302 Centenary Boulevard, Shreveport, LA 71104 . . . (318) 868-0180
Joyner, Eric 227 Kentucky Street, Petaluma, CA 94952 . . . (707) 769-1344
Judd, Andrew 18 Neepawa Avenue, Toronto, ON Canada M6R 1V2 . . . (416) 537-0700
Juhasz, Victor Represented By: The Newborn Group . . . (212) 260-6700
Julien, Terry Represented By: Lisa Freeman . . . (317) 920-0068
Just, Hal Represented By: Anita Grien Represents . . . (212) 697-6170
Justinsen, Lars Represented By: Jerry Leff Associates, Inc. . . . (212) 697-8525

KABAKER, GAYLE
13 Norman Road, Ashfield, MA 01330
Represented By: Joanne Palulian
e-mail: gkabaker@crocker.com • Website: www.crocker.com/~gkabaker • Specialty: Editorial
Pages 67,442
(413) 625-2529
(212) 581-8338

Kachantones, Robin Represented By: Suzanne Craig Represents, Inc. . . . (918) 749-9424
Kachik, John 3000 Chestnut Avenue, Baltimore, MD 21211 . . . (410) 467-7916
Kaczman, James 16 Acron Road, Brookline, MA 02146-7738 . . . (617) 738-9924
Kafanov, Vasily 320 W 89th Street #6B, New York, NY 10024 . . . (212) 242-4668
Kahn, Don Represented By: Penny & Stermer Group . . . (212) 505-9342
Kahn, Jane Hoellman 241 Central Park West, New York, NY 10024 . . . (212) 787-4421
Kai Bateman, Aaron 92 Maple Street, Colonia, NJ 07067-1608 . . . (732) 388-5913
Kalafat, Loris Represented By: American Artists . . . (212) 682-2462
Kalback, Jerry Represented By: Creative Connection . . . (410) 360-5981

KALLENBACH, GARRETT
3121 N Richmond Street, Chicago, IL 60618 • Fax (773) 604-4219
e-mail: garrettk@earthlink.net • Specialty: Humour
Page 298
(773) 604-4201

Kaloustian, Rosanne 208-19 53rd Avenue, Bayside, NY 11364 . . . (718) 428-4670
Kamalova, Hurshida 18 E 33rd Street, Apt. 3R, New York, NY 10016 . . . (212) 481-5779
Kamena, Marina Represented By: Artworks . . . (212) 627-1554
Kaminski, Karol 664 Southbridge Boulevard, Brunswick, OH 44212 . . . (330) 225-8195
Kamstra, Angela 529 S Seventh Street, Ste. 440, Minneapolis, MN 55415 . . . (612) 332-1832
Kanayama, Nobee 5141 E Anaheim Road, Long Beach, CA 90815 . . . (562) 597-9974
Represented By: Langley & Associates . . . (847) 670-0912
Kane, Nathan Represented By: Martha Productions . . . (310) 390-8663
Kane, Sean 1729 12th Avenue #115, Seattle, WA 98122 . . . (206) 720-6206

KANGAS, DAN
22 Twelve Oaks Drive, Aurora, ON Canada L4G 6J5
e-mail: dkangas@interlog.com • Specialties: Digital; Product; Technical
Page 224
(905) 726-4226

KANIA, MATT
1945 Saunders Avenue, St. Paul, MN 55116 • Fax (651) 698-7144
e-mail: maphero@aol.com • Specialties: Maps & Charts; Science; Wildlife
Pages 76-77,456
(651) 698-6960

Kanner, Catherine Represented By: Martha Productions . . . (310) 390-8663
Kanzler, John 15 Carrington Road, Bethany, CT 06524 . . . (203) 393-1634
Kaplan, Kari 110 Lovato Lane, Santa Fe, NM 87505 . . . (505) 989-8483
Kaplan, Sandra Represented By: Vicki Morgan Associates . . . (212) 475-0440

Karchin, Steve Represented By: Artists Associates . . . . . (212) 755-1365
Karl Studio, Kevin 12437 Court Drive, Sunset Hills, MO 63127 . . . . . (888) 802-8111
Karn, George 6601 Fifth Avenue S, Ste. 11, Minneapolis, MN 55423 . . . . . (612) 798-5977
Karsen, Ken 11440 Oak Drive, P.O. Box 174, Shelbyville, MI 49344-0174 . . . . . (616) 672-5756
Kasinger/Mastel Represented By: Fox Art, Inc. . . . . . (213) 662-0020

KASSIAN, OLENA
Page 235
Represented By: Sharpshooter Creative Representation, Inc.
(416) 703-5300
e-mail: shooter@the-wire.com • Website: www.portfolios.com/illustrators
Specialties: Advertising; Food; Gardens/Flowers; Illustrative; Pastels; Poster; Product; Realism; Still Life; Wildlife

Kastaris, Rip Represented By: Harriet Kastaris & Associates . . . . . (314) 773-2600
Kasun, Mike Represented By: Munro Goodman . . . . . (312) 321-1336
Katayama, Mits 1904 Third Avenue, Ste. 630, Seattle, WA 98101 . . . . . (206) 625-6946
Katchen, Carole Represented By: Carol Bancroft & Friends . . . . . (203) 748-4823
Kathari, Harsha 3632 Gatewood Lane, Aurora, IL 60504 . . . . . (630) 851-9726
Katsulis, Tom 333 N Michigan Avenue, Chicago, IL 60601 . . . . . (312) 553-2244
Katz, Aliona Represented By: Lilla Rogers Studio . . . . . (781) 641-2787
Katz, Les 451 Westminster Road, Brooklyn, NY 11218 . . . . . (718) 284-4779
Kaufman, Mark Represented By: Buck & Kane . . . . . (212) 631-0009
Kay, Stanford 39 Central Avenue, Nyack, NY 10960 . . . . . (914) 358-0798

KAYGANICH, BOB
Page 356
43533 Karli Lane, Canton, MI 48188 • Fax (734) 397-0571
(734) 397-0571
e-mail: itche123@Mich.com • Website: www.mich.com/~itche123
Specialties: Airbrush; Digital; Fantasy; Icons; Illustrative; Poster; Product; Realism

Kaylor, Lori 1739 W Division Road, Huntington, ID 46750 . . . . . (219) 468-2870
Kazuhiko, Sano 105 Stadium Avenue, Mill Valley, CA 91307 . . . . . (415) 381-6377
Kearns Inc., Cliff 392 Murray Street, London, ON Canada N6C 4X4 . . . . . (519) 672-9090
Kecman, Milan Represented By: Cliff Knecht . . . . . (412) 761-5666
Keeley, John Represented By: RKB Studios, Inc. . . . . . (612) 339-7055
Keenan, Joy Dunn Represented By: Carol Bancroft & Friends . . . . . (203) 748-4823
Keeter, Susan Represented By: HK Portfolio . . . . . (212) 675-5719
Kegler, Thomas 147 Briarhill Drive, West Seneca, NY 14224 . . . . . (716) 824-2463
Kehl, Richard Represented By: Jorgensen & Barrett Reps . . . . . (206) 634-1880

KEITH, GARY
Pages 385,442
1419 Parrott Drive, San Mateo, CA 94402 • Fax (650) 358-9327
(650) 358-9398
e-mail: gary@tintoycreative.com • Website: www.tintoycreative.com
Specialties: Advertising; Conceptual; Corporate; Digital; Editorial; Packaging

Keleney, Earl Represented By: Fran Seigel . . . . . (212) 486-9644
Keller, Laurie 4022 Loomis Drive, Muskegon, MI 49441 . . . . . (616) 798-1394

KELLER, MERLE
Page 277
Represented By: Famous Frames
(310) 642-2721
e-mail: info@famousframes.com • Website: www.famousframes.com • Specialties: Animation; Storyboards

Keller, Phil Represented By: Motion Artists, Inc. . . . . . (213) 851-7737
Keller, Steve Represented By: Martha Productions . . . . . (310) 390-8663
Kelley, Barbara 533 Main Street, Northport, NY 11768 . . . . . (516) 754-7374
Kelley, Gary Represented By: Richard Solomon . . . . . (212) 683-1362
Kelley, Patrick 1040 Veto Street NW, Grand Rapids, MI 49504 . . . . . (616) 458-5925
Kendall, Gideon 408 Seventh Street #4, Brooklyn, NY 11215 . . . . . (718) 788-8993
Kendall, Jane Represented By: Cornell & McCarthy, LLC . . . . . (203) 454-4210
Kennedy, Anne 3850 Pine Ridge Drive, Lewis Center, OH 43035 . . . . . (614) 548-5837
Kennedy, Dean Represented By: Carol Guenzi Agents, Inc. . . . . . (800) 417-5120
Kennedy, Kelly 1025 Idaho Avenue #6, Santa Monica, CA 90403 . . . . . (310) 394-2239
Represented By: Dolby Represents . . . . . (312) 855-9336
Kennedy, Victor 514 Meadowfield Court, Lawrenceville, GA 30243 . . . . . (770) 339-0345
Represented By: Steve Edsey & Sons . . . . . (312) 527-0351
Kennevan, Steve Represented By: Lulu Creatives . . . . . (612) 825-7564
Kenny, Mike Represented By: SI International . . . . . (212) 254-4996
Kenyon, Liz 4225 N 36th Street #3, Phoenix, AZ 85018 . . . . . (602) 224-6103

Kern, Michael 2320 La Paz Street, Oceanside, CA 92054 . . . . (760) 757-3336
Kerschl, Karl Represented By: Marvel Entertainment . . . . (212) 696-0808
Kervevan, Jean-Yves Represented By: Hankins & Tegenborg Ltd. . . . . (212) 867-8092
Kest, Kristin Represented By: HK Portfolio . . . . (212) 675-5719
Ketler, Ruth Sofair 101 Bluff Terrace, Silver Spring, MD 20902 . . . . (301) 593-6059
Key De-zyn Studio 4417 Pine Street, Bldg. A, Philadelphia, PA 19104 . . . . (215) 222-3223
Kidd, Diana Represented By: Carol Bancroft & Friends . . . . (203) 748-4823
Kidd, Jeremy 615 ½ Victoria Avenue, Venice, CA 90291-4834 . . . . (310) 314-9832
Kidd, Tom 59 Cross Brook Road, New Milford, CT 06776 . . . . (860) 355-1781
Kiefer, Alfons Represented By: Mendola Ltd. . . . . (212) 986-5680
Kilfoy, Michael Represented By: Harriet Kastaris & Associates . . . . (314) 773-2600
Kilgore, Susi 2804 Averill Avenue, Tampa, FL 33611 . . . . (813) 837-9759
Kilmer, David Represented By: Hankins & Tegenborg Ltd. . . . . (212) 867-8092
Kim, Joung Un Represented By: Kirchoff/Wohlberg, Inc. . . . . (212) 644-2020
Kim, Kimberly Represented By: Artco . . . . (212) 889-8777
Kim, Miran P.O. Box 1506, New York, NY 10159 . . . . (212) 777-4951
Kimber, Murray Represented By: Richard Solomon . . . . (212) 683-1362
Kimble, David Represented By: Kirsch & Associates . . . . (213) 651-3706
Kimble Pondicton Mead Represented By: Artco . . . . (212) 889-8777
Kimura, Hiro 237 Windsor Place, Brooklyn, NY 11215 . . . . (718) 788-9866
Kinder, Jim Represented By: Leyden Diversified . . . . (215) 663-0587
King, Greg Represented By: Michele Manasse . . . . (215) 862-2091
King, J.D. P.O. Box 91, Stuyvesant Falls, NY 12174 . . . . (518) 822-0225
King, Jerry Represented By: Wiley Group . . . . (415) 442-1822
King, Kathleen Represented By: Leyden Diversified . . . . (215) 663-0587
King, Manuel Represented By: Sheryl Beranbaum . . . . (401) 737-8591
King, Mary Represented By: Sheryl Beranbaum . . . . (401) 737-8591
King, Patrick 117 S Cook Street, Ste. 333, Barrington, IL 60010 . . . . (847) 842-0222
King Illustration, Fiona P.O. Box 232722, Encinitas, CA 92023 . . . . (760) 942-1121
Kingsley, D. 525 W 22nd Street #3-E, New York, NY 10011 . . . . (212) 645-7379
Kinkopf, Kathleen 12805 Calle del Oso Place NE, Albuquerque, NM 87111 . . . . (505) 856-2942
Represented By: Those 3 Reps . . . . (214) 871-1316
Kirby, Jill 1559 S 16th Street, Milwaukee, WI 53205 . . . . (715) 345-2161
Kirk, Daniel 207 Baldwin Street, Glen Ridge, NJ 07028 . . . . (201) 748-6997
Represented By: Bernstein & Andriulli, Inc. . . . . (212) 682-1490
Kirk, Rainey Represented By: The Neis Group . . . . (616) 672-5756
Kirkeeide, Deborah Represented By: Spectrum Studio, Inc. . . . . (612) 332-2361
Kirkland, James Represented By: Artco . . . . (212) 889-8777
Kirkman, Rick 2432 W Peoria Avenue #1191, Phoenix, AZ 85209 . . . . (602) 997-6004
Kirtz, Nancy Represented By: Tiffany Represents . . . . (206) 441-7701
Kissinger, Gordon 801 NW Ninth Street, Betonville, AR 72712 . . . . (501) 271-8015
Kitchell, Joyce 2755 Eagle Street, San Diego, CA 92103 . . . . (619) 291-1378
Represented By: Melissa McCallum . . . . (847) 441-8993
Represented By: Mendola Ltd. . . . . (212) 986-5680
Kitchell, Peter Represented By: Joanne Palulian . . . . (212) 581-8338
Kittelberger, Eric 1772 Bramblebush Avenue NW, Massillon, OH 44646 . . . . (330) 830-0893
Kiwak, Barbara Represented By: Barbara Gordon Associates Ltd. . . . . (212) 686-3514
Klanderman, Leland 118 E 26th Street #302, Minneapolis, MN 55404 . . . . (612) 871-4539
Klare, Tom P.O. Box 370561, San Diego, CA 92137 . . . . (619) 565-6167
Klauba, Douglas 9741 S Hamlin Avenue, Evergreen Park, IL 60805 . . . . (708) 229-2507
Klauderman, Leland Represented By: Ceci Bartels Associates . . . . (314) 781-7377
Kleber, John Represented By: Martha Productions . . . . (310) 390-8663
Represented By: Randi Fiat & Associates . . . . (312) 663-5300
Represented By: Marla Matson Represents . . . . (602) 252-5072
Klein, Christopher A. 1145 17th Street NW, Washington, DC 20036 . . . . (202) 857-7678
Klein, David 408 Seventh Street, Brooklyn, NY 11215 . . . . (718) 788-1818

KLEIN, HEDY Page 75
111-56 76th Drive #B3, Forest Hills, NY 11375 **(718) 793-0246**
e-mail: hfklein@mindspring.com • Specialties: Advertising; Conceptual; Editorial; Humour; Water Color

Klein, Michael 22 Edgewater Road, Madison, NJ 07940 . . . . (973) 765-0623
Kleinman Design P.O. Box 552, Valley Cottage, NY 10989 . . . . (718) 281-6874
Klementz-Harte, Lauren P.O. Box 4006, Meriden, CT 06450 . . . . (203) 235-6145
Klickovich, Robert V. 1626 Eastern Parkway, Louisville, KY 40204 . . . . (502) 459-0295

Kliros, Thea Represented By: Bernstein & Andriulli, Inc. .... (212) 682-1490
Klug, David 2304 James Street, McKeesport, PA 15132 .... (412) 754-5584
Kluglein, Karen Represented By: Mattelson Associates .... (516) 487-1323
Knaack, Jennifer Represented By: Air Studio .... (513) 721-1193
Knaak, Dale 901 Superior Avenue #329/331, Sheboygan, WI 53081 .... (920) 457-1915

KNAFF, J.C.
Represented By: Sharpshooter Creative Representation, Inc.
Page 236
(416) 703-5300
e-mail: shooter@the-wire.com • Website: www.portfolios.com/illustrators • Specialties: Commercial; Corporate; Editorial; Graphic Design/Illustration; Illustrative; Murals; People; Poster; Public Relations; 3D

Knier, Maria Represented By: Tiffany Represents .... (206) 441-7701
Knighton, Laurence 7101 W Saxton Drive, Boise, ID 83703 .... (208) 344-0335
Knoll, Kimberly 3850 Eddingham Road, Calabasas, CA 91302 .... (818) 222-5445
Knowles, Philip Represented By: Repertory .... (213) 931-7449

KNOX, BERNEY
Represented By: The Neis Group
Pages 299-300,455
(616) 672-5756
e-mail: neisgroup@wmis.net • Website: www.neisgroup.com • Specialty: Maps & Charts

Knox, Charlotte Represented By: Sally Heflin .... (212) 366-1893
Knutson, Kristin Represented By: Susan & Company .... (206) 232-7873
Kochakji, Patrick 6820 Shoshone Avenue, Van Nuys, CA 91406 .... (818) 708-2240
Koegel, Jeff 1141 Summit Place, Laguna Beach, CA 92651 .... (714) 376-5880
Huntington Beach, CA 92648 .... (714) 969-1775
Koelsch, Michael Represented By: Shannon Associates .... (212) 831-5650
Koen, Viktor 112 E 11th Street #1C, New York, NY 10003 .... (212) 254-3159
Koenig, Judy 1152 Rambling Road, Simi Valley, CA 93065 .... (805) 526-9978
Koerber, Nora Represented By: Das Grup .... (310) 540-5958
Kogan, Pamela Jo Represented By: The Arts Counsel .... (212) 777-6777
Kolacz, Jerzy Represented By: Reactor Art & Design Ltd. .... (416) 703-1913
Kolosta, Darrel Represented By: Marla Matson Represents .... (602) 252-5072
Konopka, Kim P.O. Box 22344, Santa Barbara, CA 93121-2344 .... (805) 965-0430
Konves, B.A. 3302A E Bottsford Avenue, Cudahy, WI 53110 .... (414) 483-5210
Konz, Stephen Represented By: Jaz & Jaz .... (206) 633-3445
Koopsman, Loek Represented By: Carol Bancroft & Friends .... (203) 748-4823
Koren, Edward Represented By: Riley Illustration .... (212) 989-8770
Kortz & Company, Dave 100 W Franklin Avenue, Minneapolis, MN 55402 .... (612) 874-9566
Korusiewicz, Maria Represented By: Janice Stefanski Represents .... (415) 928-0457
Koslow, Howard 1592 Goldspire Road, Toms River, NJ 08755 .... (732) 473-1847
Kosolapov, Alexander Represented By: American Artists .... (212) 682-2462
Kossin, Sandy Represented By: Creative Freelancers .... (800) 398-9544
Kotik, Kenneth Represented By: Rosenthal Represents .... (818) 222-5445
Represented By: Barbara Gordon Associates Ltd. .... (212) 686-3514
Kotzky, Brian Represented By: Artworks .... (212) 627-1554

KOVACH, JOSEPH PAGE
Represented By: Deborah Wolfe
Pages 252-253
(215) 232-6666
Website: www.deborahwolfeltd.com
Specialties: Advertising; Conceptual; Editorial; Mixed Media; People; Portraiture; Stock

Kovalcik, Terry New York, NY 10011 .... (212) 620-7772
Haledon, NJ 07508 .... (973) 942-9359
Kowalski, James Represented By: Donna Rosen Artists' Rep .... (301) 384-8925
Kowalski, Mike 826 56th Street, Port Townsend, WA 98368 .... (360) 379-9691
Kramer, David 3910 Bowser Avenue, Dallas, TX 75219 .... (214) 526-3881
Kramer, Moline Represented By: Jae Wagoner .... (310) 392-4877
Kramer, Peter Represented By: Bernstein & Andriulli, Inc. .... (212) 682-1490
Kratter, Paul 1128 Sanders Drive, Moraga, CA 94556 .... (415) 376-1869
Kraus, Annette 530 31st Avenue E, Seattle, WA 98112 .... (206) 860-6113
Represented By: Leighton & Company, Inc. .... (978) 921-0887
Kraus, James F. 195 W Canton Street, Boston, MA 02116 .... (617) 437-1945
Kray, Robert Represented By: Carol Bancroft & Friends .... (203) 748-4823

KREBS, KURT Pages 338-339
3393 Leewood Drive, Lake Orion, MI 48360 • Fax (248) 393-2204 **(248) 393-2204**
Represented By: The Roland Group **(301) 718-7955**
Website: www.therolandgroup.com • Specialties: Airbrush; Digital; Graphic Design/Illustration; Woodcut

Kreffel, Mike Represented By: Berendsen & Associates . . . . . (513) 861-1400
Kreigh Vander Pluym, Todd 425 Via Anita, Redondo Beach, CA 90277 . . . . . (310) 378-5559
Krejca, Gary 1203 S Ash Avenue, Tempe, AZ 85281 . . . . . (602) 829-0946
Krieger, Richard Represented By: American Artists . . . . . (212) 682-2462
Krieger, Salem 126 W 22nd Street, 2nd Flr., New York, NY 10011 . . . . . (212) 271-4341
Represented By: Creative Freelancers . . . . . (800) 398-9544
Represented By: Connie Koralik Associates Represents . . . . . (312) 944-5680
Kriegshauser, Shannon 12421 W Grafelman Road, Hanna City, IL 61536 . . . . . (309) 565-7110
Krimzer, Herb 1125 Landwehr Road, Northbrook, IL 60062 . . . . . (708) 498-8936
Krizmanic, Tatjana 2303 Bluff Street, Boulder, CO 80304 . . . . . (303) 442-2949
Kroencke, Anja Represented By: Kate Larkworthy Artist Rep. Ltd. . . . . . (212) 633-1310
Krogle, Robert Represented By: Mendola Ltd. . . . . . (212) 986-5680
Represented By: Renee Kalish . . . . . (847) 864-6127
Kroll, Kari 858 Eaton Drive, Pasadena, CA 91107 . . . . . (818) 795-9292
Krommes, Beth 310 Old Street Road, Peterborough, NH 03458 . . . . . (603) 924-8790

KRONEN, JEFF Page 277
Represented By: Famous Frames **(310) 642-2721**
e-mail: info@famousframes.com • Website: www.famousframes.com • Specialties: Animation; Storyboards

KROVATIN, DAN Page 408
2157 Pennington Road, Ewing, NJ 08638 • Fax (609) 882-6181 **(609) 882-6181**
e-mail: dkrovatin@aol.com • Specialty: Scratchboard

Krubs, Kurt Represented By: Mendola Ltd. . . . . . (212) 986-5680
Krudop, Walter 246 W 73rd Street, New York, NY 10023 . . . . . (212) 769-3819
Krumlauf, Vicky 2305 Ashland Street #C, Ashland, OR 97520 . . . . . (800) 435-6509

KUBE, DEAN Pages 252-253
Represented By: Deborah Wolfe **(215) 232-6666**
Website: www.deborahwolfeltd.com • Specialties: Advertising; Celebrity; Children; Conceptual; Editorial; Painterly; Pastels; People; Portraiture; Stock

Kuchar, Karen Represented By: Connie Koralik Associates Represents . . . . . (312) 944-5680
Kueker, Donald L. 829 Gingerwood Court, Manchester, MO 63021-8439 . . . . . (314) 225-1566
Kuhn, Grant M. 233 Bergen Street, Brooklyn, NY 11217 . . . . . (718) 596-7808
Kuhtic, Chares Represented By: SI International . . . . . (212) 254-4996
Kulman, Andrew Represented By: Jacqueline Dedell, Inc. . . . . . (212) 741-2539
Kundas, Leo 2330 Voorhies Avenue #5-O, Brooklyn, NY 11235 . . . . . (718) 769-4864
Kung, Lingta Represented By: Jerry Leff Associates, Inc. . . . . . (212) 697-8525
Kunitake, Tani Represented By: Motion Artists, Inc. . . . . . (213) 851-7737
Kunstler, Mort Represented By: Frank & Jeff Lavaty . . . . . (212) 427-5632
Kunz, Anita 230 Ontario Street, Toronto, ON Canada M5A 2V5 . . . . . (416) 364-3846
Kunze, Helen 1800 S Maple Street, Carthage, MO 64836 . . . . . (417) 359-5233
Kuramoto, John Represented By: Allen Spiegel & Associates . . . . . (408) 372-4672
Kurie, Elaine Represented By: American Artists. . . . . . (212) 682-2462
Kurisu, Jane 97 Airdrie Road, Toronto, ON Canada M4G 1M4 . . . . . (416) 424-2524
Represented By: SI International . . . . . (212) 254-4996
Kurrasch, Toni Represented By: Sylvia Franks . . . . . (310) 276-5282
Kurtz, John Represented By: SI International . . . . . (212) 254-4996
Kurtz, Mara 322 Central Park W, New York, NY 10025 . . . . . (212) 666-1453
Kurtz, Nancy A. 6113 W Stevenson Street, Milwaukee, WI 53213 . . . . . (414) 476-1587
Represented By: Yolanda Burnett Represents . . . . . (770) 967-0039
Kurtzman, Ed Represented By: Lott Representatives . . . . . (212) 953-7088
Kwas, Susan Represented By: Lisa Freeman . . . . . (317) 920-0068
Laan Graphic Art Studio, Cor 414 Crest Drive, Redwood City, CA 94062 . . . . . (650) 365-0953
Laas, Leslie C. 32102 NE 136th Street, Duvall, WA 98019 . . . . . (206) 788-6337
Labadie, Ed 1655 Fairview Avenue, Ste. 206, Boise, ID 83702 . . . . . (208) 388-0411
Labanda, Jordi Represented By: Art Department . . . . . (212) 925-4222

Labatt, Dianne 515 Roselawn Avenue, Toronto, ON Canada M5N IK2 . . . . . (416) 485-9829
Labbe, John 97 Third Avenue #2E, New York, NY 10003 . . . . . (212) 529-2831
LaCava, Vincent Represented By: Shannon Associates . . . . . (212) 831-5650
Lacey, Joe 1137 N 19th Street, Allentown, PA 18104 . . . . . (610) 433-4696 • (800) 715-7510
Lack, Donald J. 216 Sunnyside Road, Temple Terrace, FL 33617 . . . . . (813) 989-0079

LACKNER, PAUL Pages 299,302
Represented By: The Neis Group **(616) 672-5756**
e-mail: neisgroup@wmis.net • Website: www.neisgroup.com • Specialties: Editorial; People

Lackow, Andy 7004 Boulevard E #29C, Guttenberg, NJ 07093 . . . . . (201) 868-9585

LACOSTE, GARY Page 320
Represented By: PG Representatives **(413) 967-9855**
e-mail: pgreps@aol.com • Specialties: Colored Pencil; Pastels

Lada, Elizabeth Represented By: Bruck & Moss . . . . . (212) 980-8061
Lada, Mir Represented By: Suzy Johnston & Associates, Inc. . . . . . (416) 285-8905
Ladas, George 225 W Sixth Avenue, Roselle, NJ 07203 . . . . . (908) 298-3730
Laden, Nina 1517 McLendon Avenue NE, Atlanta, GA 30307 . . . . . (404) 371-0052
LaFave, Kim 121 Lyall Avenue, Toronto, ON Canada M4E 1W6 . . . . . (416) 691-3242
Represented By: Rep Art . . . . . (604) 684-6826
LaFever, Greg Represented By: Scott Hull Associates . . . . . (937) 433-8383
LaFleur, Dave Represented By: Scott Hull Associates . . . . . (937) 433-8383
Lafrance, Claude 1030 St. Alexandre #305, Montreal, PQ Canada H2Z 1P3 . . . . . (514) 393-4104
Lafrance, Laurie 94 Dorset Street W, Port Hope, ON Canada L1A 1G2 . . . . . (905) 885-6633
Lagerstrom, Wendy Represented By: Sylvia Franks . . . . . (310) 276-5282
Laird, Campbell 162 E 23rd Street #5-B, New York, NY 10010 . . . . . (212) 505-5552
Laish, James 55 Charles Street W, Ste. 2604, Toronto, ON Canada M5S 2W9 . . . . . (416) 921-1709
Lallky-Seibert, Bonnie 1675 NE 36th Street, Ft. Lauderdale, FL 33334 . . . . . (954) 564-3259
Lam, Joty 65 N Michigan Avenue #6, Pasadena, CA 91106 . . . . . (818) 577-0113
Lambase, Barbara 2705 Via Anita, Palos Verdes, CA 90274-1012 . . . . . (310) 373-4993
Lambert, John L. 1727 N Warren Avenue, Milwaukee, WI 53202 . . . . . (414) 643-5205
Represented By: Shekut Communications Network . . . . . (312) 977-9171
Represented By: Wilson-Zumbo Illustration . . . . . (414) 271-3388
Represented By: Tiffany Represents . . . . . (206) 441-7701
Lamberto Illus. & Associates 2612 Galemeadow Drive, Ft. Worth, TX 76123 . . . . . (817) 346-6971
Lambrenos, James 803 Salem Court, Atco, NJ 08004 . . . . . (609) 768-0580
Lamut, Sonja Represented By: Barbara Gordon Associates Ltd. . . . . . (212) 686-3514
Landers, Roberta Holmes Represented By: Square Moon . . . . . (510) 253-9451
Landikusic, Katherine 201 Wyandotte #405, Kansas City, MO 64116 . . . . . (816) 471-5950
Lane Caricatures, Sherry 155 Bank Street Studio 404, New York, NY 10014 . . . . . (212) 675-6224
Lane Illustration, Tammie 413 Independence Place, Aspen, CO 81611 . . . . . (970) 925-9213
Lang, Donna 564 Madrone Avenue, Sunnyvale, CA 94086 . . . . . (408) 739-4731
Langdon, John Represented By: Leyden Diversified . . . . . (215) 663-0587
Lange, Jim Represented By: Connie Koralik Associates Represents . . . . . (312) 944-5680
Langenderfer, Tim Represented By: Joel Harlib Associates, Inc. . . . . . (312) 573-1370
Represented By: Air Studio . . . . . (513) 721-1193
Langer, D.C. Brookline, MA 02146 . . . . . (888) 606-3232

LANGLEY ILLUSTRATION, STEPHANIE Page 402
619 Maybell Avenue, Palo Alto, CA 94306 • Fax (650) 857-0445 **(650) 857-9539**
Represented By: Jorgensen & Barrett Reps **(206) 634-1880**
Specialties: Line Art; Whimsical

Lanino, Deborah 170 W 23rd Street #2V, New York, NY 10011 . . . . . (212) 366-7212
Lansaw, J. Lea 7018 Braeburn Place, Bethesda, MD 20817 . . . . . (301) 564-9565
Lantz, David Represented By: Irmeli Holmberg . . . . . (212) 545-9155
Lapadula, Tom Represented By: SI International . . . . . (212) 254-4996
LaPick, John Represented By: Sam Brody . . . . . (203) 854-0805
LaPine, Julia Represented By: Sharon Dodge & Associates . . . . . (206) 284-4701
Represented By: Carolyn Potts & Associates, Inc. . . . . . (773) 935-8840
Represented By: Marla Matson Represents . . . . . (602) 252-5072
Lapinski, Joe Represented By: Carol Chislovsky Design, Inc. . . . . . (212) 677-9100
Lardy, Phillipe 478 W Broadway #5-A, New York, NY 10012 . . . . . (212) 473-3057

Larsen, Eric Represented By: Susan & Company . . . . . (206) 232-7873
Larson, Esther Represented By: Erika Becker . . . . . (212) 757-8987
Larson, Paul 1125 Sixth Street #9, Santa Monica, CA 90403 . . . . . (310) 458-9140

LARSON, SETH Pages 283,292,426
Represented By: John Brewster Creative Services **(203) 226-4724**
e-mail: creative.svcs@snet.net • Website: www.brewstercreative.com • Specialties: Collage; Paper Sculpture; 3D

Larson, Ted 62 Whitehall Road, Toronto, ON Canada M4W 2C7 . . . . . (416) 928-2324

LASCARO, RITA Page 297
75 E Seventh Street, Apt. 6A, New York, NY 10003 • Fax (212) 260-6076 **(212) 677-6494**
e-mail: britonia@aol.com • Specialties: Digital; Illustrative

Lasher, Mary Ann Represented By: Bernstein & Andriulli, Inc. . . . . . (212) 682-1490
Laslo, Rudy Represented By: Artworks . . . . . (212) 627-1554
Latto, Sophia 723 President Street, Brooklyn, NY 11215 . . . . . (718) 789-1980
Laubach, Rainer 19800 White Oaks, Clinton Township, MI 48036 . . . . . (810) 954-0418
Represented By: Art Staff, Inc. . . . . . (248) 583-6070
Represented By: The Roland Group . . . . . (301) 718-7955

LAURENCE, KAREN Pages 32,422
531 Main Street #1002, Roosevelt Island, NY 10044 • Fax (212) 759-0511 **(212) 751-8215**
Specialties: Caricature; Mixed Media

Lawlor, Terrence Represented By: Ivy Glick & Associates . . . . . (925) 944-0304
Lawrason, June 43 Springbrook Gardens, Etobicoke, ON Canada M8Z 3B8 . . . . . (416) 234-0540
Lawrence, John Represented By: Bernstein & Andriulli, Inc. . . . . . (212) 682-1490
Lawson, Robert Represented By: Connie Koralik Associates Represents . . . . . (312) 944-5680
Lazar, Zohar Represented By: Kate Larkworthy Artist Rep. Ltd. . . . . . (212) 633-1310
Lazure, Catherine 593 Riverside Drive #6D, New York, NY 10031 . . . . . (212) 690-1867
Le Moult, Dolph 597 Riverside Avenue, Westport, CT 06880 . . . . . (203) 226-4724
Le-Tan, Pierre Represented By: Riley Illustration . . . . . (212) 989-8770
Leadbetter, Diana Represented By: Alan Lynch Artists . . . . . (908) 813-8718
Leary, Catherine Represented By: Martha Productions . . . . . (310) 390-8663
Leary, T. Pat 883 E 11150 South, Sandy, UT 84094 . . . . . (801) 572-2753

LEBARRE, ERIKA Pages 299,302,424
Represented By: The Neis Group **(616) 672-5756**
e-mail: neisgroup@wmis.net • Website: www.neisgroup.com • Specialties: Book Jackets; Children; Editorial

LEBARRE, MATT Pages 299,307,435
Represented By: The Neis Group **(616) 672-5756**
e-mail: neisgroup@wmis.net • Website: www.neisgroup.com • Specialties: Digital; Editorial; People

Lebbad, James A. 24 Independence Way, Titusville, NJ 08560 . . . . . (609) 737-3458
Lebel, Ed 8927 Beckon Avenue S, Seattle, WA 98118 . . . . . (206) 722-4694
Lebenson, Richard 253 Washington Avenue, Apt. 4D, Brooklyn, NY 11205 . . . . . (718) 857-9267
Lebo, Narda 1004 N Montclair Avenue, Dallas, TX 75208 . . . . . (214) 941-2156
LeBold Studios 365 Highview Circle, Woodland Park, CO 80863 . . . . . (719) 687-2693
Lechien, Philippe 22 W 19th Street, 4th Flr., New York, NY 10011 . . . . . (212) 777-6777
Lederman, Marsha 107 N Columbus Street, Arlington, VA 22203 . . . . . (703) 243-5636
Lee, Bill 792 Columbus Avenue, New York, NY 10025 . . . . . (212) 866-5664
121 Mudge Pond Road, Box 659, Sharon, CT 06069 . . . . . (860) 364-0413
Lee, Charmain 752 Manning Avenue, Toronto, ON Canada M6G 2W4 . . . . . (416) 534-1461
Lee, Eric J.W. 444 W 35th Street #11A, New York, NY 10001 . . . . . (212) 695-4093
Lee, Hector Represented By: Barbara S. Kouts . . . . . (516) 286-1278

LEE, JARED D. Pages 370,448
2942 Hamilton Road, Lebanon, OH 45036 • Fax (513) 932-9389 **(513) 932-2154**
Specialty: Humour

Lee, Jim Represented By: Shooting Star . . . . . (213) 469-2020
Lee, Katie Represented By: Carol Bancroft & Friends . . . . . (203) 748-4823

Lee, Lilly Represented By: Pat Hackett Artist Representative . . . . (206) 447-1600

LEE, MICHAEL
Page 277
Represented By: Famous Frames
(310) 642-2721
e-mail: info@famousframes.com • Website: www.famousframes.com • Specialties: Animation; Storyboards

Lee, Paul Represented By: Allen Spiegel & Associates . . . . (408) 372-4672
Lee, Sander Alan 9099 Golf Road, Des Plaines, IL 60016 . . . . (847) 635-1336
Lee, Steve 121 N Eighth Street, Manhattan, KS 66502 . . . . (785) 539-3931

LEE, TIM
Pages 47,429
Represented By: Renard Represents
(212) 490-2450
e-mail: renardreps@earthlink.net • Website: www.renardrepresents.com
Specialties: Conceptual; Corporate; Editorial

LEE, WALTER
Page 277
Represented By: Famous Frames
(310) 642-2721
e-mail: info@famousframes.com • Website: www.famousframes.com • Specialties: Animation; Storyboards

Lee, Yuan 31 W 31st Street, 10th Flr., New York, NY 10001 . . . . (212) 268-0280

LEECH & ASSOCIATES, KENT
Pages 133,139
16 El Rincon, Orinda, CA 94563 • Fax (925) 254-3242
(925) 254-5748
Represented By: Sweet Represents
(415) 433-1222
e-mail: kentleech@hotmail.com • Specialties: Advertising; Airbrush; Architecture/Interiors; Computer; Digital; Medical; Product; Realism; Science; Technical

Leeds, Beth Whybrow Represented By: Janice Stefanski Represents . . . . (415) 928-0457
Leer, Rebecca J. 440 West End Avenue #12-E, New York, NY 10024 . . . . (212) 595-5865
Legnami, Susan Represented By: Ann Koeffler Represents . . . . (213) 957-2327
Lehner & Whyte 8-10 S Fullerton Avenue, Montclair, NJ 07042 . . . . (973) 746-1335
Leigh, Wells Represented By: Munro Goodman . . . . (312) 321-1336
Leiner, Alan Represented By: American Artists . . . . (212) 682-2462

LELOUP, GENEVIEVE
Page 328
Represented By: Michele Manasse
(215) 862-2091
e-mail: mmanasse@new-work.com • Website: www.voicenet.com/~mmanasse
Specialties: Advertising; Black & White; Cartoon; Children; Editorial; Greeting Cards; Humour; Lettering; Whimsical

Lemant, Albert Represented By: HK Portfolio . . . . (212) 675-5719
Lemley, David 1904 Third Avenue #920, Seattle, WA 98101 . . . . (206) 682-9480
LeMonnier, Joe Represented By: Melissa Turk & The Artist Network . . . . (914) 368-8606
Lempa, Mary Flock Represented By: Ceci Bartels Associates . . . . (314) 781-7377
Lempkee, Doug Represented By: Berendsen & Associates . . . . (513) 861-1400
Lendway, Andy Represented By: Deborah Wolfe . . . . (215) 232-6666

LENGYEL, KATHY
Pages 216,220
2306 Jones Drive, Dunedin, FL 34698 • Fax (813) 736-0835
(813) 734-1382
Represented By: Alexander/Pollard, Inc.
(800) 347-0734
Specialties: Advertising; Children; Collage; Editorial; Fabric; Greeting Cards; Maps & Charts; Stock; 3D

Lenker, John P.O. Box 48598, Minneapolis, MN 55448 . . . . (800) 671-2979
Represented By: Tom Maloney . . . . (312) 704-0500
Lensch, Chris Represented By: Liz Sanders Agency . . . . (714) 495-3664
Lentz, Jon Warren P.O. Box 396, Carlsbad, CA 92008 . . . . (760) 730-3554
Leon, Thomas 314 N Mission Drive, San Gabriel, CA 91775 . . . . (818) 458-7699
Leonard, Alex Represented By: Dane Sonneville . . . . (973) 744-4465
Leonardo, Todd Represented By: Lehmen/Dabney, Inc. . . . . (206) 325-8595
Leong, Shelton Represented By: Sharon Morris Associates . . . . (415) 362-8280

LEOPOLD, SUSAN
Pages 86-87,95
Represented By: Lindgren & Smith
(212) 397-7330
e-mail: inquiry@lindgrensmith.com • Website: www.lindgrensmith.com • Specialties: Collage; Conceptual; 3D

LePautremat, Bertrand Represented By: Jerry Leff Associates, Inc. . . . . . (212) 697-8525
Lesh, David 5693 N Meridian Street, Indianapolis, IN 46208 . . . . . (317) 253-3141
Leslie, Neil Represented By: American Artists . . . . . (212) 682-2462
Lesser, Ron Represented By: Jerry Leff Associates, Inc. . . . . . (212) 697-8525
Lester, Michelle 15 W 17th Street, 9th Flr., New York, NY 10011 . . . . . (212) 989-1411

LESTER, MIKE Pages 390-391,419,421,451,468
17 E Third Avenue, Ste. 2, Rome, GA 30161 • Fax (706) 234-0086 **(706) 234-7733**
e-mail: mlester101@aol.com • Website: www.mikelester.com
Specialties: Advertising; Animals; Animation; Black & White; Cartoon; Humour; People; Wildlife

Letelier, Francisco 711 ½ Sixth Avenue, Venice, CA 90291-3061 . . . . . (310) 396-0136
Lethaby/Grinning Graphics, Brad 3831 Donahue Road, Erie, PA 16506 . . . . . (814) 838-5050
Lettering Services, Inc. 40 Wynford Drive #210, Toronto, ON Canada . . . . . (416) 449-7278

LEVAN, JEFF Pages 252-253
Represented By: Deborah Wolfe **(215) 232-6666**
Website: www.deborahwolfeltd.com
Specialties: Advertising; Black & White; Cartoon; Children; Editorial; Humour; Whimsical

LeVan, Susan 30 Ipswich Street #211, Boston, MA 02215 . . . . . (617) 536-6828
Levee, Gayle Represented By: Sheryl Beranbaum . . . . . (401) 737-8591

LEVEL 5 LTD. Page 225
2722 Munson Street, Wheaton, MD 20902 • Fax (301) 942-4590 **(301) 933-6203**
e-mail: level_5_ltd@earthlink.net • Specialties: Advertising; Black & White; Computer; Digital; Graphic Design/Illustration; Photoillustration; Poster; Realism; Technical; 3D

Levert, Mireille Represented By: HK Portfolio . . . . . (212) 675-5719
Levin, Sergio Represented By: Dane Sonneville
Levin, Steven J. 6900 Meadowbrook Boulevard, #471, St. Louis Park, MN 55426
Levine, Andy 23-30 24th Street, Astoria, NY 11105 . . . . . (718) 956-8539
Levine, Bette 639 S Highland Avenue, Los Angeles, CA 90036 . . . . . (213) 925-4340
Levine, Laura 444 Broome Street, New York, NY 10013 . . . . . (212) 431-4787
Levine, Melinda 456 61st Street, Oakland, CA 94609 . . . . . (510) 658-4355
Represented By: Cliff Knecht . . . . . (412) 761-5666
Levinson, David 86 Parson Road #2, Clifton, NJ 07012 . . . . . (973) 614-1627
Levy, Barbara Represented By: Evelyne Johnson Associates . . . . . (212) 532-0928
Lewin, Lori Represented By: Alani Represents . . . . . (212) 465-3355
Lewis, Anthony Represented By: HK Portfolio . . . . . (212) 675-5719
Lewis, Buck 16 Canonchet Road, Hope Valley, RI 02832 . . . . . (800) 522-1377
Lewis, Janet Represented By: Creative Connection . . . . . (410) 360-5981
Lewis, Karen Represented By: Diane Boston Group . . . . . (212) 283-3401
Lewis, Maribeth 1471 Bobolink Place, Brentwood, MO 63144 . . . . . (314) 918-0410

LEWIS, MAURICE Pages 168,187
Represented By: American Artists **(212) 682-2462**
e-mail: info@amerartists.com • Website: www.amerartists.com • Specialties: Children; People; Realism

Lewis, Miles Represented By: Melissa Hopson . . . . . (214) 747-3122
Lewis, Stephen Represented By: HK Portfolio . . . . . (212) 675-5719
Lewis, Tim 184 St. Johns Place, Brooklyn, NY 11217 . . . . . (718) 857-3406
Lewis Art & Design, Andrew 7237 Norman Lane, Brentwood Bay, BC Canada V8M 1C6 . . . . . (250) 652-9581
Leyonmark, Roger Represented By: Beth O'Neill Artists Rep . . . . . (716) 473-0384
Lezinsky, Jon Represented By: Scott Hull Associates . . . . . (937) 433-8383
Li, Xiao Jun Represented By: Barbara S. Kouts . . . . . (516) 286-1278
Liao, Sharmen 314 N Mission Drive, San Gabriel, CA 91775 . . . . . (818) 458-7699
Liaw, Anson Represented By: Suzy Johnston & Associates, Inc. . . . . . (416) 285-8905
Lickona, Cheryl 210 E 63rd Street, Apt. 10-A, New York, NY 10021 . . . . . (212) 688-2562
Liddy, Mike 30 Charles Street #42, New York, NY 10014 . . . . . (212) 255-5539
Liedahl, Bryan 15628 S Eden Drive, Eden Prairie, MN 55346 . . . . . (612) 906-3797
Lieder, Rick Represented By: Hankins & Tegenborg Ltd. . . . . . (212) 867-8092
Lies, Brian 31 North Street, Norfolk, MA 02056 . . . . . (508) 528-8293
Ligasan, Darryl 422 E 77th Street, Apt. 5-W, New York, NY 10021 . . . . . (212) 737-4393
Lightburn, Ron Represented By: Artco . . . . . (212) 889-8777

Lillash, Richard Represented By: Air Studio . . . . . (513) 721-1193
Limer, Tina Bela Represented By: Irmeli Holmberg . . . . . (212) 545-9155
Lind, Monica Represented By: Watson & Spierman . . . . . (212) 431-4480
Lindberg, Dean 4023 14th Avenue S #7-A, Minneapolis, MN 55407 . . . . . (612) 823-1977
Lindberg, Jeffrey Represented By: Bill & Maurine Klimt . . . . . (212) 799-2231
Lindgren, Cindy 4957 Oliver Avenue S, Minneapolis, MN 55409 . . . . . (612) 929-0657
Lindner, Verne Represented By: Linda De Moreta Represents . . . . . (510) 769-1421
Lindquist, Roger Represented By: Spectrum Studio, Inc. . . . . . (612) 332-2361
Ling, Lauren Represented By: Cliff Knecht . . . . . (412) 761-5666
Lingta, Kung Represented By: Jerry Leff Associates, Inc. . . . . . (212) 697-8525
Linley, Michael 1504 W First Avenue #301, Columbus, OH 43212 . . . . . (614) 486-2921
Linn, Warren Represented By: Riley Illustration . . . . . (212) 989-8770
Lisi, Johanna 115 E Ninth Street, New York, NY 10003 . . . . . (212) 228-8657
Lisi, Victoria Represented By: Carol Bancroft & Friends . . . . . (203) 748-4823
Lisinski, Norbert 11 Moulton Court, Courtice, ON Canada L1E 2W4 . . . . . (905) 783-3311
Littman, Rosemary 299 Rutland Avenue, Teaneck, NJ 07666 . . . . . (201) 833-2417
Littman, Wally 299 Rutland Avenue, Teaneck, NJ 07666 . . . . . (201) 833-2417
Liu, Davy 2204 Sherwood Place, Glendale, CA 91206 . . . . . (818) 952-3869

LIVINGSTON, FRANCIS Page 107
Represented By: Lindgren & Smith **(212) 397-7330**
Represented By: Freda Scott, Inc. **(415) 398-9121**
e-mail: inquiry@lindgrensmith.com • Website: www.lindgrensmith.com • Specialties: Oil; Water Color

Ljungkvist, Laura Represented By: Art Department . . . . . (212) 925-4222
Llewellyn, Michael Represented By: Renee Hersey . . . . . (213) 666-3310
Llewelyn, Janis 2318 Mapleton Avenue, Boulder, CO 80304 . . . . . (303) 545-9380
Lloyd, Mary Anne 147 Wolcott Street, Portland, ME 04102 . . . . . (207) 773-4987
Represented By: Leighton & Company, Inc. . . . . . (978) 921-0887
Lloyd, Peter Represented By: Buck & Kane . . . . . (212) 631-0009
Lo, Rich Represented By: Art Bunch, The . . . . . (312) 368-8777
Lobo, Cesar Represented By: SI International . . . . . (212) 254-4996
Loccisano, Karen Represented By: Carol Bancroft & Friends . . . . . (203) 748-4823

LOCHRAY, TOM Page 142
5645 10th Avenue S, Minneapolis, MN 55417 • Fax (612) 824-8421 **(612) 823-7630**
e-mail: tomlochray@tomlochray.com • Website: www.tomlochray.com
Specialties: Advertising; Annual Report; Food; Graphic Design/Illustration; People; Poster; Product; Sports

Lockart, Lynne Represented By: Carol Bancroft & Friends . . . . . (203) 748-4823
Locke, Gary Represented By: Suzanne Craig Represents, Inc. . . . . . (918) 749-9424
Locke, Keith Represented By: Suzanne Craig Represents, Inc. . . . . . (918) 749-9424
Lockwood, Chris 1210 W Clay Street #19, Houston, TX 77019 . . . . . (713) 524-1860
Represented By: Schumann & Company . . . . . (512) 481-0907
Lockwood, Todd Represented By: Carol Guenzi Agents, Inc.. . . . . . (800) 417-5120
Loew, David Represented By: Artco . . . . . (212) 889-8777

LOFARO, JERRY Pages 168,170-171
Represented By: American Artists **(212) 682-2462**
e-mail: info@amerartists.com • Website: www.amerartists.com

Loffel, Hans 1038 B Queen Street, Honolulu, HI 96814 . . . . . (808) 593-2205
Loftus, David Represented By: Jacqueline Dedell, Inc. . . . . . (212) 741-2539
Logic Error 609 N Edinburgh Avenue, Los Angeles, CA 90048 . . . . . (213) 422-9105
LoGrippo, Robert Represented By: Frank & Jeff Lavaty . . . . . (212) 427-5632

LOHSTOETER, LORI Pages 86-87,92
Represented By: Lindgren & Smith **(212) 397-7330**
e-mail: inquiry@lindgrensmith.com • Website: www.lindgrensmith.com

Loken, Stein Represented By: Wanda Nowak . . . . . (212) 535-0438
Lomax, Carmen Represented By: Marla Matson Represents . . . . . (602) 252-5072
Lomele, Bachrun 1348 71st Street, Brooklyn, NY 11228 . . . . . (718) 837-0007
Lomprey, Steve 5474 Boyd Avenue, Oakland, CA 94618 . . . . . (510) 597-1157
Lonestar Studio 1931 Lexington, Houston, TX 77098 . . . . . (713) 520-1298

Long, Jim 4415 Briarwood Court N #16, Annandale, VA 22003-4783 . . . . . (703) 256-1718
Long, Loren Represented By: Mary Larkin . . . . . (212) 832-8116
Longacre, Jimmy P.O. Box 1199, Dripping Springs, TX 78620 . . . . . (512) 288-7477
Longtemps, Kenneth 362 Clinton Street, Brooklyn, NY 11231 . . . . . (718) 852-2178
Lonsdale, Ashley Represented By: Mendola Ltd. . . . . . (212) 986-5680
Lopez, Emmanuel 192 Spadina Avenue, Ste. 510, Toronto, ON Canada M5T 2C2 . . . . . (416) 359-0024
Lopez, Rafael Represented By: Conrad Represents, Inc. . . . . . (415) 921-7140
Lorenz Studio, Albert 49 Pine Avenue, Floral Park, NY 11001 . . . . . (516) 354-5530
Lorusso, Joseph 4600 J.C. Nichols Parkway, Kansas City, MO 64112 . . . . . (816) 756-5723
Lotts, Dan Represented By: Mason Illustration . . . . . (612) 729-1774
Loudon, Greg Represented By: Renee Kalish . . . . . (847) 864-6127
Lougee, Michelle 2 Lothian Road #3, Brighton, MA 02135 . . . . . (617) 254-7252
Represented By: Chip Caton . . . . . (860) 523-4562
Louis, Fishauf Represented By: Reactor Art & Design Ltd. . . . . . (416) 703-1913
Lounsberry, Charles 610 Seventh Street, Somers Point, NJ 08244 . . . . . (609) 601-1690

LOURDES, CANDACE Pages 256-257
99 Coleman Avenue #208, Toronto, ON Canada M4C 1P8 • Fax (416) 690-0689 **(416) 698-3304**
e-mail: lourdes@netcom.ca • Website: www.zeta-media.com/lourdes

Love, Sara Represented By: Lisa Freeman . . . . . (317) 920-0068
Loveless, Roger 1199 S Main Street, Ste. 200, Centerville, UT 84014 . . . . . (801) 292-0943
Lovell, Rick 2860 Lakewind Court, Alpharetta, GA 30005 . . . . . (770) 442-3943
Lovitt, Anita Represented By: Melissa Turk & The Artist Network . . . . . (914) 368-8606

LOW, WILLIAM Pages 124-125
Represented By: Vicki Morgan Associates **(212) 475-0440**
e-mail: vmartrep@aol.com • Website: www.vickimorganassociates.com • Specialties: Advertising; Architecture/Interiors; Children; Computer; Digital; Editorial; Greeting Cards; Landscape; Oil; People

Lowe, Vicki Represented By: Bernstein & Andriulli, Inc. . . . . . (212) 682-1490
Lowery, Denise C. 35 Flatt Road, Rochester, NY 14623 . . . . . (716) 292-5435
Lowney, Judith Represented By: Creative Connection . . . . . (410) 360-5981
Lowry, Janice 1116 N French Street, Santa Ana, CA 92701 . . . . . (714) 569-0476
Lozano, Armandina 2 Buckthorn, Irvine, CA 92604 . . . . . (714) 559-1397
Lu, Kung Represented By: Lehmen/Dabney, Inc. . . . . . (206) 325-8595
Lucas, Sheila Represented By: The Art Agency . . . . . (503) 203-8300
Lucero, Andre Represented By: Bruck & Moss . . . . . (212) 980-8061
Lucido, Cody Represented By: Melissa Hopson . . . . . (214) 747-3122
Luck, John Represented By: Berendsen & Associates . . . . . (513) 861-1400
Luczak, Laurie 223 E 35th Street #2WR, New York, NY 10016 . . . . . (212) 479-7366
Ludeke, Chuck Represented By: Connie Koralik Associates Represents . . . . . (312) 944-5680
Ludtke, Jim 163 N Formosa Avenue, Los Angeles, CA 90036 . . . . . (213) 936-5477
Luikart, Erika 1550 Ninth Avenue #7, San Francisco, CA 94122 . . . . . (415) 242-1770
Lumley, Diana Represented By: Alan Lynch Artists . . . . . (908) 813-8718
Lun-Koem, Anita 40 Freshmeadow Drive, Toronto, ON Canada M2H 2T1 . . . . . (416) 493-4150
Lund, David Represented By: Jorgensen & Barrett Reps . . . . . (206) 634-1880
Represented By: Carol Chislovsky Design, Inc. . . . . . (212) 677-9100
Lund, Gary Represented By: Nancy George . . . . . (805) 688-3772
Lund, Jon C. 124 Streetsboro Road, Hudson, OH 44236 . . . . . (330) 864-1762
Lundgren, Alvalyn 274 Mariposa Drive, Newbury Park, CA 91320 . . . . . (805) 480-9600
Lundgren, Tim Represented By: Barbara Gordon Associates Ltd. . . . . . (212) 686-3514
Lundman, Julia 853 W Washington Boulevard #1B, Oak Park, IL 60302 . . . . . (708) 386-2608
Lung, Y.W. 3300 Don Mills Road #2404, Willowdale, ON Canada M2J 4X7 . . . . . (416) 497-4359

LUNSFORD, ANNIE Pages 388,450,467
515 N Hudson Street, Arlington, VA 22201 • Fax (703) 527-3099 **(703) 527-7696**
e-mail: lunsfordarts@earthlink.net • Specialties: Advertising; Digital; Editorial; Fantasy; Humour: Whimsical

Lustig, Loretta 330 Clinton Avenue, Brooklyn, NY 11205 . . . . . (718) 789-2496

LUTZOW, JACK Page 243
906 A Noe Street, San Francisco, CA 94114 • Fax (415) 648-6032 **(415) 641-5800**
Represented By: Rita Gatlin Represents **(800) 924-7881**
Website: www.ritareps.com • Specialties: Food; Product; Water Color

Luzuriaga, Denis 1123 Broadway #1006, New York, NY 10010 . . . . . (212) 242-3818
Lyall, Dennis Represented By: Artworks . . . . . (212) 627-1554
Lydecker, Laura Represented By: Carol Bancroft & Friends . . . . . (203) 748-4823
Lyhus, Randy 4853 Cordell Avenue #3, Bethesda, MD 20814 . . . . . (301) 986-0036
Lynch, Bob Represented By: Marla Matson Represents . . . . . (602) 252-5072
Lynch, Chris Bakersfield, CA . . . . . (805) 297-7195
Lynch, Jeffrey 85 Roosevelt Street, Garden City, NY 11530 . . . . . (516) 328-6709
Lynch, Sean P. 297 Ronald Avenue, Cumberland, RI 02864 . . . . . (401) 333-6467
Lytle, John P.O. Box 5155, Sonora, CA 95370 . . . . . (209) 928-4849

LYUBNER, BORIS Pages 154-155
9015 Flint Way, Park City, UT 84098 • Fax (435) 649-8803 **(435) 649-2129**
e-mail: boris@borisart.com • Website: www.borisart.com
Specialties: Advertising; Annual Report; Corporate; Stock

MABLY, GREG Page 261
Toronto, ON Canada M5N 2Y7 **(416) 410-8744**
e-mail: greg@the-wire.com • Specialty: Computer

MacAdam, Dean 110 SW 91st Avenue #201, Plantation, FL 33324 . . . . . (954) 423-9444
Macanga, Steve 20 Morgantine Road, Roseland, NJ 07068 . . . . . (973) 403-8967
MacCombie, Turi Represented By: Evelyne Johnson Associates . . . . . (212) 532-0928
MacDonald, Greg Represented By: Jorgensen & Barrett Reps . . . . . (206) 634-1880

MACDONALD, JOHN Pages 57,463
Represented By: Renard Represents **(212) 490-2450**
e-mail: renardreps@earthlink.net • Website: www.renardrepresents.com
Specialties: Digital; Editorial; Scratchboard

MacDonald, Ross 56 Castle Meadow, Newton, CT 06470 . . . . . (203) 270-6438
Represented By: Reactor Art & Design Ltd. . . . . . (416) 703-1913
MacDougall, Rob Represented By: Mendola Ltd. . . . . . (212) 986-5680
Maceren, Jude 92 Kossuth Street, Piscataway, NJ 08854 . . . . . (908) 752-5931
Mach, Steven 87 E Elm Street, Chicago, IL 60611 . . . . . (312) 280-0071
Mackall, Debbie 2133 Ginger Circle, Palatine, IL 60074 . . . . . (847) 359-0289
MacKinnon, Mark 135 W 26th Street #8A, New York, NY 10001 . . . . . (201) 854-1711
MacLachlan, Neil Represented By: Sharpshooter Creative Representation, Inc. . . . . . (416) 703-5300
MacLeod, Ainslie P.O. Box 640575, San Francisco, CA 94164 . . . . . (415) 256-4649
Represented By: Empress Bowling League, The . . . . . (404) 705-9776
MacLeod, Lee Represented By: Bernstein & Andriulli, Inc. . . . . . (212) 682-1490

MACNICOL, GREGORY Page 336
2557 Branciforte Drive, Santa Cruz, CA 95065 • Fax (408) 426-0403 **(408) 459-0880**
e-mail: gregorym@beema.com • Specialties: Animation; Digital Imaging/3D; Mixed Media

MACPHERSON, BRUCE Pages 392-393,449
Represented By: Donna Rosen Artists' Rep **(301) 384-8925**
e-mail: djrosen@erols.com • Website: www.aaarrt.com/donnasgallery
Specialties: Advertising; Black & White; Character; Children; Editorial; Humour; Whimsical

MacQuarrie, Lynn 101 Vaughn Road #18, Toronto, ON Canada M6C 2L9 . . . . . (416) 658-3390
Macrae, Doug Represented By: Denise Azzopardi . . . . . (416) 429-2840
Madan, Dev 2814 NW Golden Drive, Seattle, WA 98117 . . . . . (206) 789-2601
Maddox, Kelly Represented By: Jerry Leff Associates, Inc. . . . . . (212) 697-8525
Mader, Stephen 38C Shank Street, Toronto, ON Canada M6J 3T9 . . . . . (416) 345-8983
Madrick, David 10 Savarin Street, Toronto, ON Canada M1J 1Z8 . . . . . (416) 266-0159
Magdalen's Temple of Art, Mary Green Bay, WI . . . . . (414) 654-7758
Maggard, John P. 102 Marian Lane, Terrace Park, OH 45174 . . . . . (513) 248-1550
Represented By: Scott Hull Associates . . . . . (937) 433-8383
Magiera, Rob 9636 Ruskin Circle, Sandy, UT 84092 . . . . . (801) 943-3650
Represented By: Steve Edsey & Sons . . . . . (312) 527-0351
Represented By: Torrey Spencer . . . . . (818) 505-1124
Magine, John Represented By: Cornell & McCarthy, LLC . . . . . (203) 454-4210

Magnes, Ron Represented By: Cliff Knecht . . . . . (412) 761-5666

MAGOVERN, PEG — Pages 299,306,459
Represented By: The Neis Group — **(616) 672-5756**
e-mail: neisgroup@wmis.net • Website: www.neisgroup.com • Specialties: People; Realism

Magsig, Stephen Represented By: Skidmore, Inc. . . . . . (248) 353-7722
Maguire, Bob Represented By: Hankins & Tegenborg Ltd. . . . . . (212) 867-8092
Mahan, Ben Represented By: Cornell & McCarthy, LLC . . . . . (203) 454-4210
Mahan, Benton P.O. Box 66, Chesterville, OH 43317 . . . . . (419) 768-2204
Mahoney, Dick Represented By: Jennifer Embler Represents, Inc. . . . . . (954) 760-4195
Mahoney, Jennifer F. 1170 Camelia Street, Berkeley, CA 94702 . . . . . (510) 524-9773
Mahoney, Katherine 60 Hurd Road, Belmont, MA 02178 . . . . . (617) 868-7877
Mahoney, Kit Hevron 2682 S Newport Street, Denver, CO 80224 . . . . . (303) 757-0689
Mahoney, Ron Represented By: Steve Edsey & Sons . . . . . (312) 527-0351
Mahurin, Matt 666 Greenwich Street, PH #16, New York, NY 10014 . . . . . (212) 691-7616
Maier, Mychael Represented By: Alani Represents . . . . . (212) 465-3355
Mair, Jacqueline Represented By: Bernstein & Andriulli, Inc. . . . . . (212) 682-1490
Major Designs P.O. Box 8727, Reno, NV 89507 . . . . . (702) 784-6187
Makowski, Stan Represented By: W/C Studio, Inc./Allan Comport . . . . . (410) 349-8669
Maldonado, Alexandra 28-23 42nd Street #1-D, Astoria, NY 11103 . . . . . (718) 545-3828

MALE, ALAN — Pages 168,191
Represented By: American Artists — **(212) 682-2462**
e-mail: info@amerartists.com • Website: www.amerartists.com

MALEK, KIM — Pages 268,430
1620 SW Taylor, Ste. 100, Portland, OR 97205 • Fax (503) 223-2719 — **(503) 223-4250**
Represented By: Christine Prapas — **(503) 658-7070**
e-mail: malekstudio@id-inc.com
Specialties: Annual Report; Corporate; Digital; People; Scratchboard; Whimsical

Malinowki, Andrzej Represented By: American Artists . . . . . (212) 682-2462
Mallouf, Christine 4232 Franklin Avenue, Los Angeles, CA 90027 . . . . . (213) 664-4674
Malone, Peter Represented By: Sally Heflin . . . . . (212) 366-1893
Malysa, Bartek Represented By: Wanda Nowak . . . . . (212) 535-0438
Mammano, Julie 15315 Alondra Boulevard, La Mirada, CA 90638 . . . . . (714) 522-0477
Manara, Milo Represented By: Alan Lynch Artists . . . . . (908) 813-8718
Manchesi, Steve Represented By: Carol Bancroft & Friends . . . . . (203) 748-4823
Manchess, Gregory 13358 SW Gallop Court, Beaverton, OR 97008 . . . . . (503) 590-5447
Represented By: Richard Solomon . . . . . (212) 683-1362
Manda, Antonia 6215 SE 22nd, Portland, OR 97202 . . . . . (503) 236-5826
Manders, John 6058 Stanton Avenue, Pittsburgh, PA 15206 . . . . . (412) 362-6580

MANDIO, MERIDEE — Page 277
Represented By: Famous Frames — **(310) 642-2721**
e-mail: info@famousframes.com • Website: www.famousframes.com • Specialties: Animation; Storyboards

Mandrachio, Richard 2275 Sutter Street, Apt. 7, San Francisco, CA 94115 . . . . . (415) 921-5938
Mangiat, Jeff Represented By: Mendola Ltd. . . . . . (212) 986-5680
Mankus Digital Imaging, Gary 835 N Wood Street #101, Chicago, IL 60622 . . . . . (800) 439-0313
Manley, Matt 840 First Street NW #1, Grand Rapids, MI 49504 . . . . . (616) 459-7595
Represented By: Corey Graham Represents . . . . . (415) 956-4750
Represented By: Air Studio . . . . . (513) 721-1193
Manna, Connie 49 Old Stage Coach Road, Andover, NJ 07821 . . . . . (973) 786-7409
Mannes, Don 345 E 76th Street #2A, New York, NY 10021 . . . . . (212) 288-1392
Manning, Garrian Chicago, IL 60611 . . . . . (312) 337-7770

MANNING, LISA — Page 126
12 Ledge Lane, Gloucester, MA 01930 • Fax (978) 927-9991 — **(978) 927-9990**
Represented By: Leighton & Company, Inc. — **(978) 921-0887**
Website: www.leightonreps.com • Specialty: Editorial

Manning, Michelle Represented By: Jan Collier Represents, Inc. . . . . . (415) 383-9026

Represented By: Jerry Leff Associates, Inc. .... (212) 697-8525
Manojlovic, Branko 2700 Bathurst, Ste. 304, Toronto, ON Canada M6D 2Z7 .... (416) 784-0007
Manoli, Georgios 397 Whalebone Lane, Essex, England RM6 6RH 44 181 599 3408
Mansfield, Renee 468 Queen Street E #104, Toronto, ON Canada M5A 1T7 .... (416) 367-2446
Mansoor, Mohammad Represented By: Berendsen & Associates .... (513) 861-1400
Mantel, Richard Represented By: Lindgren & Smith .... (212) 397-7330
Mantha, John 567 King Street W, Toronto, ON Canada M5V 1M1 .... (416) 591-9133
Mantha, Nancy Represented By: Carol Bancroft & Friends .... (203) 748-4823
Manton, Helen 99 Pleasant Street, Plainville, MA 02762 .... (508) 695-5862
Manus, Charles Represented By: Woody Coleman Presents, Inc. .... (216) 661-4222
Represented By: Image Mill .... (515) 490-6110

MANZ, PAUL Pages 338-339
Represented By: The Roland Group **(301) 718-7955**
Website: www.therolandgroup.com • Specialty: Corporate

Manzo, Kate Represented By: Bill & Maurine Klimt .... (212) 799-2231
Maratta, Kate & Peter Represented By: Flannery Lane Ltd. .... (914) 631-1413
Marchese, Carole Red Bee Cottage, 77 Lyons Plain Road, Weston, CT 06883 .... (203) 226-4535
Marchese, Frank 236 W 26th Street #805, New York, NY 10001 .... (212) 463-7025
Marchesi, Stephen Represented By: Carol Bancroft & Friends .... (203) 748-4823
Marconi, Gloria 2525 Musgrove Road, Silver Spring, MD 20904 .... (301) 890-4615
Marcotte, Tom Represented By: Berendsen & Associates .... (513) 861-1400
Mardaga, Dana 1780 Frobisher Way, San Jose, CA 95124 .... (888) 476-7786
Mardarosian, Mark Represented By: SI International .... (212) 254-4996
Marden, Phil New York, NY 10011 .... (212) 777-6777
Mardon, John 27 Colonsay Road, Thornhill, ON Canada L3T 3E9 .... (416) 881-5854
Marelich Artworks, Jeffrey 3251 Countryside Drive, San Mateo, CA 94403 .... (650) 578-8635
Margeson Illustration, John 46-147 Hinapu Street, Kaneohe, HI 96744 .... (808) 247-3830
Margolis, Don Represented By: Langley & Associates .... (847) 670-0912
Margulies, Robert 1408 Brickell Bay Drive #203, Miami, FL 33139 .... (305) 372-1046
Marion, Kate 85 Columbus Avenue, Greenfield, MA 01301 .... (413) 774-4862
Mark, Mona Represented By: Anita Grien Represents .... (212) 697-6170
Mark, Roger Represented By: American Artists .... (212) 682-2462
Marks, David 726 Hillpine Drive, Atlanta, GA 30306 .... (404) 872-1824
Represented By: Cary & Company .... (404) 296-9666
Marrero, Carlos 161 NE 89th Street, Miami, FL 33138 .... (305) 757-5776
Marsh, Dilleen Represented By: Pema Browne Ltd. .... (914) 985-2936
Marsh, Gary 30 Tottenham Street, London, England W1 9PN 44 171 636 1064
Marsh, James 21 Elms Road, London, England SW4 9ER 44 181 622 9530
Represented By: The Newborn Group .... (212) 260-6700
Marsh, Roni 1709 Howell Avenue, Medford, OR 97501 .... (541) 770-6826 • (800) 435-6509
Marshall, Craig 425 Hugo Street, San Francisco, CA 94122 .... (415) 661-5550
Marshall, Felicia Represented By: Carol Bancroft & Friends .... (203) 748-4823
Martens & Keifer 853 Broadway, Ste. 1201, New York, NY 10003 .... (212) 677-9100
Martin, Doug Represented By: Suzy Johnston & Associates, Inc. .... (416) 285-8905
Martin, Gregory S. 1307 Greenlake Drive, Cardiff, CA 92007 .... (760) 753-4073
Represented By: Frank Lux & Associates, Inc. .... (312) 222-1361
Martin, James Represented By: Creative Freelancers .... (800) 398-9544
Martin, Jeff 133 Brooks Street, East Boston, MA 02128 .... (617) 569-0335
Martin, John Represented By: Renard Represents .... (212) 490-2450
Martin, Larry Represented By: Scott Hull Associates .... (937) 433-8383
Martin, Lyn Represented By: Cliff Knecht .... (412) 761-5666
Martin, Mike 900 Royal Street, New Orleans, LA 70116 .... (504) 392-7519
Martin, Richard P.O. Box 268, Wantagh, NY 11793 .... (516) 377-3844
Martinelli, Robert Represented By: Art Source/Diane Barkley .... (914) 747-2220
Martinez, Edward Represented By: Mendola Ltd. .... (212) 986-5680
Martinot, Claude 1133 Broadway, Ste. 1614, New York, NY 10010 .... (212) 229-2249
Martucci, Stanley 34 Twin Light Terrace, Highlands, NJ 07732 .... (908) 291-5945
Marvin, Fred Represented By: SI International .... (212) 254-4996
Mascio, Tony Represented By: Leyden Diversified .... (215) 663-0587
Masla, Robert Represented By: Barbara Gordon Associates Ltd. .... (212) 686-3514
Maslen, Barbara 55 Bayview Avenue, Sag Harbor, NY 11963 .... (516) 725-3121
MASS Engineered Design, Inc. 510 Front Street W, Ste. 300, Toronto, ON Canada M5V 1B8 .... (416) 593-4663
Masuda, Coco 300 E 51st Street #6E, New York, NY 10022 .... (212) 753-9331

MATCHO, MARK Pages 332-333
2410 Eighth Avenue, Oakland, CA 94606 • Fax (510) 836-8928 **(510) 836-4462**
Represented By: Maslov/Weinberg **(415) 641-1285**
e-mail: suparocka@aol.com • Specialty: Digital

Mateu, Franc Represented By: SI International . . . . . (212) 254-4996
Mather, Daniel Represented By: Skidmore, Inc. . . . . . (248) 353-7722
Matje, Martin Represented By: Wanda Nowak . . . . . (212) 535-0438
Matsick, Anni Represented By: Cornell & McCarthy, LLC . . . . . (203) 454-4210

MATSU ILLUSTRATION Pages 45,436
Represented By: Renard Represents **(212) 490-2450**
e-mail: renardreps@earthlink.net • Website: www.renardrepresents.com • Specialties: Conceptual; Digital

Mattelson, Marvin Represented By: Mattelson Associates . . . . . (516) 487-1323
Matthews, Bonnie 848 W 35th Street, Baltimore, MD 21211 . . . . . (410) 243-3514
Matthews, Scott 7530 Ethel Avenue, St. Louis, MO 63117 . . . . . (314) 647-9899
Mattioli, Mark Represented By: Janice Stefanski Represents . . . . . (415) 928-0457
Mattotti, Lorenzo Represented By: Richard Solomon . . . . . (212) 683-1362
Maughan, William Represented By: Mendola Ltd. . . . . . (212) 986-5680
Mauterer, Erin 51 Ascot Drive, Ocean, NJ 07712 . . . . . (800) 258-9287
Maxey, Betty Represented By: Steve Edsey & Sons . . . . . (312) 527-0351
Maxwell, Misty Wheatley Represented By: Berendsen & Associates . . . . . (513) 861-1400
May, Jody 5413 Willowmere Way, Baltimore, MD 21212 . . . . . (410) 435-8864
Mayabb, Darrell 10180 W 73rd Place, Arvada, CO 80005 . . . . . (303) 420-7200
Maydak, Michael 2780 Wildwest Trail, Cool, CA 95614 . . . . . (530) 889-8118
Represented By: Conrad Represents, Inc. . . . . . (415) 921-7140

MAYER, BILL Pages 86-87,93,364-365
240 Forkner Drive, Decatur, GA 30030 • Fax (404) 373-1759 **(404) 378-0686**
Represented By: Lindgren & Smith **(212) 397-7330**
e-mail: skitzoartiste.juno.com • Website: www.lindgrensmith.com
Specialties: Advertising; Airbrush; Animation; Cartoon; Children; Conceptual;
Graphic Design/Illustration; Humour; Scratchboard; 3D

Mayforth, Hal RR #1, Box 4135, Montpelier, VT 05602 . . . . . (802) 229-2716
Maze, Deborah Represented By: Cornell & McCarthy, LLC . . . . . (203) 454-4210
Mazzetti, Alan Represented By: Freda Scott, Inc. . . . . . (415) 398-9121

MCADAMS, BARBARA Pages 252-253
785 San Bruno Avenue, San Francisco, CA 94107 **(415) 821-1379**
Represented By: Deborah Wolfe **(215) 232-6666**
Specialties: Advertising; Editorial; Greeting Cards; Icons; Lettering

MCAFEE, STEVE Page 345
P.O. Box 54272, Atlanta, GA 30308 • Fax (770) 925-2481 **(770) 925-2481**
e-mail: mcafees@mindspring.com • Website: www.stevemcafee.com
Specialties: Advertising; Collage; Corporate; Digital; Editorial

McAllaney, Susan Represented By: Tiffany Represents . . . . . (206) 441-7701
McAllister, Chris 3080 Highland Scenic Drive S, Baxter, MN 56425 . . . . . (218) 828-8786
McBain, Emmett Represented By: Art Bunch, The . . . . . (312) 368-8777
McBride, Clay Patrick 133 W 22nd Street #3, New York, NY 10011 . . . . . (212) 989-2712
McCall, Bruce 327 Central Park West, New York, NY 10025 . . . . . (212) 749-1392
McCampbell, Rachael Represented By: Sweet Represents . . . . . (415) 433-1222
McCash, Beth Represented By: Marion Moskowitz Represents . . . . . (212) 517-4919
McCauley, Adam 2400 Eighth Avenue, Oakland, CA 94606 . . . . . (510) 832-0860
McCloskey, Bill 1215 18th Street, Sacramento, CA 94124 . . . . . (415) 467-9676
McCollum, Rick Represented By: Hedge Graphics . . . . . (818) 244-0110
McCollum, Sudi 3244 Cornwall Drive, Glendale, CA 91206 . . . . . (818) 243-1345
McConnell, Jim Represented By: Square Moon . . . . . (510) 253-9451
McConney, Ken 436 E 75th Street, New York, NY 10021 . . . . . (212) 734-9432
McCormack, Daphne Represented By: Karen Wells Represents . . . . . (800) 778-9076
McCormack, Donna 46-26 247 Street, Douglaston, NY 11362 . . . . . (718) 229-7939

McCormack, Geoffrey Represented By: Mendola Ltd. .... (212) 986-5680
McCoy, Dave 8 Rillo Drive, Wayne, NJ 07447 .... (973) 305-8053
McCue, Lisa Represented By: Publishers' Graphics .... (203) 797-8188
McCusker, Helen 97 Eaglewood Boulevard, Mississauga, ON Canada L5G 1V8 .... (905) 278-4714
McCusker, Paul 97 Eaglewood Boulevard, Mississauga, ON Canada L5G 1V8 .... (905) 278-4714
McDaniel, Jerry Represented By: Anita Grien Represents .... (212) 697-6170

MCDERMOTT, JOE Pages 146-147
Represented By: Carol Guenzi Agents, Inc. **(800) 417-5120**
e-mail: artagent@artagent.com • Website: www.artagent.com
Specialties: Advertising; Airbrush; Caricature; Celebrity; Computer; People; Portraiture; Realism; Sports

McDonald, Jerry 180 Clipper Street, San Francisco, CA 94114 .... (415) 824-1377
McDonald, Mercedes 4349 Cahuenga Boulevard #105, Toluca Lake, CA 91602 .... (818) 505-8085
McDonald, Patricia Represented By: Creative Connection .... (410) 360-5981
McDonald Design, Jim 5703 E Evans Drive, Scottsdale, AZ 85254 .... (602) 494-0747
Represented By: Kimberley Boege .... (602) 265-4389
McDonnell, Patrick 3420 Westmore, Montreal, PQ Canada H4B 1Z8 .... (514) 483-5489
McDonnell, Peter Represented By: Linda De Moreta Represents .... (510) 769-1421
McDougall, Scott 712 N 62nd Street, Seattle, WA 98103 .... (206) 783-1403
McElrath/Eslick, Laura Represented By: Carol Bancroft & Friends .... (203) 748-4823

MCELROY, DARLENE Page 271
2414 Calle Zaguan, Santa Fe, NM 87505 • Fax (505) 471-3959 **(505) 471-8300**
Represented By: Christine Prapas **(503) 658-7070**
Represented By: Rhyne Represents **(303) 871-9166**
e-mail: macbruja@aol.com • Website: www.theartshow.com/darlene

McEntire Illustration, Larry 1931 Lexington, Houston, TX 77098 .... (713) 520-1298
McEvoy, Greg 219 Front Street, Toronto, ON Canada M5A 1E8 .... (416) 863-0093
McFarland, Tom 7300 Bellview Avenue, Kansas City, MO 64114 .... (816) 363-5699
McGee, Warner 2183 Edisto Avenue, Charleston, SC 29412 .... (843) 762-6649

MCGEEHAN, DAN Page 149
Represented By: Connie Koralik Associates Represents **(312) 944-5680**
Specialties: Humour; Illustrative

McGinty, Mick Represented By: The Pate Company .... (805) 529-8111
McGonagle, Russell 221 E Cullerton, Chicago, IL 60616 .... (312) 225-5557
McGovern, Michael Represented By: Artworks .... (212) 627-1554
McGovern, Tara Represented By: Artco .... (212) 889-8777
McGowan, Daniel 6318 15th Avenue NE, Seattle, WA 98115 .... (206) 526-8927
Represented By: Pat Hackett Artist Representative .... (206) 447-1600
McGrail, Rollin Represented By: Ceci Bartels Associates .... (314) 781-7377

MCGURL, MICHAEL Pages 54,428
Represented By: Renard Represents **(212) 490-2450**
e-mail: renardreps@earthlink.net • Website: www.renardrepresents.com • Specialties: Conceptual; Digital

MCINDOE, VINCE Pages 86-87,91
Represented By: Lindgren & Smith **(212) 397-7330**
e-mail: inquiry@lindgrensmith.com • Website: www.lindgrensmith.com

MCINTYRE, BRIAN Page 201
Represented By: American Artists **(212) 682-2462**
Represented By: Ian Flemming Associates
e-mail: info@amerartists.com • Website: www.amerartists.com

McIntyre, Mark J. 330 Sterling Lake Drive, Ocoee, FL 34761 .... (407) 294-9408
McKay, Craig 15 Parkway Avenue, Cincinnati, OH 45216 .... (513) 821-8052
McKean, Dave Represented By: Allen Spiegel & Associates .... (408) 372-4672
McKee, Tom Represented By: Steve Edsey & Sons .... (312) 527-0351

MCKELVEY, SHAWN Pages 168,199
Represented By: American Artists **(212) 682-2462**
Represented By: Cary & Company **(404) 296-9666**
e-mail: info@amerartists.com • Website: www.amerartists.com

McKeon, Kate 1516 Deerhaven Drive, Crystal Lake, IL 60014 . . . . . (815) 477-8518
McKie, Roy 164 Old Clinton Road, Flemington, NJ 08822 . . . . . (908) 788-7996
McKinnell, Michael Represented By: Rep Art . . . . . (604) 684-6826
McKowen, Scott Represented By: Marlena Agency . . . . . (609) 252-9405

MCLACHLAN, STUART Page 237
Represented By: Sharpshooter Creative Representation Inc. **(416) 703-5300**
e-mail: shooter@the-wire.com • Website: www.portfolios.com/illustrators • Specialties: Acrylic; Black & White; Book Jackets; Caricature; Cartoon; Conceptual; Editorial; Painterly; Scratchboard; Woodcut

McLarnan, Beth Represented By: Deborah Snyder Creative Representative . . . . . (612) 922-3462
McLaughlin, Gary Represented By: Rep Art . . . . . (604) 684-6826
McLaughlin, Paul Represented By: Alan Lynch Artists . . . . . (908) 813-8718
McLean, Don Represented By: The Neis Group . . . . . (616) 672-5756
McLean, Wilson Represented By: The Newborn Group . . . . . (212) 260-6700
McLennan, Connie Represented By: Ann Koeffler Represents . . . . . (213) 957-2327
McLimans, David 426 Clemons Avenue, Madison, WI 53704 . . . . . (608) 249-0180
McLoughlin, Wayne Represented By: Renard Represents . . . . . (212) 490-2450
McMacken Graphics 19481 Franquelin Place, Sonoma, CA 95476 . . . . . (707) 996-5239
Represented By: Hedge Graphics . . . . . (818) 244-0110
Represented By: Bernstein & Andriulli, Inc. . . . . . (212) 682-1490
Represented By: Tom Maloney . . . . . (312) 704-0500
McMahon, Brad 1949 S Manchester Avenue, Anaheim, CA 92802 . . . . . (714) 733-0489
Represented By: Carol Chislovsky Design, Inc. . . . . . (212) 677-9100
McMahon, Mark Represented By: Steve Edsey & Sons . . . . . (312) 527-0351
Represented By: Mendola Ltd. . . . . . (212) 986-5680
McMenemy, Sarah Represented By: Sally Heflin . . . . . (212) 366-1893
McMillan, Ken Represented By: Tania Kimche . . . . . (212) 529-3556
McMillen, Mike Represented By: Sell Inc. . . . . . (312) 578-8844
McMullan, James 207 E 32nd Street, New York, 10016 . . . . . (212) 689-5527
McNeely, Tom 63-A Yorkville Avenue, Toronto, ON Canada M5R 1B7 . . . . . (416) 925-1929
McNeill, Jim 3 Peru Street, Edison, NJ 08820 . . . . . (732) 548-9168

MCOWAN, ALEX Page 277
Represented By: Famous Frames **(310) 642-2721**
e-mail: info@famousframes.com • Website: www.famousframes.com • Specialties: Animation; Storyboards

McParlane, Michael Represented By: Three in a Box . . . . . (416) 367-2446
McPheeters, Neal Represented By: Hankins & Tegenborg Ltd. . . . . . (212) 867-8092
McShane, Frank Represented By: Creative Freelancers . . . . . (800) 398-9544
MDC Art Studio Represented By: Mendola Ltd. . . . . . (212) 986-5680
Mead, Kimble Pendleton 125 Prospect Park W, Brooklyn, NY 11215 . . . . . (718) 768-3632
Represented By: Artco . . . . . (212) 889-8777
Meaker, Mike Represented By: Martha Productions . . . . . (310) 390-8663
Media Alternatives 2200 N Lamar #110, Dallas, TX 75202 . . . . . (214) 979-0504
MediVisuals, Inc. 1820 Regal Row, Ste. 150, Dallas, TX 75235 . . . . . (214) 634-3996 • (800) 899-2154
9211 Forest Hill Avenue, Ste. 103, Richmond, VA 23235 . . . . . (804) 323-6124
Meek, Genevieve Represented By: Suzanne Craig Represents, Inc. . . . . . (918) 749-9424
Meek, Kitty 1405 Hillcrest Lane, Fallbrook, CA 92028 . . . . . (760) 731-6416
Meek, Steve 743 W Buena Avenue, Chicago, IL 60613 . . . . . (773) 477-8055
Meers, Tony Represented By: Artworks . . . . . (212) 627-1554
Meganck, Robert Represented By: Cliff Knecht . . . . . (412) 761-5666
Megowan, Daniel P. Represented By: Mendola Ltd. . . . . . (212) 986-5680
Megowan, John 23 E Colorado Boulevard PH, Pasadena, CA 91105 . . . . . (626) 795-7278
Mehalko, Donna 515 E 82nd Street #5C, New York, NY 10028 . . . . . (212) 794-6297
Meicle, Charisa 1527 W Chicago Avenue, Chicago, IL 60622
Meier, Melissa Represented By: Sharon Dodge & Associates . . . . . (206) 284-4701
Meisel, Ann 270 Park Avenue S #10-C, New York, NY 10010 . . . . . (212) 777-5707
Represented By: Mendola Ltd. . . . . . (212) 986-5680
Meisel, Paul 2 N Pheasant Ridge Road, Newtown, CT 06470 . . . . . (203) 270-6692

MELEGARI, CARL
Page 201
Represented By: American Artists
(212) 682-2462
Represented By: Ian Flemming Associates
e-mail: info@amerartists.com • Website: www.amerartists.com

Melendez, David Represented By: Carol Bancroft & Friends .... (203) 748-4823
Melendez, Robert Represented By: Buck & Kane .... (212) 631-0009
Melia, Paul G. 3121 Atherton Road, Dayton, OH 45409 .... (937) 294-0669
Mell, Sue 285 Texas Street, San Francisco, CA 94107 .... (415) 431-6865
Mellon, Kristen 692A Moulton Avenue, Los Angeles, CA 90031 .... (213) 223-4242
Melmon, Deborah Represented By: Sharon Morris Associates .... (415) 362-8280
Melrath Illustration, Susan 28506 NE 63rd Way, Carnation, WA 98014 .... (425) 880-4353
Meltzer, Ericka 829 Jamestown Road, East Windsor, NJ 08520 .... (732) 438-8402
Menchin, Scott 640 Broadway, New York, NY 10012 .... (212) 463-0600

MENDELSSON, JONNY
Pages 86-87,112
Represented By: Lindgren & Smith
(212) 397-7330
e-mail: inquiry@lindgrensmith.com • Website: www.lindgrensmith.com • Specialties: Collage; Digital

Mercado, Jay 4754 California Street, San Francisco, CA 94118 .... (415) 751-4232
Meredith, Bret 5916 Fairwood Lane, Minnetonka, MN 55345 .... (612) 949-9838
Represented By: Bruck & Moss .... (212) 980-8061

MERIDITH, SHELLY
Pages 362,425,447,453,467
55 Mercer Street, 4th Flr., New York, NY 10013 • Fax (212) 226-3227
(212) 941-1905
e-mail: leocat@spacelab.net • Specialties: Book Jackets; Children; Fantasy; Fashion;
Graphic Design/Illustration; Greeting Cards; Icons; Whimsical

Merkley, David Represented By: Creative Freelancers .... (800) 398-9544
Merrell, David Represented By: Suzanne Craig Represents, Inc. .... (918) 749-9424
Merrell, Patrick 80 Eighth Avenue #1308, New York, NY 10011 .... (212) 620-7777

MESHON, AARON
Page 35
269 E 10th Street, Apt. 3, New York, NY 10009 • Fax (212) 253-1350
(212) 253-1350 • (800) 753-7513

Messenger, Marc Represented By: Famous Frames .... (310) 642-2721
Messi & Schmidt Represented By: Conrad Represents, Inc. .... (415) 921-7140
Messier, Linda Represented By: Hankins & Tegenborg Ltd. .... (212) 867-8092
Messina, Charles Represented By: Corporate Art Planning .... (212) 242-8995
Mets, Marilyn Represented By: Publishers' Graphics .... (203) 797-8188
Meyer, Bill Represented By: Pat Hackett Artist Representative .... (206) 447-1600
Meyer, Claudia 3726 SE Morrison Street, Portland, OR 97214 .... (503) 232-4720

MEYER, CLAY
Pages 341,441,450,452
1020 N Jefferson, Ste. E, Jackson, MS 39202
(601) 969-5720
e-mail: clayton@netdoor.com • Website: www.claymeyer.com • Specialties: Editorial; Humour; Icons

Meyer, Jeff Represented By: Mason Illustration .... (612) 729-1774
Represented By: Langley & Associates .... (847) 670-0912
Meyer, Kerry 16 E Dartmouth, Kansas City, MO 64113
Meyers, Mike 5319 Ramsdell Avenue, La Crescenta, CA 91214 .... (818) 248-6386
Michaels, Serge 123 N Madison Avenue, Monrovia, CA 91016 .... (626) 357-1416

MICHEL, JEAN-CLAUDE
Pages 168,178
Represented By: American Artists
(212) 682-2462
e-mail: info@amerartists.com • Website: www.amerartists.com

Michel, June Represented By: Those 3 Reps .... (214) 871-1316
Micich, Paul Represented By: Bernstein & Andriulli, Inc. .... (212) 682-1490
Mickelsen, Ken 2200 N Lamar Street #114, Dallas, TX 75202 .... (214) 871-7667
Middendorf, Nikki 200 E 28th Street #2B, New York, NY 10016 .... (212) 683-2848
Middleton, Carol Represented By: Creative Connection .... (410) 360-5981
Mikec, Larry Represented By: Nachreiner Boie Art Factory .... (414) 785-1940
Mikos, Mike Represented By: Mendola Ltd. .... (212) 986-5680

Milam, Larry 3530 SE Hawthorne #3, Portland, OR 97214 . . . . . (503) 236-9121
Represented By: Jaz & Jaz . . . . . (206) 633-3445
Milbourn, Patrick Represented By: Artworks . . . . . (212) 627-1554
Miles, Chris 160 Garfield Place, Brooklyn, NY 11215 . . . . . (718) 622-6907
Mille, Mark Represented By: Langley & Associates . . . . . (847) 670-0912
Represented By: Yolanda Burnett Represents . . . . . (770) 967-0039
Represented By: Tiffany Represents . . . . . (206) 441-7701
Miller, A.J. 2207 Bay Boulevard #201, Indian Rocks Beach, FL 33785 . . . . . (813) 596-6384
Miller, Cliff Represented By: Hankins & Tegenborg Ltd. . . . . . (212) 867-8092

MILLER, DAVE Pages 168,181
Represented By: American Artists **(212) 682-2462**
e-mail: info@amerartists.com • Website: www.amerartists.com • Specialty: Airbrush

MILLER, DAVE L. Page 163
11318 S Forrestville Avenue, Chicago, IL 60628 • Fax (773) 264-0916 **(773) 264-1152**
Specialties: Acrylic; Scratchboard

Miller, David Represented By: Wanda Nowak . . . . . (212) 535-0438
Miller, Don Represented By: Patti Shaw . . . . . (416) 361-3184
Miller, Edward Represented By: Alan Lynch Artists . . . . . (908) 813-8718
Miller, Frank Represented By: Jacqueline Dedell, Inc. . . . . . (212) 741-2539
Miller, Jack Paul 1331 N Lincoln Street, Burbank, CA 91506 . . . . . (818) 841-4668
Miller, Judy L. 801 N Shepherd Hills, Tucson, AZ 85710 . . . . . (520) 296-5323
Represented By: Mary Holland & Company . . . . . (602) 263-8990
Miller, Kristen Represented By: Gretchen Harris & Associates . . . . . (612) 822-0650
Represented By: The Schuna Group . . . . . (612) 631-8480
Miller, Max Represented By: Jacqueline Dedell, Inc. . . . . . (212) 741-2539
Miller, Maxine 2110 Holly Drive, Los Angeles, CA 90068 . . . . . (213) 461-1091
Miller, Ron Represented By: Fran Seigel . . . . . (212) 486-9644
Miller, Susan Represented By: Carol Bancroft & Friends . . . . . (203) 748-4823
Miller, Tom 7314 Cannon Court, West Chester, OH 45069 . . . . . (513) 779-9818
Represented By: Berendsen & Associates . . . . . (513) 861-1400
Millet, Cathy Represented By: Marlena Agency . . . . . (609) 252-9405

MILLICENT, MARK Page 277
Represented By: Famous Frames **(310) 642-2721**
e-mail: info@famousframes.com • Website: www.famousframes.com • Specialties: Animation; Storyboards

Millsart Studio 230 N Michigan Avenue #1505, Chicago, IL 60601 . . . . . (312) 236-1044
Milne, Jonathan Represented By: Mendola Ltd. . . . . . (212) 986-5680

MILOT, RENE Pages 40,466
Represented By: Renard Represents **(212) 490-2450**
e-mail: renardreps@earthlink.net • Website: www.renardrepresents.com
Specialties: Painterly; Pastels; Watercolor

Minor, Wendell 15 Old North Road, Washington, CT 06793 . . . . . (860) 868-9101
Minot, Karen 26 Deuce Court, Fairfax, CA 94930 . . . . . (415) 457-7559
Minshull, Steve 7208 W 80th Street, Ste. 208, Overland Park, KS 66204 . . . . . (913) 341-6090

MINTZ, MARGERY Pages 162,420,444,447,461,466
108 Albemarle Road, Newton, MA 02160 • Fax (617) 332-8858 **(617) 332-8858**
Represented By: Tom Maloney **(312) 704-0500**
Specialties: Architecture/Interiors; Book Jackets; Food; Greeting Cards; Oil; Painterly;
Pastels; Product; Watercolor

Miracle, Michael 61 Rutland Street, Boston, MA 02118 . . . . . (888) 393-3779
Miralles, Jose-Maria Represented By: SI International . . . . . (212) 254-4996
Misak, Kevin Represented By: Melissa Hopson . . . . . (214) 747-3122
Mistretta, Andrea 135 E Prospect Street, Waldwick, NJ 07463 . . . . . (201) 652-7531
Mitchel, Jean-Claude Represented By: American Artists . . . . . (212) 682-2462
Mitchell, Anastasia Represented By: The Schuna Group . . . . . (612) 631-8480
Mitchell, Angelo 1561 Camino Alto, San Marcos, TX 78666 . . . . . (830) 964-2825

Mitchell, Charlie 1034 Pepper Wood Trail, Norcross, GA 30093 . . . . . (770) 564-2896
Represented By: Cary & Company. . . . . (404) 296-9666
Represented By: Dolby Represents . . . . . (312) 855-9336
Mitchell, Tracy Represented By: Lisa Freeman . . . . . (317) 920-0068
Mitchelson, Terri Represented By: Deborah Snyder Creative Representative . . . . . (612) 922-3462
Mitsui, Glenn 1512 Alaskan Way, Seattle, WA 98101 . . . . . (206) 682-6221
Mitta, Eugene Represented By: Ann Koeffler Represents . . . . . (213) 957-2327
Miyake, Yoshi Represented By: Carol Bancroft & Friends . . . . . (203) 748-4823
Miyamoto, Mas Represented By: Square Moon . . . . . (510) 253-9451
Mizell, Judy Represented By: Creative Connection . . . . . (410) 360-5981

MJOLSNESS, JANE Page 161
101 Kitty Hawk Bay Drive, Kill Devil Hills, NC 27948 • Fax (252) 480-0401 **(252) 480-0165**
Represented By: Tonal Values **(214) 943-2569**
e-mail: tonalvalues@mindspring.com
Specialties: Black & White; Conceptual; Editorial; Fashion; Food; Greeting Cards; Lettering

Mohr, Mark 5106 Reinhardt Parkway, Roeland Park, KS 66205. . . . . (913) 631-0943

MOLINA, LUIS Page 277
Represented By: Famous Frames **(310) 642-2721**
e-mail: info@famousframes.com • Website: www.famousframes.com • Specialties: Animation; Storyboards

Moline, Robin Represented By: Conrad Represents, Inc.. . . . . (415) 921-7140
Mollering, David Represented By: Hedge Graphics . . . . . (818) 244-0110
Molloy, Jack A. Represented By: Munro Goodman. . . . . (312) 321-1336
Represented By: Joanie Bernstein Art Rep. . . . . (612) 374-3169
Molnar, Albert Represented By: Sheryl Beranbaum . . . . . (401) 737-8591
Monahan, Leo Represented By: Pat Hackett Artist Representative . . . . . (206) 447-1600
Mones, Isidre Represented By: SI International. . . . . (212) 254-4996

MONGEAU, MARC Pages 26-27
Represented By: Marlena Agency **(609) 252-9405**
e-mail: marzena@bellatlantic.net • Website: http://members.bellatlantic.net/~marzena
Specialties: Conceptual; Corporate; Editorial; Whimsical

Monlux Illustration 7622 S Yakima Avenue, Tacoma, WA 98408-5315 . . . . . (800) 574-6275
Represented By: Susan & Company . . . . . (206) 232-7873
Monroe, Chris Represented By: Mason Illustration. . . . . (612) 729-1774
Montecalvo, Bruce Represented By: Jennifer Embler Represents, Inc. . . . . . (954) 760-4195
Monteiro, Marcos Represented By: Leyden Diversified . . . . . (215) 663-0587
Monteleone, John Represented By: Bill & Maurine Klimt. . . . . (212) 799-2231
Montesan, Sam 23 Hugh Park Boulevard #2, Toronto, ON Canada. . . . . (416) 531-7901
Represented By: Artworks. . . . . (212) 627-1554
Montgomery, Linda 20 D'Arcy Street, Toronto, ON Canada M5T 1J7 . . . . . (416) 977-4002
Represented By: Jacqueline Morin & Associates. . . . . (416) 506-1411
Represented By: Irmeli Holmberg . . . . . (212) 545-9155
Montiel, David 453 Fourth Street #2-L, Brooklyn, NY 11215 . . . . . (718) 788-6118
Montoliu, Ralph Represented By: Jan Collier Represents, Inc. . . . . . (415) 383-9026
Montoya, Priscilla Represented By: Carol Guenzi Agents, Inc. . . . . . (800) 417-5120
Mooney, Gerry 2 Main Street #3N, Dobbs Ferry, NY 10522 . . . . . (914) 693-8076
Moonlight Press Studio 362 Cromwell Avenue, Ocean Breeze, NY 10305 . . . . . (718) 979-9695

MOORE, ANGELA Page 72
790 Riverside Drive, Apt. 7N, New York, NY 10032 • Fax (212) 690-7011 **(212) 690-7011**
Represented By: The Pred Group **(913) 438-7733**
Website: www.predgroup.com
Specialties: Advertising; Conceptual; Editorial; Graphic Design/Illustration; Oil; Painterly; People; Poster

Moore, Chris Represented By: Bernstein & Andriulli, Inc. . . . . . (212) 682-1490
Moore, Jay Represented By: Steve Edsey & Sons . . . . . (312) 527-0351
Moore, Larry Represented By: Carol Chislovsky Design, Inc. . . . . . (212) 677-9100
Moore, Scott 1203 Harris Street, Eden, NC 27288 . . . . . (336) 627-1559
Moore, Stephen 1077 Country Creek Drive, Lebanon, OH 45036 . . . . . (513) 932-4295
Moore, Susan Represented By: Lisa Freeman. . . . . (317) 920-0068

Moores, Jeff Represented By: Pamela Korn & Associates . . . (717) 595-9298
Moraes Studio, Greg 4760 Columbus Avenue, Sherman Oaks, CA 91403 . . . (818) 905-5267
Represented By: Sharpe & Associates . . . (310) 641-8556
Morales, Elizabeth Represented By: Square Moon . . . (510) 253-9451
Morales, Manuel Represented By: Steve Edsey & Sons . . . (312) 527-0351
Mordan, C.B. Represented By: Ravenhill Represents . . . (816) 333-0744
Represented By: Repertoire . . . (972) 761-0500
Mordan, Linda Represented By: Sheryl Beranbaum . . . (401) 737-8591
Moreno, David P.O. Box 12362, San Antonio, TX 78212-0362
Morgan, Jacqui Represented By: France Aline Associates . . . (213) 933-2500
Morgan, Leonard 730 Victoria Court, Bolingbrook, IL 60440 . . . (630) 739-7705
Morgan Rogers, Stephanie Represented By: Sharon Dodge & Associates . . . (206) 284-4701
Morgenstern, Michael 429 E 73rd Street, Apt. 5E, New York, NY 10012 . . . (212) 861-7391
Morin, Josee 4030 St. Ambroise #400, Montreal, PQ Canada H4C 2C7 . . . (514) 937-2363

MORO, ROBIN Page 78
Represented By: Laurie Lambert **(513) 841-0073**
Specialties: Advertising; Editorial; People

MORRIS, ALEX Page 277
Represented By: Famous Frames **(310) 642-2721**
e-mail: info@famousframes.com • Website: www.famousframes.com • Specialties: Animation; Storyboards

Morris, Anton Represented By: Sally Heflin . . . (212) 366-1893
Morris, Burton 2215 Harmain Road, Pittsburgh, PA 15235 . . . (412) 682-7963
Represented By: Lori Nowicki & Associates . . . (212) 243-5888
Represented By: David Montagano & Associates . . . (312) 527-3283
Represented By: Ann Koeffler Represents . . . (213) 957-2327
Morris, Don Represented By: Alexander/Pollard, Inc. . . . (800) 347-0734
Morris, Frank Represented By: Bill & Maurine Klimt . . . (212) 799-2231
Morris, Julie Represented By: Renard Represents . . . (212) 490-2450
Morris, Rick 425 Juniper Drive, Pasadena, CA 91105 . . . (213) 255-6615
Morrison, Bill 68 Glandore Road, Westwood, MA 02090 . . . (617) 329-5288
Represented By: Martha Productions . . . (310) 390-8663
Morrison, Don Represented By: Anita Grien Represents . . . (212) 697-6170
Morrison, Jeff 315 Pocahontas Trail, Oxford, MI 48371 . . . (248) 969-0069
Morrow, Christopher Represented By: Beth O'Neill Artists Rep . . . (716) 473-0384

MORROW, J.T. Pages 252-253
220 Kavanaugh Way, Pacifica, CA 94044 **(650) 335-7899**
Represented By: Deborah Wolfe **(215) 232-6666**
Website: www.deborahwolfeltd.com
Specialties: Advertising; Children; Computer; Conceptual; Digital; Editorial; Mixed Media; People

Morse, Bill Represented By: Deborah Wolfe . . . (215) 232-6666
Represented By: Will Sumpter & Associates . . . (770) 460-8438
Morse, Deborah Represented By: Square Moon . . . (510) 253-9451
Morse, Tony Represented By: Ivy Glick & Associates . . . (925) 944-0304
Morser, Bruce Represented By: Pat Hackett Artist Representative . . . (206) 447-1600
Mortensbak, Jack Represented By: Leighton & Company, Inc. . . . (978) 921-0887
Mosberg, Hilary Represented By: Friend & Johnson . . . (214) 559-0055
Moschell, Paul Represented By: Lisa Freeman . . . (317) 920-0068
Moscowitz, Stephen Represented By: Beth O'Neill Artists Rep . . . (716) 473-0384
Moses, David Represented By: Will Sumpter & Associates . . . (770) 460-8438

MOSES, DUFF Page 277
Represented By: Famous Frames **(310) 642-2721**
e-mail: info@famousframes.com • Website: www.famousframes.com • Specialties: Animation; Storyboards

Moss, Meranda 252 First Avenue N, Minneapolis, MN 55401 . . . (612) 375-0180
Motoyama, Keiko 1607 E Glenhaven Drive, Phoenix, AZ 85048 . . . (602) 460-2743
Motzkus, Roger 889 W Huntington Drive, Arcadia, CA 91007 . . . (626) 447-8293
Represented By: Mendola Ltd. . . . (212) 986-5680

MOUNT, KRISTIN Pages 226,465
2123 W Warner Avenue, Chicago, IL 60618 **(800) 455-9717**
e-mail: kmount@wwa.com • Specialties: Computer; Medical; People; Portraiture; Technical

Mounts, Paul Represented By: Marvel Entertainment . . . . . (212) 696-0808
Moyer, Lee Represented By: Donna Rosen Artists' Rep . . . . . (301) 384-8925
Moyers, David 106 Grenfell Road, Dewitt, NY 13214. . . . . (315) 682-1099
Moyle, Eunice 535 One Center Boulevard #305D, Altamonte Spring, FL 32701 . . . . . (407) 895-1847
Muchmore, Pat Represented By: Leyden Diversified. . . . . (215) 663-0587
Represented By: Image Mill . . . . . (515) 490-6110
Mueller, Derek Represented By: Sweet Represents . . . . . (415) 433-1222
Mueller, Ellen 314 11th Street, Petaluma, CA 94952. . . . . (707) 778-6221
Mueller, Kate 844 E Atlantic Street, Appleton, WI 54911 . . . . . (920) 738-9437
Mueller, Mark Represented By: Mendola Ltd. . . . . . (212) 986-5680
Mueller, Pete Represented By: Liz Sanders Agency . . . . . (714) 495-3664
Represented By: Bernstein & Andriulli, Inc. . . . . . (212) 682-1490
Mukai, Dennis Represented By: Martha Productions . . . . . (310) 390-8663
Mull, Christy 3182 Holly Mill Run, Atlanta, GA 30062 . . . . . (404) 255-1430
Represented By: Susan Wells & Associates. . . . . . (404) 255-1430
Mullane, John Represented By: Fran Seigel. . . . . . (212) 486-9644
Muller, Rudy Represented By: Hankins & Tegenborg Ltd. . . . . . (212) 867-8092
Mulligan, Donald 418 Central Park West, Ste. 81, New York, NY 10025 . . . . . (212) 666-6079
Mullin, Lana Represented By: Square Moon . . . . . (510) 253-9451
Mulnar, Albert 1875 Hialeah, Orleans, ON Canada K4A 3F7 . . . . . (613) 841-7901

MULOCK, JULIAN Pages 252-253
Represented By: Deborah Wolfe **(215) 232-6666**
Website: www.deborahwolfeltd.com • Specialties: Advertising; Architecture/Interiors; Editorial; Greeting Cards; Landscape; Murals; Product; Still Life

Munck, Paula Represented By: Jacqueline Dedell, Inc.. . . . . (212) 741-2539
Munro, Steve 405 N Wabash, Ste. 3112, Chicago, IL 60611 . . . . . (312) 321-1350
Muns, Marjorie 501 Obispo Avenue, Long Beach, CA 90814 . . . . . (562) 438-2165
Represented By: Hedge Graphics . . . . . (818) 244-0110
Murai, Hitomi 373 Park Avenue S, 7th Flr., New York, NY 10016 . . . . . (212) 684-7060
Murakami, Tak Represented By: Art Bunch, The. . . . . . (312) 368-8777
Murphy, Chris Represented By: The Ivy League of Artists . . . . . (212) 243-1333
Murphy, Liz 319 W 22nd Street, Ste. 3C, New York, NY 10011 . . . . . (212) 691-2286
Murphy, Mark Represented By: Cliff Knecht . . . . . (412) 761-5666

MURPHY, SHAWN Pages 168,186
Represented By: American Artists **(212) 682-2462**
e-mail: info@amerartists.com • Website: www.amerartists.com

Murray, Barbara 23 Oakdale Court, Sterling, VA 20165 . . . . . (703) 450-9634
Murray, Darin Represented By: Harriet Kastaris & Associates . . . . . (314) 773-2600
Murton, Simon Represented By: Motion Artists, Inc. . . . . . (213) 851-7737
Musselman, Chris 5517 N Lakewood Avenue, Chicago, IL 60640. . . . . . (773) 989-8506
Represented By: Harriet Kastaris & Associates . . . . . (314) 773-2600
Represented By: Langley & Associates. . . . . . (847) 670-0912
Represented By: Wilson-Zumbo Illustration . . . . . (414) 271-3388
Muth, Jon J. Represented By: Allen Spiegel & Associates . . . . . (408) 372-4672
Mutrux, Alicemarie 1107 Broadway, San Francisco, CA 94109 . . . . . (415) 474-1336
Muzick, Terra 1805 Pine Street #21, San Francisco, CA 94109 . . . . . (415) 346-6141
Myer, Andy Represented By: Deborah Wolfe . . . . . (215) 232-6666
Myers, Glenn 5935 N BeltWest, Belleville, IL 62223. . . . . . (618) 277-6288
Mysakov, Leonid Represented By: Irmeli Holmberg . . . . . (212) 545-9155
Myshka, Christine 1 Gentore Court, Edison, NJ 08820 . . . . . (908) 754-1138
Nachreiner, Tom Represented By: Nachreiner Boie Art Factory . . . . . (414) 785-1940

NACHT, MERLE Pages 342-343
374 Main Street, Wethersfield, CT 06109 **(860) 563-7993**
Specialties: Cartoon; Children; Corporate; Editorial; Humour; Maps

Nagata, Mark 1948 Leavenworth Street, San Francisco, CA 94133 . . . . . (415) 922-6612

Nahigian, Alan 33-08 31st Avenue, Long Island City, NY 11106 . . . . . (718) 274-4042
Najaka, Marlies Merk 241 Central Park West, New York, NY 10024 . . . . . (212) 580-0058
Nakai, Michael 218 Madison Avenue #5-F, New York, NY 10016 . . . . . (212) 213-5333
286 Old Broadway, Hastings on Hudson, NY 10706. . . . . (914) 478-1605
Nakamura, Joel 72 Bobcat Trail, Santa Fe, NM 87505. . . . . (505) 989-1404
Nakata, Hiroe Represented By: HK Portfolio . . . . . (212) 675-5719
Namaye, Darren 373 Park Avenue S, 7th Flr., New York, NY 10016 . . . . . (212) 684-7060
Napoleon Art 460 W 42nd Street, 2nd Flr, New York, NY 10036 . . . . . (212) 967-6655
Narizhy, Ilya 168 Marion Street, Toronto, ON Canada M6R 1E8 . . . . . (416) 538-4173

NASCIMBENE, YAN Pages 86-87,113
Represented By: Lindgren & Smith **(212) 397-7330**
e-mail: inquiry@lindgrensmith.com • Website: www.lindgrensmith.com

Nash, Scott Represented By: Leighton & Company, Inc. . . . . . (978) 921-0887
Nass, Rhonda Represented By: Harriet Kastaris & Associates . . . . . (314) 773-2600
Nass, Rick Represented By: Image Mill . . . . . (515) 490-6110
Nasta, Vincent Represented By: Lindgren & Smith. . . . . (212) 397-7330
Nathan, Cheryl Represented By: Evelyne Johnson Associates . . . . . (212) 532-0928
Nation, Tate 719 Bradburn Drive, Mt. Pleasant, SC 29464. . . . . (843) 884-9911
Nau, Steven Represented By: Deborah Wolfe . . . . . (215) 232-6666
Naugle, Diane 3665 Thousand Oaks Boulevard, Westlake Village, CA 91362 . . . . . (805) 374-1174
Represented By: Linda De Moreta Represents . . . . . (510) 769-1421
Nazz, James 41 Union Square #628, New York, NY 10003 . . . . . (212) 366-5684
Nead, Beck 9478 N 67th Street, Milwaukee, WI 53223. . . . . (414) 365-2540
Represented By: Chris Glenn . . . . . (312) 670-7737
Neely, Keith R. 2232 Glenn Street, Los Osos, CA 93402. . . . . (805) 528-4058
Nees, Susan 450 McDuffie Drive, Athens, GA 30605 . . . . . (706) 543-3985
Negrin, Fabian Represented By: Bernstein & Andriulli, Inc. . . . . . (212) 682-1490
Neibart, Wally Represented By: Buck & Kane . . . . . (212) 631-0009
Neider, Alan Represented By: Jennifer Embler Represents, Inc. . . . . . (954) 760-4195
Represented By: Anita Grien Represents . . . . . (212) 697-6170
Neil, Tim 7614 Willoughby Avenue, Los Angeles, CA 90046 . . . . . (213) 651-4773
Nelms, Cynthia 12468 Oak Brook Place, Dubuque, IA 52001 . . . . . (319) 557-8970
Nelsen, Randy Represented By: Carol Guenzi Agents, Inc.. . . . . (800) 417-5120
Nelson, Annika Represented By: Sally Heflin. . . . . (212) 366-1893
Nelson, Bill Represented By: Richard Solomon . . . . . (212) 683-1362
Nelson, Craig Represented By: Bernstein & Andriulli, Inc.. . . . . (212) 682-1490
Nelson, Donna Kay 749 Sherman Avenue, Evanston, IL 60202 . . . . . (847) 492-0366
Nelson, Hilber 2045 Bitterroot Drive, Twin Falls, ID 83301 . . . . . (208) 733-5447
Represented By: Kolea Baker Artists Representative. . . . . (206) 784-1136
Nelson, Jerry 500 Aurora N #203, Seattle, WA 98109 . . . . . (206) 292-9186
Nelson, John 36 W Palmdale Drive, Tempe, AZ 85282. . . . . (602) 829-8992
Represented By: Irmeli Holmberg . . . . . (212) 545-9155
Represented By: Corey Graham Represents . . . . . (415) 956-4750
Represented By: Kimberley Boege . . . . . (602) 265-4389

NELSON, JOHN KILLIAN Page 277
Represented By: Famous Frames **(310) 642-2721**
e-mail: info@famousframes.com • Website: www.famousframes.com • Specialties: Animation; Storyboards

Nelson, Jon Represented By: Ceci Bartels Associates . . . . . (314) 781-7377
Nelson, Linda 25 Commerce Avenue SW, Grand Rapids, MI 49503 . . . . . (616) 774-0510
Nelson, Lynne 910 J Street #C-10, Salida, CO 81201 . . . . . (719) 539-8660
Nelson, R. Kenton 12 S Fair Oaks Avenue, Pasadena, CA 91105 . . . . . (626) 792-5252

NELSON, WILL Pages 133,138
Represented By: Sweet Represents **(415) 433-1222**
Specialties: Animals; Computer; Wildlife

Nelson & Son, Scott 22 Rayburn Drive, Millbury, MA 01527. . . . . (508) 865-5045
Nelson-Weis, Inc. P.O. Box 1183, Salina, KS 67402-1183 . . . . . (785) 825-6789
Nessim, Barbara 63 Greene Street, New York, NY 10012. . . . . (212) 219-1111
Neubecker, Robert 505 E Third Avenue, Salt Lake City, UT 84103 . . . . . (801) 531-6999
Neumann, Ann 1101 Garden Street, Hoboken, NJ 07030. . . . . (201) 653-8927

Newbold, Greg 1231 E 6000 South, Salt Lake City, UT 84121 . . . . . (801) 268-2209
Newell, Claudia 151 First Avenue, New York, NY 10003 . . . . . (212) 969-0795
Newell & Associates 11139 117th Way N, Largo, FL 33778. . . . . (813) 398-7809
Newman, Barbara Johansen 45 S Street, Needham, MA 02192 . . . . . (617) 449-2767
Newman, Dave P.O. Box 11762, Prescott, AZ 86304. . . . . (888) 771-9878
Newman, Kathleen 12325 S 90th Avenue, Palos Park, IL 60464. . . . . (708) 361-0679
Newman, Kevin 1128 Ocean Park Boulevard #314, Santa Monica, CA 90405 . . . . . (310) 394-0322
Represented By: Daniele Collignon . . . . . (212) 243-4209
Represented By: Ceci Bartels Associates . . . . . (314) 781-7377
Represented By: Liz Sanders Agency . . . . . (714) 495-3664
Newman, Leslie 1904 Third Avenue, Ste. 635, Seattle, WA 98101 . . . . . (206) 622-3025
Represented By: Jaz & Jaz . . . . . (206) 633-3445
Newman DBA Manual-Matic Co., Robert 4461 Independence Avenue N, New Hope, MN 55428 . . . . . (612) 537-3627
Newsom, Carol Represented By: Mendola Ltd. . . . . . (212) 986-5680
Newsom Illustration 7713 Red Rock Circle, Larkspur, CO 80118 . . . . . (303) 681-2472
Newson, Gregory G. 754 St. Nicholas Place, New York, NY 10032. . . . . (212) 926-0363
Newton, Debbie 1200 Romeria Drive, Austin, TX 78757 . . . . . (512) 459-2299
Newton, Richard Represented By: Renard Represents . . . . . (212) 490-2450
Newton Design, Brett 604 W Addison, Chicago, IL 60613 . . . . . (312) 528-2728
Ng, Michael 130-39 60th Avenue, Flushing, NY 11355 . . . . . (718) 461-8970
Ng, Simon Represented By: Reactor Art & Design Ltd. . . . . . (416) 703-1913
Nguyen, Richard Quan Represented By: Jim Lilie . . . . . (415) 441-4384
Nicholas, Jess Represented By: Buck & Kane . . . . . (212) 631-0009
Nicholls Design Inc., Calvin 48 Bond Street, Lindsay, ON Canada K9V 3R2 . . . . . (705) 878-1640
Nichols, Garry 1449 N Pennsylvania Street, Indianapolis, IN 46202 . . . . . (317) 637-0250

NICHOLS, JAMES — Pages 133,140-141,432
Petaluma, CA 94952 • Fax (707) 762-6699 — **(707) 762-4455**
Represented By: Sweet Represents — **(415) 433-1222**
Website: www.jnpainter.com • Specialties: Digital; Icons; Painterly

Nicholson, Norman 132 Leona Court, Alamo, CA 94507 . . . . . (925) 837-0695
Nickle, John 298 Seventh Avenue #1, Brooklyn, NY 11215 . . . . . (718) 788-7310
Nicodemus, Stephen 11972 Weatherby Road, Los Alamitos, CA 90720. . . . . (888) 493-7595

NIDENOFF, MICHELE — Pages 309,424
100 Roehampton Avenue #1215, Toronto, ON Canada M4P 1R3 • Fax (416) 932-9297 — **(416) 482-5348**
Specialties: Children; Editorial; Food

Nielsen, Cliff Represented By: Shannon Associates . . . . . (212) 831-5650
Nielsen, Terese 6049 Kauffman Avenue, Temple City, CA 91780. . . . . (626) 451-0454
Niemeyer, Paul E. 6800 Woodridge Drive, Woodridge, IL 60517 . . . . . (630) 969-1199
Nihoff, Tim 470 Commonwealth Avenue #2F, Boston, MA 02215 . . . . . (617) 536-7279 • (888) 823-0602
Niklewicz, Adam 44 Great Quarter Road, Sandy Hook, CT 06482 . . . . . (203) 270-8424
Nikosey Design, Tom 188 Dapplegray Road, Bell Canyon, CA 91307 . . . . . (818) 704-9993
Represented By: Photocom Inc. . . . . . (214) 720-2272
Nimoy, Nancy 10534 Clarkson Road, Los Angeles, CA 90064. . . . . (310) 202-0773
Represented By: Freda Scott, Inc.. . . . . . (415) 398-9121
Nine, Carlos Represented By: SI International . . . . . (212) 254-4996
Ning, Amy 3966 Gaviota Avenue, Long Beach, CA 90807 . . . . . (562) 989-9509
Represented By: Liz Sanders Agency . . . . . (714) 495-3664
Nishibeppu, Mariko 4527 ½ Finley Avenue, Los Angeles, CA 90027. . . . . (213) 664-9579
Nishinaka, Jeff Represented By: Langley & Associates. . . . . . (847) 670-0912
Nitta, Kazushige Represented By: David Goldman Agency . . . . . (212) 807-6627
Nitto, Tomio Represented By: Reactor Art & Design Ltd. . . . . . (416) 703-1913

NIXON, MARIAN — Page 401
2867 W Leland, Chicago, IL 60625 • Fax (773) 588-7640 — **(773) 588-8640**
e-mail: nixonm@enteract.com • Specialties: Advertising; Architecture/Interiors; Children; Fashion; Food; Graphic Design/Illustration; Greeting Cards; Product; Water Color; Whimsical

Nixon Art Studio, Tony 7210 Robinson Street, Overland Park, KS 66204 . . . . . (913) 384-5444
Njaa, Reuben Represented By: Vicki Prentice Associates, Inc. . . . . . (212) 332-3460

NOBLE, STEVEN Pages 133,136-137
47 Andreas Circle, Novato, CA 94945 • Fax (415) 892-4449 **(415) 897-6961**
Represented By: Sweet Represents **(415) 433-1222**
Specialty: Scratchboard

Noche, Mario Represented By: Clare Jett & Associates . . . . . (502) 228-9427
Nocito, James M. 1219 W Lewis Street, San Diego, CA 92103 . . . . . (619) 491-0433
Noffin, Landon Represented By: Nachreiner Boie Art Factory . . . . . (414) 785-1940
Noiset, Michele 279 Twin Lakes Drive, Halifax, MA 02338. . . . . (617) 294-0206
Nolan, Dennis 106 Nash Hill Road, Williamsburg, MA 01096 . . . . . (413) 268-3443
Nolan, Patricia 3525 Mockingbird Lane, Dallas, TX 25205 . . . . . (214) 521-5156
Noll, Cheryl Kirk 19 Hooker Street, Providence, RI 02908 . . . . . (401) 861-5869
Norby, Carol H. 112 S Main, Alpine, UT 84004 . . . . . (801) 756-1096
Nordell, Dale Represented By: Jaz & Jaz . . . . . (206) 633-3445

NORDLING, TODD Pages 133-134,436
315 First Avenue S, 2nd Flr., Seattle, WA 98104 **(206) 624-4996**
Represented By: Sweet Represents **(415) 433-1222**
Specialties: Advertising; Airbrush; Caricature; Cartoon; Children; Digital; Editorial; Humour; Whimsical

Nordstrom, Joe 7340 Fourth Avenue S, Richfield, MN 55423. . . . . (612) 866-7356
Represented By: The Schuna Group . . . . . (612) 631-8480
Noreika, Robert Represented By: Evelyne Johnson Associates . . . . . (212) 532-0928
Normandin, Luc 4030 St. Ambroise #400, Montreal, PQ Canada H4C 2C7 . . . . . (514) 937-2363
North, Ann P.O. Box 17024, Irvine, CA 92623-7024 . . . . . (714) 501-5055
North, Jan Represented By: Creative Freelancers . . . . . (800) 398-9544
Northeast, Christian Represented By: Reactor Art & Design Ltd. . . . . . (416) 703-1913
Norton, Larry 1918 N Craig Avenue, Altadena, CA 91001. . . . . (626) 797-9837
Norwell Illustration, Jeffery 63A Yorkville Avenue, Toronto, ON Canada M5R 1B7 . . . . . (416) 928-1010
Notarile, Chris Represented By: Mendola Ltd. . . . . . (212) 986-5680
Novak, Tony Represented By: Lulu Creatives . . . . . (612) 825-7564
Noyes, David Represented By: American Artists . . . . . (212) 682-2462
NY Film & Animation Represented By: Mendola Ltd. . . . . . (212) 986-5680
O'Brien, John Represented By: Evelyne Johnson Associates. . . . . (212) 532-0928
O'Brien, Tim Represented By: Lott Representatives. . . . . (212) 953-7088
O'Connell, Dave Represented By: Skidmore, Inc. . . . . . (248) 353-7722
O'Connell, Kathy 1494 Cold Springs Road, Pottstown, PA 19465 . . . . . (610) 326-8038
O'Connell, Mitch Chicago, IL 60601 . . . . . (312) 704-0500
O'Connor, Jeff 331 S Taylor Street, Oak Park, IL 60302. . . . . (708) 383-6698
Represented By: Langley & Associates. . . . . (847) 670-0912
Represented By: Yolanda Burnett Represents . . . . . (770) 967-0039

O'FARRELL, LIAM Page 201
Represented By: American Artists **(212) 682-2462**
Represented By: Ian Flemming Associates
e-mail: info@amerartists.com • Website: www.amerartists.com

O'FRIEL, PATTY Pages 308,445,453,467,468
1112 N Hoyne Avenue, Ste. 2, Chicago, IL 60622 • Fax (773) 384-3496 **(773) 384-3496**
Specialties: Advertising; Animals; Children; Editorial; Fantasy; Food; Icons; Product; Stock; Whimsical

O'Gorman, Molly Represented By: Artworks . . . . . (212) 627-1554
O'Keefe, David 3520 Buckboard Lane, Brandon, FL 33511 . . . . . (813) 684-4099

O'LEARY, CHRIS Pages 86-87,99
Represented By: Lindgren & Smith **(212) 397-7330**
e-mail: inquiry@lindgrensmith.com • Website: www.lindgrensmith.com

O'Leary, Daniel Represented By: Artworks . . . . . (212) 627-1554
O'Malley, Kathleen Represented By: Christina Tugeau . . . . . (203) 438-7307
O'Malley, Kevin Represented By: Melissa Turk & The Artist Network . . . . . (914) 368-8606

O'NEIL & ASSOCIATES, INC. Page 227
425 N Findlay Street, Dayton, OH 45404-2203 • Fax (937) 228-0135 **(937) 461-1852**
e-mail: oneilmkt@oneil.com • Website: www.oneil.com/html/gallery.html
Specialties: Conceptual; Industrial; Product; Technical

O'Neil Illustration, Sharron 15795 Adams Ridge Road, Los Gatos, CA 95033 . . . . . (800) 818-6187
Represented By: Karen Wells Represents . . . . . (800) 778-9076
O'Neill, Fran Represented By: Lulu Creatives . . . . . (612) 825-7564
O'Regan, Bernice 95 Bergen Street #4F, Brooklyn, NY 11201 . . . . . (718) 243-2824
O'Shea, Kevin Represented By: Lori Nowicki & Associates . . . . . (212) 243-5888
Represented By: Ann Koeffler Represents . . . . . (213) 957-2327
Oakes, Jim Represented By: Mary Holland & Company . . . . . (602) 263-8990
Oakes, Terry Represented By: Alan Lynch Artists . . . . . (908) 813-8718
Ochagavia, Carlos Represented By: Frank & Jeff Lavaty . . . . . (212) 427-5632
Ochsner, Dennis Represented By: Pat Hackett Artist Representative . . . . . (206) 447-1600
Odom, Mel 252 W 76th Street #B-1, New York, NY 10023 . . . . . (212) 724-9320
Ogai, Masaaki Represented By: Vicki Prentice Associates, Inc. . . . . . (212) 332-3460
Ogami, Nancy 1825 Lombard Street, San Francisco, CA 94123 . . . . . (888) 778-2323
Ogdemli/Feldman Design 11911 Magnolia Boulevard #39, North Hollywood, CA 91607 . . . . . (818) 760-1759
Ogle, Shawn Represented By: Jaz & Jaz . . . . . (206) 633-3445
Ogline, Tim E. P.O. Box 26786, Elkins Park, PA 19027 . . . . . (215) 886-5251
RR #2, Box 100, Hallstead, PA 18822-9651 . . . . . (717) 879-4717
Oh, Jeffrey Represented By: Janice Stefanski Represents . . . . . (415) 928-0457
Olbinski, Rafal 142 E 35th Street, New York, NY 10016 . . . . . (212) 532-4328
Represented By: Tania Kimche . . . . . (212) 529-3556
Oldroyd, Mark 11 Kings Ridge Road, Long Valley, NJ 07853 . . . . . (908) 813-8718
Olds, Scott Represented By: Skidmore, Inc. . . . . . (248) 353-7722
Olivere, Raymond L. 1435 Lexington Avenue #110, New York, NY 10128 . . . . . (212) 831-0598

OLIVIA Page 271
2414 Calle Zaguan, Santa Fe, NM 87505 • Fax (505) 471-3959 **(505) 471-8300**
Represented By: Christine Prapas **(503) 658-7070**
Represented By: Rhyne Represents **(303) 871-9166**
Represented By: Bernstein & Andriulli, Inc. **(212) 682-1490**
e-mail: macbruja@aol.com • Website: www.theartshow.com/olivia

Olmstead, David 1300 Nicollet Mall, Ste. 3046, Minneapolis, MN 55403 . . . . . (612) 339-2112
Represented By: Steven Kenny . . . . . (800) 789-9389
Olson, Rik 12869 Occidental Road, Sebastopol, CA 95472 . . . . . (707) 874-1299
Olson, Terri Represented By: Steve Edsey & Sons . . . . . (312) 527-0351
On The Mark P.O. Box 1455, Boulder, CO 80306-1455 . . . . . (303) 442-3936
Opie, David 293 Camp Street, Providence, RI 02906 . . . . . (401) 861-3706
Oppenheimer, Jennie 330 Sir Francis Drake Blvd. #C, San Anselmo, CA 94960 . . . . . (415) 488-1047
Ordaz, Frank Represented By: Berendsen & Associates . . . . . (513) 861-1400
Organ-Kean, Margaret 1916 Pike Place #12-177, Seattle, WA 98101 . . . . . (206) 527-5097
Orleman, Duff Represented By: Berendsen & Associates . . . . . (513) 861-1400

OROSZ, ISTVAN Pages 22-23
Represented By: Marlena Agency **(609) 252-9405**
e-mail: marzena@bellatlantic.net • Website: http://members.bellatlantic.net/~marzena
Specialties: Conceptual; Corporate; Editorial; Whimsical

Ortega, Jose 131 Charlie Parker Place, New York, NY 10009 . . . . . (212) 228-2606
Ortiz, Jose Luis 66 W 77th Street, Ste. 45, New York, NY 10024 . . . . . (212) 877-3081
Osaka, Richard 1693 N Craig Avenue, Altadena, CA 91001 . . . . . (626) 794-0993
Osborn, Kathy Represented By: Riley Illustration . . . . . (212) 989-8770
Osher, Glynnis Represented By: Penny & Stermer Group . . . . . (212) 505-9342

OSIECKI, LORI Page 148
123 W Second Street, Mesa, AZ 85201 • Fax (602) 962-5233 **(602) 962-5233**

Osser, Stephanie 150 Winding River Road, Needham, MA 02192 . . . . . (781) 237-1116
Ossip, Jay 2020 SW 13th Avenue, Miami, FL 33145 . . . . . (305) 854-2983
Ostrowski, Edie Represented By: Creative Connection . . . . . (410) 360-5981
Osuna, Hank Represented By: Lori Nowicki & Associates . . . . . (212) 243-5888

Otnes, Fred 26 Chalburn Road, West Redding, CT 06896 . . . . . (203) 938-2829
Otto, Brian 2072 Palace Avenue, St. Paul, MN 55105 . . . . . (612) 699-9017
Represented By: Alexander/Pollard, Inc. . . . . . (800) 347-0734
Overdrive Design Ltd. 37 Hanna Avenue, 2nd Flr. #3, Toronto, ON Canada M6K 1W9 . . . . . (416) 537-2803
Owens, Jim 121 S Fremont Street #312, Baltimore, MD 21201 . . . . . (410) 528-1131
Represented By: Terry Squire . . . . . (919) 772-1262

OWNBEY, SCOTT Page 277
Represented By: Famous Frames **(310) 642-2721**
e-mail: info@famousframes.com • Website: www.famousframes.com • Specialties: Animation; Storyboards

Pace, Annie Represented By: Art Source/Diane Barkley . . . . . (914) 747-2220
Pace, Julie 678 Wellsley Drive, Lake Arrowhead, CA 92352 . . . . . (909) 337-0731
Represented By: Tom Maloney . . . . . (312) 704-0500
Represented By: Nancy George . . . . . (805) 688-3772
Represented By: Carol Chislovsky Design, Inc. . . . . . (212) 677-9100

PACIULLI, BRUNO Pages 86-87,102
Represented By: Lindgren & Smith **(212) 397-7330**
e-mail: inquiry@lindgrensmith.com • Website: www.lindgrensmith.com • Specialty: Oil

Packer, Neil Represented By: Bernstein & Andriulli, Inc. . . . . . (212) 682-1490
Padial, Omar 244 Fifth Avenue, Ste. 2139, New York, NY 10001 . . . . . (212) 802-9498
Pagano, Peter Represented By: Mendola Ltd. . . . . . (212) 986-5680
Page, Scott 565 Avenue Road #903, Toronto, ON Canada M4V 2JN . . . . . (905) 454-1979
Page, Splash 1125 Landwehr Road, Northbrook, IL 60062 . . . . . (708) 498-8936
Pagowski, Filip 113 W 106th Street #4-B, New York, NY 10025 . . . . . (212) 665-7553
Pahl, Peter Represented By: Sharon Morris Associates . . . . . (415) 362-8280

PAILLOT, JIM Pages 73,448
4907 Holly Street, Kansas City, MO 64112 • Fax (816) 561-6201 **(816) 561-8045**
Represented By: The Pred Group **(913) 438-7733**
e-mail: paillot@gvi.net • Website: www.jimpaillot.com • predgroup.com
Specialties: Black & White; Children; Conceptual; Digital; Editorial; Humour; Maps & Charts; Water Color

Palazzo, Cathlene 3850 Reklaw Drive, Studio City, CA 91604 . . . . . (818) 505-1774
Palen, Debbie 2043 Random Road, Ste. 209, Cleveland, OH 44106 . . . . . (216) 421-2656
Palencar, John Jude 249 Elm Street, Oberlin, OH 44074 . . . . . (440) 774-7312
Palermino Studio, Patricia 9029 Greylock Street, Alexandria, VA 22308 . . . . . (703) 360-4757
Palko, Vincent 3468 Edgewood Drive, Stow, OH 44224 . . . . . (330) 688-2198
Palmer, Gary 414 Wonderwood Drive, Charlotte, NC 28211 . . . . . (704) 366-1750
Palmer, Jan Represented By: HK Portfolio . . . . . (212) 675-5719
Palmer-Preiss, Leah 2709 Vanderbilt Avenue, Raleigh, NC 27607 . . . . . (919) 833-8443
Palombo, Lisa A. Represented By: Artworks . . . . . (212) 627-1554
Palulian, Dick Represented By: Joanne Palulian . . . . . (212) 581-8338
Panda Ink P.O. Box 5129, West Hills, CA 91308 . . . . . (818) 340-8061
Pando, Leo Represented By: Vicki Prentice Associates, Inc. . . . . . (212) 332-3460
Pandora Illustration 4950 Yonge Street, Ste. 2200, North York, ON Canada M2N 6P1 . . . . . (416) 250-0235
Pansini, Tom Represented By: Liz Sanders Agency . . . . . (714) 495-3664
Pantuso, Michael 1000 W Washington Boulevard, Chicago, IL 60607 . . . . . (312) 850-1802
Pao, Derick 23 Becca Hall Trail, Scarborough, ON Canada M1V 2T7 . . . . . (416) 321-5009
Papi, Liza 231 W 25th Street #3D, New York, NY 10001-7113 . . . . . (212) 627-7438
Papp, Robert Represented By: Bill & Maurine Klimt . . . . . (212) 799-2231
Pappalardo, Dean 561 Broadway, Rm. 4D, New York, NY 10012 . . . . . (212) 431-4354
Pappas, Chris 1164 E Cunningham Drive, Palatine, IL 60067 . . . . . (847) 359-5621
Represented By: Shekut Communications Network . . . . . (312) 977-9171
Parada, Roberto New York, NY . . . . . (212) 889-8777
Represented By: Artco . . . . . (212) 889-8777

PARASKEVAS, MICHAEL Pages 86-87,104
Represented By: Lindgren & Smith **(212) 397-7330**
e-mail: inquiry@lindgrensmith.com • Website: www.lindgrensmith.com

Pardini, Patricia 88 Lexington Avenue #1F, New York, NY 10016 . . . . . (212) 683-2010
Pardo, Jackie Represented By: The Arts Counsel . . . . . (212) 777-6777

Pardue, Jack 2307 Sherwood Hall Lane, Alexandria, VA 22306 . . . . . (703) 765-2622
Pardy, Cindy Represented By: Daniele Collignon . . . . . (212) 243-4209
Paris, Pat Represented By: Gwen Walters-Goldstein . . . . . (781) 235-8658
Pariseau, Pierre-Paul Represented By: Jerry Leff Associates, Inc. . . . . . (212) 697-8525
Park, Chang Represented By: Bruck & Moss . . . . . (212) 980-8061
Park, Charlie 25930 Rolling Hills Road #420, Torrance, CA 90505 . . . . . (310) 325-4177
Park, Elliott Represented By: The Art Source . . . . . (817) 481-2212

PARK, TRIP Pages 66,423,450
38 Lenox Road, Summit, NJ 07901 • Fax (908) 522-9588 **(908) 522-0167**
Represented By: Joanne Palulian **(212) 581-8338**
Specialties: Cartoon; Humour

Park, W.B. Represented By: Sell Inc. . . . . . (312) 578-8844
Parker, Curtis Represented By: Scott Hull Associates . . . . . (937) 433-8383
Parker, Earl Kenneth Represented By: Regina Brown . . . . . (610) 539-1130
Parker, Garth 400 Merrimac Way #36, Costa Mesa, CA 92626 . . . . . (714) 435-0150
Parker, Robert Andrew P.O. Box 114, West Cornwall, CT 06796 . . . . . (860) 672-0152
Represented By: Riley Illustration . . . . . (212) 989-8770
Parman, Michael Represented By: Sam Brody . . . . . (203) 854-0805
Parmenter, Wayne Represented By: Cliff Knecht . . . . . (412) 761-5666
Parnell, Jay Represented By: Lisa Freeman . . . . . (317) 920-0068

PARNELL, MILES Pages 283,288-289,443
Represented By: John Brewster Creative Services **(203) 226-4724**
e-mail: creative.svcs@snet.net • Website: www.brewstercreative.com
Specialties: Book Jackets; Character; Editorial; Humour; Product

Parrow, Neal Represented By: Famous Frames . . . . . (310) 642-2721
Partners By Design Represented By: American Artists . . . . . (212) 682-2462
Paschkis, Julie 309 NE 94th Street, Seattle, WA 98115 . . . . . (206) 525-5205
Pascos, Greg 102 Bloor Street W #809, Toronto, ON Canada M5S 1M8 . . . . . (416) 968-0513
Passantino, Robert Represented By: Buck & Kane . . . . . (212) 631-0009
Passarelli, Chuck Represented By: American Artists . . . . . (212) 682-2462
Passey, Kim Represented By: Liz Sanders Agency . . . . . (714) 495-3664
Passow, Faye Represented By: The Schuna Group . . . . . (612) 631-8480
Pasternak, Robert 114 W 27th Street, New York, NY 10001 . . . . . (212) 675-0002
Pastrana, Robert M. 473-A Riverdale Drive, Glendale, CA 91204-1513 . . . . . (818) 548-6083
Pastucha, Ron 121 ½ N Glassell Street #14, Orange, CA 92866 . . . . . (714) 744-1505
Pate, Judith Arlene 1614 Hillhaven Road, Browns Summit, NC 27214 . . . . . (800) 6JU-DITH
Pate, Rodney Represented By: Carol Bancroft & Friends . . . . . (203) 748-4823
Patnode, Lou 1525 First Avenue #5, Seattle, WA 98101 . . . . . (206) 622-2950
Patrick, Cyndy 5 Dresden Street, Apt. 1, Boston, MA 02130 . . . . . (617) 522-4433
Patrick, John Represented By: Scott Hull Associates . . . . . (937) 433-8383

PATRICK, TOM Page 74
4726 Fairmount Avenue, Kansas City, MO 64112 • Fax (816) 531-4853 **(816) 531-4853**

Patterson, Stuart Represented By: Art Department . . . . . (212) 925-4222

PATTI, JOYCE Pages 124-125
Represented By: Vicki Morgan Associates **(212) 475-0440**
e-mail: vmartrep@aol.com • Website: www.vickimorganassociates.com
Specialties: Animals; Children; Fantasy; Landscape; Oil; Realism; Still Life; Stock

Patton, Edd 295 19th Avenue #6, San Francisco, CA 94121 . . . . . (415) 387-3126
Represented By: Kohl & Associates, Inc. . . . . . (312) 759-5920
Patton Brothers Illustration 3768 Miles Court, Spring Valley, CA 91977 . . . . . (619) 463-4562
Paul, Keith Represented By: Barbara Gordon Associates Ltd. . . . . . (212) 686-3514
Pauling, Galen T. 17704 Wormer Street, Detroit, MI 48219 . . . . . (313) 533-7674
Paulsen, Larry Represented By: Bernstein & Andriulli, Inc. . . . . . (212) 682-1490
Paulsrud, Pamela 923 Amherst, Wilmette, IL 60091 . . . . . (847) 251-5228

PAVLOVITS, IVAN Page 277
Represented By: Famous Frames **(310) 642-2721**
e-mail: info@famousframes.com • Website: www.famousframes.com • Specialties: Animation; Storyboards

Payne, Adair 5921 E Inca Street, Mesa, AZ 85205 . . . . (602) 641-7345
Payne, C.F. Represented By: Richard Solomon . . . . (212) 683-1362
Payne, Liane Represented By: Alan Lynch Artists. . . . . (908) 813-8718
Payne, Tom Represented By: Penny & Stermer Group . . . . (212) 505-9342
Peake, Kevin Represented By: Tonal Values. . . . . (214) 943-2569
Pearson, Claudia Represented By: Art Department . . . . (212) 925-4222
Pearson, Paul 1406 Gloria, Palatine, IL 60067 . . . . (847) 358-9981
Peck, Everett Represented By: Salzman International . . . . (415) 285-8267
Peck, Marshall 10 Larch Lane, Londonderry, NH 03053. . . . . (603) 432-2108

PECK, SCOTT Page 159
2701 Thorndale Circle, Plano, TX 75074 **(972) 422-7438**
e-mail: scottpeck@juno.com • Specialties: Cartoon; Editorial; Humour; Illustrative

Peck, Virginia Represented By: Lulu Creatives . . . . (612) 825-7564
Pedersen, Judy 16 McEwen Street, Warwick, NY 10990 . . . . (914) 987-1090
Peebles, Peter Represented By: Artworks . . . . (212) 627-1554
Pelavin, Daniel 80 Varick Street #3B, New York, NY 10013. . . . . (212) 941-7418
Peled, Einat Represented By: Lisa Freeman . . . . (317) 920-0068
Pelham-Foulke, Nancy A. 2828 Superior Street, Bellingham, WA 98226. . . . . (360) 671-0234
Pelka, Eric Represented By: The Arts Counsel . . . . (212) 777-6777
Represented By: Lisa Grafton Represents . . . . (714) 582-2081

PELO, JEFFREY Pages 56,436
Represented By: Renard Represents **(212) 490-2450**
e-mail: renardreps@earthlink.net • Website: www.renardrepresents.com • Specialties: Conceptual; Digital

Pembroke, Richard Represented By: American Artists . . . . (212) 682-2462
Penca, Gary Represented By: Hankins & Tegenborg Ltd. . . . . (212) 867-8092
Pencil Mill Graphics Box 264, RR #1, Castleton, VT 05735 . . . . (802) 273-2069

PENG, LEIF Pages 252-253
Represented By: Deborah Wolfe **(215) 232-6666**
Website: www.deborahwolfeltd.com • Specialties: Advertising; Black & White; Cartoon; Children; Computer; Digital; Editorial; Humour; People; Stock

Pennington, Jack Represented By: Berendsen & Associates. . . . . (513) 861-1400
Pepera, Fred Represented By: Joel Harlib Associates, Inc. . . . . (312) 573-1370
Peppard, Jackie Box 1134, 110 Tomboy Road, Telluride, CO 81435. . . . . (970) 728-3373
Pepper, Bob 157 Clinton Street, Brooklyn, NY 11201 . . . . (718) 875-3236
Pepper, Brenda 157 Clinton Street, Brooklyn, NY 11201 . . . . (718) 875-3236
Percivalle, Rosanne 450 W 31st Street, New York, NY 10001 . . . . (212) 295-7763
161 W 15th Street, New York, NY 10011
Perez, Theirry Represented By: Michelle Filomeno USA . . . . (212) 965-1000
Perez, Vincent 1279 Weber Street, Alameda, CA 94501 . . . . (510) 521-2262
Perkins, Ken 235 Agate Way, Broomfield, CO 80212 . . . . (303) 465-4346
Perringer, Stephen Represented By: Susan & Company . . . . (206) 232-7873
Perry, Bill Represented By: Famous Frames . . . . (310) 642-2721

PERSIANI, TONY Page 132
31 Magnolia Street, Framingham, MA 01701 **(508) 872-8180**
Represented By: Lori Nowicki & Associates **(212) 243-5888**
e-mail: tony@lorinowicki.com • Website: www.lorinowicki.com
Specialties: Advertising; Children; Corporate; Editorial

Persky, Lisa Jane 419 N Larchmont Boulevard #161, Los Angeles, CA 90004 . . . . (213) 461-9738
Represented By: France Aline Associates . . . . (213) 933-2500

PERTILE, PAULA — Page 62
419 22nd Avenue, San Francisco, CA 94121 • Fax (415) 668-0883 — **(415) 668-7156**
Represented By: Lynne LeCouvre Communications — **(805) 963-2859**
e-mail: ppertile@aol.com • Specialties: Children; Editorial; Whimsical

Petach, Heidi Represented By: Evelyne Johnson Associates . . . . . (212) 532-0928
Petan, Greg Represented By: Bernstein & Andriulli, Inc. . . . . . (212) 682-1490
Peters, David 2141 Walnut Avenue, Venice, CA 90291 . . . . . (310) 390-3528

PETERS DESIGN & ILLUSTRATION, GEORGE — Pages 316,423
209 Turners Crossroad S, Minneapolis, MN 55416 • Fax (612) 595-8063 — **(612) 546-4808**
e-mail: zeeinkster@aol.com • Specialties: Cartoon; Character; Children; Humour; People; Retro

Petersen, Don 3451 Guido Street, Oakland, CA 94602 . . . . . (510) 482-3808
Peterson, Bryan 2200 N Lamar Street, Ste. 310, Dallas, TX 75202 . . . . . (214) 954-0522

PETERSON, CHAD — Page 247
Represented By: Dimension — **(612) 884-4045**
e-mail: jkoltes@dimensioncreative.com • Website: www.dimensioncreative.com
Specialties: Oil; Water Color; Woodcut

Peterson, Eric Represented By: Conrad Represents, Inc. . . . . . (415) 921-7140
Peterson, Julie Represented By: Square Moon . . . . . (510) 253-9451

PETERSON, RICK — Pages 86-87,101
Represented By: Lindgren & Smith — **(212) 397-7330**
e-mail: inquiry@lindgrensmith.com • Website: www.lindgrensmith.com

Peterson Illustration, Tim P.O. Box 521296, Salt Lake City, UT 84152-1296 . . . . . (801) 466-9870
Represented By: Holly Hahn Artist Rep (H2 + Co.). . . . . . (312) 633-0500

PETRAUSKAS, KATHY — Page 405
1660 N LaSalle, Ste. 2001, Chicago, IL 60614 • Fax (312) 642-6391 — **(312) 642-4950**
Specialty: Pastels

Petrone, Valeria Represented By: HK Portfolio . . . . . (212) 675-5719
Petruccio, Steven James Represented By: Evelyne Johnson Associates . . . . . (212) 532-0928
Pettis, Ruth Represented By: The Schuna Group . . . . . (612) 631-8480
Pettit, David Represented By: Motion Artists, Inc. . . . . . (213) 851-7737

PEYCHA, ANDREW — Pages 324,442
91 Cowan Avenue, Toronto, ON Canada M6K 2N1 • Fax (416) 516-8104 — **(416) 725-8122**
Toronto, ON Canada — **(416) 516-4857**
Specialties: Acrylic; Conceptual; Editorial; Humour; Illustrative; People

Pfeiffer, Judith Represented By: Gwen Walters-Goldstein . . . . . (781) 235-8658
Phalen, Mary Jo 2048 Birch Avenue, San Carlos, CA 94070 . . . . . (650) 631-8173
Represented By: Hankins & Tegenborg Ltd. . . . . . (212) 867-8092
Phaneuf, Kathleen Represented By: Famous Frames . . . . . (310) 642-2721
Pharr, Bob 98402 Kristin, Houston, TX 77031 . . . . . (713) 771-4700
Philbrook, Diana 20927 Wolfe Way, Woodland Hills, CA 91364 . . . . . (818) 348-4255
Philippidis, Evangelia Represented By: Scott Hull Associates . . . . . (937) 433-8383
Phillips, Chet 6527 Del Norte, Dallas, TX 75225 . . . . . (214) 987-4344
Phillips, Jared 2305 Ashland Street #C, Ashland, OR 97520 . . . . . (800) 435-6509
Phillips, Laura Represented By: Hedge Graphics . . . . . (818) 244-0110
Phillips, Liz 4957 N Newhall Street, Whitefish Bay, WI 53217 . . . . . (414) 332-6344

PHILLIPS, MATT — Pages 373,378,448
121 Village Court, Woodstock, GA 30188 — **(770) 926-8385**
Represented By: Susan Wells & Associates — **(404) 255-1430**
Specialties: Cartoon; Children; Greeting Cards; Humour; Lettering; Whimsical

Phillips, Michael 53 Albemarle Avenue, Tampa, FL 33606 . . . . . (813) 821-2523

PICA, STEVE Pages 392,397,449
Represented By: Donna Rosen Artists' Rep **(301) 384-8925**
e-mail: djrosen@erols.com • Website: www.aaarrt.com/donnasgallery
Specialties: Advertising; Black & White; Children; Editorial; Humour; People; Water Color; Whimsical

Picasso, Dan Represented By: Joanie Bernstein Art Rep . . . . . (612) 374-3169
Pierazzi, Gary Grass Valley, CA 95945 . . . . . (530) 477-1950

PIERCE, LINDA Page 151
Represented By: Connie Koralik Associates Represents **(312) 944-5680**
Specialties: Advertising; Editorial; People

Pijet, Andre 3221 Bernard Street, Brossare, PQ Canada J4Z 2B7 . . . . . (514) 676-6423
Pillo, Cary Represented By: Publishers' Graphics . . . . . (203) 797-8188
Pilon, Alain Represented By: Reactor Art & Design Ltd. . . . . . (416) 703-1913
Pinkney, Debbie Represented By: Cliff Knecht . . . . . (412) 761-5666
Pinkney, Jerry 41 Furnace Dock Road, Croton-on-Hudson, NY 10520 . . . . . (914) 271-5238
Pinkney, Myles 1355 N Union Boulevard, Colorado Springs, CO 80909 . . . . . (719) 635-8848
Pinn, Alan 457 Mark Street, Peterborough, ON Canada K9H 1W1 . . . . . (705) 741-4729
Pippin, Matthew Represented By: Sheryl Beranbaum . . . . . (401) 737-8591

PIRMAN, JOHN Page 243
330 W 76th Street, New York, NY 10023 • Fax (212) 721-9787 **(212) 721-9787**
Represented By: Rita Gatlin Represents **(800) 924-7881**
Website: www.ritareps.com • Specialties: Computer; Corporate; Digital; Fashion; Icons

Pittman, Jackie Represented By: Will Sumpter & Associates . . . . . (770) 460-8438
Pitts, Ted Represented By: Scott Hull Associates . . . . . (937) 433-8383
Piven, Hanoch Represented By: Sally Heflin . . . . . (212) 366-1893
Pizzo, Robert 288 E Devonia Avenue, Mt. Vernon, NY 10552-1234 . . . . . (914) 664-4423
Place, Bob P.O. Box 541, Saugerties, NY 12477 . . . . . (914) 246-0180
Placek, Michael T. 3140 N New England Street, Chicago, IL 60634 . . . . . (312) 237-2577
Plank, Michael Represented By: Jerry Leff Associates, Inc. . . . . . (212) 697-8525
Plasse, Ami Represented By: Leighton & Company, Inc. . . . . . (978) 921-0887
Plate, Leticia 275 Bleecker Street #4, New York, NY 10014 . . . . . (212) 807-9728
Platz III, H. Rusty 15922 118th Place NE, Bothell, WA 98011-4152 . . . . . (425) 488-9171

PLAVEC, ALAN Page 245
2224 W Potomac Avenue, Chicago, IL 60622 **(773) 772-3789**

Plotkin, Barnett 100 Woods Road, North Babylon, NY 11703-3004 . . . . . (516) 586-9549

PLUNKERT C/O SPUR DESIGN, DAVID Pages 406-407
3647 Falls Road, Baltimore, MD 21211 • Fax (410) 235-4674 **(410) 235-7803**
e-mail: dave@spurdesign.com • Website: www.spurdesign.com
Specialties: Corporate; Editorial; Graphic Design/Illustration; Illustrative

Plyman, Dennis Represented By: Claudia Miller Artists Unlimited . . . . . (561) 995-9444
Podevin, Jean-Francois 5812 Newlin Avenue, Whittier, CA 90601 . . . . . (562) 945-9613
New York, NY . . . . . (212) 964-4244
Represented By: Artco . . . . . (212) 889-8777
Podrebarac, Charlie Represented By: Ceci Bartels Associates . . . . . (314) 781-7377
Podwil Studios 108 W 14th Street, New York, NY 10011 . . . . . (212) 255-9464
Poedtke, C.K. Represented By: Pat Clark Studio
Pohl, David 1629 Rhine Street, Pittsburgh, PA 15212 . . . . . (412) 231-0838
Represented By: Tonal Values . . . . . (214) 943-2569
Poladian, Elena Represented By: Creative Freelancers . . . . . (800) 398-9544
Polenghi, Evan 141 W 28th Street, Apt. 8-R, New York, NY 10001 . . . . . (212) 971-9215
Polfus, Roberta 226 N Lombard Avenue, Oak Park, IL 60302 . . . . . (708) 383-3651

POLLACK, SCOTT Page 280
78 Hidden Ridge Drive, Syosset, NY 11791 • Fax (516) 921-1908 **(516) 921-1908**
Specialties: Humour; Water Color

Polonsky Studio, Gabriel 274 LaGrange Street, Chestnut Hill, MA 02167 . . . . . (617) 965-3035

POMERANTZ, LISA Pages 252-253
Represented By: Deborah Wolfe **(215) 232-6666**
Website: www.deborahwolfeltd.com
Specialties: Advertising; Computer; Conceptual; Digital; Editorial; Humour; Whimsical

Poole, Colin Represented By: Linda De Moreta Represents . . . . . (510) 769-1421
Represented By: American Artists . . . . . (212) 682-2462
Represented By: Jennifer Embler Represents, Inc. . . . . . (954) 760-4195
Poole, Tony Represented By: Berendsen & Associates . . . . . (513) 861-1400

POPE, KEVIN Pages 58,450
Represented By: Renard Represents **(212) 490-2450**
e-mail: renardreps@earthlink.net • Website: www.renardrepresents.com
Specialties: Cartoon; Conceptual; Humour

Popeo, Joanie 230 Arriba Drive #8, Sunnyvale, CA 94086 . . . . . (650) 964-1733
Represented By: Jane Klein . . . . . (888) ART-1008
Porazinski, Rob Represented By: Jim Hanson Artist Agent . . . . . (312) 337-7770
Porfirio, Guy Represented By: Ceci Bartels Associates . . . . . (314) 781-7377
Porter, Walter Represented By: Marla Matson Represents . . . . . (602) 252-5072
Portfolio 221 N LaSalle 51500, Chicago, IL 60610 . . . . . (888) 88F-OLIO
711 Boylston Street, Boston, MA 02116 . . . . . (617) 535-5000
Post, Howard Represented By: Carol Bancroft & Friends . . . . . (203) 748-4823
Represented By: Kimberley Boege . . . . . (602) 265-4389
Potter, Giselle Represented By: Friend & Johnson . . . . . (214) 559-0055
Potts, Carolyn 1872 N Clybourn #404, Chicago, IL 60614 . . . . . (312) 944-1130
Potts, Charlene 30-20 43rd Street, Astoria, NY 11103 . . . . . (718) 274-6813
Powell, Andrew Represented By: Scott Hull Associates . . . . . (937) 433-8383

POWELL, TANA Page 243
531 Hugo Street, San Francisco, CA 94122 • Fax (415) 759-6380 **(415) 759-6453**
Represented By: Rita Gatlin Represents **(800) 924-7881**
Website: www.ritareps.com • Specialties: Acrylic; Conceptual; Editorial; Medical

Power, Stephanie Represented By: Reactor Art & Design Ltd. . . . . . (416) 703-1913
Powers, Christine Represented By: Cornell & McCarthy, LLC . . . . . (203) 454-4210
Powers, Tom Represented By: The Ivy League of Artists . . . . . (212) 243-1333
Pratt, Christine Joy Represented By: Carol Bancroft & Friends . . . . . (203) 748-4823
Pratt, George Represented By: Allen Spiegel & Associates . . . . . (408) 372-4672
Pratt, Pierre Represented By: Link . . . . . (416) 530-1500
Pravato, Victor 14 Emily Avenue, Weston, ON Canada M9L 2R1 . . . . . (416) 742-4764
Prescott, Harry J. Represented By: Ellen Harmon . . . . . (312) 829-8201
Preslicka Studio 5000 Edgewater Drive, Savage, MN 55378-5614 . . . . . (612) 447-8436
Previn, Stacey Represented By: Hedge Graphics . . . . . (818) 244-0110
Price, Amy 213 Antisdel Place NE, Grand Rapids, MI 49503 . . . . . (616) 459-7595
Price, David 6101 Bel-Air Avenue, Texarkana, TX 75503 . . . . . (903) 832-5552
Price, Heather Represented By: Mendola Ltd. . . . . . (212) 986-5680
Price, Jim Represented By: Frank Lux & Associates, Inc. . . . . . (312) 222-1361
Price, Tom Represented By: Connie Koralik Associates Represents . . . . . (312) 944-5680
Primal Screen/Animation Represented By: Terry Squire . . . . . (919) 772-1262

PRIMEAU, CHUCK Page 319
Represented By: PG Representatives **(413) 967-9855**
e-mail: pgreps@aol.com • Specialty: Digital

PRINCE, ROBERT L. Pages 283,286-287,448
Represented By: John Brewster Creative Services **(203) 226-4724**
e-mail: creative.svcs@snet.net • Website: www.brewstercreative.com • Specialties: Computer; Digital; Humour

Pritchett, Karen Represented By: Cliff Knecht . . . . . (412) 761-5666
Pritchett, Shelley Represented By: Artworks . . . . . (212) 627-1554
Probert, Jean Represented By: Ceci Bartels Associates . . . . . (314) 781-7377
ProGraphics 435 N Michigan Avenue #930, Chicago, IL 60611
Proulx, Art Represented By: American Artists . . . . . (212) 682-2462

Prud'Homme, Jules 24 Mont-Royal O #900A, Montreal, PQ Canada H2T 2S2 . . . . (514) 849-9496
Przewodek, Camille 522 D Street, Petaluma, CA 94952 . . . . (707) 762-4125
PT Pie Illustrations 33 Stonegate Drive, Southbury, CT 06488 . . . . (203) 264-0908
Pudekerk, Doug 2003 Goodrich Avenue, St. Paul, MN 55105 . . . . (612) 699-9258
Pulver Jr., Harry 105 Meadow Lane N, Minneapolis, MN 55422 . . . . (612) 377-1797

PUNIN, NIKOLAI Pages 371,438,440,452,464
311 Greenwich Street #9B, New York, NY 10013 **(212) 227-7863**
Represented By: Chip Caton **(860) 523-4562**
e-mail: nikolaip@aol.com • Website: www.nikolaiillustration.com
Specialties: Digital; Editorial; Icons; Medical; Technical

PYLE, CHARLES S. Pages 86-87,90
Represented By: Lindgren & Smith **(212) 397-7330**
e-mail: inquiry@lindgrensmith.com • Website: www.lindgrensmith.com
Specialties: Oil; People; Realism; Water Color

Pyle, Chris Represented By: Lisa Freeman . . . . (317) 920-0068
Pyle, Liz Represented By: Riley Illustration . . . . (212) 989-8770
Pyner, Marcia Represented By: Artworks . . . . (212) 627-1554

QUACK COMM./STEPHEN MACEACHERN Page 259
1024 Enola Avenue, Mississauga, ON Canada L5G 4A9 • Fax (905) 271-5922 **(905) 271-7410**
e-mail: quack@inforamp.net • Specialties: Cartoon; Digital; Maps & Charts

Quackenbush, Robert 460 E 79th Street, New York, NY 10021 . . . . (212) 744-3822
Quan, Richard Represented By: Hankins & Tegenborg Ltd. . . . . (212) 867-8092
Quanrud Illustration & Design 6987 Cadmar Lane, Seabeck, WA 98380 . . . . (360) 830-0662
Queen of Arts 12325 S 90th Avenue, Palos Park, IL 60464 . . . . (708) 361-0679
Quidley, Peter T. Represented By: Woody Coleman Presents, Inc. . . . . (216) 661-4222
Quinlan Illustration Ltd., Stephen 3062 Silverthorn Drive, Oakville, ON Canada L6L 5N7 . . . . (905) 469-0525
Quinlivan, Mary Represented By: Deborah Snyder Creative Representative . . . . (612) 922-3462
Quist, Glen Represented By: Deborah Snyder Creative Representative . . . . (612) 922-3462
Rabinowitz, Lauren Rachel P.O. Box 2283, Edison, NJ 08818-2283 . . . . (732) 549-1455
Rabl, Lorraine 629 Glenwood Avenue, Teaneck, NJ 07666 . . . . (201) 836-4283
Racer, Tim 3059 Richmond Boulevard, Oakland, CA 94611 . . . . (510) 451-0303
Rachko, Barbara 208 W 29th Street #605, New York, NY 10001 . . . . (212) 463-7060
1311 W Braddock Road, Alexandria, VA 22302 . . . . (703) 998-7496
Radencich, Mike Represented By: Mendola Ltd. . . . . (212) 986-5680
Rader, Laura Represented By: Cornell & McCarthy, LLC . . . . (203) 454-4210
Radigan, Bob Represented By: Jennifer Embler Represents, Inc. . . . . (954) 760-4195
Represented By: Susan Wells & Associates . . . . (404) 255-1430
Radmilovich, Joanne Portland, OR 97210 . . . . (503) 232-3409
Represented By: The Art Agency . . . . (503) 203-8300
Raetz, Kyle Represented By: Ceci Bartels Associates . . . . (314) 781-7377
Ragland Design & Illustration 2500 Lucky John Drive, Park City, UT 84060 . . . . (435) 645-9232

RAGLIN, TIM Pages 86-87
Represented By: Lindgren & Smith **(212) 397-7330**
e-mail: inquiry@lindgrensmith.com • Website: www.lindgrensmith.com • Specialty: Humour

Raleigh, Don 7520 Blaisdel Avenue S, Ridgefield, MN 55423 . . . . (612) 866-1023
Ralph Kelliher Illustration 11 Sequoia Road, Fairfax, CA 94930 . . . . (415) 457-4535
Ramazan, Seid Represented By: Leighton & Company, Inc. . . . . (978) 921-0887
Ramon, John Represented By: Art Source/Diane Barkley . . . . (914) 747-2220
Ramos, Ruben Represented By: Wilson-Zumbo Illustration . . . . (414) 271-3388
Rancorn, Chuck 2638 47th Street S, St. Petersburg, FL 33711 . . . . (813) 321-4990
Randall, Gail Greenfield 1912 Comstock Avenue, Los Angeles, CA 90025 . . . . (310) 556-9770
Represented By: Vincent Kamin & Associates . . . . (312) 787-8834
Randall, Mike Represented By: David Montagano & Associates . . . . (312) 527-3283

RANDAZZO, TONY Pages 168,202-203
Represented By: American Artists **(212) 682-2462**
e-mail: info@amerartists.com • Website: www.amerartists.com • Specialties: Cars; Product

Raner, Walter Represented By: Hankins & Tegenborg Ltd. (212) 867-8092
Rangne, Monica 210 First Avenue #11, New York, NY 10009 (212) 260-5121
New York, NY 10009 (212) 714-7023
Rasa Illustration Represented By: R. Fischer & Company (312) 368-1441
Rasmussen, K.C. Represented By: Sharpshooter Creative Rep Inc. (416) 703-5300
Raszka, Brian 1385 Clay Street #26, San Francisco, CA 94109 (415) 673-4479
Rattin, Mark 2043 W Wabansia Avenue, Chicago, IL 60647 (773) 384-8888
Rauf, Jeff Represented By: Skidmore, Inc. (248) 353-7722
Ravanelli, Terry Represented By: Harriet Kastaris & Associates (314) 773-2600
Ray, David Represented By: Carol Bancroft & Friends (203) 748-4823
Ray, Kit Represented By: Evelyne Johnson Associates (212) 532-0928
Rayevsky, Robert 1120 Swedesford Road, North Wales, PA 19454 (215) 661-9566
Raymer, Louis 200 Second Avenue NE, Minneapolis, MN 55413 (612) 627-9619
Raymond, Victoria 265 River Road, Apt. 6, Nyack, NY 10960 (914) 359-5631
Rea, Tracy Represented By: Harriet Kastaris & Associates (314) 773-2600
Represented By: Lulu Creatives (612) 825-7564
Read, Elizabeth 9310 NE 138th Street, Kirkland, WA 98034 (206) 821-0891
Represented By: Pat Hackett Artist Representative (206) 447-1600

REAGAN, MIKE Pages 326,456
Represented By: Michele Manasse **(215) 862-2091**
e-mail: mmanasse@new-work.com • Website: www.voicenet.com/~mmanasse • Specialties: Advertising; Black & White; Children; Corporate; Editorial; Icons; Lettering; Maps & Charts; Water Color; Wildlife

Ream, Kristine 616 Dewalt Drive, Pittsburgh, PA 15234 (412) 531-9487
Rebelo, Tanya Represented By: The Ivy League of Artists (212) 243-1333
Rechin, Kevin 7602-I Lakeside Village Drive, Falls Church, VA 22042 (703) 560-1209
Recio, Marta 836-A 18th Street, Santa Monica, CA 90403 (310) 829-4070
Red Owl, Richard Represented By: Art Source/Diane Barkley (914) 747-2220

REDGRAFIX DESIGN & ILLUSTRATION Pages 128,423,425,446,452
19750 W Observatory Road, New Berlin, WI 53146 • Fax (414) 542-5322 **(414) 542-5547**
e-mail: redgrafx@execpc.com • Specialties: Advertising; Animation; Caricature; Cartoon; Children; Corporate; Digital; Graphic Design/Illustration; Greeting Cards; Icons; Lettering

Redl, Dave Represented By: Buck & Kane (212) 631-0009
Reed, Charlie Represented By: Artline (704) 376-7609
Reed, Dave Represented By: Berendsen & Associates (513) 861-1400
Reed, Lynn Rowe Represented By: Lisa Freeman (317) 920-0068
Represented By: Mendola Ltd. (212) 986-5680
Reed, Mike Represented By: HK Portfolio (212) 675-5719
Represented By: Artline (704) 376-7609
Reeves, Patrick 2280 N Greenville Avenue, Richardson, TX 75802 (972) 699-6807
Regan, Dana C. Represented By: Publishers' Graphics (203) 797-8188
Rehbein, Richard 33-A S Union Avenue, Cranford, NJ 07016 (908) 931-1017
Reid, Michael Represented By: HK Portfolio (212) 675-5719
Reingold, Alan Represented By: Anita Grien Represents (212) 697-6170
Reinhardt, Dorothy 466 Melrose Avenue, San Francisco, CA 94127 (415) 584-9369
Reitz, Kathy Represented By: Langley & Associates (847) 670-0912
Rendeiro, Charlene 94 W Green Street, Westminster, MD 21157 (410) 848-8276
Render Group Inc., The 16 Burnham Road, Toronto, ON Canada M4G 1C1 (416) 467-8024
Renfro, Edward Represented By: Conrad Represents, Inc. (415) 921-7140
Renlie, Frank 4726 NE 178th Street, Lake Forest Park, WA 98155 (206) 362-0967
Renwick Illustration Represented By: Rita Marie & Friends (312) 222-0337
Rep Art 1201 First Avenue S #336, Seattle, WA 98134 (206) 467-9156
Reppel, Aletha Tulsa, OK (512) 454-2275
Represented By: Suzanne Craig Represents, Inc. (918) 749-9424
Reynolds, Donna 3059 Richmond Boulevard, Oakland, CA 94611 (510) 451-0303
Rhodes, Barbara 7114 Columbine Drive, Carlsbad, CA 92009 (619) 929-1049
Ricceri, David 505 Court Street #4H, Brooklyn, NY 11231 (718) 852-8987
Riccio, Frank Represented By: Mendola Ltd. (212) 986-5680
Rice, John Represented By: The Ivy League of Artists (212) 243-1333
Rich, Mary 3057 Lewis Street, Placerville, CA 95667 (530) 622-2892

RICHARD, PUTIEN Pages 116,430
516 Marine View Avenue, Belmont, CA 94002 • Fax (650) 591-2341 **(650) 591-2341**
e-mail: putien@pacbell.net • Specialties: Annual Report; Corporate

Richards, Dan Represented By: Sharpe & Associates . . . . . (310) 641-8556
Richards, Linda Represented By: Mendola Ltd. . . . . . (212) 986-5680
Richardson, Gary Represented By: Berendsen & Associates . . . . . (513) 861-1400
Richer, Paul 2109 45th Avenue, Long Island City, NY 11101 . . . . . (718) 472-0859
Rickabaugh Graphics 384 W Johnstown Road, Gahanna, OH 43230 . . . . . (614) 337-2229
Riding, Lynne 7 Gadsden Street, Charleston, SC 29401 . . . . . (803) 853-5746
Represented By: Susan Wells & Associates. . . . . (404) 255-1430
Riedy, Mark Represented By: Scott Hull Associates . . . . . (937) 433-8383
Riegel, Margaret 160 E Third Street #4G, New York, NY 10009 . . . . . (212) 254-8240

RIEGLER, JENNIFER Pages 20,445,452,458
3025 N Clifton, Chicago, IL 60657 **(773) 327-7489**
Specialties: Advertising; Food; Icons; People; Product; Whimsical

Rieser, Bonnie Represented By: Jaz & Jaz . . . . . (206) 633-3445
Rieser, William R2 361 Magee Avenue, Mill Valley, CA 94941. . . . . (415) 389-0332
Rigie, Mitchell Represented By: David Goldman Agency . . . . . (212) 807-6627
Riley, Brent Represented By: Berendsen & Associates . . . . . (513) 861-1400
Riley, Frank 108 Bamford Avenue, Hawthorne, NJ 07506 . . . . . (973) 423-2659
Ringnalda, Lisa Represented By: Sharpshooter Creative Rep Inc. . . . . . (416) 703-5300
Ristau, Paul Represented By: Dolby Represents . . . . . (312) 855-9336
Ritchie, Adam 3508 43rd Avenue S, Minneapolis, MN 55406. . . . . (612) 729-5834
Represented By: Janet Virnig . . . . . (612) 926-5585
Ritchie, Scott Represented By: Motion Artists, Inc. . . . . . (213) 851-7737
Rivard, Lisa Represented By: Artco . . . . . (212) 889-8777
Rivera, Ambrose 51215 N O'Connor #760, Irving, TX 75039. . . . . (972) 869-8282
Represented By: Repertoire. . . . . (972) 761-0500
Rivers, Bart 4043 Eisenhower Drive, Indianapolis, IN 46254 . . . . . (317) 328-8229

RIVERS, JO Pages 392,399,427,442
Represented By: Donna Rosen Artists' Rep **(301) 384-8925**
e-mail: djrosen@erols.com • Website: www.aaarrt.com/donnasgallery
Specialties: Black & White; Conceptual; Editorial; Humour; Mixed Media; Scratchboard; Whimsical

Rivoche, Paul Represented By: Link . . . . . (416) 530-1500
Roads, Andrea Represented By: K&K Art & Associates . . . . . (612) 338-9138
Robbins, David Represented By: Kolea Baker Artists Representative. . . . . (206) 784-1136
Roberts, Bruce 75 Hallowell, Montreal, PQ Canada H3Z 2E8 . . . . . (514) 849-1001
Roberts, Greg Represented By: Image Mill . . . . . (515) 490-6110
Roberts, Ken Represented By: West End Studio . . . . . (310) 664-9200
Roberts, Renata Represented By: Donna Rosen Artists' Rep. . . . . . (301) 384-8925
Roberts, Scott 6 N Main Street, Ste. 200, Bel Air, MD 21014. . . . . (410) 879-3362
Represented By: Conrad Represents, Inc.. . . . . (415) 921-7140
Roberts, Tom Represented By: Bill & Maurine Klimt . . . . . (212) 799-2231
Roberts, Victoria Represented By: Riley Illustration . . . . . (212) 989-8770
Roberts Illustration, Ray 13075 N 75th Place, Scottsdale, AZ 85260 . . . . . (602) 991-8568
Robertson, Jain 52 Hettersley Drive, Ajax, ON Canada L1T 1V4 . . . . . (905) 683-7594

ROBINETTE, ILENE Page 152
Represented By: Connie Koralik Associates Represents **(312) 944-5680**
Specialties: Advertising; Annual Report; Editorial; Fashion; People

Robinette, John 5889 Ewing Drive, Memphis, TN 38119. . . . . (901) 681-9668
Represented By: The Williams Group . . . . . (404) 873-2287
Represented By: Planet Rep . . . . . (800) 847-5101
Robinson, Mark Represented By: Virginia Boggie & Associates . . . . . (604) 943-6414
Robinson, Paul S. Represented By: Bernstein & Andriulli, Inc. . . . . . (212) 682-1490
Robinson, Tim 18 Schermerhorn Street #2, Brooklyn, NY 11201 . . . . . (718) 243-2263
Roche, Denis Represented By: Art Department . . . . . (212) 925-4222
Rockwell, Richard Represented By: Art Source/Diane Barkley. . . . . (914) 747-2220
Rockwell, Tom 90 Loden Lane, Rochester, NY 14623. . . . . (716) 359-9590

RODA, BOT Pages 168,198
Represented By: American Artists **(212) 682-2462**
e-mail: info@amerartists.com • Website: www.amerartists.com • Specialty: Cartoon

Roderick, James Represented By: Rep Art. . . . . (604) 684-6826
Rodriguez, Doris 7 ½ Jane Street #4F, New York, NY 10014 . . . . . (212) 388-7336
Rodriguez, Edel 16 Ridgewood Avenue, Mt. Tabor, NJ 07878-0102 . . . . . (973) 983-7776
Rodriguez, Francisco Represented By: Ceci Bartels Associates . . . . . (314) 781-7377

RODRIGUEZ, ROBERT Pages 46,462
Represented By: Renard Represents **(212) 490-2450**
e-mail: renardreps@earthlink.net • Website: www.renardrepresents.com • Specialties: Portraiture; Realism

Roffo, Sergio Represented By: Hankins & Tegenborg Ltd. . . . . . (212) 867-8092
Rofheart-Pigott, Irene P.O. Box 420, Garrison, NY 10524. . . . . (914) 424-8304
Rogers, Buc 1025 W Madison, Chicago, IL 60607 . . . . . (312) 421-4132
Represented By: Joel Harlib Associates, Inc. . . . . . (312) 573-1370
Rogers, Dennis Represented By: Dimension. . . . . (612) 884-4045
Rogers, Joe 2 N 112 Virginia, Glen Ellyn, IL 60137-3142 . . . . . (630) 682-0515
Rogers, Lilla Represented By: Lilla Rogers Studio . . . . . (781) 641-2787

ROGERS, NIP Pages 216,219,428
212 S Front Street, Philipsburg, PA 16866 • Fax (814) 342-6572 **(814) 342-6572**
Represented By: Alexander/Pollard, Inc. **(800) 347-0734**
Specialties: Advertising; Black & White; Conceptual; Editorial; Icons; Maps & Charts; People; Scratchboard; Stock; Wildlife

Rogers, Paul 12 S Fair Oaks Avenue #208, Pasadena, CA 91105 . . . . . (626) 564-8728
Represented By: Rita Marie & Friends . . . . . (312) 222-0337
Rogers, Randy Represented By: Mason Illustration . . . . . (612) 729-1774
Rogerson, Zebulon 10171 Hillington Court, Vienna, VA 22182. . . . . (703) 319-4035

ROGNESS, KATHLEEN Page 249
Represented By: Dimension **(612) 884-4045**
e-mail: jkoltes@dimensioncreative.com • Website: www.dimensioncreative.com
Specialties: Animals; Children; People; Realism

Rohani, Michael Sours Represented By: Mushka Rohani . . . . . (425) 771-2905
Rohr, Dixon 155 W 68th Street #26E, New York, NY 10023 . . . . . (212) 580-4065
Roldan, Jim 141 E Main Street, East Hampstead, NH 03826 . . . . . (603) 382-1686
Rolfe, David Represented By: Three in a Box. . . . . (416) 367-2446
Roma, Ursula Represented By: Berendsen & Associates . . . . . (513) 861-1400

ROMAN, IRENA Pages 252-253
Represented By: Deborah Wolfe **(215) 232-6666**
Website: www.deborahwolfeltd.com • Specialties: Advertising; Architecture/Interiors; Editorial; Greeting Cards; People; Product; Still Life; Stock; Water Color

Roman, John 575 Washington Street, Canton, MA 02021. . . . . (781) 830-9490
Rombola, John 3804 Farragut Road, Brooklyn, NY 11210. . . . . (718) 434-4870
New York, NY . . . . . (212) 645-8000
Romeo Studio, Richard 1380 Avon Lane, Ste. 3-35, Ft. Lauderdale, FL 33068 . . . . . (954) 724-7786
Roolaart, Harry 1318 Central Avenue, Ste. A-11, Charlotte, NC 28205. . . . . (704) 376-1100
Roper, Marty 6115 Brookside Boulevard, Kansas City, MO 64113 . . . . . (816) 361-8589
Represented By: The Williams Group . . . . . (404) 873-2287
Represented By: Planet Rep . . . . . (800) 847-5101
Roraback, Robin Represented By: Carol Bancroft & Friends . . . . . (203) 748-4823
Rosandich, Dan P.O. Box 410, Chassell, MI 49916-0410 . . . . . (906) 482-6234
Rosborough, Tom Represented By: Mason Illustration . . . . . (612) 729-1774
Rosco, Delro 91-822B Pohakupuna Road, Ewa Beach, HI 97606 . . . . . (808) 689-4635
Represented By: Joel Harlib Associates, Inc. . . . . . (312) 573-1370
Represented By: Rita Gatlin Represents . . . . . (800) 924-7881
Rose, Drew Represented By: Will Sumpter & Associates. . . . . (770) 460-8438
Rose, Jim 313 S McArthur, Macomb, IL 61455 . . . . . (309) 833-5745
Rosebush Co., Judson 154 W 57th Street #826, New York, NY 10019. . . . . (212) 581-3000

Roseman-Hall, Ronni RR #2, Box 1258, Beach Lake, PA 18405 . . . . (717) 729-7403
Rosemary's Cakes Inc. 299 Rutland Avenue, Teaneck, NJ 07666 . . . . (201) 833-2417

ROSEN, ELIZABETH Pages 124-125
Represented By: Vicki Morgan Associates **(212) 475-0440**
e-mail: vmartrep@aol.com • Website: www.vickimorganassociates.com
Specialties: Advertising; Collage; Computer; Editorial; Greeting Cards; Illustrative; Mixed Media; People

ROSENBAUM, JON & GEORGINA Pages 252-253,283,288-289,445
Represented By: John Brewster Creative Services **(203) 226-4724**
Represented By: Deborah Wolfe **(215) 232-6666**
e-mail: creative.svcs@snet.net • Website: www.brewstercreative.com • deborahwolfeltd.com
Specialties: Advertising; Computer; Digital; Food; Product; Realism

ROSENBAUM, SAUL Pages 252-253
Represented By: Deborah Wolfe **(215) 232-6666**
Website: www.deborahwolfeltd.com • Specialties: Advertising; Computer; Conceptual; Digital; Editorial; Humour; Icons; Maps & Charts; Technical; Whimsical

Rosenberg, Ben Killen 3734 SE Stephens Street, Portland, OR 97214 . . . . (503) 230-7735
Rosenberg, Ken 9710 Lemon Avenue, Arcadia, CA 91007 . . . . (626) 574-1631
Rosenfeld, Eileen Represented By: Creative Connection . . . . (410) 360-5981
Rosenheim, Cindy Salans Represented By: Square Moon . . . . (510) 253-9451
Rosenhouse, Irwin 256 Mott Street, New York, NY 10012 . . . . (212) 226-2848
Rosenthal, Marc 21 Church Street, Lenox, MA 01240-2504 . . . . (413) 637-1879
Rosenthal, Roberta 182 E 210th Street, New York, NY 10467 . . . . (718) 881-8024
95A Shawanga Lodge Road RR #2, Bloomingburg, NY 12721 . . . . (914) 733-1848
Rosenwald, Laurie 45 Lispenard Street #7E, New York, NY 10013 . . . . (212) 966-6896

ROSOLEK, MICK Pages 157,446
Represented By: Lexington Ashworth House **(414) 290-4313**
e-mail: mick@lexash.com • Website: www.lexash.com • Specialty: Graphic Design/Illustration

ROSS, DOUG Pages 130,427,434
Represented By: Lori Nowicki & Associates **(212) 243-5888**
e-mail: doug@lorinowicki.com • Website: www.lorinowicki.com
Specialties: Advertising; Conceptual; Corporate; Digital; Editorial

Ross, Larry 53 Fairview Avenue, Madison, NJ 07940 . . . . (201) 377-6859
Ross, Luke Represented By: Glass House Graphics . . . . (304) 232-5641

ROSS, MARY Pages 242-243,419,424,448,452
327 Hugo Street, San Francisco, CA 94122 • Fax (415) 661-2930 **(415) 661-2930**
Represented By: Rita Gatlin Represents **(800) 924-7881**
Website: www.ritareps.com • Specialties: Advertising; Animation; Black & White; Cartoon; Children; Digital; Editorial; Humour; Icons; Whimsical

ROSS, SCOTT Pages 252-253
Represented By: Deborah Wolfe **(215) 232-6666**
Website: www.deborahwolfeltd.com • Specialties: Advertising; Black & White; Cartoon; Children; Computer; Digital; Editorial; Greeting Cards; Humour; Whimsical

Rossi, Pam 908 Main Street #3, Evanston, IL 60202 . . . . (847) 475-2533
Rossignol & Associates, Larry 77 Mowat Avenue #507, Toronto, ON Canada M6K 3E3 . . . . (416) 588-9094
Rossiter, Nan Represented By: American Artists . . . . (212) 682-2462
Rotella, Maria 259 Manning Avenue, Toronto, ON Canada M6J 2K8 . . . . (416) 603-9829
Roth, Rob Represented By: Carol Bancroft & Friends . . . . (203) 748-4823
Roth, Robert Represented By: Jerry Leff Associates, Inc. . . . . (212) 697-8525
Roth, Roger Represented By: Marion Moskowitz Represents . . . . (212) 517-4919
Rother, Sue Represented By: Jerry Leff Associates, Inc. . . . . (212) 697-8525

ROTONDO, NICK Pages 252-253
Represented By: Deborah Wolfe **(215) 232-6666**
Website: www.deborahwolfeltd.com
Specialties: Advertising; Computer; Digital; Editorial; Product; Realism; Science; Still Life; Stock; Technical

Rotunda, Matthew Represented By: Artworks . . . . . (212) 627-1554
Roux, Jimminy Represented By: Three in a Box . . . . . (416) 367-2446
Rovira, Francesco Represented By: Carol Bancroft & Friends. . . . . (203) 748-4823
Rowe, Gregg Alan 517 N El Molino Avenue #8, Pasadena, CA 91101 . . . . . (626) 796-3175
Rowe, John Represented By: Mendola Ltd. . . . . . (212) 986-5680
Rowe Studio, Charles 133 Aronimink Drive, Newark, DE 19711 . . . . . (302) 738-0641
University of Delaware, Newark, DE 19716 . . . . . (302) 831-2857
Rowell, Clare 3 Florence Terrace, Falmouth, Cornwell, England TR11 3RR 44 132 621 1055
Rownd, Jim Represented By: Spectrum Studio, Inc. . . . . . (612) 332-2361
Roy, Doug Represented By: Square Moon . . . . . (510) 253-9451
Rubess, Balvis Represented By: Sharpshooter Creative Rep Inc. . . . . . (416) 703-5300
Rubin, Marvin 201 Ocean Avenue, Ste. 708-B, Santa Monica, CA 90402 . . . . . (310) 458-6616
Rubino, Cornel Represented By: Mendola Ltd. . . . . . (212) 986-5680

RUDNAK, THEO Pages 39,429
Represented By: Renard Represents **(212) 490-2450**
e-mail: renardreps@earthlink.net • Website: www.renardrepresents.com • Specialty: Conceptual

Ruegger, Rebecca Represented By: Bruck & Moss. . . . . . (212) 980-8061
Ruff, Donna 12 Topsail Road, Rowayton, CT 06853 . . . . . (203) 866-8626
Ruffins, Reynold 51 Hampton Street, Sag Harbor, NY 11963 . . . . . (516) 725-3480
Rugh, Doug 37 Gosnold Road, Woods Hole, MA 02543 . . . . . (508) 548-6684
Ruppert, Larry Represented By: Spectrum Studio, Inc. . . . . . (612) 332-2361

RUSH, JOHN Page 33
123 Kedzie Street, Evanston, IL 60202-2509 **(847) 869-2078**
Specialties: Advertising; Historical; Murals; Mythology; Oil; People; Realism

Russel, Kristian Represented By: Art Department . . . . . (212) 925-4222
Russell, Bill Represented By: Reactor Art & Design Ltd. . . . . . (416) 703-1913
Russell, David M. 823 Seamaster Drive, Houston, TX 77062-5103 . . . . . (281) 488-2302
Russell, Mike 427 First Street, Brooklyn, NY 11215. . . . . . (718) 499-3436
303 Park Avenue S #308, New York, NY 10010 . . . . . (212) 598-9707
Russo, Anthony 51 Fogland Road, Tiverton, RI 02878 . . . . . (401) 624-9184
Russo/Mazemaster Illustration, David Anson Represented By: David Goldman Agency . . . . . (212) 807-6627
Rutkowski, John Represented By: Schumann & Company . . . . . (512) 481-0907
Represented By: Deborah Wolfe . . . . . (215) 232-6666

RUTTER, DALE Pages 392,394
Represented By: Donna Rosen Artists' Rep **(301) 384-8925**
e-mail: djrosen@erols.com • Website: www.aaarrt.com/donnasgallery
Specialties: Advertising; Editorial; Fantasy; Humour; Whimsical

RV2 Represented By: Joel Harlib Associates, Inc. . . . . . (312) 573-1370
Ryan, Cheri Represented By: Jorgensen & Barrett Reps. . . . . . (206) 634-1880
Ryan, Lorraine Represented By: Creative Connection . . . . . (410) 360-5981
S.F. Society of Illustrators 493 Eighth Avenue, San Francisco, CA 94118-3007 . . . . . (415) 221-6840
Saari, Rijalynne Represented By: Fortuni Illustration . . . . . (414) 964-8088
Saas, Susan Represented By: Kate Larkworthy Artist Rep. Ltd. . . . . . (212) 633-1310
Sabanosh, Michael 433 W 34th Street, Apt. 18-B, New York, NY 10001. . . . . . (212) 947-8161
Sabella, Jill 2607 Ninth Avenue W, Seattle, WA 98119 . . . . . (206) 285-4794
Sabin, Bob Represented By: Hankins & Tegenborg Ltd. . . . . . (212) 867-8092
Sabin, Tracy 13476 Ridley Road, San Diego, CA 92129. . . . . . (619) 484-8712
Sadowski, Wictor Represented By: Marlena Agency. . . . . . (609) 252-9405
Saecker, Tom Represented By: Joanne Palulian . . . . . (212) 581-8338
Saffold, Joe Represented By: Renard Represents . . . . . (212) 490-2450
Saint James, Synthia P.O. Box 27683, Los Angeles, CA 90027 . . . . . (213) 769-4298
Saito, Yukari 861 N Fourth Avenue, Covina, CA 91723 . . . . . (626) 331-2797
Sakahara, Dick 28826 Cedarbluff Drive, Rancho Palos Verdes, CA 90275-3118 . . . . . (310) 541-8187
Represented By: Kathee Toyama Represents . . . . . (626) 440-0333

Sakmar, Eva Represented By: Buck & Kane . . . . . (212) 631-0009
Sakstrup, Kim Represented By: Spectrum Studio, Inc. . . . . . (612) 332-2361
Salazar, Miro P.O. Box 421443, San Francisco, CA 94142 . . . . . (415) 647-5660
Salem, Kay 14222 Dallas Parkway #1088, Dallas, TX 75240 . . . . . (281) 469-0996
Salentine, Katherine Represented By: Janice Stefanski Represents . . . . . (415) 928-0457

SALERNO, STEVEN Pages 86-87,114
Represented By: Lindgren & Smith **(212) 397-7330**
e-mail: inquiry@lindgrensmith.com • Website: www.lindgrensmith.com

Salgian, Mitzura Represented By: Hankins & Tegenborg Ltd. . . . . . (212) 867-8092
Salvati, Jim 6600 Royer Avenue, West Hills, CA 91307 . . . . . (818) 348-9012
Salzillo-Shields, Sandra Represented By: Cornell & McCarthy, LLC . . . . . (203) 454-4210
Salzman, Yuri Represented By: Cornell & McCarthy, LLC . . . . . (203) 454-4210

SAMANICH, BARBARA Page 70
188 E Vista Del Cerro, Tempe, AZ 85281 • Fax (602) 966-6082 **(602) 966-3070**
Represented By: Vargo Bockos **(312) 661-1717**
Represented By: Marla Matson Represents **(602) 252-5072**
e-mail: sammyart@aol.com • Specialties: Advertising; Black & White; Conceptual; Editorial; Food; Icons; Illustrative; Pastels; Scratchboard; Whimsical

Sammel, Chelsea 482 S Street, Hollister, CA 95023 . . . . . (408) 636-7443
Sams, B.B. P.O. Box A, Social Circle, GA 30279 . . . . . (770) 464-2956
Samsovich, Jim Represented By: RKB Studios, Inc. . . . . . (612) 339-7055
Samul, Cynthia 15 Pacific Street, New London, CT 06320 . . . . . (860) 444-7060
Sancha, Jeremy Represented By: Bernstein & Andriulli, Inc. . . . . . (212) 682-1490
Sanchez, Carlos Represented By: Harriet Kastaris & Associates . . . . . (314) 773-2600
Sandbox Digital Playground 203 N Wabash Avenue #1602, Chicago, IL 60601 . . . . . (312) 372-1170
Sanders, Bruce Represented By: Leighton & Company, Inc. . . . . . (978) 921-0887
Sanders, Jane 465 Lexington Avenue,Studio 33, New York, NY 10017 . . . . . (212) 986-1827
Sandford, John Represented By: Pema Browne Ltd. . . . . . (914) 985-2936
Sandro, Cindy 662 Medlock Road, Decatur, GA 30033 . . . . . (404) 633-3321
Represented By: The Williams Group . . . . . (404) 873-2287
Represented By: Planet Rep . . . . . (800) 847-5101
Sanford, Susan 19 Los Amigos, Orinda, CA 94563 . . . . . (510) 253-3131
Represented By: Maslov/Weinberg . . . . . (415) 641-1285

SANO, KAZUHIKO Pages 41,466
Represented By: Renard Represents **(212) 490-2450**
e-mail: renardreps@earthlink.net • Website: www.renardrepresents.com
Specialties: Conceptual; Painterly; Pastels; Watercolor

Santa Lucia, Francesco Represented By: Mendola Ltd. . . . . . (212) 986-5680
Santiago, Rafael 306 E Sixth Street, Apt. 16, New York, NY 10003 . . . . . (212) 505-6296
Santiago, Rose Mary 515 Vista Grande Avenue, Daly City, CA 94014 . . . . . (650) 756-8975
Sanz, Jocelyn D. 120 Knoll Circle S, San Francisco, CA 94080 . . . . . (415) 583-8628
Saputo, Joe Represented By: Kathleen Cornell & Company . . . . . (310) 301-8059
Represented By: Mendola Ltd. . . . . . (212) 986-5680

SARDELLA, FERRUCCIO Pages 28-29
Represented By: Marlena Agency **(609) 252-9405**
e-mail: marzena@bellatlantic.net • Website: http://members.bellatlantic.net/~marzena
Specialties: Conceptual; Corporate; Editorial; Whimsical

Sardinha Illustration & Design 16 Sparta Road, Toronto, ON Canada M6L 2M5 . . . . . (416) 249-0285
Sargent, Claudia Karabaic 15-38 126th Street, College Point, NY 11356 . . . . . (718) 461-8280
Sasaki, Ellen Joy Represented By: Cornell & McCarthy, LLC . . . . . (203) 454-4210
Sasaki, Goro Represented By: Bernstein & Andriulli, Inc. . . . . . (212) 682-1490
Sasaki, Yutaka K. 3435 19th Avenue S, Seattle, WA 98144 . . . . . (206) 723-2003

SAUBER, ROBERT Pages 124-125
Represented By: Vicki Morgan Associates **(212) 475-0440**
e-mail: vmartrep@aol.com • Website: www.vickimorganassociates.com
Specialties: Children; Computer; Digital; Greeting Cards; People; Realism; Stock; Water Color; Wildlife

Sauk, Mark 5401 Martin Lane, Hanover Park, IL 60103 . . . . (630) 837-6114
Saunders, Fred Represented By: Jaz & Jaz . . . . (206) 633-3445

SAUVE, GORDON Page 238
Represented By: Sharpshooter Creative Representation, Inc. **(416) 703-5300**
e-mail: shooter@the-wire.com • Website: www.portfolios.com/illustrators
Specialties: Acrylic; Advertising; Airbrush; Black & White; Children; Illustrative; People; Realism; Wildlife

Savage, Patricia Represented By: Melissa Turk & The Artist Network . . . . (914) 368-8606
Savely, Rod 30 Pierce Avenue, Beverly, MA 01915 . . . . (508) 921-0887
Savink, Alex Represented By: Marvel Entertainment . . . . (212) 696-0808

SAWYER, DAVID Page 34
2471 Franklin Avenue, Louisville, CO 80027 • Fax (303) 604-2936 **(303) 666-5581**
Specialties: Airbrush; Technical

Sawyer Illustration, Scott Represented By: Bobbi Wendt/Parallel Universe . . . . (415) 487-2160

SAYLES, ELIZABETH Page 207
60 Brookside Avenue, Valley Cottage, NY 10989 **(914) 267-4127**
Represented By: Cornell & McCarthy, LLC **(203) 454-4210**
Specialties: Book Jackets; Children; Editorial; Food; Pastels; People; Still Life; Travel

Sayles, John Represented By: Jerry Leff Associates, Inc. . . . . (212) 697-8525
Saylor, Steven P.O. Box 204, 400 Main Street, Dayton, NV 89403 . . . . (702) 246-0232
Scanlan, David 1600 18th Street, Manhattan Beach, CA 90266 . . . . (310) 545-0773
Scardova, Jaclyne Fairfax, CA 94930 . . . . (415) 721-0707
Scarpulla, Caren P.O. Box 4303, Burbank, CA 91503-4303 . . . . (213) 913-2458
Schaare, Harry Represented By: Hankins & Tegenborg Ltd. . . . . (212) 867-8092
Schaedler, Sally Represented By: Gwen Walters-Goldstein . . . . (781) 235-8658
Schaeffer, Debra Represented By: Envoy Creative Consultants . . . . (703) 706-5729
Schaeppi, Kristi Represented By: RKB Studios, Inc. . . . . (612) 339-7055
Schaffer, Amanda 445 Hanson Lane, Ramona, CA 92065 . . . . (760) 788-0388
Schatner, Gille Represented By: Mendola Ltd. . . . . (212) 986-5680
Scheffler, Harlan Represented By: Mason Illustration . . . . (612) 729-1774
Scherman, John 310 E 12th Street, New York, NY 10003
Scheuer, Philip A. 126 Fifth Avenue, New York, NY 10011 . . . . (212) 620-0728
Schiettino, Joe 49 W 45th Street, New York, NY 10036 . . . . (212) 921-1199 • (800) 243-2667
Schill, George Represented By: Cliff Knecht . . . . (412) 761-5666
Schindler, Steven D. Represented By: Publishers' Graphics . . . . (203) 797-8188
Schiwall, Linda Represented By: Irmeli Holmberg . . . . (212) 545-9155
Schleinkofer, David Represented By: Mendola Ltd. . . . . (212) 986-5680
Schlowsky Digital Studios 73 Old Road, Weston, MA 02193 . . . . (781) 899-5110
Schmid, Paul Represented By: Lulu Creatives . . . . (612) 825-7564
Schmidbauer, Terry 37H Terrace Lane, Lake Zurich, IL 60047 . . . . (847) 438-7141
Schmidt, Bill Represented By: Hankins & Tegenborg Ltd. . . . . (212) 867-8092
Schmidt, George 183 Steuben Street, Brooklyn, NY 11205 . . . . (718) 857-1837
Schneebalg, Martin 272 Carroll Street #2, Brooklyn, NY 11231 . . . . (718) 624-6022

SCHNEIDER, CHRISTINE M. Page 1
2100 Heatherwood Drive F6, Lawrence, KS 66047 • Fax (785) 865-5706 **(785) 838-7630**
e-mail: schneider@cjnetworks.com • Website: www.cjnetworks.com/~schneider
Specialties: Advertising; Caricature; Children; Conceptual; Editorial; Humour; Poster

Schneider, Doug 9016 Danube Lane, San Diego, CA 92126 . . . . (619) 695-6796

SCHNEIDER, R.M. Pages 283,286-287,426,430
Represented By: John Brewster Creative Services **(203) 226-4724**
e-mail: creative.svcs@snet.net • Website: www.brewstercreative.com
Specialties: Annual Report; Collage; Corporate; Mixed Media

Schochet, Bob Represented By: Pema Browne Ltd. . . . . (914) 985-2936
Schofield, Den Represented By: Philip M. Veloric Associates . . . . (610) 520-3470
Scholl, Heather Represented By: Jaz & Jaz . . . . (206) 633-3445
Scholl, Oliver Represented By: Motion Artists, Inc. . . . . (213) 851-7737

Schongut, Emanuel 2855 Bush Street #302, San Francisco, CA 94115 . . . . . (415) 440-9074
Schrader, Brian Represented By: Connie Koralik Associates Represents . . . . . (312) 944-5680
Schreiner, John Represented By: Spectrum Studio, Inc. . . . . . (612) 332-2361
Schrier, Fred Represented By: Lisa Freeman . . . . . (317) 920-0068
Schrier, Jim Represented By: Air Studio . . . . . (513) 721-1193
Schroder, Mark 1927 E Bendix Drive, Tempe, AZ 85283 . . . . . (602) 897-1097
Represented By: Lori Nowicki & Associates . . . . . (212) 243-5888
Represented By: Terry Squire . . . . . (919) 772-1262
Schuett, Stacey P.O. Box 15, Duncans Mills, CA 95430 . . . . . (707) 632-5123
Represented By: Christina Tugeau . . . . . (203) 438-7307
Schug/Studio West, Sonny 15424 N 63rd Street, Scottsdale, AZ 85254 . . . . . (602) 998-1927
Schulenburg, Paul 185 Main Street, Orleans, MA 02653 . . . . . (508) 255-9554
Schulte, Eliza Represented By: Mendola Ltd. . . . . . (212) 986-5680
Schulte Design, Lynn 126 N Third Street, Ste. 510, Minneapolis, MN 55401 . . . . . (612) 334-3440
Schumacher, Michael Represented By: Pat Hackett Artist Representative . . . . . (206) 447-1600
Schumaker, Ward 466 Green Street, San Francisco, CA 94133-4067 . . . . . (415) 398-1060
Schurr, Gerry Represented By: Buck & Kane . . . . . (212) 631-0009
Schuster, Rob Represented By: Berendsen & Associates . . . . . (513) 861-1400
Schwab, Bill 31 Park Place, Brooklyn, NY 11217 . . . . . (718) 399-8021
Schwab, Michael Represented By: Renard Represents . . . . . (212) 490-2450
Schwartz, Daniel Represented By: Richard Solomon . . . . . (212) 683-1362
Schwartz, John Represented By: Bill & Maurine Klimt . . . . . (212) 799-2231
Schwartz, Judith 231 E Fifth Street, New York, NY 10003 . . . . . (212) 777-7533

SCHWARZ, JOANIE Pages 124-125
Represented By: Vicki Morgan Associates **(212) 475-0440**
e-mail: vmartrep@aol.com • Website: www.vickimorganassociates.com • Specialties: Book Jackets; Children; Computer; Digital; Editorial; Greeting Cards; People; Photography; Realism; Stock

SCHWARZ, TERRI SHAY Pages 296,424,441,445,467
St. Louis, MO 63117 **(314) 644-0091**
Specialties: Children; Editorial; Food; Whimsical

SCHWARZE, EVAN Page 5
104 S Home Avenue, Oak Park, IL 60302 • Fax (708) 445-0154 **(708) 445-0154**
Represented By: Frank Lux & Associates, Inc. **(312) 222-1361**
Specialties: Architecture/Interiors; Editorial; Graphic Design/Illustration; Landscape; Murals; Oil; Painterly; People; Water Color

Schweitzer, David Represented By: Hedge Graphics . . . . . (818) 244-0110
Schwinger, Larry Represented By: Artworks . . . . . (212) 627-1554
Sciacca, Thomas 11005 Bristol Bay #623, Brandenton, FL 34209 . . . . . (941) 795-6323
Represented By: Anne Albrecht & Associates . . . . . (312) 595-0300
Scible, Betsy Gosheff 3161 Gosheff Lane, Gambrills, MD 21054 . . . . . (410) 451-2855
Scoggins, Tim 1919 Huntington Lane #1, Redondo Beach, CA 90278 . . . . . (310) 798-3774
Represented By: Hall & Associates . . . . . (213) 962-2500
Scott, Bernard Represented By: Creative Connection . . . . . (410) 360-5981
Scott, Bill Represented By: Nachreiner Boie Art Factory . . . . . (414) 785-1940
Scott, Maren Represented By: Pema Browne Ltd. . . . . . (914) 985-2936
Scott Illustration, Greg 11800 Montgomery NE, Albuquerque, NM 87111 . . . . . (505) 294-4063

SCROFANI, JOE Pages 168,182
Represented By: American Artists **(212) 682-2462**
e-mail: info@amerartists.com • Website: www.amerartists.com

Scruton, Clive Represented By: HK Portfolio . . . . . (212) 675-5719
Seabaugh, Max Represented By: Conrad Represents, Inc. . . . . . (415) 921-7140
Sealock, Rick 2217 10th Avenue SW, Calgary, AB Canada T2M 0M6 . . . . . (403) 276-5428
Seaver, Jeff 130 W 24th Street #4B, New York, NY 10011-1938 . . . . . (212) 741-2279
Seed, Susan Represented By: Sheryl Beranbaum . . . . . (401) 737-8591
Seeley, Laura 2617 Sharondale Drive, Atlanta, GA 30305 . . . . . (404) 262-2868
Seifer, Les 261 Kingsland Avenue, Brooklyn, NY 11222 . . . . . (718) 389-3766
Seiffer, Alison 7 Deforest Road, Montauk, NY 11954 . . . . . (516) 668-0326

Seigel, Mark Represented By: Melissa Turk & The Artist Network . . . . . (914) 368-8606
Selby, Andrea 31 Walker Street #3, New York, NY 10013-3595 . . . . . (212) 334-9367
Selby, Andrew 9 Perryfield, Matching Green, Essex, England CM17 OPY 44 127 973 1452
Sempe, Jean Jacques Represented By: Riley Illustration . . . . . (212) 989-8770
Senties, Charles 1349 N Oakley Boulevard, Chicago, IL 60622 . . . . . (773) 252-5119
Represented By: Steve Edsey & Sons . . . . . (312) 527-0351
Serafin, Marsha 690 Washington Street #3A, New York, NY 10014 . . . . . (212) 206-9212
Severn, Jeffrey Represented By: Square Moon . . . . . (510) 253-9451
Shadle, Kathlyn 827 NW 64th Street, Seattle, WA 98107 . . . . . (206) 783-2908
Represented By: Pat Hackett Artist Representative . . . . . (206) 447-1600
Shaffer, Desiree Represented By: Creative Connection . . . . . (410) 360-5981
Shakirov, Fathulla New York, NY 10016 . . . . . (212) 481-5779
Shanahan, Danny Represented By: Riley Illustration . . . . . (212) 989-8770
Shannon, David 1328 W Morningside Drive, Burbank, CA 91506 . . . . . (818) 563-6763

SHAP, SANDRA Page 156
Represented By: Carol Chislovsky Design, Inc. **(212) 677-9100**
Specialty: Comic

Shapton, Leanne Represented By: Reactor Art & Design Ltd. . . . . . (416) 703-1913
Sharp, Bruce Represented By: Donna Rosen Artists' Rep . . . . . (301) 384-8925
Sharp, Chris Represented By: Wanda Nowak . . . . . (212) 535-0438
Shasky, Jane Represented By: Jorgensen & Barrett Reps . . . . . (206) 634-1880
Shaul, Wendy Rudick 7556 Rio Mondego Drive, Sacramento, CA 95831 . . . . . (916) 429-0288

SHAVER, MARK Pages 372, 435
2334 Oak Street #C, Santa Monica, CA 90405 • Fax (310) 392-9978 **(310) 450-4336**
Represented By: Liz Sanders Agency **(714) 495-3664**
e-mail: mshaver@aol.com • Specialties: Computer; Digital; Editorial; Illustrative

Shaw, Barclay 170 East Street, Sharon, CT 06069 . . . . . (203) 364-5974
Shaw, Kendra Represented By: Fortuni Illustration . . . . . (414) 964-8088
Shaw, Ned Represented By: Conrad Represents, Inc. . . . . . (415) 921-7140
Shaw, Stan Represented By: Lehmen/Dabney, Inc. . . . . . (206) 325-8595
Shaw & Associates, David 108 Ranleigh Avenue, Toronto, ON Canada M4N 1W9 . . . . . (416) 487-2019
Shawver, Natasha 2750 Adeline, Berkeley, CA 94703 . . . . . (510) 548-5349
Represented By: Barbara Mizuno . . . . . (310) 472-1446
Shay, R.J. Represented By: Harriet Kastaris & Associates . . . . . (314) 773-2600
Represented By: Repertoire . . . . . (972) 761-0500
Sheban, Chris 1807 W Sunnyside Avenue #1-G, Chicago, IL 60640 . . . . . (773) 271-2720
Sheehy, Michael Represented By: Bernstein & Andriulli, Inc. . . . . . (212) 682-1490
Shega, Marla 4401 Edinburg Lane, Hanover Park, IL 60103 . . . . . (630) 830-4745
Shein, Bob 15 Glenfield Lane, Nesconset, NY 11767 . . . . . (516) 265-0064
Sheldon, Paul Represented By: Artco . . . . . (212) 889-8777
Shelley, Ronald 6880 SW 80th Street, Miami, FL 33143 . . . . . (305) 667-0154

SHELLY, JEFF Pages 344,448
2330 San Marco Drive, Los Angeles, CA 90068 • Fax (213) 464-6630 **(213) 460-4604 • (800) 318-3244**
e-mail: jlshelly@aol.com • Website: www.theispot.com/artist/shelly
Specialties: Advertising; Cartoon; Children; Editorial; Greeting Cards; Humour; People; Whimsical

Shelly, Roger Represented By: Sweet Represents . . . . . (415) 433-1222
Shelton, Daniel 4333 St.-Catherine W, Montreal, PQ Canada H3Z 1P9 . . . . . (514) 630-7810
Shelton, Darryl Represented By: Ravenhill Represents . . . . . (816) 333-0744
Shepard & Associates 2303 Gilbert Avenue, Cincinnati, OH 45206 . . . . . (513) 559-9356
Shephard, Tom Represented By: Woody Coleman Presents, Inc. . . . . . (216) 661-4222
Shepherd, James Represented By: Fortuni Illustration . . . . . (414) 964-8088
Shepherd, Mark Represented By: Berendsen & Associates . . . . . (513) 861-1400
Sheppard, Richard Represented By: Linda De Moreta Represents . . . . . (510) 769-1421
Sherbo, Dan 4208 38th Street NW, Washington, DC 20016 . . . . . (202) 244-0474
Sherbowich, Mary 87 Tape Avenue, Toronto, ON Canada M1E 4A2 . . . . . (416) 469-3816
Sherman, Oren Represented By: Artco . . . . . (212) 889-8777
Sherman, Whitney 5101 Whiteford Avenue, Baltimore, MD 21212 . . . . . (410) 435-2095
Sherrill, Robert 3207 ½ Foothill Boulevard, Pasadena, CA 91107 . . . . . (626) 796-1468
Sherwood, Stewart 625 Yonge Street #303, Toronto, ON Canada M4Y 1Z5 . . . . . (416) 925-8528

SHIDLA, JOY MASSEN Page 251
6037 11th Avenue S, Minneapolis, MN 55417 • Fax (612) 866-0358 **(612) 866-0358**
Specialties: Children; Food; Nature; Pastels; People; Portraiture; Product; Realism; Water Color

Shiff, Andrew 153 Clinton Street, Hopkinton, MA 01748 . . . (508) 435-3607
Shigley, Neil 17696 Montero Road, San Diego, CA 92128 . . . (619) 451-1101
Shimamoto, Michiko Represented By: Barbara Gordon Associates Ltd. . . . (212) 686-3514
Shiragi, Fariba Represented By: Berendsen & Associates . . . (513) 861-1400
Shock, Steve Represented By: Munro Goodman . . . (312) 321-1336
Shoffner, Terry 11 Irwin Street, Toronto, ON Canada M4Y 1L1 . . . (416) 967-6717

SHOHET, MARTI Pages 86-87,103
Represented By: Lindgren & Smith **(212) 397-7330**
e-mail: inquiry@lindgrensmith.com • Website: www.lindgrensmith.com • Specialties: Computer; Cutouts

SHORROCK, PAUL Page 201
Represented By: American Artists **(212) 682-2462**
Represented By: Ian Flemming Associates
e-mail: info@amerartists.com • Website: www.amerartists.com

Short, Kevin A. 34562 Via Catalina, Capistrano Beach, CA 92624-1346 . . . (714) 240-6979
Represented By: Kimberley Boege . . . (602) 265-4389

SHORT, ROBBIE Page 321
Represented By: PG Representatives **(413) 967-9855**
e-mail: pgreps@aol.com • Specialty: Water Color

Sibayan, Noel P.O. Box 680061, Corona, NY 11368 . . . (718) 595-0812
Siboldi, Carla Represented By: Carol Chislovsky Design, Inc. . . . (212) 677-9100
Siciliano Studio, Gerald 9 Garfield Place, Brooklyn, NY 11215 . . . (718) 636-4561
Sienkiewicz, Bill Represented By: Shannon Associates . . . (212) 831-5650
Signorino, Slug P.O. Box 387, Michigan City, IN 46361 . . . (219) 879-5221
Silver, Judy Reed 1808 Manning Avenue #103, Los Angeles, CA 90025 . . . (310) 474-7701
Represented By: Sharpe & Associates . . . (310) 641-8556
Silver, Stanley 701 N Arden Drive, Beverly Hills, CA 90210 . . . (310) 285-0800
Represented By: Mendola Ltd. . . . (212) 986-5680
Silver Moon Represented By: Scott Hull Associates . . . (937) 433-8383
Silvers, Bill Represented By: Mendola Ltd. . . . (212) 986-5680
Simanson, Greg Represented By: Susan & Company . . . (206) 232-7873
Simard, Remy Represented By: HK Portfolio . . . (212) 675-5719
Simeone, Lauren E. 855 Windsor-Perrineville Road, Hightstown, NJ 08520 . . . (609) 426-4490
Simon, Angela Represented By: Black Inc. Creative Rep. . . . (602) 381-1332
Simon, Susan 962 E State Street, Ithaca, NY 14850 . . . (607) 277-5903
Simon, William 9431 Bonhomme Woods Drive, St. Louis, MO 63132-3404 . . . (314) 993-3522
Simpson, Craig 1546 Powell Street, Norristown, PA 19401 . . . (610) 279-0991
Simpson, Gretchen Dow Represented By: Riley Illustration . . . (212) 989-8770
Simpson, John Miles Represented By: Leyden Diversified . . . (215) 663-0587
Sims, Blanche Represented By: Carol Bancroft & Friends . . . (203) 748-4823
Sims, Lisa Represented By: Robin Ogden Represents . . . (612) 925-4174
Sims, Ronald 10609 Sandpiper Drive, Houston, TX 77096 . . . (713) 271-3703

SINCLAIR, VALERIE Pages 53,429
Represented By: Renard Represents **(212) 490-2450**
e-mail: renardreps@earthlink.net • Website: www.renardrepresents.com • Specialty: Conceptual

Singer, Alan 3021 Elmwood Avenue, Rochester, NY 14618 . . . (716) 473-4115
Singer, Phillip Represented By: Mattelson Associates . . . (516) 487-1323
Sinovcic, Miro Represented By: Hankins & Tegenborg Ltd. . . . (212) 867-8092
Sipley, Donald Represented By: Hankins & Tegenborg Ltd. . . . (212) 867-8092
Siracusa, Catherine 112 W 74th Street, Apt. 4R, New York, NY 10023 . . . (212) 580-8084
Sirrell, Terry Represented By: Pema Browne Ltd. . . . (914) 985-2936
Sis, Peter 252 Lafayette Street #5E, New York, NY 10012 . . . (212) 226-2203
Sisdale, Bob Represented By: Mendola Ltd. . . . (212) 986-5680

Siu, Peter Represented By: Artworks . . . . . (212) 627-1554
Represented By: Martha Productions . . . . . (310) 390-8663
Siudmak, Wojtek Represented By: Marlena Agency . . . . . (609) 252-9405
Sivavec, Diane Represented By: Hankins & Tegenborg Ltd. . . . . . (212) 867-8092
Sizemore, Ted Represented By: Hankins & Tegenborg Ltd. . . . . . (212) 867-8092
Skeen, Keith D. Represented By: Yolanda Burnett Represents . . . . . (770) 967-0039
Represented By: Langley & Associates . . . . . (847) 670-0912
Skelton, Steve Represented By: Ravenhill Represents . . . . . (816) 333-0744
Skillicorn, Mark 1655 N Damen, Chicago, IL 60647 . . . . . (773) 549-9548
Skivington, Janice 1017 E Willow Avenue, Wheaton, IL 60187
Represented By: Gwen Walters-Goldstein . . . . . (781) 235-8658
Represented By: Carol Bancroft & Friends . . . . . (203) 748-4823
Slackman, Chas B. 320 E 57th Street, New York, NY 10022 . . . . . (212) 758-8233
188 Suffolk Street, Sag Harbor, NY 11963 . . . . . (516) 725-3696
Slark, Albert 109 Jameson Avenue #714, Toronto, ON Canada M6K 2X2 . . . . . (416) 536-3865

SLEMONS, JEFF Pages 240-241
2555 Walnut Street, Ste. LF, Denver, CO 80205 • Fax (303) 298-0807 **(303) 298-0807**
Specialties: Black & White; Caricature; Cartoon; Editorial; Fantasy; Humour; Mixed Media; Painterly; People; Water Color

Sloan, Michael 32 Gramercy Park S #13K, New York, NY 10003 . . . . . (212) 253-2047
Sloan Design & Illustration, Rick 9432 Appalachian Drive, Sacramento, CA 95827 . . . . . (916) 364-5844
Slonim, David 232 South Street, Chesterfield, IN 46017 . . . . . (765) 378-6511
Small, David 25626 Simpson Road, Mendon, MI 49072 . . . . . (616) 496-7491
Smallish, Craig Represented By: Jim Hanson Artist Agent . . . . . (312) 337-7770
Smallwood, Steve 4702 Summer Creek Lane SE, Grand Rapids, MI 49508-7502 . . . . . (616) 249-2845
Smith, Anne Represented By: Lilla Rogers Studio . . . . . (781) 641-2787
Smith, Audrey Represented By: Mark Sherrah . . . . . (416) 972-6161
Smith, Dan Represented By: American Artists . . . . . (212) 682-2462
Smith, Debbie Represented By: Terry Squire . . . . . (919) 772-1262
Smith, Douglas Represented By: Richard Solomon . . . . . (212) 683-1362
Smith, Elwood H. Represented By: Maggie Pickard . . . . . (914) 876-2358
Smith, Gary Represented By: Bill & Maurine Klimt . . . . . (212) 799-2231
Smith, Genine Represented By: Planet Rep . . . . . (800) 847-5101
Smith, Geoff Represented By: Scott Hull Associates . . . . . (937) 433-8383

SMITH, GRAHAM Pages 294-295
3510 Front Street #3D, San Diego, CA 92103 • Fax (619) 293-3824 **(619) 296-9323**
e-mail: smithbrain@aol.com • Website: www.artmasters.net
Specialties: Collateral; Design; Fashion; Illustrative; Packaging; Product

Smith, James Noel Represented By: Friend & Johnson . . . . . (214) 559-0055
Smith, Jamie Represented By: HK Portfolio . . . . . (212) 675-5719
Smith, Jay Represented By: Yolanda Burnett Represents . . . . . (770) 967-0039
Smith, Jere Represented By: Kolea Baker Artists Representative . . . . . (206) 784-1136
Smith, Jos. A. 159 John Street, 6th Flr., New York, NY 10038-3523 . . . . . (212) 825-1475
Smith, Laura 6545 Cahuenga Terrace, Hollywood, CA 90068 . . . . . (213) 467-1700
Smith, Marcia Represented By: Beth O'Neill Artists Rep . . . . . (716) 473-0384
Smith, Marty 3033 Scott Road, Burbank, CA 91504 . . . . . (818) 845-3945
Represented By: Barb Hauser . . . . . (415) 647-5660
Represented By: Chip Caton . . . . . (860) 523-4562

SMITH, MEG Page 250
Represented By: Dimension **(612) 884-4045**
e-mail: jkoltes@dimensioncreative.com • Website: www.dimensioncreative.com
Specialties: Food; Water Color

Smith, Philip Represented By: Cornell & McCarthy, LLC . . . . . (203) 454-4210
Smith, Rick 1236 Tranquilla Drive, Dallas, TX 75218 . . . . . (214) 321-6264
Smith, Roger W. 239 NW 13th #205, Portland, OR 97209 . . . . . (503) 226-8252

SMITH, RYLE
Pages 146-147
Represented By: Carol Guenzi Agents, Inc.
(800) 417-5120
e-mail: artagent@artagent.com • Website: www.artagent.com
Specialties: Advertising; Animation; Black & White; Caricature; Cartoon; Editorial; Humour; People; Whimsical

Smith, Theresa Represented By: HK Portfolio . . . . . (212) 675-5719

SMITH, TREVOR
Page 201
Represented By: American Artists
(212) 682-2462
Represented By: Ian Flemming Associates
e-mail: info@amerartists.com • Website: www.amerartists.com

Smock, Doug 741 Astor Street, Norristown, PA 19401 . . . . . (610) 272-3182
Smola, Jim 94 Maple Hill Avenue, Newington, CT 06111 . . . . . (860) 665-0305
Smollin, Michael Represented By: Mendola Ltd. . . . . . (212) 986-5680
Smyth, Fiona Represented By: Reactor Art & Design Ltd. . . . . . (416) 703-1913
Smythe, Danny Represented By: Rita Marie & Friends . . . . . (312) 222-0337
Snave, Karen Represented By: Renee Kalish . . . . . (847) 864-6127
Sneberger, Dan Represented By: Fran Seigel . . . . . (212) 486-9644
Sneed, Brad 5112 W 72nd Street, Prairie Village, KS 66208 . . . . . (913) 362-6699

SNIDER, JACKIE
Pages 322-323
800 Concession 2W RR1, Warkworth, ON Canada K0K 3K0
(705) 924-1487
Specialties: Children; Editorial; Humour

SNIDER, STEPHEN
Pages 322-323
800 Concession 2W RR1, Warkworth, ON Canada K0K 3K0
(705) 924-1487
Specialties: Architecture/Interiors; Aviation; Historical; Landscape; Transporatation

Snodgrass Illustration, Steve Represented By: Holly Hahn Artist Rep (H2 + Co.) . . . . . (312) 633-0500
Snow c/o Royter Snow Design, Scott 1537 S Main Street, Salt Lake City, UT 84115 . . . . . (801) 484-0419
Snyder, Teresa 25727 Mountain Drive, Arlington, WA 98223 . . . . . (360) 435-8998
Snyder, Wayne 25727 Mountain Drive, Arlington, WA 98223 . . . . . (360) 435-8998
Sobey, Mike Represented By: Steve Edsey & Sons . . . . . (312) 527-0351
Represented By: Mason Illustration . . . . . (612) 729-1774
Soderlind, Kirsten Represented By: Vicki Morgan Associates . . . . . (212) 475-0440

SODERSTROM, DENNIS
Page 150
Represented By: Connie Koralik Associates Represents
(312) 944-5680
Specialties: Cartoon; Character; Product

Soetarman, Lily Los Gatos, CA 95032 . . . . . (408) 356-3187
Sofo, Frank R. 34 Strattion Square, East Hampton, NY 11937 . . . . . (516) 324-6119
Sohaei, Iraj P.O. Box 4613, Orange, CA 92863-4613 . . . . . (800) 735-2922

SOKOLOVA, VALERIE
Pages 86-87,111
Represented By: Lindgren & Smith
(212) 397-7330
e-mail: inquiry@lindgrensmith.com • Website: www.lindgrensmith.com

Sokolowski, Ted Road #2 Box 408, Lake Ariel, PA 18436 . . . . . (717) 937-4527
Sola, Luis Represented By: Langley & Associates . . . . . (847) 670-0912
Represented By: Yolanda Burnett Represents . . . . . (770) 967-0039
Soliz, Roy 601 Stadium Road, Port Arthur, TX 77642 . . . . . (409) 982-6323
Soloman, Debby 1 Hudson Street, 3rd Flr., New York, NY 10013-3674 . . . . . (212) 619-7900
Soltis, Linda DeVito P.O. Box 462, Woodbury, CT 06798 . . . . . (203) 263-4019
137 Barn Hill Road, Woodbury, CT 06798
Somerville, Kevin Represented By: Spencer Church . . . . . (206) 860-9239
Sona Communications 10 Grenoble Drive #202, North York, ON Canada M3C 1C6 . . . . . (416) 429-0410
Sorensen, Henri Represented By: Evelyne Johnson Associates . . . . . (212) 532-0928

SORENSEN, MARCOS
Page 357
3531 25th Street, San Francisco, CA 94110 • Fax (415) 282-5681
(415) 282-5796
e-mail: marcos@astrocat.com • Website: www.astrocat.com
Specialties: Animation; Conceptual; Humour; Websites

Sorra, Kristin Represented By: Carol Bancroft & Friends . . . . (203) 748-4823
Sorren, Joe Represented By: Joanie Bernstein Art Rep . . . . (612) 374-3169
SOS Represented By: The Arts Counsel . . . . (212) 777-6777
Soukup, James Represented By: Alexander/Pollard, Inc. . . . . (800) 347-0734
South, Randy 4226 Fair Avenue, Studio City, CA 91602 . . . . (818) 769-6900
Spaatz, Seymor 1125 Landwehr Road, Northbrook, IL 60062 . . . . (708) 498-8936
Spackman, Jeff Represented By: Publishers' Graphics . . . . (203) 797-8188
Spaulding, Kevin Represented By: Ann Koeffler Represents . . . . (213) 957-2327
Spear, Chuck 456 Ninth Street, Unit 2, Hoboken, NJ 07030 . . . . (201) 798-9117
Speer, Steve Represented By: Tricia Joyce . . . . (212) 962-0728
Speers, Pauline 5393 SE Bulman Avenue, Port Orchard, WA 98366 . . . . (360) 871-2800
Spellman, Susan Represented By: Gwen Walters-Goldstein . . . . (781) 235-8658
Spencer, Joe Represented By: Betsy Hillman . . . . (415) 381-4728
Spencer Studios, Mary 7816 Connie Drive, Huntington Beach, CA 92648 . . . . (714) 848-4954

SPENGLER, KENNETH Page 363
2668 17th Street, Sacramento, CA 95818 • Fax (916) 441-3490 **(916) 441-1932**
Specialties: Advertising; Children; Editorial

Spengler, Margaret 2668 17th Street, Sacramento, CA 95818 . . . . (916) 441-1932
Spilsbury, Simon Represented By: Bernstein & Andriulli, Inc. . . . . (212) 682-1490
Spirin, Gennady 621 Brickhouse Road, Princeton, NJ 08540 . . . . (609) 497-1720
Splash Page Represented By: Langley & Associates . . . . (847) 670-0912
Spohn, Cliff Represented By: Hankins & Tegenborg Ltd. . . . . (212) 867-8092
Spoke Illustration, Lena 70 Nina Street, Toronto, ON Canada M5R 1Z6 . . . . (416) 535-5508
Spollen, Chris 362 Cromwell Avenue, Staten Island, NY 10305-2304 . . . . (718) 979-9695
Spom, Jessica Represented By: Creative Connection . . . . (410) 360-5981
Sposato, John 43 E 22nd Street, New York, NY 10010 . . . . (212) 477-3909
Spransy, Tim Represented By: Yolanda Burnett Represents . . . . (770) 967-0039
Represented By: Langley & Associates . . . . (847) 670-0912
Spreitz, Sandy B. P.O. Boxe 1803, New York, NY 10009 . . . . (212) 254-0809
Springer, Sally 1510 N Thumb Point Drive, Ft. Pierce, FL 34949 . . . . (561) 467-0095
Sprouls, Kevin 1 Schooner Lane, Sweetwater, NJ 08037 . . . . (609) 965-4795
Sprull, Barbara 366 Adelaide Street E, Toronto, ON Canada M5A 3X9 . . . . (416) 594-6594
Spurlock, J. David 170 Wildwood Avenue, Upper Montclair, NJ 07043 . . . . (973) 744-1135
Square, Carl Represented By: Donna Rosen Artists' Rep . . . . (301) 384-8925
Squire, Nina Green Valley, Raleigh, North Devon, England EX31 4HY 44 127 137 8939
St. Pierre, Joe Represented By: Artco . . . . (212) 889-8777
Staake, Bob 726 S Ballas Road, St. Louis, MO 63122 . . . . (314) 961-2303
Stabin, Victor 84-21 Midland Parkway, Jamaica, NY 11432 . . . . (212) 243-7688
Stabler, Barton 419 Tremont Avenue, Westfield, NJ 07090 . . . . (908) 789-7415
Stadler, Greg 2706 10th Avenue, Seattle, WA 98119 . . . . (206) 284-2231
Stagg, James Represented By: Ann Koeffler Represents . . . . (213) 957-2327
Stagg, Pamela 3 Bennington Heights Drive, Toronto, ON Canada M4G 1A7 . . . . (416) 423-0477
Stahl, Ben Represented By: Bill & Maurine Klimt . . . . (212) 799-2231
Stahl, Nancy 470 West End Avenue #8G, New York, NY 10024 . . . . (212) 362-8779
Stallard, Peter Represented By: Harriet Kastaris & Associates . . . . (314) 773-2600
Stamm, Jan 4808 Hawley Boulevard, San Diego, CA 92116 . . . . (619) 280-6205
Stampatori, Riccardo 60 Wadsworth Crescent, Cambridge, ON Canada N7S 5A3 . . . . (519) 624-8202
Stanford, Walter 102 Piedmont Drive, Kannapolis, NC 28081 . . . . (704) 933-8787
Represented By: Kerry Reilly Reps . . . . (704) 372-6007
Stanicek, John 1900 Richard Street, Aurora, IL 60506 . . . . (708) 859-0506
Stankiewicz, Steve 44 Gramercy Park N, New York, NY 10010 . . . . (212) 477-4229
Represented By: Leighton & Company, Inc. . . . . (978) 921-0887
Stanley, Anne 5 Kent Road, Toronto, ON Canada M4L 2X5 . . . . (416) 463-6614
Represented By: Three in a Box . . . . (416) 367-2446

STARR, JIM Pages 168,184
Represented By: American Artists **(212) 682-2462**
e-mail: info@amerartists.com • Website: www.amerartists.com
Specialties: Airbrush; Graphic Design/Illustration; Scratchboard

Starrett, Terri 22425 Ventura Boulevard #101, Woodland Hills, CA 91364 . . . . (818) 342-8501
Represented By: Connie Koralik Associates Represents . . . . (312) 944-5680
Represented By: Penny & Stermer Group . . . . (212) 505-9342

Stasiak, Krystyna Represented By: Square Moon . . . . . (510) 253-9451
Stasolla, Mario 37 Cedar Hill Avenue, South Nyack, NY 10960 . . . . . (914) 353-3086
Stasys Represented By: Marlena Agency . . . . . (609) 252-9405
Statema, John Represented By: Marvel Entertainment . . . . . (212) 696-0808
Statts, Jason Howard P.O. Box 16626, Savannah, GA 31416 . . . . . (912) 355-8398
Steadman, Barbara Represented By: Evelyne Johnson Associates . . . . . (212) 532-0928
Steadman, Lee Represented By: Cliff Knecht . . . . . (412) 761-5666

STEAM INC. Pages 124-125
Represented By: Vicki Morgan Associates **(212) 475-0440**
e-mail: vmartrep@aol.com • Website: www.vickimorganassociates.com
Specialties: Advertising; Airbrush; Animation; Cartoon; Character; Digital; Icons

Stearney, Mark 621 S Plymouth Court #202, Chicago, IL 60605 . . . . . (312) 360-9033
Steccati-Tanovitz, Eve 6300 Estates Drive, Oakland, CA 94611 . . . . . (510) 339-0182
Steck, Jim Represented By: Anne Albrecht & Associates . . . . . (312) 595-0300
Steele, Marlene Represented By: Berendsen & Associates . . . . . (513) 861-1400

STEELE, ROBERT GANTT Pages 86-87,105
Represented By: Lindgren & Smith **(212) 397-7330**
e-mail: inquiry@lindgrensmith.com • Website: www.lindgrensmith.com
Specialties: Architecture/Interiors; Historical; Landscape; People; Realism; Water Color

Stehrenberger Illustration, Michiko New York, NY 10011 . . . . . (212) 979-0490
Steiger, Cheryl 1790 Spruce Avenue, Highland Park, IL 60035 . . . . . (847) 831-2294
Steiger, Keith Represented By: Melissa Hopson . . . . . (214) 747-3122
Stein, August 3841 Fourth Avenue #110, San Diego, CA 92103 . . . . . (619) 299-8999
Represented By: Leighton & Company, Inc. . . . . . (978) 921-0887
Stein, Mark 73-01 Juniper Valley Road, Middle Village, NY 11379 . . . . . (718) 326-4839
Steinberg, James 115 Montague Road, Amherst, MA 01002 . . . . . (413) 549-1932
Steiner, Frank Represented By: Hankins & Tegenborg Ltd. . . . . . (212) 867-8092
Represented By: Teenuh Foster Represents . . . . . (314) 647-7377
Steininger, Otto 636 Broadway, New York, NY 10012 . . . . . (212) 982-5222
Steiny, J.T. Represented By: Shooting Star . . . . . (213) 469-2020
Steirnagle, Michael 2116 Rock Glen, Escondido, CA 92026 . . . . . (760) 736-4015
Stemp, Tiffany Represented By: Art Department . . . . . (212) 925-4222

STENSTROM, REBECCA Page 246
Represented By: Dimension **(612) 884-4045**
e-mail: jkoltes@dimensioncreative.com • Website: www.dimensioncreative.com • Specialty: Water Color

Stentz, Nancy Represented By: Jerry Leff Associates, Inc. . . . . . (212) 697-8525
Represented By: Jorgensen & Barrett Reps . . . . . (206) 634-1880
Stepanek, Mike Represented By: Daniele Collignon . . . . . (212) 243-4209
Stephens, John Represented By: Jeff Palmer . . . . . (203) 222-8777
Stergulz, Richard 2051 Geneva Street #8, Oceanside, CA 92054 . . . . . (760) 754-8154
Stermer, Dugald Represented By: Jim Lilie . . . . . (415) 441-4384
Sterrett, Jane 160 Fifth Avenue #700, New York, NY 10010 . . . . . (212) 929-2566

STEVENS, DARYL Pages 358-359,438,443
6 Jones Street, Apt. 5D, New York, NY 10014 • Fax (212) 620-4145 **(212) 741-1610**
e-mail: dstevens@studio202.com • Website: www.studio202.com
Specialties: Advertising; Animation; Cartoon; Children; Computer; Corporate; Digital; Editorial; Icons

Stevens, Heidi 22 10th Street, Petaluma, CA 94952 . . . . . (707) 769-1252
Stevenson, David 733 Owl Drive, Vacaville, CA 95687 . . . . . (707) 447-5720
Represented By: Conrad Represents, Inc. . . . . . (415) 921-7140
Stewart, Bryan SS 2 Site 27 Comp #58, Penetanguishene, ON Canada L0K 1P0 . . . . . (705) 549-7045

STEWART, DON Pages 252-253
117 W Green Court, Greensboro, NC 27407 **(336) 854-2769**
Represented By: Deborah Wolfe **(215) 232-6666**
Website: www.deborahwolfeltd.com
Specialties: Airbrush; Children; Editorial; Greeting Cards; People; Realism

STEWART, J.W. Pages 86-87,100
Represented By: Lindgren & Smith **(212) 397-7330**
e-mail: inquiry@lindgrensmith.com • Website: www.lindgrensmith.com

Stewart, Jenny 18 First Avenue #17, New York, NY 10009 . . . . . (212) 228-5618
Stewart, John 11323 Blythe Street, Sun Valley, CA 91352-4432 . . . . . (213) 875-2012
Stewart, Michelle Represented By: Ken Barboza . . . . . (212) 505-8635
Stewart, Pat Represented By: Evelyne Johnson Associates . . . . . (212) 532-0928
Stickman Studios 54 Wilton Drive, Brampton, ON Canada L6W 3A1 . . . . . (905) 450-9928
Stiglich, Joyce 727 Forest Glen Court, Maitland, FL 32751 . . . . . (407) 644-5294
Stiles, Geoffrey R. 1 Lazy Brook Drive, Waterboro, ME 04061 . . . . . (617) 247-8680
Still, Wayne Anthony Represented By: American Artists . . . . . (212) 682-2462
Stillman, Susan White Plains, NY 10606 . . . . . (914) 682-3771
Stilwell, Jim Represented By: Jennifer Embler Represents, Inc. . . . . . (954) 760-4195
Stine, Richard Represented By: Jaz & Jaz . . . . . (206) 633-3445
Stinson, Don Represented By: Steve Edsey & Sons . . . . . (312) 527-0351
Stirnweis, Shannon 116 Perry Road, New Ipswich, NH 03071 . . . . . (603) 878-9841
Stivell, Alain Represented By: Jan Collier Represents, Inc. . . . . . (415) 383-9026
Stock, Jeffrey 10 Doaks Lane Little Harbor, Marblehead, MA 01945 . . . . . (781) 639-8384
Stockworks/Stock Illustration Represented By: Martha Productions . . . . . (310) 390-8663
Stocky, Tom Represented By: Nachreiner Boie Art Factory . . . . . (414) 785-1940
Stoddard, Paul 524 Main Street, Stoneham, MA 02180 . . . . . (781) 438-0266

STOLPER, KAREN Pages 338-339
160 W 16th Street, Apt. 1-M, New York, NY 10011 **(212) 675-5150**
Represented By: The Roland Group **(301) 718-7955**
Website: www.therolandgroup.com • Specialties: Conceptual; Painterly

Stone, Holly 244 Friar Tuck Drive, Baton Rouge, LA 70815 . . . . . (504) 273-0257
Stong, Michel Represented By: Planet Rep . . . . . (800) 847-5101
Storey, Lee 6565 Green Valley Circle #306, Culver City, CA 90230 . . . . . (310) 670-3477
Storozuk, Walter Represented By: Creative Freelancers . . . . . (800) 398-9544
Stottlemyer, John 445 Suzanne Avenue, Shoreview, MN 55126 . . . . . (612) 241-3256
Stout, Tim 135 W Dorothy Lane, Dayton, OH 45429 . . . . . (937) 298-5133
Represented By: Joel Harlib Associates, Inc. . . . . . (312) 573-1370
Stout, William 1468 Loma Vista Street, Pasadena, CA 91104 . . . . . (626) 798-6490

STRAUB, MATT Page 409
207 Avenue B, Apt. 3A, New York, NY 10009 **(212) 995-9359**
Website: www.erols.com/okstraub • Specialties: Animals; Book Jackets; Digital; Humour; Icons; Illustrative; Maps & Charts; People; Wildlife

Straub, Philip W. 50 Laurel Drive, Monroe, CT 06468 . . . . . (203) 261-4334
Represented By: Fran Seigel . . . . . (212) 486-9644
Street, David & Renee 13908 Marblestone Drive, Clifton, VA 20124 . . . . . (703) 631-1650
Streeter, Katherine 530 Stockton Street #103, San Francisco, CA 94108 . . . . . (415) 788-0492

STRELECKI, KAREN Pages 216,223
4019 Rockmill Drive, Marietta, GA 30062 • Fax (770) 998-0137 **(770) 998-0137**
Represented By: Alexander/Pollard, Inc. **(800) 347-0734**
Specialties: Advertising; Cartoon; Children; Editorial; Fantasy; Humour; Stock; 3D; Whimsical

Strizek & Associates, Inc. 333 E Ontario Street #713B, Chicago, IL 60611-4862 . . . . . (312) 266-4900
Stroster, Maria 2057 N Sheffield Avenue, Chicago, IL 60614 . . . . . (773) 525-2081
Struthers, Doug Represented By: Artco . . . . . (212) 889-8777
Struzan, Drew 624 Eaton Drive, Pasadena, CA 91107 . . . . . (626) 578-7291
Stuart, Walter Represented By: Salzman International . . . . . (415) 285-8267
Stubbs, Tommy 4628 Mossburg Court, Atlanta, GA 30066 . . . . . (770) 924-2382
Represented By: Susan Wells & Associates . . . . . (404) 255-1430

STUDIO 212 Pages 310-311,433
1605 Stemmons Freeway, Dallas, TX 75207 • Fax (214) 720-0080 **(214) 744-4421**
e-mail: billjenkins@studio212.com • Website: www.studio212.com • Specialty: Digital

Studio Liddell Represented By: Frank & Jeff Lavaty . . . . . (212) 427-5632

Studio M 3088 Walnut Avenue, Long Beach, CA 90807 . . . . . . (562) 426-1888
Studio Macbeth Represented By: Artco . . . . . . (212) 889-8777
Represented By: Jeff Palmer . . . . . . (203) 222-8777

STUDIO NORTH/CATHY LOCKE Pages 274,453
7595 Redwood Boulevard #215, Novato, CA 94945 • Fax (415) 893-9464 **(415) 893-9292**
e-mail: cathy@studionorthnet.com • Website: www.studionorthnet.com
Specialties: Book Jackets; Digital; Food; Gardens/Flowers; Icons; Medical; Portraiture; Websites

Studio West, Inc. Represented By: RKB Studios, Inc. . . . . . . (612) 339-7055
Sturman, Sally Mara Represented By: The Arts Counsel . . . . . . (212) 777-6777

STUTZMAN, LAURA Pages 254-255,459,466
100 G Street, Mountain Lake Park, MD 21550 • Fax (301) 334-4186 **(301) 334-4086**
e-mail: eloqui@aol.com • Website: www.eloqui.com
Specialties: Advertising; Corporate; Editorial; Food; People; Portraiture; Product; Realism; Sports; Water Color

STUTZMAN, MARK Pages 254-255,460,462
100 G Street, Mountain Lake Park, MD 21550 • Fax (301) 334-4186 **(301) 334-4086**
e-mail: eloqui@aol.com • Website: www.eloqui.com
Specialties: Advertising; Airbrush; Celebrity; Fantasy; People; Portraiture; Poster; Product; Realism

Stymest, Brian 7 Eaglerock Way, Montclair, NJ 07042 . . . . . . (973) 509-2490
Suchit, Stu 117 Jayne Avenue, Port Jefferson, NY 11777 . . . . . . (516) 928-6775
Represented By: Renard Represents . . . . . . (212) 490-2450
Suddick, Bill 20 Highcroft Road, Toronto, ON Canada M4L 3G2 . . . . . . (416) 469-0843
Sudo, Masato 278 12th Street #1L, Brooklyn, NY 11215 . . . . . . (718) 768-0679
Suhrie, Rhonda 2851 Francis Avenue, La Carescenta, CA 91214 . . . . . . (818) 248-6376

SULLIVAN, DON Pages 146-147
Represented By: Carol Guenzi Agents, Inc. **(800) 417-5120**
e-mail: artagent@artagent.com • Website: www.artagent.com • Specialties: Advertising; Editorial

Sullivan, Robert Represented By: Artco . . . . . . (212) 889-8777
Sullivan, Steve Represented By: Creative Freelancers . . . . . . (800) 398-9544
Suma, Doug Santa Monica, CA 90405 . . . . . . (310) 392-4877
Sumichrast, Jozef Represented By: Renard Represents . . . . . . (212) 490-2450
Summers, Ethan 5512 Landmark Lane, Charlotte, NC 28270 . . . . . . (704) 365-4554
Summers, Mark Represented By: Richard Solomon . . . . . . (212) 683-1362

SURGE GRAPHIX, LLC Page 315
57 Stanton Street, New York, NY 10002 • Fax (212) 388-0276 **(212) 995-5290**
e-mail: fusion@escape.com • Website: www.surgegraphix.com
Specialties: Maps & Charts; Medical; Mixed Media; Technical; 3D

Sutton, Jim Represented By: Renee Kalish . . . . . . (847) 864-6127
Sutton, Judith 41 W Ferry Street, New Hope, PA 18938 . . . . . . (215) 862-9771
Sutton, Ward 104 MacDougal Street #19, New York, NY 10012 . . . . . . (212) 460-9527
Suzan, Gerardo Represented By: Gwen Walters-Goldstein . . . . . . (781) 235-8658
Suzuki, Bob 192 Spadina Avenue, Ste. 502, Toronto, ON Canada M5T 2C2 . . . . . . (416) 504-8739
Swaine Design & Illus., Michael 6735 N 10th Place, Phoenix, AZ 85014 . . . . . . (888) 264-5400
Swan, Joan Represented By: Tonal Values . . . . . . (214) 943-2569
Swan, Sara Represented By: Holly Hahn Artist Rep (H2 + Co.) . . . . . . (312) 633-0500

SWANSON, JAMES Pages 144-145
15 Richmond Avenue, La Grange Park, IL 60526 • Fax (708) 352-3082 **(708) 352-3081**
Specialties: Animals; Digital; Entertainment; Food; Sports

Swanson, Robert Represented By: Hankins & Tegenborg Ltd. . . . . . . (212) 867-8092
Swanson Studio, Harry US Route 1, P.O. Box 60, Lincolnville, ME 04849 . . . . . . (207) 789-5559
Swarts, Jeff 308 S Cedar Street, Danville, OH 43014-0289 . . . . . . (740) 599-6516
Sweeney, Jerry 1644 Beryl Drive, Pittsburgh, PA 15227 . . . . . . (412) 884-5704
Sweeney, Mark W. 35 Macopin Avenue, Upper Montclair, NJ 07043 . . . . . . (973) 744-9158
Sweet, Brian Represented By: Alan Lynch Artists . . . . . . (908) 813-8718

Sweet, Melissa 29 W Street, Portland, ME 04102 . . . . . (207) 772-4850
Sweny, Steve Represented By: Donna Rosen Artists' Rep . . . . . (301) 384-8925
Swerdlow, Trina P.O. Box 23987, Pleasant Hill, CA 94523 . . . . . (925) 687-6499
Swierzy, Waldemar Represented By: Marlena Agency . . . . . (609) 252-9405
Swift, Elvis Represented By: Joanie Bernstein Art Rep . . . . . (612) 374-3169
Swift, Michael Represented By: Famous Frames . . . . . (310) 642-2721
Sylvain Represented By: Motion Artists, Inc. . . . . . (213) 851-7737
Symank, Yvonne Represented By: Creative Connection . . . . . (410) 360-5981
Syme, Hugh Represented By: The Pate Company . . . . . (805) 529-8111

SYME ILLUSTRATION, ALEC Page 384
Represented By: Geoffrey Stewart **(612) 824-8914**
e-mail: geo@scc.net • Website: www.stewartartists.com • Specialties: Animation; Digital; 3D

Symington, Gary Represented By: Sheryl Beranbaum . . . . . (401) 737-8591
Syverson, Lisa M. 1740 W Sunnyside Avenue, Chicago, IL 60640 . . . . . (773) 989-9670
Szegedy, Esther Represented By: Cornell & McCarthy, LLC . . . . . (203) 454-4210

SZPURA, BEATA Page 69
48-02 69th Street, Woodside, NY 11377 • Fax (718) 424-8440 **(718) 424-8440**
Website: www.halcyon.com/artstock • Specialties: Advertising; Children; Conceptual; Corporate; Food; Greeting Cards; Humour; Lettering; Maps & Charts; People

Taback, Simms Represented By: The Newborn Group . . . . . (212) 260-6700
Tachiera, Andrea El Cerrito, CA 94530 . . . . . (510) 525-3484
Tagel, Peggy Represented By: HK Portfolio . . . . . (212) 675-5719
Talalla, Doug Represented By: Nancy Bacher . . . . . (612) 786-1200
Talbot, Jim Represented By: Mendola Ltd. . . . . . (212) 986-5680
Talcott, Julia 74 Elmhurst Road, Newton, MA 02158 . . . . . (617) 964-6556
Taleporos, Plato 333 E 23rd Street, New York, NY 10010 . . . . . (212) 689-3138
Tamura, David Represented By: Creative Freelancers . . . . . (800) 398-9544
Tanabe, Hiroshi Represented By: Kate Larkworthy Artist Rep. Ltd. . . . . . (212) 633-1310
Tanaka, Lynn 4018 W 44th Street, Edina, MN 55424-1033 . . . . . (612) 926-8923
Tanaka, Yasuo 1 Irving Place #U-12B, New York, NY 10003 . . . . . (212) 995-8489
Tanenbaum, Robert Represented By: Mendola Ltd. . . . . . (212) 986-5680
Tanhauser, Gary Represented By: Salzman International . . . . . (415) 285-8267
Tank, Darrel Represented By: Sweet Represents . . . . . (415) 433-1222
Tanning, Jim 10 E 66th Street, Kansas City, MO 64113 . . . . . (816) 361-5191
Tanovitz, Ron 6300 Estates Drive, Oakland, CA 94611 . . . . . (510) 339-0182
Tar, Laszlo P.O. Box 2088, Halesite, NY 11743 . . . . . (516) 673-1235
Tarabay, Sharif Represented By: John Brewster Creative Services . . . . . (203) 226-4724
Targete, Jean Pierre Represented By: Hankins & Tegenborg Ltd. . . . . . (212) 867-8092
Tarlofsky, Malcolm P.O. Box 786, Glen Allen, CA 95442 . . . . . (707) 833-4442
Tarnowski, Glen P. Represented By: Creative Freelancers . . . . . (800) 398-9544
Tate, Clarke Represented By: Frank Lux & Associates, Inc. . . . . . (312) 222-1361
Represented By: Mason Illustration . . . . . (612) 729-1774
Tatjana Represented By: Carol Guenzi Agents, Inc. . . . . . (800) 417-5120
Tatopoulos, Patrick Represented By: Motion Artists, Inc. . . . . . (213) 851-7737
Tauss, Herbert South Mountain Pass, Garrison, NY 10524 . . . . . (914) 424-3765
Taxali, Gary Represented By: Conrad Represents, Inc. . . . . . (415) 921-7140
Taylor, Bridget Starr Represented By: Melissa Turk & The Artist Network . . . . . (914) 368-8606
Taylor, C. Winston 17008 Lisette Street, Granada Hills, CA 91344 . . . . . (818) 363-5761

TAYLOR, DAHL Pages 124-125
Represented By: Vicki Morgan Associates **(212) 475-0440**
e-mail: vmartrep@aol.com • Website: www.vickimorganassociates.com • Specialties: Advertising; Architecture/Interiors; Black & White; Corporate; Greeting Cards; People; Portraiture; Poster; Realism; Sports

Taylor, Jody Represented By: Evelyne Johnson Associates . . . . . (212) 532-0928

TAYLOR, JOSEPH Page 312
1217 Church Street, Evanston, IL 60201 • Fax (847) 328-2485 **(847) 328-2454**
Represented By: David Montagano & Associates **(312) 527-3283**
e-mail: josepht280@aol.com • Specialty: Digital

Taylor, Terry 24 Eldredge Street, Port Chester, NY 10573 . . . . (914) 937-7730
Taylor, Tim P.O. Box 34, Parsippany, NJ 07054 . . . . (973) 267-7081
Taylor, Tom 240 Wychwood Avenue, Toronto, ON Canada M6C 2T3 . . . . (416) 654-5906
Tcichman, Mary Represented By: Melissa Turk & The Artist Network . . . . (914) 368-8606
Teare, Brad Represented By: Artworks . . . . (212) 627-1554

TEDESCO, BOB Page 355
8 Payne Road, Bethel, CT 06801 **(203) 778-3206**
e-mail: greycheek@aol.com • Specialties: Conceptual; Digital; Illustrative; Realism; 3D

Teemley, Trudy 3671 Bear Street, Apt. E, Santa Ana, CA 92704 . . . . (714) 850-1964
Teisher, Anne 977 Via Del Monte, Palos Verdes, CA 90274 . . . . (310) 375-0575

TELLOK, MARK Page 81
4060 St. Laurent, Ste. 309, Montreal, PQ Canada H2W 1Y9 • Fax (514) 281-7616 **(514) 288-6918**
Represented By: Anna Goodson **(514) 983-9020**

Temple, Chuck 67 Dawn Ridge Drive, Kitchener, ON Canada N2N 3J5 . . . . (519) 744-5945
Templeton, Sandra 924 E Red Road, Independence, MO 64055 . . . . (816) 833-1523
Ten, Arnie 37 Forbus Street, Poughkeepsie, NY 12601 . . . . (914) 485-8419
Tennant, Craig P.O. Box 7058, Golden, CO 80403 . . . . (303) 642-3286
Tenud, Tish 447 Amhurst Circle, Folsom, CA 95630 . . . . (916) 355-8511
Terreson, Jeffrey Represented By: Mendola Ltd. . . . . (212) 986-5680
Terry, Erin Represented By: Sheryl Beranbaum . . . . (401) 737-8591
Terry, Will 180 S 300 West, Apt. 3, Springville, UT 84663 . . . . (800) 489-9488
Teves, Miles 1428 Ontario Street, Burbank, CA 91505 . . . . (818) 848-2028
The CIA Represented By: Bernstein & Andriulli, Inc. . . . . (212) 682-1490
The Garret, Inc. 9322 Olive Boulevard, St. Louis, MO 63143 . . . . (314) 645-6480
Thelen, Mary 5907 Llano Street, Dallas, TX 75206 . . . . (214) 827-8073
Represented By: Jerry Leff Associates, Inc. . . . . (212) 697-8525
Thermes, Jennifer Represented By: Leighton & Company, Inc. . . . . (978) 921-0887
Thewes Jr., Thomas Represented By: Bernstein & Andriulli, Inc. . . . . (212) 682-1490
Thole, Cathleen Represented By: American Artists . . . . (212) 682-2462
Thomas, Charles Represented By: Ann Koeffler Represents . . . . (213) 957-2327
Thomas, Fred 2128 NW 197th Street, Shoreline, WA 98177 . . . . (206) 546-5249
Thompson, Bryon 6132 Billingham Lane, Ft. Wayne, IN 46835 . . . . (219) 486-5941
Represented By: Lori Nowicki & Associates . . . . (212) 243-5888
Thompson, Darren Represented By: Steven Kenny . . . . (800) 789-9389
Thompson, Del & Dana 108 Montis Drive, Greenville, SC 29609 . . . . (803) 246-6407
Thompson, Emily 433 W 43rd Street #3E, New York, NY 10036 . . . . (212) 245-2543
Thompson, George 433 W 43rd Street #3E, New York, NY 10036 . . . . (212) 245-2543
Thompson, John 206 Haddonfield Drive, Dewitt, NY 13214 . . . . (315) 449-1241
Thompson, M. Kathryn 333 Cascade Drive, Fairfax, CA 94930 . . . . (415) 459-8835
Thompson, Margot 62 Pearson Avenue, Toronto, ON Canada M6R 1G1 . . . . (416) 537-1887
Thompson, Marina 31 Willow Road, Nahant, MA 01908 . . . . (781) 581-1725
Thompson, Stephen Represented By: Ceci Bartels Associates . . . . (314) 781-7377
Thompson, Thierry 212 Dorchester Lane, Alamo, CA 94507 . . . . (510) 210-0155 • (800) 643-0029
Represented By: Mendola Ltd. . . . . (212) 986-5680
Thompson Bros. 331 W Stone Avenue, Greenville, SC 29609 . . . . (864) 241-0810
Thomssen, Kate 1336 Scheffer Avenue, St. Paul, MN 55116 . . . . (612) 698-9129
Represented By: Alexander/Pollard, Inc. . . . . (800) 347-0734
Thoner, Dan 3485 Copley Avenue, San Diego, CA 92116 . . . . (619) 282-0031
Thorborg, Lisa Represented By: Beth O'Neill Artists Rep . . . . (716) 473-0384

THORNBURGH, BETHANN Pages 86-87,108
Represented By: Lindgren & Smith **(212) 397-7330**
e-mail: inquiry@lindgrensmith.com • Website: www.lindgrensmith.com
Specialties: Acrylic; Black & White; Pen & Ink; Water Color; Whimsical

Thornburgh, Rebecca Represented By: Publishers' Graphics . . . . (203) 797-8188
Thornley, Blair 1251 University Avenue, San Diego, CA 92103 . . . . (619) 299-3874
Thornton, Blake 126 Main Street S #B7, Hailey, ID 83333 . . . . (208) 788-1434
Represented By: Rita Marie & Friends . . . . (312) 222-0337
Thornton, Jeremy Represented By: Betsy Hillman . . . . (415) 381-4728
Thorpe, Jim Represented By: Image Mill. . . . . (515) 490-6110

Thrun, Thomas 8 Courtney Drive, Flanders, NJ 07836 . . . . . (973) 927-7316
Thurston, Russell 17-B Caminito de Pinon, Santa Fe, NM 87505 . . . . . (505) 466-1168
Tiani, Alex 9401 Ivy Ridge Place, Charlotte, NC 28269 . . . . . (704) 599-0414
Represented By: Daniele Collignon . . . . . (212) 243-4209
Tibbles, Jean-Paul Represented By: Bernstein & Andriulli, Inc. . . . . . (212) 682-1490
Tieber, Simone 161 Hudson Street, 5th Flr., New York, NY 10013 . . . . . (212) 925-9119
Tierney, Tom Represented By: Evelyne Johnson Associates. . . . . . (212) 532-0928

TILLEY, DEBBIE
608 S Grape Street, Escondido, CA 92025 • Fax (760) 738-8019
Represented By: Salzman International
Specialty: Humour
Page 293
(760) 432-6282
(415) 285-8267

Tillinghast, David 1003 Diamond Avenue, Ste. 200, South Pasadena, CA 91030. . . . . . (626) 403-0991
Timmes, Patrick 5 Oakmere Drive, Baldwin, NY 11510. . . . . . (516) 377-8907
Timmons, Bonnie Represented By: Joanne Palulian . . . . . (212) 581-8338
Tinkelman, Murray 75 Lakeview Avenue W, Peekskill, NY 10566-6430 . . . . . (914) 737-5960
Tirolese, Ana 268 Grosvenor Street, London, ON Canada N6A 4V2. . . . . . (519) 646-6170
Titleman, Lynn Represented By: Cornell & McCarthy, LLC. . . . . . (203) 454-4210
Tjandra, Kristin 23-17 26th Street, Astoria, NY 11105 . . . . . (718) 726-7990
To, Bonnie Represented By: Allen Spiegel & Associates . . . . . (408) 372-4672
Tobert, Willie Represented By: Ken Barboza . . . . . (212) 505-8635
Tobin, Nancy Represented By: Square Moon. . . . . . (510) 253-9451
Tocchet, Mark J. 225 Weldy Avenue, Oreland, PA 19075 . . . . . (215) 885-1292
Todd, Mark 123 Prospect Place #1, Brooklyn, NY 11217 . . . . . (718) 783-1488
Todd, Susan Represented By: Three in a Box. . . . . . (416) 367-2446
Toelke, Cathleen P.O. Box 487, Rhinebeck, NY 12572 . . . . . (914) 876-8776
Tolagson, Jamie Represented By: Allen Spiegel & Associates . . . . . (408) 372-4672
Tolonen, Susan Represented By: Nachreiner Boie Art Factory . . . . . (414) 785-1940
Tomek, Tom G. 943 N Winchester Avenue, Chicago, IL 60622 . . . . . (773) 227-7845
Tomlinson, Richard 319 E 24th Street, New York, NY 10010 . . . . . (212) 685-0552
Tomonari, Itsuko Represented By: Carol Bancroft & Friends . . . . . (203) 748-4823
Toomer, George 3923 Cole Avenue, Dallas, TX 75204 . . . . . (214) 522-1171
Represented By: Those 3 Reps . . . . . (214) 871-1316
Torline, Kevin Represented By: Berendsen & Associates . . . . . (513) 861-1400
Tormey, Carlotta A. 819 Grosvenor Place, Oakland, CA 94610 . . . . . (510) 451-3423
Torp, Cynthia Represented By: Lindgren & Smith. . . . . . (212) 397-7330

TORREJON, MONICA
Toronto, ON Canada
Toronto, ON Canada
e-mail: alterna@istar.ca • Website: www.home.istar.ca/~alterna • Specialties: Editorial; People
Page 210
(416) 878-6225
(416) 922-6662

Torres, Carlos 60 Hagen Avenue, North Tonawanda, NY 14120. . . . . . (716) 695-9440
Represented By: Shannon Associates . . . . . (212) 831-5650

TORRES, DANIEL
Represented By: Alan Lynch Artists
Pages 368-369
(908) 813-8718

Tosch, Jaime 8732 Fair Oaks Boulevard, Carmichael, CA 95608 . . . . . (916) 944-2097

TOWNER, BOB
Represented By: Famous Frames
e-mail: info@famousframes.com • Website: www.famousframes.com • Specialties: Animation; Storyboards
Page 277
(310) 642-2721

Towns, Krista Braukmann 6N 777 Palomino Drive, St. Charles, IL 60175 . . . . . (630) 513-9525

TOYAMA, KEN
Represented By: Wiley Group
e-mail: dww@wco.com • Website: www.dwrepresents.com • Specialty: Digital
Page 121
(415) 442-1822

TP Design 7007 Eagle Watch Court, Stone Mountain, GA 30087 . . . . . (770) 413-8276
Trachok, Cathy 2928 San Antonio Drive, Walnut Creek, CA 94598 . . . . . (510) 933-6619
Travers, Jana Represented By: Creative Connection . . . . . (410) 360-5981
Travis, Janet 2531 B McKinney Avenue, Dallas, TX 75201 . . . . . (214) 871-6064

Traynor, Elizabeth 702 Nottingham Road, Wilmington, DE 19805 .... (302) 658-6637
Treadway, Todd Represented By: Leyden Diversified .... (215) 663-0587
Represented By: Image Mill .... (515) 490-6110
Treatner, Meryl 2 Daisy Lane, Maple Glen, PA 19002 .... (215) 540-9993
Tremlett, Mark Represented By: Tonal Values .... (214) 943-2569
Tripson, Elizabeth Represented By: Carol Bancroft & Friends .... (203) 748-4823
Trojanowski, Dorothy 237 E 33rd Street #3A, New York, NY 10016 .... (212) 679-5442
Troller, Michael 201 Gates Street, San Francisco, CA 94110 .... (415) 206-0605
Trudlaw, Dick 6404 W 125th Street, Overland Park, KS 66209 .... (913) 338-4224

TRUEMAN, MATTHEW Page 325
Represented By: Michele Manasse **(215) 862-2091**
e-mail: mmanasse@new-work.com • Website: www.voicenet.com/~mmanasse • Specialties: Black & White; Children; Conceptual; Editorial; Greeting Cards; Medical; People; Portraiture; Poster; Water Color

TrueOrder Architecture+Design Represented By: Marla Matson Represents .... (602) 252-5072
Truman, Sue 226 Havelock Street, Toronto, ON Canada M6H 3B9 .... (416) 531-2656
Trusilo, Jim Represented By: Cliff Knecht .... (412) 761-5666
Tsemach, Shaul Represented By: Aurelia Papitto .... (617) 742-3108
Tsuchiya, Julie 423 Washington Street, San Francisco, CA 94111 .... (415) 986-5365
Tucci, Dominick 26 Tremont Place, Nutley, NJ 07110 .... (973) 284-0755
Tucker, Ezra Represented By: France Aline Associates .... (213) 933-2500
Represented By: Richard Solomon .... (212) 683-1362
Tucker, Greg 1915 Lakeview Road SW, Albuquerque, NM 87105 .... (505) 873-3727
Represented By: Carol Chislovsky Design, Inc. .... (212) 677-9100
Tull, Bobbi 6103 Beachway Drive, Falls Church, VA 22041 .... (703) 998-9292
Tunnell, Eric Represented By: Donna Rosen Artists' Rep .... (301) 384-8925
Tunstull, Glenn Represented By: Buck & Kane .... (212) 631-0009
Turchyn, Sandy Represented By: American Artists .... (212) 682-2462
Turgeon, Jim 403 N Wabash Avenue, Chicago, IL 60611 .... (312) 781-9512

TURGEON, POL Pages 86-87,98
Represented By: Lindgren & Smith **(212) 397-7330**
e-mail: inquiry@lindgrensmith.com • Website: www.lindgrensmith.com • Specialties: Advertising; Animation; Collage; Conceptual; Corporate; Editorial; Graphic Design/Illustration; Greeting Cards; Mixed Media; Poster

Turk, Natasha 3827 E Indian School Road #18, Phoenix, AZ 85018 .... (602) 954-8116
Turk, Steve 927 Westbourne Drive, Los Angeles, CA 90069 .... (310) 788-0682
Turner, Dona Represented By: Betsy Hillman .... (415) 381-4728
Turner, Patrick Represented By: Jaz & Jaz .... (206) 633-3445
Turner, Ray Represented By: Corey Graham Represents .... (415) 956-4750
Tusa, Tricia 619 Asbury, Houston, TX 77007 .... (713) 864-8864
Tusan, Stan Represented By: Square Moon .... (510) 253-9451
Tuschman, Richard Represented By: Jacqueline Dedell, Inc. .... (212) 741-2539
Tuttle, Jean 145 Palisade Street, Ste. 406, Dobbs Ferry, NY 10522 .... (914) 693-7681
Twinem, Neecy Represented By: Melissa Turk & The Artist Network .... (914) 368-8606

TYLDEN-WRIGHT, JENNY Pages 368-369
Represented By: Alan Lynch Artists **(908) 813-8718**
Represented By: Arena **44 171 267 9661**

Ueland, John 1281 Riesling Circle, Livermore, CA 94550 .... (510) 449-9169

UHL STUDIOS, DAVID Pages 208-209
1261 Delaware Street, Denver, CO 80204 • Fax (303) 534-2056 **(303) 534-2054**
e-mail: daviduhl@sni.net

Ulrich, George Represented By: HK Portfolio .... (212) 675-5719
Ulriksen, Mark 841 Shrader Street, San Francisco, CA 94117 .... (415) 387-0170
Ulve, Kirsten Represented By: Holly Hahn Artist Rep (H2 + Co.) .... (312) 633-0500
Unger, Elaine 23650 Via Beguine, Valencia, CA 91355 .... (805) 259-2174
Unger, Judy Represented By: Barb Hauser .... (415) 647-5660
Represented By: Penny & Stermer Group .... (212) 505-9342
Represented By: Langley & Associates .... (847) 670-0912
Unruh, Jack 2706 Fairmount, Dallas, TX 75201 .... (214) 871-0187

Represented By: Susan Wells & Associates . . . . (404) 255-1430
Uram, Lauren Represented By: Richard Solomon . . . . (212) 683-1362

URBANOVIC, JACKIE Page 85
420 N Fifth Street, Ste. 950, Minneapolis, MN 55401 • Fax (612) 333-4823 **(612) 673-9323**
Website: www.maggieinc.com • Specialties: Advertising; Children; Humour; Public Relations

Urquijo, Clara Represented By: Carol Bancroft & Friends . . . . (203) 748-4823
Ursino, John 8 New Street, North Reading, MA 01864 . . . . (978) 664-1365
Utley, Tom Represented By: Woody Coleman Presents, Inc. . . . . (216) 661-4222
Uyehara, Elizabeth Represented By: Lisa Freeman . . . . (317) 920-0068
Vaccarello, Paul Represented By: Tom Maloney . . . . (312) 704-0500
Vaccaro, Lou Represented By: Creative Freelancers . . . . (800) 398-9544
Vaccaro, Victor 6 Sunny Drive, Bellport, NY 11713 . . . . (516) 286-6266
Vahrameev, Vadim 570 26th Avenue #3, San Francisco, CA 94121 . . . . (415) 751-5471
Vainisi, Jenny Represented By: Ann Koeffler Represents . . . . (213) 957-2327
Valencia, Carlos 353 Palmerston Boulevard, Toronto, ON Canada M6G 2N5 . . . . (416) 963-9070
Valenti, Lisa 964 Pelhamdale Avenue, Pelham, NY 10803 . . . . (914) 738-1995
Valko, Diane 235 S Beach Boulevard #93, Anaheim, CA 92804 . . . . (714) 826-3440
Vallejo, Boris Represented By: Joel Harlib Associates, Inc. . . . . (312) 573-1370
Valley, Gregg 144 Jonathan Drive, McMurray, PA 15317 . . . . (724) 941-4662
Represented By: Lori Nowicki & Associates . . . . (212) 243-5888
Van Eck, Guus Represented By: Tonal Values . . . . (214) 943-2569

VAN ES, CHRIS Pages 252-253
Represented By: Deborah Wolfe **(215) 232-6666**
Website: www.deborahwolfeltd.com
Specialties: Advertising; Black & White; Collage; Conceptual; Editorial; Mixed Media; People

Van Horn, Michael RD 2 Box 442, Red Hook, NY 12571 . . . . (914) 758-8407
Van Kampen, Vlasta 206 Glenview Avenue, Toronto, ON Canada M4R 1R3 . . . . (416) 483-2678
Van Leeuwen, Terrel 14257 Edson Road, Poplar Grove, IL 61065 . . . . (815) 765-3834
Van Meter, Sam Represented By: Image Mill . . . . (515) 490-6110
Van Rynbach, Iris Represented By: Evelyne Johnson Associates . . . . (212) 532-0928
Van Ryzin, Peter Represented By: Hankins & Tegenborg Ltd. . . . . (212) 867-8092
Van Valkenburgh, Sherilyn 102 Sidney Green Street, Chapel Hill, NC 27516 . . . . (919) 968-1496
Van Vort, Don 19823 Gulf Boulevard, Indian Shores, FL 33785 . . . . (813) 595-6211
Vanacore, Clare Glen Ellen, CA 95442 . . . . (707) 996-2688
New York, NY 10019 . . . . (212) 245-3632
Vance, Steve Represented By: Martha Productions . . . . (310) 390-8663
Vander Houwen, Greg P.O. Box 498, Issaquah, WA 98027 . . . . (206) 999-2584
Vanderbos, Joe 15840 Vanderbos, Guerneville, CA 95446 . . . . (707) 869-1414
Vanderdasson, Bill Represented By: Claudia Miller Artists Unlimited . . . . (561) 995-9444
Vangsgard, Amy 517 N Beachwood Drive, Los Angeles, CA 90004 . . . . (213) 461-3094
Vann Studio, Bill 1706 S Eighth Street, St. Louis, MO 63104 . . . . (314) 231-2322
Varah, Monte Represented By: Mary Holland & Company . . . . (602) 263-8990
Vargo, Kurt Represented By: David Goldman Agency . . . . (212) 807-6627
Vasconcellos, Daniel 225 Old Washington Street, Pembroke, MA 02359 . . . . (781) 829-8815
Vasquez, Madeline 3627 Niblick Drive, La Mesa, CA 91941 . . . . (619) 465-8683

VASS, ROD Pages 168,196
Represented By: American Artists **(212) 682-2462**
e-mail: info@amerartists.com • Website: www.amerartists.com

Vaughan, Thomas 5 Birch Terrace, West Lebanon, NH 03784 . . . . (603) 298-5330
Vaughn, Derrick 514 Kenyon Street NW, Washington, DC 20010 . . . . (202) 829-6229
Veach, Steven 657 20th Street, San Diego, CA 92102 . . . . (619) 238-4537
Vecchio, Riccardo 1 Christopher Street, Apt. 12G, New York, NY 10014 . . . . (212) 647-9390
Villaggio Dei Pini, 34, Usmate, MI Italy 20040 . . . . 39 39 67 30 89
Vega Design, Paul 1215 18th Street, Sacramento, CA 95814 . . . . (916) 441-1330
Velasco, Jerry Represented By: Lisa Freeman . . . . (317) 920-0068
Vellekoop, Maurice Represented By: Reactor Art & Design Ltd. . . . . (416) 703-1913

VENO, JOE Pages 131,428,440
Represented By: Lori Nowicki & Associates **(212) 243-5888**
e-mail: joe@lorinowicki.com • Website: www.lorinowicki.com
Specialties: Advertising; Conceptual; Corporate; Editorial

Ventura, Andrea Represented By: Richard Solomon . . . . . (212) 683-1362
Ventura, Marco Represented By: Sally Heflin. . . . . (212) 366-1893
Verdaguer, Raymond Represented By: Richard Solomon . . . . . (212) 683-1362
Verkaaik, Ben Represented By: Frank & Jeff Lavaty . . . . . (212) 427-5632
Verman, Marcia G. Represented By: Buck & Kane . . . . . (212) 631-0009
Verzaal, Dale C. Represented By: The Williams Group . . . . . (404) 873-2287
Vibbert, Carolyn 3911 Bagley Avenue N, Seattle, WA 98103 . . . . . (206) 634-3473
Victor, Ron Represented By: Buck & Kane. . . . . (212) 631-0009
Vilchez, Armando 829 S 7th, La Grange, IL 60525 . . . . . (708) 352-4264
Villa, Roxana P.O. Box 260485, Encino, CA 91426 . . . . . (818) 906-3355
Villani, Ron Represented By: Joel Harlib Associates, Inc. . . . . . (312) 573-1370
Villerreal, Bill Represented By: Claudia Miller Artists Unlimited . . . . . (561) 995-9444
Vincent, Wayne Represented By: Mendola Ltd. . . . . . (212) 986-5680
Vismara, Paul Chicago, IL 60657 . . . . . (888) 847-6272
Visual Logic 722 Yorklyn Road, Ste. 150, Hockessin, DE 19707 . . . . . (302) 234-5707

VITALE, STEFANO Pages 86-87,94
Represented By: Lindgren & Smith **(212) 397-7330**
e-mail: inquiry@lindgrensmith.com • Website: www.lindgrensmith.com

Vitali, Dominique Represented By: Kate Larkworthy Artist Rep. Ltd. . . . . . (212) 633-1310
Viva, Frank 1216 Yonge Street #203, Toronto, ON Canada M4T 1W1 . . . . . (416) 923-6355
Vivarelli, Annalisa Represented By: The Arts Counsel . . . . . (212) 777-6777
Viviano, Sam 25 W 13th Street, New York, NY 10011-7955 . . . . . (212) 242-1471

VIVIT, JERRY Page 277
Represented By: Famous Frames **(310) 642-2721**
e-mail: info@famousframes.com • Website: www.famousframes.com • Specialties: Animation; Storyboards

Vollman, Bryan 2320 W Fourth Street, Duluth, MN 55806 . . . . . (218) 722-9491
Voltz, Ralph 1101 Westchester Boulevard, Charlotte, NC 28205. . . . . (704) 566-8283
Von Buhler, Cynthia 16 Ashford Street, Boston, MA 02134. . . . . (617) 783-2421
Represented By: Maslov/Weinberg . . . . . (415) 641-1285
Von Hagen, Arden 6430 Charlotte Pike, Nashville, TN 37209 . . . . . (615) 352-1700
Von Ulrich, Mark 920 Broadway, Ste. 402, New York, NY 10010 . . . . . (212) 995-8781

VOO, RHONDA Pages 168,200
Represented By: American Artists **(212) 682-2462**
e-mail: info@amerartists.com • Website: www.amerartists.com
Specialties: Advertising; Children; Collage; Fantasy; Food; Graphic Design/Illustration; Greeting Cards; Humour; Icons; Product

Voo Doo Airbrushing 717 Finley Avenue, Units 9/10, Ajax, ON Canada L1S 3T1 . . . . . (905) 686-7554
Voo Doo Arts 20 Marie-Anne W, 3e, Montreal, PQ Canada H2W 1B5. . . . . (514) 982-6022
Vorobik, Linda Represented By: Melissa Turk & The Artist Network . . . . . (914) 368-8606
Voth, Greg 67 Eighth Avenue #40, New York, NY 10014 . . . . . (212) 807-9766
Voth, Pam 372 Bleecker Street, New York, NY 10014 . . . . . (212) 243-9003
Vye, Mike 308 Prince Street #414, St. Paul, MN 55101 . . . . . (612) 290-2587
Wack, Jeff 3614 Berry Drive, Studio City, CA 91604 . . . . . (818) 508-0348
Represented By: Mendola Ltd.. . . . . (212) 986-5680
Wagner, Brett 1085 Hickory View Circle, Camarillo, CA 93012 . . . . . (805) 987-1123
Wagner, Marijke Paquay 1085 Hickory View Circle, Camarillo, CA 93012 . . . . . (805) 987-1123

WAGNER, MARK Page 277
Represented By: Famous Frames **(310) 642-2721**
e-mail: info@famousframes.com • Website: www.famousframes.com • Specialties: Animation; Storyboards

Wagner, Stephen 110 Menefee Mountain Lane, Washington, VA 22747 . . . . . (703) 675-3046

WAGT, ROBERT Page 109
Represented By: Lindgren & Smith **(212) 397-7330**
e-mail: inquiry@lindgrensmith.com • Website: www.lindgrensmith.com

Wainscott, Jim Represented By: Air Studio .... (513) 721-1193
Waldman, Bruce 18 Westbrook Road, Westfield, NJ 07090 .... (908) 232-2840
Waldman, Neil 54 Rockingchair Road, White Plains, NY 10607 .... (914) 949-5257

WALDREP, RICHARD L. Pages 252-253
Represented By: Deborah Wolfe **(215) 232-6666**
Represented By: Donna Rosen Artists' Rep **(301) 384-8925**
Website: www.deborahwolfeltd.com • aaarrt.com/donnasgallery
Specialties: Advertising; Children; Conceptual; Editorial; Mixed Media; People; Portraiture; Sports

Waldron, Sarah M. 24 Western Avenue, Ste. 1, Petaluma, CA 94952 .... (707) 778-0848
Walker, Jason Represented By: Sharpshooter Creative Rep Inc. .... (416) 703-5300
Walker, Jeff Represented By: Hankins & Tegenborg Ltd. .... (212) 867-8092
Walker, John 4423 Wilson Avenue, Downers Grove, IL 60515 .... (603) 963-8359
Represented By: Frank Lux & Associates, Inc. .... (312) 222-1361
Walker, Lawrence 1740 W 120th Street, Apt. C, Los Angeles, CA 90047 .... (213) 777-5526
Walker, Mark 3840 Arroyo Road, Ft. Worth, TX 76109 .... (817) 920-9430
Walker, Rory 16 Gathorne Road, Headington, Oxford, England OX3 8NF 44 186 576 1875
Walker, Russell Represented By: Bernstein & Andriulli, Inc. .... (212) 682-1490
Walker, Sylvia Represented By: Evelyne Johnson Associates .... (212) 532-0928
Walker, Tracy Represented By: Scott Hull Associates .... (937) 433-8383
Wallace, Janet P.O. Box 6495, Malibu, CA 90264 .... (310) 589-9622
Wallace, John Represented By: HK Portfolio .... (212) 675-5719

WALLACE, LAURA Page 239
Represented By: Sharpshooter Creative Representation, Inc. **(416) 703-5300**
e-mail: shooter@the-wire.com • Website: www.portfolios.com/illustrators • Specialties: Advertising; Black & White; Communications; Computer; Conceptual; Corporate; Editorial; Humour; People; Public Relations

Wallace, Nina Represented By: Philip M. Veloric Associates .... (610) 520-3470
Wallace, Sean Represented By: Air Studio .... (513) 721-1193
Wallis, Rebecca Cordowr, 5 Nancevallon, Cornwall, England TR14 9DE 44 120 971 4849
Walton, Brenda Represented By: Suzanne Craig Represents, Inc. .... (918) 749-9424
Walton, Matt Represented By: Ravenhill Represents .... (816) 333-0744
Wanagat, Carol Represented By: Peter Kuehnel & Associates .... (312) 642-6499
Wanta, Theresa 433 Holly Avenue, St. Paul, MN 55102 .... (612) 298-9636
Ward, John Represented By: Bobbi Wendt/Parallel Universe .... (415) 487-2160
Ward, Keith Represented By: Yolanda Burnett Represents .... (770) 967-0039
Represented By: Langley & Associates .... (847) 670-0912
Ward, Sam 6829 Murray Lane, Annandale, VA 22003 .... (703) 256-8313

WARD, TOM Pages 146-147
Represented By: Carol Guenzi Agents, Inc. **(800) 417-5120**
e-mail: artagent@artagent.com • Website: www.artagent.com • Specialty: Digital

Ware, Richard 339 First Avenue, Ste. 2F, New York, NY 10003-2917 .... (212) 673-9102
Wariner, David Represented By: Kerry Reilly Reps .... (704) 372-6007
Warner Illustration & Design, Linda 28 Sherman Drive, Hilton Head, SC 29928 .... (843) 689-5044
Warnick, Elsa 636 NW 20th Avenue #7, Portland, OR 97209 .... (503) 228-2659
Warren, Amanda Represented By: Harriet Kastaris & Associates .... (314) 773-2600
Warren, Dave Represented By: Berendsen & Associates .... (513) 861-1400
Warren, Jim Represented By: Alan Lynch Artists .... (908) 813-8718
Warren, Kirk 617 Silverstone Avenue, Winnepeg, MB Canada R3T 2V6 .... (204) 261-7404
Represented By: Rita Gatlin Represents .... (800) 924-7881
Warrick, Roger Represented By: Berendsen & Associates .... (513) 861-1400
Warshaw, Jerry 800 Hinman Avenue, Ste. 708, Evanston, IL 60202-2325 .... (847) 866-6667
Washburn, Lucia Represented By: Publishers' Graphics .... (203) 797-8188
Washington, Sharon Represented By: Mark Sherrah .... (416) 972-6161
Wasson, Cameron 1118 Sir Francis Drake Blvd., Kentfield, CA 94904 .... (415) 455-8874
Represented By: Liz Sanders Agency .... (714) 495-3664
Waters, Susy Pilgrim Represented By: Lilla Rogers Studio .... (781) 641-2787

Watford, Wayne Represented By: Martha Productions . . . . . (310) 390-8663
Watkins, Leslie 25 Grove Street #3, New York, NY 10014 . . . . . (212) 989-2616
Watkins, Liselotte Represented By: The Arts Counsel . . . . . (212) 777-6777
Watkinson, Brent 6849 Mastin, Merriam, KS 66203 . . . . . (913) 677-0062
Represented By: Hedge Graphics . . . . . (818) 244-0110
Watling, James Represented By: Publishers' Graphics . . . . . (203) 797-8188
Watson, Esther 123 Prospect Place, Apt. 1, Brooklyn, NY 11217 . . . . . (718) 783-1488
Watson, Paul Represented By: Three in a Box . . . . . (416) 367-2446
Watson, Richard Jesse 2305 Ivy Street, Port Townsend, WA 98368-6825 . . . . . (360) 385-9777

WATTS, STAN Pages 168,204
Represented By: American Artists **(212) 682-2462**
e-mail: info@amerartists.com • Website: www.amerartists.com • Specialty: Illustrative

Wawiorka, Matt Represented By: Lisa Freeman . . . . . (317) 920-0068

WEAKLEY, MARK Pages 216-217,452,463
105 N Alamo, Rm. 602, San Antonio, TX 78205 • Fax (210) 222-0283 **(210) 222-9543**
Represented By: Alexander/Pollard, Inc. **(800) 347-0734**
Specialties: Advertising; Black & White; Food; Icons; People; Portraiture; Product; Realism; Scratchboard; Stock

Webb, David 2100 Morris Avenue, Birmingham, AL 35203 . . . . . (205) 252-9998
Webb, Quentin Represented By: Creative Freelancers . . . . . (800) 398-9544
Webb, Tim Represented By: Lori Nowicki & Associates . . . . . (212) 243-5888

WEBER, MARK Pages 338-339
113 E 29th Street, Erie, PA 16504 • Fax (814) 453-2050 **(814) 453-2050**
Represented By: The Roland Group **(301) 718-7955**
Website: www.therolandgroup.com • Specialties: Conceptual; Editorial; Lettering; Mixed Media

WEEKS, BRENDA Pages 36,440,444,447,461
35 Jane Street, Ste. 5, Toronto, ON Canada M6S 3Y3 • Fax (416) 766-9315 **(416) 766-2942**
Specialties: Advertising; Book Jackets; Children; Editorial; Food; Greeting Cards; Mixed Media; Oil; Product; Still Life; 3D

Wehler, Lisa Represented By: Creative Connection . . . . . (410) 360-5981
Wehrman, Richard 247 N Goodman Street, Rochester, NY 14607 . . . . . (716) 271-2280
Wehrman, Vicki P.O. Box 146, East Bloomfield, NY 14443 . . . . . (716) 657-7910
Wehrstein, David Represented By: Frank Lux & Associates, Inc. . . . . . (312) 222-1361
Weidner, Bea 621 St. George's Road, Philadelphia, PA 19119 . . . . . (215) 753-1915
Weidner, Teri Represented By: Publishers' Graphics . . . . . (203) 797-8188
Weil, Cindy Represented By: David Montagano & Associates . . . . . (312) 527-3283
Weiner, Paul 14 Cypress Street #2, Brookline, MA 02146 . . . . . (617) 738-0446

WEINMAN, BRAD Pages 266,460
5268 Lindley Avenue, Encino, CA 91316 • Fax (818) 342-9985 **(818) 342-9984**
Represented By: Christine Prapas **(503) 658-7070**
e-mail: brado@linkonline.net • Specialties: Advertising; Book Jackets; Celebrity; Corporate; Editorial; Fantasy; People; Portraiture; Wildlife

Weinstein, Ellen 1 Union Square W #512, New York, NY 10003 . . . . . (212) 675-4360
Weinstein, Morey 807 Larkwood Drive, Greensboro, NC 27410 . . . . . (336) 854-5161
Weisbecker, Philippe Represented By: Riley Illustration . . . . . (212) 989-8770
Weisberg, Glen 140 West End Avenue, Apt. 2G, New York, NY 10023 . . . . . (212) 724-1872
Weisberg, Pamela 2588 El Camino Real #349, Carlsbad, CA 92008 . . . . . (760) 720-5328
Weiss, Charles 39 Seal Cove Drive, Toronto, ON Canada M9C 2C7 . . . . . (416) 534-4456
Weissman, Bari Represented By: Publishers' Graphics . . . . . (203) 797-8188
Weller, Don Represented By: Daniele Collignon . . . . . (212) 243-4209
Weller, Linda Represented By: Carol Bancroft & Friends . . . . . (203) 748-4823
Welles Design Core, Toby Represented By: Shannon Associates . . . . . (212) 831-5650
Welliver, Norma Represented By: Claudia Miller Artists Unlimited . . . . . (561) 995-9444
Wells, Leigh 250 W 22nd Street #4D, New York, NY 10011 . . . . . (212) 627-8518
Wells, Peter Represented By: Wilson-Zumbo Illustration . . . . . (414) 271-3388

WELLS, STEPHEN Pages 216,222,466,468
14027 Memorial Drive #125, Houston, TX 77079 • Fax (281) 579-3220 **(281) 579-3220**
Represented By: Alexander/Pollard, Inc. **(800) 347-0734**
Represented By: Karen Wells Represents **(800) 778-9076**
Specialties: Advertising; Editorial; Painterly; People; Portraiture; Realism; Sports; Still Life; Water Color; Wildlife

WELSH, PATRICK J. Page 84
59 Bryant Road, Turnersville, NJ 08012 • Fax (609) 232-6050 **(609) 232-3130**
e-mail: welshdesign@p3.net • Specialties: Advertising; Caricature; Cartoon; Children; Digital; Editorial; Graphic Design/Illustration; Icons; Mixed Media; People

Wend Art, Dan 4300 Sunset Boulevard NE #J5, Renton, WA 98059 .... (206) 430-1025
Wenngren, Anders Represented By: Art Department .... (212) 925-4222
Wepplo, Michael Represented By: Das Grup .... (310) 540-5958
Werblun, Steve Represented By: Famous Frames .... (310) 642-2721
Werner, Honi 132 Pacific Street, Brooklyn, NY 11201 .... (718) 237-2256

WERTZ, MICHAEL S. Page 11
385 1/2 Jersey Street, San Francisco, CA 94114 • Fax (415) 695-1839 **(415) 824-5542**
e-mail: michael@wertzateria.com • Website: www.wertzateria.com • Specialties: Advertising; Architecture/Interiors; Computer; Editorial; Greeting Cards; Icons; Lettering; Pastels; People; Portraiture

West Design, Jeffery 283 Pine Forest Drive, Aptos, CA 95003 .... (408) 688-6075

WESTBROOK, ERIC Pages 387,428,442,460,467
2325 42nd Street NW #419, Washington, DC 20007 • Fax (202) 328-8593 **(202) 328-8593**
Specialties: Advertising; Conceptual; Corporate; Editorial; People; Portraiture; Realism; Science; Sports; Still Life; Whimsical; Wildlife

Westerberg, Rob Represented By: Mendola Ltd. .... (212) 986-5680
Westmark, John Represented By: Jennifer Embler Represents, Inc. .... (954) 760-4195
Westphal, Ken 9208 Roe Avenue, Prairie Village, KS 66207 .... (913) 381-8399
Westwood, William 915 Broadway, Albany, NY 12207 .... (518) 432-5237
Wetmore, Barry 1003 Diamond Avenue, Ste. 207, South Pasadena, CA 91030 .... (626) 254-5438
Wexler, Ed 4701 Don Pio Drive, Woodland Hills, CA 91364 .... (818) 888-3858
Wharton, Jennifer Heyd 218 N Washington Street #1, Easton, MD 21601 .... (410) 770-9190

WHATLEY, JULIA Page 201
Represented By: American Artists **(212) 682-2462**
Represented By: Ian Flemming Associates
e-mail: info@amerartists.com • Website: www.amerartists.com

Wheaton Illustrations, Liz 16780 Dry Creek Court, Morgan Hill, CA 95037 .... (408) 776-1325
Wheeler, Rick P.O. Box 673, Moab, UT 84532 .... (435) 259-6204
Whelan, Michael 23 Old Hayrake Road, Danbury, CT 06811 .... (203) 792-8089
Whim Whams Illustration Studio 3314 Oberon Street, Kensington, MD 20895 .... (301) 933-4912
Whipple, Rick Represented By: The Art Source .... (817) 481-2212
White, B.P. 6913 Whitaker Avenue, Van Nuys, CA 91406 .... (818) 785-9363

WHITE, BRIAN Page 340
2108 Sul Ross, Houston, TX 77098 • Fax (713) 522-4220 **(713) 522-4220**
e-mail: brian@twinpix.com • Website: www.twinpix.com
Specialties: Children; Digital; Editorial; Humour

WHITE, CRAIG Page 340
161 Lower Terrace, San Francisco, CA 94114 • Fax (415) 522-1912 **(415) 522-1875**
e-mail: craig@twinpix.com • Website: www.twinpix.com
Specialties: Book Jackets; Collage; Digital; Editorial; Photoillustration

White, Eric 1142 Castro Street, San Francisco, CA 94114 .... (415) 821-3839
White, Jane 6245 E McDonald Drive, Paradise Valley, AZ 85253 .... (602) 905-2628
White, Jenny Represented By: Publishers' Graphics .... (203) 797-8188

WHITE, JOHN Pages 299,303,445
Represented By: The Neis Group **(616) 672-5756**
e-mail: neisgroup@wmis.net • Website: www.neisgroup.com • Specialty: Food

White, Keinyo Represented By: Publishers' Graphics . . . . . (203) 797-8188
White, Meg Represented By: Buck & Kane . . . . . (212) 631-0009
White Lie Design, Roger 160 West End Avenue #3K, New York, NY 10023 . . . . . (212) 362-1848
Whiteside Design Studio 1533 East Avenue #J3, Lancaster, CA 93535 . . . . . (805) 940-5953
Whitesides, Kim Represented By: Renard Represents . . . . . (212) 490-2450
Whiting, Jim 222 Country Haven Road, Encinitas, CA 92024 . . . . . (760) 944-4530
Whitney, Bill 116 W Illinois Street #5-W, Chicago, IL 60610 . . . . . (312) 527-2455
Whitney, Jack Represented By: Linda Ramin & Associates . . . . . (314) 781-8851
Whitney, Richard Studios at Crescent Pond, 100 Chalet Drive, Stoddard, NH 03464 . . . . . (603) 446-7476
Whitver, Harry 409 Brook Hollow Road, Nashville, TN 37205-3505 . . . . . (615) 352-2400

WICKART, MARK Page 337
6293 Surrey Ridge Road, Lisle, IL 60532 • Fax (630) 369-4004 **(630) 369-0164**
Specialties: Advertising; Airbrush; Cartoon; Fantasy; Food; Graphic Design/Illustration; Greeting Cards; Humour; Product; Still Life

WICKSTROM, SHARI Page 277
Represented By: Famous Frames **(310) 642-2721**
e-mail: info@famousframes.com • Website: www.famousframes.com • Specialties: Animation; Storyboards

WIDENER, TERRY Page 329
Represented By: Michele Manasse **(215) 862-2091**
e-mail: mmanasse@new-work.com • Website: www.voicenet.com/~mmanasse
Specialties: Advertising; Children; Conceptual; Corporate; Editorial; Greeting Cards; Murals; People; Poster; Sports

Wieland, Don Represented By: Mendola Ltd. . . . . . (212) 986-5680
Wiemann, Roy P.O. Box 271, New York, NY 10012 . . . . . (212) 431-3793
Represented By: Clare Jett & Associates . . . . . (502) 228-9427
Wiemer, Dan Represented By: Mason Illustration . . . . . (612) 729-1774
Wiener, Mark 164 E 37th Street, New York, NY 10016 . . . . . (212) 696-1792

WIENS, CARL Page 166
2255 B Queen Street E #1176, Toronto, ON Canada M4E 1G3 **(613) 476-2500**
e-mail: wiens@ican.net • Website: http://home.ican.net/~wiens
Specialties: Animation; Black & White; Cartoon; Comic; Corporate; Editorial; Icons; Websites

Wiggins, Bryan Represented By: Jennifer Embler Represents, Inc. . . . . . (954) 760-4195
Represented By: Carol Guenzi Agents, Inc. . . . . . (800) 417-5120
Wilburn, Kathy Represented By: Creative Connection . . . . . (410) 360-5981
Wilcox, David Represented By: The Newborn Group . . . . . (212) 260-6700
Wilgus, David P.O. Box 971, Davidson, NC 28036 . . . . . (704) 892-7738
Represented By: Bernstein & Andriulli, Inc. . . . . . (212) 682-1490
Wilkin, Charles Represented By: Kimberley Boege . . . . . (602) 265-4389
Wilkins, Sarah Represented By: Riley Illustration . . . . . (212) 989-8770

WILKINSON, COREY Pages 60-61,427,453,460,463
855 Joyce Avenue, Melrose Park, IL 60164 • Fax (708) 562-2512 **(708) 562-2512**
e-mail: csw@juno.com • Specialties: Celebrity; Conceptual; Icons; Portraiture; Scratchboard; Water Color

Will, David Represented By: Jeannie Will . . . . . (847) 755-1351
Willardson, Dave Represented By: Vicki Morgan Associates . . . . . (212) 475-0440
Willardson & Associates 103 W California Avenue, Glendale, CA 91203 . . . . . (818) 242-5688
Williams, Brad 99 Albury Way, North Brunswick, NJ 08902 . . . . . (732) 398-0129
Williams, Donald Represented By: Evelyne Johnson Associates . . . . . (212) 532-0928
Williams, Eric Represented By: Hankins & Tegenborg Ltd. . . . . . (212) 867-8092
Williams, Garry K. 7045 California Avenue, Hammond, IN 46323 . . . . . (219) 989-0350
Williams, Jim K. 436 Liberty Hill, Cincinnati, OH 45210 . . . . . (513) 241-0068
Williams, Karin Represented By: Creative Connection . . . . . (410) 360-5981
Williams, Kent 102 Sidney Green Street, Chapel Hill, NC 27516 . . . . . (919) 968-1496

Represented By: Allen Spiegel & Associates . . . . . (408) 372-4672
Williams, Kurt Alan Represented By: Air Studio . . . . . (513) 721-1193
Williams, Lorraine 36 Plaza Street E #4B, Brooklyn, NY 11238 . . . . . (718) 638-7203
Williams, Lucinda 88 Shipston Road, Stratford, Warwickshire, England CV37 7LR 44 178 929 4738
Williams, Nicholas 33 Chestnut Drive, Wanstead, London, England E11 2TA 44 181 923 4875
Williams, Oliver Represented By: Jerry Anton . . . . . (212) 633-9880
Williams, Renee 537 Stahr Road, Apt. 1, Elkins Park, PA 19027 . . . . . (215) 635-4142
Williams, Sam Represented By: HK Portfolio . . . . . (212) 675-5719

WILLIAMS, SUSAN NOVAK Pages 383,435,441,445,453
221 W Elmwood Place, Minneapolis, MN 55419 • Fax (612) 824-2896 **(612) 824-6103**
e-mail: raywilliams@worldnet.att.net • Specialties: Digital; Editorial; Food; Icons; People; Product

Williams, Toby 82 Fifers Lane, Boxboro, MA 01719 . . . . . (978) 263-8106
Willoughby Design Group 602 Westport Road, Kansas City, MO 64111 . . . . . (816) 561-4189
Willy, April G. Represented By: Harriet Kastaris & Associates . . . . . (314) 773-2600
Wilsbach, Mary Represented By: Leyden Diversified . . . . . (215) 663-0587
Wilson, Ann Represented By: Carol Bancroft & Friends . . . . . (203) 748-4823
Wilson, Janet 127 York Street, Eden Mills, ON Canada N0B 1P0 . . . . . (519) 856-2811
Wilson, Jim Represented By: Yolanda Burnett Represents . . . . . (770) 967-0039
Wilson, John A. 1907 Newton Street, Austin, TX 78704 . . . . . (512) 448-1615

WILSON, LEE Page 277
Represented By: Famous Frames **(310) 642-2721**
e-mail: info@famousframes.com • Website: www.famousframes.com • Specialties: Animation; Storyboards

Wilson, Lin P.O. Box 8572, Madison, WI 53708 . . . . . (608) 224-1910
Wilson, Phil Represented By: Cliff Knecht . . . . . (412) 761-5666
Wilson, Russ 2215 S Third Street #201-C, Jacksonville Beach, FL 32250 . . . . . (904) 249-0060
Wilson, Ty 7 Cornelia Street, Ste. 1B, New York, NY 10014 . . . . . (212) 627-5703
Wilton, Nicholas 330 Sir Francis Drake Blvd., Ste. 2C, San Anselmo, CA 94960 . . . . . (415) 488-4710

WILTSE, KRIS Pages 124-125
Represented By: Vicki Morgan Associates **(212) 475-0440**
e-mail: vmartrep@aol.com • Website: www.vickimorganassociates.com
Specialties: Black & White; Editorial; Fantasy; Food; Icons; People; Still Life; Wildlife; Woodcut

Wimmer, Mike Represented By: Mendola Ltd. . . . . . (212) 986-5680

WINBORG, LARRY Pages 252-253
Represented By: Deborah Wolfe **(215) 232-6666**
Website: www.deborahwolfeltd.com • Specialties: Advertising; Black & White; Children; Mixed Media; People; Portraiture; Sports; Stock; Water Color; Wildlife

Winger, Jody Represented By: Gretchen Harris & Associates . . . . . (612) 822-0650
Wingert, Theresa Represented By: Jorgensen & Barrett Reps . . . . . (206) 634-1880

WINK, DAVID Page 361
678 King Avenue, Marion, OH 43302 • Fax (740) 383-4040 **(740) 387-8267**
e-mail: davewink@on-ramp.net • Website: www.theispot.com • Specialties: Advertising; Conceptual

Winston, Jeannie 2549 Patricia Avenue, Los Angeles, CA 90064 . . . . . (310) 837-8666

WINTER, DAVE Page 334
54 W Hubbard #101, Chicago, IL 60610 • Fax (312) 527-3327 **(312) 527-3900**
Specialties: Advertising; Cartoon; Humour; Icons; Whimsical

Winter Digital Arts 240 E 90th Street #4B, New York, NY 10128 . . . . . (888) 831-0058

WINTERBOTTOM, JILL Page 277
Represented By: Famous Frames **(310) 642-2721**
e-mail: info@famousframes.com • Website: www.famousframes.com • Specialties: Animation; Storyboards

Winters, Greg 6722 Dume Drive, Malibu, CA 90265 . . . . . (310) 589-0456
Winters, Lorne 6131 Fullerton Crescent, Mississauga, ON Canada L5N 3A3 . . . . . (905) 824-4743

Winton, Mary Dahl P.O. Box 60487, Colorado Springs, CO 80960-0487 . . . . (719) 575-9230
Wiseman, Helen Pinkneys Manor, Wimbish, Essex, England CB10 2XD 44 179 959 9215

WISENBAUGH, JEAN Pages 86-87,457
Represented By: Lindgren & Smith **(212) 397-7330**
e-mail: inquiry@lindgrensmith.com • Website: www.lindgrensmith.com • Specialties: Digital; Maps & Charts

Wisniewski, Jim Represented By: Steve Edsey & Sons . . . . (312) 527-0351
Witmer, Keith Represented By: Anne Albrecht & Associates . . . . (312) 595-0300
Represented By: Sharon Dodge & Associates . . . . (206) 284-4701
Witus, Ted Represented By: Pat Hackett Artist Representative . . . . (206) 447-1600
Wohnoutka, Michael Represented By: Deborah Snyder Creative Representative . . . . (612) 922-3462

WOKSA, MARSHALL Page 248
Represented By: Dimension **(612) 884-4045**
e-mail: jkoltes@dimensioncreative.com • Website: www.dimensioncreative.com
Specialties: Advertising; Children; Conceptual; Editorial; Humour; People; Poster; Product; Sports

Wokuluk, Jon 1301 S Westgate Avenue, Los Angeles, CA 90025-1481 . . . . (310) 473-5623
Wolf, Elizabeth 3303 N Mountain Lane, Boise, ID 83702 . . . . (208) 387-0031
Wolf, Lee Edward 41 Belknap Street #3, Somerville, MA 02144 . . . . (617) 776-3523
Wolf, Paul Represented By: Clare Jett & Associates . . . . (502) 228-9427
Wolf-Hubbard, Marcie 1507 Ballard Street, Silver Spring, MD 20910 . . . . (301) 585-5815
Wolfe, Ashley 98 Cortland Avenue, San Francisco, CA 94110 . . . . (415) 826-7345
Wolfe, Bruce Represented By: Sweet Represents . . . . (415) 433-1222
Wolfe, Corey R. Represented By: Nancy George . . . . (805) 688-3772
Wolff, Punz 457 Herkimer Avenue, Haworth, NJ 07641 . . . . (201) 385-6028
Wolgemuth, Stephan Represented By: Mendola Ltd. . . . . (212) 986-5680
Wolk-Stanley, Jessica 590 Seventh Avenue, 3rd Flr., Brooklyn, NY 11215 . . . . (718) 965-2706
Wollman, Paul Represented By: Tania Kimche . . . . (212) 529-3556

WOLOSCHINOW, MICHAEL Pages 30-31
Represented By: Marlena Agency **(609) 252-9405**
e-mail: marzena@bellatlantic.net • Website: http://members.bellatlantic.net/~marzena
Specialties: Conceptual; Corporate; Editorial; Whimsical

Wolter, Ted 1243 W Sherri Drive, Gilbert, AZ 85234 . . . . (602) 545-9349
Wolynski, Wojciech Represented By: Mendola Ltd. . . . . (212) 986-5680
Wood, Judith Represented By: Sharon Morris Associates . . . . (415) 362-8280
Wood, Rob 17 Pinewood Street, Annapolis, MD 21401 . . . . (410) 266-6550
Wood, Tracey Represented By: Reactor Art & Design Ltd. . . . . (416) 703-1913
Woodman, Dave 750 Kings Road #224, Los Angeles, CA 90069 . . . . (213) 782-0116
Represented By: Elizabeth Poje . . . . (310) 556-1439
Woodman, Nancy Represented By: Square Moon . . . . (510) 253-9451
Woods, Noah 927 Westbourne Drive, Los Angeles, CA 90069 . . . . (310) 659-0259
Woods, Paul 414 Jackson Street, San Francisco, CA 94111 . . . . (415) 399-1984
Woods, Rosemary Represented By: Susan & Company . . . . (206) 232-7873
Represented By: Alan Lynch Artists . . . . (908) 813-8718
Woodward, Theresa Represented By: Ann Koeffler Represents . . . . (213) 957-2327
Woodworth, Viki Represented By: Evelyne Johnson Associates . . . . (212) 532-0928
Woolery, Lee Represented By: Berendsen & Associates . . . . (513) 861-1400
Woolf, Jeanette 1164 E 820, North Provo, UT 84606 . . . . (801) 377-3958
Woolf, Marie Ward 3601 Old Highway, Catheys Valley, CA 95306 . . . . (209) 966-3535

WOOLLEY, JANET Pages 366-367
Represented By: Alan Lynch Artists **(908) 813-8718**
Represented By: Arena **44 171 267 9661**

Worcester, Mary Represented By: Gretchen Harris & Associates . . . . (612) 822-0650
Worley, Zoe 2 Kirsten Place, Weston, CT 06883 . . . . (203) 222-9421
Worthington, Bruce 472 Cedar Park Drive SW, Calgary, AB Canada T2W 2J7. . . . . (403) 281-7295
Woska, Marshall Represented By: Dimension . . . . (612) 884-4045

WRAY, WENDY Pages 124-125
Represented By: Vicki Morgan Associates **(212) 475-0440**
e-mail: vmartrep@aol.com • Website: www.vickimorganassociates.com
Specialties: Black & White; Children; Medical; People; Product; Realism; Still Life; Technical

Wright, Erin Whittier 256 Archif Road, Jasper, GA 30143 . . . . (706) 692-3222
Wright, Ian Represented By: Heart 44 171 833 4447
Wright, Jane Chambless Represented By: Melissa Turk & The Artist Network . . . . (914) 368-8606

WRIGHT, JONATHAN Pages 168,179
Represented By: American Artists **(212) 682-2462**
e-mail: info@amerartists.com • Website: www.amerartists.com • Specialties: Technical; Water Color

Wright, Julie Represented By: Beth O'Neill Artists Rep. . . . . (716) 473-0384
Wright, Paul Represented By: Alan Lynch Artists . . . . (908) 813-8718
Wright, Ted Represented By: Ceci Bartels Associates . . . . (314) 781-7377
Wright Creative Group, Inc., Bob 247 N Goodman Street, Rochester, NY 14607 . . . . (716) 271-2280
Wrobel Design/Illustration, Cindy 415 Alta Dena Court, St. Louis, MO 63118 . . . . (314) 721-4467
Wu, Leslie 36 Harwood Lane, East Rochester, NY 14445 . . . . (716) 385-3722

WUMMER, AMY Pages 252-253
Represented By: Deborah Wolfe **(215) 232-6666**
Website: www.deborahwolfeltd.com • Specialties: Advertising; Black & White; Cartoon; Children; Greeting Cards; Humour; Mixed Media; People; Water Color; Whimsical

Wyatt, Carol 1835 Colina Drive, Glendale, CA 91208 . . . . (818) 240-8641
Xavier, Roger 23200 Los Codona Avenue, Torrance, CA 90505 . . . . (310) 373-7049
XPlane Corp. 809 Geyer Avenue, St. Louis, MO 63104 . . . . (314) 436-0505
Yaccarino, Dan 95 Horatio Street, Ste. 204, New York, NY 10014 . . . . (212) 675-5335
Yalowitz, Paul 3416 Baugh Drive, New Port Richey, FL 34655 . . . . (813) 372-9444
New York, NY . . . . (718) 857-9267
Yamashiro, Allen Represented By: Lehmen/Dabney, Inc. . . . . (206) 325-8595
Yamashita, Nob Represented By: Famous Frames . . . . (310) 642-2721
Yang, Eric 213 La France Avenue #F, Alhambra, CA 91801 . . . . (626) 284-4727
Yang, James Represented By: David Goldman Agency . . . . (212) 807-6627
Yang, Jung Kyu Represented By: Air Studio . . . . (513) 721-1193
Yanish, Mary 204 S Olive Avenue, Apt. 7, Alhambra, CA 91801 . . . . (626) 457-5143
Yankus, Marc 190 W 10th Street #3C, New York, NY 10014 . . . . (212) 242-6334
Yanson, John Michael 211 Eighth Street NE, Washington, DC 20002 . . . . (202) 546-0600
Yarnall, Nancy E. 8 Morris Street, Merchantville, NJ 08109 . . . . (609) 488-2292

YATES, MARK Page 277
Represented By: Famous Frames **(310) 642-2721**
e-mail: info@famousframes.com • Website: www.famousframes.com • Specialties: Animation; Storyboards

Yayo Represented By: Wanda Nowak . . . . (212) 535-0438
Ybarra, Frank Represented By: Marla Matson Represents . . . . (602) 252-5072
Yealdhall, Gary Represented By: American Artists . . . . (212) 682-2462

YEARINGTON, TIM Page 63
4709 Northwoods Drive, Box 811 RR3, Woodlawn, ON Canada K0A 3M0 • Fax (613) 832-0879 **(613) 832-0879**
Represented By: Imagination/Carmen Grenier **(613) 253-0063**
Represented By: Mary Holland & Company (U.S.) **(602) 263-8990**
e-mail: yearington@sympatico.ca • imagin@magi.com • Specialties: Acrylic; Advertising; Annual Report; Conceptual; Editorial; Environmental; Greeting Cards; Landscape; Nature; Realism

Yeasting, Nancy Represented By: Virginia Boggie & Associates . . . . (604) 943-6414
Yee, Josie 39 Walker Street, Apt. 3, New York, NY 10013 . . . . (212) 334-3907
Yemi Represented By: Creative Freelancers . . . . (800) 398-9544
Yeomans, Jeff Represented By: Lehmen/Dabney, Inc. . . . . (206) 325-8595
Yerkes, Lane 11471 Persimmon Court, Ft. Myers, FL 33913 . . . . (941) 561-1055
Yiannias, Vicki Represented By: Daniele Collignon . . . . (212) 243-4209
Yip, Filip Represented By: Lulu Creatives . . . . (612) 825-7564
Represented By: Freda Scott, Inc. . . . . (415) 398-9121

Yip, Jennie 1417 W Ninth Street, Brooklyn, NY 11204 . . . . . (718) 331-3350
Represented By: Mendola Ltd. . . . . . (212) 986-5680
Yoe Studio! 209 Chateau Rive, Peekskill, NY 10566 . . . . . (914) 734-4756
York, Jeff 1445 N State Parkway #1902, Chicago, IL 60610 . . . . . (312) 664-8849
York, Judy 500 E 83rd Street, Apt. 2L, New York, NY 10028 . . . . . (212) 988-1290
Youll, Paul Represented By: Hankins & Tegenborg Ltd. . . . . . (212) 867-8092
Young, Bob 1003 Diamond Avenue, Ste. 209, South Pasadena, CA 91030 . . . . . (626) 441-8955

YOUNG, EDDIE Pages 168,189
6108 Pageantry Street, Long Beach, CA 90808 • Fax (562) 429-1400 **(562) 429-2513**
Represented By: American Artists **(212) 682-2462**
e-mail: youngeddie@earthlink.net • info@amerartists.com • Website: www.amerartists.com
Specialties: Cartoon; Character; Digital; Humour

Young, Paul P.O. Box 344, Champaign, IL 61824 . . . . . (217) 398-1923
Youssi, John 17N943 Powers Road, Gilbert, IL 60136 . . . . . (847) 428-7398
Yuan, Lisa 530 Molino Avenue #205, Los Angeles, CA 90013 . . . . . (213) 626-6763
Yule, Susan Hunt 176 Elizabeth Street, New York, NY 10012 . . . . . (212) 226-0439
Zacharow, Christopher Represented By: The Newborn Group . . . . . (212) 260-6700
Zador, Lisa Represented By: The Arts Counsel . . . . . (212) 777-6777
Zahares, Wade Represented By: Edana Reps . . . . . (617) 437-9760
Zaharuk, Michael 61 Alvin Avenue, Toronto, ON Canada M4T 2A8 . . . . . (416) 538-7410
Zalme, Ron 936 Country Road 619, Newton, NJ 07860 . . . . . (973) 383-1392

ZAMAN, FARIDA Page 244
18 Norman Road, Upper Montclair, NJ 07043 • Fax (973) 744-9191 **(973) 744-9377**
70 Erskine, Ste. 303, Toronto, ON Canada M4P 1Y2 **(416) 489-3769**
e-mail: fzaman@cybernex.net • Specialties: Advertising; Book Jackets; Corporate; Editorial; Fashion; Food; Greeting Cards; Lifestyle; People; Product

Zamic, Rene Represented By: Reactor Art & Design Ltd. . . . . . (416) 703-1913
Zammarchi, Robert P.O. Box 1147, Boston, MA 02134 . . . . . (617) 787-9513
Zann, Nicky 155 W 68th Street, New York, NY 10023 . . . . . (212) 724-5027
Zaretzki, Andreas Represented By: Reactor Art & Design Ltd. . . . . . (416) 703-1913
Zaruba, Ken 703 Wildlife Court, Westminster, MD 21157 . . . . . (410) 876-8447
Zastrow, Stuart Represented By: Nachreiner Boie Art Factory . . . . . (414) 785-1940
Zavesky Productions 8990 Shepard Road, Macedonia, OH 44056-1958 . . . . . (216) 467-5917
Zeller, Cori 1885 N Oak Hills Drive, Meridian, ID 83642 . . . . . (208) 888-3273
Zeltner, Tim 203 Ellsworth Avenue, Toronto, ON Canada M6G 2K7 . . . . . (416) 653-2065
Zemke Illustration, Deborah 5 S Ninth Street, Columbia, MO 65201 . . . . . (573) 443-4903
Zermeno, Joe Cabrera 21920 Seine Avenue, Hawaiian Gardena, CA 90716 . . . . . (310) 393-5431

ZERNITSKY, LEON Page 127
605 Finch Avenue W, Apt. 716, North York, ON Canada M2R 1P1 • Fax (416) 638-9271 **(416) 638-9271**
Specialties: Advertising; Corporate; Editorial; Illustrative

Zettler, Rick Represented By: Sharpshooter Creative Rep Inc. . . . . . (416) 703-5300
Zgodzinski, Rose Represented By: Three in a Box . . . . . (416) 367-2446
Zhang, Xiang Represented By: Artco . . . . . (212) 889-8777
Zherdin, Boris 91 Washington Avenue, Leonardo, NJ 07737 . . . . . (908) 291-8226
Zhu, Hua Represented By: Pat Foster . . . . . (212) 661-4557

ZICK, BRIAN Pages 86-87
Represented By: Lindgren & Smith **(212) 397-7330**
e-mail: inquiry@lindgrensmith.com • Website: www.lindgrensmith.com

Ziegelman, Terry Represented By: Connie Koralik Associates Represents . . . . . (312) 944-5680
Zielinski, John 1529 Montana Street #100, Chicago, IL 60614 . . . . . (773) 549-4944
Represented By: Steve Edsey & Sons . . . . . (312) 527-0351
Represented By: Sal Barracca Associates . . . . . (212) 889-2400
Ziemienski, Dennis Represented By: Daniele Collignon . . . . . (212) 243-4209

ZIMMERMAN, ROBERT Pages 16-17,434,449,453,461
Asheville, NC **(828) 252-9689**
e-mail: zimm@circle.net • Website: www.zimm.net
Specialties: Digital; Greeting Cards; Humour; Icons; Product

Zingone, Robin 24 Old Depot Road, Chester, CT 06412 . . . . . (860) 526-1755
Zinkowski, Dale 66-31 Saunder Street, Forest Hills, NY 11374 . . . . . (718) 793-1295
Zito, Andy 135 S La Brea Avenue, Los Angeles, CA 90036 . . . . . (213) 931-1182
Zlotsky, Boris Represented By: Mendola Ltd. . . . . . (212) 986-5680
Zuarenstein, Alex Represented By: Anita Grien Represents . . . . . (212) 697-6170
Zuckerman, Craig Represented By: Spencer Church . . . . . (206) 860-9239
Zudeck, Darryl 35 W 92nd Street #5G, New York, NY 10025 . . . . . (212) 663-9454
Zumbo, Matt Represented By: Yolanda Burnett Represents . . . . . (770) 967-0039
Represented By: Langley & Associates . . . . . (847) 670-0912
Zuniga, Joseph 8903 Dunlap Crossing Road, Pico Rivera, CA 90660. . . . . . (562) 949-1101
Zunk, Ingrid R. 758 Wildomar Street, Pacific Palisade, CA 90272. . . . . . (310) 454-2662
Zuzalek, Michele 611 W Sola Street #1, Santa Barbara, CA 93101 . . . . . (805) 962-3367
Zwarenstein, Alex Represented By: Anita Grien Represents . . . . . (212) 697-6170
Zwicker, Sara Mintz 98 Stetson Street, Braintree, MA 02184 . . . . . (781) 848-8962
Zwinger, Jane Represented By: The Art Agency . . . . . (503) 203-8300
Zwingler, Randall 1106 Greenway Road, Wilmington, DE 19803 . . . . . (302) 478-6063

ZWOLAK, PAUL Pages 28-29
Represented By: Marlena Agency **(609) 252-9405**
e-mail: marzena@bellatlantic.net • Website: http://members.bellatlantic.net/~marzena
Specialties: Conceptual; Corporate; Editorial; Whimsical

ARTIST REPRESENTATIVES

A.R.T.S. Resource 545 Sutter Street, Ste. 305, San Francisco, CA 94102 . . . . . (415) 775-0709
Air Studio 203 E Seventh Street, Cincinnati, OH 45202. . . . . (513) 721-1193
AKA Reps, Inc. 153 Waverly Place, 5th Flr., New York, NY 10014 . . . . . (212) 620-4777
Alani Represents 580 Broadway, Ste. 502, New York, NY 10012 . . . . . (212) 465-3355
Albrecht, Anne 405 N Wabash Avenue, Ste. 4410, Chicago, IL 60611. . . . . (312) 595-0300

ALEXANDER/POLLARD, INC. Pages 214-223
848 Greenwood Avenue NE, Atlanta, GA 30306 • Fax (404) 875-9733 **(404) 875-1363 • (800) 347-0734**
1841 Lake Cypress Drive, Safety Harbor, FL 34695 **(813) 725-4438**

Aline, France 7507 Sunset Boulevard #10, Los Angeles, CA 90046. . . . . (213) 933-2500

AMERICAN ARTISTS Pages 167-206
353 W 53rd Street #1W, New York, NY 10019 • Fax (212) 582-0090 **(212) 682-2462**
New York, NY 10019 **(212) 582-0023**
e-mail: info@amerartists.com • Website: www.amerartists.com

Anderson, Anita 637 Swarthmore Avenue, Pacific Palisade, CA 90272 . . . . . (310) 281-1963
Anton, Jerry 119 W 23rd Street, Ste. 203, New York, NY 10011 . . . . . (212) 633-9880
Apple Agency, The No. 1 Holly Tree Lodge, South Humberside, England DN15 8SS 44 172 428 9081
Arbour Artist Rep, Adrienne 17 Atlantic Avenue #3, Toronto, ON Canada M6K 3E7 . . . . . (416) 410-9828

ARENA Pages 366-369
144 Royal College Street, London, England NW1 0TA • Fax 44 171 284 0486 **44 171 267 9661**
Represented By: Alan Lynch Artists **(908) 813-8718**

Art Agency, The 2405 NW Thurman Street, Portland, OR 97210. . . . . (503) 203-8300
Art Bunch, The 230 N Michigan Avenue, Chicago, IL 60601 . . . . . (312) 368-8777
Art Collection, The 95 Great Titchfield Street, London, England W1P 7FP. 44 171 580 2978
Art Department 48 Greene Street, 4th Flr., New York, NY 10013 . . . . . (212) 925-4222
Art Rep Services 123 N Third Street, Ste. 402, Minneapolis, MN 55401 . . . . . (612) 672-9940
Art Source, The P.O. Box 2193, Grapevine, TX 76051 . . . . . (817) 481-2212
Art Source/Diane Barkley Box 257, Pleasantville, NY 10570. . . . . (914) 747-2220
Artco 232 Madison Avenue, Ste. 402, New York, NY 10016 . . . . . (212) 889-8777
227 Godfrey Road, Weston, CT 06883 . . . . . (203) 222-8777
Artisan Creative Solution 850 Montgomery Street, San Francisco, CA 94118 . . . . . (800) 213-4278
Artists Associates 4416 La Folla Drive, Bradenton, FL 34210 . . . . . (941) 756-8445
211 E 51st Street, Ste. 5F, New York, NY 10022 . . . . . (212) 755-1365
Artists Development Group 21 Emmett Street, Providence, RI 02903-4503. . . . . (401) 521-5774
Artists Rep of Texas 11601 Katy Freeway, Houston, TX 77079 . . . . . (281) 558-6665
Artline 439 S Tryon Street, Charlotte, NC 28202-1191. . . . . (704) 376-7609
Arts Counsel, The 853 Broadway, Ste. 606, New York, NY 10003. . . . . (212) 479-7744
Artworks 89 Fifth Avenue, Ste. 901, New York, NY 10003 . . . . . (212) 627-1554
Asciutto Art Representatives 1712 E Butler Circle, Chandler, AZ 85225 . . . . . (602) 899-0600
Atchley, Cindy 1001 Greenbay Road, Winnetka, IL 60093 . . . . . (847) 441-9848
Bacher, Nancy 2654 Rodeo Drive NE, Blaine, MN 55449. . . . . (612) 786-1200
Bahm, Bob 25488 Bryden Road, Beachwood, OH 44122. . . . . (440) 542-0145
Baker Artists Representative, Kolea 2814 NW 72nd Street, Seattle, WA 98117 . . . . . (206) 784-1136
Bancroft & Friends, Carol 121 Dodgingtown Road, Bethel, CT 06801 . . . . . (203) 748-4823
Barasa & Associates, Inc. 2001 E Fremont Court, Arlington Hghts., IL 60004 . . . . . (847) 253-5795
Barboza, Ken 853 Broadway, Ste. 1603, New York, NY 10003 . . . . . (212) 505-8635

BARRACCA ASSOCIATES, SAL Pages 346-353
381 Park Avenue S, New York, NY 10016 • Fax (212) 889-2698 **(212) 889-2400**

Bartels Associates, Ceci 3286 Ivanhoe Avenue, St. Louis, MO 63139. . . . . (314) 781-7377
Chicago, IL 63139 . . . . . (312) 786-1560
New York, NY 10010 . . . . . (212) 912-1877
Baugher & Associates, Liz 300 N State Street, Ste. 4511, Chicago, IL 60610 . . . . . (312) 832-9888
Becker, Erika 150 W 55th Street, PH NE, New York, NY 10019 . . . . . (212) 757-8987
Becker Artists Rep, Ann Dunphy 9131 Westview, Houston, TX 77055 . . . . . (713) 465-3037
Beckett, Rosie 55 Rochester Place, London, England NW1 9JU 44 171 482 3400

Bender, Brenda 309 E Paces Ferry Road, Ste. 140, Atlanta, GA 30305 .... (404) 842-1913
4170 S Arbor Circle, Marietta, GA 30066 .... (770) 924-4793 • (800) 488-9781
Bennett Associates, R.J. 319 Avenue C, Ste. 8C, New York, NY 10009 .... (212) 673-5509
Beranbaum, Sheryl 934 Williamsburg Circle, Warick, RI 02886 .... (617) 437-9459
Berendsen & Associates 2233 Kemper Lane, Cincinnati, OH 45206 .... (513) 861-1400
Berg, Carmen 2005 W Division Street, Chicago, IL 60622 .... (513) 861-1400
Bernstein & Andriulli, Inc. 60 E 42nd Street, Ste. 822, New York, NY 10165 .... (212) 682-1490
Bernstein Art Rep, Joanie 817 S Westwood Drive, Minneapolis, MN 55416-3354 .... (612) 374-3169
Biernat, Anna Sterling Heights, MI 48312 .... (248) 545-2363
Bina 632 Broadway, 8th Flr., New York, NY 10012 .... (212) 533-1734
Birenbaum, Molly 7 Williamsburg Drive, Cheshire, CT 06410 .... (203) 272-9253
Black & White Illustration Co. 72-74 Brewer Street, London, England W1R 3PH 44 171 734 7007
Black Hat Ltd. 4 Northington Street, London, England WC1N 2JG 44 171 430 9146
Black Inc. Creative Rep. 2512 E Thomas, Ste. 2, Phoenix, AZ 85016 .... (602) 381-1332
Boege, Kimberley P.O. Box 7544, Phoenix, AZ 85011-7544 .... (602) 265-4389
Boggie & Associates, Virginia 4924 2A Avenue, Vancouver, BC Canada .... (604) 943-6414
Bookmakers Ltd. P.O. Box 1086, Taos, NM 87571 .... (505) 776-5435
Boston Group, Diane 175 Fifth Avenue, Ste. 2453, New York, NY 10010 .... (212) 283-3401
Brady, Evelyn M. 1641 Third Avenue #29A, New York, NY 10128 .... (212) 427-9600
Brauer, Laura 3325 N Lincoln Avenue #202, Chicago, IL 60657 .... (773) 525-8803
Breitmayer Marketing Commun. 1306 Summit Avenue, Lakewood, OH 44107 .... (216) 226-1455

BREWSTER CREATIVE SERVICES, JOHN — Pages 283-292
597 Riverside Avenue, Westport, CT 06880 • Fax (203) 454-9904 — **(203) 226-4724**
e-mail: creative.svcs@snet.net • Website: www.brewstercreative.com

Brody, Sam 77 Winfield Street, Ste. 4, East Norwalk, CT 06855-2138 .... (203) 854-0805
Brown, Regina 307 S Trooper Road, Norristown, PA 19403 .... (610) 539-1130 • (800) 217-6121
Brown & Company, Charlie 1221 Campbell Road, Houston, TX 77055 .... (713) 468-8161
Brown Ink 801 Edgewood Lane, Fort Lee, NJ 07024 .... (201) 224-9562
Bruck & Moss 333 E 49th Street #3J, New York, NY 10017 .... (212) 980-8061
New York, NY 10012 .... (212) 982-6533
Bruml, Kathy New York, NY .... (212) 874-5659
Buchner, Linda 1720 Wyandotte Street, Kansas City, MO 64108 .... (816) 472-4546
Buck & Kane 481 Eighth Avenue #1530, New York, NY 10001 .... (212) 631-0009
Burg Artist Representative, Kathleen 228 S First Street, Milwaukee, WI 53204 .... (414) 273-5555
Burnes, Velynda 2918 Pond Run Lane, New Richmond, OH 45157 .... (513) 553-6762
Burnett Represents, Yolanda 6478 Chestnut Hill Road, Flowery Branch, GA 30542 .... (770) 967-0039
Bussler, Tom 1733 W Pierce Avenue, Chicago, IL 60622 .... (312) 649-5553
CAPIC 100 Broadview Avenue, Ste. 322, Toronto, ON Canada M4M 2E8 .... (416) 462-3677

CARY & COMPANY — Page 199
666 Bantry Lane, Stone Mountain, GA 30083 • Fax (404) 296-1537 — **(404) 296-9666**

Catbird Represents 1045 Sansome Street #345, San Francisco, CA 94111 .... (415) 399-1540

CATON, CHIP — Page 371
15 Warrenton Avenue, Hartford, CT 06105 • Fax (860) 231-9313 — **(860) 523-4562**

Cerise, Jeff 16421 Olivine Street, Ramsey, MN 55303 .... (612) 753-1115
Che Sguardo Represents 500 N Wells Street, Chicago, IL 60610 .... (312) 440-1616
Chicago Artist Representatives P.O. Box 11902, Chicago, IL 60611-0902 .... (312) 409-6211

CHISLOVSKY DESIGN, INC., CAROL — Page 156
853 Broadway, Ste. 1201, New York, NY 10003 • Fax (212) 353-0954 — **(212) 677-9100**

Church, Spencer 425 Randolph Avenue, Seattle, WA 98122 .... (206) 860-9239
Clare Associates, Pam 7535 Bradley Boulevard, Bethesda, MD 20817-1450 .... (301) 424-9298
Clark Studio 333 N Michigan Avenue #315, Chicago, IL 60601 .... (312) 263-3754
Coleman Presents, Inc., Woody 490 Rockside Road, Cleveland, OH 44131 .... (216) 661-4222 • (800) 486-1248

COLLIER REPRESENTS, INC., JAN — Pages 88-89
P.O. Box 470818, San Francisco, CA 94147 • Fax (415) 383-9037 — **(415) 383-9026**
Website: www.collierreps.com

Collignon, Daniele 200 W 15th Street, New York, NY 10011 .... (212) 243-4209
Command Arts 308 Prince Street #410, St. Paul, MN 55101 .... (612) 291-1954
Comp Art Plus 311 W 34th Street, New York, NY 10001 .... (212) 279-0800
Conrad Represents, Inc. 2149 Lyon Street #5, San Francisco, CA 94115 .... (415) 921-7140
Contestabile, Carol 3500 Maple, Dallas, TX 75219 .... (214) 599-5075
Continuity Studios 4710 W Magnolia Boulevard, Burbank, CA 91505 .... (818) 980-8852
Cornell & Company, Kathleen 737 Milwood Avenue, Venice, CA 90291 .... (310) 301-8059

CORNELL & MCCARTHY, LLC — Page 207
2-D Cross Highway, Westport, CT 06880 • Fax (203) 454-4258 — **(203) 454-4210**

Corporate Art Planning 27 Union Square W, Ste. 407, New York, NY 10003 .... (212) 242-8995
Cowan, Pat 68 E Division Road, Valparaiso, IN 46383 .... (219) 462-0199

CRAIG REPRESENTS, INC., SUZANNE — Page 9
4015 E 53rd Street, Tulsa, OK 74135 • Fax (918) 749-9424 — **(918) 749-9424**

Craven Design Studios, Inc. 234 Fifth Avenue, 4th Flr., New York, NY 10001 .... (212) 696-4680
Creations Unlimited 3612 Buckeye Court, Fairfax, VA 22033 .... (703) 435-0005
Creative Advantage, The 620 Union Street, Schenectady, NY 12305 .... (518) 370-0312
Creative Connection P.O. Box 253, 614 Stillwater Road, Gibson Island, MD 21056-0253 .... (410) 360-5981
Creative Freelancers 99 Park Avenue, Ste. 210A, New York, NY 10016 .... (800) 398-9541
Creative Network, Inc. 1089 Broch Road, Milton, MA 02186 .... (617) 698-1968 • (800) 309-1102
Cuccia, Michelle 742 Yale Drive, Allen, TX 75002 .... (972) 390-2209
Danz, Sandy 4680 Demyhig Lane, Placerville, CA 95667 .... (530) 622-3218
Darby, Nancy 5050 Helix Terrace, La Mesa, CA 91941 .... (619) 440-6265
Darling, Lisa P.O. Box 619, Mattawan, MI 49071 .... (800) 412-2722

DAS GRUP/CARRIE PERLOW — Page 10
311 Avenue H, Ste. D, Redondo Beach, CA 90277 • Fax (310) 792-9161 — **(310) 540-5958**
e-mail: dasgrup@earthlink.net

Dauman Pictures 4 E 88th Street, New York, NY 10128 .... (212) 860-3804
Davick, Linda 4805 Hilldale Drive, Knoxville, TN 37914 .... (423) 546-1020
Davidson/Dogstar, Rodney 626 54th Street S, Birmingham, AL 35212 .... (205) 591-BARK
Davis, Brooke 4323 Bluffview Boulevard, Dallas, TX 75209 .... (214) 352-9192
Day Otis & Associates, Inc., Dorothy 373 S Roberston Boulevard, Beverly Hills, CA 90211 .... (310) 652-8855
De Moreta Represents, Linda 1839 Ninth Street, Alameda, CA 94501 .... (510) 769-1421
Dedell, Inc., Jacqueline 58 W 15th Street, Ste. 6, New York, NY 10011 .... (212) 741-2539
Delphinium 6435 Blenheim Road, Baltimore, MD 21212 .... (410) 377-6777
Dice, Ron 1700 North Park, Ste. 3F, Chicago, IL 60614 .... (312) 266-6313

DIMENSION — Pages 246-250
9801 Dupont Avenue S #168, Minneapolis, MN 55431 • Fax (612) 884-3450 — **(612) 884-4045**
e-mail: jkoltes@dimensioncreative.com • Website: www.dimensioncreative.com

Dodge & Associates, Sharon 3033 13th Avenue W, Seattle, WA 98119 .... (206) 284-4701
Dolby Represents 333 N Michigan Avenue #1100, Chicago, IL 60601 .... (312) 855-9336
Drost, Cindy 1829-2 Grove, Glenview, IL 60025 .... (847) 729-0957
Dwyer & O'Grady P.O. Box 239, East Lempster, NH 03605 .... (603) 863-9347
Edana Reps 174 W Brookline Street #1, Boston, MA 02118 .... (617) 437-9760
Edberg Photo Rep, Grace 835 Moraga Drive, Ste. 2, Los Angeles, CA 90049 .... (310) 471-2288

EDSEY & SONS, STEVE — Page 270
401 N Wabash Avenue, Ste. 635, Chicago, IL 60611 • Fax (312) 527-5468 — **(312) 527-0351**

Elliott/Oreman Artists Rep 25 Drury Lane, Rochester, NY 14625 .... (716) 586-6041
Elsesser, Karen 650 E Bay Point Road, Bayside, WI 53217 .... (414) 352-7786
Embler Represents, Inc., Jennifer 10 Fairway Drive, Deerfield Beach, FL 33441 .... (954) 760-4195
Empress Bowling League, The 2402 Glenridge-Stratford Drive, Atlanta, GA 30342 .... (404) 705-9776 • (888) 705-9776
Enste-Jaspers, Marion Hamburg, Germany 49 40 22 23 26
Extreme Connection Salt Lake City, UT 84158 .... (801) 363-2170
Falcon, Ron 13618 Clifford Avenue, Cleveland, OH 44135 .... (216) 252-8869
Falken, Linda C. 65 Hawthorne Place, Montclair, NJ 07042 .... (973) 746-0898

FAMOUS FRAMES Page 277
5855 Green Valley Circle #308, Culver City, CA 90230 • Fax (310) 642-2728 **(310) 642-2721 • (800) 530-3375**
247 E 57th Street, 2nd Flr., New York, NY 10022 • Fax (212) 980-6556 **(212) 980-7979**
e-mail: info@famousframes.com • Website: www.famousframes.com

FAURE, LAURENCE Pages 214-215
Paris, France **33 1 46 06 29 36**

Fiat & Associates, Randi 1727 S Indiana Avenue, Chicago, IL 60616 . . . . . (312) 663-5300
Filomeno USA, Michelle 155 Spring Street, 2nd Flr., New York, NY 10012 . . . . . (212) 965-1000
Fiorenzo & Associates 25 E 20th Street #3, New York, NY 10003 . . . . . (212) 982-1747
First Image West 104 N Halsted Street, Ste. 200, Chicago, IL 60661 . . . . . (312) 733-9875 • (800) 433-4765
Fischer & Company, R. 333 N Michigan Avenue, Chicago, IL 60601 . . . . . (312) 368-1441
Fishback Illustrations, Inc., Lee Englewood, NJ 07631 . . . . . (201) 568-4868
New York, NY . . . . . (212) 929-2951
Fisher Represents, Bunny 730 N Franklin #605, Chicago, IL 60610 . . . . . (312) 280-1961
Flannery Lane Ltd. 12 Birch Close, North Tarrytown, NY 10591 . . . . . (914) 631-1413
Fleming, Laird Tyler 12240 Montana Avenue, Los Angeles, CA 90049 . . . . . (310) 442-1078

FLEMMING ASSOCIATES, IAN Pages 168,201
c/o American Artists, New York, NY 10019 • Fax (212) 582-0090 **(212) 682-2462**
e-mail: info@amerartists.com • Website: www.amerartists.com

Fortuni Illustration 2508 E Belleview Place #41, Milwaukee, WI 53211 . . . . . (414) 964-8088
Foster, Pat 310 Madison Avenue, Ste. 1225, New York, NY 10017 . . . . . (212) 661-4557

FOSTER REPRESENTS, TEENUH Pages 6-7
1051 S Big Bend Boulevard, Ste. 210, St. Louis, MO 63117 • Fax (314) 647-0177 **(314) 647-7377**

Fox Art, Inc. 3033 Fernwood Avenue, Los Angeles, CA 90039 . . . . . (213) 662-0020
Francisco Creative Services 419 Cynwyd Road, Bala Cynwyd, PA 19004 . . . . . (610) 667-2378
Franks/The Creative Resource, Sylvia 12056 Summit Circle, Beverly Hills, CA 90210-1300 . . . . . (310) 276-5282
Freelance Hotline 119 N Fourth Street, Ste. 409, Minneapolis, MN 55401 . . . . . (612) 341-4411
Freeman, Lisa 740 E 52nd Street, Ste. 8, Indianapolis, IN 46205 . . . . . (317) 920-0068
Friend & Johnson New York, NY 10011 . . . . . (212) 337-0055
Larkspur, CA 94939 . . . . . (415) 927-4500
4606 Cedar Springs #1527, Dallas, TX 75219 . . . . . (214) 559-0055
Chicago, IL 60604 . . . . . (312) 435-0055
Fullmoon Artists Rep 1000 S Alhambra Circle, Coral Gables, FL 33146 . . . . . (305) 667-1557
Furet Art Consultants 4355 Maryland Avenue, Ste. 302, St. Louis, MO 63108 . . . . . (314) 531-0940
Gaffney Agency, The 6166 Leesburg Pike #D-105, Falls Church, VA 22044 . . . . . (703) 533-2440
Gardiner, David 21-B Endlesham Road SW, London, UK England SW12 8JX 44 181 675 3055

GATLIN REPRESENTS, RITA Pages 242-243
P.O. Box 7080, Corte Madera, CA 94925 • Fax (415) 924-7891 **(415) 924-7881 • (800) 924-7881**
e-mail: gatlin@ritareps.com • Website: www.ritareps.com

George, Nancy 1259 Highland Road, Santa Ynez, CA 93460 . . . . . (805) 688-3772
George Reps 256 Horizon Avenue, Venice, CA 90291 . . . . . (310) 399-1664
Giavedoni, Paola 1179 A King Street W, Ste. 206, Toronto, ON Canada M6K 3C5 . . . . . (416) 588-0326
Glass House Graphics 11 Hawk Court North Park, Wheeling, WV 26003 . . . . . (304) 232-5641
Glenn, Chris 520 N Michigan Avenue #620, Chicago, IL 60611 . . . . . (312) 670-7737
Glick & Associates, Ivy San Francisco, CA 94598 . . . . . (415) 543-6056
Godfrey, Dennis 201 W 21st Street #10G, New York, NY 10011 . . . . . (212) 807-0840
Goldman Agency, David 41 Union Square W, Ste. 918, New York, NY 10003 . . . . . (212) 807-6627
Goldstein, Gwen Walters 50 Fuller Brook Road, Wellesley, MA 02181 . . . . . (781) 235-8658

GOMBERG, SUSAN Page 234
New York, NY 10003 **(212) 206-0066**

Goodman, Inc., Tom 626 Loves Lane, Wynnewood, PA 19096 . . . . . (610) 649-1514

GOODSON, ANNA Page 81
C.P. 325 Succ. Westmount, Montreal, PQ Canada H3Z 2T5 • Fax (514) 482-0686 **(514) 983-9020**

GORDON, TAMI Pages 214-215
P.O. Box 4112, Montebello, CA 90640 **(213) 887-8958**

Gordon Associates Ltd., Barbara 165 E 32nd Street, New York, NY 10016 . . . . . (212) 686-3514
Gordon-Clarke, Susan 60 Riverside Drive, Ste. 1GH, New York, NY 10024 . . . . . (212) 580-1928
Gorton Group, The 14900 Landmark Boulevard #540, Dallas, TX 75206 . . . . . (972) 233-3163
Graham Represents, Corey Pier 33 North, San Francisco, CA 94111 . . . . . (415) 956-4750

GRIEN REPRESENTS, ANITA Page 282
155 E 38th Street, New York, NY 10016 • Fax (212) 697-6177 **(212) 697-6170**
e-mail: agrien@aol.com • Website: www.anitagrien.com

Grimm, Mike 1537 N Bell, Chicago, IL 60622 . . . . . (773) 862-4742
Groeschel, Erika 15 E 32nd Street, New York, NY 10016 . . . . . (212) 685-3291

GUENZI AGENTS, INC., CAROL Pages 146-147
865 Delaware Street, Denver, CO 80204 • Fax (303) 820-2598 **(303) 820-2599 • (800) 417-5120**
e-mail: artagent@artagent.com • Website: www.artagent.com

Guided Imagery Productions 2995 Woodside Road #400, Woodside, CA 94062 . . . . . (650) 324-0323
Hackett Artist Rep, Pat 1809 Seventh Avenue, Ste. 1710, Seattle, WA 98101-1328 . . . . . (206) 447-1600
Hahn, Andrew J. 45 E 25th Street #30A, New York, NY 10010 . . . . . (212) 889-7899
Hahn Artist Rep (H2 + Co.), Holly 837 W Grand Avenue, 4th Flr., Chicago, IL 60622 . . . . . (312) 633-0500
Hall & Associates 606 N Larchmont Boulevard, Los Angeles, CA 90004 . . . . . (213) 962-2500
Halley Resources 37 W 20th Street #603, New York, NY 10016 . . . . . (212) 206-0901
Hankins & Tegenborg Ltd. 60 E 42nd Street, New York, NY 10165-1940 . . . . . (212) 867-8092
Hanson Artist Agent, Jim 777 N Michigan Avenue #706, Chicago, IL 60611 . . . . . (312) 337-7770

HARLIB ASSOCIATES, INC., JOEL Page 139
10 E Ontario Street #4708, Chicago, IL 60611-2736 • Fax (312) 573-1445 **(312) 573-1370**
e-mail: harlibhq@aol.com

Harmon, Ellen 950 W Lake Street, Chicago, IL 60607 . . . . . (312) 829-8201
Harriet, Diane Beverly Hills, CA . . . . . (310) 275-2620
Harris, Lisa 722 Yorklyn Road, Ste. 150, Hockessin, DE 19707 . . . . . (302) 234-5707
Harris & Associates, Gretchen 5230 13th Avenue S, Minneapolis, MN 55417 . . . . . (612) 822-0650 • (800) 765-0617
Hart, Vikki 780 Bryant Street, San Francisco, CA 94107 . . . . . (415) 495-4278
Hauser, Barb P.O. Box 421443, San Francisco, CA 94142-1443 . . . . . (415) 647-5660
Hawkins Group 1505 Bella Vista, Dallas, TX 75218 . . . . . (214) 327-6828
Hayes Associates, Kathy 131 Spring Street, New York, NY 10012 . . . . . (212) 925-4340
Heart 1 Tysoe Street, 2nd Flr., London, England EC1R 4SA 44 171 833 4447
Hedge, Joanne 1415 Garden Street, Glendale, CA 91201 . . . . . (818) 244-0110
Heflin, Sally 455 W 23rd Street #8D, New York, NY 10011 . . . . . (212) 366-1893
Hersey, Renee 1923 Preston Avenue, Los Angeles, CA 90026 . . . . . (213) 666-3310

HILL, DEBORAH page 260
14211 SW Teal, Apt. A, Beaverton, OR 97008 **(503) 590-6767**
e-mail: DebinOr@aol.com

Hillman, Betsy Pier 33 N, San Francisco, CA 94111 . . . . . (415) 381-4728
HK Portfolio 666 Greenwich Street, Ste. 860, New York, NY 10014 . . . . . (212) 675-5719
Hoch & Associates 101 N Wacker Driver #CM190, Chicago, IL 60606 . . . . . (312) 689-8077
Hoffman, Kim 2020 Airport Way S, Seattle, WA 98125 . . . . . (206) 343-7118
Holland & Company, Mary 6638 N 13th Street, Phoenix, AZ 85014 . . . . . (602) 263-8990
Holmberg, Irmeli 280 Madison Avenue, Ste. 1110, New York, NY 10016 . . . . . (212) 545-9155
Hopson, Melissa 1605 C Stemmons, Studio 212, Dallas, TX 75207 . . . . . (214) 747-3122
Horwath, Diane 5192 Durnham Drive, Waterford, MI 48327 . . . . . (810) 738-1330
House, Jennifer 2419 Daybreak, Dallas, TX 75287 . . . . . (214) 807-7212
Howell Reps 301 Poplar Grove Court, Woodstock, GA 30189 . . . . . (770) 592-0058
Hull Associates, Scott 68 E Franklin Street, Dayton, OH 45459 . . . . . (937) 433-8383
New York, NY 10001 . . . . . (212) 966-3604
Hunter, Nadine 80 Wellington Avenue, P.O. Box 307, Ross, CA 94957 . . . . . (415) 456-7711
Iconomics 155 N Collins Avenue, Ft. Collins, CO 80524 . . . . . (800) 297-7658

IEZZI, MIKE Page 258
1237 Chicago Road, Troy, MI 48083 • Fax (248) 583-3216 **(248) 583-5540**

Image Mill 2800 University Avenue #303, West Des Moines, IA 50266 . . . . (515) 490-6110

IMAGINATION/CARMEN GRENIER Page 63
202 Crampton Road RR#1, Carleton Place, ON Canada K7C 3P1 • Fax (613) 253-3183 **(613) 253-0063**
e-mail: imagin@magi.com

Inman, E.W. 6723 N Lightfoot Avenue, Chicago, IL 60646. . . . . (773) 792-9169
Ishizuka, Shinobu 11835 W Olympic Boulevard, Ste. 825, Los Angeles, CA 90064. . . . . (310) 478-4454
Ivy League of Artists, The 18 W 21st Street, 7th Flr., New York, NY 10010 . . . . (212) 243-1333
Iwen, Fred 2413 N Clybourn, Chicago, IL 60614 . . . . (773) 296-4131
Jacobs, Howard 333 N Michigan Avenue #1410, Chicago, IL 60601. . . . . (312) 263-0950
Jakeman Illustration, Kathy 20 Trefoil Road, London, England SW1 2EQ 44 181 875 9525
Jaz & Jaz 4033 Aurora Avenue N, Seattle, WA 98103 . . . . (206) 633-3445
Jenni Representative, Jane 472 Portland Avenue, St. Paul, MN 55102. . . . . (612) 224-6763
Jett & Associates, Clare 7118 Upper River Road, Prospect, KY 40059 . . . . (502) 228-9427
Johnson Associates, Evelyne 201 E 28th Street, New York, NY 10016. . . . . (212) 532-0928

JOHNSON ASSOCIATES, ROGER Page 282
116 Mohican Court, West Layfayette, IN 47906 • Fax (765) 497-2180 **(765) 497-7504**
e-mail: rjassoc29@aol.com

Johnston Artists Rep, Suzy 39 Cranfield Road, Toronto, ON Canada M4B 3H6 . . . . (416) 285-8905
Jorgensen & Barrett Reps P.O. Box 19412, Seattle, WA 98109 . . . . (206) 634-1880
Joyce, Tricia 79 Chambers Street, New York, NY 10007 . . . . (212) 962-0728
K&K Art & Associates 401 Second Avenue, Ste. 800, Minneapolis, MN 55401 . . . . (612) 338-9138
Kalish, Renee 1707 Keeney Street, Evanston, IL 60602 . . . . (847) 864-6127
Kamin, Vincent 260 E Chestnut, Ste. 3005, Chicago, IL 60611 . . . . (312) 787-8834
Karpe, Michele 11959 Woodbridge Street, Studio City, CA 91604 . . . . (818) 760-0491
Kastaris & Associates, Harriet 3301A S Jefferson Avenue, St. Louis, MO 63118. . . . . (314) 773-2600
Keating, Peggy 30 Horatio Street, New York, NY 10014. . . . . (212) 691-4654
Kellogg-Cirino Creative 525 E Flower Street, Phoenix, AZ 85012 . . . . (602) 241-1828
Kelly Reps 112 S Glen Avenue, Tampa, FL 33609 . . . . (813) 872-9996
Kenney & Weinberg 286 Spring Street, 5th Flr., New York, NY 10012. . . . . (212) 807-7774
Kenny, Steven 3557 Slate Mills Road, Sperryville, VA 22740 . . . . (800) 789-9389
Kimche, Tania 137 Fifth Avenue, 11th Flr., New York, NY 10010 . . . . (212) 529-3556
Kimmel, Lily 12 E 86th Street #1522, New York, NY 10028 . . . . (212) 794-1542
Kirchoff/Wohlberg, Inc. 866 United Nations Plaza, New York, NY 10017 . . . . (212) 644-2020
Kirsch & Associates 218 Elm Court, Rhinelander, WI 54501. . . . . (715) 369-2130
Los Angeles, CA 90048 . . . . (213) 651-3706

KLEIN, JANE Pages 6-7, 164-165
1635 E 22nd Street, Oakland, CA 94606 • Fax (510) 535-0437 **(888) ART-1008**
e-mail: jkleinr@aol.com

Klimt Represents 15 W 72nd Street, New York, NY 10023 . . . . (212) 799-2231
Knable & Associates, Ellen 1233 S La Cienega Boulevard, Los Angeles, CA 90035 . . . . (310) 855-8855
Knutsen, Jan 527 Marquette Avenue, Minneapolis, MN 55422. . . . . (612) 288-9925
Koeffler Represents, Ann 5015 Clinton Street, Ste. 306, Los Angeles, CA 90004 . . . . (213) 957-2327
Kohl & Associates, Inc. 203 N Wabash Avenue, Chicago, IL 60601 . . . . (312) 759-5920

KORALIK ASSOCIATES REPRESENTS Pages 149-153
900 W Jackson Boulevard #7W, Chicago, IL 60607 • Fax (312) 421-5948 **(312) 944-5680**

Korn & Associates, Pamela P.O. Box 521, Canadensis, PA 18325 . . . . (717) 595-9298
Kouts, Barbara S. P.O Box 560, Bellport, NY 11713-0560 . . . . (516) 286-1278
Kramer + Kramer 156 Fifth Avenue, New York, NY 10010 . . . . (212) 645-8787
Kramer, Ina Survival Group 36 E 20th Street, New York, NY 10003 . . . . (212) 614-0616
Kuehnel & Associates, Peter 30 E Huron Plaza, Chicago, IL 60611 . . . . (312) 642-6499
Kurlansky Associates, Sharon 192 Southville Road, Southborough, MA 01772. . . . . (508) 872-4549
Kwak, Sunny 1045 Sansome Street #345, San Francisco, CA 94111. . . . . (415) 399-1540

LAMBERT, LAURIE — Pages 78-79
2870 Romana Place, Cincinnati, OH 45209 • Fax (513) 841-0017 — **(513) 841-0073**

Langley & Associates 4300 N Narragansett, Chicago, IL 60634 . . . . . (847) 670-0912
111 E Wacker Drive, 26th Flr., Chicago, IL 60601 . . . . . (312) 540-9470
Larkin, Mary 220 E 57th Street, Ste. 5-J, New York, NY 10022 . . . . . (212) 832-8116
Larkworthy Artist Rep. Ltd., Kate 32 Downing Street, Ste. 4D, New York, NY 10014-4781 . . . . . (212) 633-1310
Lavaty, Frank & Jeff 217 E 86th Street, Box 212, New York, NY 10028 . . . . . (212) 427-5632
Lawrence Represents, Robert 25 Bucaneer, Marina del Rey, CA 90292 . . . . . (310) 827-0457
LeCouvre Communications, Lynne 605 Litchfield Lane, Santa Barbara, CA 93109 . . . . . (805) 963-2859
Lee, Beth 35 W 90th Street, Ste. 4-G, New York, NY 10024 . . . . . (212) 362-6732
Leff Associates, Inc., Jerry 420 Lexington Avenue, Rm. 2760, New York, NY 10170 . . . . . (212) 697-8525
Lehmen/Dabney, Inc. 1431 35th Avenue S, Seattle, WA 98144 . . . . . (206) 325-8595

LEIGHTON & COMPANY, INC. — Page 126
7 Washington Street, Beverly, MA 01915 • Fax (978) 921-0223 — **(978) 921-0887**
e-mail: leighton@leightonreps.com • Website: www.leightonreps.com

LEXINGTON ASHWORTH HOUSE — Page 157
1220 S 25th Street, Milwaukee, WI 53204 — **(414) 290-4313**
Website: www.lexash.com

Leyden Diversified 976 Old Huntingdon Pike, Huntingdon Vlly, PA 19006 . . . . . (215) 663-0587
Lilie, Jim 110 Sutter Street, Ste. 706, San Francisco, CA 94104 . . . . . (415) 441-4384

LINDGREN & SMITH — Pages 86-115
250 W 57th Street, Rm. 521, New York, NY 10107 • Fax (212) 397-7334 — **(212) 397-7330**
San Francisco, CA — **(415) 788-8552**
e-mail: inquiry@lindgrensmith.com • Website: www.lindgrensmith.com • stockillustrated.com

LINK — Pages 18-19
2 Silver Avenue, Ste. 205, Toronto, ON Canada M6R 3A2 • Fax (416) 530-1401 — **(416) 530-1500**

Lock Source 6202 N Neva, Chicago, IL 60631 . . . . . (773) 631-0064
Lorraine & Associates 2311 Farrington Street, Dallas, TX 75207 . . . . . (214) 688-1540
Lott Representatives 60 E 42nd Street, Ste. 1146, New York, NY 10165 . . . . . (212) 953-7088
Ludlow, Catherine Artists Rep 750 N Stanley Avenue, Los Angeles, CA 90046 . . . . . (213) 658-6920
Lulu Creatives 4645 Colfax Avenue S, Minneapolis, MN 55409 . . . . . (612) 825-7564
Lux & Associates, Inc., Frank 401 N Wabash Avenue, Ste. 532, Chicago, IL 60611 . . . . . (312) 222-1361

LYNCH ARTISTS, ALAN — Pages 366-369
11 Kings Ridge Road, Long Valley, NJ 07853 • Fax (908) 813-0076 — **(908) 813-8718**

M.A.R.S. Reps P.O. Box 1197, Lake Zurich, IL 60047 . . . . . (847) 438-7128
Magnet Artists 33 Eswyn Road, London, England SW17 8TR 44 181 767 2618

MALONEY, TOM — Pages 143,162
307 N Michigan Avenue #1006, Chicago, IL 60601 • Fax (312) 704-0501 — **(312) 704-0500**

Malooly Represents, Mary 703 McKinney Avenue, Ste. 206, Dallas, TX 75202 . . . . . (214) 922-9292

MANASSE, MICHELE — Pages 325-331
2134 Aquetong Road, New Hope, PA 18938 • Fax (215) 862-2641 — **(215) 862-2091**
e-mail: mmanasse@new-work.com • Website: www.voicenet.com/~mmanasse

Marek & Associates 170 Fifth Avenue, 7th Flr., New York, NY 10010 . . . . . (212) 924-6760
Marie & Friends, Rita Highland Park, IL 60035 . . . . . (773) 222-0337

MARLENA AGENCY — Pages 22-31
278 Hamilton Avenue, Princeton, NJ 08540 • Fax (609) 252-1949 — **(609) 252-9405**
New York, NY — **(212) 289-5514**
e-mail: marzena@bellatlantic.net • Website: http://members.bellatlantic.net/~marzena

Martha Productions 11936 W Jefferson Boulevard, Ste. C, Culver City, CA 90230 . . . . (310) 390-8663
Martini, Charlie P.O. Box 5811, Austin, TX 78763 . . . . (512) 328-8881
Marvel Entertainment 387 Park Avenue S, New York, NY 10016 . . . . (212) 696-0808
Maslov/Weinberg 608 York Street, San Francisco, CA 94110 . . . . (415) 641-1285
Mason Illustration 3810 Edmund Boulevard, Minneapolis, MN 55406 . . . . (612) 729-1774

MATSON REPRESENTS, MARLA — Pages 70,270
1429 N First Street, Phoenix, AZ 85004 • Fax (602) 252-5073 — **(602) 252-5072**
e-mail: mmreps@primenet.com • Website: www.primenet.com/~mmreps

Mattelson Associates 37 Cary Road, Great Neck, NY 11021 . . . . (516) 487-1323
Mazziota, Beth 2809 Ross Avenue, Ste. 305, Dallas, TX 75201 . . . . (214) 871-9191
McCallum, Melissa 1020 Elm Street, Winnetka, IL 60093-2119 . . . . (847) 441-8993
McCusker, Kathleen E. 3178 Belgrade Street, Philadelphia, PA 19134 . . . . (215) 427-6114
McElroy, Robert 38-42 E First Street, New York, NY 10003 . . . . (212) 505-6195
McKay, Linda 5728 Live Oak, Dallas, TX 75206 . . . . (214) 826-6055
McLean & Friends 2060 Peachtree Road NW #1705, Atlanta, GA 30305 . . . . (404) 881-6627
McMahon, Brian 1535 N Western Avenue, Chicago, IL 60622 . . . . (773) 227-6778
McManus & Associates 3100 Gulf Boulevard, Belleair Beach, FL 33786 . . . . (813) 595-2893
Mead Associates, Robert 421 Park Avenue, Rye, NY 10580 . . . . (212) 688-7474 • (800) 717-1994
Meininger, Vicki 2618 Hanover Avenue, Richmond, VA 23220 . . . . (804) 359-8583

MENDOLA LTD. — Page 139
420 Lexington Avenue, PH, New York, NY 10170 • Fax (212) 818-1246 — **(212) 986-5680**
Website: www.mendolaart.com

Miller Artists Unlimited, Claudia 6679 NW 24th Terrace, Boca Raton, FL 33496 . . . . (561) 995-9444
Miller, Patrick & Associates 300 N State Street, Ste. 5035, Chicago, IL 60610 . . . . (312) 595-1555
Mizuno, Barbara 622 S Barrington Avenue #306, Los Angeles, CA 90049 . . . . (310) 472-1446
Moffet, Maureen 121 Lyall Avenue, Toronto, ON Canada M4E 1W6 . . . . (416) 691-3242

MONTAGANO & ASSOCIATES, DAVID — Pages 312-313
11 E Hubbard Street, 7th Flr., Chicago, IL 60611 • Fax (312) 527-2108 — **(312) 527-3283**
e-mail: dmontag@aol.com

Moore Represents, Tammy 3942 Valeta Street, Ste. 246, San Diego, CA 92110 . . . . (619) 222-5773

MORGAN ASSOCIATES, VICKI — Pages 124-125
194 Third Avenue, New York, NY 10003 • Fax (212) 353-8538 — **(212) 475-0440**
e-mail: vmartrep@aol.com • Website: www.vickimorganassociates.com

Morin & Associates, Jacqueline 51 Bulwer Street #200, Toronto, ON Canada M5T 1A1 . . . . (416) 506-1411
Morris Associates, Sharon 580 Washington Street #204, San Francisco, CA 94111 . . . . (415) 362-8280
Moskowitz Represents, Marion 315 E 68th Street, New York, NY 10021 . . . . (212) 517-4919
Motion Artists, Inc. 1400 N Hayworth Avenue #36, Los Angeles, CA 90046 . . . . (213) 851-7737

MUNRO GOODMAN — Pages 214-215
5 E 17th Street, 6th Flr., New York, NY 10003 • Fax (212) 633-1844 — **(212) 691-2667**
e-mail: cgoodman@blast.net
405 N Wabash, Ste. 2405, Chicago, IL 60611 • Fax (312) 321-1350 — **(312) 321-1336**

Nachreiner Boie Art Factory 925 Elm Grove Road, Elm Grove, WI 53122 . . . . (414) 785-1940

NEIS GROUP, THE — Pages 299-307
11440 Oak Drive, P.O. Box 174, Shelbyville, MI 49344 • Fax (616) 672-5757 — **(616) 672-5756**
e-mail: neisgroup@wmis.net • Website: www.neisgroup.com

Nelson, Cindy 270 W 91st Street, New York, NY 10024 . . . . (212) 965-1090
Nevill, Charlene/Vis-A-Vis 717 Capp Street, San Francisco, CA 94110 . . . . (415) 824-4772
Newborn Group, The 270 Park Avenue S, Ste. 8E, New York, NY 10010 . . . . (212) 260-6700
Newman & Associates, Carole 2503 Main Street, Santa Monica, CA 90405 . . . . (310) 394-5031
Northern Art Collection, The 23 New Mount Street, Manchester, England M4 4DE 44 161 953 4034

NOWAK, WANDA — Page 129
231 E 76th Street, Ste. 5D, New York, NY 10021 • Fax (212) 535-1624 — **(212) 535-0438**

NOWICKI & ASSOCIATES, LORI Pages 130-132
37 W 20th Street, Ste. 902, New York, NY 10011 • Fax (212) 243-5955 **(212) 243-5888**
e-mail: lori@lorinowicki.com • Website: www.lorinowicki.com

Nygreen, Ann 250-A Seaview Avenue, Piedmont, CA 94610 . . . . (510) 652-1744
O'Leary, Gin Boston, MA . . . . (617) 924-4802
O'Neill Artists Rep, Beth 208 Antlers Drive, Rochester, NY 14618 . . . . (716) 473-0384
Oasis Art Studio 10551 Greenbrier Road, Minnetonka, MN 55305 . . . . (612) 927-0955
Ogden Represents, Robin 4409 Washburn Avenue S, Minneapolis, MN 55410 . . . . (612) 925-4174
Orbit/Denise Azzopardi 2 Everett Crescent, Toronto, ON Canada M4C 4P2 . . . . (416) 429-2840
Palmer, Jeff 232 Madison Avenue, New York, NY 10016 . . . . (212) 889-8777

PALULIAN, JOANNE Pages 65-67
18 McKinley Street, Rowayton, CT 06853 • Fax (203) 857-0842 **(203) 866-3734**
New York, NY **(212) 581-8338**

Papitto, Aurelia 300 Commercial Street #807, Boston, MA 02109 . . . . (617) 742-3108
Parvis/Milani 270 Lafayette, Ste. 1300, New York, NY 10012 . . . . (212) 965-0676
Pass Productions, Agate 15566 Sandy Hook Road, Poulsbo, WA 91031 . . . . (206) 621-9069
Pate Company, The 2510-G Las Posa Road, Camarillo, CA 93010 . . . . (805) 529-8111
Payne Associates 32 W 31st Street, 5th Flr., New York, NY 10001 . . . . (212) 239-4283
Pema Browne Ltd. Pine Road, H.C.R., Box 104-B, Neversink, NY 12765 . . . . (914) 985-2936

PENNY & STERMER GROUP Page 269
19 Stuyvesant Oval, Ste. 2D, New York, NY 10009-2021 **(212) 505-9342**
e-mail: clstermer@aol.com • Website: www.pennystermergroup.com

PG REPRESENTATIVES Pages 317-321
211 Monson Turnpike Road, Ware, MA 01082 • Fax (413) 967-3293 **(413) 967-9855**
e-mail: pgreps@aol.com

Phillips, Diedra 14 Skinner Path, Marblehead, MA 01945 . . . . (781) 639-1600
Photocom Inc. 3005 Maple Avenue #104, Dallas, TX 75201 . . . . (214) 720-2272
Pickard, Maggie 2 Locust Grove Road, Rhinebeck, NY 12572 . . . . (914) 876-2358
Pickford, Noelle 27 Britton Street, London, UK England EC1M 5NQ 44 171 584 0908
Pinnacle Creative 8136 Mullen Road, Lenexa, KS 66215-4198 . . . . (913) 438-1888
Planet Rep 5 Tower Drive, Mill Valley, CA 94941 . . . . (415) 388-9391 • (800) 847-5101
Poje, Elizabeth 1001 S Alfred Street, Los Angeles, CA 90035 . . . . (310) 556-1439
Pomegranate Pictures 5 W 19th Street, 5th Flr., New York, NY 10011 . . . . (212) 633-2313
Potts & Associates, Inc., Carolyn 1872 N Clybourne, Ste. 404, Chicago, IL 60614 . . . . (773) 935-8840

POWDITCH ASSOCIATES Page 139
863 Hartglen Avenue, Westlake Village, CA 91361 **(805) 497-0069**

Powell, Alan Dean 655 N Harper, Los Angeles, CA 90048 . . . . (213) 653-7041
Powell, Anne 1641 Bathurst Street #101, Toronto, ON Canada M5P 3J6 . . . . (416) 484-9430

PRAPAS, CHRISTINE Pages 262-271
12480 SE Wiese Road, Boring, OR 97009 • Fax (503) 658-3960 **(503) 658-7070**
e-mail: cprapas@teleport.com

PRED GROUP, THE Pages 71-73
10012 Perry Drive, Overland Park, KS 66212 • Fax (913) 438-7734 **(913) 438-7733**
e-mail: predgrp@gvi.net • Website: www.predgroup.com

Prentice Associates, Inc., Vicki Rockefeller Center, 630 Fifth Avenue, Ste. 2000, New York, NY 10111 . . . . (212) 332-3460
Pribble, Laurie 653 Pomfret Road, Hampton, CT 06247 . . . . (860) 455-0811
Pritchett, Tom 80-20 Grenfell Street, Kew Gardens, NY 11415 . . . . (212) 688-1080
Private View 26 Leavendale Road, London, England SE23 2TW 44 181 291 1110
Production Arts Ltd. 3707 Barry Avenue, Los Angeles, CA 90066 . . . . (310) 915-5610
Publishers' Graphics 251 Greenwood Avenue, Bethel, CT 06801 . . . . (203) 797-8188
Putscher, Terry P.O. Box 461, Narberth, PA 19072 . . . . (610) 667-8890
Rabin & Associates, Bill 680 N Lake Shore Drive, Chicago, IL 60611 . . . . (312) 944-6655

Ramin & Associates, Linda 6239 Elizabeth Avenue, St. Louis, MO 63139 . . . . (314) 781-8851
Ravenhill Represents 1215 W 67th Street, Kansas City, MO 64113 . . . . (816) 333-0744
Reactor Art & Design Ltd. 51 Camden Street, Toronto, ON Canada M5V 1V2 . . . . (416) 703-1913

REILLY REPS, KERRY — Pages 214-215
1826 Asheville Place, Charlotte, NC 28203 — **(704) 372-6007**
e-mail: reillyreps@aol.com

Remen Willis Design Group 2964 Colton Road, Pebble Beach, CA 93953 . . . . (408) 655-1407

RENARD REPRESENTS — Pages 38-59,411
501 Fifth Avenue, Ste. 1407, New York, NY 10017-6103 • Fax (212) 697-6828 — **(212) 490-2450**
e-mail: renardreps@earthlink.net • Website: www.renardrepresents.com

Rep Art 2491 W 22nd Avenue, Vancouver, BC Canada V6L 1M3 . . . . (604) 684-6826

REPERTOIRE — Page 213
2029 Custer Parkway, Richardson, TX 75080 • Fax (972) 761-0501 — **(972) 761-0500**
e-mail: repertoire@onramp.net

Reps, Ty 920 1/4 N Formosa Avenue, Los Angeles, CA 90046 . . . . (213) 850-7957
Rhyne Represents, Paulette 2075 S University Boulevard, Denver, CO 80210 . . . . (303) 871-9166
Riley Illustration 155 W 15th Street, Ste. 4C, New York, NY 10011 . . . . (212) 989-8770
Rittenberg, Michelle 1210 Washinton Avenue #B, Santa Monica, CA 90403. . . . . (310) 458-1917
RKB Studios, Inc. 420 N Fifth Street, Ste. 920, Minneapolis, MN 55401 . . . . (612) 339-7055
Roche Represents, Diann 705 W 90th Terrace, Kansas City, MO 64114 . . . . (816) 822-2024
Rogers Studio, Lila 6 Parker Road, Arlington, MA 02174 . . . . (781) 641-2787
Rohani, Mushka 9229 215th Street SW, Edmonds, WA 98020 . . . . (425) 771-2905

ROLAND GROUP, THE — Pages 338-339
4948 St. Elmo Avenue, Ste. 201, Bethesda, MD 20814 • Fax (301) 718-7958 — **(301) 718-7955**
e-mail: npnrolgp@erols.com • Website: www.therolandgroup.com

ROSEN ARTISTS' REP, DONNA — Pages 392-399
15209 Rockport Drive, Silver Spring, MD 20905 • Fax (301) 879-9854 — **(301) 384-8925**
e-mail: djrosen@erols.com • Website: www.aaarrt.com/donnasgallery

Rosenthal Represents 3850 Eddingham Avenue, Calabasas, CA 91302 . . . . (818) 222-5445
Rutt Associates, Dick 234 Shoreline Drive Yacht Cove, Columbia, SC 29212 . . . . (803) 407-2030
Saba 116 E 16th Street, 8th Flr., New York, NY 10003 . . . . (212) 477-7722

SALZMAN INTERNATIONAL — Page 293
New York, NY 10022 — **(212) 997-0115**
716 Sanchez Street, San Francisco, CA 94114 • Fax (415) 285-8268 — **(415) 285-8267**
Chicago, IL 60622 — **(312) 782-2244**

Sampson, Corinna 303 30th Avenue, San Francisco, CA 94121 . . . . (415) 386-5982

SANDERS AGENCY, LIZ — Page 372
16 Phaedra, Laguna Niguel, CA 92677 • Fax (714) 495-0129 — **(714) 495-3664**
e-mail: lizsanders@aol.com

Sands Artist Rep, Trudy 1230 Golden Trophy, Dallas, TX 75232 . . . . (214) 905-9037
Saunders, Michele 84 Riverside Drive, New York, NY 10024 . . . . (212) 496-0268
Saylor, Brooks 201 Beeston Court, Morrisville, NC 27560 . . . . (919) 481-6500
Schell, Jeff 222 Northwind Drive, Stockbridge, GA 30281 . . . . (770) 507-2951
Schenker, Michael 126 Fifth Avenue, New York, NY 10011-5606 . . . . (212) 691-0122
Schlager, Inc., Barbara 225 Lafayette Street #902, New York, NY 10012. . . . . (212) 941-1777
Schumann & Company 1009 W Sixth Street, Ste. 207, Austin, TX 78703 . . . . (512) 481-0907
Schuna Group, The 1503 Briarknoll Drive, Arden Hills, MN 55112 . . . . (612) 631-8480
Schwager Productions, Linda 1081 E Fifth Avenue, Chico, CA 95926 . . . . (916) 345-6464

SCOTT, INC., FREDA — Page 107
1015-B Battery Street, San Francisco, CA 94111 • Fax (415) 398-6136 — **(415) 398-9121**

SELL, INC. Pages 214-215
333 N Michigan Avenue #800, Chicago, IL 60601-3901 • Fax (312) 578-8847 **(312) 578-8844**
e-mail: sellinc@aol.com • Website: http://members.aol.com/sellinc

SF Society of Illustrators 493 Eighth Avenue, San Francisco, CA 94118 .... (415) 221-6840
Shannon Associates 327 E 89th Street, Ste. 3E, New York, NY 10128 .... (212) 831-5650
1306 Alabama Street, Huntington Beach, CA 92648 .... (714) 969-7766
Sharpe & Associates 7536 Ogelsby Avenue, Los Angeles, CA 90045 .... (310) 641-8556
25 W 68th Street, Ste. 9A, New York, NY 10023 .... (212) 595-1125

SHARPSHOOTER CREATIVE REPRESENTATION, INC. Pages 229-239
49 Bathurst Street, Ste. 400, Toronto, ON Canada M5V 2P2 • Fax (416) 703-0762 **(416) 703-5300**
e-mail: shooter@the-wire.com • Website: www.portfolios.com/illustrators

Shaw, Patti 192 Spadina Avenue, Ste. 312, Toronto, ON Canada M5T 2C2 .... (416) 361-3184
Shekut, Linda 980 N Michigan Avenue, Chicago, IL 60611 .... (312) 977-9171
Sherrah, Mark 460 Parliament Street #2, Toronto, ON Canada M5A 3A2 .... (416) 972-6161
Shooting Star 1441 N McCadden Place, Los Angeles, CA 90028 .... (213) 469-2020
1178 Broadway, 4th Flr., New York, NY 10001 .... (212) 447-0666
SI International 43 E 19th Street, 2nd Flr., New York, NY 10003 .... (212) 254-4996
Sicilia/Sharpe P.O. Box 95273, Seattle, WA 98145 .... (206) 547-5334
Sillen, Florence 55 W 11th Street, New York, NY 10011-8662 .... (212) 243-9490
Skidmore, Inc. 29580 Northwestern Highway, Southfield, MI 48034-1031 .... (248) 353-7722
Smiddy, Catherine 1419 Swallow Circle, Dallas, TX 75067 .... (214) 317-7427
Snyder Creative Representative, Deborah 5321 W 62nd Street, Minneapolis, MN 55436-2660 .... (612) 922-3462
Sobol, Lynne 3039 N Marengo, Altadena, CA 91001 .... (626) 791-9214
Solomon, Richard 121 Madison Avenue, Ste. 5F, New York, NY 10016 .... (212) 683-1362
Solutions Group, The 4116 Hawthorne, Dallas, TX 75219 .... (214) 522-3312
Spectrum Studio, Inc. 1503 Washington Avenue S, 3rd Flr., Minneapolis, MN 55454 .... (612) 332-2361
Spencer, Torrey 11201 Valley Spring Lane, Studio City, CA 91602 .... (818) 505-1124
Spiegel & Associates, Allen 221 Lobos Avenue, Pacific Grove, CA 93950 .... (408) 372-4672
Spitzer, Russ 70 Beech Street, Paterson, NJ 07501 .... (973) 279-0066
Square Moon 6 Monterey Terrace, Orinda, CA 94563 .... (510) 253-9451
Squire, Terry 4233 Mountainbrook Road, Apex, NC 27502 .... (919) 772-1262
Starwatcher Agency, The P.O. Box 17270, Encino, CA 91416 .... (818) 343-9922
Stefanski Represents, Janice 2022 Jones Street, San Francisco, CA 94133 .... (415) 928-0457
Stevens, Robin 3950 N Lake Shore Drive #1707B, Chicago, IL 60613 .... (312) 689-3442

STEWART, GEOFFREY Page 384
615 W 34th Street, Minneapolis, MN 55408 • Fax (612) 827-3870 **(612) 824-8914**
e-mail: geo@scc.net • Website: www.stewartartists.com

Still Life Studios 1886 Thunderbird Road, Troy, MI 48084 .... (248) 362-3111
Storyboards 1426 Main Street #F, Venice, CA 90291 .... (310) 581-4050
Straiges, Denise Philadelphia, PA 19119 .... (800) 916-1293
Studio & Artist Rep South Pasadena, CA 91031 .... (213) 461-4969
Style Architect 733 Amsterdam Avenue #24A, New York, NY 10025 .... (212) 749-0284
Sullivan & Associates 3805 Maple Court, Marietta, GA 30066 .... (770) 971-6782
Sumpter & Associates, Will 179 Massengale Road, Brooks, GA 30205 .... (770) 460-8438
Susan & Company 5002 92nd Avenue SE, Mercer Island, WA 98040 .... (206) 232-7873
SWAN P.O. Box 440, Paramus, NJ 07653-0440 .... (201) 967-1313

SWEET REPRESENTS Pages 133-141
716 Montgomery Street, San Francisco, CA 94111 • Fax (415) 433-9560 **(415) 433-1222**

T-Square etc. 1426 Main Street, Ste. F, Venice, CA 90291 .... (310) 581-2200
Taylor, Laura 286 Fifth Avenue #401, New York, NY 10001 .... (212) 279-2838
Taylor, Teresa 3278 Wilshire Boulevard, Los Angeles, CA 90010 .... (213) 812-8755
Team Agency, Inc., The 63 Endicott Street #407, Boston, MA 02113 .... (617) 742-3444
Thorogood Illustration 5 Dryden Street, London, England WC2E 9NW 44 171 829 8468
Those 3 Reps 2909 Cole Avenue, Ste. 118, Dallas, TX 75204 .... (214) 871-1316
Threadgold, Suzie 5585 Green Valley Circle, Culver City, CA 90230 .... (310) 642-2721
Three in a Box 468 Queen Street E #104, Toronto, ON Canada M5A 1T7 .... (416) 367-2446
Tiffany Represents 2000 Second Avenue, Ste. 906, Seattle, WA 98121 .... (206) 441-7701

TIS Publishing Corp. Box 2088, Halesite, NY 11743 . . . . . (800) 334-3201
Tise, Katherine 200 E 78th Street, New York, NY 10021 . . . . . (212) 570-9069
Tiziana 44A Honeck Street, Englewood, NJ 07631 . . . . . (212) 921-1899

TONAL VALUES Pages 160-161
131-133 N Montclair Avenue, Dallas, TX 75208 • Fax (214) 942-6771 **(214) 943-2569 • (800) 484-8592**
e-mail: tonalvalues@mindspring.com

Torus Management 15 E 10th Street, Ste. 1D, New York, NY 10003 . . . . . (212) 353-0680
Toyama Represents, Kathee 1994 San Pasqual Street, Pasadena, CA 91107 . . . . . (626) 440-0333
Tugeau, Christina 110 Rising Ridge Road, Ridgefield, CT 06877 . . . . . (203) 438-7307
Tuke, Inc., Joni 325 W Huron Street #515-A, Chicago, IL 60610 . . . . . (312) 787-6826
Turk & The Artist Network, Melissa 9 Babbling Brook Lane, Suffern, NY 10901 . . . . . (914) 368-8606

VARGO BOCKOS Page 70
211 E Ohio Street, Ste. 2404, Chicago, IL 60611 • Fax (312) 661-0043 **(312) 661-1717**

Veloric Associates, Philip M. 200 Roberts Road, Ste. F-6, Bryn Mawr, PA 19010 . . . . . (610) 520-3470
Vincent, Barbara 140 Bentwood Drive, Stamford, CT 06902 . . . . . (203) 322-2332
Virnig, Janet 5236 W 56th Street, Minneapolis, MN 55436 . . . . . (612) 926-5585
Volz, Marney 433 W 45th Street, Ste. 4C, New York, NY 10036 . . . . . (212) 262-7795

W/C STUDIO, INC./ALLAN COMPORT Pages 214-215
208 Providence Road, Annapolis, MD 21401 • Fax (410) 349-8632 **(410) 349-8669**
e-mail: acomport@aol.com • Website: www.theispot.com

Wagoner, Jae 654 Pier Avenue Unit C, Santa Monica, CA 90405 . . . . . (310) 392-4877
Waldin, Deb 5300 Vernon Avenue, Minneapolis, MN 55436 . . . . . (612) 922-4953
Wallace, Hannah 137 W 14th Street, Ste. 204, New York, NY 10011 . . . . . (212) 337-0055
Warner & Associates 1425 Belleview Avenue, Plainfield, NJ 07060 . . . . . (908) 755-7236
Warshaw Blumenthal 104 E 40th Street, Ste. 201, New York, NY 10016 . . . . . (212) 867-4225
Washington-Artist Rep 22727 Cielo Vista, Ste. 2, San Antonio, TX 78255 . . . . . (210) 698-1409

WELLS & ASSOCIATES, SUSAN Pages 373-381
5134 Timber Trail NE, Atlanta, GA 30342-2148 • Fax (404) 255-3449 **(404) 255-1430 • (888) 255-1490**
e-mail: swells@mindspring.com

Wells Illustration, Steven P.O. Box 651, London, England SE25 5PS 44 181 689 1427

WELLS REPRESENTS, KAREN Page 222
14027 Memorial Drive, Ste. 125, Houston, TX 77079 • Fax (281) 579-3220 **(281) 579-3220 • (800) 778-9076**

Wendt/Parallel Universe, Bobbi 1045 Sansome Street #402, San Francisco, CA 94111 . . . . . (415) 487-2160
West End Studio 1501 Main Street #201, Venice, CA 90291 . . . . . (310) 664-9200
Whalen, Judy 5551 Vanderbilt Avenue, Dallas, TX 75206 . . . . . (214) 821-4550
Wiest Group P.O. Box 760037, Lathrup Village, MI 48076-0037 . . . . . (313) 865-7777

WILEY GROUP Pages 119,121
94 Natoma Street, Ste. 200, San Francisco, CA 94105 • Fax (415) 442-1823 **(415) 442-1822**
e-mail: dww@wco.com • Website: www.dwrepresents.com

Will, Jeannie 1104 Plum Grove Road #202, Schaumburg, IL 60173 . . . . . (847) 755-1351
Williams Group, The 731 Stovall Boulevard, Atlanta, GA 30342 . . . . . (404) 873-2287 • (800) 791-1189
Wilson Zumbo Illustration 301 N Water Street, Milwaukee, WI 53202 . . . . . (414) 271-3388

WOLFE LTD., DEBORAH Pages 252-253
731 N 24th Street, Philadelphia, PA 19130 • Fax (215) 232-6585 **(215) 232-6666**
Website: www.deborahwolfeltd.com

Wolter & Associates, Bob 440 N Wabash, Ste. 1909, Chicago, IL 60611 . . . . . (312) 670-8770
Zaccaro & Associates, Jim 315 E 68th Street, New York, NY 10021 . . . . . (212) 744-4000
Zari International 853 Broadway, Ste. 1516, New York, NY 10003 . . . . . (212) 388-8541
Zarley, Tim 3800 Waterworks Parkway, Des Moines, IA 50312 . . . . . (515) 270-1987